BASIC TACTICS

MAO TSE-TUNG

BASIC TACTICS

TRANSLATED AND WITH AN INTRODUCTION BY

Stuart R. Schram

FOREWORD BY

Brigadier General Samuel B. Griffith, II
USMC (Ret.)

FREDERICK A. PRAEGER, *Publishers*

New York • Washington • London

1966

FREDERICK A. PRAEGER, PUBLISHERS
111 Fourth Avenue, New York, N.Y. 10003, U.S.A.
77–79 Charlotte Street, London W. 1, England

Published in the United States of America in 1966
by Frederick A. Praeger, Inc., Publishers

Second printing, 1967

© 1966 by Frederick A. Praeger, Inc.

All rights reserved

Library of Congress Catalog Card Number: 66–18912

This book is Number 186 in the series of
Praeger Publications in Russian History and World Communism

Printed in the United States of America

ACKNOWLEDGMENTS

Two contributions, different in nature but equally indispensable, have made it possible to produce this volume. The first of these, logically and chronologically, consisted in providing the Chinese text. The only known copy of this little book is to be found in the library of the Ministry of Justice near Taipei. A handwritten copy obtained from this source is deposited at Harvard University. Mr. Eugene Wu, the Librarian of the Harvard-Yenching Library, very kindly supplied reproductions of this copy for the use of General Griffith and myself. For this I am under the deepest obligation.

My debt to General Griffith is equally great. Not only did he generously agree to write a Foreword evaluating the interest and significance of *Basic Tactics* from the standpoint of a professional soldier long noted for his competence in this domain. He also was good enough to devote considerable time and effort to the examination of my translation, and made a number of very valuable suggestions for improving it. Without his collaboration, I should not have felt justified in venturing into the complex and highly technical field of guerrilla warfare, even though it is obviously central both to Mao's revolutionary methods and to his personality. It is a pleasure to express my gratitude here.

S. R. S.

CONTENTS

FOREWORD

GENERAL SAMUEL B. GRIFFITH

Mao Tse-tung's extensive military writings, habitually described by Peking's propagandists as "The Glorious Military Thought of Comrade Mao Tse-tung," have been required reading in the People's Republic of China for almost twenty years. But only during the last ten has Mao's canon begun to receive the attention it deserves elsewhere. This situation (which on a number of counts may be mildly described as deplorable) derives from the fact that some of Mao's more obscure military essays have only recently attracted the interest of competent translators. Fortunately, the series of lectures collected under the title *Basic Tactics* was discovered by one of our more perceptive students of Chairman Mao's turbulent career. His welcome translation of this primer on guerrilla warfare marks the latest significant addition to the growing corpus of Mao's work now available in Western languages.

It would be difficult to find another observer of the contemporary Chinese scene so well equipped for this demanding task as Stuart Schram. During a year at Harvard, where he was associated with the East Asian Research Center, and more recently in Paris, at the Centre d'Etude des Relations Internationales, Dr. Schram has concentrated on digging out, translating, and analyzing works by Mao hitherto neglected, if not, indeed, unknown to most Westerners interested in contemporary China and in the man who more than any other is responsible for the creation of the People's Republic.

Mao Tse-tung's thesis on the protracted, agrarian-based revolutionary war—a war in which man, not weapons, is the decisive factor—is now neatly packaged. But the evolution of this thesis was a gradual process. Mao arrived at his conclusions progressively, and patiently built up a formula suitable to the Chinese milieu as he observed it and to conditions as they existed. In doing so, he created an original theory of war.

To be sure—and this is apparent in *Basic Tactics*—he drew heavily on China's historical experience and on her ancient writers. (He is particularly indebted to Sun Tzu.) He levied a contribution on Lenin as well. But the resulting synthesis is his own. Armed with it, Mao reshaped China. He believes that others so armed will reshape the world.

During the summer and autumn of 1926, millions of impoverished peasants in Hunan province, driven to desperation by the rapacity of tax collectors, the oppressions of the military, the manipulation of grain prices by greedy merchants, and the ruthless exactions of gentry landlords, determined to take matters into their own hands. The tidal progress of this spontaneous agrarian movement was closely observed by the chief of the recently created Peasant Department of the Chinese Communist Party, Mao Tse-tung.

From January 4 to February 5, 1927, Mao traveled

extensively in his native province, where he conducted an on-the-spot investigation of this incipient peasant revolt. In retrospect, this experience proved to be one of the most decisive in his career—and in the history of the Party he would one day lead. For what Mao saw and heard in the five counties he visited during those thirty-two days persuaded him, first, that buried in the inchoate and inarticulate rural masses lay an inherently invincible potential for organized revolutionary action, and second, that only the peasantry of China, and not the urban proletariat, could provide the base for the revolution that would transform his country.

In his report, Mao described the dynamic movement he witnessed in Hunan as a "colossal event." Comparing it to a "tornado or tempest," he wrote that this irresistible force would "break all trammels" and "send all imperialists, warlords, corrupt officials, local bullies, and bad gentry to their graves." What position was the Party to take? "To march at their head and lead them? Or to follow at their rear, gesticulating at them and criticizing them? Or to face them as opponents?" In the event, the Party (still obedient to the line generated in Moscow) continued to place its hopes in a revolution led by the proletariat, and chose none of the alternatives offered by Mao. For the first (but not the last) time in his career, he was to be stigmatized as a "deviationist."

Mao's search for a successful formula for the revolutionary process in China led him next, in 1928, to recognition that an armed force, disciplined, literate, trained, politically loyal, and inculcated with revolutionary zeal, was an indispensable instrument for the conquest of power:

> . . . the existence of a regular Red Army of adequate strength is a necessary condition for the existence of the Red political power. . . . Unless we have regular armed forces of adequate strength, even though we have won the mass support of the workers and peasants, we certainly cannot create an independent regime, let alone an independent regime that lasts long and develops daily.*

Ten years later, he would write in "Problems of War and Strategy":

> Every Communist must grasp the truth: "Political power comes out of the barrel of a gun." Our principle is that the Party commands the gun, and the gun will never be allowed to command the Party. . . . Anything can grow out of the barrel of a gun. According to the Marxist theory of the state, the army is the chief component of the political power of a state. Whoever wants to seize the political power of the state and to maintain it must have a strong army.

As the series of lectures assembled in *Basic Tactics* shows, Mao conceived it to be one of his many responsibilities to contribute what he could to creating for the Party a reliable and effective "gun."

Although in *Basic Tactics* Mao is talking about an ambiguous war, the reader will discover that there is no

---

* "Why Can China's Red Political Power Exist?" (1928).

ambiguity in what he has to say on the subject. Mao's political theorizing has sometimes been criticized as amateurish, verbose, tendentious, repetitious. These charges cannot be laid to *Basic Tactics*, which is thoroughly professional, usually laconic, objective, and to the point.

As Dr. Schram observes, in the Introduction to his felicitous translation, Mao had to speak in simple terms, for he was speaking to an audience that consisted largely of young and inexperienced peasant soldiers and political cadres. But this directness and simplicity, which the translator has preserved, enhances rather than detracts from the impact of the essays. After all, to a guerrilla soldier, killing one's enemy, or possibly being killed by him, is a very practical matter indeed.

Throughout these lectures, several basic themes are evident. One of them is the absolute requirement for political indoctrination; another, the expectation that the properly motivated soldier will behave under all circumstances with unflinching fortitude and will meet his fate courageously. Such soldiers, says Mao, are invincible. Two other important points stressed by Mao are unity within the army and unity of the army with the people. This is not a Leninist concept, as some have presumed, but derives from China's enviable martial tradition.

Basic Tactics reflects the calculated prudence characteristic of Chinese Communist military and political methods. This was expressed operationally in their habitual refusal to accept combat unless victory was certain. One of the insuring factors was accurate intelligence, of both the enemy and the terrain; a second, the ability secretly to concentrate vastly superior forces at the point of contact so that enemy units could be annihilated "one by one."

In all warfare, each commander seeks to gain and retain freedom of action—by one means or another, to maneuver the opponent into a situation where he can do no more than react to blows falling upon him with unexpected force and from unexpected directions. Because guerrillas are invariably weaker in material terms than are their adversaries, it becomes all the more essential to their success in combat—and, indeed, to their ultimate preservation—never to permit the initiative to pass to their enemy.

Centuries ago, Sun Tzu wrote: "Now war is based on deception. Move when it is advantageous, and create changes in the situation by dispersal and concentration of forces." This dynamic pattern of alternating dispersal and concentration keeps a guerrilla situation fluid, and fluidity, in turn, conduces to exercise of the initiative. The interplay is complicated, but never static.

In Chapter VI of *Basic Tactics*, Mao writes that the first principle of guerrilla action "lies in careful and secret preparations, and in rapid and sudden attack." Nothing is more calculated to unnerve an opponent, for "the thunderclap leaves no time to cover one's ears."

Mention should be made of Mao's organizational concepts. It will be obvious to the reader of *Basic Tactics* that Mao was searching for a formula that would ensure maximum operational flexibility with economy of force.

In the West, we attempt to attain this happy combination by an *ad hoc* process in which we form "task forces" or smaller "task groups," "units," or "elements," each appropriate in strength and composition to successful execution of the specific mission assigned. In this particular context, Dr. Schram has used Western terminology to convey Mao's meaning with greater accuracy.

As an operational handbook for guerrillas, as well as for those who have to cope with them, *Basic Tactics* leaves little to be desired. But wider application of some of the elementary precepts set forth in it will also be obvious. Flexibility, deception, maneuver, indirection, surprise: all are components of strategic and tactical patterns designed to gain and retain freedom of action, and hence are as appropriate to total strategy as they are to the more limited sphere of military operations.

One may hope that *Basic Tactics* will be studied at all echelons of our defense establishment as well as in other government agencies that are now, and will doubtless for some time to come, be involved in combating "ambiguous war."

INTRODUCTION

STUART R. SCHRAM

Mao Tse-tung's methods for employing guerrilla warfare as a political weapon were developed in the dual
context of the civil war against the Kuomintang (1927–
37 and 1945–49) and the war of resistance against Japan
(1937–45). Although the propaganda themes and the
methods for mobilizing the masses were somewhat different in each case, the two enterprises were closely
linked. The theme of resistance to the foreign invader
was more important than that of social revolution, for it
was by establishing his image as the staunchest defender
of the Chinese nation that Mao laid the foundations of
his ultimate triumph over Chiang Kai-shek. Today, it is
hardly necessary to add, the national-liberation theme
is basic to the manner in which Mao's guerrilla model is
presented and applied by the Chinese and by their partisans throughout Asia, Africa, and Latin America.

In addition to a large number of orders, directives, and
other brief topical writings dealing with military problems, Mao has produced five major works on guerrilla
warfare. Two of them date from the period of civil war
against the Kuomintang, prior to the establishment in
1937 of the "Second United Front." The first is a resolution written by Mao for a congress of the Communist
Party organizations in the Red Army in December,
1929, frequently known (from the name of the place

where the congress was held) as the "Kut'ien Resolution." Only the first third of this has been retained in the current canon of the *Selected Works*, under the title "On Correcting Mistaken Ideas in the Party";[1] the remaining two-thirds, dealing primarily with problems of organization and propaganda, has never been translated into English. The second item from the civil-war period is "Problems of Strategy in China's Revolutionary War," written in December, 1936; with the usual textual changes,* this is included in the *Selected Works*.[2]

Mao's three works on guerrilla warfare dating from the period of the war against Japan were all produced during the first half of 1938. Two of them have long been familiar: "Strategic Problems of the Anti-Japanese Guerrilla War"[3] (a chapter in a collective work entitled *All the Problems of the Anti-Japanese Guerrilla War*) and "On Protracted War."[4] General Griffith has translated the whole of *All the Problems* . . . , the other chapters of which were revised and approved by Mao even if he did not write them all himself.† Only the present volume has hitherto remained entirely unknown and untranslated.

---

* For a discussion of the nature and motives of Mao's rewriting of his works for the current official version, and a variety of examples of the changes he has made, see my *Political Thought of Mao Tse-tung* (New York: Frederick A. Praeger, 1963), *passim*.

† See *Mao Tse-tung on Guerrilla Warfare*, trans. Samuel B. Griffith (New York: Frederick A. Praeger, 1961). The text from which General Griffith made his translation was published in 1937 under the title *Yu-chi chan*. It was apparently a preliminary version of the book published in 1938 under the title *All the Problems of the Anti-Japanese Guerrilla War* (*K'ang-Jih yu-chi chan-cheng ti i-pan wen-t'i*).

Basic Tactics, like "On Protracted War," was originally presented as a course of lectures. But, whereas the lectures comprising "On Protracted War" were given before the Association for the Study of the War of Resistance Against Japan in Yenan (apparently a relatively small and select body), those constituting *Basic Tactics* were given at the Anti-Japanese Military-Political University (K'ang-Jih Chün-cheng Ta-hsüeh, known as "K'ang-ta" for short). This university was divided into four sections, one of which was designed to train guerrilla leaders.* Presumably Mao's lectures were given before the 300 students of this section. Judging by the state of the Chinese text, the book is probably based on the stenographic report of what he said, rather than on a copy completely written out by Mao himself,† but there can be no doubt that he checked the result and that the content closely reflects his thinking.

The nature of the audience Mao was addressing explains the two points that set *Basic Tactics* apart from all his other writings: the discussion deals almost exclusively in concrete terms with problems of military tactics, rather than with the larger political and ideological issues raised by the anti-Japanese war, and it is conducted

---

* For a brief account of its organization and curriculum, see my biography, *Mao Tse-tung* (Harmondsworth: Penguin Books, 1966; New York: Simon and Schuster, 1967), pp. 206–7. (The pagination cited here and elsewhere is that of the Penguin edition.)

† Particularly noticeable because a character is sometimes wrongly replaced by another character pronounced the same way but with a totally different meaning. There are also one or two sentences that appear out of place. On the whole, though, the text is in reasonably good condition.

on an extremely rudimentary level. The emphasis on practical matters was natural in lecturing to future guerrilla commanders. As for the level of the presentation, the minimum academic requirement for admission to K'ang-ta was a diploma from a higher primary school (roughly equivalent to an American junior high school diploma), and the course lasted only six months. It was, therefore, necessary to speak in simple and easily understandable terms.

Apart from the level of sophistication of his audience, Mao had another reason for avoiding Marxist jargon in these lectures. In the context of the war of resistance against Japan, he wanted this little book to reach not only the Communist cadres trained in Yenan, but the Kuomintang or nonparty leaders of the guerrilla bands that were springing up all over the occupied areas of China to fight the invader. Consequently, it was not desirable to inject any ideological content other than the nationalism that constituted the lowest common denominator among all the participants in this struggle.*

Thus, the text here made available is a simple and down-to-earth discussion, in fundamentally nonideological terms, of the manner in which one goes about waging guerrilla warfare against a foreign occupant. It is my conviction that by its very simplicity and concreteness

* The book was published and put on sale in Hankow in March, 1938. The name of the publisher—Tzu-ch'iang Ch'u-pan-she, or "Self-Strengthening Publishing House"—deliberately echoes the slogan of the conservative reformers of the late nineteenth century, who called for "self-strengthening" (*tzu-ch'iang*) in the face of growing foreign domination.

the book helps to fill out our image of Mao's personality and of his political style. But before discussing what can be learned from it in this respect, I shall first endeavor to put it in the context of Mao's political experience and his gradual development of a revolutionary strategy based on guerrilla warfare in the countryside.

From Politician to Guerrilla: Mao's Evolution Before 1938

Mao Tse-tung was born among the Chinese peasantry. From his earliest youth, his imagination was stirred by tales of military heroism—both the triumphant wars of past emperors and the feats of arms of peasant rebels. His first published article, which appeared in 1917, when he was twenty-three, described a system of exercises calculated to strengthen the bodies of the Chinese and, thereby, make them more capable of defending their country. "The principal aim of physical education," he wrote, "is military heroism."[*]

It might have been assumed that, because he started with both an intimate knowledge of the peasantry and a deep interest in martial affairs, Mao would have come very rapidly to the idea that guerrilla warfare waged by peasants could play a decisive role in Chinese politics. In fact, Mao's experience as a student in Changsha detached

* Schram, *Political Thought of Mao Tse-tung*, p. 99. For an analysis of the sources of Mao's thought and the factors that shaped his personality at this period, see *ibid.*, pp. 3–11; for a more detailed discussion, see the introduction to my complete French translation of Mao's 1917 article: *Mao Ze-dong, Une étude de l'éducation physique* (Paris: Mouton, 1963).

him from his rural background, and Marxism—as he and most of the other founding members of the Chinese Communist Party understood it in the early 1920's—reinforced his prejudices against the peasantry. For a time, it seemed to him that only the proletariat was capable of effective revolutionary action, and he devoted himself primarily to work among the labor unions. Subsequently, in 1923–25, he distinguished himself by his extreme zeal working in and with the Kuomintang bureaucracy.

A better understanding of Lenin's theories about the alliance between the workers and the peasants in backward countries, added to his own concrete experience of the revolutionary force inherent in the peasantry, led Mao—beginning in the summer of 1925—to look once more toward the countryside. But an orientation toward the peasantry did not as yet mean an orientation toward guerrilla warfare. On the contrary, during the years 1925–27, Mao remained more sincerely committed than almost any other leading figure in the Chinese Communist Party to carrying out the "national revolution" in alliance with the Kuomintang. At the second Kuomintang Congress in January, 1926, he spoke up in favor of a flexible attitude toward the most extreme right-wingers in the Kuomintang—the so-called Western Hills Faction—because, he said, he still hoped that those comrades would return to the revolutionary path. And although, in the summer of 1926, on behalf of the Kuomintang, he trained peasant agitators who, in fact, would later be used against the Kuomintang, he favored collaboration with the "Left Kuomintang"—if not with

Chiang Kai-shek—until the open rupture between the Communists and the Nationalists in the summer of 1927.[5]

In January and February, 1927, during his famous investigation of the peasant movement in Hunan, Mao at last felt the full force of the revolutionary potential of the peasantry. In the summer of 1927, he suddenly swung far to the left, and was one of the first to recommend an open break with the Kuomintang and the use of the Communists' own red flag. He was also one of the first to grasp the decisive importance of organized military forces in the new political situation created by Chiang Kai-shek's rupture with the Communists.[6] But it was only very gradually that he came to develop the concept of waging guerrilla warfare from territorial base areas as the primary form of revolutionary struggle in China over a long period. The stages in his development of this strategy are fundamental to an understanding of the originality of his contribution to the methods of Communist revolution.

Mao's guerrilla experience began in the so-called Autumn Harvest Uprising of September, 1927. This uprising, which was to take place in Hunan and in three neighboring provinces, got its name from the fact that it was designed to enlist the participation of the peasants by exploiting their resistance to rent collection following the harvest. It was the Chinese Communists' answer to the severe repression then being carried out by Chiang Kai-shek and the other military leaders enjoying *de facto* control in various parts of the country. In a situation that threatened the very existence of the Communist Party—

and the peasant associations and other mass organizations
the Party to a large extent controlled—the only solution
that the Central Committee could conceive was apocalyptic. It consisted of "uninterrupted uprisings" by the
popular masses until the Kuomintang was finally overthrown in all of China. This line, later stigmatized (not
altogether unjustly) as "putschist," differed in three important respects from the revolutionary model that Mao
was ultimately to adopt:

1) It postulated that the essential fighting would be
done by the masses themselves in arms, not by organized
armed units.

2) Although recognizing that, for the moment, it was
easier to carry out uprisings in the countryside than in
the city, it still regarded the urban proletariat as the only
class capable of striking really decisive blows in favor of
the revolution.

3) It assumed that everything would be decided relatively quickly and that the revolutionary struggle would
spread almost immediately to the whole territory of
China.

In contrast to this original concept, Mao came to envisage a revolutionary process that (1) would give a Red
Army a central role, (2) would rely essentially on the
peasantry and would encircle the cities from rural base
areas, and (3) would involve a prolonged struggle from
gradually expanding territorial bases. The second and
third of these principles he discovered only somewhat
later. In September, 1927, as Special Commissioner of the
Party to carry out the uprisings in Hunan, he found him-

self in conflict with the Central Committee (dominated, since the "August 7th Emergency Conference," by Ch'ü Ch'iu-pai) only regarding the respective roles of organized military forces on the one hand and the masses in arms on the other.

In his exchanges with the Central Committee at the time, Mao claimed that he quite agreed with the official viewpoint, according to which regularly constituted military units could be only "auxiliary forces," and the success of the uprising would be assured by the intervention of the masses. But, in fact, he had already grasped that one could not expect poorly armed and virtually untrained peasants to overcome hostile armies capable of shooting them down at will. In his planning, therefore, he relied essentially on the four regiments at his disposal. When these proved in part unreliable and, in any case, insufficient to defeat the Kuomintang forces in the area, he refused to continue the battle against hopeless odds— to the great indignation of the Central Committee—and withdrew with the remnants of his forces to the mountainous area known as the Chingkangshan, on the border between Hunan and Kiangsi.[7]

On the Chingkangshan, where he was joined by Chu Te in April, 1928, Mao discovered the second of the three fundamental ideas in his road to power—the importance of base areas. He explained this concept in picturesque terms to his soldiers, as one of them has since recalled:

In speaking of the relation between armed struggle and revolutionary base areas, Chairman Mao used an amusing popular metaphor. A revolution's need for a base area, he said, was just like an individual's need for buttocks. If an individual didn't have buttocks, he wouldn't be able to sit down. He would have to run around or stand around all the time, and would certainly not be able to hold out long. His legs would get tired and collapse under him, and he would fall down. It was only when a revolution had a base area that there was a place to rest and recuperate, to regain strength, to recruit new forces, and thus to continue the struggle on an ever wider basis until final victory.[8]

Although Mao, by 1928, had already grasped both the importance of organized military units in the Chinese revolution and the utility of base areas, he had scarcely begun to develop a long-term strategy for achieving power by this means. In his report of November, 1928, now known under the title "The Struggle in the Chingkang Mountains," he complained that the masses were "cold and aloof," to such an extent that Mao and his comrades suffered from "an acute sense of isolation." In the original version of this text, he went so far as to state that his own adventure on the Chingkangshan did not merit the name of an insurrection, but was merely "contending for the empire" (*ta chiang-shan*), in the manner of those candidates for the throne who, in the past, had started out from a limited territorial basis.[9]

What Mao was doing on the Chingkangshan could indeed not be called an insurrection, but that did not mean it was nothing more than an old-fashioned revolt aiming to conquer the country by military power. If Mao himself saw it at the time in such a light, it was for the most part because, like Moscow and the Central Committee, he still expected victory to result largely from the action of the masses, in the course of a nationwide "revolutionary high tide." In this perspective, his own activities on the Chingkangshan could only be regarded as a holding operation until the high tide at last appeared. His little army would then act as a catalyst in promoting the revolutionary conflagration.

In order to move from this position to the full-blown model of revolution by protracted guerrilla warfare from rural base areas, it was necessary for Mao to grow both more optimistic regarding the possibilities of his own action and more pessimistic regarding the hope of a nationwide revolutionary high tide. Optimism regarding the potentialities of the rural base areas came in the course of the second half of 1929 and the first half of 1930. On the one hand, Mao and his comrades moved from the poor and remote mountain fastnesses of the Chingkangshan to a new base in southwestern Kiangsi Province, and there, he altered the highly radical and sectarian land policies that had alienated a large part of the peasantry on the Chingkangshan and had contributed greatly to the "coldness" from which he had suffered in the past. On the other hand, the Red Army grew in size, and Mao, Chu Te, P'eng Te-huai, and the other commanders developed more effective tactics for guerrilla combat, resulting in a number of victories over the local armies during the winter of 1929–30.

Thus, the base areas were strengthened, both politically and militarily. But Mao would hardly have clarified his own conceptions so quickly if Li Li-san, the dominant figure in the Central Committee since Ch'ü Ch'iu-pai's disgrace early in 1928, had not ordered the Red Army to attack several major cities in Central China in the late summer of 1930. Li, who had hitherto shown the greatest contempt for Mao's guerrilla methods—and indeed for everything that went on in the countryside—suddenly decided that the Red Army could make a powerful contribution to the victory of the revolution, provided its offensive was coordinated with strikes and other activities by the urban workers. Although P'eng Te-huai succeeded in taking Changsha and holding it for ten days, he was driven out again, and a second assault, by the combined forces of Mao, P'eng, and Chu Te, failed to achieve its aim in nearly two weeks of bloody fighting. This demonstration that the cities could not readily be taken was a decisive factor in the development of the strategy of revolution from rural bases. Mao ultimately persuaded his comrades to abandon the hopeless battle—for the second time, as in September, 1927, defying the orders of the Central Committee to take the capital of his native Hunan province—and returned to the base in Kiangsi.*

* For an account of these battles, see Jerome Ch'en, *Mao and the Chinese Revolution* (London and New York: Oxford University Press, 1965), pp. 156–59. Regarding the "Li Li-san line" and its relation to that of Moscow, see Benjamin I. Schwartz, *Chinese Communism and the Rise of Mao* (Cambridge, Mass.: Harvard University Press, 1958), pp. 127–63; Hsiao Tso-liang, *Power Relations Within the Chinese Communist Movement, 1930–1934* (Seattle: University of Washington Press, 1961), pp. 14–38; and the controversy between Schwartz and Hsiao in *The China Quarterly*, No. 12 (1962), pp. 231–34, and No. 15 (1963), pp. 160–64; also my own account of this period in *Mao Tse-tung*, chaps. 6 and 7.

In the wake of the catastrophic defeat of Li Li-san's policy of immediate assaults on the cities, both Moscow and the new leadership of the Chinese Communist Party, installed in power with Stalin's backing, began to devote more and more attention to Mao's rural base areas. At the direct instigation of the Comintern, a "Chinese Soviet Republic" was established on the symbolic date of November 7th, 1931 (the anniversary of the Russian Revolution), with its capital at Juichin in southwest Kiangsi. But this new interest of Stalin and his protégés in the "Soviet Areas" meant less rather than more freedom for Mao to develop his own revolutionary model, because, to the extent that the development of these territorial bases became the principal activity of the Chinese Communist Party, the Central Committee began to devote a large part of its time and energy to deciding how the work should be done. And the ideas of the Soviet-supported leadership on this subject were very different from those of Mao.

It must be admitted that Mao's own conceptions, although they were beginning to take shape as a coherent system, did not trace any clear pathway to ultimate victory. By this time, he had definitely adopted the three essential principles of the central role of the army, the importance of rural base areas, and the protracted character of the struggle. In the fall of 1931, after the failure of three Kuomintang "encirclement and annihilation" campaigns, it appeared that Mao's methods would permit the Communists to hold out indefinitely. However, the nature of his military strategy offered little hope of consolidating and expanding the Central Soviet Area much beyond its existing limits.

The reason is simple. An essential feature of all guerrilla strategy and tactics is to concentrate one's own forces in order to destroy the enemy units one by one. To achieve this result, accurate information on the enemy's movements and secrecy regarding one's own movements are indispensable, and both depend in turn on the support of the population. It is therefore advantageous to fight on the territory of the revolutionary bases, where the population has been thoroughly indoctrinated, rather than in the surrounding "white" areas, where the inhabitants may still be influenced by the enemy's counterpropaganda. In addition, it is advantageous to fight in areas where one knows the terrain, but the enemy does not. All this is exactly what Mao advocated, under the slogan of "luring the enemy deep" (into Soviet territory), and what he actually did during Chiang's first three campaigns. The results were excellent—although the third campaign might not have ended so well for Mao if Chiang had not been called away in September, 1931, by the Japanese aggression in Manchuria. But it was understandable that the Central Committee—the viewpoint of which was strongly defended at the time by Chou En-lai—should have seen little hope of ultimate victory in such a strategy. For how could one stabilize and enlarge the "Chinese Soviet Republic" if this would-be state within a state could not even protect the inhabitants already living under its authority from the constant incursions of enemy armies?

In fact, there probably was no escape from this dilemma within the context of the situation as it then existed. Only the Japanese invasion, which enabled the Communists to appeal to the nationalism of the Chinese peasants as well as to their hunger for the land, would ultimately create the conditions in which victory was possible.* Moreover, the tactics of encircling the "Soviet Areas" with a constantly shrinking ring of blockhouses and barbed wire, adopted by Chiang under the guidance of his German advisers in the fifth encirclement and annihilation campaign beginning in the late summer of 1933, would have been extremely difficult to counter in any case. But, by rejecting Mao's flexible guerrilla tactics as a relic of an earlier stage and by behaving as though they were the rulers of a full-fledged state capable of fighting Chiang Kai-shek on equal terms, Stalin's protégés hastened the catastrophic defeat from which the Chinese Communists only extricated themselves, in a greatly weakened condition, after the 6,000-mile "Long March" to the barren northwest province of Shensi.

As early as July, 1934, the Communists announced their intention of going northward to fight the Japanese.† But, although the Chinese Soviet Republic had

---

* Although I think he overstates his case, there is no doubt that Chalmers Johnson is correct in affirming (*Peasant Nationalism and Communist Power* [Stanford, Calif.: Stanford University Press, 1962]) that Mao would never have come to power if he had not been able to mobilize the Chinese peasantry by exploiting their nationalist sentiments. I would dispute his contention that the land hunger of the peasantry played an altogether negligible role in Mao's triumph, but there is no doubt that nationalism was the decisive factor.

† See the extracts from their proclamation to this effect in Schram, *Political Thought of Mao Tse-tung*, pp. 152–54.

declared war on Japan in April, 1932, until early 1936 Communist propaganda explained that nothing could be done against Japan until the "chief traitor," Chiang Kai-shek, had been overthrown and Soviet Power established throughout the country. The agreement finally concluded between the Communists and the Kuomintang in September, 1937, after the commencement of the second wave of Japanese aggression against China in July, gave Mao the opportunity he had been waiting for. It was in this context that Mao gave the lectures that comprise this book.

Mao's Policies and Political Style in 1938

Considerable discussion has been devoted to the question of whether Mao was, in fact, interested in fighting the Japanese or whether he was not concerned exclusively with building up his own strength for the inevitable civil war against the Kuomintang in the future. Quite obviously neither Mao nor Chiang ever thought that China could offer a place for both of them indefinitely. This much being granted, it is my opinion that, when he wrote this text in 1938, Mao had resigned himself to playing a more subordinate role for a longer period than turned out to be the case. The key to his attitude is to be found in a passage from his essay "On New Democracy," published in January, 1940. At that time, Mao wrote:

Today, whoever can lead the people in driving out Japanese imperialism, and introducing democratic government, will be the savior of the people. *If the Chinese bourgeoisie is capable of carrying out this responsibility, no one will be able to refuse his admiration; but if it is not capable of doing so,* the major part of this responsibility will inevitably fall upon the shoulders of the proletariat [italics added].*

The italicized words, which have been eliminated from the current version of this text, are exceedingly clear. If the Kuomintang—which Mao regarded as the political incarnation of the bourgeoisie—had been able to establish its prestige as the party capable of leading China to independence and progress, Mao would not have been in a position to challenge Chiang Kai-shek directly in the foreseeable future. A variety of indications, including certain of Mao's contemporary statements,† suggest that, in the early years of the anti-Japanese war, Mao expected Chiang to be more successful in establishing his image as the savior of China. In any case, as regards Mao's behavior in 1938, the year he wrote *Basic Tactics,* the question of whether he was primarily concerned with fighting the Japanese or with establishing his own power is of little significance. Even if the future conflict with the Kuomintang was never absent from his thoughts, the indispensable first step toward satisfying his ambi-

* For a translation based on the original text, see H. Carrère d'Encausse and S. Schram, *Le Marxisme et l'Asie 1853–1964* (Paris: Armand Colin, 1965), p. 355. (An English-language edition of this book is scheduled for publication by Penguin Books in 1967.) Compare with *Selected Works,* II, 350.

† See, in particular, his prediction in October, 1938, of a "brilliant future" for the Kuomintang (Schram, *Political Thought of Mao Tsetung,* pp. 159–60).

tions was to demonstrate the sincerity and effectiveness of the Communist-led guerrillas as fighters against Japan. This Mao and his comrades proceeded to do, as Chalmers Johnson shows conclusively on the basis of the records of the Japanese Army itself. Two or three years later, when their reputation had been established and when, also, the Kuomintang was beginning to adopt a more hostile attitude toward them, the Communists devoted themselves increasingly to extending their own influence at the expense of their Nationalist allies. In 1938, however, guerrilla warfare against the Japanese invader was not only Mao's professed aim but also his effective concern.

This preoccupation finds succinct but striking expression in Mao's lectures to future guerrilla leaders translated here. As indicated earlier, the only ideological content of these lectures is an appeal to all Chinese to struggle unremittingly for the salvation of their nation. "We must inspire ourselves," Mao declared, "with the most resolute spirit of unyielding struggle, with the most burning patriotic sentiments, and with the will to endurance, and carry out a protracted struggle with the enemy." This struggle, he emphasizes in the introductory chapter, is justified not merely by national pride but also by the elemental need for survival:

> We must know that, although the circumstances and the duration of the war are cruel and protracted, this situation is nothing compared to what would happen if the war were lost; if our country were destroyed, and the whole of our people reduced to a position of irretrievable ruin,

the suffering would be even more cruel and would never come to an end. Therefore, however cruel the war may be, we must absolutely and firmly endure until the last five minutes of struggle.

These words, spoken a few weeks after the wanton rape of Nanking by the Japanese, were fully justified by sober reality. But they also corresponded to the warrior's temperament, which is no doubt the most fundamental aspect of Mao's personality. He expressed this quality in full measure in the following paragraph entitled "We must not fear the enemy":

When we see the enemy, simply because he has a weapon in his hands, we must not be frightened to death like a rat who sees a cat. . . . We are men; our enemies are also men; we are all men, so what should we fear? The fact that he has weapons? We can find a way to seize his weapons. All we are afraid of is getting killed by the enemy. But when we undergo the oppression of the enemy to such a point as this, how can anyone still fear death? And if we do not fear death, then what is there to fear about the enemy?

This passage irresistibly calls to mind another exhortation penned by Mao nearly twenty years earlier, in a newspaper he edited during the May Fourth Movement of 1919:

What is the greatest force? The greatest force is that of the union of the popular masses. What should we not fear? We should not fear heaven. We should not fear ghosts. We should not fear the dead. We should not fear the bureaucrats. We should not fear the militarists. We should not fear the capitalists.[10]

Mao's conviction that a fearless attitude is one of the indispensable keys to victory also finds eloquent expression in the model harangues for unit commanders contained in Chapter XV, 4, as does his vision of war as the supreme form of drama. The guerrillas are called upon to consider themselves as an "invincible iron army," to "summon up" their "awe-inspiring reputation" and "preserve" their "glory," to "shed" their "last drop of blood," and to "die rather than surrender."

If the guerrilla must be courageous, this does not mean that he should be foolhardy. On the contrary, the essence of Mao's tactics here, as in all of his other writings, consists in avoiding battle at almost any cost unless there is the strongest possible assurance of victory. But even in a victorious battle there will be sacrifices. Mao advocates a combination of extreme prudence in planning operations and extreme daring in carrying them out. Thus, prior to every action, all officers are to appoint a replacement, "in order to express their resolution to sacrifice themselves" (Chap. VII, 2).

If *Basic Tactics* reflects Mao's warlike temperament, it also illustrates how deeply he is rooted in Chinese culture and traditions. Naturally enough, the classical text most frequently cited is Sun Tzu's *The Art of War.* Mao's very definition of guerrilla tactics as consisting in "avoiding strength and striking at weakness" echoes the language of Sun Tzu and, in fact, sums up the whole essence of that master strategist's teaching.* In many other places, Mao's Chinese text contains word-for-word citations from *The Art of War* and the associated commentaries—as in the case of his injunction to appear "when the enemy does not expect it,"† and to "cause an uproar in the East, strike in the West."‡ He also takes from Sun Tzu in slightly modified form the metaphor "The thunderclap leaves no time to cover one's ears."§

The methods recommended by Mao are inspired not only by Sun Tzu's precepts, but also by the tricks and stratagems that had been employed in China for many centuries and are recounted both in the standard dynastic histories and in the popular novels Mao knows so well. When we read of hurling stones down at the enemy in a mountain defile (Chap. II, 14), or of feigning defeat and luring the enemy into an ambush (Chap. IX, 1), literally dozens of passages call themselves to mind—especially from the famous novel of war and statecraft *Romance of the Three Kingdoms*, which had nourished Mao's youthful imagination.

One of the distinguishing characteristics of the Communist movement in China, as it has taken shape under

* Compare Chap. I, 4, with Sun Tzu, *The Art of War*, trans. Samuel B. Griffith (Oxford: Clarendon Press, 1963), Chap. V, 4, and Chap. VI, esp. 6 and 10.

† Compare Chap. II, 9, with *Art of War*, Chap. I, 26. (Here, and in the following two examples, there are differences in the English translations, but the Chinese is the same.)

‡ Compare Chap. II, 12, with *Art of War*, Chap. III, 13, commentary of Chang Yu (p. 80 of Griffith's translation.)

§ Compare Chap. II, 12, with *Art of War*, Chap. I, 26, commentary of Ho Yen-hsi (p. 70 of Griffith's translation).

Mao Tse-tung's leadership, is the extraordinary role of the army as the vanguard of the revolution. It would be going too far to say that Mao has replaced the Communist Party with the Red Army as the incarnation of the people's revolutionary will. On the contrary, Mao has always insisted on the fact that the Party retains its unique and privileged position. "Our principle is that the Party commands the gun, and the gun must never be allowed to command the Party," he wrote in November, 1938.[11] And, of course, the Party organizations and representatives in the Red Army (or the "Eighth Route Army," as it had been renamed for the purposes of the United Front at the time *Basic Tactics* was written) exercised a considerable degree of control over the Communist military forces. The fact remains that, since the days on the Chingkangshan, the Army has been a symbol of disciplined loyalty, devotion, and self-sacrifice and has played its critical role as a revolutionary instrument, not only by fighting but also by conducting propaganda and mobilizing the masses.

If the Army is thus to play, conjointly with the Party, the role of a revolutionary vanguard, it must be subjected to intensive indoctrination designed to endow it with the appropriate political consciousness. Thus, it was natural that Mao's very first writing on guerrilla problems, the Kut'ien Resolution of 1929, was very largely devoted to problems of political training and thought reform. The same concerns figure extensively in *Basic Tactics*.

A central problem in this respect is that posed by

Mao's insistence on what he himself has called "conscious activity." As a young man in his twenties, at the time of the May Fourth Movement, Mao had become convinced that only individual initiative, freed from the trammels of traditional society, could provide the energy necessary to get China moving once more. After his conversion to Leninism, he naturally expected salvation to come not from the individual but from the revolutionary action of the masses. But, at the same time, he considered it essential that all those participating in revolutionary action do so consciously, not by rote.

In Mao's view, the supreme manifestation of conscious activity is provided by man at war.[12] Whether one agrees with this or not, the simultaneous insistence on spontaneity and discipline appears less blatantly contradictory on the level of military tactics dealt with in this book than in the more general political context wherein Mao also introduces the notion. On the one hand, he calls for the maintenance of an "iron military discipline" (Chap. XV, 6) and, as a theme for propaganda during a retreat, puts forward the injunction "Execute resolutely to the end the orders of your superiors" (Chap. XV, 8). On the other hand, he declares that "in the case of the independent actions carried out in the course of guerrilla operations, there is generally no way to verify whether or not their tasks are executed in accordance with orders, and frequently they act beyond the knowledge of the responsible commander" (Chap. IV, 2). Hence, he recognizes the necessity for commanders to have "a lively intelligence and the ability to

adapt rapidly to changing circumstances" (Chap. IV, 2)
and the importance of increasing "the spirit of initiative"
(Chap. XIV, 5).

The relationship here postulated between the top commanders of a guerrilla unit and their subordinates illustrates the way in which Mao envisages the relationship
between the leaders of the Communist Party and the
revolutionary masses: the former establish the objectives, and the latter carry them out with a combination
of fidelity and initiative. Indeed, an essential aspect of
the drama of China today is the fact that Mao continues
to behave as though the objectives of Chinese foreign
and domestic policy were as self-evident as in 1938,
when the aim was "simply to kill the enemy," and as
though the available resources could be adapted to the
ends of the regime as simply as a wooden stool could
then be turned into a weapon for killing a Japanese
soldier.

This oversimplification of present realities to fit them
into the pattern of Mao's guerrilla experience is the more
striking in view of the considerable realism exhibited in
this text of 1938. Not only did he recognize that there
were "a good many among the popular masses" (Chap.
II, 18) who were prepared to betray the cause of China
for the sake of personal advantage, but, even within the
guerrilla forces themselves, the soldiers were seen as so
prone to desert that a whole system of "committees
against desertion" was necessary to discourage them
from doing so (Chap. IV, 9). In other words, the world
—except for the Japanese invader, who, understandably,

was seen exclusively in a hostile light—was not black and white, but gray. Even in the camp of those who were fighting for China's independence, shortcomings and backslidings were to be expected, should be dealt with in a down-to-earth manner, and should not be overdramatized. How have the current doctrinaire policies grown out of a heritage originally so pragmatic?

The Guerrilla Heritage Today

It is universally recognized that the experience of guerrilla warfare, which Mao shares with his comrades of the generation now in power, has profoundly marked the style and content of all of Peking's policies, both internal and external. We have Mao's own testimony that, at the time of the "Great Leap Forward," there were those within the Chinese Communist Party who regarded the attempt to produce steel by mobilizing the masses as "a guerrilla habit."[13] Mao then stigmatized such criticisms as "obviously incorrect." But, in more recent years, the guerrilla ethos has been deliberately brought into the foreground of the effort to forge a generation of heirs worthy of the revolution, through study of Mao Tse-tung's thought and assimilation of the experience of their elders.

During the first half of 1966, the attempt to remold the whole of Chinese society in terms of the thought of Mao Tse-tung reached new heights of frenzy. Mao's thought, which has always been marked by a certain subtlety, despite its dogmatic character, was reduced to a handful of crudely simplified slogans, and, in the name of this orthodoxy, all those who dared to think or feel for themselves were cast into darkness.

Whether this campaign has been inspired primarily by Mao himself, or by others speaking in the name of an aging leader, the excesses that accompany it no doubt result in part from a struggle for succession engendered by the prospect of Mao's disappearance in the near future. But, at the same time, if the political scene in China today appears as an extravagant and absurd caricature of all the most extreme tendencies in Mao's thought, nevertheless, it is a recognizable caricature, which grows out of—even as it distorts—the past. It is Mao gone mad, but it is Mao just the same.

In particular, we find in Chinese doctrine today three basic strands that have always been part of Mao's thought and personality: the guerrilla component, the Communist component, and the component of Chinese nationalism. The current hysteria is fed by the guerrilla's belief in the primacy of the human will, by the nationalist's fury against the Soviet "revisionists," who are believed to have betrayed their Asian comrades, and by a cult of "proletarian" virtue analogous to that which existed in the Soviet Union during the worst periods of the 1920's and 1930's.

The Red Guard movement, which marks (as of September, 1966) the culminating stage in the current "great cultural revolution," also clearly displays the influence of these three factors. The military and guerrilla imprint is too obvious to require comment. As for ideological content, the activity of these zealots is accompanied by an extraordinary muddle of Leninist (or pseudo-Leninist) and nationalist ideas. Museums are invaded, statues smashed, and the whole of China's traditional culture rejected as "bourgeois" and therefore foreign to socialism —and at the same time the mobs of adolescents scream their hatred of the "foreign devils." The whole enterprise is carried out in the name of Marxism and of Mao Tsetung's thought (which, as everyone knows, is the pinnacle of Marxism in our day), and yet its first result has been to strike a blow at the primacy of the Party, which is the very keystone of Marxist orthodoxy as Mao learned it from his masters, Lenin and Stalin. The atmosphere and methods owe something to Stalinist techniques of ideological regimentation as practiced twenty or thirty years ago in the Soviet Union. They also show considerable resemblance to the spontaneous outbursts of mass violence against foreign and corrupt elements which have marked Chinese history in the nineteenth and twentieth centuries, including those experienced and promoted by Mao in his youth.

These tendencies in Chinese internal politics, if they continue to gather momentum, can hardly fail to have important repercussions in the domain of foreign policy. Although such a development is obviously a matter of vital concern to the world at large, it is impossible to deal seriously with it in the compass of this brief work. Here I can only consider in general terms the impact of Mao's personality on China's attitude toward the outside world. In this respect, what are the implications for the present—and for the future—of the mentality and experience so vividly communicated in *Basic Tactics*?

The lessons that Mao drew from the struggle against Japan, and which he regards as applicable to the present-day struggle against "U.S. imperialism," can be summed up in three basic propositions:

1) The enemy is wholly evil and implacably hostile.

2) The very existence of the Chinese nation (and of the other nations of Asia, Africa, and Latin America to which Mao recommends the Chinese example) is at stake.

3) Man is the decisive factor; no weapons, however terrible, can triumph over the revolutionary will of the aroused masses.

In considering the present-day influence of this tradition, a fourth factor must be added—Mao's passionate desire to believe in the relevance of his own experience. He fought his way to power in the course of nearly a quarter of a century of warfare against seemingly overwhelming odds. It is manifestly intolerable to him that these exploits, which have so profoundly influenced the history of China and of the world, should cease to inspire the revolutionary struggles of the present.

Mao and his spokesmen, such as Lin Piao, apply the principles summarized above in three contexts: (1) Sino-American relations; (2) the struggle of other peoples, such as that currently being waged by the National Liberation Front in South Viet-Nam, against "U.S. imperialism"; (3) the world struggle between revolution and counterrevolution as a whole (Lin Piao's notorious thesis of people's wars, which posits encirclement of the "cities of the world"—Europe and North America—by the agrarian nations constituting the world's "rural areas").

These three "fronts" are closely connected. In Mao's view, the national liberation struggle of each separate people throughout the world will contribute to the goal of the final overthrow of imperialism by nibbling away here and there at the U.S. colossus. The sum of these struggles of the peoples of the world adds up to the over-all battle of the revolutionary "countryside" against the imperialist "cities." And China remains in the center of the whole process—as guide and mentor of the anti-imperialist peoples and because each additional front in the global struggle for liberation pins down part of the forces of "U.S. imperialism," thereby deterring it from the accomplishment of its principal goal, which Mao sees as the destruction of the Chinese revolution. In other words, China is in the center of things both as inspirer and as beneficiary of all revolutionary efforts.

Which role takes priority in Mao's mind? Is world revolution for him above all China's mission—or China's opportunity? Obviously, this is one of the crucial questions of our day. Upon the answer to it depend both an over-all judgment regarding the probable actions of the Chinese regime and the conclusions one may draw regarding an appropriate American policy to meet this challenge.

The same question can be put in other terms by asking whether Mao is motivated primarily by the interests of

China or by the interests of the world revolution. On this subject, divergence of opinion is very wide. There are those who would make of him, in effect, the successor of all the Chinese emperors of the past. Others regard him as a revolutionary fanatic whose mentality and behavior are virtually unaffected by the fact that he is Chinese. In my opinion, it is quite impossible to make any sense of this problem unless one recognizes that Mao takes very seriously both Chinese aims and revolutionary aims. This combination in itself—whatever the precise weight one may attribute to either factor*—has important implications. Because Mao is a Chinese profoundly concerned with the destiny of his own country, he might conceivably be influenced in certain circumstances by the advantages to be gained for China from a modification in her attitude toward the United States. Because, at the same time, he is genuinely committed to certain revolutionary dogmas, it would scarcely be possible simply to "make a deal" with him on a basis of sheer *Realpolitik*. He has already shown himself prepared to bend his revolutionary principles in the interests of China, but he could not be expected to abandon them altogether. Nor are his successors likely to do so in the foreseeable future.

If Mao is committed not only to China but also to revolution, what is the nature of this commitment? One

---

* On the relative importance of these two aspects of Mao's personality—and the way in which they combine and interact—see my contribution to the symposium "What Is Maoism?" in *Problems of Communism*, September–October, 1966, pp. 1–30.

can get at the answer to this question by asking what he
—or his successors—will do when confronted by certain
unpalatable facts that do not fit in with their view of the
world. Mao still professes to believe in world proletarian
revolution. Although he is convinced that, for the moment, the principal "zone of revolutionary tempests" is
to be found in Asia, Africa, and Latin America, he still
holds that the European and American working classes
nonetheless constitute a revolutionary force—albeit a
subordinate one. Sino-Albanian collaboration is presented
as an alliance between the Chinese Communists, who
have "been making most valuable contributions to the
international Communist movement and the working-
class movement," and the Albanians, who are "holding
high the revolutionary banner of Marxism-Leninism in
Europe," thus earning the undying gratitude of the
European proletariat.[14] Chinese diplomats and ideolo-
gists commonly declare that the exploited proletarians in
Sweden, England, or the United States—not to mention
the Soviet Union and Yugoslavia—are about to rise up
and overthrow their capitalist or neo-capitalist oppressors.

The Chinese Communists clearly cannot abandon this
perspective in the current climate of ideological witch-
hunts and insistence on "proletarian" leadership in the
political, cultural, economic, and military spheres. But
one day Mao, or his successors, will be forced to recognize and acknowledge that the workers of the advanced
industrial nations, however discontented they may be
with their fate, no longer represent a revolutionary force

capable or desirous of challenging the existing order head on. What will happen then?

Two reactions are conceivable. The leaders in Peking, concluding that world revolution is a myth, may, consequently, feel that they might as well do the best they can for themselves in direct negotiations with the United States. Or, abandoning all pretense of the class character of the world struggle, they may present it simply as a conflict between the rich nations and the poor nations, between the handful of privileged in Europe and North America and the exploited masses of Asia, Africa, and Latin America. In other words, recognition of an unpalatable reality could lead either to a less ideological approach to world politics or to the transformation of the Chinese ideological framework from a "Sinified" but nonetheless recognizable Marxism-Leninism into an unadulterated doctrine of national, cultural, or even racial conflict.

For the time being, Mao and those who speak in his name present themselves as the champions both of China's national interests and of the world revolution. In theory at least, China still maintains a link with the outside world in the form of Afro-Asian solidarity. But, in the face of recent events in Indonesia and elsewhere, Mao may well be tending toward the conclusion that if the white "imperialists" and "revisionists" of the United States and the Soviet Union constitute the worst enemies of the Chinese people, black and brown men are not much good either. No lessening in the attitude of self-righteous xenophobia that prevails in Peking, and no real breach in the intellectual and moral isolation of the Chinese leaders, is likely in the near future. Indeed, the situation will probably get worse before it gets better. The desire, expressed by responsible spokesmen for the U.S. Government, to open channels of communication between the two countries has been received, as might have been expected, only with insults.

The Chinese have little experience in dealing with foreigners on equal terms. In accepting Leninism as universal truth and the Soviet Union as a model and a guide, Mao likewise accepted the idea that at least certain Europeans—his comrades in the Communist Parties of other countries—were genuine friends of China. Today, despite the brave declarations emanating from Peking, affirming that Communist China enjoys the support of the overwhelming majority of the people of the world, little remains of the dream of "proletarian internationalism" or of the hope that national differences would lose all importance in a great socialist commonwealth. "Hate America" campaigns constitute the most important single theme for the political mobilization of the Chinese masses, but the "hate Russia" theme is not far behind.

The struggle in Viet-Nam is today in first place on Mao's list of "people's liberation wars." And yet, although it is obvious that only the Soviet Union is in a position to give effective military assistance to North Viet-Nam, Mao did not shrink from launching his Red Guards against the Soviet Embassy in a demonstration that could only be regarded by the leaders in Moscow as a deliberate challenge to them to break off diplomatic relations if they dared. The slogans call for ideological purity and proletarian internationalism, but in fact, as I have already pointed out, revolutionary obscurantism all too reminiscent of Stalin's purges goes hand in hand with a narrow-minded xenophobia reminiscent of the Boxers. Neither of these tendencies has much appeal abroad. Even those who support Peking as the only force on the world scene uncompromisingly hostile to "U.S. imperialism" do so with increasing embarrassment and increasing mental reservations. Mao's China is isolated today as it has never been since 1949.

It would be strange and ironical if one day, when the current madness in Peking has abated and the war in Viet-Nam has come to an end, "imperialist" America should contribute to leading China away from a state of moral guerrilla warfare with other nations toward participation in the world community. But irony is the stuff of history.

Meanwhile, what is the best method for dealing with Communist China? Surely, no one would deny the need for firmness. The guerrilla mentality that characterizes Mao and his comrades, as the reading of *Basic Tactics* reminds us once more, is a tough mentality—even when this toughness is not exacerbated by a political atmosphere such as prevails in Peking at the present time. The adversary who appeared to lose his nerve would earn only contempt. But, at the same time, there is unquestionably a point of no return beyond which it is not profitable to push either Mao the guerrilla or Mao the Chinese nationalist. Mao the nationalist is prepared to make apparently irrational and dangerous choices when China's dignity seems to him to be at stake. And such desperate attitudes are encouraged by the mentality and experience of Mao the guerrilla, who is accustomed to fighting against impossible odds and finds a certain exhilaration in doing so.

Notes to the Introduction

1. Mao Tse-tung, *Selected Works* (Peking; Foreign Languages Press, 1964), I, 105–16. The translations of the first three volumes of the Chinese edition of Mao's works published in the 1950's under the auspices of the British and American Communist parties (New York: International Publishers; London: Laurence and Wishart) have now been repudiated by Peking, which has published its own translation of the four Chinese volumes. (Vol. IV appeared in April, 1961; Vol. I in September, 1964; Vol. III in September, 1965; and Vol. II in December, 1965.) This new version has the double advantage of being the official version and of corresponding volume for volume to the Chinese text. (In the earlier translation, the second volume of the original, longest of the four, was split up into Vols. II and III of the translation, so that Vol. III of the Chinese edition became Vol. IV of the English edition.) Consequently, it seems preferable to refer henceforth only to the Peking edition, which is freely available both in the United States and in the United Kingdom. From here on, I shall designate it simply by the abbreviated title *Selected Works*, followed by the volume number.

2. *Ibid.*, 179–254.

3. *Selected Works*, II, 79–112.

4. *Ibid.*, 113–94.

5. For details and references regarding these various phases in Mao's career, see Schram, *Mao Tse-tung*, pp. 60–93.

6. See Schram, "On the Nature of Mao Tse-tung's 'Deviation' in 1927," *The China Quarterly*, No. 18 (1964), pp. 55–66.

7. For a more detailed account of the "Autumn Harvest Uprising," see Schram, *Mao Tse-tung*, pp. 119–25.

8. *Hui-i Ching-kang-shan ch'ü ti tou-cheng (Reminiscences of the Struggle on the Chingkangshan)* (Peking: Jen-min Ch'u-pan-she, 1956), p. 11.

9. Compare *Selected Works*, I, 97–98, with the original unbowdlerized text in *Mao Tse-tung Hsüan-chi, hsü-pien* (supplement), Chin-Ch'a-Chi Hsin-hua Shu-tien, 1947, p. 82.

10. Schram, *Political Thought of Mao Tse-tung*, p. 105.

11. *Selected Works*, II, 224.

12. Schram, *Political Thought of Mao Tse-tung*, p. 207.

13. Statement of September 29, 1958, to a reporter of the New China News Agency, quoted in Schram, *Political Thought of Mao Tse-tung*, p. 254.

14. See "Joint Statement of China and Albania," *Peking Review*, No. 21 (May 20, 1966), pp. 5–12.

BASIC TACTICS

MAO TSE-TUNG

Chapter I

INTRODUCTORY REMARKS

1. How the popular masses carry out military action.

How is it that the bare-handed masses, banded together in ill-armed military units without guns or bullets, are able to charge the enemy, kill the enemy, and resolutely carry out effective action in the war? This is a very widespread and very reasonable query. But if we know the function of the weapons used by an army and the aim of an army's action, we can then understand how our popular masses, although bare-handed, still have weapons and can engage in action to subdue the enemy.

The principal function of an army's weapons is simply to kill the enemy, and an army's final aim is simply to reduce or destroy the enemy's fighting strength. Well, in our daily life, is there any object that cannot be used to kill the enemy or any type of action that cannot reduce or destroy his fighting strength? For example, a kitchen knife, a wooden cudgel, an axe, a hoe, a wooden stool, or a stone can all be used to kill people. Such actions as cutting electric lines, destroying bridges, starting rumors, spreading poison, or cutting off supplies can everywhere inconvenience the enemy or reduce his fighting strength. All these are methods we may be unwilling to utilize or unable to employ. If we really want to kill and exterminate the enemy, there are weapons for us everywhere and work for us to be doing at all times, in order to ensure effective united action by the army and the people.

2. *Points for special attention.*

Apart from this, we must pay special attention to the present war on the national level, which has become cruel beyond our imagining and has also lasted a long time. We must not, because we are undergoing the suffering of a war more cruel than any seen in the past, immediately capitulate; nor must we, under the influence of a long war, suddenly lose our endurance and give way to lassitude. We must inspire ourselves with the most resolute spirit of unyielding struggle, with the most burning patriotic sentiments, and with the will to endurance, and carry out a protracted struggle against the enemy. We must know that, although the circumstances and the duration of the war are cruel and protracted, this is nothing compared to what would happen if the war were lost; if our country were destroyed and the whole of our people reduced to a position of irretrievable ruin, the suffering would be even more cruel and would never come to an end. Therefore, however cruel the war may be, we must absolutely and firmly endure until the last five minutes of struggle. This is especially the case with our present enemy, who finds his advantage in a rapid decision in the war, whereas our advantage is to be found in the strategy of a protracted war.

3. We must not fear the enemy.

When we see the enemy, simply because he has a weapon in his hands, we must not be frightened to death like a rat who sees a cat. We must not be afraid of approaching him or infiltrating into his midst in order to carry out sabotage. We are men; our enemies are also men; we are all men, so what should we fear? The fact that he has weapons? We can find a way to seize his weapons. All we are afraid of is getting killed by the enemy. But when we undergo the oppression of the enemy to such a point as this, how can any one still fear death? And if we do not fear death, then what is there to fear about the enemy? So when we see the enemy, whether he is many or few, we must act as though he is bread that can satisfy our hunger, and immediately swallow him.

The above points should all also be taken into account when we wage a war of resistance.

4. Definition of guerrilla warfare.

When it is not advantageous for our main land army to meet the enemy in large-scale engagements and we, therefore, send out commando units, or guerrilla units, which employ the tactics of avoiding strength and striking at weakness, of flitting about and having no fixed position, and of subduing the enemy according to circumstances, and when we do not oppose the enemy according to the ordinary rules of tactics, this is called employing guerrilla tactics.

Chapter II

TACTICS

At a time when our country's national defense preparations are not completed, and when our weapons are inferior to the excellent equipment with which the enemy has provided himself, we must observe the following principles whenever we wish to wage a battle with the enemy:

1. Precautions when on the march.

When we are on the march, we must send plainclothes units armed with pistols ahead of our vanguard, behind our rear guard, and to the side of our lateral defenses, in order to spy out the situation and to forestall unexpected attacks by the enemy, or superfluous clashes.

2. Precautions during halts.

When we encamp, if there is a presumption that the enemy may be near, we should send every day a guerrilla company—or at least a platoon—toward the enemy's defenses to carry out reconnaissance at a distance (from 20 to 30 li*) or to join up with the local forces and carry out propaganda among the masses, in order to inspire them to resist the enemy. If this unit discovers the enemy, it should, on the one hand, resist him and, on the other hand, report to us so that we can prepare to meet the foe or to retreat without being drawn into an unnecessary battle.

3. We must not attack strong positions.

If the enemy guards his position firmly or defends a strong strategic point, then, unless we have special guarantees of success, we must *not* attack him. If we attack him, we will waste considerable time, and our losses in killed and wounded will certainly be many times those of the enemy. Moreover, in guerrilla warfare, our artillery is not strong; if we recklessly attack a strong position, it will be very difficult to take it rapidly, at one stroke, and, meanwhile, it will be easy for the enemy to gather his forces from all sides and surround us. On this point, the army and the people must be absolutely firm of purpose and cannot act recklessly in a disorderly fashion because of a moment's anger.

4. Do not fight hard battles.

If we do not have a 100 per cent guarantee of victory, we should not fight a battle, for it is not worth while to

---

* One li is approximately one-third of a mile.—Ed.

kill 1,000 of the enemy and lose 800 killed ourselves. Especially in guerrilla warfare such as we are waging, it is difficult to replace men, horses, and ammunition; if we fight a battle and ourselves lose many men, and horses, and much ammunition, this must be considered a defeat for us.

5. We must not fight if the situation of the enemy is not clear.

When we are encamped in a certain place and suddenly discover the enemy but are not informed regarding his numbers or where he is coming from, we must absolutely not fight, but must resolutely retreat several tens of li. It is only if we are right up against the enemy that we should send covering units, for, if the enemy comes to attack us, it is certainly because his forces are superior or he has a plan, and we must under no circumstances fall into his trap. If the enemy is in force, it is obviously advantageous to retreat. If his numbers are small and we retreat, nothing more than a little extra fatigue is involved, and there will always be time to return and attack him again later.

6. We must organize the masses and unite with them.

Modern warfare is not a matter in which armies alone can determine victory or defeat. Especially in guerrilla combat, we must rely on the force of the popular masses, for it is only thus that we can have a guarantee of success. The support of the masses offers us great advantages as regards transport, assistance to wounded, intelligence, disruption of the enemy's position, etc. At the same time, the enemy can be put into an isolated position, thus further increasing our advantages. If, by misfortune, we are defeated, it will also be possible to escape or to find concealment. Consequently, we must not lightly give battle in places where the masses are not organized and linked to us.

7. *Using the masses to make a surprise attack and break a blockade.*

When the enemy surrounds us and blockades us, we should rouse the popular masses and cut the enemy's communications in all directions, so that he does not know that our army is already near him. Then, we should take advantage of a dark night or of the light of dawn to attack and disperse him.

8. *Surprise attacks on isolated units.*

When we have reconnoitered the enemy's position and have kept our men at a distance of several li, and when he has unquestionably relaxed his precautions, then we advance rapidly with light equipment, before dawn when the enemy does not expect us, and exterminate him.

9. *Using the popular masses to harry the enemy.*

On the basis of a decision by the main force of the army, in time of battle, we send out part of our forces, divided into several units—the smallest element being a platoon—to lead the local militia, police, volunteer army, or other popular masses of the peasantry and the workers. These groups use a great variety of flags, occupy mountaintops or villages and market towns, use brass gongs, spears, rudimentary cannon, swords and pikes, trumpets, etc. They scatter all over the landscape and yell, thus distracting the enemy's eyes and ears. Or, both night and day, on all sides, they shoot off isolated shots to cause panic among the enemy soldiers and fatigue their spirit. Then, afterward, our army appears in full strength when the enemy does not expect it and disperses him by a flank attack.

10. Circling around to get away from the enemy.

When we are faced with a large enemy force and do not have sufficient strength to meet its attack, we use the method of circling around. We hasten to a place where there are no enemy troops, and we use mountain trails so that the enemy cannot catch up with us. At the same time, along the way, we utilize the popular masses, getting them to carry on reconnaisance work in the front and the rear, so that we are not attacked by the enemy from either direction.

11. Getting out of difficult situations.

Presume that in the rear there is a pursuing army and in the front an obstacle, or that the pursuing army is too strong for us. As a plan to get out of such a difficult situation, we can send a part of our forces 4 or 5 li off, to lure the enemy up a big road, while our main force follows a side road and escapes the enemy. Or we can make a detour around to the enemy's rear and attack him there by surprise. Or we can use the local militia and the police to go along another route, leaving some objects, making footprints in the road, sticking up notices, etc., so as to induce the enemy to follow them. Then, our main force suddenly rushes out from a side road, striking at the enemy from the front and the rear, encircles him on all sides, and annihilates him.

12. "Cause an uproar in the east, strike in the west."

When the army wants to attack a certain place, it does not advance there directly but makes a detour by some other place and then changes its course in the midst of its march, in order to attack and disperse the enemy. "The thunderclap leaves no time to cover one's ears."

13. Concealed attacks from ambush.

When the enemy is pursuing us in great haste, we select a spot for an ambush and wait until he arrives. Thus, we can capture the enemy all at one stroke.

14. Ambushing the enemy in the course of his march.

When we learn from reconnaissance that the enemy plans to advance from a certain point, we choose a spot where his path is narrow and passes through confusing mountainous terrain and send a part of our troops—or a group of sharpshooters—to lie hidden on the mountains bordering his path, or in the forest, to wait until his main force is passing through. Then we throw rocks down on his men from the mountains and rake them with bullets, or shoot from ambush at their commanding officers mounted on horseback.

15. Making a strong defense by emptying the countryside.

When our spies have informed us that the enemy is about to arrive, and if our force is not sufficient to give battle, we should then carry out the stratagem of "making a strong defense by emptying the countryside." We hide the food, stores, fuel, grain, pots and other utensils, etc., in order to cut off the enemy's food supply. Moreover, as regards the popular masses of the area in question, with the exception of old men, women, and children, who are left behind to provide reconnaissance information, we lead all able-bodied men to hiding places. Thus, the enemy has no one to serve as porters, guides, and scouts. At the same time, we send a few men to the enemy's rear communication lines, to cut off his supplies, capture his couriers, and cut or sabotage his communications facilities.

16. Meeting a superior enemy.

(1) When the enemy advances, we retreat. If the enemy's forces were weaker than ours, he would not

dare advance and attack us. So, when he advances toward us, we can conclude that the enemy is certainly coming with a superior force and is acting according to plan and with preparation. It is, therefore, appropriate for us to evade his vanguard, by withdrawing beforehand. If we meet with the enemy in the course of our march and either do not have clear information regarding him or know that his army is stronger than ours, we should, without the slightest hesitation, carry out a precautionary withdrawal.

As to the place to which we should withdraw, it is not appropriate to go long distances on the main roads, so that the enemy follows us to the end. We should move about sinuously in the nearby area, winding around in circles. If the enemy appears ahead of us, we should circle around to his rear; if the enemy is on the mountains, we should descend into the valleys; if the enemy is in the middle, we should retreat on the two sides; if the enemy is on the left bank of the river, we should retreat on the right bank; if the enemy is on the right bank, we should retreat on the left bank.

Moreover, in withdrawing, when we come to a crossroads, we can deliberately leave some objects in the branch of the road we do not take or send a small fraction of our men and horses that way, in order to leave some tracks or write some notices or symbols. Or we can write some distinguishing marks on the road we do take to indicate that it is closed. Thus, we induce the enemy to direct his pursuit and attack in the wrong direction.

At such times, it is best to evacuate the popular masses

and such armed forces as the militia, police, volunteer army, etc., by various routes in all directions, in order to confuse the enemy's eyes and ears. We can leave behind part of our men, who bury their uniforms and weapons and disguise themselves as merchants, street vendors, etc. They spread rumors or pretend to be obliging in order to spy out information regarding the enemy's numbers, his plans, the location and routine of his camps, and the precautions he is taking. If the enemy questions them about the direction in which we have withdrawn and the strength of our force, they should talk incoherently, pointing to the east and saying the west, pointing to the south and saying the north, replacing big by small and small by big, talking at random and creating rumors. They wait until our army is about to attack, and then they dig up their uniforms and put them on, take out their weapons, and attack the enemy from his midst, thus completely routing him and leaving him with nowhere to turn.

(2) When the enemy retreats, we pursue. When the enemy army retreats, it is appropriate to take advantage of the situation to advance. On such an occasion, the enemy's military situation must have undergone a change, otherwise he would not have retreated, and he is certainly not prepared to join battle against us with any resolution. If we take advantage of the situation and make a covering attack on his rear, the enemy's covering units will certainly not be resolved to fight, and in the context of the enemy's over-all plan it will be difficult for his forward units to return and join in the fray. In rough moun-

tainous terrain, where the paths are narrow and rivers and streams intertwined so that there are many bridges, even if the enemy's forward forces were to turn back, this move would require much time. So, by the time he turns back, his rear will already have been annihilated and he will already have been disarmed.

At this time, the organizations of the popular masses should devise methods for destroying the bridges on the route over which the enemy is retreating, or cutting the wires of his communications system. Or, best of all, they should wait until the bulk of the enemy's army have retreated and, taking advantage of the protection afforded by our guards and army, block the enemy's path of retreat, so that, although his forces may want to turn back, they cannot do it, and, although they yearn for help, they cannot obtain it.

But, at such a time, the most important task of the popular masses is to spy out the direction in which the enemy is withdrawing, in order to ascertain whether or not there may be an ambush or a feigned retreat intended to encircle us from two sides, and report to us immediately so that our army can pluck up courage and pursue the enemy or devise a method of evading him.

(3) When the enemy halts, we harass him. When the enemy is newly arrived in our territory, is not familiar with the terrain, does not understand the local dialect, and is unable to gain any information from the scouts he sends out, it is as though he had entered a distant and inaccessible land. At such a time, we should increase our harassment—shooting off guns everywhere,

to make him ill at ease day and night, so exercising a great influence on both his mind and body. Under such circumstances, I fear that any army, however overbearing, will begin to waver and will become weary. We need only await the time when his spirits are wavering and his body weary, and then, if our armies rush in all together, we can certainly exterminate him completely.

17. Dealing with a weak enemy.

Fighting as we are for the existence of our nation and the achievement of the aims of guerrilla warfare—which are to destroy the enemy and to stir up the courage of the popular masses—when we are faced with a weak enemy, naturally we should unite with the popular masses of the place in question to surround him and exterminate him at one stroke.

18. Arousing the masses.

There are always a good many among the popular masses who forget the great cause for the sake of petty advantage. Frequently, having received great favors from the enemy, they act contrary to conscience and aid the forces of evil. For this reason, before the arrival of the enemy in a given place, we must do our utmost to whip up the spirits of the popular masses, to rouse their will to resist, and to endow them with an unshakable resolve to fight to the end, without seeking advantage, without compromise or surrender. We must induce them to follow our orders sincerely and to cooperate with our army to resist the enemy. At the same time, we should also organize "resist-the-enemy associations," "associations for national salvation," and other types of professional bodies to facilitate the transmission of orders and the evacuation of villages in time of necessity and to clean out traitors and prevent their utilization by the enemy.

Chapter III

THE AIM OF THE WAR

The ultimate aim of guerrilla warfare is certainly to disarm the enemy, to destroy his fighting strength, to get back the territories he has occupied, and to save our brethren whom he is trampling under foot! But when, because of objective circumstances and other factors of various kinds, it is impossible to attain this goal, it sometimes happens that the areas unaffected by the fighting are controlled by the enemy in all tranquillity. This should not be. Because of this possibility, we must think up methods for inflicting economic and political damage in these areas and destroying communication facilities, so that, although the enemy has occupied our territory, it is of no use to him and he decides to withdraw on his own initiative.

In guerrilla warfare, we must observe the principle "To gain territory is no cause for joy, and to lose territory is no cause for sorrow." To lose territory or cities is of no importance. The important thing is to think up methods for destroying the enemy. If the enemy's effective strength is undiminished, even if we take cities we will be unable to hold them. Conversely, when our own forces are insufficient, if we give up the cities, we still have hope of regaining them. It is altogether improper to defend cities to the utmost, for this merely leads to sacrificing our own effective strength.

Chapter IV

ORGANIZATION

1. Opportunities for organization.

(1) When we are devoting ourselves to warfare in an open region, it is the sparsely populated areas, with a low cultural level, where communications are difficult and facilities for transmitting correspondence are inadequate, that are advantageous.

(2) Narrow mountainous regions, rising and falling terrain, or areas in the vicinity of narrow roads—all of which are inconvenient for the movement of large bodies of troops—are also advantageous.

Opportunities also exist:

(3) When the people in the enemy's rear are in sympathy with our army.

(4) When the enemy is well-armed, and his troops numerous and courageous, so that we have to evade direct clashes.

(5) When the enemy has penetrated deeply into our territory and we are preparing everywhere to carry out measures of harassment and obstruction against him.

(6) Dense forests or reedy marshes, in the depths of which we can disappear, are most advantageous for this purpose, especially in the late summer and autumn, when we find ourselves behind a curtain of green.

2. *Forms of organization.*

The action of a guerrilla unit takes one of the following forms:

(1) We send out a large cavalry unit from our main force, together with mounted artillery, or cavalry accompanied by a platoon or more armed with light automatic weapons. They penetrate as rapidly as possible into the enemy's rear, destroy there all his communications links, and carry out the thorough and complete destruction of all his storehouses of food, grain for his horses, and ammunition. Moreover, they send out a small group of their forces to destroy all places of military significance in the enemy's rear. Once these forays have been carried out, the group fights its way out in another direction and rejoins the main force.

(2) We send out cavalry or a special task group of infantry. Their strength should be from a platoon to a few companies. They should penetrate as deeply as possible into the enemy's rear and, moving rapidly and unpredictably, should carry the battle from one place to another. When there is no alternative, or when the enemy is not expected to arrive before a certain time, they can also dwell temporarily in secret where they are. As required by the exigencies of the situation, they can employ either

all or a part of their forces. They return when the time comes that they can no longer stay in the enemy's rear, or when the task entrusted to them is completed, or because the enemy has already discovered our traces and our intentions, and has taken effective measures of defense.

(3) In the enemy's rear, we choose some young, strong, and courageous elements among the local population and organize some small groups who will accept the leadership of the experienced and trained persons we send out or of experienced persons whom we had trained previously in the place in question. The secret activity of these small groups involves moving from their own area to another one, changing their uniforms, unit numbers, and external appearance, and using every method so as to cover their tracks to the utmost.

(4) Or we seek volunteers from our army and provide them with high-quality light weapons, in order to form them into special guerrilla units under the leadership of such officers as have benefited from experience and study.

(5) Guerrilla units can be classified according to their nature. Those formed of selected volunteers are called special guerrilla units. Those organized generally from a part of our army are called basic guerrilla units. Those organized from the local population are called local guerrilla units. When basic and local guerrilla units engage in combined actions, they are subject to the unified command of the commander of the basic unit.

(6) As for the choice of the members of a guerrilla unit, the members of a basic guerrilla unit should be taken

from among those soldiers who are healthy, firm of purpose, patient, courageous, and quick-witted. Moreover, the soldiers should themselves be willing to join the group in question. In the case of the independent actions carried out by these men in the course of guerrilla operations, there is generally no way to verify whether or not their tasks are executed in accordance with orders, and frequently they act beyond the knowledge of the responsible commander. For this reason, the choice and training of members of guerrilla units should have as its central theme "faithfully carrying out one's task."

(7) The choice and the nomination of the commander of a guerrilla task group or small group requires even greater forethought and reflection. The capacity of the commanders for faithful and courageous action, their military knowledge—especially their knowledge of guerrilla tactics—their possession of a lively intelligence and the ability to adapt rapidly to changing circumstances, their loyalty, and their daring are indispensable conditions for carrying out plans and completing our tasks.

3. Number of troops.

The number of men belonging to a guerrilla unit is determined by the tasks, but it commonly ranges from five or ten men to something over a thousand. However, the maximum strength of such a unit may not exceed one regiment. If the number of soldiers is too large, the movements of our forces will be encumbered, there will be greater difficulties regarding food supply, and it will be difficult to conceal the troops by the use of false uniforms. Because of these problems, our plans may be discovered or revealed before they have been carried out. Moreover, replenishing our supplies of ammunition will be a problem. Furthermore, we will often have difficulties because of poor roads, with the result that not only will all our plans prove merely illusory, but also we will often fall into difficulties to no good purpose in going and returning.

The great superiority of a small guerrilla unit lies in its remarkable mobility. With very little expenditure of time and effort, one can get food, and it is also easy to find a place to rest, for one does not need much in the way of rations or a place of shelter to camp. Still less is one held up by bad roads, and supplies of ammunition and medicine are also easy to replenish. If we do not succeed in our operation, we can retreat in good order.

4. Types of soldiers.

As for the type of soldiers employed in guerrilla units, cavalry, engineers, and highly mobile infantry troops are excellent. Cavalry is entrusted with the task of creating disorder on the enemy's flanks, and also, when we are pursuing the enemy, with that of maintaining pressure on his rear guard and creating confusion on his flanks and in his rear. Moreover, at all times, cavalry is the guerrilla unit's only instrument for transmitting correspondence and for reconnoitering. Hence, the cavalry is indispensable to any guerrilla unit. Engineers are used for destroying communications in the enemy's rear (such as railroads, telephone and telegraph lines, bridges, etc.) As for the highly mobile infantry units, they are useful to startle the enemy and produce in him a feeling of insecurity night and day.

5. Weapons.

Apart from the rifles of the infantry and the cavalry, light machine guns, hand grenades, etc., guerrilla units should also be supplied with pistols and submachine guns.

To the extent that the terrain permits it, one can also add heavy machine guns, mortars, and small cannons.

6. Men and baggage.

Convenience of movement and agility being the characteristics of a guerrilla unit, the baggage train, cases of equipment and ammunition, etc., should all be kept as simple as possible for the sake of convenience. The combatant and noncombatant members of the unit should all be organized as most appropriate for guerrilla warfare, and all other persons who are not indispensable should be kept to the strict minimum.

(1) The officers and men in each guerrilla squad should not exceed 8; each platoon should not exceed 26; and each company should not exceed 100.

(2) When automatic weapons are somewhat more numerous, the number of men can be still further reduced, and guerrilla units composed of 5 or 6 men can be sent

out repeatedly, in order to achieve the greatest result in terms of harassing the enemy or securing intelligence.

(3) Each commanding officer of a unit should have only one orderly at most. Apart from this, according to the complexity of the tasks, two or three officers should share the services of one orderly. Even more attention should be accorded to not abusing this rule by unnecessarily increasing the number of couriers as a substitute for orderlies and to seeing that an unnecessarily large number of men are not sent to carry out a given task, thereby reducing the fighting strength of one's own unit. Hence, when one sends out couriers, one must reflect carefully on whether they can accomplish their task or not.

(4) It is preferable that each mess unit should not carry bundles of food. When the dry rations carried separately by each soldier are exhausted, one should take advantage of opportunities to borrow the pots and pans of the population so as to prepare supplementary rations. If it is necessary to carry bundles, each unit should not carry more than two.

(5) Bundles of writing materials should not be carried in excess of needs. Normally, two bundles per regiment, one per battalion, and one per company are permissible. The weight of each bundle should not exceed 40 kilograms.

(6) Each officer and soldier should carry his own bedding, knapsack, etc. Bearers should not be engaged to transport these items. This rule should be firmly established in advance.

7. *Objects to be carried.*

A guerrilla unit preferably should have the following things:

(1) Equipment and explosives for destroying railroads, telephone and telegraph lines, arsenals, etc.

(2) Medicines. Those needed in case of emergencies should be carried according to the season, but dressings, etc., should be provided on a permanent basis.

(3) A compass, and maps of the area in which the guerrilla unit operates.

(4) Light radio equipment, which is especially important in order to be able to report at all times on the situation of the enemy and to listen in on the enemy's reports.

(5) A certain quantity of gold coins, to provide for unexpected needs and for buying food.

8. *Discipline.*

Whether or not the military discipline of a guerrilla unit is good influences the reputation of our whole army and its ability to secure the sympathy and support of the popular masses. Only strict discipline can assure the complete victory of all our independent actions. Consequently, our attitude toward those persons who violate military discipline, harm the people's interests, and do not resolutely execute the orders of their superiors, should consist in punishing them severely without the slightest regard for politeness. The application of military discipline in a partisan unit does not aim exclusively at punishment. Rather, it aims at strengthening the political instruction of the officers and men and raising their level of political consciousness, thereby indirectly eliminating a large number of actions contrary to military discipline and causing the officers and soldiers to understand the psychology of the masses, so that at appropriate times they can unite effectively with the common people.

9. Political organization.

(1) Each guerrilla task group and small group should have a political director, and in the headquarters of the guerrilla unit there should be a political training department, for directing the political work of officers and soldiers and dealing with the human problems of all the political instructors.

(2) Each mess unit of a guerrilla unit should establish a special commissioner in order to guard against the infiltration and activity of reactionary elements and to encourage those soldiers without clear ideological consciousness who are wavering in their purpose.

(3) In order to prevent desertion by the soldiers, a committee against desertion, as well as "groups of ten," should be organized in each guerrilla unit. The groups of ten and the committee against desertion are negative methods for preventing desertion. Their organization and work should be carried out roughly as follows:

a. In order to prevent desertion, every guerrilla unit should establish a desertion committee and every mess unit should organize a group of ten.

b. The committee against desertion should be composed of from seven to nine people, one of them being the chairman and the others members. It should be composed of lower-level cadres who can endure difficulties and whose thinking is firm, as well as heads of the groups of ten. The groups of ten are composed of ten men in all, one of them being the head and the others members. They are made up of faithful and reliable soldiers.

c. The over-all activity of the groups of ten is subordinated to the committee against desertion. As regards military matters, it is subordinated to the commander of the unit and to the committee against desertion. In other work, it is subordinated to the political training department. Both groups of ten and committees against desertion must accept the guidance of their commanding officer.

d. The work of the group of ten should take account of all the actions and talk of the officers and soldiers, especially of "camp idlers" and such. Unstable elements should be secretly watched, even if they are members of the group of ten or their friends.

Meetings should be held once a week to review the work and to report to the commanding officer and the committee against desertion regarding the situation in general at all times. After each extreme difficulty or when our army has suffered a slight defeat and is staying in its base camp, special attention should be paid to unfavorable attitudes that may develop among the soldiers and to conversations that may endanger the morale of the soldiers.

e. The work of the committee against desertion consists above all in reviewing the work of the groups of ten and in admonishing and guiding them at the appropriate times. The committee may also call conferences of the heads of all the groups of ten, or plenary conferences of all the members of the groups, to discuss the progress of the work as a whole.

The soldiers' life is rather like living in the desert, and every day the men undergo the fatigue of political study and training in the art of combat. This may easily engender feelings of disgust and opposition. In order to provide entertainment for the army and to compensate for a dull life, one should establish in a guerrilla unit clubs or amusement rooms. (For details of the organization and activities of such clubs, see the account in Chap. XV, 10.)

10. Special forms of military organization.

(1) In order to make up for insufficient supplies of ammunition and poor marksmanship, every company should have from three to nine sharpshooters, to be employed exclusively for shooting from ambush at long distances or for shooting at special targets (enemy officers, machine-gunners or artillerymen, couriers, etc.).

(2) The commander of each task group and small group should choose particularly sharp-eyed couriers to serve as observers. Normally, a task group commander should have two of these, and a small group commander one. These men serve exclusively to remedy the insufficiency of battlefield observation.

(3) Each task group and small group of a guerrilla unit should have two nurses, who devote themselves exclusively to emergency care of sick officers and soldiers and to instruction in hygiene.

(4) In order to obtain reliable information regarding the enemy's dispositions, so as to be able to oppose him without losing any opportunities, all guerrilla units should establish groups of scouts. Normally, it will be sufficient if each unit has one platoon, each task group has one squad, and each small group a smaller element. A network of local scouts should also be established by the group of scouts wherever they go, or by scouts concealed in advance.

Chapter V

TASKS

The principal object of the action of a guerrilla unit lies in dealing the enemy the strongest possible blows to his morale, and in creating disorder and agitation in his rear, in drawing off his principal force to the flanks or to the rear, in stopping or slowing down his operations, and ultimately in dissipating his fighting strength so that the enemy's units are crushed one by one and he is precipitated into a situation where, even by rapid and deceptive actions, he can neither advance nor retreat.

(1) Destroy railroads and highways within the area of action, as well as important structures along the roads. Telephone lines and telegraph systems are especially important.

(2) Destroy the enemy's principal or secondary supply depots.

(3) Destroy the enemy's storehouses of food and military equipment.

(4) Strike in the enemy's rear, at his baggage train, or at his mounted and unmounted couriers, as well as at his mounted scouts, etc. Also seize the provisions and am-

munition that the enemy is bringing up from the rear to the front.

(5) Strike at the enemy's independent task groups and at the inhabited areas that he has not yet solidly occupied.

(6) Mobilize and organize the popular masses everywhere and aid them in their own self-defense.

(7) Destroy airfields and military depots of the air force in the enemy's rear.

Chapter VI

OPERATIONS

1. *Action.*

(1) The first principle lies in careful and secret preparations, and in rapid and sudden attack. Fierce wind and heavy rain offer a favorable occasion for a guerrilla attack, as do thick fog, the darkness of night, or circumstances in which it is possible to strike at an exhausted enemy.

(2) The operations of a guerrilla unit should consist in offensive warfare. Whether its numbers be great or small, such a unit can nonetheless appear where it is not expected and, in its attacks, take advantage of the enemy's lack of preparations. But when there are indications that the situation is unfavorable, or when there is no certainty of victory, it is appropriate to withdraw rapidly, so as not to suffer damaging losses. If the attack originally planned by the guerrilla unit fails to give an advantageous result, and the enemy goes over to the offensive, a guerrilla unit should withdraw quickly. Only when the enemy pursues us, and it is impossible to evade

his attacks, can we fight a defensive action and then gradually withdraw.

2. *The use of tactics.*

(1) The redoubtable force of a guerrilla unit definitely does not depend exclusively on its own numerical strength, but on its use of sudden attacks and ambushes, so as to "cause an uproar in the east and strike in the west," appearing now here and now there, using false banners and making empty demonstrations, propagating rumors about one's own strength, etc., in order to shatter the enemy's morale and create in him a boundless terror. In addition, we must pay attention to such principles as: "The enemy advances, we retreat, the enemy retreats, we advance, the enemy halts, we harass him," camouflaged attacks, etc.

(2) A really excellent stratagem for bringing the enemy to his destruction lies in mobilizing the popular masses, in making a strong defense by emptying the countryside, in luring the enemy to penetrate our lines deeply, in cutting his communications, in placing him in a position where he has difficulties with his food supply, where his men are weary and the terrain is unfavorable —and then launching an attack.

(3) By such tactics as sudden attacks, ambushes, making a strong defense by emptying the countryside, etc., a guerrilla unit should make every effort to avoid positional warfare, and all frontal engagements. Before the local guerrilla units have received regular military training, they should not be launched against the enemy in a

regular and prolonged battle. For this reason, when local guerrilla units are first formed, they should be used only in conjunction with actions by basic or special guerrilla units. It is only after a certain period that they can act independently.

(4) If we strike at the point where the enemy feels the greatest difficulties, in order to draw his main force to come to the relief of the position, then, afterward, we send our main force somewhere else, either to attack other isolated and weak forces of the enemy or to attack his reinforcements on the march.

3. Advantageous and disadvantageous terrain.

(1) Because open terrain affords very little good cover, it is slightly disadvantageous for us when guerrilla units operate there. Covered, mountainous, or broken terrain are advantageous for us.

(2) A guerrilla unit should be thoroughly familiar with the terrain in its region of action and should think frequently about the ways in which it can appear from a place where the enemy army does not expect it, following secret and hidden routes such as valleys, forests, or narrow winding paths, so as to approach close to the enemy army and take advantage of a situation in which the enemy, persuaded he is quite secure, has taken no measures of defense whatsoever. Then, following the principle that the "thunderclap leaves no time to cover one's ears," the unit can strike sudden blows and then vanish into hiding without a trace, thus reducing the enemy to a level where he does not feel secure whether

he is withdrawing or advancing, attacking or defending, moving or remaining still, sitting or lying down.

(3) Relatively large villages, market towns, and places where there is a reasonably large amount of grain and other moveable property are frequently the objects of enemy attack and harassment. A guerrilla unit should regularly spy out the enemy's traces, and prepare an ambush so as to attack him when he is in the midst of his march.

(4) A guerrilla unit should use every method, within its area of action, to prevent the enemy's small units from entering, and his main force from concealing itself there. In case of necessity, a guerrilla unit should also strive to unmask the military strength, disposition, and plans of the enemy operating outside its area of action.

4. Seasons.

A guerrilla unit must consider the seasons (winter, summer, or autumn are suitable for operations), with reference to the strength of our forces and those of the enemy, and especially with reference to the weapons of war; it must also be thoroughly familiar with the organization of the enemy's rear. Whether or not each season is favorable to us is also determined with reference to the terrain.

5. Secret action.

The peculiar quality of the operations of a guerrilla unit lies entirely in taking the enemy by surprise. Consequently, we must take every possible measure to preserve military secrecy, as described in detail below:

(1) The commander of the unit should explain to his subordinates their tasks and the plan for the operation only just before the action begins, or while they are advancing. In case of necessity, he should explain the whole plan only by stages, so that others learn about each stage only when required.

(2) The best method for the transmission of orders in a guerrilla unit is by oral explanations from the commander to his subordinates. It is necessary to limit written orders insofar as possible, in order to avoid leakage of military secrets.

(3) One should not discuss the whole of one's actions and plans with guides or the local population. This is the case even with regard to local populations favorable to us; it is even more necessary to forbid such talk when we are about to attack a certain place.

(4) We should send out faithful and reliable scouts in advance to observe the point where we are going to camp or to lie in ambush along important roads in the enemy's rear, in order to cut off his information.

(5) When we advance, our rear guard should take full responsibility for obliterating and removing all secret signals and road signs. We should also advance by a circuitous route, so that the enemy does not know the direction of our advance.

(6) Fixed code names should be used in place of all unit designations, and the use of the real names of units should be strictly prohibited.

(7) Except in case of necessity, all documents should be burned immediately after they have been read.

(8) Apart from the methods already enumerated, the true plans of a guerrilla unit can also be obscured in certain cases by using the local population for the deliberate propagation of false information about the operations of the guerrilla unit, in order to deceive the enemy.

6. *Arrangements and preparations for movement.*

In order that our movements may be rapid, apart from doing our utmost to simplify all our organization, we should at all times maintain excellent preparations for action (investigation and intelligence regarding the front, care of sick soldiers, preparation for guides, preferably employing local peasants whose sympathies lie with the guerrillas, or other reliable persons), and we should also preferably carry three days' dry rations. If this is done, then when we want to move, we move, and when we want to stop, we stop, and there is no need for special arrangements.

7. *The conditions for victory.*

(1) A condition for the victory of a guerrilla unit is that the officers and soldiers have an absolutely courageous and resolute spirit. They must also be filled with a spirit of action in common, and be thoroughly alert and resolved to carry out their own tasks. Apart from this, they must have healthy bodies and be able to endure

boundless hardships, be good at the use of their weapons, etc.

(2) A guerrilla unit should not lose heart in difficult times, nor should it cease its activity if it encounters difficult circumstances. As regards their confidence in ultimate victory, their confidence in the success of their cause, and especially their hatred of our national enemy, such circumstances should only strengthen their purpose to advance courageously in spite of all obstacles.

8. United actions.

If a small guerrilla unit, because its numbers are insufficient, cannot carry out a task assigned to it, it can unite temporarily with a few other guerrilla units, in order to fulfill its task.

Guerrilla operations are best carried out under cover of night.

Chapter VII

SURPRISE ATTACKS

1. Points that should be carefully considered regarding our tasks before a surprise attack.

When a guerrilla unit has finished concentrating for an attack, and when plans for scouts, courier service, etc., have all been satisfactorily completed, and one is preparing a surprise attack on a certain inhabited place, the commander of the guerrilla unit must first form a clear idea about each of the following points:

(1) What is the strength of the military forces defending the given inhabited place? How are they deployed? How are they armed? What is their fighting capacity? How many scouts to sound a warning have they sent out?

(2) Is there any other enemy nearby? If there is, how far away is he? Can he quickly come to the aid of the defending forces? Can we imagine how he would come to aid them? From what direction he would come?

(3) What sort of roads are there that could be followed by the guerrillas and by the enemy? What hidden

roads are there in the vicinity of the place we intend to attack by surprise? What route will we take to get to the place we are attacking? The preceding three points are not only things we should know in view of carrying out a surprise attack; we must also not fail to consider them with reference to our withdrawal after the attack.

(4) As for fixing the time of a surprise attack, it is best to carry it out at night, for, under the cover of darkness, even if the attack should fail, it can still inspire panic in the enemy. But we can attack at night only if we are thoroughly familiar with the terrain, and have clearly understood the enemy's dispositions or have extremely good guides. Otherwise, we should choose instead to carry out such surprise attacks at daybreak. If a surprise attack is to be directed against a supply depot, it should be carried out in the dead of night, for the men, horses, and military equipment in such a depot will be on the move again very early, at daybreak.

(5) Can the population of the given inhabited place aid the enemy or not? How can we prevent the population from bringing trouble on itself in this way?

While we should think through our plans at length, we should avoid overly subtle plans.

2. Points for attention before setting out.

(1) Before setting out, a guerrilla unit should complete all its preparations for the march (see below). Moreover, it should consider taking stretchers for transporting wounded soldiers.

(2) The method for a surprise attack on the enemy should be thoroughly understood beforehand not only by the commander of the unit and the commanders of each task group, but also by all the members of each independent task group. The best mode of transmitting this information is through oral explanations by the commander and his staff. Written orders of all kinds should be held to a minimum, in order to avoid having their contents divulged by loss or mistake.

(3) Prior to setting out, all officers at every level should appoint a replacement, in order, on the one hand, to express their resolution to sacrifice themselves and, on the other hand, to avoid the risk that, if they are wounded or killed, the action of the guerrilla unit may fail to attain its objective because of them, thus influencing the whole situation.

3. Points for attention while on the move.

(1) We must make the greatest efforts to conceal the movements of a guerrilla unit and to prevent discovery by the enemy. Consequently, while advancing, we must leave the highroads and avoid large villages, and choose out-of-the-way places or even places where there are no roads at all, advancing along narrow winding trails. But we should keep away from miry roads, so as to avoid excessive fatigue.

(2) When advancing, we should not proceed for a long time on the same road, for this makes it easy for the enemy to discover our tracks. From the standpoint of

keeping our movements secret, it is also generally appropriate to move by night, even when we are advancing a long distance.

(3) When we are advancing, for the sake of concealing ourselves, we should hold the number of people we send out for reconnaissance to the very lowest level. In general, it will be sufficient to send just a few scouts along the road, but we must have very good guides.

(4) If we are not absolutely certain that there are no enemy spies coming to observe us, it is best to divide our forces into small groups, which advance separately in different directions and then concentrate at a point which has been secretly designated.

(5) When a guerrilla unit is on the move, it should be constantly prepared for a meeting with the enemy. For this reason, the commanding officer of a guerrilla unit generally advances, accompanied by his staff, just behind the scouts, behind the élite soldiers, or ahead of the staff of the unit (the staff is entrusted to the leadership of the second in command). Thus, it is easy to obtain a clear picture of the situation, and decisions can be taken very rapidly. If the commander sees that it is possible to advance, he advances; if he becomes aware of difficulties, he withdraws. All that is required is for two or three officers to hold a discussion, and then the decision can be made. Thus, we avoid sending orders back and forth, with the consequent wasting of opportunities, and we diminish command from the rear, and its attendant evil of taking action not in keeping with the circumstances.

(6) Apart from the scouts sent out along the road, the soldiers of the guerrilla unit should not load their rifles, so as to avoid accidental discharges during the march and discovery by the enemy.

4. *Measures to be taken if the enemy is encountered while on the march.*

(1) Under no circumstances should a guerrilla unit provoke a pointless battle before it has reached its objective. Even though a guerrilla unit may encounter the enemy in the course of its march, it should devise a way for getting around him—if necessary, departing from the original plan. If there is no way of avoiding battle, we should emerge from ambush, after rapid preparations, so as to appear where the enemy does not expect us and annihilate him by a surprise attack. At the same time, when we are carrying out such a maneuver, we should pay attention to whether the enemy halts or advances, and send out scouts to reconnoiter from all directions. If the enemy army is not prepared for battle or if, although he is in some strength, he is not on the alert, we should charge him immediately. Otherwise, we should remain in hiding and quietly await an opportunity.

(2) When, in the course of our march, we encounter enemy outposts or scouts, we should avoid being seen by them and circle past them in strict silence. But if we encounter a situation in which we judge there is an opportunity to be grasped, we should act rapidly and capture them without firing a shot.

5. *Disposition of troops during a surprise attack.*

When a guerrilla unit carries out a surprise attack, the disposition of its troops should be more or less as follows:

(1) We should launch a fierce attack by our main force on the point in the enemy's disposition where it hurts the most—a really swift and resolute sudden blow. We should also send another force around to carry out energetic action on the enemy's flanks and in his rear, in order to confuse his judgment, and prevent him from fathoming where our main force is located.

(2) We should attack one point in the enemy's disposition with all our might, but we should also carry out feigned deployments in other places and make an empty demonstration with a few scattered soldiers, so as to confuse the enemy's eyes and ears, and disperse his forces.

(3) If we can determine beforehand the enemy's line of retreat, then we should, within the limits of what is possible, send a part of our forces to intercept him. If the enemy has his heavy artillery and logistic supply installed outside the village, then we should designate a special small group to seize them.

(4) If the guerrilla unit is numerically strong, it should be divided into several columns and should carry out the attack from two, three, or several directions, attempting to cut off the enemy's retreat. But we should consider the matter thoroughly, so as to avoid causing confusion in our own ranks, which might result in erroneously taking our own troops for those of the enemy. Because

of this possibility, it is necessary, in advance of the action, to agree on signals.

(5) In the case of a surprise attack on the enemy, if there is reason to fear that enemy reinforcements may arrive from a certain direction, we should send a small body of troops in advance of the action to the route where the reinforcements may arrive, so as to obstruct their advance, or report this peril to the main force.

(6) At the time of a surprise attack, the choice of the point on which the brunt of the attack will fall, and the geographical distribution of our forces (in general, two-thirds of our men are used for the principal direction of attack, and only one-third for the auxiliary directions of attack) must absolutely be such as to prevent the enemy forces from spreading out or receiving reinforcements and to make it possible for us to smash them one by one.

(7) The various task groups making up a guerrilla unit should divide their forces within a very short distance of the point where the attack is to be made, and from there make a separate but coordinated advance. The best place for this is the point from which the charge will be made. In this way, we can avoid such misfortunes as losing our way, or the premature division of our forces, and we can also guard against the danger of surprise attacks by the enemy. For the farther apart are the various independent columns or groups, the more likely they are to be separated by the terrain, and the more difficult it will be to expect them all to strike at the same moment.

6. *The success of a surprise attack.*

In general, we charge the enemy when he is not prepared, in circumstances where he is frightened and flustered. If we really want to strike when the enemy is not expecting us and attain success, the following points should be attended to:

(1) We must act rapidly and secretly and not allow our plans to be revealed prematurely.

(2) We must strike at a time when the enemy's warning system is not very alert.

(3) We must make an empty display, and attack in several places at once, so that the enemy's reaction is confused, his forces are frightened and hamper one another, and he cannot use all his strength to resist us stubbornly.

(4) In carrying out the surprise attack, we must attack at the appointed hours; there must be no noise; no shots must be fired; there must be no battle cries. We must make every soldier understand the use of the arms employed in a surprise attack, which are the bayonet and the hand grenade. We must not return fire simply because we hear the gunfire of the enemy. It is only when we have an opportunity to take advantage of the situation to attack the enemy that we should launch our attack, with our vanguard well supported by our rear guard, choosing frontal, flanking, or direct blows.

7. *Dispositions following the success of a surprise attack.*

(1) As soon as the tasks of a surprise attack have been carried out, a guerrilla unit should rapidly withdraw.

Before withdrawing, it is best to go a few li, in a false direction, and then afterward turn and go in our true direction, so that the enemy will be unable to discover our tracks, and will not be able to follow us.

(2) It is not appropriate for a guerrilla unit to take along prisoners, or to acquire large amounts of booty, which hinder our movement. It is best to require the prisoners first to hand over their weapons, and then to disperse them, or to execute them. As for booty, it should be dispatched by the local government, or by the population.

(3) During the battle, three officers and men out of every company should be given the exclusive task of picking up and gathering together abandoned rifles and ammunition. After a victorious battle, we should devote all our efforts to collecting everything on the battlefield, and we can also call upon the population of nearby areas to gather such things together, so that not the smallest trifle is left behind.

8. Dispositions following the defeat of a surprise attack.

If a surprise attack is defeated, we should rapidly withdraw to the place of assembly designated in advance. The usual assembly point is in the place where we encamped the previous night. If our forces are sufficient, we can leave a reserve unit along the designated withdrawal route, to look out for prisoners and wounded men.

Chapter VIII

ESPIONAGE

1. Points for attention when carrying out espionage.

(1) All reports on the situation should be transmitted without loss of time to one's superiors or to friendly armies.

(2) The reports which we collect absolutely must be in full detail. All sloppy and negligent reporting must be severely prohibited.

(3) The scope of espionage is not limited merely to the situation of the enemy; spies should also pay attention to the terrain. We should be informed of all aspects of the terrain that are disadvantageous to us, especially those aspects favorable to the enemy, such as narrow roads, river crossings, circuitous routes for avoiding these river crossings and narrow roads, etc.

(4) We should bend every effort to obtain complete and detailed information regarding all matters having any relation to our guerrilla unit; our efforts should never cease until we understand the situation thoroughly.

(5) We should pay attention to the sentiments of the

people toward ourselves and the enemy. Are the people actively aiding us? How is their positive attitude manifested?

2. *Methods of espionage.*

Apart from sending out courageous and intelligent individuals (i.e., spies) to carry out espionage on every hand, a guerrilla unit must unite closely with the popular masses of the place in question. Moreover, in strategically important places, we use reliable local inhabitants or those among the people who sympathize with the guerrilla unit (for example, we can make use of feudal relationships and find a relative, or someone belonging to the family of a person who has been executed by the enemy; we can also employ those among the people who hate the enemy, etc.). We give these people a relatively good salary, establish a secret espionage network, as well as a system of sentries, so that we can transmit information with facility.

3. *Espionage regarding the number of the enemy's troops, his tactical skill, and his armament.*

(1) Where are so and so many enemy infantrymen, cavalrymen, artillerymen, and other units to be found? How many armored cars and trains, tanks and airplanes does the enemy have? And where are they?

(2) What kind of defensive works does the enemy have in his front, in his rear, and around his cities and other places? What kind of forces are defending?

(3) Where are the enemy's encampments and arsenals?

(4) What about the enemy's reserves and flanking troops? Where are they?

(5) How is the morale of the enemy soldiers? Are they prepared to fight or not? What are their relations with the people and with their own officers?

(6) What about the enemy army's supplies of military equipment, bedding and clothes, food, and other items?

4. Espionage regarding the terrain.

(1) First of all, we must pay attention to the important roads within this area, as well as their direction, their width, their type of surface, whether or not they are muddy, etc., and whether or not they are suitable for use by all types of forces.

(2) Are there any forests or not? If there are, we must pay attention to the kinds of trees, and to their area.

(3) We must consider rivers, their width and depth, their rate of flow, the slope and type of soil of the banks. Are there bridges, ferries, or other means for crossing the river? If there are bridges, will they bear up under artillery, the baggage train, and other types of unit?

(4) Are there any marshes? Where? What is their area? Can they be crossed or not? If so, we must note what kinds of troops can get through them.

Chapter IX

AMBUSHES

1. Types of Ambush.

When we emerge suddenly from hiding, and strike a sudden blow at the enemy who is just passing by, this is called an ambush. The sole habitual tactic of a guerrilla unit is the ambush. By means of an ambush it is extremely easy to obtain a good result, and as a general rule they are always advantageous. Such action is divided into the following types:

(1) Ambush by luring the enemy. This occurs when our troops, so to speak, prostrate themselves and hold out both arms, enticing the enemy to penetrate deeply. It is carried out by first placing our main force in ambush along the two sides of the road, or in a hiding place on one side, and then attacking the enemy with a small force. This force then feigns defeat and withdraws, luring the enemy deep into our lines, after which the main force rushes out from one side or both sides and carries out a surprise attack.

(2) Waiting ambushes. These are very similar to am-

bushes by luring the enemy, but it is not necessary for a part of our forces to feign defeat. Instead, we establish an observation post on some height, to observe the movements of the enemy army, and when his main force has reached the appropriate point, we rush out and attack him by surprise.

2. Spots for carrying out ambushes, and objectives to be attacked.

Ambushes can be carried out against a variety of objectives such as isolated enemy soldiers, couriers, whole mobile units, logistic convoys, transport columns, trains, etc. Further details are given below.

(1) When ambushing the enemy's cavalry or infantry, we should choose a spot where they cannot use their weapons and where it is not easy for them to manifest their full strength.

(2) Ambushes against logistic convoys or transport columns should be carried out in the midst of a forest or in the countryside.

(3) Ambushes of small enemy units, or whole mobile units or motorized transport columns are most valuable. But we must first understand their plans, the direction in which they are advancing, and the time it will take them to pass. We must also reflect in detail on the location for the ambush and carefully seek out a place likely to contribute to a favorable result. At the same time, we must carefully select in advance the route for our own withdrawal.

(4) When a guerrilla unit carries out an ambush against a railroad train, our forces can be split into three parts. The first part should take up battle positions near the railroad, to guard against resistance from the train. The second part should take up a position on the two sides of the train, and shoot into the carriages. The third part has the task of charging and boarding the train to make a search, unloading the cargo, taking charge of the weapons, etc.

3. *The terrain in ambushes.*

The point at which an ambush is carried out must have the following features:

(1) It must have good cover, in order to prevent our being observed by the enemy and, at the same time, permit us to observe the enemy.

(2) It must permit us to employ our maximum fire power.

(3) It must allow us to leap out rapidly at one bound from ambush and come to grips with the enemy. Hence, between the point where we lie in ambush and the enemy, there should be a dense forest, a damp depression, a narrow road, or some other intervening ground.

4. *The distance from which an ambush should be carried out.*

If the guerrilla unit which carries out a surprise attack is in sufficient strength so that it wants to come to grips with the enemy at one bound, then it should stage its ambush near the side of the road. If, on the other hand, the enemy is in considerable strength, and our plan is merely to harass him and cause confusion, then we should remain in a place some distance from the road.

5. *Important tricks for an ambush.*

(1) An ambush can most advantageously be carried out in silence. Whether by day or night, loud talking should be absolutely forbidden, as should patrolling along the front.

(2) Remaining a long time in ambush can easily lead to discovery of our plans and an increase in the danger. Because of remaining too long in ambush, the state of tension of our men is gradually weakened, and they can no longer maintain their vigilance. Hence, one can easily be discovered by the enemy. A point that especially merits attention is that, if we have already been discovered by the enemy, we should immediately either launch our attack or withdraw.

Chapter X

SURPRISE ATTACKS ON THE ENEMY'S FORAGING UNITS

1. Occasions for surprise attacks.

A charge against the enemy's foraging units should be carried out under the following circumstances:

(1) It can be executed when the enemy unit is nearing a village.

(2) We can wait until the enemy enters a village and has scattered in all directions to forage from door to door, and then carry it out.

(3) We can wait until the enemy has finished foraging and is returning loaded with booty, and then attack by surprise from ambush.

(4) Which of the above types of attack is most appropriate should be determined with reference to the circumstances, by the persons who are responsible for the guerrilla unit. They should carefully evaluate all the factors and make arrangements adapted to circumstances.

2. Surprise attacks in a village.

It is most advantageous to attack the enemy's foraging units in a village. At such a time the greater part of the enemy's foraging unit is scattered all over the place, and it is not easy for them to gather together quickly. But, in carrying out this type of surprise attack, we must steal by the enemy's warning outposts or capture his sentinels without the slightest sound; only then can we make our attack.

3. Surprise attacks outside a village.

If the force carrying out a surprise attack is especially weak, it must wait until the foraging is completed and until the foraging column has reached a place favorable to a surprise attack—such as when it is passing through a forest, across a bridge, or along a narrow road—before attacking.

4. The objectives of the surprise attack.

When a guerrilla unit has attacked and dispersed the enemy unit covering a foraging operation, it can reckon only that it has completed part of its attack. It must also destroy or capture all of their wagons. Consequently, the guerrilla unit should first engage the enemy covering unit in combat and then attack the logistic convoy with its main force and capture it.

5. Points to which the guerrilla unit should pay attention.

It is easy to obtain the assistance of the local population when attacking one of the enemy's foraging units. Hence, within the limits of what is possible, part of the property seized should be given to the popular masses, to heighten their courage.

Chapter XI

SURPRISE ATTACKS ON THE ENEMY'S TRANSPORT UNITS

An attack on a transport column is one of the most advantageous forms of action for a guerrilla unit, since we can obtain in this manner the weapons, food, and supplies we need.

1. Sudden surprise attacks.

With such attacks, we can frighten the enemy out of his wits, and precipitate him into a state of complete confusion. The coolies of the transport units are, in large part, timid peasants forcibly impressed. Moreover, the size of the covering force is limited, and it is generally spread out over a very long distance. If we overturn one of the wagons, we can make all the wagons behind it stop too.

2. Methods of attack.

(1) The guerrilla unit must not forget that its task is not to defeat the enemy, but to capture the enemy's

wagons. Consequently, we should detail only a part of our forces to do battle with the enemy's covering unit. The rest of our men should be ordered to plunder, pursue, and demolish the materials he is transporting. Hence, whenever we carry out such a surprise attack, we should do our best to contrive matters so as to open fire rapidly against the transport unit and cause them to stop, in order to increase their confusion and fear.

(2) In order to stop the whole transport column, it is only necessary to shoot at the front part of it, because, under conditions of mass anxiety and bewilderment, when the wagons in front stop, they will interfere with one another, fall over on the side of the road, and bring about a situation of extreme confusion. If there are a large number of transport wagons, and if, because the front of the column is under fire, the wagons at the rear endeavor to turn around and escape, the guerrilla unit should send out a small number of riflemen to shoot furiously from cover at the tail end of the column, so that it does not dare turn around.

(3) If the unit carrying out the surprise attack is in an inferior position, and the covering unit is taking active precautionary measures, the guerrilla unit should exhaust the enemy by incessant false alarms, and then, when the transport column is passing through a forest or valley or along a narrow road in some other type of terrain, where the enemy's logistic convoy cannot easily turn around, the attack should be swiftly carried out.

It is not often advantageous to carry out a surprise attack on a baggage train in a village, for the covering unit and the logistic convoy can easily make use of the houses and other cover, and offer strong resistance.

(4) If the covering unit has already been dispersed by our attack, the resistance of the transport unit has also been overcome, and enemy reinforcements cannot arrive in time, the guerrilla unit can then destroy the wagons and the goods they are carrying or destroy completely whatever the guerrillas cannot carry away or have no use for.

Chapter XII

THE CORRESPONDENCE NETWORK OF A GUERRILLA UNIT AND THE DESTRUCTION OF COMMUNICATIONS FACILITIES IN THE REAR

1. *The object of the network.*

So that they may be able to call upon one another for aid and receive information at all times regarding the situation of the enemy, guerrilla units should do their utmost to maintain the closest and most solid relations with the local population for the exchange of correspondence.

2. *Means for maintaining relations.*

In order to set up such a correspondence network, we should, in addition to utilizing the telephone in the greatest possible measure, employ all means at hand. These include runners, messengers on horseback, messengers on bicycles, secret couriers posted in advance for transmitting information, as well as transmittal by sentries, and even signals and pre-established signs, etc.

3. *Methods for transmitting reports.*

(1) A network for important correspondence should be set up. Reports of an urgent character can best be transmitted by messengers on horseback. When this is impossible, we should send out reliable individuals particularly good at going on foot. It is also possible to arrange in advance for the transmittal of secret letters. There are times, too, when we must send out several men, each of them taking a different route, to make certain that the report in question will reach its destination. (This method should be limited to the most important reports.)

(2) As for ordinary reports that are not particularly important, they are commonly transmitted by runners or messengers on bicycles. There are times when one can also use faithful individuals from among the local population who are thoroughly familiar with the routes to carry such reports.

4. *Signals for communications.*

For the sake of convenience in guiding each guerrilla group or unit by day or by night, in its actions in mountainous terrain or in forests, the commander of a guerrilla unit should establish in advance a certain number of basic signals and signs (such as signal fires at night, smoke signals by day, colored pennants, flags, semaphore signaling by flags, paper signals, whistles, bugle calls, etc.).

5. Dispositions regarding routes of communication in the rear.

Should we or should we not destroy the routes of communication in the enemy's rear? We must reflect in detail about this problem. If we conclude that, in the future, our own army will not need to utilize these roads, or will not be able to utilize them, then we can destroy them.

6. Points for attention in destroying routes of communication.

If we want to destroy routes of communication, we must be thoroughly familiar with the terrain. It is only then that, moving rapidly and elusively, we appear suddenly and quickly withdraw. In eliminating the enemy's sentries, we must not fire a shot, in order not to alert them and give them a chance to flee.

7. Precautions when beginning the destruction of routes of communication.

When we begin the destruction of routes of communication, we must first send out a detachment to the place where the presence of the enemy has been reported, in order to keep an eye on the enemy's patrols and his small detachments, so that they cannot quickly and secretly get close to the point where our own unit is at work. If, while beginning work, we are discovered by the enemy, we should shoot at him to keep him from coming nearer.

8. *Methods for destroying works on the ground.*

(1) Railroads should be destroyed at the points where they are most difficult to repair, such as at curves, at points where the railway is hidden from view, where the enemy's precautions are lax, where we can work under cover, or where we can destroy a large length of track. When destroying the rails, we should bend them, or hollow out the ground beneath them. In low-lying places we should dig ditches. As for tunnels, we should obstruct them.

(2) Railroad ties, wooden bridges, telegraph and telephone poles, etc., should be burned up. Wires should be carried away or dropped into the water.

(3) Signals, switches, semaphores, railroad carriages, etc., located in the stations should be destroyed, preferably by blowing them up with explosives.

(4) In destroying cobblestone roads, highways, bridges, and other constructions, we must in all cases choose a method of destruction appropriate to the nature of the construction.

Chapter XIII

REGULAR HIDING PLACES AND PRECAUTIONS TO BE TAKEN WHEN WE HALT

1. Marshaling our troops.

The problem is not merely one of resting and marshaling our troops. We require a place that can also be used for conserving ammunition and food and for receiving and looking after wounded and sick soldiers. Hence, the place in question commonly serves also as a supporting point in time of battle. As soon as we are the objects of the enemy's pursuit and attack, we withdraw there, and secretly hide, so as to await an opportunity to act or to begin resisting the enemy again.

2. The choice of a spot.

(1) A hiding place where we can rest for a long time may conveniently be found deep in the forest, in a thatched hut near a marsh, in a cave under the ground or in a mountainside, on a lonely farm, or in a small and secluded hamlet. Because of the sympathy it enjoys, a small guerrilla unit normally has no difficulty at all in finding a regular hiding place.

(2) A guerrilla unit must absolutely maintain the strictest secrecy regarding the hiding places it has selected. Even one's closest friends and relatives must not be informed if they have no connection with the guerrilla unit in question. If our original hiding place has been discovered by the enemy, then, in general, we should not wait for the enemy to come and attack us but must quickly remove elsewhere.

(3) Sometimes such hiding places also serve as storehouses for military equipment, powder, and provisions, and also for receiving wounded and sick soldiers. More often, a separate secret location in the vicinity of the hiding place is selected for each type of storehouse because there are people continually going in and out of a hiding place and it can very easily be discovered by the enemy.

(4) The more individuals there are among the people who support the guerrillas, so that the guerrilla unit can also maintain a communications network among the people, the easier it is for the guerrilla unit to find a hiding place. There are times when, in order to evade the enemy's pursuit and attack, and find a good place to hide, a given guerrilla unit must be split up, each of its members being obliged to find a way to hide himself in one of the houses of the local population. In such circumstances, the local population is the only hope of salvation of the members of the guerrilla unit.

3. *The question of provisions.*

In places where the local population is hostile to the guerrillas, there is no alternative to foraging backed by

force, but one should send reliable people from among
the detachment, in order to guard against pillaging.

When the guerrilla unit does not fear discovery, it can
send out a special small unit to forage for food, to collect
contributions of food, or to demand food supplies from
the local authorities.

4. Changing one's halting place.

The best method by which a guerrilla unit can maintain its own security is through the agility of its action.
In case of necessity, the unit can make a habit of changing its halting place every night (if, during the day, it
has been in village A, at twilight it moves to village B).

5. Occupying a halting place.

When a guerrilla unit encamps, the arrangement of its
forces should be determined entirely by the nature of
its action, but it should not occupy a large village that its
own forces are insufficient to hold. If a guerrilla unit
cannot do otherwise, and finds itself in such a place, it
should occupy only a few collective dwellings situated
apart and convenient for defense. The best thing is to be
located in a village where one can keep a lookout in
all directions, especially on the road along which the
enemy might come. We must absolutely not disperse the
members of the unit to stay in different houses, acting,
for the sake of individual convenience, in a way of
which the enemy could take advantage. In order to keep
the enemy from knowing where we are staying, the best
method is to enter the village only late at night. More-

over, we should look about carefully on all sides of the village and not allow anyone at all to come out.

6. *The degree of precautions.*

In order to avoid excessive fatigue to the members of a guerrilla unit, and to assure them of a real rest, it is not necessary to send out large numbers of scouts to sound a warning. It suffices to arrange for military outposts and concealed scouts in all adjoining places and along all roads (those which the enemy must take, or those related to us). We should also send out spies to places from 2 to 4 li away. This distance will be sufficient.

Whether or not the enemy attacks us, we must always fix an assembly point at a distance of from 10 to 16 li, for use in case of withdrawal. Moreover, the roads leading to the assembly point should be designated and marked in advance (but there must be at least two roads giving access to such a place).

7. *Preparations.*

When a guerrilla unit is staying in a place, all its members, whether they be officers or soldiers, must at all times take measures to prepare for battle. Especially after twilight, every officer and soldier must gather together the arms and other equipment he carries with him, and arrange them in proper order, so that it will be convenient, in case there is an alarm in the dark, for him to go out quickly and meet the attack.

8. When there is anxiety about a surprise attack by the enemy.

(1) If the guerrilla unit itself is especially alert, if its intelligence network is organized with exceptional discretion, and if the people of the area are in sympathy with us, so that they regularly report all movements to us, then it is extremely difficult for the enemy to mount sudden surprise attacks. But whatever the circumstances may be, we must always exercise due caution.

(2) In order to prevent the enemy relying on a hostile population from coming and making a surprise attack on us, we must take special precautionary measures. Thus, by methods of intimidation we warn the local population, we arrest and detain people. But at the same time, the unit must exercise caution and be prepared.

(3) If there is an alarm, we should assemble the whole unit in a building that has been prepared for defense. We should dispatch to this building advance sentries and observers as required. The entrance to the building should be closed by movable obstacles, and we should establish in advance signals for the defense. Weapons and other equipment should be properly prepared and placed within reach of each man.

(4) When circumstances are extremely critical, part of a friendly unit should take over responsibility for the security of our position and the place in which our army is staying, as well as for sending out spies far and wide to add to the warning system. They report constantly to

the guerrilla task group on the situation of nearby enemy forces.

(5) When we use artificial obstacles to block the roads, we must make provision for communication with our first line and reserves, as well as with the local population and our correspondence network.

(6) In case of necessity, the roads within villages can be completely blocked off, or we can leave a way through. Whenever possible, each guerrilla task group should have a prepared position.

9. Dispositions in case of an enemy surprise attack.

(1) When we discover that the enemy is moving toward us, if we find out from reconnaissance that he is not in strength, we should annihilate him with one sudden blow. If the enemy forces are several times more numerous than ours, we should rapidly withdraw. But while we are withdrawing we should give the enemy a false impression of the direction in which we are moving, so as to conceal our actual route of withdrawal.

(2) If the enemy attacks us by surprise and we do not succeed in evading him, we should exploit in full measure the advantages of a village for defensive action, resist him firmly, and then later take advantage of an opportunity to withdraw.

(3) If we have already lost a village, we should reply by a counterattack or counterblows in order to take it back quickly and save our captured comrades, or those comrades who are clinging to a position and defending it

stubbornly to the death. If our action is rapid, we can always attain such objectives, because after a victory the enemy is often in great confusion and lax in his precautions.

(4) The best occasion for carrying out such counterblows, or such a counteroffensive, is just after the victory of the enemy's surprise attack. The sacrifices of a charge under such circumstances are less than those from running away, or from stopping and giving battle in unfavorable terrain following the enemy's attack.

Chapter XIV

TRAINING

1. *The scope of training.*

Training is not limited to the military arts; we must also pay attention to political training, to the literacy movement, to training in hygiene, etc. Consequently, when a guerrilla unit is engaged in drill, literacy training should represent an appropriate part of the whole, and can be given in all places and at all times.

For the purpose of achieving a full and satisfactory result from all the kinds of training carried out in a guerrilla unit, we must increase the will to study on their own initiative among the officers and soldiers. Apart from the political aspect, and in addition to increasing political consciousness, we must also promote amusements for the army, mitigate a painful and tedious existence, assist the people in their own self-defense, and cause the armed force of the popular masses to unite closely with us.

2. *Training in all subjects.*

The consequence of training in all subjects, though it is difficult to reduce it to uniformity, is, as regards methods in general, to proceed from the superficial to the profound, first the broad and then the rigorous, from the simple and easy to the complex and difficult, first the partial and then the universal. In all fields, one must demonstrate one's theories by concrete experience, so as to strengthen the students' confidence.

3. Cultivating the people's capacity for self-defense.

The most pressing and most important task of a guerrilla unit is to carry out guerrilla attacks without ceasing in the places occupied by the enemy, to seize and kill all traitors and reactionaries, and to protect the popular masses. At the same time, a guerrilla unit must investigate the concrete offenses of the enemy and use every possible method to discover and smash his tricks and plots. Therefore:

(1) It is advantageous to make known our good government, to make great efforts to unite with the popular masses, and to support the forces of the popular masses. Such actions can also be carried out on the territory of the enemy. We should also use every possible method and devote all our strength to encourage the people to imitate our own actions, stimulate them to fight the enemy actively, and guide their combat.

(2) Our action in supporting the people's capacity for self-defense should be of long duration, and not ephemeral. We must do the best we can to let people know that, at all times, a guerrilla unit struggles and sacrifices itself for the popular masses and, even in the

case of the most dangerous crisis, will absolutely not harm the popular masses. If the local population meets with a defeat in its first military action, after we have drawn it into the war, its spirit of struggle will necessarily be dissipated to some extent. When the masses falter in this way, we must devise a way to rouse their enthusiasm and to bring their spirit of struggle to a high level once more.

(3) A guerrilla unit constitutes the most conscious and advanced segment of the people. Hence, they should first unite those among the popular masses who are dissatisfied with the enemy and who accept the leadership of those we send among them. We must also aid the people to establish plans, to get arms, and to establish liaison and mutual assistance with mass organizations in neighboring villages and even in other cities that are victims of the enemy's oppression. But, in carrying out all such work, we must maintain the strictest secrecy.

4. Training in hygiene.

(1) In order to strengthen its own fighting capacity, every mess unit should designate one or two soldiers as nurses, to treat the ailments of the officers and soldiers when they arise and, also, to explain the rudiments of hygiene, as well as to assist, direct, supervise, and encourage all matters of hygiene in the unit.

(2) Replenishing stocks of medicines is an extremely difficult matter in a guerrilla unit. Hence we should, in accordance with the seasons, etc., prepare certain medi-

cines especially for emergency care, and other normally indispensable medicines. As regards wounded and seriously ill members of the unit, when there is no alternative, they are entrusted to fellow soldiers with some slight medical knowledge or to local inhabitants sympathetic to us.

5. Military training.

Military training all relates to the enemy army. Its purpose is to create greater skill than that of the enemy in each specialized art.

(1) Subjects. The items requiring particular attention are dispersing, assembling, marksmanship, maneuvering an army, mountain climbing, construction of military works, night fighting, mountain fighting, fighting on narrow roads, espionage and security measures, searches, liaison, and other such actions.

(2) Methods. In carrying out military instruction, particular attention should be paid to all methods of teaching and explanation, which should be more or less as described below:

a. For theoretical instruction, one can employ the method of giving suggestions and the method of questions and answers. All methods of teaching that adopt the style of speechmaking and injecting [ideas into the students' heads] should be eliminated in so far as possible.

b. When explaining actions, we should pay attention to linking our talks with the living reality, so that it will be easy for the soldiers to understand us.

c. We should devote more time to concrete demonstrations of actions and less time to talking about empty theories. Consequently, the greatest effort should be made to diminish the duration and number of classroom sessions, and the number of practical exercises should be increased.

d. All explanations in the classroom should in so far as possible correspond to the exercises outside.

e. All demonstrations of actions should be carefully prepared in advance before they are executed. All negligent and perfunctory behavior—doing things any old way—must absolutely be eliminated.

f. With respect to all activities, we should devise a way to incite the officers and soldiers to carry out a competition, in order to increase the spirit of initiative and the positive attitude they manifest in their work, and to speed up the work.

g. Increase applied training, diminish training according to a fixed pattern, and correct the erroneous idea that training according to a fixed pattern is useful in maintaining military discipline.

h. The plan of training should be suited to the circumstances, time, and place in which it is to be carried out. The training plan must absolutely not be rigid; we must seize every occasion and strive to give training adapted to the circumstances. This is done more or less as indicated below:

(i) We utilize the time when the army is on the march to carry on direction finding, recognizing differences in terrain, estimating distances, reconnaissance action, and designating objectives and the utilization of terrain.

(ii) When we are in camp, we utilize preparations for security measures in order to carry out exercises in all kinds of observation and precautions, beginning with the role of advanced sentries. We also provide training in construction of military works.

(iii) We utilize the opportunity provided by a battle, and before setting out or before the fighting begins, we explain, on the basis of the tasks we have been ordered to perform, such forms of action as ambushes, surprise attacks, main attacks, and supporting attacks, etc.

(iv) We utilize the opportunity, when we are awaiting the moment for action, to explain in practical terms how we resist the charges of the enemy, as well as shooting and other such military actions.

(v) We utilize post-battle exposition and criticism (such exposition and criticism should be based on a minute investigation of the facts, carried out beforehand) to point out the strengths and weaknesses in our actions during the battle and what was appropriate and inappropriate in the individual commands, thus giving a concrete lesson to all officers and men.

(vi) We utilize the time offered by morning and evening roll calls to give various kinds of talks.

(vii) We utilize the occasion offered by the recreation period to put on games, dances, and modern-style plays, having military significance, thus imperceptibly increasing the officers' and soldiers' desire to correct themselves, and increasing their willingness to follow good examples.

(viii) We utilize each occasion of reward and punishment to carry out thorough propaganda among the officers and soldiers, in order to increase the soldiers' sense of achievement and their shame in doing evil, and thus, little by little, fostering a good military discipline.

6. Political training.

In order to assure that all the independent actions of a guerrilla unit attain complete victory, apart from reinforcing military training, the most important thing is that we must make certain that the officers and soldiers have a high level of "political consciousness" and of "devotion" to their own cause. Political training is the only method by which this objective can be attained. Its content is described in detail later on.

7. The literacy movement.

In order to increase the cultural level of the officers and soldiers, so that they may more easily absorb all kinds of training, each mess unit must carry out literacy training. The methods are as follows:

(1) The "A" class includes all those who know about fifty characters.

(2) The "B" class includes those who know about twenty characters.

(3) The "C" class includes those who know no characters at all.

(4) The teachers of the various classes consist of those in the unit with a relatively high cultural level.

(5) When we halt, there should be an hour each day devoted to the study of characters. When we are on the march, we can carry out instruction either while moving or during rest periods. In such training, the important thing is regularity rather than speed. In general, if the soldiers learn two words a day, it is excellent.

Chapter XV

POLITICAL WORK

1. The aim of the political work of a guerrilla unit.

This aim lies in strengthening and raising to a higher level the fighting capacity of each member of the unit. The fighting capacity of a guerrilla unit is not determined exclusively by military arts, but depends above all on political consciousness, political influence, setting in motion the broad popular masses, disintegrating the enemy army, and inducing the broad popular masses to accept our leadership. All the plans of a guerrilla unit, whether they be political, military, or of any other nature, are all directed toward this single end.

2. The main content of political work.

We must carry out political instruction directed toward the resurrection of our people (stimulate the soldiers' national consciousness, their patriotism, and their love for the people and for the masses) and see to it that every officer and soldier in a guerrilla unit understands not only the national tasks for which he is responsible but also the necessity of fighting in defense of our state.

We must also pay attention to supporting the leaders, to maintaining the solidarity of the unit with real sincerity, to carrying out to the end the orders of one's superiors, and to maintaining an iron military discipline. We must see to it that the multitude of the soldiers are of a single mind and endowed with the resolve and the will to save our country together.

Apart from strengthening its own fighting capacity, a guerrilla unit must also carry out propaganda among the masses regarding the plots of the invaders and of the enemy.

3. Discussions in small groups.

These are excellent activities to unite our wills, to strengthen confidence, and to proclaim our doctrine.

(1) We collect the views of all the comrades, in order to avoid feelings of alienation and to achieve the effect of gathering together ideas and obtaining greater advantage.

(2) By training the cadres, we increase their capacity for work and give them more practice in techniques for holding meetings and in methods of speaking. We will also be able to solve problems more quickly, investigate the past, and transform the future.

(3) We can thus verify the fellowship existing among the members of the unit, and draw new comrades into the party.

(4) This method is convenient for training, and makes it possible to understand completely each comrade's circumstances, capacity, and knowledge.

(5) According to their character, these activities can be divided into discussion meetings, review meetings, and criticism meetings.

4. Methods.

Before the meeting we must prepare for it. These preparations consist in informing the members of the group, establishing the essential subject matter of the discussion, and, at the same time, reporting to the next higher echelon.

(1) As regards the number of participants, from three to five represents the optimum.

(2) One should not be bound by any rigid pattern. Discussion meetings can be held at all times and in all places.

(3) As for the time limit, it is not desirable that the meetings should last too long. One hour is the maximum permissible.

(4) It is appropriate to hold one meeting a week. The order of procedure consists in a report by the chairman, discussion of the report by the participants, and a conclusion entrusted to the leader of the group. The record of the meeting should indicate in detail the name of the chairman, the subjects of discussion, the number of those present and absent, and the place where the meeting was held.

(5) Not more than two problems at most should be discussed. The discussion should have as its starting point the individual problems of the participants.

(6) As for the manner of speaking, it is appropriate that the remarks of the participants should deal with essentials and be simple and clear. They should be systematic and not repetitive. They should be persuasive in content and presented in a friendly and agreeable manner. In answering questions, one should avoid any hint of mockery and pay attention to what the others say. At the same time, one should arrive at a decision concerning the topic discussed.

(7) As regards the leader of the group, his report should be simple. He should not give a long and repetitive presentation but seize the occasion to induce the participants to speak.

(8) The conclusion should follow the inductive method. It should include a criticism of the whole of the discussions. If there are dissident conclusions, they may also be expressed.

5. Carrying out political work.

One should not merely rely on a few political workers. The best thing is to be able to attract and train conscious elements, or interested officers and soldiers, to participate in the work and to train the whole personnel of the unit so that they can all carry on effective political work.

6. Types of political work.

In broad terms, political work can be divided into three categories according to whether it is carried out in ordinary times, during battle, or after a battle. As for propaganda destined to encourage the troops, the various aspects are as indicated below:

(1) Political work in ordinary times. We intensify political training in order to raise the level of political consciousness, create unity in thought, word, and deed, maintain an iron military discipline, and unite closely with the popular masses. The methods are roughly as follows:

a. We must really put into practice the principles of not disturbing or harming the people (such as "Pay fairly for what you buy," "Speak politely," "Return everything you borrow," and "Pay for anything you damage").*

b. At all times and in all places, aid the popular masses and help them to solve their difficulties (for example, help the popular masses to gather the harvest or to cultivate their land and send our army doctors to prevent epidemics or treat the people's ailments, or to enquire after people who have suffered difficulties and devise methods to aid them), maintain the unity of the army and the people, and encourage the spirit of sharing both good fortune and adversity together.

c. Chat frequently with the popular masses and let them know about our military discipline and our affec-

---

* These are the first four of the "Eight Points for Attention," which governed the behavior of Red Army men from the time of the civil war against the Kuomintang in the middle 1930's down to the final victory in 1949. For the revised version of the "Three Main Rules of Discipline" and the "Eight Points for Attention," see *Selected Works*, IV, 155–56.

tion for them, and also learn in detail about the hunger and suffering among the people.

d. Frequently hold joint entertainment sessions for the soldiers and the people, so as to smooth over any feelings of alienation between the army and the people and increase the affection of the army and the people for one another.

(2) Resolving any feelings of alienation between the lower and higher ranks of officers and soldiers. The methods employed are roughly as follows:

a. Persons engaged in political training, apart from sharing the good fortune and adversity of the soldiers, should also frequently chat with the soldiers, carefully investigate all their deep griefs and report their problems at all times to their superior officers, and devise methods for improving the situation.

b. As regards all the opinions of higher and lower ranks, we should take our stand on a position of pure rational knowledge, convince them by an attitude of sincere entreaty, and explain things to them. We must make absolutely certain that higher and lower ranks unite solidly as one man, and we must strengthen their capacity to unite.

c. With respect to soldiers who violate discipline, we should use educational methods to persuade them. All corporal punishment and insults must absolutely be reduced.

d. We should frequently hold meetings at which officers and soldiers can enjoy themselves together, in order to heighten the affection between officers and soldiers.

(3) Augmenting the officers' and soldiers' hatred of the enemy, and increasing their resolve to fight to the death to kill the enemy. Increasing the common hatred of the enemy is an important factor in strengthening the soldiers' morale. Consequently, a guerrilla unit should pay particular attention to all the atrocities of the enemy, and to all the instances in which he massacres our army or our people, and carry out propaganda generally among the army regarding these atrocities, so as to heighten the courage of the officers and soldiers to fight to the death and harden their resolve to fight the enemy to the death, since either we or they must perish.

(4) Strengthening confidence in the inevitable victory of our war against the enemy. The methods are more or less as follows:

a. We must frequently avail ourselves of the tales of the glorious feats of arms in our past, in order to carry out propaganda among our officers and soldiers and inspire them.

b. We put forward examples of the enemy's defects (such as difficulties, collapses, and other problems that he has recently encountered), in order to demonstrate that in the end the enemy must be defeated.

c. We must put forward examples of our own strong points (such as the support of the popular masses, transmission of information, familiarity with the terrain) and the present victorious circumstances, in order to demonstrate that we must ultimately triumph.

d. By exposing the clever tricks habitually used by

the enemy, we make known the points to which our army should pay particular attention, in order to prevent the emergence of a mentality of fearing or underestimating the enemy.

After we have suffered an attack, we sink for a time into a situation characterized by difficulties and painful effort, and as a consequence we underestimate ourselves, exaggerate the enemy's strength, and lose our confidence in victory.

7. *Political work in time of battle.*

Political work before we set out is carried on as described below.

(1) The commander in chief of the unit first calls a meeting of the cadres. He explains in what respects the existing political situation is favorable to us, as well as the conditions of victory and the significance of the battle. He also explains the methods and points for attention in attaining our goal, but without infringing military secrecy.

(2) On the basis of the meeting of the cadres, the political training section immediately calls meetings of political workers at all levels, at which the essential points and the methods of propaganda are explained and concrete tasks are assigned.

(3) The various groups immediately call meetings of all the officers and soldiers, at which, in addition to reporting on the current political situation and the guarantees of our victory, conditions for competition are also put forward. ("He who is lightly wounded should not

leave the firing line, he who is seriously wounded should not cry out in pain"; "Let us see who can hand in the most weapons"; or "Let us see who can take the most prisoners.") At the same time, tasks are distributed to all political workers and activists (supervision, leadership, or propaganda).

(4) Political workers should be sent to the local population to gather them together, call meetings, and give talks, inspiring them to participate in the battle or to join the ranks of the porters or the transport units. As regards the organizations of the popular masses, we should guide them in methods of calling meetings, of fighting, and of preparing mobilization.

(5) After the battle has begun, the most important political training workers should be sent to inspire the units responsible for the main attack or for particularly important actions. The less important political training workers should be sent to inspire the less important fighting units.

(6) Propaganda units and groups of singers and dancers (all composed of lively and lovable boys in uniform and attractive clothing) should be sent in advance to positions along the side of the roads where the army will advance, to give short talks, sing, dance, or shout slogans, so as to inspire the maximum of courage in the officers and soldiers.

8. Political work after the battle has begun.

(1) After the battle has begun, we should pay attention to calling out slogans to the soldiers of the other

side, so as to dissipate their morale. This is one of the forms taken by our work of sabotage.

(2) When the situation on the battlefield enters the stage of an encounter at close range or from positions arrayed opposite one another, we devise a method for holding a joint meeting with the soldiers of the opposite side and take advantage of this opportunity to give them food, in order to gladden their hearts. After this, we carry on more propaganda work, which must be prepared in advance.

(3) After the battle has begun, we must assuredly carry out propaganda directed toward those outside our army. It is even more important to inspire those within our army. The methods for this work are diverse and are determined primarily by what is adapted to the circumstances. For example:

a. On the attack:

(i) When we suffer a surprise attack by the enemy while advancing to attack, we should give an explanation such as the following: "Comrades! Airplanes cannot decide a battle. We must seize this opportunity, advance rapidly, and quickly come to grips with the enemy on the ground. Charge the enemy with your bayonets!"

(ii) When firing begins, we should encourage the soldiers in the following terms: "Comrades! Don't shoot at random, shoot only when you have taken careful aim. We must try to kill an enemy with every bullet."

(iii) When we are near the enemy and are about to charge, the method for inspiring the soldiers is as follows: "Comrades! The time to dispose of the enemy has come. We shall pay no attention to sacrifice, we shall summon up our courage, defeat the enemy and annihilate him. Let our victory inspire the whole army! Forward quickly! Charge!"

(iv) When the first charge is repelled and we charge a second time, we should encourage the soldiers as follows: "Comrades! We are an invincible iron army, we are a mighty unit victorious in every battle, we are absolutely resolved to destroy this enemy and preserve our glorious reputation."

(v) When officers are wounded or killed in battle, we should exhort the troops as follows: "Comrades! Our officers (So-and-so) and (So-and-so) have already sacrificed themselves gloriously. Let us tread in their bloody footsteps, complete their task, and annihilate the enemy before us. Let us go and avenge them!"

(vi) If the enemy shows signs of wavering, we should exhort the soldiers as follows: "Comrades! The enemy is wavering. Charge quickly and capture his commander in chief alive!"

(vii) When we pursue the enemy, we should exhort the soldiers as follows: "Comrades! The enemy has retreated. Pursue him quickly! Charge and smash the enemy's holding units, finish off his main force, annihilate his whole force. Let us see who can hand in the most arms, and who can take the most prisoners. To win a battle and not to pursue the enemy is a great pity."

b. On the defense:

(i) When the order has been received, we should carry out propaganda as follows: "Comrades! The enemy has arrived. This is the best opportunity to annihilate the enemy. Make skillful use of natural obstacles, and shoot with *sang-froid*. The more of the enemy we kill and wound, the easier it will be for our main attack to progress and obtain results."

(ii) When the enemy charges, we should exhort the troops as follows: "Comrades! The enemy is about to charge. Fix your bayonets, and prepare your hand grenades. Let us summon up our awe-inspiring reputation, preserve the glory we have already won, and annihilate the enemy in front of our position."

(iii) When we are surrounded by the enemy, we should exhort the soldiers as follows: "Comrades! We are an ever-victorious unit. We are a courageous and invincible iron army. We will wage a bloody battle to the end for our people and our country, shed our last drop of blood, hold onto our rifles to the death, and die rather than surrender. To hand over one's rifle is suicide, to surrender is the supreme shame. Let us smash their lines at one point and break through."

(iv) At the time of the counterattack or when the order to go over to the offensive is received: "Comrades! We are counterattacking. Let us take away the enemy's rifles, let us capture the enemy officers, let us see who is most courageous!"

(v) Propaganda when we retreat: "Comrades! Let us keep our movements secret and baffle the enemy in his calculations. Let us open wide our arms and lure the enemy to penetrate deep. Do not break ranks, do not fall behind, do not waver, do not succumb to panic, do not fear sacrifice, execute resolutely to the end the orders of your superiors. Final victory will be ours!"

(vi) When we cover the withdrawal of our forces, the methods for exhorting them are similar to those indicated above.

9. Political work following a battle.

After the battle has been concluded, political work continues.

(1) In order to avoid the appearance of attitudes of slighting the enemy or fearing the enemy, we should pay attention to the following points:

a. We should correctly point out the causes of victory and defeat. We must not become puffed up because of a small victory; still less can we lose our confidence in victory because of a small setback.

b. We must establish the attitude that should be adopted henceforth, or the points requiring attention.

(2) We should collect materials and anecdotes concerning our victory, as well as the names of units, individual officers, and soldiers who have fought courageously. We should then use these materials to compose propaganda outlines, songs, dances, old- and new-style plays, etc.

(3) We should print large numbers of victory announcements and slogans and stick them up everywhere.

At the same time, we should organize a roving propaganda unit, which spreads out toward areas established in advance, to carry out propaganda and to call the popular masses together and hold meetings to celebrate the victory.

(4) When meetings are held to celebrate the victory, one should pay attention to the following points:

a. Report on the significance of the victory, and the tasks now before us, as well as the concrete methods to be employed to carry out these tasks.

b. Report on units that have fought courageously, as well as individual officers and soldiers. As for officers and soldiers wounded or killed, one can select the most valuable among them and report about them.

c. Put on new versions of classic plays, as well as songs and dances.

While the reports indicated under a and b above are being delivered, or the play is being put on, the units participating in such a meeting should shout out slogans in accompaniment. We should also bring up the methods for providing pensions to the members of the families of the soldiers killed in battle.

Moreover, we should bring together the prisoners and the booty in the sight of the masses, thus further increasing the courage and the spirit of struggle of our soldiers and of the people.

(5) At meetings to celebrate the victory, all organizations should also launch a consolation movement. The main points for attention in this respect are:

a. As regards material consolation, the important

thing is not the quantity, but the significance; it is not the elegance and refinement of the items given, but their utility. Such things as straw sandals, face towels, pigs, sheep, chickens, and ducks are all suitable for this purpose.

b. In case there is a lack of goods for material consolation, consolation in the form of honors should be used. For example, one can make flags for presentation, or compose songs in memory of the fallen, or issue an order of the day in their praise.

c. Following a small victory, there should be no large-scale consolation. Consolation should be carried out only if we can devise means for doing it in a place near the battlefield.

(6) We should praise examples of combined operations, autonomous actions, and the resolute application of orders. Thus:

a. When there are those who, in the course of a fierce battle, have achieved victory by combined operations, autonomous action, and the resolute execution of orders, the maximum effort should be made to publicize the fact and to praise them. Those who have the misfortune to be defeated in similar circumstances should also be praised.

b. When there is punishment for those who, in order to preserve their own forces, fail to advance, or fail to carry out their tasks energetically, thus bringing about the defeat of another unit of our army, the case should also be the object of large-scale propaganda within the unit. In this way we give a lesson to the officers and soldiers of the whole unit, or of other units, and make them afraid to commit similar offenses.

10. *Work pertaining to clubs and amusement rooms.*

By virtue of the fact that it compensates for a painful and tedious existence in the army, this is also a way of preventing desertion. The essentials regarding the organization and work of clubs are dealt with below.

(1) Rules regarding organization.

a. In order to promote entertainment in the army, compensate for a tedious existence, increase interest in our work, and inspire a taste for study, each mess unit within a guerrilla unit should organize an amusement room. This should be divided into a military section, a guerrilla section, and a physical culture section. Each officer and soldier in the mess unit should choose one of these sections, in accordance with his own nature; he can, if he wishes, participate in two or three of the sections.

b. One person from among the company commanders or the particularly energetic and capable platoon commanders should be chosen to be responsible for the amusement room. Each of the three sections should have a section head, chosen at a meeting of the members of the section, for a period of six months, with the possibility of being chosen to succeed himself.

c. Each week there should be one meeting of the section heads and one meeting of the members of each section. A meeting of the leaders should be held once a month. It is called separately by the chairman of the section heads.

d. In its work, the amusement room should follow the guidance of the club of the next higher echelon. It is also subject to the supervision and guidance of the commanding officer of the unit. In military affairs, it is absolutely subordinate to the commanding officer of the unit.

e. In order to guide and unify the work of the various amusement rooms, a guerrilla battalion should establish a club. This club should have a chairman and a secretary who are responsible for all its activities.

f. The club should be attached to the political training section, because the work of the amusement rooms constitutes a kind of political training. If there is no political training section, the club is directly subordinated to the commanding officer.

g. The work of the club consists in guiding and promoting the work of the various amusement rooms. Consequently, each week there should be a meeting of the responsible heads of the various amusement rooms, and each month we should call a meeting of all the officers and soldiers or a meeting of the army and the people together.

All the work of both the clubs and amusement rooms should have as its principle not to interfere with military administration, military training, or military action.

(2) The essentials of the work of clubs and amusement rooms.

a. The work of the military section consists in

furthering a spirit of independent study among the officers and soldiers, in discussion of military questions, or in the mutual rectification of the actions of the members, in order to remedy the lacks and insufficiencies of military training. Its content is as indicated below.

(i) Bayonet section (practice, taking a hypothetical enemy country* as the object).

(ii) Grenade section (throwing a wooden hand grenade at a target).

b. Guerrilla section.

(i) Taking aim from a fixed support.

(ii) Checking one's aim.

(iii) Carriage while shooting.

(iv) Investigations when setting out.

(v) Utilization of obstacles.

(vi) Shooting at various types of objectives in the field.

(3) Physical culture section. The work of this section lies in strengthening the bodies of the officers and soldiers. It can also remedy insufficiencies in military training. Its contents is as follows:

a. Ball playing (basketball, football, volley ball, tennis, baseball, etc.).

b. Track and field sports (high jump, broad jump, races, obstacle courses).

c. Boxing and swordplay.

(4) Entertainment section. The work of this section consists in providing amusement for the members of the

* Presumably, the meaning here is to use a dummy dressed as a soldier of the country in question.—ED.

army, in compensating for a tedious existence, and in increasing the soldiers' interest in their work and their taste for study.

a. Joke section. This section can carry on its activities at any time at all, but attention should be paid to the following points:

(i) When jokes are told, we must make them easy to understand. We can take materials from joke books and such, but they should not be too obscene.

(ii) When telling stories, we should devote much time to stories about the abundant exploits and great enterprises of the ancients, and to their excellent words and admirable conduct, in order to achieve an inspirational effect.

(iii) When reporting on the news, we should devote attention to our own victories and to the atrocities of the enemy.

b. Theatrical section. This section utilizes rest periods, both in the evenings and during the day, to put on all sorts of new-style plays, traditional operas, comedy teams, story-tellers with drums, etc.—performances that have political content and are at the same time amusing, in order to improve morale.

c. Song and dance section. In accordance with the circumstances in which the unit finds itself and the nature of its tasks, this section composes all sorts of songs, in order to stimulate the interest of the officers and soldiers in singing songs, or it puts on dances in costume, assuming various comical attitudes, in order to make the onlookers laugh until they hold their sides.

d. Music section. This is divided into violin, harmonica, guitar and other groups, which can accompany the plays and dances.

e. The methods of work of all sections should be adapted to the time and circumstances. They should be employed in a lively manner, and on no account in a wooden fashion.

f. The work of all sections should be subject to strict control and supervision. We should also use methods of competition to induce all the officers and soldiers to make spontaneous efforts.

g. All kinds of songs and old and new plays, etc.

h. For the benefit of the work, all groups and sections should have specialized talents.

i. The officers and soldiers who participate in these performances should be excused from their other duties.

LOUIS NAPOLEON
AND THE SECOND EMPIRE

LOUIS NAPOLEON

AND

THE SECOND EMPIRE

by

J. M. THOMPSON

F.B.A., F.R.HIST.S.

HONORARY FELLOW OF ST. MARY MAGDALEN
COLLEGE

THE NOONDAY PRESS, *New York, 1955*

PRINTED IN THE UNITED STATES OF AMERICA

PREFACE

I WAS led on from the Revolution and Napoleon to Louis Napoleon and the Second Empire because it seemed to me that the Restoration monarchies of 1815-48, however different in temper, formed together an interlude in post-revolutionary French history; whereas the Second Empire was the direct sequel of the First Empire, and the natural transition from the First to the Third Republic. Natural, not inevitable; for if Louis Napoleon had not been there in 1848 to claim the Bonapartist succession — and the only one of his family fit to do so — the Party of Order might have succumbed, and a period of anarchy might have been followed by another posthumous Monarchy or another premature Republic. So much seemed clear; but I had no fixed idea either of the developments of French public opinion after 1848, or of the part played by Louis himself during the eighteen years of his ascendancy. I have tried to present the evidence under both these heads, as it came to me, and without any wish to force conclusions upon the reader. The historian cannot remain unopinioned, but he always hopes for readers who will form their own views: he is a judge instructing a jury: the verdict is theirs.

If I have relied more than usual upon indirect evidence, it is because Louis, after he became Emperor, talked little and wrote less: there are few historical characters about whom observation counts for so much, and experiment (if the word may be allowed) for so little. If I have seemed to rely overmuch on English authorities, that may be excused by the importance which Louis always attached to his friendship with our country, which so often entertained him in exile, and where he kept so many friends. I might have spent the rest of my life accumulating more evidence from these and other sources — here a little and there a little — but there must always be an end to this kind of retouching: so I let the picture go as an impression, the best that I can hope to produce now, of a fascinating but puzzling character. I only wish that Mr. F. A. Simpson had not found it necessary to say that he cannot now finish the two volumes needed to complete the work he began so well thirty-four years ago.

I must thank Mr. Ivor Guest for the help that his book *Napoleon III in England* has given me, and for the photograph which appears as the frontispiece; and Sir Richard Graham for the drawing of Louis on horseback. I regret that Mr. Hales' *Pio Nono* and Mr. Mack Smith's *Cavour and Garibaldi* appeared after Chapter VII was in print.

J. M. T.

CONTENTS

CONTENTS

ILLUSTRATIONS

THE HEIR (1808-1831)

Remember thee!
Ay, thou poor ghost, while memory holds a seat
In this distracted globe. Remember thee!
Yea, from the table of my memory
I'll wipe away all trivial fond records,
All saws of books, all forms, all pressures past,
That youth and observation copied there;
And thy commandment all alone shall live
Within the book and volume of my brain,
Unmix'd with baser matter.

Hamlet, I, v

I

The place; No. 17 rue Cérutti (now Lafitte), Paris: the time; the night of April 20th-21st, 1808.

THE family, the country, and the continent into which Louis Napoleon was born were dominated by a single will: that of his uncle, the Emperor Napoleon. Nine years ago the Corsican exile had made himself master of Paris. Four years ago he had been crowned Emperor of the French people. In less than ten years, by efficient autocracy and a series of military successes, he had ordered France, Italy, the Netherlands, and western Germany under his rule, and had dictated terms to Prussia, Austria, and Russia. His code of law, his economic system, his garrisons and officials, his ambassadors and spies were in action all over Europe. There was hardly a man, from general to merchant, from bishop to statesman, who must not consider, before he made a decision, what Napoleon would think of it; or, more probably, what he should do in view of some decision that Napoleon had already made. For without any question the Emperor held the initiative: his was the master mind.

Napoleon's seven brothers and sisters called him *Sire* and *Votre Majesté*. Joseph was King of Naples, and would soon be King of Spain. Louis was King of Holland, Jérôme King of Westphalia. Elisa and Pauline became Princesses, Caroline a Queen. Only Lucien refused the obedience that could have earned a crown. Napoleon dictated their marriages, their divorces, and the names of their children. They had to come when and where he summoned them, and could not travel without his leave. In return they had wealth, palaces, and flattery; but all just so long as his favour might

I

last, or his fortune hold. *Nouveaux riches* and *nouveaux royales*, they were unsure of themselves, shallow-rooted in an alien soil, and without traditions amongst some of the oldest aristocracies in Europe. When Napoleon made himself Emperor the Bonapartes became a dynasty, and quarrelled over his succession. They were already jealous of the Beauharnais — the Empress Joséphine, her son Eugène, and her daughter Hortense; and soon became doubly so, because Hortense's sons by Louis, Napoléon-Charles (1802) and Napoléon-Louis (1804), were the only male Bonapartes of the next generation in the line of succession; for Joseph Bonaparte had only daughters, and Charles-Lucien, son of Lucien Bonaparte, and Jérôme, son of Jérôme Bonaparte, were excluded, with their fathers, because their mothers were commoners.

When Hortense's third son, Louis-Napoléon, was born (1808) he stood fourth in the line of succession after his uncle Joseph, his father Louis, and his elder brother Napoléon-Louis: for his eldest brother, Napoléon-Charles, had died the year before (May 5th, 1807): but within less than three years the birth of Napoleon's legitimate son, the King of Rome (March 20th, 1811), made it unlikely that Louis' branch of the family would be needed to supply a successor; and the abdication of 1815, followed by fifteen years' reign of the restored Bourbons and eighteen of the Orleanist Louis-Philippe, might seem to end all hope of another Napoleonic Empire. Yet for thirty years Louis stubbornly believed that he was destined to fulfil his uncle's last dream at St. Helena, and took as omens of it every event that brought him nearer to that goal: the deaths of Napoleon (1821), of Napoléon-Louis (1831), of the King of Rome (1832), of Joseph Bonaparte (1844), and of his father Louis (1846); till in 1848 he remained the only legitimate heir of Bonapartism.

During these years Louis was formulating in his own mind, and using for dynastic propaganda, a view of the Napoleonic Empire not unlike that which the Emperor himself had tentatively adopted in the *acte additionnel* of 1815, and had elaborated in his conversations at St. Helena — a view which might still make a military dictatorship acceptable to a generation tired of war and demanding a constitution. This new Napoleonism was to be based on popular suffrage; it was to take form in liberal institutions; it was to stand for international peace; it would uphold the right of each people to choose

2

its own government and mind its own affairs. All this was, of course, bad history: the actual Empire had not been at all like that. But it was good propaganda. The common people lives by faith, not facts: its religions are based on myths. Louis' instinct was right when he founded his appeal to France upon a legendary, not a historical Napoleon.

It would be a mistake to suppose that he did not know what he was doing, and why he was doing it. Thirty years of dull peace, political corruption, and middle-class prosperity had produced a state of mind ready to forget all the harm that Napoleon had done and to remember only his benefits; to regret times when life at home was more exciting, and the country more respected abroad; to lament lost territories, forgetting who had lost them, and to sigh for *la gloire*, without remembering at what a cost it had been won. Indeed – and here was the inner power of Louis' appeal – the benefits had been real: life under the Empire, if more dangerous, had also been more invigorating; *la gloire* might mean suffering and death, but it added to the stature of common humanity. The Napoleonic legend was not a mere travesty of history: it was the prose of Napoleon's career turned into poetry, fiction made out of fact; and in appealing to it Louis was relying not merely upon what was false in it, but also, and even more, upon what was true. He remembered as well as any of his family or friends what it had meant to be dependent upon the Emperor's will, and to live under the Imperial regime. He had no illusions as to the real character and aims of that hard, exacting, yet popular autocracy. And in recalling personal memories he was also appealing to national experience. France for better or worse was so deeply marked with fifteen years of that one man's rule that it had not been able to accommodate itself to any other; and it would be ready, almost at the mere name of Napoleon, whilst clutching at a myth, to fall back into a way of life so well adapted to its traditions and temperament.

'The mere name of Napoleon': would that be enough? How long would the legend hold, without a Man to sustain it? Had Louis the intelligence, the character, the power of will to reimpose his uncle's regime upon a country (let alone a continent) that had changed as much as every society must change after a period of revolution and war? How far and for how long the adventure succeeded; when and why it failed: that is the story of Louis Napoleon and the Second Empire.

2

Of all the royal marriages that Napoleon devised to enlarge his dynasty and secure his succession that of Louis and Hortense seemed to be the most advantageous, and turned out to be the most unhappy. Louis, the fourth of the Bonaparte brothers, was a queer-tempered, morose, invalidish man of twenty-four, with a taste for literature: Hortense, Joséphine's daughter, was nineteen, a bright attractive girl, fond of dancing, music, and acting, a great favourite of her step-father Napoleon. It seemed both to him and to her mother a fine idea to make her a link between the Bonapartes and the Beauharnais, and perhaps the mother of a new line of heirs to the throne. She was not in love with Louis, and he did not want to marry: but they could not withstand the Emperor's will, and were made man and wife by the Papal Legate, Cardinal Caprara, on January 4th, 1802. On October 10th the same year their first son was born, and named Napoléon-Charles; on October 11th, 1804, a second son, named Napoléon-Louis. By this time everyone knew that the marriage was a failure. Louis neglected his wife, disliked her girlish tastes, sus-pected her friendships, and spied on her at every turn. She pined for Paris and Malmaison, and resented his Puritanical discipline. Whilst Napoleon protected her, and blamed his brother, Joseph and Lucien Bonaparte, aided by Caroline Murat, spread rumours of her mis-behaviour, and did their best to break up the marriage. A recon-ciliation was patched up when in June 1806 Louis became King of Holland; but that autumn Hortense spent with her mother at Mayence, and when she returned to Holland Louis' treatment of her was such that Napoleon, from the depths of Poland (he was living at Finkenstein with his mistress Marie Walewska) dispatched one of his most stinging rebukes. 'Your quarrels with the Queen (he said) are becoming public property. If only you would keep for family life the fatherly and effeminate disposition you exhibit in the sphere of government, and apply to public affairs the severity that you display at home! You drill your young wife like a regiment of soldiers . . . You have the best and worthiest wife in the world, and yet you are making her unhappy. Let her dance as much as she likes: she is just the age for it . . . Do you expect a wife of twenty, who sees her life slipping away, and dreams of all she is missing, to live in a nunnery or a nursery, with nothing to do but bath her baby? . . . Make Hortense happy — she is the mother of your child-

4

ren. The only way is to treat her with all possible trust and respect. It's a pity she is so virtuous: if you were married to a flirt, she would lead you by the nose. But she is proud to be your wife, and is pained and repelled by the mere idea that you may be thinking poorly of her.'[1]

Louis, who also had his grievances, replied that Napoleon had been listening to court gossip, for which the French ambassador at the Hague was chiefly to blame, and said that his jealous watch on his wife was due to affection — as indeed, in such a neurotic and religious nature, it may well have been.[2] Within a fortnight the marriage was put to a supreme test: the eldest son, Napoléon-Charles, was taken ill and died. Hortense was distracted with grief, and Louis shocked into a temporary solicitude. Napoleon covered his disappointment at the loss of an heir with easy exhortations to be calm and cheerful: 'They tell me (he wrote to Hortense) you have lost interest in life, and are indifferent to everything. That is not as it should be, and not what you promised me. Your son was all you cared for? What about your mother and myself?'[3] But he agreed that a change of scene would do her good, and sanctioned a holiday in the Cauterets district of the Pyrenees, where Barèges and Bagnères-de-Bigorre had been frequented as watering-places since the fifteenth century: were they not visited by Montaigne, Froissart, Henri IV, and Madame de Maintenon? Louis followed Hortense (he had tried a cure at Barèges before his marriage), and they were together at Cauterets from June 23rd to July 6th. There followed a month during which Hortense and her friends carried through a round of excursions, ending with the well-known mountain route from Cauterets to Gavarnie by the Lac de Gaube and the Col de Vignemale, even now a ten hours' affair ('guide advisable'), and at that time thought impossible for a woman. On August 12th Hortense rejoined her husband at Toulouse: she had worked off her sorrow and recovered her health. It was an affectionate reunion: *Je me jettai dans vos bras*, Louis wrote afterwards; and in a letter to her brother Eugène ten days later Hortense said: 'I am with the King, and we are getting on well together. I don't know whether it will last, but I hope so, for he wants to treat me better, and you know I have never deserved ill treatment.'[4]

This episode has been given in more detail than it might seem to deserve because of its bearing on the birth of Hortense's third son, Louis-Napoléon, on April 21st, 1808. Apparently for no better

reason than that this date fell less than nine months after Louis and Hortense came together again at Toulouse, the gossip which had never spared Hortense discovered a reason for accusing her of misconduct with one or another of her companions during the holiday in the Pyrenees. Louis himself, in later moments of suspicion, would assert that Louis-Napoléon was not his son. The matter is not unimportant, because it makes a considerable difference to one's estimate of Louis' character whether he was a Bonaparte as well as a Beauharnais, and in one's judgment of his career whether Bonapartism was an idea that he adopted or an inheritance that he could not avoid.

The temporary reconciliation at Toulouse did not last. When Louis returned to the Hague in September, Hortense, who was now with child, refused to go with him, and insisted on remaining in Paris till its birth the following April. Louis' grievances against his wife were not made easier to bear by a double disagreement with Napoleon: he refused to accept the crown of Spain, and he insisted upon ruling Holland in his own way. Another letter from the Emperor reproaching him with his treatment of his wife (August 17th, 1808) seemed to his suspicious mind a proof that Hortense was plotting against the family, and drove him to the extreme measure of disowning her. 'Madame, (he wrote on August 29th) our unhappy quarrels have been the cause of all my family troubles . . . My only consolation is to live away from you, to have nothing to do with you and nothing to expect of you . . . Adieu, Madame . . . Adieu for ever.' Nothing came of this move at the moment; but later in the year he visited Paris (but not his wife) to ask Napoleon's approval of a separation, with an allowance for Hortense, and his own custody of the elder child. The question was put to a family council at the Tuileries on December 24th, 1809, ten days after a similar gathering had sanctioned Joséphine's divorce, and Louis' request was refused: one divorce was sufficiently damaging to the Imperial prestige. For two months in the following year (April 11th-June 1st, 1810) Hortense tried once more to live with her husband, now at Amsterdam; but the Dutch climate and the King's conduct drove her away again, for a cure at Plombières. A month later Louis, harassed by Napoleon's criticisms and demands, abdicated the Dutch throne, and fled to Toplitz in Bohemia, appointing Hortense Regent for her elder son. When she asked Napoleon what she should do, he replied that he intended to annex Holland to France, and that she

was now free to live quietly in Paris, where he arranged that she should enjoy a settlement of £100,000.

She saw no more of her husband for three years. The later part of that summer she spent at Aix-les-Bains with Charles de Flahaut, the romantic soldier son of Talleyrand and Mme de Souza; and the next year gave birth under mysterious circumstances (the only date known is that of the registration of birth, October 22nd, 1811), to his son, Charles-August-Louis-Joseph 'Demorny'. The Duc de Morny was thus just seven months younger than the King of Rome, and three and a half years younger than Louis-Napoléon. This proof, as he might well take it to be, of his suspicions of Hortense no doubt induced Louis to make a fresh claim for the possession of his elder son. It came before the courts in January 1815. The case was decided in his favour; but before the three months' time-limit was up the return of Napoleon from Elba enabled Hortense to take the boy with her during the Hundred Days, and during her flight from Paris: he was not handed over to Louis' emissaries till October 1815.

A year later Louis made another attempt to secure an ecclesiastical annulment of his marriage, but received so little encouragement from the family, whose influence was by this time powerful at Rome, that he once more gave up the attempt. Finally in 1817 an arrangement was reached by which Louis made over to Hortense a sum of money, and allowed the elder boy to visit her at Augsburg. Though they never lived together again, they were on friendly terms during Hortense's winter visits to Rome between 1822 and 1831, and remained nominally husband and wife till Hortense died in 1837. But this reconciliation, for what it was worth, came too late to efface the impression of an estrangement which had lasted from the time of Louis-Napoléon's birth till his fourteenth year. He knew of his father only as an enemy during the most sensitive time of his life, and became, more than was good for any growing boy, his mother's pet, a partisan in a family quarrel, and with only half a home.[5]

3

The young Louis inherited his father's moodiness and his mother's manners. 'He was a charming child,' says Hortense Lacroix, 'as gentle as a lamb, affectionate, caressing, generous (he would even give away his clothes to anyone in need), witty, quick in repartee, and with the sensibility of a girl; but easily puzzled,

and intellectually lazy ... He had not a trace of arrogance, and would throw himself unreservedly into the arms of the first person he met, overwhelming him with caresses beyond rhyme or reason, so that people said he must have a warm and loving heart. But there was nothing in it: he forgot you as soon as you were out of his sight.'⁶ He was always a dreamy child, sensitive to passing impressions, but with unfathomed depths of reserve. When his brother said he wanted to be a soldier, Louis declared his ambition was to sell flowers, like the boy at the door of the Tuileries. His grandmother, Joséphine, who loved her garden, made a favourite of him: his first tutor, the abbé Bertrand, allowed him to shirk his lessons: and his mother's friends could refuse him nothing when 'his light blue lacklustre eyes turned on them with a look of kindness and goodwill'.⁷

Louis had his father's eyes, and as he grew up lost the slight resemblance to Napoleon that could be seen in his infancy: this failure to inherit the Napoleonic features — especially when contrasted with his cousins Jérôme and Mathilde — was to prove a stumbling-block to his early career. But it is too easily assumed that the Emperor Napoleon's was the typical Bonaparte face. Louis Bonaparte was not much like him, nor were Louis and Hortense's other sons. It is the evidence of Hortense Lacroix, who was brought up with him, and knew him perhaps better than anyone else, that Louis 'had many little bodily tricks resembling his father', which she believed to have been inherited, not acquired. She at least would not hear a word of his supposed illegitimacy.⁸

Louis' resident father, during his early childhood, was his uncle the Emperor, and his homes were the palaces where his mother was always a welcome guest, almost a second hostess. When Napoleon was away from Paris, she had a town house in the rue Cérutti and a country seat at Saint-Leu. When he was at home she was never long absent from the Tuileries, St. Cloud, Fontainebleau, or Malmaison. But during the later years of the Empire these periods became less frequent and less prolonged; for Napoleon was at home about 140 weeks out of six years — a good deal less than half the time — and only twice during the summer. Add that these periods were given up not only to constant business, but also to public functions, reviews, hunting, visits to the opera, dinners, and dances; so that there was not much time left for the quiet home life which royalty appreciates in proportion to its rarity. Louis-Napoléon would be

too young to remember more, perhaps, than the impression of a sleek, tubby, talkative little man, who took him on his knee, lifting him alarmingly by his head — a man with a menacing eye, and a habit of shouting, behind closed doors, at ministers or ambassadors. It was the rule that Hortense and her children should dine once a week at the Tuileries, when the Emperor would make them sit at the table, and tell them stories from La Fontaine, between conversations with the actors, architects, or officials who might have business to do with him. But this meant putting on their best clothes and their best manners; and no doubt they were happier running wild in the gardens of Malmaison or Saint-Leu.[9]

Napoléon-Charles, though only two at the time, played a part in the great coronation scene in Nôtre Dame in 1804; but Louis-Napoléon can have known little of the stirring events of his first five years — at home the divorce of Joséphine, the marriage with Marie-Louise, the birth of the King of Rome; abroad the Austrian campaign of 1808, the Erfurt Congress of 1809, the invasion of Russia in 1812, and the German campaign of 1813. But two stories cannot be quite discredited. When the Tsar Alexander was in Paris in 1814 he spent much time in company with Hortense, whose obligations to Napoleon did not prevent her setting her cap at his conqueror. Young Louis, aged six, was so grateful for this kindness to his mother that during one of his visits 'the little fellow sidled up to him and quietly placed on one of the Tsar's fingers a ring which his uncle Prince Eugène, the Viceroy of Italy, had given him. The boy, on being asked by his mother what he meant by this, said "I have only this ring, which my uncle gave me; but I have given it to the Emperor Alexander, because he has been so kind to you, dear Mamma." The autocrat smiled, and placing the gift on his watch-chain, said he would never part with it, but would keep it in remembrance of the noble trait of generosity shown by one so young'.[10]

The other story appears in Persigny's propagandist *Lettres de Londres* (1840), and therefore at least bears Louis' *imprimatur*. It is that on the eve of Napoleon's departure for the Waterloo campaign of 1815, when he was saying goodbye to Hortense, the boy exclaimed, 'Sire, I don't want you to go to the war: those wicked Allies will kill you!' The Emperor is said to have turned to Soult, who was with him, with the words 'Embrace the child, Marshal: he has a good heart. Perhaps one day he will be the hope of my race.'[11]

4

Carefully as she had played her cards in 1814, Hortense was over-whelmed by the disaster of 1815. At the first news of Napoleon's landing in France she was suspected of having worked for him: she had in fact been intriguing, perhaps with Fouché, for the return of Marie-Louise and 'Napoleon II' from Austria, and her brother Eugène's appointment as *Lieutenant-général* of the Empire. The knowledge of this ingratitude for his kindness lost her the friendship of the Tsar, without reconciling the Emperor to her flirtations with the Allies, and it was only old affection, and family feeling, which kept her by Napoleon during the days before and after Waterloo; most of all, perhaps, the memory of her mother, for Joséphine had died at Malmaison on May 29th, 1814. It was here, before starting on June 29th, 1815, for his last journey into exile, that Napoleon said goodbye to Hortense and her two sons, as well as to his illegitimate children by Marie Walewska and Eléonore Denuelle. She never saw him again. But she was vowed to the cult of his memory; and in the mind of the boy of seven who was with her he was already beginning to shine as the patron saint of a Second Empire.

Louis may not have known of the Tsar's refusal to answer his mother's letters, or of the order issued (July 17th) for her expulsion from Paris: but he must have remembered the flight to Dijon and Geneva; then, again expelled, to Aix-les-Bains, where (early in October) his elder brother was claimed and taken away by his father, and then by Morat, Berne, and Zürich to Constance (December 7th), which was to be his home for the next twenty years. For after a residence at Augsburg, Hortense purchased (January 11th, 1817) a country house called Arenenberg overlooking the 'lower lake' between Constance and the Falls of the Rhine; and there in 1820 she settled down, like Napoleon at Longwood, to commemorate the First Empire, and to prepare her son for the Second.[12]

Louis' education falls into three stages: 1817-19 (aet. 9-11), when he was at Augsburg or in Italy, with the abbé Bertrand as tutor; 1820-23 (aet. 12-15) which he spent under the intensive tuition of Le Bas at Augsburg and Arenenberg; and 1823-27 (aet. 15-19) when Le Bas' tuition was broken off and finally ended by visits to Marien-bad and to Italy, and Louis began to educate himself.

'Every man', wrote Louis at thirty-one, 'is the slave of the

memories of childhood. He obeys all his life, without question, the impressions he received when he was a boy, the trials and influences which he had to face.'[13] 'You are right', he told his friend of childhood, Hortense Lacroix, a few years later, 'in saying that childhood and youth are two great saints canonized by death: but allow me to add that the people one knew during the first years of life are like the precious relics of these great saints, and share their atmosphere of affection and adoration.'[14] The grandest figure of all these, to every member of the Bonaparte family, was of course Napoleon: his memory overshadowed Louis all his life. 'How can pygmies like ourselves', he wrote to his cousin Jérôme in 1865, 'really appreciate at its full worth the great historical figure of Napoléon? It is as though we stood before a colossal statue, the form of which we are unable to grasp as a whole.'[15] But there were the lesser saints of his childhood: his mother and her friends, his brother Napoléon-Louis, Hortense Lacroix, his tutors, and more than one old servant of the family.

His mother Hortense, *toute femme* like Joséphine, with a full share of the Beauharnais charm and *insouciance*, had been deserted by her husband and deprived of her elder (his favourite) son. It is not surprising that she consoled herself with a lover (Flahaut), surrounded herself with friends (especially such as could flatter her taste for music and painting), and spoilt her remaining (and favourite) child. Not that this was difficult. Spoiling implies a tendency to be spoilt; and Louis had always been a docile, sentimental little boy, almost girlish in his ways, with his mother's looks and moral likenesses; temperamentally lazy and self-indulgent, but capable of heroic moods and adventurous decisions; he would never be a wilful man, like the great Napoleon, who insisted that his 'star' had led him in the direction he intended to go, but a sleep-walker, who believed that he was fated to follow the ghost of Napoleon wherever it might lead. Hortense, the prize pupil of Saint-Germain and the spoilt favourite of Malmaison, living on memories of the 'good old days' against a background of family portraits and Napoleonic relics, inevitably filled the boy's mind with day-dreams, in which regret for lost glories mixed with hopes for their restoration. Such feelings would be strengthened by the visits of his uncle Eugène, who soon settled near Arenenberg, and of Charles de Flahaut, himself a fellow-soldier and admirer of Napoleon, as well as by the presence of Hortense's series of companions – Louise Cochelet,

Elisa de Courtin, and Valérie Masuyer. When Mlle Cochelet in 1822 married Colonel Parquin, a soldier of the Grand Army, and they settled down close by, his battle-stories brought to life the Napoleonic relics which filled the show-cases of Arenenberg.[16] There were old servants of his mother, too, with whom Louis kept in touch all his life, such as the Mme Guibout to whom he sent 200 francs when he was in prison in 1842, or Florenton, his mother's coachman in 1815, who was still in his service in 1857.[17] Above all, there was Hortense Lacroix, the daughter of his mother's *femme-de-chambre*, born a year after Louis, and brought up with him; for her mother was an ambitious woman, who gave the girl an education above her station, and started her on a literary career which won her a reputation as an art critic, and when she died, a eulogy from the pen of Ernest Renan. Louis loved her as a sister — he had no other: they were together at Arenenberg; she was *en pension* at Augsburg when he attended the *Gymnasium* there; and she was with Hortense for some years before her marriage to the artist Sébastien Cornu took her out of his life. Louis had not seen her for twelve years before his imprisonment, which brought them together again, in 1840. Their friendship was, as his letters make plain, an attraction of like minds but opposite temperaments. 'I wish you were a man!' he exclaims: 'you understand things so well, and, details apart, I think as you do.' But in twelve years he has passed through more than a century of experiences which she cannot share;[18] and she has a patient and persistent application which she can instil into his writing of a *Manuel d'Artillerie* and a *Life of Caesar*, but not into his political career.

As to Louis' tutors, the influence of the abbé Bertrand, who held that position till 1819, was by common consent negligible, or worse. The boy's father, who would not have disapproved of the abbé on religious grounds, insisted, when he had discovered the facts, that Louis must have a new tutor; and Le Bas, as soon as he was appointed, reported that though his pupil had a good head and heart, he was backward, ignorant, lazy, and with a dislike for working (*dégout complet pour l'étude*); at twelve years of age, he might be no more than seven.[19]

5

The tutorship of Philippe Le Bas needs more serious consideration than it has generally been given. He was the son of the Jacobin

and regicide friend of Robespierre and Saint-Just, and of Elisabeth, the younger daughter of Robespierre's friend and landlord Duplay; he was born within a few days of his father's suicide at the Hôtel de Ville (July 27th, 1794), and spent his early weeks with his mother in prison. When she was released she made a living as a laundress, and succeeded in giving her son a good education. He served in the Napoleonic navy, then in the army (in the campaigns of 1813-14), became *sous-chef de bureau* in the Prefecture of the Seine, married Clémente, a grand-daughter of Duplay, and had one child. He was trying to increase his income by teaching at the Collège de Sainte-Barbe when his character and talents brought him to the notice of the Baron Devaux; and it was Devaux who recommended him as resident tutor to Hortense.

Philippe Le Bas was a Jacobin, but not of the Left. His father had been a member of the *comité de sûreté générale*, most of whose members regarded with some dislike the Robespierrist *comité de salut public*; his decision to throw in his lot with Robespierre at Thermidor was due more to personal than to political loyalty, and his suicide the only alternative to arrest and certain execution. His wife was more attached to Robespierre's memory than to her grand-parents, whose political intransigence Philippe did not share. In Bertrand's view he was not an Ultra, hardly a Liberal. He was in fact a 'man of '89'. We have his own word for this; for when in 1827 he became acquainted with Félix Lepeletier, the brother of the *conventionnel* Michel Lepeletier, he wrote home saying 'He is one of the very small number of those who have lived through every phase of our Revolution without disloyalty to their principles or change in their opinions. He is very fond of my good mother, and never speaks of her without enthusiasm. You can imagine how much I like him and seek his company.'[20] But Le Bas' essential interests were not political; he was a scholar through and through; a capable teacher of Greek and Latin, of Italian and mathematics; and a bibliophile — the kind of man, Bertrand said, whose first question, in any town he visited, was 'Where is the library?' and who knew every librarian from the Baltic to the Rhine. What he mainly owed to his Jacobin upbringing (as so many did) was an austerity of purpose, and a methodical way of life. Bertrand's tutorship had never imposed a time-table: within a month of Le Bas' arrival Louis found that he must get up at 6, go for a walk till 7, study grammar till 8.30, Latin from 9 to 10.30, mathematics from

11.30 to 1, then German and Greek till 3, and history and geography from 4 to 6; still to be followed by an hour's revision before bedtime at 9. In other words, nine and a half hours' work a day, with five and a half hours for meals and recreation. Four months later the time-table is revised, but the proportion of work and play remains the same. The severity of this regime, for a boy of twelve to thirteen, was increased by the fact that his tutor was always by his side: they had their specially dieted meals alone, they went walking alone, with edifying conversation; only for an hour a day, before going to bed, was Louis allowed to break their continuous tête-à-tête, and to share the company and talk of his mother's *salon* — 'the most dangerous hour in the day', Le Bas called it.[21]

Evidently the tutor did not share the mother's belief in her good influence on Louis' mind and morals. 'I made it my chief care (Hortense wrote in 1832) to mould his character. A man can learn much good under the influence of a woman: her words produce more effect than a man's; they come from the heart, and speak to it.' But Hortense was not at all the person she thought herself to be. Every page of her *Mémoires* convicts her of self-deception. She was sentimental, emotional, self-righteous; a *poseuse*, always thinking of her misfortunes and of her ailments. Louis was fond of her, but he wanted to live his own life.

The discipline imposed by Le Bas succeeded beyond expectation. Louis accommodated himself to his new tutor's ways with *douceur et docilité*: soon he was showing more keenness about his work: within six months Le Bas could report (in one of the solemn letters in which he discussed his work with his friends) 'My young pupil becomes more interesting every day, and every day his progress is more evident. His mother is very satisfied, indeed amazed, for he has really changed in every respect.' But one is hardly surprised to hear that when the boy slept alone (he commonly shared a room with his tutor) he was subject to 'night fears', due to his *faible complexion*; so that Le Bas thought it best for a time to put him off violent or exciting forms of exercise — riding, dancing, swimming and fencing.[22] At Easter 1821 Louis was entered as a day boy at the Augsburg *Gymnasium*, where he learnt German (there exists a short letter to Hortense Lacroix in that language), soon raised himself from 54th to 24th, and within a year was fourth in a class of 94.[23] Le Bas supplemented the school curriculum with home teaching: we hear that Louis has taken to reading such English classics as *Robinson*, *Sandfort et Merton*,

le petit Grandison, and that his tutor hopes to get him on to the *Bibliothèque des voyages* and Plutarch: he is making good progress in Latin, but is still (unlike Napoleon) weak in mathematics. During the school terms he is living with Le Bas and his wife in Hortense's house at Augsburg, and no doubt the regular routine of life is kept up. The summer vacations of two months in August and September are spent in 1821 and 1822 at Arenenberg.

They were at Augsburg when, on July 14th, 1821, Le Bas received a letter from Bertrand, asking him to break to Louis the news of Napoleon's death at St. Helena. Hortense, he said, was deeply affected by the loss of one 'who had been like a father to her, and who left to all his descendants a name that would be immortal'. Louis was to go into mourning for six months. The news produced a vivid impression upon the boy, said his tutor, who did not fail to improve the occasion by pointing out 'how much he would have to do to win a position and reputation worthy of the name he bore and of the man who had given it him'. Nor can it be doubted that he had something to do with the composition of the letter Louis wrote to his mother three days later: regretting that he had not seen Napoleon before his death ('at Paris I was so young that I hardly remember him except in my heart'); and ending 'When I do wrong, I have only to think of this great man, and I seem to feel his shade in me telling me to be worthy of the name Napoleon'.[24]

6

Louis' education was always threatened by his mother's unsettled way of life. There is talk of a fresh journey to Italy in letters of February 22nd, June 4th, and July 13th, 1823. Le Bas admits that he would enjoy seeing the antiquities of Rome and Florence; but he dreads the interruption of Louis' studies and way of life, and he dislikes the prospect of meeting the boy's father. However, before the Italian plan can be carried out, Louis Bonaparte himself arrives on a visit to Marienbad, with the elder boy Napoléon-Louis, and invites Le Bas and the younger boy to join him there (August 1823). They could not refuse. Le Bas found Louis pleasant enough, but *inconstant, instable*. 'We live', he told his wife, 'in almost complete idleness'; he can only contrive (at his pupil's own suggestion) two or three hours' tuition a day. He was glad to get back to Augsburg after 'one of the most disagreeable months' of his life: Louis Bona-

parte had indeed grown querulous, and suspicious, and he was upset by the news of the death of the Pope Pius VII (August 20th, 1823).

No sooner back from Marienbad than off to Italy. On November 3rd they were at Verona, three days later at Bologna, and by December 22nd they reached Rome. There they remained till the middle of April 1824. Hortense enjoyed meeting Mme Récamier, and they went sight-seeing together. Le Bas was enthusiastic about the Roman remains, the galleries and libraries (though his Jacobin taste would have sacrificed a surplus of sacred pictures for a few of David's republican masterpieces); he even enjoyed Rossini at the Opera. But he deplored the reduction of his pupil's work-time to a bare three or four hours a day. 'We have lost a whole year,' he laments, and says that, if Louis were not so fond of him, and the stipend so necessary, he would resign his tutorship. The boy spends too much time with his father and mother; 'goes to bed late, gets up late, does a little slack work before lunch, goes riding at midday, and comes back tired out at 3, yawns over his lessons till 5, and goes off to spend the rest of the day with his father. You can imagine how I tremble at what this portends for the future!' But in March the news of Eugène's death changed Hortense's plans; and by May 14th they were all back at Bologna, on the way to Arenenberg. By the end of June Le Bas is making up for lost time by giving Louis eight hours' tuition a day. They are still at Arenenberg in October, when Hortense's departure means the end of frivolity (*les ris et les jeux*); and if things go on as at present his pupil will 'not only have made up for lost time, but made provision for the future'. In fact Le Bas thinks he can fairly claim a holiday; and in August 1825, takes Clémence for a two months' trip to Paris. In October he is back at Augsburg with Louis; but tuition is held up by plans for another winter in Italy: the passports are delayed, whilst the books have been sent ahead. However by Christmas they are settled in at Florence, which Le Bas prefers to Rome, for the government of Tuscany 'is at least paternal and tolerant', whereas 'the magnificent memories of Rome are poisoned by its present condition'.

This second long stay in Italy was really the death of Le Bas' tutorship. The party remained in Rome till the autumn of 1827, after moving into the lovely Villa Paolina, which Hortense inherited on the death of Pauline Bonaparte (June 1825), and which Le Bas describes with unwonted enthusiasm. But the excitements of the Carnival season distract him from the study of 'an unedited philo-

sophical treatise by a certain Nicephorus' on the duties of kingship:
he complains that the libraries are closed for religious festivals half
the days of the year; and latterly, when they are open, he walks all
the way from the Villa to the Vatican to pursue his studies. Evidently he is giving little time to Louis. It is almost as an afterthought
that he refers to him in a letter of March 9th, 1826: 'His character is
as good and lovable as ever. His mind is developing, his ideas are
widening. But life here is very distracting, and his work suffers. I
can hardly find one or two hours a day to get him to read a few fine
extracts from Tacitus. All the rest of our work is held up.' A year
later (May 23rd, 1827), 'Prince Louis is still as good as he has always
been', but little can be done unless he can be got away from his
father, and back to Arenenberg. It was at this time, too, that Louis
began a life friendship with Francesco, Conte di Arese, whose
mother, an old friend of Hortense, arrived in Rome in 1827. Arese
was almost of his own age, and shared his views about Austria and
1815. It was his influence, perhaps, more than any other, which led
Louis into the 'Resistance' movement of 1831.

His tutor could hardly approve: but meanwhile, in spite of illness,
Le Bas has been able to prepare editions of two Greek books, and to
translate a third: his own literary career is well under way. They
return home at last in July; but within two months he writes to
say that he has been dismissed by Hortense from his tutorship, on
the ground of economy, and because there is no more that he can do
for his pupil.[25]

One cannot be surprised that the affair ended so. But it remains
beyond doubt that during the six years that they had been together
Louis had grown from a sickly and sentimental child into an independent and athletic young man; that his tutor's friendship stood for
a self-discipline and a devotion to study which enabled him to
carry on for the next nine years some degree of self-education, and
to make good use of the other six most formative years of his imprisonment (1840-46); and that it remained with him as an occasional
reminder and motive all his life.

The letter in which Le Bas announced his dismissal by Hortense
was dated from Arenenberg, October 4th, 1827. That winter, and
the spring and summer of 1828, Louis spent at home, or not far
afield. In spite of a bout of illness, he put in a month's serious reading
(he praises Carnot's *Eloge de Vauban*, and disagrees with Napoleon's
verdict on it);[26] celebrated his birthday (April 21st, 1828) with a

display of fireworks, added bayonet-fencing to his athletic exercises, tried (but too late in the season) to be admitted to the Swiss Artillery Training Camp at Thun, and paid two visits: one to his cousin Mathilde, Jérôme's daughter, at Ulm (there had been sentimental passages between them at Arenenberg), and another to his Baden relations — the Duchess Stéphanie (Beauharnais) and her daughters Joséphine and Marie — at Fribourg. Some drawings of sentimental and romantic subjects, showing more of his mother's influence than of any original talent, have survived from this period.[27]

But Louis' heart was still in Rome, and he wrote more than once to his dear *filleule* Hortense Lacroix (living there with her mother), sending greetings to his friends, and messages from his mother asking her to recover a loaned portrait of Pauline and to secure the delivery of 'three barrels of red wine ordered a year ago'.[28] At last (October 6th, 1828) he is off again to the city of his destiny.

7

It has been a subject of controversy from the age of Mazzini to that of Mussolini how much Italian unity owed to the French Revolution and the Napoleonic Empire. Recent historians, headed by Gentile, have tried to show that not only Mazzini (whose dislike of the Revolution was obvious) but also Gioberti and Cavour owed nothing to French influences, everything to the Italian tradition, and that the Risorgimento was an authentic nationalist movement. But the verdict of history seems to be that Italian nationalism always needed some force from outside to counteract the feudalism, clericalism, and municipalism which prevented its self-expression. And this was supplied, at the end of the eighteenth century, as at the end of the fifteenth, by France.

Granted that the essential policy, both of the Republic and of the Empire, was to exploit the resources of Italy for the benefit of France, yet that country began, during the years of French occupation, to be less parochial, less feudal, and less ecclesiastical: the new code and courts, the new tax system, the new secular administration, together with a national flag and a national army, provided a scaffolding within which might be erected the Italian nation and state of the following century. But it must not be supposed that more than a few wise men understood the needs of their country sufficiently to appreciate what Napoleon had done for it. To the

mass of the people, who had suffered so long under the misrule of Spain, Austria, and the Papacy (only broken during the reforming regimes of Joseph II in Lombardy, Leopold in Tuscany, and Charles III in Naples), Bonaparte's programme of 1796–97 brought hopes of republicanism which he encouraged as far as he dared without danger to his military resources: but with the establishment of the Napoleonic Kingdom of Italy it soon became clear that, whilst the French government was more efficient than the Austrian, it was hardly less oppressive; and the secret societies which since 1796 (the probable birth-date of Carbonarism) had plotted against foreign domination, whether Austrian, French, or Spanish, now concentrated their attacks on the Napoleonic regime. When it broke up in 1814, the quarrels of these revolutionary parties contributed to the failure of Murat in the south and Eugène in the north to save Italian unity; and when the Congress of Vienna re-established the pre-revolutionary small state system under Austrian suzerainty it unwittingly gave new life and a new objective to the cause of Italian freedom and nationality. The Risorgimento was conceived in 1815, though it did not come to birth till 1848. The long period of gestation was marked by a series of revolts — at Naples in 1820, in Piedmont in 1821, and in the Papal States in 1831 — and by a series of repressions.[29]

Napoleon never saw Rome; and perhaps the crudity of his attitude towards the Papacy was based as much upon his ignorance of Roman feeling as upon his reading of the history of Charlemagne and Leo III. In designing a palace there for the King of Rome he was unconsciously preparing for his nephew's life-long preoccupation with the Roman problem — a knot which he had failed to cut, and which his successor must painfully untie.

Pius VII and Cardinal Consalvi, whose lives and policies were in effect those of a single person, bore no grudge against Napoleon for his sharp practice in the matter of the Concordat, or his attempt to force the Papal States into the Continental System. They were grateful to him for re-establishing the Catholic Church in France, and they realized the affinity of his administrative aims to those of the Papacy: they were as ready to borrow new ideas of government from a republican Empire as the despots of the previous century had been ready to borrow enlightenment from the Encyclopaedists. As soon as Pius was back in the Quirinal (June 1814), Consalvi wrote to his friend Pacca: 'It would have been absurd for Noah, when he left the ark after the Flood, to try to act as he had done before entering

it; he had to deal with a world entirely changed by the deluge. Yet those were only physical changes, and he had the few survivors on his side.' We, he implied, have to introduce changes which will be resented by those who should support them. And so they were. The decree of July 6th, 1816, swept away the short-lived French regime, but substituted for it a system of administration, justice, finance, and even industry and agriculture, based on 'the unity and uniformity designed by God to be the foundation of a strong and happy government'; a system which was centralized, efficient (if it had been carried out), and with some recognition of secular control, but which left all the ultimate authority in the hands of ecclesiastics. It was this system which, backed by the prestige of Pius VII, and carried on with all the pertinacity of Consalvi, outlived them both, and was the real cause of the insurrection of 1831.[30]

It was attacked both from the Right and from the Left. From the Right, where the reactionary ecclesiastics (*zelanti*) and the aristocratic laity complained of the loss of privileges and power inflicted on them by the policy of the reformist ecclesiastics (*politicanti*); whilst the Left, represented amongst the upper classes by the *Guelfs* and amongst the lower classes by the *Carbonari*, fought against *étatisme* and ecclesiastical control: violently opposed, in their turn, by the pro-papal and anti-liberal *Sanfedisti*.

Leo XII, who succeeded Pius VII in 1823 (Consalvi died the same year), gave the administrative reforms of 1816 an even more reactionary turn; and with increasing economic troubles, and violent but ineffective measures against brigands and *Carbonari*, the situation moved towards the crisis of 1830-31.

8

It is not to be thought that Rome — the meeting-place of all civilizations, the museum of all ages, the burial-place (as Chateaubriand said) of liberty and of tyranny — meant no more for Louis than it did for his tutor. To Le Bas the Carnival might be worth a letter home to amuse Clémence; but the only buildings that interested him were the libraries — and that on account of the books which they contained; his neat Jacobin mind rejected as superstitious mummery the lights and incense of the Catholic church, and despised the luxurious frivolity of a society of *émigrés* and *aristos*. During the occasional visits of 1822-27 his pupil may in part have

shared these views: but when he was free to go his own way, and to form his own mind, it is evident that other influences were at work — influences which had a critical effect on his Italian sympathies and policies in later years.

The Napoleonic deluge had left a deposit of republicanism all over Europe. It was impossible any longer for revolutionary movements to be localized. The fall of Charles X in July 1830 was followed by revolutionary risings in Belgium, in Germany (Brunswick, Hesse, and Saxony), in Poland, and in Italy. Louis, now twenty-two, was at Thun, attending the Swiss Artillery Training camp, when news came of the events in Paris. What it meant to him is clear enough from a letter to his mother: 'We get a series of accounts here, and the remarkable thing is the universal rejoicing ... At this moment France is flying the tricolour. How I envy those who have been the first to restore her old renown!' For, as Hortense wrote to a friend about the same time, 'You will have seen that my sons' enthusiasm could not be restrained, in spite of my wish that they should not appear in the business. They have been brought up to admire what is noble and fine: they are proud of their country, and would have been glad to be of service to her; and they are in the twenties!' But now came a bitter set-back; for on September 2nd the Chamber of Deputies, terrified of any foreign intrigue, reaffirmed the law of January 12th, 1816, which exiled from France all members both of the Bourbon and of the Bonaparte families. Joseph, the titular head of the Bonapartes, and Louis' father, their pledge of orthodoxy and conservatism, protested in vain. When, that autumn, Louis accompanied his mother back to Rome, he was in a mood to take part in any revolutionary movement that might offer itself.

Waterloo and the abdication of 1815 had brought across the Alps, like birds migrating to the warm south, a flight of Bonaparte refugees. Lucien, who had so unexpectedly thrown in his lot with Napoleon, was formally exiled to Italy. The charity of Pius VII, who forgave his ill-treatment for the sake of the Concordat, attracted others of the proscribed family: *Madame Mère*, Cardinal Fesch, Louis, Pauline; later Jérôme and his family, Julie with her daughters (her husband Joseph was by now in America), Caroline Murat after her husband's execution, and Elisa's daughter Napoléone, Countess Camerata. Most of them were rich with the pensions and plunder of the Empire, and lived in style: *Madame Mère* in the Palazzo Rinuccini, Fesch in the Palazzo Falconieri, with a vast col-

lection of pictures which he traded with foreign visitors. Pauline, separated from her husband, built herself the Villa Paolina; Lucien spent most of his time on a country estate at Canino, but also owned two villas, and a big palace in Rome; this last he let to Jérôme, who was always running into debt. King Louis had the Palazzo Mancini in Rome, and a villa at Albano, but preferred to live at Florence. They lived *incognito*: Julie as Comtesse de Survilliers, Louis as Comte de Saint-Leu, Jérôme as Comte de Montfort, Caroline as Comtesse de Lipona (an anagram for Napoli), Lucien as Prince de Canino: only *Madame Mère* remained Madame Bonaparte and Pauline (in her own right) Princess Borghese. When Hortense visited Rome with her sons she lived in the Palazzo Ruspoli, till the Villa Paolina came to her by the death of Pauline.[31]

Thus the Bonapartes formed a considerable and influential society; but though under the protection of the Pope, they could not be exempt from the suspicious supervision of the spies of Metternich or the French representative at the Vatican. By the law of January 1816 they could not travel outside Italy without the leave of the Allies' representatives in Paris, and so long as Napoleon was alive they were under constant suspicion of conniving in plots (supposed to be hatched by Joseph in America) for his rescue from St. Helena, as they had been in 1814 for his escape from Elba. After his death in 1821 suspicion shifted to his son the Duc de Reichstadt; and when revolution broke out both in Italy and France in 1830 it was assumed that some of the Bonapartes were behind a plot to invite the Duc de Reichstadt, failing his call to the French throne, to make his title 'King of Rome' a reality, and, until he arrived there, to appoint Louis his Regent. One is at first surprised that the choice should have fallen on the younger brother, not the elder — the dreamy and indolent son of his mother, not the father's favourite, four years his elder, whom Valérie Masuyer described as a strikingly handsome young man, with a well-balanced mind, logical and eloquent, 'every inch the Emperor'. But Napoléon-Louis was newly married to Charlotte, the daughter of Joseph: he lived at Florence, not Rome, and was interested in the manufacture of paper, and in ballooning: these occupations may have held him back, until his younger brother arrived at Florence with news of an abortive rising at Rome.

Pius VIII died on November 30th, 1830. The Conclave to elect his successor could not meet before December 14th. During

the interregnum the cardinals believed a rising had been planned for December 10th, several arrests had already been made, and on the following day the city Governor called on Fesch, and asked him to see that Louis left Rome; for, he said, the young man had been seen riding about the streets with a cavalryman's saddle-cloth (*chabraque*) in red, white, and blue, the revolutionary colours. When Fesch demurred, three officers of the Papal army promptly escorted Louis across the frontier into Tuscany; and next day the Secretary of the Sacred College informed the representatives of foreign powers that in consequence of the discovery of a plot (*dessein pervers follement conçu par quelques individus dévoyés*) some thirteen persons had been expelled from the territory of the Holy See, amongst them *M. le Comte Louis Bonaparte, second fils de M. le Comte de Saint-Leu.* Amongst those threatened with expulsion was Jérôme Bonaparte's eldest son Jérôme-Napoléon, a boy of sixteen; but thanks to the intervention of the Russian minister and the *chargé d'affaires* for Wurttemberg he was allowed to remain. Some of the highest families in Rome were supposed to be implicated in the plot, and it was said that *Madame Mère* herself had promised, if it were successful, her financial help.

According to papers which fell into the hands of the Vatican there was to be a gathering on December 10th in the square of St. Peter's: Louis himself, carrying the tricolour, was to head a body of Papal dragoons, who had been bribed to follow him in a march on the armoury attached to the castle of St. Angelo, where two artillery officers had been bribed to admit them. Having thus armed themselves, some of the rebels would make their way to the slum districts across the Tiber, and call on the people to join them, distributing money provided by *Madame Mère*; the main body, dividing into four columns, would attack the castle of St. Angelo, seize the bank of Santo Spirito, arrest the leading cardinals and the city Governor, and throw open the prisons. This done, they would mount the Capitol, and proclaim Louis as Regent for the King of Rome. The same night they would join hands at Civita-Castellana with the rebel forces in the Marches.

Such was said to be the plan; and it had only failed because when Louis arrived before St. Peter's he heard that his followers at Bologna were not ready, that the dragoons had returned to duty, and that the authorities had closed the gates of St. Angelo. The interesting thing about it — and this is perhaps evidence that the story was true — is

the likeness of the plot to those which Louis certainly tried to carry out at Strasbourg in 1836 and at Boulogne in 1840. There are the same elements of a military *coup* followed by an appeal to the people; of an attack on the headquarters of the garrison; and of the attempts to win over officers and men to the insurgent cause. As for the Duc de Reichstadt, there is no evidence that he knew about the plot, or was the least likely to welcome the important part assigned to him — any more than he was to challenge Louis-Philippe's right to the crown of France. But this would not seriously trouble such conspirators.

When Louis arrived at Florence he wrote (January 4th, 1831) to Félix Baciocchi at Bologna: 'You will have heard that I have been forced to leave Rome: apparently the Cardinals were afraid of me. Some people say that I am much hurt by this insult; but they are mistaken. There are governments by which it is an honour to be persecuted.' If this is not an avowal of guilt, it is still less a denial of it; and the sequel bears out the suggestion that Louis was already regarded as one of the leaders of the insurrection. For within three weeks (January 25th) he left Florence with his elder brother, Napoléon-Louis, to join the rebels in Umbria: a month later they were at Terni, 100 miles south-east of Florence, with Colonel Sercognani, who had once fought under Eugène Beauharnais; and from Civita-Castellana Louis had addressed a species of ultimatum to the Pope; while at Bologna, fifty miles north of Florence, the command was in the hands of Colonel Armandi, another of Eugène's officers, and recently tutor to Napoléon-Louis. When Lucien's sixteen-year-old son Pierre Bonaparte was arrested on his way to join them it may well have seemed that the whole Bonaparte family was involved in the plot; though Lucien, himself in his younger days a friend of P.-J. Briot, the founder of French Carbonarism,[32] disowned his son, and agreed to his exile to America; though Jérôme protested that his boy had nothing to do with the rising; and though King Louis (partly as a good Catholic and partly as an unnatural husband and father) was bitterly opposed to his sons' adventure, and would not even take steps to win back the elder brother, who was his particular care.

It is not easy to determine the part played by Hortense in all this. There can be no doubt that she encouraged her son's claims to the Bonapartist succession in France, and welcomed the opportunity that seemed to be offered by the July revolution in Paris. But why should she favour an anti-Papal revolt in Italy, or encourage her

sons to take part in it? Perhaps, so long as the affair seemed to be going well, from pride in their prowess; perhaps from habitual opposition to her husband, who was a partisan of the Papacy? Nor would this be inconsistent with her change from approbation to anxiety, when her sons lost their command, and were fugitives before the Austrian army. She had always been a Beauharnais as well as a Bonaparte — the first by instinct, the second by habit: now the second nature gave way to the first. It is not necessary, as one of her biographers does, to talk of *double jeu* or *hypocrisie*.[33]

She had followed Louis from Rome to Florence. Now she would follow him from Florence, wherever he might be; for she had found there a letter saying that the two brothers felt bound by their name, and by their promise to help the cause of a suffering people, to join the rebels, and that they were at last seeing life and enjoying the adventure. Two things particularly alarmed her. Whether or not she sympathized with the Bonapartist background of the insurrection, she hated and feared the idea of any association with the *Carbonari*; and she knew that since the election of the new Pope, and the calling in of the Austrian troops, no quarter would be given to rebels. A letter from Terni, dated February 26th, gave her a clue as to her sons' whereabouts, and on March 11th she set out, with a passport provided by the British Minister to Tuscany in the name of 'Mrs. Hamilton', on the difficult and at that time dangerous journey across country to Foligno, the reputed headquarters of the rebel army. But just at this time Armandi's plans had changed. Up to the beginning of March there had been hopes of French intervention on behalf of the rebels; and it was feared that this help might be refused if Louis-Philippe heard of the prominent part being played by the Bonapartes. Accordingly Armandi recalled the two boys to Bologna, rewarded them with military honours, and deprived them of command in the field. But it was soon clear that no help was coming from France, whilst, on the other hand, Austrian troops had reoccupied Modena (March 9th), and were advancing southwards.

When Hortense arrived at Foligno (March 14th) her sons had gone north: all she could hear was that they had distinguished themselves in the fighting at Terni and Spoleto, and were now with Armandi, retreating before the Austrian advance along the Via Emilia from Bologna to Imola, Faenza, Forli, and Ancona. She sent a messenger to Forli, who on his return reported an epidemic of measles there. She set out for Ancona on the 19th, but soon heard that Napoléon-

Louis had caught the infection; and she arrived at Pesaro only to find Louis there, himself ill and disheartened, and to learn that Napoléon-Louis had fallen ill at Forli on the 11th, died on the 17th, and been buried in the Cathedral.[34]

On March 23rd they reached Ancona, but only three days before the town capitulated to the Austrians. Louis had been excluded from the amnesty granted to most of Armandi's followers, and the house in which they had taken refuge was commandeered by an Austrian officer. The story of Louis' concealment there, the pretence of escape by sea to Corfu, the journey by road to Loretto, with Louis and Zappi (another young proscript, carrying an appeal from Bologna to Paris) disguised as footmen, the risky passage past Austrian outposts at Tolentino and Papal guards at Foligno, the midnight crossing of the Tuscan frontier, the ruse by which Louis passed through Siena, the adoption of English disguises at Pisa, the visit to Napoléon-Louis' paper factory at Serra-Vezza, the halt at Spezia — Louis was interested in its possibilities as a naval base; then Genoa, Savona, Nice; and at last Cannes, and the road to Paris — all this loses no touch of romance in the narrative of Valérie Masuyer, who, with Louis' faithful valet Thélin, shared the adventure. Perhaps to Louis himself it was only an exciting end to a youthful escapade: but to Hortense, an invalidish woman of forty-seven, accustomed to a life of self-indulgent ease, it was an act of heroism that gave greater stature to her character, and a fresh belief in her favourite son's newly discovered vocation. If he was henceforth to play the Bonaparte, at least a Beauharnais would not be wanting.[35]

9

'Newly discovered vocation' — is the phrase justifiable? What had been in Louis' mind when, at sixteen, he knelt on the bank of the Rubicon, and filled a bottle with water from a stream as ominous to Caesar as the Niemen to Napoleon? Or when at twenty-two he treasured a bullet picked up by the bridge of Arcola? Three years later, when he wrote his *Considérations politiques et militaires sur la Suisse*,[36] he would envisage all Switzerland as a Napoleonic battlefield, and every European movement for independence as led by old soldiers of the Grand Army. Did he already believe (as he put it in 1833) that the government of Napoleon, 'the People's Emperor',

had offered the world a regime from which no classes were excluded, and institutions which gave equal favour to all? If so, then to join in an Italian agitation for national freedom and constitutional government was a truly Napoleonic task. Put in this way, even his father Louis might not have objected to it: but the proper place for a Napoleonic crusade (he would hold) was France, from which the Bonapartes had been expelled; not Italy, where the Papacy had protected them. And so, when his elder boy's body was brought from Forli to be buried in the church of San Spirito at Florence, the epitaph which Louis Bonaparte set over it said nothing of his dying for Italy, but only of his living for France:

FRANÇAIS DE CŒUR ET D'AME
IL NE SE RAPPELAIT L'EXIL ET LE MALHEUR DES SIENS
QUE POUR EN AIMER DAVANTAGE SA PATRIE[37]

It was, then, as a French patriot, not as an Italian refugee, that Louis Napoleon entered France in April 1831, and arrived, after a sentimental visit to Fontainebleau, at Paris (March 23rd). His mother reckoned that King Louis-Philippe, whom she had befriended in 1815, would overlook their defiance of the ban against which her husband had protested. They travelled incognito, and put up at the Hôtel de Hollande, in the rue de la Paix. On the 25th Louis fell ill again, and took to his bed. On the 26th Hortense had a friendly interview with the King and the royal family, in every circumstance of secrecy, at the Palais-Royal. But of course their presence in the capital was soon known; and Parisian rumour reported that they were involved in a plot which broke out at Strasbourg that May to put the Duc de Reichstadt on the throne. Was it by accident that their rooms at the hotel had a balcony that overlooked the Place Vendôme, and that their departure from Paris was delayed until after the popular demonstration (May 5th) at the foot of the Vendôme Column on the tenth anniversary of Napoleon's death, with cries of *Vive Napoléon II*? Louis was at any rate thinking of a possible change of dynasty: not many months later (December 15th) he wrote to his father that if there were another revolution in France, it would end 'either in a Republic, or a Bourbon restoration, or Napoleon II': the first two would not concern him; as for the third, he could only wait to see what the head of the family at Vienna would do. In a letter to the King on his arrival in Paris he had protested that his only ambition was to serve in the ranks

of the French army, and that he would die happy if he laid down his life fighting for his country. With singular or intentional blindness he persevered for some years in this attitude; as though it were possible for a Bonaparte, and a nephew of Napoleon, to *serve*, and not to *command*.[38]

At the moment nothing was to be gained by further delay; and a few days later, under official pressure from Casimir-Perier, the King's *premier ministre*, the refugees crossed the Channel. 'Prince Louis Napoleon Bonaparte, second son of Louis Bonaparte, has arrived in London (reported *The Times* a month later), and is staying with his mother, Hortensia, Duchess of St. Leu, formerly Queen of Holland.' They remained in England nearly three months.[39]

This visit to London was the first of five during the years that Louis was a claimant to the French throne; and it began a connection which lasted till the death of the dethroned Emperor, at Chislehurst, an honoured guest, once feared, but now pitied, forty years later. The refugees — Hortense, Louis, and Mlle Masuyer — landed at Dover on May 10th, and travelled to London by Canterbury, where they found themselves in the excitements of a General Election on the issue of Parliamentary Reform. They put up at Fenton's Hotel in St. James' Street for a few days, before moving to a house in George Street, Hanover Square. They were not well off, for Hortense was still waiting for the £50,000 that she had claimed from her mother's inheritance; and they lived quietly, hoping for passports which would enable them to return to Switzerland. But they had relations and friends in England: Charlotte, the widow of Napoléon-Louis, Christine, daughter of Lucien Bonaparte by his first wife, and married since 1824 to Lord Dudley Stuart, Achille Murat from America, the Comte de Montrond, an old friend of Pauline Bonaparte, and a Plombières acquaintance, Lady Glengall. They made new friendships too: with the Duchess of Bedford, Lord Mahon, Lady Tankerville, Lady Davy, Baron Neumann. They dined at Holland House (July 8th) to be charmed by Lord Holland and bullied by his lady. They went sight-seeing to the Zoological Gardens, the Tower of London, and the Thames Tunnel. They saw a 'new Grand Historical and Military Spectacle' called 'Napoleon Buonaparte' at the Theatre Royal, Covent Garden, and went to the opera and the ballet. Louis enjoyed dancing and flirting at Vauxhall and Almack's, and witnessing William IV open Parliament. Nor did he lose sight of his political ambitions;

for he listened to proposals from Mirandoli, an Italian refugee, that he should subscribe to the revolutionary plans of Comte Lennox, the proprietor of a Paris newspaper, *La Révolution de 1830*. It was perhaps partly to break this dangerous connection (Mirandoli was arrested along with other 'Bonapartist' plotters in November) that Hortense moved on July 9th to the Royal Kentish Hotel at Tunbridge Wells, and then, as in town, to a private house there. Here Louis transferred his easy affections to the lovely Miss Godfrey, and for a time forgot to be a conspirator.[40]

At the end of July the passports they had been waiting for – Talleyrand, the French ambassador, and Sébastiani, the Foreign Minister, had done nothing to expedite them – came to hand; and after another short stay in town they left Dover (August 7th) for Boulogne, where, at the foot of the *Colonne de la Grande Armée*, Hortense described Napoleon's distribution of crosses of the Legion of Honour there in August 1804: then, avoiding Brussels and Paris, passed through France, with sentimental excursions to Mortefon- taine and Malmaison, to the Swiss frontier and Arenenberg.[41]

THE PRETENDER (1831-1840)

HOR. He waxes desperate with imagination.
MAR. Let's follow; 'tis not fit thus to obey him.
HOR. Have after. To what issue will this come?
MAR. Something is rotten in the state of Denmark.
HOR. Heaven will direct it.
MAR. Nay, let's follow him.   *Hamlet*, I, iv

I

THE five years between Louis' return from London to Arenenberg in August 1831 and his Strasbourg adventure of October 1836 were no doubt 'the least eventful period of his life'; but they were the most important for the growth of his life's purpose – his dedication to the cause of Bonapartism. Why was this, and what is the evidence for it?

First, the matter of physical and legal succession in the Bonaparte family. For twenty years Louis had been barred from the Napoleonic heritage by his cousin the Duc de Reichstadt and by his elder brother Napoléon-Louis. But now, almost suddenly, both obstacles disappeared. Napoléon-Louis died at Forli in March 1831, the Duc de Reichstadt at Vienna on July 22nd, 1832. Up to the end of 1831 Louis was waiting, as he told his father, to see what the head of the family would do; he rejected an invitation to lead a rebellion in Poland, and he gave publicity to a supposed refusal to offer himself for the Belgian throne in 1831. But from 1832 onwards he is set on a course which more and more clearly aims at another 'return from Elba', the overthrow of Louis-Philippe, and the restoration of a Napoleonic Empire.[1]

The evidence for this lies in Louis' own published works: for he made no secret of his ambitions, knowing well that France was deeply discontented with the Orleanist rule, and that Paris at least would always welcome an escape from the double apprehension of a Bourbon restoration or a Red Republic to the security of a Bonapartist regime. In May 1832 Louis published, under the title of *Rêveries politiques*,[2] a pamphlet in which he discussed the best means of regenerating his country. Different suggestions had been made: 'My own belief (he wrote) is that it can only be done by combining those two popular causes, Napoleon II and the Republic. The great

30

man's son is the sole representative of supreme glory, as the Republic is of supreme liberty. The name Napoleon excludes all fear of a return of the Terror: the word Republic excludes all fear of a return of Absolutism.' Nothing could be clearer or more uncompromising. By 'Napoleon II' Louis meant the Duc de Reichstadt, who was still alive when he wrote; but in a 'Sketch of a Constitution' added to the pamphlet – it defines an Empire based on national sovereignty and a despotism emerging from a Declaration of Rights – he provided (failing a legitimate heir) for the popular election of a successor who was, no doubt, to be himself.[3]

That his thoughts still turned upon his family heritage was shown by another pamphlet in 1833 called *Considérations politiques et militaires sur la Suisse*; for here Switzerland is little more than a stage-setting for the Napoleonic armies and Empire. He is already outlining the *Idées napoléoniennes* which he was to put into final shape six years later. What, he wonders, was Napoleon's ruling aim? And he replies: 'the defeat of Russia, and the overthrow of the whole system of England'. He would have made Warsaw, Westphalia, and Italy national states. In France he would have turned his dictatorship into a constitutional regime. Stability, liberty, independence would have been everywhere the marks of his rule. 'The government of Napoleon, the People's Emperor, offered the world perhaps the first example of a regime in which all classes were welcomed, none rejected, and in which institutions were set up equally favourable to all.' As to how Louis would forward this ideal, there is evidence in letters to his father and to Vieillard, his brother's former tutor. To his father (May 10th, 1833) he writes: 'I have no ambition but that of returning some day to my country'; but he can only do it by help of a national party; and so he will openly associate himself with *tout ce qui se fait de patriotique en France*.[4] To Vieillard he laments (February 18th, 1834) that 'the greatest man of modern times' has no party in France; and explains (January 30th, 1835) the difficulties of his own position: 'I know that my name is everything, but that my personality still counts for nothing. By birth I am an aristocrat, in temperament and opinion a democrat. I owe everything to heredity, indeed to having been designated as Napoleon's heir (*réellement tout à l'élection*). Some flatter me for my name's sake, some for my title. If I take a step outside my ordinary place in life I am charged with ambition: if I stay quietly in my corner, I am accused of apathy and indifference. In a word, my name inspires

similar fears both in the Liberals and in the Absolutists. My only political friends are to be found amongst those habitual gamblers who think that, of all possible chances, I may be a lucky bet.' Aware of all this, 'I have made it my rule to follow no guidance but the intuitions of my heart, my reason, and my conscience ... in short, to pursue the straight line ahead, whatever difficulties I may encounter: for so I may succeed in raising myself to a height at which I may still be lit by an expiring ray from the sunset of St. Helena'.[5]

Rhetoric, perhaps, but fine and genuine: Hortense Lacroix always said that Louis was meant to be a poet; his imagination pictured himself as the claimant to a heroic inheritance. And at Arenenberg his dream was indulged: Madame Récamier, who came to stay there when Paris was attacked by cholera in 1832, says that all the household treated him as royalty (*en souverain*): he always took precedence. So, when the rumour got about in 1834 that he aspired to the hand of the Queen of Portugal, his disclaimer was well advertised in the press: how could he look abroad for a recognition he expected from his own countrymen?[6] 'The hope of some day serving France as a citizen and a soldier (he said) fortifies my heart, and counterbalances in my estimation all the thrones in the world.'[7] Rhetoric again, but rhetoric well adapted to the troubles in France, where a second republican insurrection at Lyon this year was only put down after much bloodshed, and was followed by Fieschi's attempt to assassinate the King, and by the repressive 'Laws of September', 1835.

As for a bride, it was in November 1835, that Jérôme Bonaparte came to stay with Hortense at Arenenberg, and brought with him his fifteen-year old daughter Mathilde: in character and looks an undoubted Bonaparte, a classical and rather boyish beauty not unlike her aunt Pauline, but with more sense and wit. There, and at Florence where they met again the next year, Louis fell in love with his cousin, as he did with any pretty girl he met, and she with him: they parted in tears, and with hopes of marriage. His father was at first opposed to the engagement; when he relented, her father raised difficulties – as usual, financial.[8] It was the Strasbourg affair which outraged Jérôme, disillusioned Mathilde, and brought the romance to an end. She was offended because Louis kept her in the dark as to his plans: he explained afterwards (in a letter to Charlotte, May 1837) that he reckoned, if his attempt succeeded she would forgive him, and if it failed she would have no more to do with him.[9]

It seems to have been about this time, too, that Louis first made the acquaintance of a man who decisively influenced his career: Victor Fialin, better known as Comte later Duc de Persigny, — a man of his own age and temperament, an adventurer and a 'gambler', who had sacrificed a career in the army to join in the 1830 revolution, and was now a Paris journalist, the editor of the short-lived *l'Occident français*, and a partisan of a Bonapartist restoration. His influence was perhaps more decisive than any other in the Strasbourg adventure of 1836.[10]

On August 16th, 1832, Louis' uncle Joseph Bonaparte had landed at Liverpool after seventeen years' American exile, determined to uphold in person, as he had done in writing, the claims of his family against the ban imposed on the Bonapartes by Louis-Philippe. When he landed in England, it was to hear of the death of the Duc de Reichstadt, which left him the indisputable head of the Bonaparte family. He at once summoned Lucien, Jérôme, and Louis Napoleon (whose father was too ill to travel) to meet him in London. Louis took with him his Italian friend and fellow-plotter Francesco Arese. They travelled, as Louis usually did, by the Batavier line from Rotterdam, arrived in London in mid-November and stayed with Joseph Bonaparte.

It was in the course of this journey that Louis visited the battle-field of Waterloo, went over the ground, map in hand, and stood where his uncle had stood, at La Belle Alliance, sixteen years ago.[11] Did he share the mood in which Napoleon had refused to under-stand failure or to accept defeat? At any rate he would not shrink from staking everything he had on the chance of success. For he was a gambler, too; but a gambler without a system, who left too much to luck.

Less is known of Louis' doings during this winter visit than of his earlier and later residences in England. Some time was taken up by family councils, in which he grew impatient of his uncles' caution; he even visited Paris to meet his supporters there. Some time too was given to such social activities as he could afford, in the company of Joseph's daughter and his sister-in-law (Napoléon-Louis' widow) Charlotte, or of Achille Murat; and there were jaunts to Brussels and Liverpool. In May 1833 he returned to Arenenberg, determined to carry on with his plan for active intervention in France, whatever his father and uncles might think of it.

Joseph, who was still refused permission to enter France or Italy,

remained for three years more in England, a centre of Bonapartist hopes, and a source of propaganda, but not of conspiracy: he would be a moderating influence, if he could, upon the nephew's extravagances of behaviour as he had tried to be upon those of the uncle. After another short visit to America in 1835, he returned to England six months after the death of *Madame Mère* in Rome at the age of eighty-six (February 2nd, 1836); and he was still in England when he heard of Louis' attempted *coup* at Strasbourg — an adventure of which he wholly disapproved; Louis, he said, had 'ignored his father and uncles as though they were already in their graves'.[12]

2

Why did Louis think that France was in a condition to welcome a Bonapartist attempt on the throne? Why did he time it for 1836? Why did he choose, as his starting-point, Strasbourg?

The answer to the first question is in all the histories of the period. The revolution of 1830 was an echo of that of 1789, and set up a constitutional monarchy which was as unlikely to last as that of 1791: Louis-Philippe was not put on the throne by the nation which had deposed Charles X, and his government was not that which the people desired. An Orleans king who based his rule on a plutocracy was little better than a Bourbon king who based his rule on an aristocracy. He was in fact in a far weaker position. In 1789 there had been no republican party, no socialist movement, no Bonapartism; a past to be repudiated, not idealized; a future all fluid and optimistic, not prejudged and compromised by the experiences of a Jacobin republic, a Girondin oligarchy, a Napoleonic despotism, and a Bourbon reaction. In 1830 Louis-Philippe ruled, under constant threats of assassination, by favour of the *pays légal*, that less than a quarter of a million well-to-do Frenchmen (out of a population of 32 millions) whose £10 tax-payment gave them the vote: such was the result of half a century's agitation for a universal franchise. Parliamentary government on the pre-Reform English model was disliked and despised for its corruption and its disregard of popular needs. The beginnings of an Industrial Revolution, which increased the wealth of the commercial and financial middle class, left the small land-owners, the chief inheritors of the Revolution, unmoved, whilst it created a new self-consciousness and solidarity amongst the industrial workers, and played into the hands of the

Socialists. The Jacobins by necessity and Napoleon by choice had been able to distract public attention from home to foreign affairs by successful wars, and by flaunting captured flags at the Invalides. Louis-Philippe, by temperament a man of peace, by experience of exile a good European, and well aware that he held his throne by leave of the 'legitimate' sovereigns who had remodelled the world in 1815, quite failed to win respect for his timid foreign policy at home or abroad.

If for six years after his accession he had shrewdly avoided disaster, few doubted that it was sure to come. Tocqueville's increasingly gloomy forecasts — so like those of d'Argenson during the long decline of Louis XV's reign — are perhaps the best evidence of this. Writing in 1836, which he admits to be a time of increased prosperity, he says: 'All our past experience teaches us that this repose may itself become fatal to the Government', which will never understand 'the susceptibilities of the country': ten years later 'one feels ashamed of being led by a vulgar and corrupt aristocracy; and if this feeling should prevail among the lower classes it may produce great calamities'. When at last the end came, his reflection was that Louis-Philippe had set a dangerous precedent in being put on the throne by the Paris mob, and then relying, not on the people as a whole, but on the bourgeoisie, who were at once electors and elected, patrons and pensioners, law-makers and administrators: the king's corrupt use of them made 'the middle classes objects of hatred and contempt', and 'I never thought him during the latter years of his reign safe from a revolution'.

Louis Napoleon had not the political insight of a Tocqueville; but he had been sufficiently in touch with anti-government opinion in Paris since 1831 to read the 'signs of the times': in November 1830 a Polish insurrection to which Louis-Philippe gave sympathy, but no support; the anti-papal Italian rising of 1831, in which Louis himself had taken part, which collapsed through lack of French help, and ended in the strengthening of Austrian control over the Papacy; the acceptance in 1831 and the enforcement in 1832 of the independence of Belgium under the rule of the British nominee, Leopold I; the cholera epidemic, the Vendée rising, and the Lamarque funeral demonstration in Paris in 1832; the April *affaire* and second Lyon insurrection in 1834, and the Fieschi plot in 1835. He knew, too, that though Pius VIII had recognized Louis-Philippe as *Roi très Chrétien*, the king had been driven by his distrust of the Legitimist leanings of

most of the clergy and by the anti-clericalism of his government into measures against the Church, of which the removal of the crucifix from the law-courts was a sign that no one could mis-read.[13]

There is sufficient evidence, then, that by 1836 the main current of French revolutionary and national feeling was no longer flowing along the choked-up channel of bourgeois Orleanism. But what grounds had Louis Napoleon for thinking that it could be diverted into a new course of Bonapartism? He would know well enough what educated people were reading about Napoleon – both the works of serious historians and the propaganda of the legend-makers. He would hardly be in a position to judge how far, and in what proportions, either of these affected the uninstructed mass of public opinion – indeed it still remains problematical.

The Revolution of 1830 had largely been the work of historians, and, in the person of Louis-Philippe, an ex-Jacobin and ex-*émigré*, a cousin of the king whom his father had condemned to death, it had put a historical monument on the throne. There followed a notable rebirth of historical studies, which had been depressed during the Empire and Restoration: but they were more concerned with the events of the ten years after 1789 than with the fifteen that followed 1799. In 1830 at least four writers published popular histories of the Revolution, and one (Reybaud) thought it worth while to compose fabricated *Mémoires* of Robespierre, which led to the revival of his cult by Laponneraye a few years later. More works on the same lines appeared in 1832 and 1833; and in 1834, whilst Labaume turned from Napoleon's invasion of Russia to write a 'monarchical and constitutional' history of the Revolution, Buchez and Roux began the publication of their great *Histoire parlementaire*, a quarry from which all later historians have hewn material for their structures.

But though the Revolution held the first place in historical studies, it would not be fair to belittle the pioneer work that was being done at this time on the career of Napoleon – fugitive attempts, perhaps, for the most part, too soon overwhelmed by the tide of propaganda from St. Helena: military memoirs, such as those of Dumas, Beauvais, de Ségur, or Pelet; and political lives by Arnault, Laurent, de Norvins, above all Thiers and Thibaudeau. But the death of Napoleon in 1821 let loose a double flood of more or less legendary adulation: the poetry of Hugo (*Lui*, 1829, *Ode à la Colonne*, 1830) and Béranger (*Le Cinq Mai*, *Le Vieux Sergeant*, 1831), the novels of Stendhal, Vigny, and Musset, on one side; on the other

36

the records of Napoleon's conversations and sufferings at St. Helena by O'Meara (1822), Las Cases (1823), Antommarchi (1825); and the long series of *Mémoires* dictated by the ex-Emperor himself to give his own version of his career. Of these books Las Cases' *Mémorial* had an immense vogue in several languages, and many editions: its sentiments and rhetoric so obscured the real figure of Napoleon (the balance of truth was not restored till the publication of Gourgaud's *Journal* in 1899 and of Bertrand's in 1951) that it was easy to obtain credence for the theory that the Napoleonic regime had been founded on the principles of liberalism, pacifism, nationalism, and religious toleration. This was the opinion to which Louis Napoleon had hoped to appeal in his *Rêveries* and *Considérations*, and which he was to exploit still further in the *Idées napoléoniennes* of 1839.

But how far were Béranger's verses, Las Cases' rhetoric, or Louis' interpretations shared or understood by the general public in 1836? A nation commonly remembers of its past what it wants to remember: the Pole his oppression, the Irishman his grievances, the Spaniard his pride, and the Frenchman not the sufferings of the Napoleonic age, but its glories. Louis, as he already recognized, had one great asset—the name 'Napoleon'. It provided a text both for the historian and for the legend-maker. It appealed above all to the vast majority who had forgotten the history and had never learnt the legend. The name was enough. The difficulty was to get this national appeal past the barrier of royalism and ecclesiasticism, of army and politicians, and of a money-making middle class entrenched in power. There could be no effective appeal to national pride until the *volonté générale* once more asserted itself in a Paris revolution, and swept aside all the obstacles in the way of another 'Emperor of the People'. But now, as then, there must be the use of force in order to make way for the use of persuasion: the route to Paris lay viâ the army.

3

For such a design Strasbourg was an ideal starting-point. What the Channel was to Londoners the Rhine was to Parisians. Strasbourg, the most important city and fortress on the upper Rhine frontier, was also the bridgehead of the road to western Germany and the Danube valley. To a continental country any frontier town is what a port is to an island: a place where foreign influences are

felt, and where sentiments hostile to the capital and government (especially if the capital is not itself a port) may make headway. Still half German in language and religion, with inhabitants whom geography and temperament had made Rhinelanders rather than Frenchmen, Strasbourg had been a centre of opposition to every recent Paris government: to the Jacobins, to the Empire, to the Restoration, and now to Louis-Philippe. For though there survived, as in every large town, and particularly in so prosperous an industrial and commercial centre, a business and official society ready to support any government that secured its profits and its stipends, and though at heart Alsace was more French than German in its loyalties, yet, ever since July 1889, when Arthur Young watched the mob breaking the windows of the Town Hall, and still more since July 1830, when the tricolour was again hoisted on the tower of the Cathedral, there had existed at Strasbourg a party of young revolutionaries and republicans ready to show the sympathy of a bilingual population with fellow-partisans beyond the Rhine. When Louis-Philippe visited Strasbourg in 1831 he was publicly reminded of his duty to defend the *liberté* which had placed him on the throne; and if the attempts on his life, culminating in that of Fieschi in 1835, won him some popularity, this was more than outweighed by the repressive and unpopular Laws of September which followed.

To Louis Strasbourg was not merely a centre of opposition to the government, and a link between republicans in Paris and constitutionalists in Frankfort or Berlin: it was also the most important garrison town on the upper Rhine, and the nearest to Switzerland. Its garrison at this time consisted of one Infantry regiment, the 46th, and two Artillery regiments, the 3rd and 4th: to the 3rd was also attached a battalion of Engineers. The officers of these regiments were accustomed to spend their leave at Baden and other German resorts of fashion; and here Louis had cultivated their allegiance. But they were no longer the republican patriots who had fought at Arcola or Marengo: they were professional soldiers, heirs of the Grand Army, with a regimental *esprit de corps* and a habit of loyalty to the government of the day. A few of the older officers, no doubt, had served under Napoleon, and still regretted the fall of the Empire; and some of the younger men might hope for quicker promotion and better pay under a Bonapartist restoration. As for the rank and file, most would follow their officers; but some might desert to the magic of the name Napoleon.

Magic would be needed; for there was not much appeal to the professional soldier in this Italian Irregular, this Swiss Volunteer, who looked so little like a Bonaparte, and spoke French with a German accent. They may well have been more amused than impressed to hear that he had written a learned work on the use of artillery, and had sent copies to the heads of the service — he, a mere amateur! His approaches to their senior officers were not hopeful. General Voirol answered a letter of August 14th by ordering Louis' messenger back across the Rhine, and passing the letter on to the Minister of War at Paris. General Excelmans to a similar invitation sent no reply. Raindu, an infantry officer, in the course of an interview at Kehl, warned Louis against relying on the Strasbourg garrison, who were no more likely to desert their duty, or join in a popular rising, than those of Lyon, Grenoble, or Paris. Only a few junior officers, of whom the most prominent was Lieut. Laity of the Engineers, pledged themselves to take part in the attempt. It was not until his new friend Persigny brought Colonel Vaudrey of the 4th Artillery Regiment to see him that Louis secured the support of a really important ally: a fine soldier, who had fought at Waterloo, whose friend, the Paris singer Eléonore Brault or Gordon (for she had buried a British husband) was a keen Bonapartist, and whose regiment, by a happy chance, was that which had served Bonaparte's guns at Toulon in 1793, and had welcomed Napoleon at Grenoble on his return from Elba in 1815. Now the plan could proceed, with some hope of success.[14]

4

Historians are fortunate in having Louis' own account of the affair, as he wrote it down for his mother a few weeks afterwards: only some sentimental reflections which interrupt and some unimportant details which complicate the narrative are here omitted.[15]

'You know the reason I gave for leaving Arenenberg: what you did not know was my inner intention at that moment. I was so confident that Bonapartism (*la cause napoléonienne*) was the only creed that could civilize Europe, and so satisfied as to the nobility and purity of my aims, that I had fully made up my mind to raise the Imperial standard (*aigle*), and to perish for my political faith... On the 27th (of October) I arrived at Lahr, a small village in the Grand Duchy of Baden, where I expected news ... On the morning of the 28th I left Lahr, retraced my steps, passed through Fribourg, Neuf-

Brisach, and Colmar, and arrived at Strasbourg, without any difficulty, at 11 p.m. My carriage went to the Hôtel de la Fleur, whilst I put up for the night in a small room reserved for me in the rue de la Fontaine. There, next day, I saw Colonel Vaudrey, and handed him the plan of operations I had drawn up: but the Colonel, whose noble and generous feeling deserved a better reward, said to me: "This is no occasion for an armed rising. Your cause is too French and too pure to be stained by a single drop of French blood. There is only one procedure worthy of you, only one which will avoid any clash of force (*collision*). As soon as you are at the head of my regiment we will all march to General Voirol's quarters. An old soldier such as he will never stand out against the sight of you and the Imperial eagle, when he knows that the garrison is behind you." I agreed with his views, and everything was fixed accordingly for the next morning. A house had been taken in a street near the Austerlitz barracks; there we were all to assemble, and thence to move to the barracks as soon as the infantry regiment was on parade.

'At 11 p.m. on the 29th one of my friends came to take me to this meeting-place; we crossed the city together. The streets were lit by bright moonlight. I took this fine weather as a good omen for the next day. I carefully noted the points we passed. I was impressed by the silence everywhere. How different it might be tomorrow! . . . When we arrived at the house in the rue des Orphelines I found my friends assembled in two rooms on the ground floor. I thanked them for their devotion to my cause, and told them that from this moment we would share our fortunes, good and bad alike. One of the officers brought a flag (*aigle*): it was that of the old 7th regiment of the line: "It is Labédoyère's!" they all exclaimed; and each of us pressed it to his heart with deep emotion. (Labédoyère was the Napoleonic general who welcomed him at Grenoble on the return from Elba in 1814, and was shot by the royalists on August 19th, 1815.) . . . All the officers were in full uniform; I wore an artillery uniform and a general officer's head-dress (i.e. a Napoleonic *tricorne*). The night passed very slowly; I spent it writing my proclamation, which I had not liked to print beforehand, for fear of some indiscretion. It was agreed that we should remain in the house until the Colonel told me to come to the barracks. We counted every hour, every minute, every second. The time fixed upon was 6 a.m. . . . A few minutes later a message came that the Colonel was ready. Full of hope I hurried into the street. M. Parquin, in a

Brigadier-general's uniform, and a battalion commander carrying the eagle were by my side; two officers followed. It was not far, and did not take long. The regiment was drawn up in battle order in the barrack square inside the railings; on the grass plot (*parterre*) were forty mounted gunners... Colonel Vaudrey stood alone in the centre of the parade-ground and I advanced towards him. At once the Colonel – and there was something magnificent at that moment in his fine looks and figure – drew his sword and cried: "Men of the 4th Artillery Regiment! Today a great revolution is in making. You see before you the nephew of the Emperor Napoleon. He comes to concern himself with the rights of the people. People and Army can trust him. Let all who love the glory and the liberty of France rally round him. My men! you will feel, as I your commander do, all the grandeur of the enterprise you are attempting, all the sanctity of the cause you are going to defend. Can the nephew of the Emperor Napoleon count on you?"... His voice was drowned by unanimous shouts of *Vive l'Empereur!*

'Then I spoke. "I am resolved (I said) to conquer or to die for the cause of the French people. It is to you that I made up my mind to appeal first of all, because you and I share great memories. It was in your regiment that my uncle, the Emperor Napoleon, served as captain: it was with you that he won renown at the siege of Toulon; and it was your brave regiment which opened the gates of Grenoble to him on his return from the Isle of Elba. Soldiers! A new destiny awaits you. It is for you to begin a great enterprise; you will be the first to have the honour of saluting the eagle of Austerlitz and Wagram!" Then I took in my hands the eagle carried by M. de Querelles, one of my officers, and showed it to them, saying: "Soldiers! this is the symbol of French glory, and it is destined to become the symbol of Liberty. For fifteen years it led our forefathers to victory: it shone on every battlefield, it was borne through every capital in Europe. Rally to this noble standard that I entrust to your honour and to your courage! March with me against the traitors and oppressors of the fatherland, with the cry, *Vive la France! Vive la Liberté!*" A thousand voices answered "We will". Then we marched off, headed by the band, every face bright with joy and hope.'

(*It must have been cold and still dark in the streets, for sunrise at the end of October was not till nearly 7 o'clock, and not many people were yet*

about. On the way to the general's quarters Louis detached Laity to sum-mon the Engineers, Lombard to get the proclamations printed, one section to seize the "télégraphe aérien", and another to arrest the Préfet of the Bas-Rhin department.)

'When I arrived (the story continues) in the courtyard of the general's residence (it was near the Arsenal, in the centre of the town), I went upstairs followed by Vaudrey, Parquin, and two officers. The general was not yet dressed. "General", I said, "I come as a friend. I should be distressed if I had to raise our old tricolour again without a brave soldier like you. The garrison has declared for me. Make up your mind, and follow me." They showed him the eagle; but he thrust it aside, saying "They have deceived you, Prince. The army will do its duty, and I am going to prove it here and now." I left him then, and gave orders that an artillery picket should stay behind and keep him under arrest . . . When I left the general's house I was greeted with renewed cries of *Vive l'Empereur!* . . . but I was already deeply affected by this failure, which I had not expected, for I was certain that the mere sight of the eagle would revive the general's old memories of military fame, and would bring him to my side.

'We marched on, leaving the main street and entering the Finkmatt barracks (at the north end of the town) by the narrow lane leading to it from the faubourg de Pierre. It is a big build-ing, set in a kind of *cul-de-sac*, and the space in front is too narrow for a regimental parade in battle order. Finding myself hemmed in between the city wall and the barracks, I realized that our plan had gone wrong. When we arrived the soldiers crowded round us, and I made a speech. Most of them went off to get their arms, and returned to rally round us with cries of sympathy. But I saw amongst. them signs of hesitation, due to some officers spreading rumours that threw doubts on our identity (someone had said Louis was Vaudrey's nephew, an impostor); and as in any case we were wasting valuable time in an unfavourable position, instead of hurrying on at once to the other regiments that were expecting us, I suggested to the Colonel that we should leave. He advised me to stay, and I took his advice. A few minutes afterwards it was too late. Some infantry officers arrived, shut the gates, and strongly reprimanded their men. They hesitated: I tried to arrest the officers: their men released them. This led to general confusion, and the space was so restricted that we were all lost in the crowd. Civilians standing on the city wall threw stones at the troops. The gunners wanted to use their guns, but we pre-

vented them, for we saw at once that we should have caused a number of casualties. I saw the Colonel at one moment arrested by the infantry and at another rescued by our men. I myself was nearly killed in the middle of a mass of men who, when they recognized me, struck at me with their bayonets; and I was parrying their blows with my sword, and trying to quiet them down, when the gunners came up, rescued me from their muskets, and surrounded me. Then I dashed with several non-commissioned officers towards the mounted gunners in order to secure a horse, all the infantry following me. I found myself hemmed in between the horses and the wall, unable to move. At that moment the soldiers came up from every direction, and seized me, and took me to the guard-room. As I went in I found M. Parquin there. I grasped his hand. He greeted me with a calm and resigned air, saying, "We shall be shot, Prince, but we will make a good end." — "Yes, I replied, we have failed, but it was a fine and noble attempt." ' (*It was barely 8 o'clock: the whole affair was over in two hours.*)

5

Owing to the inefficiency of the semaphore system (*télégraphe aérien*) in foggy weather, it took thirty-six hours for the news of the Strasbourg *putsch* to reach Paris, two hundred and fifty miles away. When it was realized that the attempt had failed, what might have been an epic became, under the shrewd management of Louis-Philippe, almost a farce. Whilst Louis in prison spoke readily of his intention to 'establish a government based on popular election' and to 'summon a National Congress', Vaudrey, persuaded that it was really a Bourbon plot, surrendered the Arsenal, Lombard destroyed the proclamations, and Persigny, after burning some compromising papers, made his escape, still threatening violence. He need not have done so; nor need Hortense have feared for her son's life, and hurried off to Paris to save him. The one object of the government, as in the case of the Duchesse de Berry two years before, was to avoid undue publicity, and to prevent the affair being exploited by the political opposition. After spending ten days in prison at Strasbourg, Louis was bustled off on November 9th to Paris, and within four days found himself, not (as he may have feared), like a second d'Enghien, at Vincennes, but at Lorient, to be shipped off unpunished, indeed untried, to North America. No one saw him,

unless it was on November 12th, in the *salle-à-manger* of the *Préfecture de Police* at Paris, where a Spanish girl of ten, Eugenia de Montijo, playing there with the Delessert children, caught a glimpse of her future husband sitting at table, refreshing himself with biscuits and a glass of champagne.[16] He was given no opportunity to deny the misleading accounts of his conduct and bearing handed out to the ambassadors of foreign powers, or to answer the insults and caricatures of the Paris Press.

For his mother he had drafted two letters, one announcing success, the other failure. It was the first which reached her on October 31st, but she soon heard the truth (Valérie Masuyer had relations at Strasbourg), and set out for Paris. From Viré, where she stayed with the Duchesse de Ragusa, she sent on her companion, Mme Salvage, to see Count Molé, the *président du conseil*. He assured her that Louis was in no danger, and she returned to Arenenberg. From his Strasbourg prison, from the Paris Prefecture, and from Lorient, whilst waiting to sail, Louis wrote to his mother, urging her not to try to follow him; whilst to his old friend Vieillard and to Odilon Barrot he said that he took full responsibility for what had been done, and was very sorry he was not to be able to share the punishment of his fellow-conspirators. But in fact there was nothing to share. The twelve days' trial at Strasbourg in January 1837 ended in the acquittal of all the accused; and local opinion was so obviously on their side that no attempt was made to reverse the verdict or to penalize the regiments which had taken part in the rising. Indeed the government must have regretted ever allowing the trial to come on; for it gave the prisoners an opportunity to advertise the aims of the conspiracy; whilst the sale of five thousand copies of a hastily compiled biography of their leader suggested that Bonapartism had vitality enough to survive this temporary set-back.

The effect of failure upon Louis' deep irrepressible optimism was to increase his romantic faith in his destiny: it was the same all through his early career. During the long voyage across the Atlantic — for (the better to silence her passenger) the *Andromède* was diverted by sealed orders to Rio de Janeiro — Louis longed for a sight of St. Helena, and repeated to himself the Bonapartist creed: 'Alas! I could never catch sight of the historic rock (he wrote to Vaudrey on April 15th); but it always seemed to me that on the breeze floated the last words of the Emperor to the companions of his exile — "I have sanctioned all the principles of the Revolution: I have infused

them into my laws, into my acts".' 'If the Emperor (he wrote to Joseph a week later) looks down from heaven, he will be satisfied with me.' He already regarded the French colony in New York and Philadelphia as he had regarded the French colony in London: it was to be a fresh centre of Bonapartist propaganda. Even at Rio, where he was not allowed to land, he managed to smuggle ashore a communiqué to the local press, giving his own version of the Strasbourg affair.

But America was no longer the serpentless Paradise of Liberty that Lafayette had helped to create sixty years before, and that the king whom Louis was trying to dethrone had visited so agreeably in 1797. A year after Lafayette landed in South Carolina there had arrived at Baltimore a successful shipowner who had made a fortune by gun-running — a prototype of the 'big business' man who was to supplant the original Puritan. William Patterson lived to be one of the richest men in the States, and to marry his daughter to the youngest brother of the Emperor Napoleon. In the letters of Elizabeth Patterson[17] — a lovely, ambitious and self-centred girl, the first of the American heiresses — can be read the contrast between the prosperous Puritan Philistinism of Baltimore and the cultured Bohemianism of Paris or Florence: the contrast also, illustrated by her own shrewd investments, between the extravagant finance of the Bonapartes — gamblers all, generous in promises, mean in fulfilment — and the solid cautious money-making of her father's business friends. America was now a plutocracy, with a national character and (whatever Elizabeth might say) a culture of its own. It was no longer so impressed by Royalty as it had been when Jérôme Bonaparte landed there in 1804.

It had indeed grown to like and respect his brother Joseph, who had arrived at New York (succeeding where Napoleon failed) in 1815; for he was a rich man who invested his money in real estate, and built at 'Point Breeze' on the Delaware a big mansion filled with the loot of Italian picture-galleries; and here the Comte de Survilliers, as he called himself (from a part of his old property at Mortefontaine), entertained French, Italian, and Spanish refugees, but without committing himself or his purse to their designs — not even that of rescuing his brother from St. Helena. Ten years later he was still an American land-owner, though a French citizen, dealing with the marriage designs of one or another of the impecunious Bonapartes upon his well-endowed daughters. But the accession of

Louis-Philippe hurt his Bonaparte pride deeply enough to take him back to Europe in 1832, the year in which Louis had met him in London: and he was still there when the nephew whose Strasbourg *coup* upset all his plans landed at Norfolk, Virginia, after four months at sea, on March 30th, 1837. Louis had written, before he sailed, asking his uncle for a letter of introduction to Philadelphia and New York society, and proposing to purchase part of Joseph's estate. The letter was unanswered, and 'Point Breeze' remained closed against him.[18]

But at New York his friend Arese (who had sailed direct) and his servant Thélin were waiting to welcome him, and soon became the centre of a group of French and Italian patriots.

It is never easy to follow the comings and goings of the exiled Bonapartes. But certainly young Jérôme Bonaparte, the son of Elizabeth Patterson, was in America at this time, with his mother: he married to Susan Williams, and founding a family, she brightening the *ennui* of Baltimore society with a store of smart clothes and jewellery brought back from Paris in 1834. Louis had been friendly enough with Jérôme when they were together in Rome in 1826, and one would expect them to have met now; but there seems to be no evidence of it. Achille and Lucien Murat had been settled in the States since 1922, the one as an officer in the army, the other in civilian employment. But again there is no evidence of contact. On the other hand the family reputation was not improved by the presence of Pierre (aged 22), the third son of Lucien Bonaparte by his second wife, Mme Jouberthon – a violent and disorderly youth who all his life, and wherever he was – Italy, America, England, Albania, Algeria – courted adventure and got into trouble with the police; he was to follow Louis to London, and embarrass him there, and to reappear at Paris more than thirty years later in a scandalous incident during the crisis of 1870.

Whatever comfort was lacking in his relations Louis found in the hospitality shown by New York society to a foreign prince with more fame than fortune, who carefully studied the American scene and had a flattering way with women. For Louis, to his credit, was interested in everyone and everything: the Brazilian librarian and French scientist who were his fellow-voyagers on the *Andromède*; the soldiers, politicians, and literary men (Washington Irving among them) whom he met in American drawing-rooms; the Hamiltons, Livingstones, Schuylers, and other 'old' families of the new world;

and the railways, steamships, farms, and warehouses of a country which (he remarked) 'possesses immense material forces, but is deficient in moral force': yet, he added, with more discernment than Elizabeth Patterson, 'the moral world begins to rise upon the physical world . . . The reign of ideas is opening on this side of the Atlantic'; and he noticed that the tyranny of authority was giving way to the tyranny of the crowd.

Louis' behaviour, if only because he had no money to indulge his fancies, was discreet, and earned the approval of General Watson Webb and his brother-in-law, the Rev. C. S. Stewart, a naval chaplain, who twenty years later wrote a vindication of him against charges apparently due to confusion between Louis and the deplorable Pierre. He was temperate in food and drink, and never gave ground for suspicion of irregular habits. What most impressed this American was his affection for his mother, and his recurrent talk about his French claims and designs: Louis (he said) regarded the failure at Strasbourg as a providential sign that his hour had not yet come: for though he sometimes talked of settling down in America, and planned a journey to investigate the country (a design carried out by his friend Arese after his departure) – he would no doubt, in his adaptable way, have made himself at home there – yet he was for ever dreaming about a bigger destiny. He had given no promise (though it was alleged against him) not to return to France. His fellow-conspirators were active in Paris and London. Even here in New York his friends were trying to secure his promise to renew the attempts of 1831 and 1836. He only awaited a call.[19]

It came unexpectedly, and in an unhappy form. His mother had long been ailing, and was none the better for her anxious journey to Paris after the Strasbourg affair. In the spring of 1837 her doctor, Conneau (a Corsican with a French head and an Italian heart, medical adviser of the Bonapartes in Rome, and since 1831 one of Hortense's household at Arenenberg), in consultation with two Swiss colleagues, diagnosed cancer, and asked Dr. Lisfranc of Paris to operate. Perhaps fearing the responsibility, he refused. Hortense wrote to Louis that she had been threatened with an operation, but that she was glad of the decision, for it would have been a great risk. She evidently did not know that it was the only hope of saving her life, or that Valérie Masuyer (or it may have been Conneau) had added at the foot of her letter the summons *Revenez, revenez*. When, on June 3rd, Louis read this ominous postscript, he booked a

passage by the next packet. He sailed on the 12th, and was in London by July 10th.[20]

There he was delayed for nearly three weeks, staying at Fenton's Hotel, and trying to get a passport for the journey on to Switzerland. Persigny was at hand to help him, and Lady Dudley Stuart dealt with the embarrassing Pierre Bonaparte, who had followed him to England. But Sébastiani, now at the French Embassy, reported his arrival to Molé in Paris, and was instructed not merely to refuse a passport, but to have Louis carefully watched. The Austrian and Prussian ambassadors would do nothing.[21] At last he got a false passport in the name of Robinson, left London on July 29th, and travelled in disguise by Rotterdam and the Rhine to Mannheim, and thence by road. So he reached Arenenberg on August 4th, in time to be with his mother for two months before she died on October 5th. She was buried a week later (but Louis could not be there) at Rueil, near Malmaison, by the side of her mother Joséphine.

It is worth while to notice, in passing, the contrast between the romantic European and the prosaic American atmospheres in their influence upon the Bonapartes. (What would have happened, for instance, if Napoleon had settled, as he wished to do, in the States?) Of all the young Bonapartes, *Napoléonides* of the second generation, Louis and Jérôme most resembled one another in the circumstances of their childhood and education. Hortense was, next to Joséphine, the woman whom the First Consul most admired: it was said of Elizabeth Patterson that, failing Joséphine, she would have been the perfect wife for Napoleon. Both were beautiful — Hortense (though half a Creole) with the conventional good looks of the old world, Elizabeth with the unfamiliar loveliness of the new. Both had been deprived of thrones — Hortense by Louis' abdication, Elizabeth by Napoleon's refusal to recognize her marriage to his brother Jérôme. Both were ambitious, self-centred, worldly-minded; but each had a son on whom every surplus of affection and ambition was expended; and both had taken care to educate these sons for the high position that might still be theirs. Jérôme had just left Harvard; Louis still felt the influence of Le Bas. They had many interests in common, many divergent opinions and impressions too to discuss. But whereas Jérôme always remained faithful to the American way of life which his mother renounced, and was to shatter all her dreams by marrying a Baltimore girl, and settling

48

down to the commonplace business life of his grandfather's family, Louis shared all his mother's cosmopolitan tastes and Bonapartist designs, laying up in his heart the supernatural voices and visions that forecast his imperial destiny. If Hortense, at the moments of crisis in 1831 and 1836, feared for his life, she never wavered in her hope of his final success. It is said that when he set out for Strasbourg she placed on his finger the marriage ring of Joséphine; at any rate the memory of his mother remained, after her death, the closest link between *le Petit* and *le Grand* Napoleon.[22]

6

If Louis in action, as in Rome in 1831 and at Strasbourg in 1836, showed an incapacity for planning or carrying out a *coup de main*, he exhibited, in the intervals of enforced inaction, something like a genius for the arts of propaganda. Nothing could have been better managed than the situation created by his presence in Switzerland in 1838. He had hardly settled down, after his mother's death, in the castle of Gottlieben, which he inherited under her will, than the French Foreign Office reminded the Swiss government of its participation in 1816 in the ban against the Bonapartes, and demanded his expulsion. Louis retaliated by encouraging his fellow-conspirator of Strasbourg, now living with him at Arenenberg, Lieutenant Laity, to publish a full account of that affair (*Relation historique des événements du 30 octobre 1836*), making it out to have been a serious insurrection, which jeopardized the French throne. Of this pamphlet five thousand copies were printed and widely distributed. Louis-Philippe now fell into the trap which he had then escaped: Laity was put on trial before the *Cour des pairs*, on a charge of *attentat contre la sûrete de l'état*, and sentenced to five years' imprisonment, a fine of five hundred pounds, and police *surveillance* for the rest of his life. Not content with making Laity a martyr and Louis a hero, the French government renewed its demands on the Swiss so tactlessly (even to threats of war) that the Pretender to the French throne became a symbol of Swiss independence. He was able to advertise his claims all over Europe, and, at the crucial moment, in collusion with his Swiss protectors, to take refuge in England, where the government would not miss a heaven-sent opportunity of humiliating, with all diplomatic correctness, a sovereign whose friendship it held so cheap.[23]

In London too, he returned with immensely increased prestige to a better centre for intrigue. By his timely withdrawal from Switzerland he had averted war: by coming to England he associated two homes of freedom, two refuges for the victims of oppression.

The two years which Louis spent in England between his return from Switzerland in October 1838 and his Boulogne adventure of August 1840 were very different from his flying visits of 1831, 1832, and 1837. Then he had been a poor adventurer, a transient refugee: now he had a suite of seven companions, including Conneau, Vaudrey and Persigny; he was rich, and almost royal. How rich, has been disputed, for he was a master of the art of living on appearances. Hortense's will contained many legacies to Valérie Masuyer, Conneau, her domestics, and her friends: she had sold pictures and jewellery to meet household expenses. The sale of Arenenberg must have brought in something, and there was part of the rent of a villa at Lucca: but Louis could no longer count on the Napoleonic pension which his mother had struggled so hard to secure. In the end, he enjoyed an income of some £5000 a year from his mother's estate, and perhaps half as much from his father's: on both securities he raised large loans.[24] During his first months in England he was content with modest quarters at Fenton's Hotel and Warren's Hotel in Regent Street; but later he set up house in expensive style, first in Carlton House Terrace (Lord Cardigan's) and then in Carlton Gardens (Lord Ripon's), with a host of servants, a stable full of horses, a box at the opera, and a coach emblazoned with the imperial eagle. His friends in town were those of Lady Blessington's circle at Gore House (she had met Hortense in Rome): Bulwer, Disraeli, Greville, d'Orsay; the Rossetti family; the Somersets, Beauforts, Hertfords, and Harringtons; and the young aristocrats who lived on the hospitality of the Scottish Lord Eglinton. In this society he set himself to live the life of an English 'man about town', riding a fine Arab (he had a good seat on a horse), or driving a cabriolet in Hyde Park, taking the Disraelis for a row on the river at Fulham (and stranding them on a mud-bank), paying a visit, as an artillery expert, to Woolwich Arsenal, seeing Charles Kean in *Hamlet* at the Haymarket, and the French plays at the St. James', and taking a picturesque and leading part in the great event of the summer of 1839, the pseudo-medieval jousting and feasting of the Eglinton Tournament.[25]

What impression did Louis produce upon those who met him at this time? There is no lack of evidence: the drawings by d'Orsay

(wearing uniform with sword and star) or John Doyle (stiff and elegant on horseback), both showing the (as yet) short moustache and small imperial, and the profile which, a few years later, became such a boon to the caricaturists; or the pen-portraits of Greville — 'a short thickish vulgar-looking man, without the slightest resemblance to his Imperial uncle, or any intelligence in his countenance' — and of William Shee — 'quiet, silent, and inoffensive ... but he does not impress one with the idea that he has inherited his uncle's talents'; but by common consent most brilliantly impersonated by Disraeli's *Prince Florestan*, 'a pretender, and not a very scrupulous one', who, though he was not insensible to the charms of society, and especially of agreeable women, was not much chagrined by 'the neglect of the *crème de la crème* of society'. Though his acquaintances were limited, they were not undistinguished, and he lived with them in intimacy ... At Carlton Gardens 'there was a dinner twice a week . . . It was an interesting and useful house for a young man, and especially a young politician, to frequent . . . The Prince encouraged conversation, though himself inclined to taciturnity. When he did speak, his terse remarks and condensed views were striking, and were remembered'.[26]

There was all the time something deep and disturbing about him. He would spend hours studying in the Reading Room of the British Museum, and consulting his friend Panizzi, once too a Carbonaro, who had been an Assistant Librarian there since 1831, and since 1837 Keeper of the Printed Books. Odd-looking foreigners would be introduced by Persigny to the study in which he sat writing. Messengers would go to and fro between London and Dover. No one objected to his resuming friendly relations with his uncles Joseph and Jérôme; but when the illegitimate son of Napoleon, the Comte Léon, arrived in London, apparently to pick a quarrel with him, and forced a challenge to a duel on Wimbledon Common (March 3rd, 1840), which ended in an appearance at Bow Street Police Station, though honour was avenged, society was a little shocked.[27] It was realized that Louis' presence in England was a *façade*, a cover for political designs on the continent that might turn an act of national hospitality into a threat to international peace.

Not that Louis himself made any secret, amongst his friends, of his ambitions, if not of his designs. Alison's *History of Europe*, published during the years 1833-42, contained some references to French history after the date at which it ended, 1815; and among them two

notes on Louis Napoleon's bearing during his last visit to England. 'Nothing can persuade him (said one friend, the Earl of W——) he is not to be the Emperor of France; the Strasbourg affair has not in the least shaken him; he is constantly thinking of what he is to do when on the throne'; (and another, the Duke of Newcastle): 'We frequently went out to shoot together; neither cared much for sport, and we soon sat down on a heathery brow of Goatfell, and began to speak seriously. He always opened these conferences by discoursing on what he would do when he was Emperor of France ... The idea that he would eventually be the Emperor of the French never for a moment left the mind of Louis Napoleon.'[28]

Louis was not content with casual talk about his destiny. He was all the time carefully preparing the ground for another attempt upon the French throne. His fashionable friends were surprised when, at Leamington, during the autumn of 1838, he had long and secret conversations with Oborski, a Polish refugee;[29] and when in January 1839 he made a round of the factories and workshops of Birmingham and Manchester, note-book in hand. They did not realize, as he did, that the country he intended to rule was beginning to share the industrial experiences which had transformed the Black Country. They had not his reason for reflecting that Louis-Philippe himself had been brought up by Mme de Genlis and by his Jacobin father as a friend of the People, and had acquired during his travels in Switzerland and Scandinavia, North America and the West Indies a wide knowledge of how the other half of the world lived, and a more realistic view than many Socialists held of the demands of the Workers. The Pretender to the throne must, then, outbid the occupant of it. He must show, in the writings he planned for propaganda, how the interests of the People coincide with the prerogatives of the Crown.

7

Such, in effect, was the text of Louis' most ambitious and effective manifesto on Bonapartism, the 50,000-word *Les idées napoléoniennes*, written in 1839. 'The Napoleonic idea', it announced, 'consists in a reconstitution of French society overturned by fifty years of revolution, and in a reconciliation of Order and Liberty, the rights of the people and the principles of authority.' Why 'Napoleonic'? it might be asked. Because 'Napoleon saw that his role was to be the testamentary executor of the Revolution. What was his aim? Liberty.

With his rule all the passions of revolution came to an end. Strong in the support of the people, he proceeded at once to abolish every unjust law, to heal every wound, to reward every merit, to exploit every achievement, and to secure the collaboration of all Frenchmen for a single end, the prosperity of France.' This he did by centralization, organization, improving the lot of the poor, encouraging industry, and holding an even balance between rich and poor, the government and the governed. 'A constitution ought to be made purely for the nation for which it is intended: it should be like a coat so well made that it fits only one man.' To meet the objection that Napoleon was a man of war, Louis urges that he always subordinated the *ordre militaire* to the *ordre civil*, and that his wars were forced upon him by the Allies: if sometimes he seemed to be the aggressor, it was because he wished for the advantage of the initiative. (As Mignet says, the real author of a war is not he who attacks but he who makes attack necessary.) And anyhow the aim of all his wars and conquests was a Holy Alliance of Europe; it was 'to substitute for *l'état de nature* amongst the nations *l'état social* — a solid League of Nations (*association européenne*) resting upon the sovereign rights of each nationality and the satisfaction of their common interests (*des nationalités complètes et des intérêts généraux satisfaits*)'. If he failed, it was because his plan was too big, and his pace too fast: 'he tried to do the work of several centuries in ten years of Empire'.

What is the moral (Louis ends by asking)? Napoleon's system will remake itself, because Europe needs it; and he hints not too obscurely that the Emperor has an heir: 'Where today can be found that amazing man who impressed his personality upon the world through its respect for the superiority of his ideas?'

Louis gave a copy of the *Idées* to his friend Bulwer Lytton, who wrote in the margin (the book is still at Knebworth): 'Prince Louis Napoleon has qualities that may render him a remarkable man if he ever returns to France. Dogged, daring, yet somewhat reserved and close, he can conceive with secrecy and act with promptitude. His faults would comprise conceit and rashness, but akin with those characteristics are will and enthusiasm. He has these in a high degree. Above all, he has that intense faith in his own destiny with which men rarely fail of achieving something great, without which all talents lack the *mens divinior*.'[30]

The *Idées* was an appeal to the politicians, as the *Manuel d'Artillerie* had been an appeal to the army. For the common people something

more human and personal was needed. This was supplied by the *Lettres de Londres* issued anonymously (but generally attributed to Persigny) early the next year. Here two points were particularly emphasized – Louis' likeness to Napoleon, the lack of which had ruined his chances at Strasbourg (it was not until he became Emperor that he cultivated an appearance of his own); and the Napoleonic austerity and activity of his daily life (as observed by the faithful Dr. Conneau). 'The Prince is a working, active man, severe towards himself, indulgent towards others. At 6 a.m. he is in his study, where he works until noon, his luncheon hour. After this repast, which never lasts longer than ten minutes, he reads the papers, and has notes taken of the more important events or opinions of the day. At 2 he receives visits; at 4 he goes out on private business; he rides at 5, and dines at 7; then generally he finds time to work again for some hours in the course of the evening. As to his tastes and habits, they are those of a man who looks only at the serious side of life; he does not understand luxury for himself. In the morning he dresses for the entire day; he is the simplest-dressed man of his household, although there is always a certain military elegance in his appearance.'[31] One would like to have Bulwer's marginal comments on this passage.

Not content with propaganda aimed from England, Louis was deeply committed also to Parisian conspiracy. He financed two papers in the Bonapartist interest – *Le Capitole* (which cost him £7000) and *Le Commerce*: he was in touch with two Clubs – a women's *Club des Cotillons*, and a military *Club des culottes de peau*. A mysterious Marquis de Crouy Chanel, *alias* Prince de Croy, acted as go-between with the Tsar of Russia; Vaudrey and Mrs. Gordon, by no means discouraged by the Strasbourg fiasco, formed a liaison with their fellow-plotters in London, and acted as an agency for distributing the *Idées*, the *Lettres*, and a third publication, printed in Paris the same year, *De l'avènement des idées impériales*, recommending 'the sublime and national doctrine of the Empire' to the attention of all Frenchmen.[32]

Four years had passed since the Strasbourg adventure when Louis decided to renew his attempt upon the French throne. The sovereign he hoped to replace was now, at sixty-seven, an old and tired man. More attempts had been made to assassinate him. In 1835 the Neuilly plot headed by Armand Barbès and the *Société des Familles* had to be

suppressed, after street fighting, by the National Guard. An attempt was made to blame the Bonapartists; and Louis wrote to *The Times* to say he had nothing to do with it. 'If I were the soul of a conspiracy (he said) I should be the leader of it in the day of danger, and I should not deny it after defeat.' In 1838 one Hüber, already implicated in the Neuilly affair, had been arrested at Boulogne carrying plans for an infernal machine to blow up the King.[33]

Besides troubles at home, Louis-Philippe had troubles abroad. The failure to secure a meeting with the young Queen Victoria in 1839 — a sign that the French King's friendliness was not trusted across the Channel — was followed the next year by the refusal of the Chamber to grant a dowry to the Duc de Nemours — a personal affront from his own people. The successes, such as they were, of the Algerian campaigns of the 'thirties were outweighed, in public opinion, by the King's refusal to find a pretext for war in the exclusion of France from the Treaty of London in 1840. By the summer of this year the prestige of the French crown had sunk very low. But, as in 1836, so in 1840 Louis needed an omen — some single event to give point and urgency to the military *coup* by which he proposed to initiate his attempt, and to the popular appeal upon which he relied to clinch it. In 1836 this had been provided by the Fieschi plot, and the repressive laws of September. Now an even better occasion was to be supplied by Louis-Philippe himself.

That clever king was well aware that Bonapartism was one of the expressions of opposition to his regime. As long ago as 1833 he had tried to conciliate it by removing Louis XVIII's *fleur-de-lys* from the summit of the Vendôme column, and restoring the figure of Napoleon — but in civilian dress. Three years later he had completed that proud monument of the victories of the Republican and Napoleonic armies, the Arc de Triomphe. The Strasbourg affair, particularly the circumstances of the trial, suggested that something more was needed — some gesture (he liked gestures) which would publicly and permanently link the memory of the Emperor of the People with loyalty to the King of the French. Ten years before, only two months after his accession (October 7th, 1830), the Chamber had discussed but refused to act upon a petition for the recovery of the body of Napoleon from British keeping at St. Helena; and Victor Hugo had apostrophized the dead Emperor:

> *Dors, nous t'irons chercher! Ce jour viendra peut-être!*

Now, in 1840, 'the day' really seemed to have come, for on May 1st the King's ministers secured his consent to the plan, on the 12th it was discussed in the Chamber, and on the 26th the proposal was adopted, and a grant voted towards the cost of carrying it out.

It is significant that it was on May 15th that Louis consulted Orsi, his financial agent in London, about raising money for his fresh attempt, which (Persigny added) was now certain of success. But how much more significant, how much more certain of success, if Louis himself had planned, not only the attempt, but also the occasion of it! For it seems that, many months before, he had urged Joseph to sound Lord Palmerston, who had replied that he had no objection — he might even propose the return of the body to the French Government; that he had then tried to improve the occasion by getting Daniel O'Connell, a less tactful agent, to intervene, threatening to raise the question in the House; that Palmerston had then informed Thiers what was going on; that Thiers, seizing a heaven-sent opportunity to distract public opinion from his foreign policy, and to discomfit the Anglophobes, persuaded Louis-Philippe hmself to make the first move (through the unwilling Guizot, then French ambassador in London), and took steps to carry the affair through the Chamber. The proposal, as finally adopted (for it met with some opposition, and occupied three sittings) included the recovery of Napoleon's body from its grave at St. Helena, and its burial in the church of the Invalides. Thiers counted on this to win over the Bonapartists, or at least to deprive them of their strongest argument: Louis believed that, when the great moment came, he, not Louis-Philippe, would be there to receive, in the name of the French nation, the body of the national hero. So the *Idées* was re-issued with a foreword dated *Londres, 1840*, and with the motto *Ce ne sont pas seulement les cendres, mais les idées de l'Empereur qu'il faut ramener* — 'that amazing man who, like a second Joshua, made the shadows retreat and the sun stand still in the sky'.[34]

But there was one detail in Thiers' programme which would never have formed part of Louis': a blunder which spoilt the gesture. In his last weeks at Longwood Napoleon had instructed Bertrand to hand over the supreme symbol of his victories, 'the sword of Austerlitz', to his son, the 'King of Rome'. Bertrand had not done so; and now he presented it to Louis-Philippe, to be deposited with Napoleon's body at the Invalides. As the 'King of Rome' was dead, it might seem the best disposal of the relic; but to good Bonapartists it

was an outrage that the sword should, even for a few weeks, be in the keeping of a dynasty that had displaced Napoleon. Joseph fell ill with chagrin; and Louis wrote to *The Times*, saying that 'The sword of Austerlitz should never be in enemy hands; it must remain where it can be brandished in the day of danger for the glory of France. Let them deprive us of our country; let them confiscate our property; let them show generosity only towards the dead; we know how to suffer, so long as our honour is not attacked. But to deprive the heirs of the Emperor of the only heritage which fate has left them, to give to a gainer by Waterloo the arms of the vanquished, is to betray the most sacred duties, to force the oppressed to go one day and say to the oppressors: Return to us those things that you have usurped.'[35] This sentimental rhetoric was meant for Paris, not for London; and it was true to the mood in which Louis embarked on his new enterprise. On May 15th he knew that his plan was in train: on July 7th the frigate *Belle-Poule* set sail for St. Helena with the Prince de Joinville and a party of Napoleon's old comrades on board: on August 4th the *Edinburgh Castle* left the Thames with Louis and his friends for the invasion of France.

8

The expedition had been planned with the same attention to detail and the same disregard of essentials as the Strasbourg affair of 1836. It was to be a military *putsch*, as before, transforming itself into a popular rising; and it seemed a good omen that the troops of the Strasbourg garrison had now been moved to the northern command. At Lille, their headquarters, General Magnan, though offered a big bribe, twice refused his support. More was to be hoped from two detachments of the 42nd Infantry Regiment stationed at Calais and Boulogne: Lieutenant Aldenize at Boulogne, the easier of the two ports for a landing, was expected (in the absence of his superior officer, Captain Col-Puygélier) to welcome the invaders. To make sure of some military show — for the handful of supporters at Strasbourg had been too easily outnumbered — Louis had collected a following of over fifty, and chartered a small steamer, under pretence of a Channel trip, to carry them and their equipment to the French coast. This consisted of two carriages and nine horses (for the march on Paris), two trunks full of uniforms of the 40th Infantry Regiment (stationed at Calais), chests of muskets

and pistols, baskets of food and drink, and packets of proclamations, which this time had been printed beforehand. As at Strasbourg, there were to be three of them: one addressed to the people of Boulogne, one to the army, and a third to the French nation. This last repeated the dominant *motif* of the whole attempt: 'The ashes of the Emperor shall not return except to a France regenerated . . . Glory and Liberty must stand by the side of Napoleon's coffin . . . I feel behind me the Emperor's shadow urging me on; and I shall not halt until I have recovered the sword of Austerlitz, replaced the eagles on our banners, and restored the people to its rights.' To the army he said: 'Soldiers! the great shade of the Emperor Napoleon speaks to you by my voice. Hasten, whilst it is still crossing the ocean, to get rid of traitors and oppressors. To arms!' To the people of the Pas de Calais he spoke more soberly of the economic advantages they might expect from his rule. To these proclamations were added decrees — to be issued, no doubt, when the expedition reached Paris — deposing Louis-Philippe, discharging the army from its oath to the crown, dissolving the Chambers, summoning a National Congress, threatening with dismissal all officers who did not join him, and offering rewards to all who did.

So the strange expedition set sail. Was it tragedy or farce? A selfish adventure or a patriotic crusade? Only the result, as far as public opinion went, could decide. But at the last moment — by a gesture which seemed to add a touch of pantomime to the whole production — a tame eagle, purchased from a boy at Gravesend, was perched on the mast, and accompanied Louis' fortunes across the Channel. The company included, besides Louis himself, Count Orsi, the Florentine banker who had financed the expedition; General Montholon, now a man of fifty-seven, who had not accompanied the other companions of Napoleon's exile on the *Belle-Poule*; Colonel Voisin, an Austerlitz veteran of sixty; Colonel Mésonan, fifty-seven, another Napoleonic veteran, and Louis' unsuccessful agent at Lille; four other veterans, Desjardins, Montauban, Laborde, and Galvani; Dr. Lombard, Dr. Conneau, and of course, Persigny; the rest of the fifty, apart from the English crew, were mostly French, with a few Poles.

The landing at Boulogne had originally been fixed for the night of August 4th-5th, when it was known that Colonel Col-Puygélier would be away from his post; but owing to delays in starting, and in picking up separate parties at London Bridge, Greenwich,

Gravesend, Margate, and Ramsgate, the *Edinburgh Castle* arrived off Wimereux, just north of Boulogne, after a rough crossing, twenty-four hours late. This was the first set-back, but does not seem to have discouraged Louis' followers, who, with £25 in their pockets, and fortified with good food and drink, were assured that within a few days they would be in Paris, the heroes of a glorious adventure. They landed in the dark on the open beach, a boat-load at a time. They were discovered by a customs-house officer, who did not believe their explanation; but he and his men were forced to march with the supposed soldiers of the 40th Regiment to Boulogne. Here, half an hour after sunrise (which was at about 4.30 a.m.) they entered the Lower Town, by the coast road, Aldenize at their head, then Lombard carrying a tricolour banner inscribed with Napoleon's victories, Arcola, Marengo, Austerlitz, Moscow, and surmounted by an Imperial eagle, then Louis and his staff in generals' uniforms, and the rank and file. When they reached the barracks of the 42nd Regiment, the sentry presented arms, and they all marched in. So far so good. But Col-Puygélier had by now returned to duty, and, warned by Lieutenant Maussion (who had met the procession, but had been allowed to go free), forced his way into the barrack-square, rallied his men, turned out Louis' followers, and shut the gates upon them — but not before Louis had wounded a man of the 42nd with a pistol-shot.

What was to be done now? It was the position that might have occurred at Strasbourg, if Louis had escaped capture at the Finkmatt barracks. Should he accept defeat, and make his escape from the trap, as he had entered it, by sea? Or should he try to occupy the strongest position in the town, and fight it out? He decided upon the second course, hoping perhaps for the popular rising that a march through the streets might encourage. The lower town of Boulogne, though much changed, is still dominated by the old Upper Town (Haute Ville) within its square of medieval walls, with their three gates, and the citadel (*château*) at the north-eastern angle. That was the objective. But Col-Puygélier had gone ahead, and they found the gates barred. There was no hope of success now; but failure might at least be graced by a Bonapartist gesture. Louis led the way up the Calais road to the hill-top where the Colonne de la Grande Armée commemorated Napoleon's attempt to invade England in 1805; and on its summit he planted his avenging tricolour. But he was not allowed a heroic martyrdom, or even a

dignified surrender. When the troops and National Guards called out by the *Préfet* arrived, his friends hurried him away across the cliffs to the nearest point on the beach; and there with a few others he waded and swam out to a boat moored off shore, only to be fired on, thrown into the water, and rescued half-drowned by the pursuers. Louis, wounded, was one of five survivors. He was carried back to the Haute Ville and imprisoned in the *château*. By 8 o'clock every member of his little army had been taken; two lay dead on the shore. The Boulogne adventure had never even come as near to success as that at Strasbourg. It had lasted an hour longer.[36]

The failure was indeed so complete that the French Government was said to have connived in the adventure, in order to trap the Pretender. This was denied some years afterwards by Rémusat, who was Minister of the Interior at the time. He admitted however that it was known that Louis was planning something of the kind, and asserted that he had paid a Paris artist to paint a portrait of Louis' agent, Mrs. Gordon, hoping that during the sittings she might reveal his plans. However this may be, it seems clear that neither Sébastiani nor Guizot, who was also in England at the time, had guessed the exact nature or destination of the expedition. They took the rhetoric about Napoleon's body to mean that Louis might attack the *Belle-Poule* on her way up the Channel — and in fact her company expected something of the kind; but if so, they would not anticipate anything happening for some months.

Whether expected or unexpected, it was not possible to ignore a second attempt in four years to undermine the loyalty of the army and to plot the overthrow of the crown. Another unpunished exile would not be enough. At the risk of giving Louis an opportunity for self-advertisement, he must be formally tried and condemned. But not before a local court, like the Strasbourg prisoners, with the risk of acquittal. The Laity affair provided a precedent: Louis would be arraigned before the supreme Court of Peers, which could be trusted to deal severely with him. And to mark the seriousness of his crime, he was transferred under strict guard first to the *château* of Ham, and then to the Conciergerie in Paris, where he was put in the cell occupied five years before by the assassin Fieschi. (His father's protest, in a letter to *Le Commerce*, was in the purest style of Bonapartist rodomontade — as though no Bonaparte could commit a crime.) He was visited in prison by Mme Récamier, and showed his

gratitude by the gift of a copy of *Fragments historiques*. Meanwhile Louis-Philippe paid a state visit to Boulogne, where the troops and (more particularly) the National Guard were thanked and rewarded for their loyalty.[37]

The trial opened on September 28th. Every French trial was, by tradition, a debate (*débats*) between the prisoner and his prosecutors. There was nothing surprising, then, in Louis being given leave to make a statement; nor, except among those who had not read his *Idées*, in the ability with which he expressed his mission. 'Fifty years ago', he said, 'the principle of popular sovereignty was consecrated in France by the most effective revolution in world-history . . . The nation has never revoked this great act of sovereign power; and the Emperor himself said that nothing done without it is legitimate.' So Louis had no personal ambition, and no Imperial aim. His father had resigned a throne rather than rule against the interests of his people: his uncle had abdicated sooner than accept terms which laid the French frontier open to attack. Louis had never for a moment forgotten these examples . . . 'One last word, Gentlemen,' he ended: 'I stand before you as the representative of a principle, a cause, and a defeat. The principle is the sovereignty of the people; the cause is that of the Empire; the defeat is Waterloo. You have acknowledged the principle; you have served the cause; as for the defeat, it is for you to avenge it.'

It was a clever attempt to identify Bonapartism with the finest moments of the Revolution and the Empire, and to point to it as the only way of escape from the doom which had threatened France ever since 1815; and none of these pleas was forgotten in the long speech for the defence by the eloquent Berryer two days later. But there was no getting away from the bare facts of the landing at Boulogne, or the wording of the proclamations, which none of the twenty prisoners — though each had his say — troubled to deny, and upon which Franck-Carré, the *procureur général*, called for the heaviest punishment, short of death. On October 6th the court pronounced its sentence: Aldenize to transportation for life; Parquin, Montholon, Lombard, and Persigny to twenty years' rigorous imprisonment; Mésonan to fifteen, Voisin and two more to ten years; the rest to lesser terms. Louis himself was sentenced to perpetual imprisonment in a fortress within the French frontiers.[38]

What Paris, if not France, thought of the whole affair may be read in the *Débats* of August 13th. 'We will acknowledge that, if there be

a popular reminiscence in France, it is that of the Great Captain whose name is associated with our immortal victories; but if there be a forgotten family, it is the Imperial family. The son of Napoleon, in dying, carried with him to the tomb the remnant of interest which was attached to the blood of the Emperor. France has pardoned in the Emperor the unsupportable harshness of his domestic government, the unheard-of rigours of conscription, the disasters of 1812 and 1813, and the evils caused by his unbounded ambition; and in the popular mind the hero has been almost deified. The image of Napoleon is everywhere, from the humble cottage to the public monuments; but Bonapartism is extinct; even the *éclat* of the glory of the Emperor crushes those who ridiculously attempt to cover themselves with it. Where was M. Louis Bonaparte arrested? At the foot of the Column of Boulogne — the column raised by the Grand Army in honour of its chief! It was reserved for Bonapartism to expire on that spot.'[39]

But it had not expired.

THE OUTLAW (1840–1848)

HAM. Denmark's a prison.

ROS. Then is the world one.

HAM. A goodly one; in which there are many confines, wards, and dungeons, Denmark being one o' the worst.

ROS. We think not so, my lord.

HAM. Why, then 'tis none to you; for there is nothing either good or bad, but thinking makes it so: to me it is a prison.

ROS. Why, then your ambition makes it one; 'tis too narrow for your mind.

HAM. O God! I could be bounded in a nutshell, and count myself a king of infinite space, were it not that I have bad dreams.

GUIL. Which dreams, indeed, are ambition.

Hamlet, II, ii

I

HALF WAY between Amiens and Laon, on the direct line from Boulogne to Reims, is a town of 3000 inhabitants called Ham. Its château, built in the thirteenth century, still in 1840 — for it suffered as a modern fortress in the war of 1914 — bore all the marks of a medieval *donjon*, with moat, drawbridge, square court enclosed by crenellated walls, and a great tower of massive stone-work 100 feet high. The country round was marshy and misty, damp in summer, cold in winter, a haunt of waterfowl. The medieval cells in the great tower, though shown to visitors before the first world war as the place of Louis' imprisonment, had long been disused; Polignac in 1830 and Louis in 1840 were confined in part of the modern barracks built inside the courtyard — two rooms on the first floor for Louis himself, two on the ground floor for old Montholon, that faithful fellow-outlaw, and one on the first floor for the clever and companionable Dr. Conneau. The windows were barred, and the only entry was through a guard-room, where a detachment of the garrison of 400 was always on duty. Louis' sitting-room was about 16 feet square: dirty and dilapidated, until May 1841, when in reply to his complaints some improvements were made. The commandant of the garrison and governor of the prison was Demarle, who had arrested Louis at Boulogne, and had no sympathy with him; but after three months' rigorous treatment, during which Louis was allowed no visitors, and regretted the comparative freedom of the Conciergerie, whilst Montholon remembered how much more comfortably he had lived at Longwood, his personal charm and good behaviour induced his gaoler to relax these conditions: he

63

could add to his dog, his flowers (grown on a small roof-garden), and his books an occasional ride round the court on horse-back; whilst his valet, Thélin, was allowed to carry letters in and out of the *château*, and visitors were admitted to his rooms.[1]

Louis' chief cause of grief during the early months of imprisonment was the news of the marriage of his cousin Mathilde (November 1st) to the rich and brutal Russian, Anatole Demidoff. She had soon to get rid of him again, and it may well be that she proved more useful to Louis as a wealthy and fashionable hostess than she could have been as a wife. His chief cause of disappointment was that Napoleon's body was received in Paris, and the sword of Austerlitz laid upon the bier, by the Sovereign he had hoped to displace (December 15th). He consoled himself by publishing a rhetorical address to the dead Emperor (*Aux mânes de l'Empereur*) which was at the same time an attack on men who honoured him with their lips whilst in their hearts they were glad that he was dead, and that his living representative was safely under lock and key.[2]

With the coming of spring, and the easing of his captivity, Louis set to work seriously on the literary propaganda which was to be the chief occupation of his six years' imprisonment. He had said, when he was told of his sentence to *emprisonnement perpétuel*, 'Is anything in France perpetual?' He knew how many governments the country had seen since 1789; how many proscriptions; how many amnesties. Louis-Philippe was an old man, his throne tottering every day. It might not be many years before the Pretender once more made a bid for the crown. Meanwhile he could prepare the ground.

In January 1841 Louis wrote, for the War Minister, a pamphlet on percussion-caps for the French artillery. In May he published a refutation of Guizot's comparison of the accession of Louis-Philippe with that of William III, calling it *Fragments historiques*: the upshot of his argument was that the history of England teaches this lesson to kings: 'March in the van of the ideas of your time, and these ideas will follow and support you: march in the rear of them, and they will drag you down: march against them, and they will destroy you': the last way, of course, was Louis-Philippe's. But Louis contemplated a real contribution to history, and also to Bonapartist propaganda — nothing less than a *Life of Charlemagne*, which was to prove that, like Napoleon, his work had left permanent marks on European civilization. He had since his imprisonment reopened a correspondence with his old friend Hortense Lacroix (now Madame

Cornu) — a correspondence to which he contributed 232 letters during five and a half years. Hortense, a bright-eyed intelligent bustling body, was always ready to do a friend a good turn; a republican, a journalist, an authoress, she had access to literary and learned circles. To her Louis explained his aim, and asked for a supply of books. 'My history of Charlemagne (he said) can be summed up as an attempt to answer three questions: What was the state of Europe before his time? What changes did he bring about? What influence did this great man have upon subsequent generations?' By telling the truth about Charlemagne he hopes to tell the truth about Napoleon inoffensively. To men like Constant, Guizot, and Lafayette, Waterloo means only the *Charte* of 1815: whereas 'to myself, as to the French people, Waterloo is a poignant memory which still makes my hair stand on end; the fall of France, the ruin of my family; a sentence of death upon that colossus of a man whose name I bear'. But when Sismondi, whom he consulted, pointed out the difficulties of the subject, and denied Napoleon's likeness to Charlemagne except as a conqueror, Louis dropped this project, and was soon at work on less embarrassing subjects.

Louis' solitude was, during the summer of 1841, relieved not only by a two days' visit of Hortense and her husband, but by the frequent company (by the complaisance of the Governor), of a local girl, Alexandrine Vergeot, a cobbler's daughter, who remained his mistress throughout his imprisonment, and bore him two sons, Eugène and Louis: he took great interest in their upbringing, and provided for their future: for Louis was as kind and conscientious about what he knew to be an unconquerable weakness as his uncle had been casual and even brutal in his more occasional *amours*. He also resumed correspondence this year with his young cousin Prince Napoleon, Jérôme's son; telling him that on the eve of the Boulogne expedition he had drawn up a will making him his heir, and saying that though prison life was not particularly gay, he was at least on French soil, and within reach of his friends.[3]

The second year of captivity, 1842, was given up to a new work on Louis' special subject — *Etudes sur le passé et l'avenir de l'Artillerie* — and to a pamphlet on a question in which the great Napoleon had taken much interest: the beet-sugar industry. This had grown up under the Empire as a result of the Continental Blockade; its continuance had created a rivalry between the beet-sugar growers of France and the sugar importers of the West Indies: the eternal ques-

tion of slavery was also involved. Louis found good reasons at this time to support the industrialists against the colonists, and even quoted Robespierre's supposed dictum, 'Let the colonies perish rather than a principle.' Not many years later he became a champion of Free Trade against Protection: he was to discover — as he did about more than one of his convictions — that it was not a principle, but a matter of political convenience. One other literary project — it came to nothing — was that of founding a *Revue de l'Empire*, about which he wrote to Vieillard on June 10th. The letter is of more interest than the project, for it contains an unusually frank apologia. 'I have been called *entêté* (pig-headed), but it is quite untrue. I listen to all the advice given me, and after weighing it in the balance I make up my mind. It is the necessity I feel for choosing and deciding that has characterized me so.' A man on a desert island must build the best boat he can, and trust himself to it: he may escape alive; if he fails, it is a better death than being devoured by wild beasts or dying of *ennui*. 'You (Vieillard) rely on method and calculation: I rely on my faith — a faith which enables one to bear anything that happens with resignation . . . a faith which alone is able to move mountains . . . The fact is, the Napoleonic cause goes to my soul (*l'âme*); it stirs and revives pulsing memories (*souvenirs palpitants*); and it is always by appealing to the heart, not to cool reason, that one moves men in the mass.'[4] Napoleon, of course, would have thought less of his feelings, and more of the next thing to be done: but he never spent six years in prison.

Louis' letters to Hortense Cornu during 1842 deal partly with his writings (he wants books on the beet-sugar industry, and figures about agricultural production), partly about their personal relations: 'How I wish you were a man! You understand things so well, and I agree with almost all your ideas. All the same, I like you as you are, and it would be a pity to change; our relations would lose their charm — for my feeling about you is something better than love, something more lasting; yet it is something better and more tender than friendship.' It is clear that Louis has a poor opinion of that *l'amour* to which he is so constantly enslaved.[5]

The next year, 1843, whilst still working on the *Manuel d'Artillerie*, he has fitted up a small room as a kind of laboratory, and has time for a communication on his electrical experiments to the Académie des Sciences — a new field for propaganda; time also for a letter to Chapuys-Montlaville defending the *coup d'état* of Brumaire against

an attack by Lamartine; ('a man wholly antipathetic to me, a regular political-sentimental Don Quichotte', he calls him, writing to Hortense).[6]

2

But Louis' chief literary work in 1843 took the form of contributions to the local press — to the *Progrès du Pas-de-Calais*, the *Journal du Loiret*, and the *Guetteur de Saint-Quentin*. He wrote on all manner of subjects, as a good journalist must: about Parliamentary procedure, about Clerical Education, about National Defence; but always (especially after he dropped his anonymity) with a view to discrediting the Government and putting forward a Bonapartist policy; and in one of these articles, in answer to a questioner, entitled *Profession de foi démocratique*, he once more outlined his programme. 'I have never believed,' he wrote, 'and I never shall believe that France is the property (*appanage*) of a particular man or family. I have never claimed any rights but those of every French citizen. I shall never desire anything but to see the People as a whole choose with complete liberty the form of government that suits its taste.' In other words Louis is seeking to dethrone Louis-Philippe, and if the nation wishes for another monarchy rather than for a republic, he will put himself forward as a candidate for popular election as his successor. He thinks poorly of hereditary succession. He will, like his uncle the Emperor, be the People's choice.[7]

In the same mood he sends Hortense some material for a biography she is writing of him, to appear in the *Encyclopédie moderne*: about his years in the Artillery Camp at Thun, and his 'act of heroism' at Constance when he stopped a runaway carriage and saved the lives of the woman and child in it; with some particulars about the visit of Madame Mère and Pauline Bonaparte to Elba in 1814. He thanks her for a supply of tobacco — this was one of his solaces in prison — and so began his later habit of constant cigarette-smoking. He has been reading Adam Smith; he has had visits from young Thibaudeau, the scientist Peletier and his son, Mme Salvage (an old friend of his mother), d'Hérouel (a local land-owner and beet-sugar grower who had leave to visit him once a month), Degeorge (the proprietor of the *Progrès du Pas de Calais*), the deputy Joly, his foster-brother and *homme de confiance* Bure, his solicitor Noël, and (best of all) Laity, just released from prison. But he complains of public indifference to his fate — how the press would agitate if he were the last of the

Bourbons instead of the Bonapartes! He tells her about his first son by Alexandrine, born at Paris on February 25th, 1843 — 'a man in solitude as I am grows fond of anything'.[8]

January 1844 finds Louis getting up to work at 6 o'clock every morning; and on April 15th he sends to the editor of *Progrès* the article afterwards published separately as *L'Extinction du Pauperisme*: an elaborate scheme for state-subsidized land-settlement, based on Mansion's *Essai sur l'extinction de Mendicité en France* (1829), and linking up similar suggestions by Saint-Simon and other Socialists with Napoleon's scheme for settling old soldiers of the Grand Army in the Landes. This pamphlet was the best piece of propaganda that Louis could have produced: it was noticed in the Paris press; it brought him appreciative letters from the poet Béranger and the novelist George Sand (a recent convert to republicanism); and it even persuaded the working-class leaders that Bonapartism was on their side of the quarrel with the bourgeois regime of Louis-Philippe. Six months later Louis exploited this success with an article in *Progrès* criticizing the foreign policy of the Government, especially the expensive Algerian war; solid peace could only be achieved, he said, by a return to Henri IV's great plan for a United States of Europe. Something like this, which he thought he had found in Napoleon's mind, remained in his own for many years.[9]

It was at the end of this year, too, that he received a three days' visit from the Socialist historian and politician Louis Blanc — a visit described in his *Révélations historiques* fifteen years later. He would never forget, Blanc said, 'our stroll on the narrow rampart assigned to his melancholy walks, and overlooked on all sides by sentinels. I think I see him yet, walking with slow steps, his head bent; I think I still hear his voice, speaking low, lest the wind should carry his words to the gaoler'. The two men had much common ground in dislike of the Government and care for the common people; and the historian of the French Revolution flattered the Pretender to Empire by describing 'the imperial light which the passion of the moment would kindle in his blue eye'. Another visitor about the same time, an old American friend from London, Henry Wikoff, tried to win sympathy for the prisoner by underlining the 'dreary and repulsive' look of the country, the bare walls and uncarpeted floor of his room, and the air of 'dreariness and melancholy which surrounded him'.[10] This is not the impression given by Louis' letters to Hortense. He has had official visits from the *Préfet* and *Sous-préfet*; *une autre*

personne (his mistress) has returned from Paris (May 9th); and Laity now comes to see him three times a week (May 20th). He gets frequent news of his son Eugène. Though the Paris papers have not treated *L'Extinction* too well (August 3rd), the editor of a Paris paper is proposing a collected edition of his writings, and he is working hard at his researches into the history of Artillery. Hortense has become indispensable to him – his librarian, his almoner, his financial adviser. 'Since you left me (he writes) I say a prayer every day for you and your husband. You will smile, I dare say; but I pray every evening for those I love. There are not more than fifteen of them, so it is a very short prayer.'[11]

Louis' letters to Prince Napoleon this year show that Jérôme had been refused permission to visit Ham (August 3rd), and that he was acting as agent for the attempted sale of some of Louis' Napoleonic relics to his sister's rich husband Demidoff: this provision for future needs suggests that the possibility of escape from prison was already in Louis' mind.[12] The death of his uncle Joseph Bonaparte (July 28th, 1844) and the serious illness of his father soon brought it home to Louis how close he was to becoming the only representative of Bonapartism *de jure* as well as *de facto*. But to enforce his claims he must be free; and he was tired of waiting for the amnesty that might some day follow the death of Louis-Philippe. ('Being in prison is like waiting for death: nobody writes to me now: they have all forgotten me', he complains to Hortense – February 14th). Would the British Government, he wondered, which had shown him kindness in 1831, intervene again?

In answer to an invitation sent to him in January 1845, Louis' English friend Lord Malmesbury visited Ham on April 20th. 'I found him little changed', he wrote in his Memoirs, 'although he had been imprisoned five years, and very much pleased to see an old friend fresh from the outer world, and that world London . . . He confessed that, although his confidence and courage remained unabated, he was weary of his prison, from which he saw no chance of escaping . . . He stated that a deputation had arrived from Ecuador offering him the Presidency of that Republic if Louis-Philippe would release him, and in that case he would give the King his parole never to return to Europe. He had therefore sent for me as a supporter and friend of Sir R. Peel, at that time our Prime Minister, to urge Sir Robert to intercede with Louis-Philippe to comply with his wishes . . . As a precedent for English official interference I was to quote

Earl Grey's in favour of Prince Polignac's release in 1830. I assured the Prince that I would do my best; but added that Lord Aberdeen was our Foreign Secretary, and that there was nothing of romance in his character ... After a stay of three hours I left the prison, and returned to London deeply impressed with the calm resolution, or rather Philosophy, of this man, but putting little faith as to his ever renouncing the throne of France.'[13]

The result of Malmesbury's visit was that a month later the Duc d'Istrie visited Ham with an unofficial statement of the terms upon which Louis' release might be considered: a formal undertaking to abstain from any action against the government, and to renounce all claims to the throne. He was not likely to sacrifice so much for so little, and nothing more came of this plan. Louis soon found a better approach. In August 1845 his father's chronic ill-health took a more serious turn, and he sent his old secretary, Poggioli, to Paris with letters for Decazes and Montalivet asking the French Government to let Louis visit him at Florence before it was too late. There was no reply. This was a situation which Louis well knew how to exploit. He waited till November: 'I am making no move (he wrote to Hortense on November 12th): but perhaps they will make some offer to me, in return for undertakings': then on December 23rd he wrote to Duchâtel, the Minister of the Interior, promising on his honour that if he were allowed to go to Florence he would return, and 'place himself at the disposal of the Government'. The ministers refused this offer. Louis wrote again on January 14th, 1846, this time to Louis-Philippe personally, 'appealing to his humanity' to overrule his ministers' decision. The only reply (again through the ministers) was that Louis must sign a renunciation of his claims and a request for pardon for his offences at Strasbourg and Boulogne: a covering letter from Odilon Barrot and other deputies urged him to comply. But again he refused. 'I do not consider it consistent with my duty (he wrote to Barrot on February 2nd) to attach my name to the letter of which you have sent me a copy ... If I signed, I should be asking for pardon without avowing the fact; I should be sheltering behind my father's request ... I consider such a course unworthy of me. If I thought it consistent with my honour to invoke the royal clemency, I should write to the King, "Sire, I ask pardon".' To Hortense he wrote on the 23rd: 'The whole thing has broken down (*tout est rompu*). I shall not leave Ham now unless it is to go to the Tuileries or to the graveyard.'[14]

3

It was in this mood that Louis suddenly found an opportunity for what he had not seriously expected for five years — escape.

Finding his prisoner so amenable and so studious, the Governor of the prison had gradually allowed discipline to be relaxed. Repairs were going on: workmen came in and out: they chatted with the sentinels at the drawbridge, who took little notice of one more or less. Thélin, who was allowed to take messages for Louis to the town, easily smuggled in a workman's blouse and cap. Louis shaved off his beard, darkened his complexion, put on his disguise, shouldered a plank, and at 6 a.m. on May 26th walked out of the castle. The pipe he had put in his mouth, for further disguise, fell and broke: he had the presence of mind to pick up the bits. His dog *Ham* would have followed and betrayed him, had not Thélin prevented it. Once he was safe away, Thélin followed: Louis threw away his disguise, and they drove off in a *cabriolet* that was waiting for them. Two hours later they were at Valenciennes, where Louis picked up a passport made out in the name of Colonel Crawford by two ladies of that name who were staying at the *Plat d'Etain* and had visited him in prison. To cross the frontier as soon as possible, Louis went on by train to Brussels, where the Crawfords caught him up next day. Meanwhile, at Ham, Dr. Conneau was playing a comedy to prevent any pursuit. He gave it out that Louis was unwell, and had been sick; he must stay in bed. To enforce the deception he put a dummy figure in Louis' place, and produced a basin of nasty-smelling chemicals. It was not till nearly twelve hours after the escape that Demarle, paying his evening visit (he had been away the previous night), insisted on seeing his prisoner, and found that he had fled. It was too late to hope to recapture him.[15]

Twenty-four hours later — it was Derby Day, May 27th — the 'Comte d'Arenenberg' had crossed the Channel and arrived in London. 'On returning home from White's Club' (so Lord Malmesbury recorded it that day) 'a man ran over the street and stopped my horse, and at first I did not recognize him, but to my great surprise I saw Prince Louis Napoleon, whom I had left two months before as a prisoner in the fortress of Ham. He had just landed after his escape, and was going into the Brunswick Hotel in Jermyn Street. On the same day we dined with the Duke of Beaufort at Hamilton House, and as the party was sitting down to dinner I saw opposite me Louis

de Noailles, who was one of the attachés at the French Embassy, and said across the table to him, "Have you seen him?" "Who?" he asked. "Louis Napoleon," I replied; "he is in London, having just escaped." De Noailles dropped the lady who was on his arm and made but one jump out of the room, for it seems that the news had not yet reached the French Embassy. I never saw a man look more frightened.'[16]

4

No one comes out of six years' imprisonment the same man as he went in. Granted that Louis had the company of two old friends, a mistress, a valet, and a dog; that the Governor treated him, in the Bastille tradition, less as a criminal than as a guest; that the Governor's wife gave hospitality to his fairly frequent visitors; that he had all the books Hortense could supply, and that his correspondence went uncensored: yet he must be, for most of the time, his own prisoner, immured in his own thoughts, with no certainty — so long as the apparently deathless Louis-Philippe remained on the throne — that he would ever escape. Though he was treated well, and could exchange ideas with people who shared his interests and sympathized with his cause, yet he felt that he was forgotten by the world outside, and that Bonapartism was making little headway in the country. He escaped from imprisonment in poor health — rheumatic, under-nourished (he put on 4 lbs. between November 1846 and February 1847),[17] and with impaired eyesight: it was a marvel that his mind was no less alert, his interest in learning undiminished, and his will to pursue his political course more determined than ever. But he had shed at Strasbourg and Boulogne the illusion that his aims could be attained by a military *coup d'état*: intrigue, not force, was the means that best suited his genius. He still believed in Napoleon's maxim that he who would succeed must rely upon the support of the people (*Les hommes qui ont changé l'univers n'y sont jamais parvenus en gagnant des chefs, mais toujours en remuant les masses*); but he would not incite a popular movement; he would wait to be invited before he marched at its head.[18]

For this waiting policy London was the ideal headquarters. But first two matters must be settled: his obligations to those who might suffer for his escape, and his duty to visit his father's death-bed: for Louis was always dutiful and considerate, especially if a show of private virtue was likely to be a help to public recognition. Mme

Cornu had disapproved of his escape, about which he had not consulted her, but which she had guessed from a mysterious letter sent on the day before it took place. Louis now wrote to her (London, May 31st), promising that their work on the *Études sur le passé et l'avenir de l'Artillerie* would go on, expressing his concern for Dr. Conneau, and saying that he hoped still to visit Florence. Conneau was in fact put on trial with the Governor of Ham and sentenced to three more months' imprisonment. When he arrived in England, Louis gave him £900 to buy a medical practice.[19] As for his father's illness, Louis lost no time in writing to the French and Austrian ambassadors, the Duke of Tuscany, and even Metternich; but none of them would offend the French Government by giving a passport to an escaped prisoner, an unpardoned Pretender to the throne. He was still hopeful when he wrote to Hortense on June 20th; but he could not risk another journey across Europe with a false passport as he had done in 1837; and on July 25th his father died without their meeting again.

Free of these obligations, Louis could resume his plans for the moment (which he thought could not be long delayed) of Louis-Philippe's end, whether by violence, or old age, or forced abdication. His two immediate concerns were agents and funds. His young cousin Jérôme (Prince Napoleon) soon met him in London, and at Bath, where he spent the late summer recuperating, they were joined early in September by Hortense and her husband. Louis had moved from the Pulteney Hotel to 55 Pulteney Street: he went to Mass at the Catholic chapel, and to entertainments in Sydney Gardens; and he was fond of country walks. On one of these excursions they all visited Clifton Downs, and Louis in sentimental mood said he would like to settle down there and live in the presence of so much beauty; but Prince Napoleon, always antipathetic to his cousin's mind, supposed that 'When you have seen a thing once, it is enough.' An older cynic, W. S. Landor, was at Bath, too, but was won over by a presentation copy of the first volume of the *Etudes sur l'Artillerie* which came out at this moment, and by the easy way in which Louis took his disapproval of Napoleon. Other friends were met when Louis moved in the autumn to the Bedford Hotel at Brighton; here he 'experienced what Liberty might mean, cantering over the Sussex Downs', and was credited with a design to marry one of his fellow-visitors, Miss Angela Burdett, who had recently inherited the Coutts millions. But, as he soon discovered,

'Miss Coutts' money was left her on condition of marrying an Englishman'.[20]

There was some justification for such rumours, for Louis was seriously thinking of marriage. The death of his father in July 1846, followed by that of Prince Napoleon's elder brother in June 1847, brought it home to him how few Bonapartes were left to carry on the dynasty. Already on April 28th, 1847, he had written to Prince Napoleon: 'it is sad indeed to think that neither you nor I have any children. There will be no Bonapartes left but Lucien's illegitimate family (*la mauvaise branche de Lucien*). So I should be very glad to marry. But there hasn't been a word from Dresden: she must be an extraordinary woman!' The 'extraordinary woman' remains anonymous; but it is known that Louis had, during his previous visit to England, been struck by the half Spanish beauty of Emily Rowles, and that she sent parcels to him during his imprisonment, and made him a loan in 1851. But she was now married. When in 1858 her husband was sentenced for embezzlement, Louis helped her by purchasing the family pictures, and giving her a pension. A Miss Seymour is also mentioned.[21]

Back in London again for the winter season, Louis renewed his old friendships with the rich and fashionable; was elected a member of the Army and Navy Club, the Junior United Services Club, and the Athenaeum; frequented the theatres and opera as an admirer of Rachel and Jenny Lind; went hunting with the Queen's Buckhounds; and captured from the protection of Kinglake, afterwards the malevolent critic of his part in the Crimean War, the fashionable courtesan of the moment, Lizzie Howard — a lady of humble origin, but of beauty and wit, whose willingness to share her wealth with a prince was to Louis not the least of her charms. She helped to finance his cause in 1848, and their *liaison* continued till his marriage with Eugénie, when he pensioned her off with the title of Comtesse de Beauregard.[22]

Louis was now living — how far, a historian may doubt — beyond his means. Most of what he had raised by savings and sales during his imprisonment had gone to help his fellow-conspirators of Strasbourg and Boulogne. His new house in King Street cost £300 a year in rent. There was a limit to what he could raise on his expectations from bankers who hoped that he might later be in a position to do them great favours (Barings allowed him an overdraft of £2000); or from friends who might trade on his financial

difficulties (like one Pollard of Crockford's Club, who cheated him of a like sum); or from a mistress who hoped perhaps to share a throne. He had applied as long ago as 1845 to another royal exile, the Duke of Brunswick, tempting him with a document in Treaty form by which each party undertook, if he returned to power, to help in the other's restoration — the Duke to 'take possession of the Imperial throne of Germany', Louis to 'restore France to the full exercise of the national sovereignty of which she was deprived in 1830'. On the eve of his escape from prison he pressed the Duke (who was a very rich man) for a loan of £7500, and apparently with success. By these and other expedients Louis lived from hand to mouth, hoping and calculating that he would not now have long to wait before he 'came into his own'.[23]

Meanwhile he missed no opportunity of keeping his name before the readers of *The Times* and its Paris correspondents: on November 10th, 1846, by a denial of the charge made in Capefigue's *History of Europe* that he had broken an undertaking in 1836 not to return to Europe — a charge already disproved at the Strasbourg trial: 'I allow no one (he wrote) to impugn my good faith, which, thank God, I have known how to keep intact amid so many cruel trials'; by another letter to the same effect, when the charge was repeated in the French Chamber, on April 23rd, 1847; or by a private letter to the Editor the same year sending him an interesting extract from a letter of one of his friends in Paris. He might hope by such means to win the support of the world's most powerful paper.[24] It was perhaps mainly to keep his name alive in another influential quarter, the City of London, that Louis revived a scheme that he had started whilst in prison — that of a Nicaraguan canal from the Atlantic to the Pacific. Then it had been designed as a bait to the French Government, which might welcome his voluntary exile to the New World. Now it was put forward as a business undertaking to which the City was invited to subscribe £4 millions to put Louis' name on the map. But the *Canal of Nicaragua* never got beyond a paper scheme, and was soon forgotten in the greater opportunities of 1848.[25]

Two events in the late summer of 1847 must have seemed to Louis' superstitious mind omens pointing towards his return. His uncle the ex-King Jérôme made his peace with Louis-Philippe, was given leave (September 27th) to reside in France, and took Prince Napoleon back with him to Paris; and the body of his father, the ex-King Louis, was allowed burial at Saint-Leu alongside that of Napoléon-

Louis, both brought back from Italy to rest in the native soil from which Louis Napoleon himself was still an exile. Louis had not approved of the terms of Jérôme's petition to Louis-Philippe; but his dislike of such a surrender was overruled by 'the touching spectacle of the sole surviving brother of the Emperor reclaiming his fatherland'.

As for King Louis, he had made amends in his will for a slander of half a life-time by recognizing the legitimacy of his surviving son. '*Je laisse tous mes autres biens* (he had written) *à mon héritier universel, Napoléon-Louis, seul fils qui me reste*.[26]

5

Although nearly a century and a half have passed since English and French troops met on a battlefield, and it is a hundred years since Louis Napoleon himself sealed the *entente cordiale* between our two countries, yet the New Elizabethan needs, no less than the Old, a Chorus to carry his imagination across the Channel to 'the vasty fields of France', to understand the two mighty Peoples

> Whose high upreared and abutting fronts
> The perilous narrow ocean parts asunder,

and to 'turn the accomplishment of many years' — two great national traditions — 'into an hour-glass' of historical narrative. France has never been as England, or Paris as London; and an Englishman or Londoner deceives himself if he thinks he can readily comprehend French ways of thought and behaviour. The superficial knowledge of a foreign country gained by the easy travel of thousands may even be a hindrance to intimate understanding; and perhaps more Englishmen talked good French and knew Paris well in 1850 than in 1950.

Lord Normanby, the British Ambassador to Paris from 1846 to 1852, was one of these men, and his *Journal of a Year of Revolution*, begun in July 1847, may serve as a prologue to the events in which Louis Napoleon was to play such an important part. 'During the course of the month of July 1847 (he wrote), many circumstances had occurred which had seemed to strengthen my unwilling conviction that we were upon the eve of a great convulsion in France.' What were the circumstances that seemed so ominous? The 'railway elections' of 1846, returning a 'great Conservative majority' to power, confirmed Normanby's opinion 'that there exists in the

present state of France no attachment to any individual, and no respect for any institution; but that the system has been maintained by its identification with the material interests of the middle classes. *Enrichissez-vous* has long been said to be the paternal admonition addressed from the throne to the people'; but this had come to mean the purchase of Ministerial seats by promises of local railway-lines, to be assisted by British capital. This recent scandal had added to the disrepute in which the Chamber of Deputies was already held – a body 'elected but by an infinitesimal portion of the vast population of France', and prevented by its large number of public functionaries and rules of debate from any effective opposition to the government. Nor had the Press freedom to criticize; for an editor could be cited for slander before a court where there was no publicity and from which there was no appeal. This would matter less if Louis-Philippe himself still commanded the support that put him on the throne seventeen years ago; but 'such has been his conduct towards every statesman whom the system has produced that there is not one at this moment who retains the slightest faith in his sincerity'. Nor had he support in the country. 'There exists but a shadow of an aristocracy, with broken fortunes and without privileges.' 'In the clubs, amongst all the young men, and in the principal *salons*, the tone in general is hostile to the present state of things.' Even the middle classes, the supposed beneficiaries of the regime, were disappointed and disillusioned. What was more serious, there were 'vague rumours as to the spread of Communism', and 'another fact which is of serious import; there has been withdrawn from the savings' banks of Paris, within the last nine months, sixteen millions of francs'.

'Under all these circumstances (Lord Normanby wrote on) it is not surprising that the anniversary of the "three glorious days" (the Revolution of July 1830) should have struck me as a popular fête without any popular feeling ... I have mixed with crowds in all parts of the world, of all colours as well as of all tempers, and I never saw so little joyous a mass as those amongst whom I mingled during the three days.'[27]

This Paris crowd was the Sovereign People that seventeen years ago had overthrown one dynasty, and in six months' time would overthrow another; the Sovereign People to which Louis Bonaparte was once more to address his appeal. Why was it so unhappy, so impotent, yet so capable of sudden violence?

The population of Paris at this time was a little over a million, as compared with the 600,000 usually attributed to it in 1789. The number of workers (*ouvriers*) was 342,000, viz., 204,000 men, 113,000 women, and 25,000 children: not an overwhelming proportion of the whole, but formidable in the mass, when it is considered that they comprised one in four of all the *ouvriers* in the country, and numbered more than twice the total population of any other city in France. The greatest number of these workers employed in any one industry was the 126,000 of the clothing trades (*vêtement, fils, tissus*): the hours of such workers were fifteen or fifteen and a half a day, and their wages at most two shillings a day for men, one shilling for women, and from sixpence to ninepence for children. This would mean, allowing for Sundays, holidays, and other interruptions of work, that the total earnings of a family of husband, wife, and two children would be about fifty pounds a year. Such a family, living in one room of a crowded tenement, would always be on the borderline between poverty and destitution; seasonal unemployment, illness, or a rise in the cost of bread would bring them within need of public assistance or private charity. There is no need to paint in the darker colours— poor food, overcrowding, occupational diseases, and the rest — for which there is ample evidence in the contemporary accounts of Guépin (1825), Villermé (1840), de Morogues (1832), or Pénot (1828). Such workers could hardly be anything but unhappy and discontented.[28]

But why were they normally so impotent? Because they were accustomed to their lot, which had never much improved during half a century of revolution. Because the law prohibiting trades unions or strikes was enforced by magistrates and police under the control of their employers and rulers. Because they were disfranchised, and had no say in the government of the country or the capital. Because they were not (as at Lyon, for instance) nearly all of one trade, but divided into more than a dozen, with different customs and interests — 40,000 in the building trade, 36,000 in furnishing, 35,000 in local luxury products, and so on. And because most of these industries were still carried on in small workshops under employers (*patrons*) of a score or two of workers.

How was it, then, that this depressed and divided population of the Paris slums was so feared by the Government, and so courted by the Opposition? Because, for so many centuries, and by such a weight of national tradition, Paris had stood for France — the

residence of royalty and aristocracy, the centre of administration, the Mecca of middle-class ambition — yes, and the pulse of the French people. Because in 1789, 1792, 1793, and now again in 1830, the people of Paris had transformed the political situation by direct action. Because in Paris alone they were in touch with the politicians, and could be instructed and led by journalists and agitators. Because they had amongst them men who remembered how to build barricades and to conduct street-fighting. And because nowhere else in the country were there in daily contact such obvious examples and advertisements of poverty and wealth, ease and oppression, authority and unrest.

There was nothing very new in all this: the considerable trans-formation in working conditions which came about in the second half of the nineteenth century had hardly begun. But there had been some signs of change between 1836 and 1847 upon which Louis Napoleon built fresh hopes. Some of these were political. The gesture by which Louis-Philippe had hoped to capture Bonapartism — the re-burial of Napoleon at the Invalides in 1840 — had turned to his disadvantage. That apotheosis of the Empire would always be an argument against the Monarchy. A fiction is more popular than a fact. The Napoleonic legend could be better exploited from a tomb than from a throne. The dead hero and the sword of Austerlitz were still waiting to be rescued from alien keeping by the living repre-sentative of the Bonapartes. Nor had the attempts of the government to assert national rights and prestige — the corollary of the gesture at the Invalides — met with much success. The long-drawn question of the Spanish marriages had, indeed, ended in a diplomatic victory over England (1846) which wiped out the defeat of 1840; but it was at the expense of Queen Victoria's friendship, and of the *entente cordiale* spoken of in connection with the royal visits of 1843 and 1845; and it was interpreted in France less as a declaration of national independence than as a dynastic triumph of the Orléans over the Coburg interest. It confirmed the impression that Louis-Philippe's foreign policy was directed mainly by personal feuds and family ambitions. To these ambitions the death in 1842 of the Duc d'Or-léans, the heir to the throne, was a serious set-back; and the Prince de Joinville's pamphlet on the French navy (1844) came as an uncom-fortable reminder of opposition to the King's colonial policy from within his own family.

To the Paris workers, no doubt, it was not the foreign but the

home policy of the government which was working a change during the years 1840-47; and not the despised politicians but the admired (if misunderstood) socialists who were creating a new outlook. Darmès, whose attempt on Louis-Philippe's life coincided with the disinterment of Napoleon's body at St. Helena (October 15th, 1840), was said to be a Communist, and his programme was 'to talk to old women about Jesus; to the workers about their exploitation by their employers; and to the poor about the hardheartedness of the rich'. This would be a fair enough summary of the propaganda by which men who were socialists in their economic outlook and republicans in their political policy organized the Paris workers into the street-fighters of 1848.[29]

For a few months after the July days of 1830 the new government, like the Jacobin party in 1793, was too uncertain of itself to suppress the *sansculottes* who had put it in power: strikes, petitions, and demonstrations went unpunished: a *Journal des ouvriers*, a *L'Artisan*, a *Le Peuple* expressed the disillusionment of the workers with a revolution which had altered the political but not the social outlook: but by the end of 1831 the failure of the Lyon revolt showed that the government (again, like the Jacobins of 1794) was in the mood and had the power to enforce the laws against the *ouvriers*. For the next few years recourse was had to republican-inspired societies such as the *Amis du Peuple* (middle class, with affiliated workers) and *Société des droits de l'homme* (partly working class), and to a number of separate trade associations, particularly those of printers and compositors, tailors and boot-makers, the most intelligent of the workers. It was not Paris but Lyon which led the way to the next development. There the silk-workers, organized as *mutuellistes*, and backed by the *L'Echo de la Fabrique* (a sign that they were factory-hands for the most part) started another strike for higher wages which led to serious street fighting with the troops, and ended in the massacre of the rue Transronain (April 1834). The Laws of September the next year made the position of workers' *associations* all over the country so precarious that they existed, for the future, mainly as secret societies, with increasingly political programmes: such in Paris were the *Société des Familles* and the *Société des Saisons*: both were suppressed in 1839, but reappeared in 1840 as an amalgamated *Société communiste*.[30]

The immediate leaders in this development were, as always in Paris, men relatively unknown outside their parish or *société* —some

of them heroes of the *trois glorieuses* of 1830, a few veterans of the last few days of the Convention. But behind these men were the new *idéologues*, the republicans whom Thiers and Lafayette had cheated out of the expected fruits of the July rebellion: some of them (to adopt a recent classification),[31] publicly opposing the government in *Le National* and in the Chamber, corresponded to the Girondin opposition in the Convention: others, corresponding rather to the Jacobins of the 1790s, co-operated with the workers through the *Amis du Peuple* and *Société des droits de l'homme*, and expressed their radical views in the columns of the *Tribune* and the *Réforme*. Their most important leader was Ledru-Rollin, a friend of Louis Blanc, and his helper in the creation of the Second Republic — 'nothing more (said de Tocqueville) than a very sensual and sanguine heavy fellow, quite without principles and almost without brains'.[32] Others were social theorists rather than political reformers, followers of Saint-Simon and Fourier: the humane scientist Raspail, whose *Réformateur* anticipated many modern socialist measures, Considérant and Leroux, popularizers of socialist theory, Cabet, the communist author of *Voyage en Icarie* and editor of the Sunday paper *Le Populaire*, and Louis Blanc, the most influential writer of them all, whose *L'Organisation du Travail* (1839) was an instalment of a Beveridge Plan for the setting up of a Welfare State. But none of these groups was for revolution by violence: this was the creed of a fourth class which, brought up on Buonarroti's *La conspiration des Égaux*, a history of the Babeuf affair of 1796, revered the prophetic Proudhon, and followed the militant Blanqui whenever he happened to be out of prison. These were 'the Reds' feared by the government and hated by the army: the men of the barricades, whose martyrdom in 1848 and 1871 was to inspire Marxism and to create the International. Their papers were the *Christ républicain*, the *Carmagnole*, the *Journal de la Canaille*, or the *Robespierre* . . . Nor would such an enumeration of sects exhaust the reality. It was an age of ' 'isms'. Thirty years later an old lady could recall that her grandmother had been an Orleanist, her grandfather a Bonapartist, her first husband a Comtist, her father a Fourierist, her best friend a Saint-Simonian; she herself was brought up on a manual entitled 'Twenty-one precepts on the duties of a Perfect Republican-Socialist'.[33]

It was not surprising, then, that Louis Napoleon, viewing the Paris scene from his prison window at Ham and his study in St. James', decided that he must wait until some event (it might come

from any source and at any moment) fired the explosive fuse of socialism and republicanism. His attempt to exploit the Lyon affair of 1834 had failed; so had his appeal to Bonapartist feeling in 1840: Strasbourg and Boulogne were too far from Paris, and the army associated the name Napoleon with *la gloire* rather than with the rights of the workers. He had therefore tried to nationalize Bonapartism in his *Idées napoléoniennes*, and to socialize it in his *L'Extinction du Paupérisme*: his agents were in touch with many of the republican and socialist leaders. More than that: during his stay in England he had been aware of the Chartist movement, and its backing by the Christian Socialism of F. D. Maurice, at once so like and so unlike Lamennais and the doctrine of *L'Avenir*. His appearance as a Special Constable in Piccadilly on April 10th, 1848, was taken by those who knew his sympathy with the People and remembered his visit to Paris two months before as a sign of opposition to the policy of violence which he had then seen in action. 'Sir,' he replied to one who questioned his action, 'the peace of London must be preserved.' But he was thinking of Paris.[34]

6

The year 1848 – the most significant date in European history between 1789 and 1914 – means for this biography the Paris revolution which began with the abdication of King Louis-Philippe on February 24th and ended on December 10th with the election of Louis Napoleon as President of the French Republic. The course of these events in Paris has often been described in outline and in detail. What is less certain and more relevant is the reflection of them in Louis' mind, and the motives which led him twice to withdraw before finally accepting a national invitation to return to the country which had for so long exiled him and outlawed the cause for which he stood.

For three years before the outbreak, of which nothing but the suddenness of its occurrence took him by surprise – Paris had as usual been expecting a revolution, but not of that kind, and not then – Louis had his agents in the French capital: Persigny, Laity, Vieillard, Ferrère, Montholon, Piat, Orsi, and his young cousin Prince Napoleon. This last, in spite of the ban against his family, had been allowed to visit his sister Mathilde in Paris in 1845. Louis had written to him from Ham, advising him whom to meet and whom

to avoid amongst the 'crowd of spies and intriguers' in the capital, and urging him to lose no opportunity of forwarding the Bonapartist cause, of which he was (after Louis himself) the only worthy representative. And every inch a Bonaparte. Lady Holland, who met him in Paris at this time, reported that, on paying a private visit to the Invalides, his Napoleonic features so astonished the sentinel that the man involuntarily presented arms; soon he was greeted with cries of *C'est le fils de l'Empereur!*, was embraced by General Petit, who had been in command of the Guards to whom Napoleon bade farewell at Fontainebleau in 1814, and left amid acclamations of *Vive l'Empereur!*

Whether or not Louis knew of such occasional incidents, he still took a despondent view of his prospects. 'Nothing can be done at the moment', he wrote on August 24th; 'the nation is asleep, and will remain asleep for a long time yet. Whatever may be said, I have tried the only means of awakening it — the army; and I have failed hopelessly. I can't and won't try again: I must wait patiently for a better opportunity.' And again on October 27th: 'No one in France pays attention to anything nowadays but boilers and locomotives: true, they often enough explode!' But when (after a visit to Florence) Jérôme returned to Paris with his father in September 1847, it was as an observer of a situation which like the locomotives, might explode without warning.[35]

It may seem strange that Louis, a man of forty, with so many adventures and so much worldly experience behind him, should have chosen as his agent a youth of twenty-five, who had never strayed far from the influence of a happy-go-lucky father dependent upon anyone who would provide him with protection and cash. The fact was, Jérôme's son and daughter were the only members of the second generation of Bonapartes who shared Louis' belief in the family destiny; the only two who looked like Bonapartes; the only two who accepted the *idées napoléoniennes* as a workable programme; the only two who were clever enough to play a part in the Second Empire. But though he liked and used his young cousin, Louis never fully understood or trusted him. His character and ideas were a caricature of his own. 'What at bottom I find at fault in him (he wrote to a friend in 1846) is his incalculability (*caractère indéchiffrable*). There are people one understands and knows at a first meeting: whether you like them or dislike them, you know at once the kind of person you are dealing with. But Prince Napoleon is sometimes

frank, loyal, and honest, sometimes stiff and underhand. At one moment he shares in heart to heart talk about your ambitions, your sufferings, your sympathies for every great and generous cause; at another moment his conversation is dry, scabrous, and futile. What am I to believe? I always hope for the best, so long as I have no proof of the opposite; and, whilst I am always on my guard, I put no curb on my impulses of kindness and friendship.' This uneasy partnership of two *caractères indéchiffrables* supplies an intriguing sub-plot to the drama of the Second Empire.[36]

On January 29th, 1848, in the Chamber, Tocqueville delivered an apocalyptic harangue which is the fittest preface to the year's events, and provides the best justification for Louis' hopes. Was there no danger, he asked, because there were no riots? No revolution, because no obvious disorder? See what is preparing amongst the working classes. 'Can you not perceive that their passions, instead of political, have become social? . . . that they are gradually forming opinions and ideas destined to upset not merely this or that law, or ministry, or form of government, but society itself? that they are questioning the right of property, as resting on injustice?' Why did the old regime fall? Not by the act of any individual. No: 'the class that was then the governing class had become, through its indifference, its selfishness, its vices, incapable and unworthy of governing the country' . . . That is the situation again now . . . Legislative changes are not enough. 'In God's name, change the spirit of the Government; for, I repeat, that spirit will lead you into the abyss.'[37]

Less than a month later Tocqueville's words came true. An apparently frivolous dispute about the time and place of a political banquet (one of a six months' series in a campaign of anti-government propaganda) gave an occasion, on February 22nd, for a students' demonstration which led to a popular insurrection and the building of barricades. When the government called on the National Guard for its traditional duty of suppressing the *sansculottes* in the name of the *bourgeoisie*, it appeared that nine out of twelve battalions would not take orders from Guizot. The King's dismissal of the unpopular minister on the 23rd might have ended the affair, but for an accidental clash between troops and demonstrators in the Boulevard des Capucins that evening, when over thirty civilians were killed. When Louis-Philippe heard of it, he dismissed Guizot's successor, Molé, and called in the regular army under Bugeaud to pacify or coerce the crowds. Both methods failed; and next day,

the 24th, he abdicated in favour of his grandson, the Comte de Paris, and escaped, as Louis XVI had done fifty years before, through the Tuileries gardens. Fortunately for France and for himself he was not recaptured; and on March 3rd, after adventures 'like one of Walter Scott's best tales', as Palmerston put it, he arrived disguised as Mr. William Smith at the Bridge Inn at Newhaven.[38]

With Louis-Philippe there passed away not only a dynasty but an age, never to return. So it must have seemed to the dying Chateaubriand, as he listened to the gunfire of February, and to Madame Récamier, who sat by his bedside, almost blind, and destined to die less than a year later.

Louis had been taken by surprise by the events of February 22–24th, and could not tell, until he was in Paris, what the situation might be. When he arrived there post-haste on the 25th, the revolution was over. In the streets the people who had put up the barricades were pulling them down again. Someone asked him to lend a hand in replacing the *pavé*. 'My good woman,' he is said to have replied, 'that is just what I have come to Paris for.' But would his help be welcomed by the Provisional Government which was already set up? At midnight, from Vieillard's lodgings in the rue de Sentier, Persigny carried a letter to the Hôtel de Ville:

Gentlemen,

The people of Paris having heroically destroyed the last traces of the foreign invasion, I hurry from exile to place myself under the banner of the newly proclaimed Republic. Having no ambition but to serve my country, I hasten to report my arrival to the members of the Provisional Government, and to assure them of my devotion to the cause they represent, and of my personal sympathy.

LOUIS NAPOLEON BONAPARTE

But the Provisional Government saw in Louis a rival to their appeal for popular support, not an ally; and he was quick to see that this was not the moment for another Bonapartist *putsch*. He returned to England, leaving behind a second letter:

Gentlemen,

After 33 years of exile and persecution, I believed I had acquired the right to find once more a refuge on the soil of

the fatherland. You think that my presence in Paris at this moment is embarrassing; I therefore withdraw for the time being. You must take this sacrifice as a sign of the purity of my intentions, and of my patriotism.

L. N. BONAPARTE[39]

For the next seven months Louis watched the course of events in Paris from across the Channel, very closely, very cautiously, estimating his chances, and refusing to be drawn by the rash advice of Laity or Persigny into any premature move.

The Provisional Government of February 24th consisted of seven nominees of the *National* (right) and three of the *Réforme* (left). They interpreted the popular rising which had put them in control, and which had expressed its desires through 171 journals and 145 clubs, as a demand for the old Republic 'one and indivisible'; for the tricolour in place of the red flag (this Lamartine insisted upon); for the abolition of capital punishment; the end of slavery in the colonies; freedom of meeting (*réunion*); liberty of the press; membership of the National Guard to be open to all; financial stability, with a minimum of taxation; and a Constituent Assembly elected by universal suffrage.

This last would perhaps give Louis his opportunity. But it would never do if he allowed his name to be canvassed without certainty of success. At present he would only allow Persigny and Ferrère to seize every opportunity to advertise him, even encouraging his adherents to put his name, though not a candidate, into the ballot-box. He knew, like any modern Communist, that his time would come when the people grew disillusioned as to the hopes of the latest revolution. 'After Strasbourg and Boulogne', he wrote to Persigny, 'the poor and the republicans showed their sympathy for me, whilst the rich and the monarchists laughed at me as a mere Pretender. The revolution has not changed these opinions, but it has altered the interests of the two parties. The republicans have no further need of me, and have become my enemies . . . We must look at things more philosophically. At present the people believes in all the fine words it hears: it thinks it is going to get Henri IV's *la poule au pot*. It is drunk with victory and hope. There must be an end of these illusions before a man who believes in discipline (*un homme d'ordre*) can get a hearing. Until that moment any initiative would be useless and impotent . . . Either the Republic will consolidate itself – then I

can re-enter it as an ordinary citizen; or it will give rise to a period of disorder and bloodshed — and then I shall go and plant the standard of my name in a place where it will stand for a good cause, plain and clear for victory.'[40]

Louis then is a republican? Yes, because that is the political form that the revolution has taken; but a republican who believes in the necessity of strong government, a republican who remembers Brumaire, the Consulship, and the Empire. In the elections of April 23rd two Bonapartes were returned —Jérôme's son and Lucien's; but Louis refused to stand, and wrote privately to the Editor of *The Times* asking him to contradict a report to the contrary: if his name appeared in the ballot-box in some working-class constituencies, it was an omen, but no more. Until the Constitution was drawn up, he told Vieillard (May 11th), he could not even be sure of personal safety. 'So long as the social condition of France remains unsettled, and so long as the Constitution remains unfixed, I feel that my position in France must be very difficult, tiresome, and even dangerous.' This caution was fully justified. Only four days later an attack by the 'Reds' on the Assembly was a failure: but it was attributed to the Bonapartists, and the deputies retaliated by renewing against Louis personally the general exclusion of both ex-reigning families from France enacted sixteen years before. Louis sent Persigny, for publication, a protest against this action, with a covering letter in which he said that nothing would now induce him to leave England for another two months.[41]

In June a fresh group of supplementary elections was due, and it was known that the Prince de Joinville, who had not shared the unpopularity of his father, was standing for Paris on the very ground that Louis had chosen for himself, as an *homme de l'ordre*. This was too much for Laity, who, without asking Louis' leave, announced his candidature in posters all over Paris. Louis unwillingly accepted the *fait accompli*; but Persigny was instructed (June 1st, 2nd) not to commit him to anything: 'I want to be outside it all,' he wrote; 'I want to go my own way, and play the part that suits me — that or nothing.' When the results of the voting were announced, Louis was found to have been elected seventh on the list for Paris, as well as in Corsica, and in three country departments.[42] Delighted but still cautious, he well knew how to make capital out of his success. First he wrote a letter of thanks to his supporters.

Citizens,

Your votes fill me with gratitude. This mark of sympathy, all the more flattering because unsolicited, reached me at a moment when I regretted my inaction; for the country needs the help of all its children to emerge from the difficult situation in which it is placed. Your confidence imposes duties on me which I shall study to fulfil. My interests, my feelings, my wishes are the same as yours. A Parisian by birth (*enfant de Paris*), and now a representative of the people, I shall collaborate with my colleagues to re-establish order, confidence, and employment, to secure peace abroad, to strengthen democratic institutions . . . Let us rally round the altar of the country under the flag of the Republic, and let us show the world the grand spectacle of a people regenerating itself without violence or civil war or anarchy.[43]

But he knew very well that a Bonaparte who had made two attempts on the throne could not easily be accepted as a fellow-republican; and he cannot have been surprised when he heard that the next day Lamartine had declared the intention of the Government to enforce the ban of 1830 against him, that all the *Préfets* in the country had received orders to apprehend him if he appeared in their departments, and that Laity and Persigny had been arrested.[44] Nevertheless his election was valid, and he might have taken his seat. But once more he preferred an ultimate to an immediate advantage, and wrote another letter which put himself in the position of a John Wilkes or a Charles Bradlaugh — a martyr to principle against the tyranny of an unpopular assembly.

Mr. President (he wrote on June 14th),

I was starting to take up my post when I heard that my election had become the pretext for deplorable disorders and misunderstandings. I did not ask for the honour of being a representative of the people, because I knew that I was the subject of insulting suspicions: still less did I seek power. If the people were to entrust me with duties, I should know how to carry them out. But I disavow those who attribute to me ambitious aims which are not mine. My name is a symbol of national renown (*de nationalité, de gloire*), and I should be sincerely grieved if it were used to worsen the disorders and

divisions of the fatherland. I would rather remain in exile. I am ready for any sacrifice for the happiness of France.

The generosity of this renunciation was a little spoilt by the sentence *Si le peuple m'imposait des devoirs, je saurais les remplir*: it meant and it was taken by the Assembly to mean that Louis' real aspirations were not republican, but imperial. Such was the effect produced by these words in the Assembly that Louis, as soon as he heard of it, wrote again next day, emphasizing his republicanism, but resigning his seat.[45]

Once more his caution was justified by events. If Louis had blundered in hinting at his real aims, it was a *felix culpa* which in the end won the salvation of his cause. Within a week of this last letter the 'Reds' who had been defeated on May 15th returned to the attack, swollen by the discharged workers from the *ateliers nationaux*, singing the *Ça ira*, crying *La liberté ou la mort!*, and once more throwing up barricades. The Assembly commissioned Cavaignac to suppress the rising: he had under his command 30,000 regular troops, 12,000 *gardes mobiles* (recruited from the lowest of the people), and National Guardsmen from the *bourgeois* sections: he would fight in France as he had fought in Africa, crush the ill-armed Parisians as he had crushed the ill-armed Algerians, show no pity, and give no quarter. The affair lasted three days, and was not over until some 3000 civilians had been killed, and 6000 rounded up for exile.

Though some cries were heard of *Vive Louis Napoléon!* the June rising was not Bonapartist in origin. Persigny and Laity were in prison: Ferrère was ill in England. It was not, indeed, the work of any political party. It was one more of those desperate outbreaks of the Paris poor, workless, foodless, and voteless, under leaders of their own choosing, against a *bourgeois* monopoly of wealth and power. If Louis had supported it he would have lost the respect of the army and of the politicians; if he had declared against it, he would have forfeited his carefully built up reputation as a friend of the workers. According to Louis Blanc, whose *Révélations historiques* gives a vivid first-hand account of the revolution, he made a clever attempt at the last minute to back both sides, by sending yet another message across the Channel addressed to Cavaignac:

> General (he wrote on June 22nd), I know your feeling for my family. If the situation now developing takes a turn in our favour, you shall be Minister of War.

In other words, whether or not Cavaignac put down the rebellion, Louis hoped to profit by it, and would make a bid for the support of the army. But perhaps it was as well for Louis' reputation that this letter was not published.[46]

There followed a three months' interlude, during which the Assembly drew up the Constitution of 1848, and Louis silently prepared the ground for his third and final intervention. There is little evidence as to his state of mind during this period. On June 16th he wrote to Prince Napoleon explaining his refusal to sit in the Assembly, and regretting that his cousin (now deputy for Corsica) had made a speech blaming the Strasbourg and Boulogne adventures: what would he think if Louis reproached him for accepting Louis-Philippe's leave to return to France (which evidently still rankled)? But, as he told Persigny on July 19th, the Prince must be consulted, and treated as though he were Louis' representative: *l'union fait la force.* Only he must not sign his name as *Napoléon Bonaparte*, for that is misleading, and indistinctive. 'For myself (Louis says) I always prefer being called *Louis N.* to distinguish me from my other relations. I wouldn't mind being called *Louis-Napoléon-Nabucho-donosor Bonaparte* if it were necessary to mark my individuality.'[47] Another letter belonging to this time is to the Russian ambassador offering the Tsar 'certain objects of which I wish to dispose' in order to raise funds for a 'return to France in the near future'. He remembered Alexander's kindness to his mother in 1814, and Nicholas' purchase of her pictures in 1825.[48]

A second group of supplementary elections was due in September for thirteen departments. Would Louis stand again? General Piat asked for instructions, and received this reply, dated August 28th.

You ask me if I would accept the post of representative of the people were I to be re-elected. I reply without hesitation, Yes! Now that it has been demonstrated that my election in four departments at once was not the result of intrigue, and that I have kept myself a stranger to all manifestations and every political manoeuvre, I should consider myself wanting in my duty if I did not respond to the call of my fellow-citizens. My name can now no longer be made a pretext for disturbances. I am anxious therefore to re-enter France, and to take my seat amongst the representatives of the people, who desire to organize the Republic upon a broad and solid basis. In order to

render the return of the late government impossible there is but one thing to do, and that is to do better than they; for you know, General, we have really not destroyed the past until we have replaced it by something else.[49]

When the elections came on, Louis' name was put up in thirteen departments. Persigny was ordered not to talk (as he was apt to do) about Louis' designs on the Presidency. He took pains to disabuse Louis Blanc of the impression, due to some loose talk by Lestre, another of his supporters, that he was aiming at the re-establishment of the Empire. Every penny that he could raise in London was sent across the Channel to pay for election addresses and posters. The burden of them all was to be: 'There is one name which is the symbol of order, of glory, of patriotism; and it is borne today by one who has won the confidence and affection of the people. Let the choice of the people be also the choice of commerce, industry, and property. Let his name be a first pledge of reconciliation. He will obtain an amnesty for the victims of June; and his knowledge of political and social questions will help to deliver you from unemployment, destitution, and anarchy.'[50]

The result showed how shrewdly Louis had judged the temper of the electorate — its material needs, its hatred of the Government, its lack of interest in theoretical socialism, its Messianic hope in the name Napoleon. He was chosen by five Departments, and polled three hundred thousand votes. His victory was celebrated in Paris by a torchlight procession, whilst the band of the National Guard played *Veillons au salut de l'Empire*. This time Louis showed no hesitation. As soon as the result of the elections was known (September 24th) he left London for France, and put up at the Hôtel de Paris in the Place Vendôme, beneath the column of Napoleon.

7

He took his seat in the Chamber on September 26th; and the occasion seemed to justify an apologia. He had been elected as a republican; but he had twice been convicted of armed rebellion against the crown, not in the name of the republic, but of the Bonapartes — a rival dynasty; and it was obvious to all who knew him that this was more than ever his ultimate aim. But how many of the deputies knew him? — either his appearance or his character?

Sheer inquisitiveness gave him a hearing which hostility might have denied.

'*Citoyens représentants* (he began; and they noticed at once his nervousness, his unfamiliarity with public speaking, and his foreign accent — he pronounced *République Ripiblique*); It would be impossible for me to keep silence after the slanders to which I have been subjected. I must in this place, and on the first day that I am allowed to take my seat amongst you, make a public statement of the opinions which I really hold, and which I have always held. I have at last regained my country and my citizenship, after thirty-three years of proscription and exile. It is to the Republic that I owe this happiness: it is to the Republic that I offer the assurance of my gratitude and devotion. I want to certify those generous fellow-countrymen who have returned me to this House that I shall do all I can to justify their confidence by working with you for the preservation of order (*tranquillité*), for that is the primary need of the country — and for the development of those democratic institutions which the people rightfully demands' (and there was some more to the same effect).[51]

The deputies listened, but did not believe. There was no look or manner of the great Napoleon in this insignificant figure, so easily caricatured, with the big nose recalling the famous Bouginier of the 'thirties,[52] and the short legs; no suggestion of power to lead or to command; nothing romantic (unless it were his imprisonment) to account for his present success, no popular appeal to inspire fear of his future. It was hardly worth insisting on the ban which might still exclude him from the House. Even so shrewd an opponent as Thiers might argue that the Bonapartes were a poor lot, even compared with the Bourbon and Orléans claimants. And so, 'partly from contempt, partly from pity, and partly from hatred of the laws of the Restoration',[53] the exclusion of 1830 was abrogated (October 11th), and Louis was allowed to retain his seat. But those who took the trouble to look below the surface were not so easily satisfied. They had to acknowledge 'the wonderful perspicuity with which Louis saw into the feelings of the French people, and the wonderful skill with which he worked on them'. 'We all (said Montalembert) thought France wedded to class divisions and constitutionalism: he saw that the equality for which the French are *passionnés* is Asiatic equality — one ruler and everything flat below him . . . that they do not wish for a chief, but for a master, under whom every man may have a

chance of becoming minister. . . He trusted in the legendary superstition with which the memory of Napoleon was worshipped . . .
All this he, who had never been in France but as a prisoner, knew,
and we who had been growing in it for thirty years did not know'.[54]

The few who knew Louis best realized that to this insight were
added imagination and passion. 'He has an inventive, original,
and powerful imagination', said Hortense Cornu . . . 'I have known
him build castles in the air and live in them for years . . . When he
was young he had two fixed ideas — to be the Emperor of France
and the liberator of Italy; and I do not believe that even now (this
was in 1858) he has abandoned the latter . . . Like most men of
imagination he lives in the future: as a child his desire was to become
a historical character': in fact to rival Napoleon. With all this 'he has
no moral sense', and he is master of the *charlatanerie* which carries
away the French people. 'He inherits all this (it is now Guizot speaking) from his uncle . . . Though the physique is not that of a Bonaparte, the mind is. But he is totally without his uncle's power of
invention. His intellect is sterile. He can copy, and has done so
successfully, but he cannot originate.'[55] With this estimate Hortense
Cornu agrees, in a passage which may be taken as the most know-
ledgeable portrait — for there was something feminine in Louis
which a woman could understand — 'His intellectual character has
great excellences and great deficiencies. He has no originality or invention: he has no power of reasoning, or rather of discussing: he has
few fixed or general principles of any kind. But he is a very acute
observer, particularly of the weaknesses and follies of those around
him. There is as much discrepancy in his moral qualities. He is
exceedingly mild and kind; his friendships are steady, though his
passions are not. He has in a high degree decision, obstinacy, dis-
simulation, patience, and self-reliance. He is not stopped or turned
out of his course by any scruples. What we call a sense of right and
wrong he calls prejudice. His courage and determination are perfect . . . But he is exceedingly indolent and procrastinating, and his
habitual suspicion deprives him of much assistance from others . . .
Everything wearies him. He gets up *ennuyé*, he passes the day *ennuyé*,
he goes to bed *ennuyé*.'[56] But once more — not to leave boredom as the
final impression — 'His silence and calm hide a passionate temperament . . . His heart is ingenuous, and yet like his mind it is tortuous.
Though he never fell in love for the sake of loving, yet his heart is
inclined to be captured by an adventure for the joy of being in a

conspiracy.' This is Valérie Masuyer, remembering the Italian adventure of 1831: but it was as true of 1836, of 1840, and now of 1848.[57]

With the completion of the elections the Assembly could begin its work – the drawing up of a Constitution. With so many doubtful precedents before them the deputies might have been excused for indecision, but in fact they summarily disposed of questions which at any other moment would have caused infinite discussion; for they were united by the double fear which was still after half a century the essential driving force of national politics: fear of monarchy and fear of 'Red' revolution. To guard against the first, the sovereignty of the people must be embodied in government by a single chamber: to prevent the second the executive must be under the control of a single individual, an American President (Tocqueville was on the Committee), with authority over the army and police. And to ensure the permanence of this system, it must be made as difficult as possible to alter the constitution. Louis took little part in the sessions which settled these points. The only thing that mattered to him was the method of electing the executive officer – the President of the Republic. For if he were the nominee of the Assembly, the choice would amost certainly fall on Cavaignac, whose repression of the June rising was the most recent reminder of the 'Red' danger, and of the way to deal with it; but if he were elected by the people, Louis had every hope that his name would carry the day; and what could such a President be (as Tocqueville said) but a pretender to the crown? Not the crown of a Bourbon or an Orléans king, but the crown of a Bonapartist Emperor; and to the general French mind there was between the two (which to the English mind might seem so much alike) an infinite difference – as infinite as the contrast between the drab days of Louis-Philippe and the legendary glories of Napoleon. There might have been more hesitation about so momentous a decision if it had not been for Lamartine, the most persuasive orator and leader in the Assembly, who was as sure that the President of a national Republic must be elected nationally as he was certain that, if Louis were elected, he would never be able to carry through a second Brumaire. And such indeed was the feeling of most of the deputies, who remembered with a smile the double fiasco of Strasbourg and Boulogne, and could see nothing to fear in the ineffective orator of September 26th.[58] It needed a poet, not a

politician, to see the truth. 'It is not a Prince who returns to the country', wrote Victor Hugo in *L'Evènement* (Louis' most eloquent supporter now, as afterwards his most eloquent enemy), 'it is an Idea. The people has been waiting for Napoleon ever since 1815. The man whom the people has just elected to represent it is not the victim of a scrimmage at Boulogne; he is the victor of Jéna . . . His candidature dates from Austerlitz!'[59]

Jeanne, the pious and innocent country girl who was the heroine of George Sand's first *roman champêtre* (1844) believed in fairies; but the three deities she prayed to were the Virgin Mary, Jeanne d'Arc, and Napoleon. It was still the same in the national crisis of 1914: the shops were full of picture postcards representing one or another of these three (according to the ecclesiastical colour of the publisher) leading the French army to victory.

Such, in effect, was the claim that Louis himself now made, in a speech in the Assembly in answer to the challenge, what right had he to stand for the Presidency? 'Am I accused (he replied) of accepting a popular call which I have not canvassed? My answer is, Yes, I accept it; and it is a call which does me honour. I accept it because a series of elections, and the unanimous decree of the Assembly annulling the proscription of my family, justify my belief that France regards my name as holding out hope of social consolidation. What the country needs above all is a solid, intelligent, strong, and wise government, a government which thinks less of punishing evil than of healing it. My one desire is to deserve the respect of the national Assembly, and of all responsible citizens (*hommes de bien*), and the trust of this great-hearted people whose views have so recently been brushed aside (*qu'on a si légèrement traité hier*). I shall always study to exhibit the imperturbability of a man resolved to do his duty.'[60]

Meanwhile Louis was pushing his candidature amongst the country electorates, appealing (as he knew would be most effective) to the memory of the great Emperor, but promising (as he knew was necessary to conciliate the politicians) to devote himself, if elected, to the consolidation of the Republic. He outlined a policy which included freedom of worship and education, protection of property, reduction of taxation, provision of employment, old age relief, improvement of industrial conditions, free enterprise, and liberty of the press. To the ecclesiastics, who preferred utility to Utopianism, he promised educational control, and protection of the Temporal

Power of the Papacy. Though, to please the business men, he had declared for peace, he added a special promise to look after the interests of the army. He promised a general amnesty for political offenders. Finally he pledged his honour to leave to his successor, at the end of his four years' term of office, 'the executive strengthened, liberty intact, and progress accomplished'.[61]

This specious programme, which included something for everybody, was backed by all the resources of a well-organized electioneering campaign, and by a personal appeal possessed by none of the other candidates. While Persigny, from the rue Montmartre, showered pamphlets on the provinces, and handed out articles to the press, Louis showed himself riding in the Bois de Boulogne (he always looked best on horseback), charmed callers at the Hôtel du Rhin, and extracted money from his cousin Mathilde and his mistress Miss Howard. But his overwhelming asset was without doubt his name, worth a thousand arguments and many millions of francs. Of the other candidates Cavaignac was the Government nominee, Ledru-Rollin and Raspail were representatives of rival socialist parties, Lamartine and Changarnier stood for themselves. Only Louis stood, as it had been the proud boast of the 'men of '89' and of the Man of Brumaire to stand, for the French nation. He was realist enough to reckon that out of every 20 voters 14 were town or country workers; he may have guessed that more than half of them were illiterate, and many as ignorant of politics, perhaps, as the Ardennes peasants who said to Taine in 1851, 'Louis-Napoleon is a very rich man; he will pay for the Government, and there will be no more taxes.'[62]

The election took place on December 10th: ten days later the result was announced:

Louis Napoleon	5,434,226 votes
General Cavaignac	1,448,107
M. Ledru Rollin	370,119
M. Raspail	36,900
M. Lamartine	17,910
General Changarnier	4,790

THE PRESIDENT (1848-1852)

His greatness weigh'd, his will is not his own,
For he himself is subject to his birth:
He may not, as unvalu'd persons do,
Carve for himself, for on his choice depends
The safety and the health of the whole state;
And therefore must his choice be circumscrib'd
Unto the voice and yielding of that body
Whereof he is the head. *Hamlet*, I, iii

I

LOUIS' induction as President was fixed for December 20th. It is said that General Changarnier, who was in command of the troops escorting the new President to his official residence, said to Molé: 'Suppose I were to take him to the Tuileries instead of the Elysée?' — 'Be sure you don't,' replied Molé, 'he will go there soon enough of his own accord.' Both buildings were almost in the same street. It was not much further from the Republican to the Imperial Palace than (as they had once warned Mirabeau) from the Capitol to the Tarpeian Rock. The enemies of the new President guessed that he had his eyes on the Tuileries; his friends were urging him to occupy it; Louis himself intended to – but not yet.

'Don't go to the Assembly,' was Persigny's advice: 'send them a message saying that you will take your oath to the Constitution provided that it first receives the ratification of the people.' Ratification by *plébiscite* was in fact consistent with democratic precedent, and had been proposed by a small number of deputies: but the majority voted against it, for they knew that the people took no interest in their Constitution, and feared that it might take the opportunity to declare for an Empire. Louis would not accept a plan which involved all the hazards of a *coup d'état*. Was he wrong? Ought he to have taken the overwhelming vote of December 10th as a national call to the throne? Were not his subsequent troubles – the broken oath to the Constitution, the bloodshed and proscriptions of December 1851, his subservience to the Liberals and to the Church, and the sacrifice of British friendship – largely due to the four years' delay between Presidency and Empire?

If ever a historical parallel is justified, it would be justified here,

between the two Napoleons. Did not Marx, who was a better historian than economist, hit upon the happy title, 'The Eighteenth Brumaire of Louis Bonaparte'? Must not Louis, who thought so much about his great uncle, have remembered that four years elapsed between the First Consulship and the Empire? May he not have thought that a similar delay was advisable for himself too? What he forgot was that the First Consul was already in effect Emperor in 1799, and that the climax of Napoleon's career was the Life Consulship of 1802, not the Empire of 1804. Or perhaps he did not forget this, and reckoned that in a few years his Presidency might mature of its own merit into Empire. But could he count on another Marengo, another Concordat, another Peace of Amiens? Was France ready in 1848, as in 1800, to accept, in return for peace at home and abroad, the suppression of political liberty; and was Louis in a position to offer such a bargain? With all his greater advantages, Napoleon had waited four years for a favourable opportunity to declare himself Emperor — a plot against his government, a threat against the life which was now, since the vote of Life Consulship, the only security of public order, a risk which pointed to the necessity of fixing the succession. Would fortune provide Louis with an equal opportunity? It had done so in 1836 and 1840: he was in the mood to hope that it would do so again.

But the immediate reason why Louis missed the chance of a *coup d'état* in 1848 was that he was not ready, He had waited five years for Strasbourg, and four for Boulogne. Though he kept his ambition alive, and pursued his propagandist campaign during his six years' imprisonment, the revolution of 1848 took him by surprise: he did not know — nobody knew — just what it might mean: he preferred to watch events from beyond the Channel. When he was elected to the Assembly, he could not be sure how far it was due to dislike of the government, and how far to belief in himself. When he was elected President he still did not know whether it was for his person and policy, or for the mere name Napoleon. In the Assembly he might stand for the Party of Order, kept in power by a Coalition of Fear between the Conservatives who feared the Liberals, the Liberals who feared the Republicans, and the Republicans who feared a military dictatorship. In the provinces his name was apparently all-powerful: but what did anyone know of the provinces? Would they support a Parisian *coup d'état*? What in any case would be the outcome, if the Parisian workers were given

another reason for barricades, and the army another excuse for shooting them down in the name of *l'Ordre*? Could he even trust the army — an army which at Strasbourg and Boulogne (he must have reflected sometimes) he had so signally failed to lead to victory?

In fact, and in short, Louis was not a man to extemporize, or to make sudden decisions. He must always hear advice, weigh the *pros* and *cons*, and work out a plan, before settling on a course of action: and the ten days from December 10th to 20th were not enough. Nor was he so unscrupulous as to go back on his word so obviously or so soon. In speech after speech, letter after letter, and in a spate of manifestoes, he had declared his intention to support and strengthen the Republic, and at the moment he meant to do so. He would take the oath required of its President. It represented his present intention. Circumstances might change; and, when circumstances change, oaths, like treaties, are no longer binding.

The Assembly met at 4 p.m. on December 20th. The result of the Presidential election was declared. Cavaignac surrendered his mandate. Louis mounted the tribune, dressed in sober black, with white gloves, and the plaque of the Legion of Honour — outwardly a civilian of the party of Order — and took the oath: 'In the presence of God and in face of the French people, I swear to remain faithful to the democratic Republic and to defend the Constitution.' He followed this up with a written declaration: 'My future conduct is determined by the national vote and the oath that I have just taken. My duty is laid down, and as an honourable man I shall fulfil it. I shall regard as enemies of the country any who try to change by unlawful means what has been established by France as a whole (*la France entière*). Your intentions and desires (he told the deputies) are the same as mine . . . We have the same great purpose to fulfil: the foundation of a Republic which is a Commonwealth (*dans l'intérêt de tous*), and of a strong and fair government, inspired by a sincere love of progress, neither reactionary nor visionary. We have only to be patriots (*les hommes du pays*), not partisans: then, with God's aid, we shall at least do well, and perhaps magnificently.'[1]

Louis had not forgotten to compliment Cavaignac; and as he left the tribune he went over to him and held out his hand. The gesture was not returned; nor was this due merely to personal pique. There were many in the House who did not trust the new head of the party of Order.

Louis' progress from Presidency to Empire was in three stages: the first, from December 20th, 1848, to July 1849, resembled the earlier period of the Directory, from October 1795 to September (Fructidor) 1797, or of the First Consulship, from Brumaire to Marengo: it was a time of uncertainty and experiment, within constitutional forms, but preparing for emancipation from them, and for a free course towards dictatorship. The second stage lasted nearly two years, till the end of April 1851: the change of ministry in October 1849 made it as certain as Fructidor or Marengo had done that dictatorship only waited for an opportunity. The third and last stage began in April 1851.[2]

'I hold that the President has six million more reasons in his favour (wrote Mme Flahaut after the vote of December 10th) than Louis-Philippe had.' Louis knew it; his friends knew it; he knew that they did. 'The Empire is the only thing that can save the situation', wrote Morny on May 16th. But the time had not yet come. On December 19th, 1848, Mazzini had written a long letter to Prince Jérôme Napoleon, whom he knew to be acting as Louis' agent in Paris, warning him against this obvious ambition. 'Whatever may be the personal qualities of your cousin, he cannot continue in the manner of Napoleon. Napoleon was a whole world in himself. A Napoleonic dynasty would belittle this historic type. Besides, new dynasties are not possible in Europe . . . In less than ten years the whole of Europe will be republican . . . Napoleon closed one historic epoch; the members of his family will open another. In the Bonaparte family there has been a Napoleon; now there shall be Washingtons.'[3] Louis never shared this visionary republicanism; but he would willingly begin as Washington, if by doing so he could end as Napoleon.

He chose a Ministry that would conciliate a touchy and suspicious Chamber: at its head Odilon Barrot, a Liberal, but not of the Left, a man acceptable to all parties, nominated after a conspiratorial night meeting with Lamartine – Louis always loved the *mis-en-scène* of intrigue; Falloux (with promise of a clerical Education Act); Drouyn de Lhuys at the Foreign Office; the economist Passy at the Treasury; Faucher as Home Secretary, Buffet as Minister of Commerce, Rulhière as War Minister; and one republican make-weight, Bixio. At meetings of this Cabinet Louis would sit silent, listening, but apparently hearing nothing. 'The words one addressed to him (said Tocqueville) were like stones thrown down a well; their sound was

heard, but one never knew what became of them.' Others besides Flahaut admitted that he 'exercised a sort of fascination' over them – the more extraordinary because it was due to 'his simplicity and candid manner'. 'A sort of immobility of features' was what struck Moltke when he first met him, 'and the almost extinct look of his eyes . . . together with a friendly and good-natured smile which has nothing Napoleonic about it. He mostly sits quietly with his head on one side.' The German thought that 'this tranquillity must be very inspiring to the restless French nation'; and that 'it was not apathy, but the sign of a superior mind and a strong will . . . *Il ne se fâche jamais*, people said of him'.[4]

Louis might appear not to be listening to his ministers: his temper was always under control. Yet Hortense Cornu once caught in his eye, 'a tiger-like expression such as I had never seen before', and was so surprised that, though not a nervous person, she 'started, and stopped speaking': but 'then his features resumed their old kind expression; he begged me to continue, and he listened to me to the end quietly: he always conquered himself'. Montalembert too once saw this look: it was so exceptional as to be worth recording. The inattention, then, was only apparent: the kind manner masked the ripening of an intention, if not of a determination to carry it out. Having heard what his ministers had to say, Louis would make up his own mind: having by his kindness invited confidences, he would use them, as the Bourbons used the *cabinet noir* (the secret censorship of the post), to discover and to confound his enemies.

Signs of an attempt to impose his will on the government were soon noticed. Within a week of becoming President (December 27th) he demanded to be shown the state papers dealing with the Strasbourg and Boulogne affairs: but when they were refused, and the ministers made it a threat of resignation, he gave way – a Napoleonic gesture that failed in mid-air. When, a month later (January 29th), the 'Reds' of Paris demonstrated against Faucher's censorship of their paper *Solidarité républicaine*, and the disbanding of the *Garde mobile*, they were dispersed by Changarnier's troops, with cries of *Vive l'Empereur!* But Louis refused to seize this second invitation to a *coup d'état*. He would still be Washington.

He made his attitude even more clear to Prince Napoleon, when at Bordeaux, on his way to be ambassador at Madrid, that embarrassing young understudy made a speech hinting at Louis' intention to throw off the yoke of constitutional government. 'You know me

well enough (Louis wrote on April 10th) to be sure that I shall never submit to any attempt to influence me, and shall always make it my business to govern in the interest of the people, not of any party. I respect those whose ability and experience enable them to give me good advice . . . But I follow only the promptings of my mind and heart . . . My first duty was to reassure the country. Well, for the last four months the feeling of security has grown steadily. Safety first; then reform . . . Nothing (he ended) nothing shall trouble the clear vision of my judgment or the strength of my resolution. I shall march straight forward, with no moral scruples (*libre de toute contrainte morale*), in the path of honour, with conscience my only guide; and when I resign my office I shall at least have done what I honestly believed to be my duty.'[5]

Young Jérôme was offended at this rebuke, threw up his embassy, returned to Paris, and was not reconciled to Louis until the attack on his life at Marseille in September 1852. He was playing, perhaps consciously, the part that Lucien Bonaparte had played towards Napoleon fifty years before, reminding him of his republican past and opposing his imperial ambitions. What hurt Louis most in his cousin's criticism was that he knew it was the voice of his own 'better self', trying to make itself heard all the time against the Morny-Persigny voices of his 'worser self': a warning of the republican tradition, the national faith which he was pledged to consolidate, against the call of a family ambition which might only lead to another 1815.

But for the present Louis' reading of the political situation was more than verified by the elections to the new Legislative Assembly in May 1849. Outside Paris and a few districts in the provinces, the Republicans were hopelessly outvoted. Whereas in the previous Assembly the party of Order had secured 34 per cent of the seats, the Moderate Republicans 55 per cent, and the 'Reds' 11 per cent, in the new House the figures were 64 per cent, 11 per cent, and 25 per cent. Once more Paris had been outvoted by the Provinces, the town workers by the country labourers.[6]

Two events, during the summer of 1849, helped to strengthen Louis' prestige (whether as President or as Emperor-designate, only he could say): an epidemic of cholera, during which he showed his sympathy and courage, distributing money and visiting the sick: and a tour of the provinces, during which he took care to study local interests and to appeal to local patriotism. At Chartres he recalled

the coronation of Henri IV, and an era of pacification; at Amiens the peace of 1802; at Nantes he saluted the recently erected statue of Cambronne, the hero of Waterloo; at Angers (where he opened the new railway to Tours) he spoke of individual enterprise; and at Havre of commercial prosperity. He even revisited his old prison at Ham, where — a triumph of tact — he praised both revolution and counter-revolution, both prisoner and President.

Paris watched this tour of the provinces with some apprehension. The President was appealing, as the Girondins had done, from the national assembly to the nation. But he had a sense, which they never had, of what the nation really needed, and an honest intention — for there is no need to doubt his sincerity — to supply it: a government under which the workers would have their just share of the national wealth. 'Don't forget (he said to the employers) to spread amongst the workers sound ideas of political economy. Give them a fair share of the dividends of their labour (*une juste part dans la distribution du travail*), and so prove to them that the interests of the rich are not opposed to those of the poor.' Louis was discovering France, and France was discovering Louis. At the next election, or the next *plébiscite*, the people would be voting not for a name, but for a man. A man who might, indeed, too easily become discouraged or diverted from his early ideals; but never an oppressor of the people, never a commonplace dictator.[7]

2

Louis was hardly less adroit in dealing with the questions of foreign policy which arose during his first year as President. His family connections, his residence in Switzerland and Rome, and his forced periods of exile in England and America had given him an understanding of foreign countries rare amongst Frenchmen; and his meditations at Ham had formulated his reading of Napoleon's testament and the *Mémorial* of St. Helena into a programme which he was at last in a position to carry out. Those who knew him best were indeed, aware, and probably he was conscious too, that he lacked the consecutiveness of mind and perseverance of will necessary for his great task. His programme would become, in musical terms, a series of linked melodies rather than the logically connected movements of a symphony. He could be diverted from the straight course of principle by the need to conciliate a political party, or the fear of

international complications. Illness would add to indecision, and indolence allow his policies to be misapplied by those whom he should have overruled. It becomes more and more difficult, as time goes on, to trace the original design which might have given unity and dignity to the foreign policy of the Second Empire. Nevertheless — and it must always be remembered to his credit — Louis never lost the affection and respect of his old friends. Conneau, writing to Arese in June 1849, after saying how little good he could find in the politicians of any party, ended: 'Amongst this swarm of corrupt egoists I can see only one man to love and respect, and that is our Prince'.

And now, in 1849, at the dawn of adventure, the peak to be climbed stood out clear from the mists that would envelop it later in the day. Louis believed himself commissioned to restore a Napoleonic regime adapted to a post-Napoleonic world. Supreme power in France must be in the hands of an individual, but it must rest on the consent of the people. It must prevail, not by the achievements of war, but by the arts of peace. France is the country best fitted to lead Europe forward from the artificial 'restoration' of 1815 towards the natural sequel of 1789, the 'United States' of Europe, in which every nation would have the government it wished, and all would share peacefully in a common exchange of goods and ideas.

The first international question that arose was that of the Principalities (Moldavia and Wallachia). Though it was impossible at the moment to prevent joint Russian and Turkish suzerainty (by the convention of May 1st), there was no doubt that Louis would support the movement for the union of the two territories already championed in Paris by Bratianu and other Rumanian nationalists — a sympathy which took practical form in 1859 and 1866. Again, when Kossuth and other Hungarian patriots took refuge in Turkey in August 1849, France supported England in backing the Sultan's refusal to give them up to Austria and Russia. Yet again, when Palmerston made the Don Pacifico case an excuse for sending a fleet to the Piraeus (January 1850), Louis intervened so actively (even recalling his ambassador from London) that the British Government had to compromise the matter by the Convention of July 18th. Persigny's mission to Prussia in January 1850 was intended to sound Frederick-William as to the plan for the unification of Germany which Louis favoured, especially if it strengthened Prussia at the expense of Austria, and raised the question of the French recovery of

the Rhine frontier. Finally Louis intervened in the attempt of Prussia in 1850 to assert her rights at Neuchâtel — a threat defeated by an international Convention of 1852.

In all these affairs Louis showed a width of view and a will to assert French rights which caught the attention of the other powers; and this was, no doubt, one of the reasons why they regarded his rise to absolute rule in 1852 with such apprehension. He was, in fact, better understood and more feared outside France than within. He might almost have adapted Metternich's saying: 'I could always rule Europe, but never France.'[8]

It is difficult to form so clear a judgment about the most embarrassing question of foreign policy which faced Louis' early Presidency — the Italian problem. Here, more than in any other aspect of his career — for it was to beset him all his life — he was the victim of a fatal double-mindedness. For there was Catholic blood in all the Bonapartes; yet Louis had spent some of the most impressionable years of his youth in Rome under the tuition of a Jacobin who saw nothing in Catholicism but antiquarianism and superstition. He had risked his life in an insurrection against the misgovernment of the Papal States. The Carbonaro of 1831 was still alive in the President of 1848. But he must now act with the responsibility of an executor of the Concordat and a trustee of the French Church.

Nor was the situation in Italy what it had been when Louis left the country in 1831. True, there had been, if anything, an intensification of Austrian and Papal misrule. Macaulay, visiting Rome in 1838, described how every part of the government was in the hands of ecclesiastics. 'Imagine what England would be if all the members of Parliament, the Ministers, the Judges, the Ambassadors, the Governors of Colonies, the very Commander-in-Chief and Lords of the Admiralty were, without one exception, bishops or priests; and if the highest post open to the noblest, wealthiest, ablest, and most ambitious layman were a Lordship of the Bedchamber! . . . The States of the Pope are, I suppose, the worst governed in the civilized world; and the imbecility of the police, the venality of the public servants, the desolation of the country, and the wretchedness of the people, force themselves upon the observation of the most heedless traveller.'[9]

But if the hatred of Austrian and Papal misrule was no less than it had been, it now took a different form. Carbonarism had given

place to Mazzinism; and Mazzini was still the prophet of Young Italy, still the idealistic nationalist and republican, not the discontented impracticable plotter who afterwards impeded the work of Victor Emmanuel and Cavour: his cause was still supported in London and Berne, and had given rise to a notable literature of freedom.

During the fifteen years' reaction under Gregory XVI (1831-1846) no serious rising had been attempted; but there were some omens of the Risorgimento to come. In 1835 the Emperor Francis II died, and was succeeded by Ferdinand, an imbecile, in whose name Metternich and Kolowrat did everything to avoid trouble in Italy. Louis-Philippe had refused to intervene in 1831, though satisfying French jealousy of Austria by occupying Ancona in 1832: he was careful not to interfere again. Charles Albert of Sardinia (1831) had to live down his dubious reputation during the rising of 1821, and could not easily accept the leadership of Italy to which the independent traditions and economic progress of Sardinia entitled her. But he was forced on by circumstances. During the early 'forties, whilst Louis was in prison, Cavour was already editing *Il Risorgimento*, and applying to his own country the lessons learnt from American democracy and English industrialism. When D'Azeglio in 1845, after touring central and northern Italy, told Charles Albert that the country was ready to fight for freedom if Sardinia would give the lead, the King replied that, when the opportunity came, he would be ready. Like Louis, he was waiting for an omen.[10]

The omen came — and all the world saw it — when in June 1846 Gregory XVI was succeeded by Pius IX. Any change at Rome was for the better; but here was a Pope who amnestied political criminals, projected railways and gas-lighting, proposed to reform the prisons and the schools, gave office to laymen, relaxed the press censorship, allowed the enlargement of the Civil Guard, and, with Gizzi as Secretary of State, inaugurated a programme of social and economic progress. Metternich retaliated by occupying papal Ferrara; but six months later (December 1846) had to withdraw. A movement for constitutional government spread from Piedmont (October 1847) all over the peninsula. In Verdi's patriotic drama *Ernani* the chorus *A Carlo Quinto sia gloria e onor* was changed to *A Pio Nono*. From Monte Cassino, the most famous and learned monastery in Italy, Dom Luigi Tosti appealed to the Pope, in the name of enlightened Catholics, to play his part as a liberal and a reformer. On March

15th, 1848, a constitution was proclaimed in Rome: on the same day Metternich fled from Vienna. A week later, after five days' street fighting, the Austrian garrison withdrew from Milan. This was Charles Albert's opportunity. On March 24th he declared war on Austria. But his own inexperience and the inferiority of his troops were no match for Radetsky and his regulars: defeated at Custozza (July 25th, 1848) he signed an armistice on August 8th, and the first blow for Italian freedom had failed. Nor was there anything to hope from Rome. Pius IX, carried further than he intended by his bid for popularity, had seen too late that he could not take part in active hostilities against Catholic Austria. His reforms did not satisfy the Romans. His reforming minister, Rossi, was assassinated (November 15th), and he fled in disguise to Gaeta, leaving the Romans to set up (February 1849) a Mazzinian Republic. What could this be, to all good Papalists, but the *Abominationem desolationis stantem in loco sancto*? What better reason could there be for a Catholic Emperor to intervene? But the complicated troubles in Austria throughout the summer and autumn of 1848, culminating in the abdication of Ferdinand in favour of young Francis Joseph on December 2nd, and not ending till the subjection of Hungary, with Russian help, in August 1849, made intervention at Rome impossible. On the other hand Charles Albert was emboldened to resist Austrian demands under the armistice of August 1848, and to renew the war in Lombardy.[11]

It was at this turn of affairs (December 1848) that Louis' old friend and fellow-conspirator Arese arrived in Paris with congratulations from Charles Albert on his election as President, and with a request for his help against Austria. Arese no doubt reminded Louis of his part in the rebellion of 1831, and of the promise he had made, when they were in America in 1837, that when the day came for him to preside over the destinies of France he would do all he could to support the claims of Italian nationalism. But what could Louis do? He did not deny — he never denied — his interest in the liberation of Italy: but he was pledged, as President, to a policy of peace. Charles Albert's cause was that of all Italians; but if France were his ally she would be fighting not merely against Austria, but against the Pope; and the President, whatever his private views about Papal misrule, could not so antagonize the clerical vote which had helped to put him in power. He could not forget that twice already — in January and December 1848 — a military expedition had nearly sailed from

Toulon to safeguard the Pope against republicanism, and that he had himself, during his electioneering for the Presidency, publicly disowned Lucien Bonaparte's son, Charles, Prince de Canino, for his part in the Roman revolution. He must at all costs keep his hold on the country and constitution, until the moment came for the *coup d'état* which he was secretly planning.[12]

In the spring of 1849 events forced his hand. On February 18th Pius issued from Gaeta an appeal to the Catholic powers; and on March 23rd Charles Albert, resuming his war on Austria, was fatally defeated at Novara, and forced to abdicate in favour of Victor Emmanuel — a disaster which concealed success, for the *Re Galantuomo* was to do what the *Re Tentenna* could never have done, and to become the creator of Italian independence. Meanwhile Louis pledged French support to Piedmont by guaranteeing the integrity of her state, and promising, if necessary, to take part in a partial and temporary occupation of Italian territory. This resulted in the favourable terms of the Treaty of Turin (August 6th). But four months previously Austrian troops had restored the Grand Duke Leopold of Tuscany; and this step, which might be followed at any moment by an Austrian occupation of Rome, roused the same suspicions which had sent a French force to Ancona in 1832 — suspicions backed by the national hatred of Austria as an executor of the settlement of 1815. On April 25th the military expedition already twice projected sailed from Toulon under the command of Oudinot, the son of Napoleon's marshal, but without his ability. On the 30th he attacked Rome prematurely, and was beaten off by Garibaldi's volunteers.

There were still nearly three weeks to go before the elections which meant so much for the future tactics of the President. Meantime he allowed Drouyn de Lhuys to send Ferdinand de Lesseps to Rome to cover up Oudinot's blunder, and to arrange an armistice and a treaty by which the French troops were to be admitted to Rome as neutrals, whilst the position of the Pope was still undetermined. But at the same time (May 9th) he used the incident for an appeal to the army, upon which he would have to rely for his *coup d'état*, publishing a letter to Oudinot in which he said: 'I will not allow our military renown to be sullied. Your men can always count upon my help and gratitude.' And when, ten days later, the elections of May 18th returned a big Catholic majority, he recalled de Lesseps, and allowed Oudinot to take advantage of an Austrian advance to-

wards Rome to make a fresh attack on the city. This was successful, and on July 3rd the tricolour at last flew on the Castello di S. Angelo.

3

Geographically Rome might seem remote from Paris; but in no other sense, least of all to a Bonaparte, a nephew of Napoleon, a cousin of the King of Rome. Louis' policy was the same in both capitals: to stand as the champion of Order between the opposite extremes of reaction and revolution. But Order, in his mind, and in the scheme of his Empire, included Law and Liberalism; it was for all parties in the state, poor as well as rich, anti-clericals as well as Catholics; yes, and for foreigners as well as Frenchmen. So, whilst the Catholics were still rubbing their hands over the occupation of Rome, he published a letter to his aide-de-camp Edgar Ney (whose name was itself a Napoleonic memory) declaring that 'the French republic had not sent an army to Rome to stifle Italian liberty', and that the help given to the Pope was conditional on his granting a general amnesty, adopting the *Code Napoléon*, and introducing a liberal administration.[13]

He followed up this attack on the Papalist party two months later (October 31st) by dismissing the by now obstructive Barrot ministry and appointing 'men of action', including two who were to play a large part under the Empire – Fould (Finance Minister) and Rouher (Minister of Justice). In a message to the Legislative Body the same day, and soon afterwards (November 11th) in a speech at the Palais de Justice, Louis declared an economic programme, promising the workers a larger share of the national wealth; and a month later (December 10th) at the Hôtel de Ville he hinted that representative government was being discredited by the quarrels and delays of the Assembly, and spoke of the high destiny of the country – presumably to be accomplished under another (in his mind an imperial) regime: 'Our aim is not to reproduce a pale copy of the past, but to combine all men of good heart and mind in establishing something finer than a charter, something more lasting than a dynasty: the eternal principles of religion and morality, together with the new rule of a healthy political system.'

Catholics and conservatives could take little exception to such sentiments, whilst they were sufficiently reminiscent of Robespierre's moralistic style to appeal to Jacobins and Socialists. Indeed they

contained something more than an electoral programme: a political ideal which never quite faded from Louis' mind, and has remained as a main hope of European civilization. 'He judged that the antagonism between bourgeoisie and people could be abolished by the creation of a strong, disciplined, and productive state, in which the workers would be content.' But it was Louis' misfortune that when he was most honest he was most suspected of deceit. The 'Reds' in fact trusted nobody but themselves; the Catholics accepted the benefits of the Loi Falloux (March 15th, 1850) and Loi Parieu as an instalment of ecclesiastical control over education, and intrigued for more; and the Men of Order welcomed the new electoral qualification of three years' residence, and the fresh restrictions on the Press (July 1850), whilst suspecting that they were instalments of an imminent dictatorship.[14]

That there were many people of this last kind in Paris, even after the failure of the demonstrations of January 29th and June 13th, was shown by the supplementary elections of March 10th the next year, when twenty out of the thirty seats left vacant by those involved in the June affair were filled by workers' candidates. Louis cleverly allowed the reactionaries in the Assembly, alarmed by this omen, to nominate fresh ministers of their own way of thinking — Thiers, Molé, Montalembert, Berryer, Broglie, Baroche — and to proceed with a repressive policy which made them more than ever unpopular amongst the workers and their leaders: the Loi Falloux, which nominally freed education from state control, but really handed it over to the Church; the Press law of July 16th, which required all articles on political or theological questions to be signed, and handicapped editors in other ways; and the Electoral law of May 31st, which, by disqualifying voters for various and often trivial political offences, and by insisting on three years' residence in the same district, disfranchised three million Jacobins, Socialists, soldiers, and poor workers.[15]

Though Louis might be able to exploit this situation in his own interests, he was, at the moment, powerless to do anything more, and sometimes lost heart. 'Although I am here,' he said to Lord Malmesbury in Paris on April 16th, 'I know nobody: the friends I have I don't know, and they don't know me even by sight. Although a Frenchman, not fifty of them had ever seen me when I came over from England. I have tried to consolidate all political parties, but I can conciliate none . . . The Chamber is unmanageable.

I stand perfectly alone, but the army and the people are with me, and I don't despair.'[16] He might have added that he had behind him the *Constitutionnel*, whose 90,000 subscribers were assured by its editor Véron, its financial supporter Morny, and its new literary contributor Sainte-Beuve that Louis was the only hope of the party of Order; whilst Veuillot of the *Univers* recommended him to Catholic voters. Not only so. He was reassured this summer by another tour of the provinces, meeting Frenchmen who were not politicians, workers who were not socialists, and republicans who might become imperialists. In his speeches he said that the common people were his friends, as they had been Napoleon's: 'When I see the influence my name still exercises over the masses – an influence due to the heroic head of my family – I am glad of it, not for myself, but for you, for France, and for Europe.' He was careful, especially in industrial centres, to proclaim himself the champion of Order and Prosperity; but when at Lyon he declared that 'One who has been elected by six million voters is bound to carry out the will of the people', some cried *Vive la République*, some *Vive le Président*, some *Vive Napoléon*, and some *Vive l'Empereur!* Louis might have quoted Antony's 'I come to bury Caesar, not to praise him'. It is at least worth noticing that he had mastered a new form of propaganda which Napoleon seldom attempted: the occasional public harangue.'[17]

The enthusiasm roused by such speeches was not entirely spontaneous; for in many parts of the country a *Société du dix décembre* was using violence to recommend Bonapartism; and its President, Louis' old friend General Piat, took care that special attention should be paid to the army. For it had of late years become a custom – and a politically dangerous one in the French army – to acclaim its commanders in person (Austrian statesmen, contrariwise, took pride in the fact that their troops were forbidden when on parade even to cheer the Emperor). This gave special point to an incident which occurred in Paris on October 11th. When at a review one regiment failed to give the expected cry at the saluting-point: *Vive Napoléon!* and Louis dismissed their commanding officer, the commander-in-chief, General Changarnier, protested, and republished an old regulation ordering silence on parade. Changarnier, who had done Louis good service in 1849, was a brave soldier, but a notorious fop ('he dresses like an old dandy', noted Malmesbury, 'with a wig, and very tight stays') and too free of speech – it was he who had invented for Louis the nickname 'the depressed parrot' (*le perroquet*

mélancholique) — and such opposition could not be tolerated at the head of the armed forces of Paris. On January 3rd, 1851, Changarnier was dismissed.[18]

To mask this attack on the Chamber — for Changarnier's double command of the Paris garrison and of the National Guard was its only safeguard against another 'Red' revolt — Louis cleverly associated the conservative leaders with his action, and again appointed new ministers, whom he described as 'men specially chosen, and determined to devote themselves to public business without any party ties . . . honourable men whose acceptance of this patriotic task will entitle them to the gratitude of the country'. But when the names of these patriots were published it might be doubted whether they stood for policy of appeasement between President and Chamber, or for a declaration of war; for they included Saint-Arnaud as Minister of War and de Maupas as Prefect of Police — men better adapted to carry out a personal policy than to conciliate the wavering opinions of a parliament.[19]

By this time there were few who doubted that Louis was aiming at Empire. Tocqueville, whose testimony is of special value both from the width of his experience and from his independent, almost English cast of mind, whilst convinced that the mass of the people — workers and *bourgeoisie* alike — wanted permanence, was still doubtful up to the end of 1850 whether Louis would be any more acceptable as a permanent ruler than (say) 'Henri V', or the Comte de Paris. 'Still, he is *there*, and has for him the fear of change.' Early in 1851 Tocqueville's choice turns more and more towards Louis, who is gaining credit in his struggle with the unpopular Assembly. If he wins, 'we have the Empire under another name'; for Louis never learnt in England the art of parliamentary government, and will rule through ministers who are clerks. He expects — as most people did — a *coup d'état* when Louis' re-election comes up in May 1852: it will end either at Vincennes or the Tuileries; but Louis will never be a constitutional king — 'a role utterly repugnant to all his prejudices and tastes . . . He is essentially Prince: the role of Washington would have no charms for him. He has believed for twenty years in his destiny to be the permanent ruler of France.'

Foreign powers were beginning to take alarm. Brünnow, the Russian ambassador, soon after Louis' election as President, proposed an Anglo-Russian alliance as a precaution against another Moscow

expedition. 'We had good information', said Disraeli, 'as to Louis Napoleon's intentions'; and he possessed a 'drawing of Louis Napoleon in full imperial robes and paraphernalia' made a month before the declaration of December 1851.[20]

Only the last step towards victory now remained: to draw up a plan of battle, and to appoint a Staff to carry it out. The parliamentary position, to continue the military metaphor, was flanked by two key positions, the capture of which would expose the centre of the line to direct assault. One was Article 45 of the Constitution, which prohibited the re-election of the President for a further term of office at the end of his four years. The other was the Franchise Law of May 31st, 1850, which had reduced the electorate by some three millions, but without altering the requirement of two million votes for the election of a new President. Against both these positions Louis could advance under republican colours: the cry of *Vive l'Empereur!* would not be raised till the final assault. For the demand for the abrogation of Article 45 only implied that Louis wished to extend his tenure of the Presidency, and the Law of May 31st was an offence against what had been a good republican principle for the last fifty years – the *Volonté générale* as expressed through universal franchise.

The revision of the Constitution, so as to allow of Louis' re-election, had been demanded by seventy-nine out of the eighty-six departments, and was of course backed by the *Société du dix décembre*. It was seriously discussed in the Chamber in 1851; for even Louis' opponents foresaw that worse things might happen if both President and Parliament disappeared together in May 1852. But the deputies could not agree, and the vote against revision in July was as good as a surrender of this key position to the enemy. Louis, who was once more touring the provinces, was well aware of this. At Dijon, on June 1st, he had said, 'A new political age is beginning. From end to end of France petitions are being signed demanding the revision of the Constitution. I await with confidence the public manifestoes and the decisions of the Assembly, which will be inspired by the single thought of the good of the state. If France holds that no one has the right to settle her affairs without consulting her she has only to say so: she can count on my courage and energy.' And at Tours on July 1st: 'I look forward to the future of the country without fear, for it will always be saved by the will of the people, freely expressed and devoutly accepted . . . I invoke in all my prayers that solemn

moment when the strong voice of the people dominates all opposition and conciliates every form of rivalry.' There could not be much doubt now that Louis intended, not an extended Presidency, but an Empire founded on an appeal to the people.[21]

The second key position to be attacked was the Law of May 31st. On November 4th Louis himself proposed its abrogation, and was defeated by only six votes; yet they were enough to sound the doom of the conservative Assembly, and to secure Louis the support of the common people. But in his message of that date – the last he addressed to the deputies – he spoke rather of the danger, which all parties now foresaw, of another 'Red' revolution at the May elections; and it was this which gave the conservatives in the Assembly the forlorn hope of a counter-offensive which might yet prevent Louis' *coup*. In the early days of the Assembly, by a decree of May 11th, 1848, the duty of defending its liberty had been invested in the President, with the right of commandeering for this purpose the armed forces of Paris: but in the Constitution, in view of the quieter situation and the objections of the military command, this right had been withdrawn: Article 50 merely said that the President 'has control of the army (*dispose de la force armée*), but cannot command it in person'; and Article 32 that the Assembly 'decides what military forces are necessary for its safety, and controls their use (*elle en dispose*)'. In view of this Louis had ordered any copies of the decree of May 11th still exhibited in the barracks to be taken down. But now the *questeurs* of the assembly (deputies charged with its internal administration) proposed that under Article 32 the Commandant of the Paris troops should be ordered to use all the armed forces of the capital to protect the Assembly against – what else could it be but the threatened *coup d'état* of the President? This *proposition des questeurs* came up for debate on November 17th, and was defeated by 100 votes. The counter-attack had failed: the role of the Assembly was played out: nothing now could prevent the final assault; whilst the assailants could claim that they were only anticipating a plot against the constitution, if not against the person of the President, by the very guardians of public order.[22]

There was another enmity with which Louis had to reckon – that of the royalists. The simultaneous disappearance of President and Parliament provided for under the constitution opened a field of adventure even to the last Bourbon, the youngest Orléans. Could they not agree to share the crown – the Comte de Chambord, who

had no son, to hand it on after him to the Comte de Paris? Such was the *fusion* talked of between the two royal families. But in fact there was no disposition to accept such a compromise between a party of Ultramontane country gentlemen, who could not forget or forgive the double fall of their divine rights, and a party of Liberal Catholics, financiers and industrialists, who intended to profit by the Spirit of the Age: a party of *droits* and a party of *titres*. Such an alliance was only thinkable as an obstacle in the way of either Empire or Republic. Even Queen Victoria, who was in sympathy and close touch with exiles of Claremont, disapproved of their designs. 'I fear (she wrote to Leopold on December 31st) that poor Joinville *had* some *mad* idea of going to France', and added '*The candidature* of Joinville was in every way unwise, and led Louis Napoleon to take so desperate a course.' Palmerston knew of it too.[23]

The clue to success lay in control of the army; Louis was well aware of it. The dismissal of Changarnier had shown his distrust of certain elements in the Paris garrison. Since April he had been recruiting supporters from amongst the younger officers in command of the forces fighting in Algeria — men, like Napoleon's generals in Italy under the Directory, with no affection for the politicians, and hardly more scrupulous as to shooting down 'Reds' in the streets of Paris than Kabyles in the African desert. The most important of these men was Saint-Arnaud, already known as an admirer of Louis, and one who had called the Assembly 'a crowd of talkers, intriguers, and revolutionaries': he came home victorious from Algeria in August 1851, and was appointed Minister of War. Magnan, who by now regretted his refusal to join Louis in 1840, was already in command of the Paris garrison, officered mainly by men from Africa, the President's partisans; Vieyron controlled the National Guard; Fleury, Espinasse, Vaudrey (of the Strasbourg affair), Canrobert, and others fresh from active service gave a military stiffening to the staff.

The inner circle, who shared Louis' confidence, were, besides Saint-Arnaud, the inevitable Persigny, de Maupas as Prefect of Police, Mocquard as Secretary, Flahaut, who came over from London early in November 1851, and above all Morny, not merely Louis' half-brother, but a man of coolness, courage, and immense talent, if he once turned his attention from sport and gambling to politics. Morny was in this affair, by most accounts, the principal planner; already in May 1849 he was seeing Louis every day, and discussing

everything with him — and how Louis must have regretted his absence at Strasbourg and Boulogne! 'He possessed', said Eugénie, 'in a high degree most of the qualities of great statesmanship: a sense of realities and possibilities, clearness of vision, readiness and subtlety of mind; he spoke temperately and to the point; stuck to his purpose, but with as little imperiousness as weakness; was cool, ingenious, and secretive in action; he had the subtle art of leading and managing men. Moral considerations apart, December 2nd, which was mainly his work, was a masterpiece . . . How far superior to Brumaire, when lack of foresight was only equalled by clumsiness, and Bonaparte himself lost his head! Machiavelli himself . . . would have had nothing but praise for the Second of December.'[24]

There were others, claiming to be well-informed, notably the anonymous author of *An Englishman in Paris* (1892) afterwards identified as A. D. Vandam, who cried down Morny's part in the affair, and cried up Persigny's. According to this view Persigny, who had been driving Louis rather unwillingly from Presidency to Empire, was in close touch with Palmerston and Walewski across the Channel; the delay in carrying out the *coup* was due to his insistence that it must wait for the laying of the submarine telegraph cable from Dover to Calais, for which the concession had been given on January 8th, 1851, and which was completed on November 13th. Three days later the *proposition des questeurs* was brought forward, and thrown out; and that was the signal for the *coup*. Louis would have postponed it; but on November 26th Persigny produced a letter from London with a draft for £2000, representing the last financial help that could be expected; and Louis gave way. That these and other rumours obtained currency is chiefly evidence of the personal jealousies that existed amongst Louis' followers. It need not be doubted either that Louis held back or that Persigny pushed him on: that Palmerston was in sympathy with the *coup* was clear enough from the sequel: but almost certainly Persigny had not the ingenuity or the patience to plan December 2nd. Eugénie knew what she was saying in attributing its success to Morny.[25]

4

The date finally chosen was itself an omen of success, a Napoleonic anniversary — Austerlitz Day, December 2nd. On the evening of the 1st Louis gave his weekly reception at the Elysée, and was

his usual kindly inscrutable self; but one sharp-eyed guest noticed him having a private word with Vieyron, the commandant of the National Guard; it was to warn him to be at his post, waiting for orders, at 6 a.m. 'Can you hear a big bit of news without change of face? — I think so — Well, it is tonight! — Can you answer for it that the drums will not beat for parade tomorrow, and that the Guard will not be in the streets? — Yes': and next day the drums were found broken, and the powder damp. Meanwhile Morny, with Cavaignac and Lamoricière, was at the Opera, and then at the Jockey Club. Afterwards he joined the inner circle of plotters at the Elysée, to distribute the final orders. Louis read them out from Morny's notes, which he had marked on the outside 'Rubicon', together with the proclamations he intended to address to the army and the nation. About 11 the meeting broke up. Louis went to bed, leaving orders that he should be called at 5. Maupas, with Béville, a trusted officer of Louis, drove to the Imprimerie Nationale, where a staff of compositors, specially summoned (as was not unusual) for Government work, was soon printing the Proclamations, whilst the building was surrounded by troops under orders to shoot anyone trying to leave. By 5 o'clock the bills were at the Préfecture de Police, and by 7.30 the first workmen to be astir found them posted up at every corner of the city.

By this time the next part of the plan was already in train. A dozen key-points in the capital had been seized by troops during the night. At 5 the Palais Bourbon was occupied. Between 6.15 and 6.45 sixteen deputies (in spite of their constitutional privilege) and some seventy other persons who might have organized opposition were simultaneously arrested in their homes by pickets of police under sergents-de-ville personally instructed by Maupas, and were interned in the prison on the Boulevard Mazas. At 7 o'clock some thirty deputies found their way by a back door into the Palais Bourbon, but failed to induce Dupin, their President, to take any action (he had an understanding with Louis' party) and were dispersed by the troops. Later as many as 300 deputies, finding the Palais Bourbon closed, met in the Mairie of the 10th arrondissement (it was convenient for many of them, who lived in the Faubourg Saint-Germain), and after long and fruitless debate were in their turn marched out by the police, and over 200 interned in the d'Orsay barracks; later in the day they were transferred in buses and cabs to the Mazas prison, Mont Valérien, or Vincennes; eight of the most important, including

Cavaignac, Changarnier, and Lamoricière, to Louis' old quarters at Ham.

On the Haute Cour, even more than on the Assembly, lay the obligation to act under Article 68 of the Constitution, which said that 'Any measure by which the President of the Republic dissolves, prorogues, or hinders the work of the National Assembly is a crime of high treason, involving deprivation of his office'. Its members met, but did no more than arrange another meeting. They would wait to see how the affair went, before committing themselves to their duty.

Meanwhile the public notices were doing their work. The *Proclamation du Président de la République* was headed in large capitals APPEL AU PEUPLE. 'Frenchmen! (it said) The present situation cannot continue. Every day that passes aggravates the danger of the country. The Assembly, which ought to be the firmest support of order, has become a centre of conspiracy ... Instead of passing laws in the public interest, it is forging weapons for civil war: it is attacking the power that I hold directly from the people; it is encouraging all kinds of evil passions; it is ruining the repose of France. I have dissolved it, and I call on the whole people to judge between it and me.' Louis went on to say that the Constitution had broken down, and that the country must choose between it and himself. He outlined a new Constitution under five heads closely similar to that of the year VIII. 'This system, created by the First Consul at the opening of the century, has already given France peace and prosperity: it will guarantee them for the future. Such is my profound conviction. If you agree with me, show it by your votes ... You will be voting for the first time since 1804, understanding why, and knowing for what and for whom ... If you believe that the cause of which my name is a symbol — France regenerated by the Revolution of 1789, France organized by the Emperor — is your cause too, then proclaim your belief by sanctioning the powers for which I ask.'

There followed, AU NOM DU PEUPLE FRANÇAIS, a Decree by the President in five articles:

Art. I   The National Assembly is dissolved.
Art. II Universal suffrage is restored. The Law of May 31st is abrogated.
Art. III The French people is summoned to the polls between December 14th and 21st inst.

Art. IV   Martial Law is declared throughout the 1st Military
Division.

Art. V   The Conseil d'Etat is dismissed.

(A sixth Article charged the Minister of the Interior, who counter-
signed it, to carry out the decree.)

The third proclamation was addressed A L'ARMÉE. 'Soldiers!' it
began — that was the Napoleonic formula — 'Be proud that it is
your mission to save the country. I am counting on you, not to
break the law, but to enforce respect for the first law of the land, the
national sovereignty, whose legitimate representative I am ... I
appeal to the loyalty of the people and army: either give me the
means of assuring your prosperity, or choose someone else in my
place.' After exhorting them to defend the right of the people to
express its opinion at the polls, Louis ended by reminding them (with
the usual oratorical pretence that he was not doing so) of the
memories his name recalled. 'Those memories are engraved on
your hearts. We are united by links that can never be broken. Your
history is mine. We share a common past of glory and suffering.
In the future we shall share the same enthusiasm and resolve for the
peace and greatness of France.'[26]

What could have been more reassuring to the people of Paris — to
the tradesmen who had been dreading another Red Revolution, to
the workmen who resented the loss of their votes, or to the army
which still prided itself on its Napoleonic victories? History was
about to repeat itself: not the lamentable history of 1793 and 1848,
but the glorious history of 1799 and 1804. It only needed a popular
vote to inaugurate a Second Empire which would resemble the First
in having on the obverse of its prestige, if not of its coinage, NAPO-
LEON EMPEREUR, and on the reverse REPUBLIQUE FRANÇAISE.

At 10 o'clock Louis thought that the time had come to test popular
feeling, and rode out from the Elysée into the Place de la Concorde
and along the *quais* by the Louvre: ex-King Jérôme, the only Bonaparte of the old generation, rode with him, and a group of generals
and officers: he was received by some of the troops with cries of
Vive l'Empereur! and some of the crowd shouted *Vive la République!*
— so ambiguous still was his role. But it was no triumphal march.
Maupas afterwards reported to Morny: 'I must admit that I don't
think we have the popular sympathy: There are no signs of enthusiasm anywhere.' Louis did not venture to leave the Elysée again

that day, or the next. He did not even appear at the diplomatic dinner that evening at the Foreign Office; and his *migraine* was taken as a political ailment. There had been demonstrations against him by students in the Place de l'Ecole de médecine, and by a well-dressed crowd (wearing not the *blouse* but the *paletot*) in the Place de la Bastille; and a procession had marched down the rue Saint-Martin singing the *Marseillaise*. Louis was faced by something as incalculable as his own mind — the temper of the Paris people. The *coup* had begun 'according to plan'; but how would it end?

Morny, who had studied to good effect the course of previous Paris *émeutes*, warned Maupas that the dangerous moment would be the third day. And so it was. On December 3rd the shops and theatres were open as usual, and the everyday life of the capital seemed to be resumed. The crowds at the street-corners read without much interest the names of the new ministers, and of the Consultative Committee that the President had appointed to help him in his work. But as the day went on, Louis at the Elysée, Morny at the Ministère de l'Intérieur, and Maupas at the Préfecture de Police gradually realized that something had gone wrong; and soon fresh notices were posted up calling for public calm, and threatening that anyone found carrying arms or building or defending barricades would be shot out of hand. What had happened?

Early in the morning a group of republican deputies, of whom the poet Victor Hugo was the ringleader, had formed a *Comité de Résistance* to organize opposition. Hugo himself signed and issued a poster *Au Peuple!* saying that Louis was an outlaw, and calling them *Aux armes!* Between 9 and 10 a crowd some 100 strong threw up a small barricade in the rue Sainte-Marguerite (Faubourg Saint-Antoine). When troops advanced against them a shot was fired, and a soldier wounded. His comrades fired back, and Dr. Baudin, a deputy, who stood on the barricade, fell dead. The crowd, which remembered 1848, had no fight in it, and was soon dispersed. But the *émeute* had its first martyr.

There were a few other clashes with the troops the same day in the narrow streets north of the Hôtel de Ville, and in one, the rue Aumaire, two civilians were killed. But at nightfall the troops were recalled to barracks; and whilst Hugo and his friends organized a public funeral of the three victims, and preached armed resistance for the morrow, Louis and his advisers considered what should be done. They had perhaps underestimated the influence of the republican

deputies; they should have arrested more. But they were not alarmed by the threat of barricades: they knew how little heart there was likely to be in their defence, after the bloodshed of 1848. Maupas, as a civilian, thought a demonstration in force would be enough; but the soldiers, Saint-Arnaud and Magnan, wanted to teach the *canaille* an Algerian lesson, and to have done once and for all with these 'Red' disorders. Louis, having put his faith in the army, could hardly withdraw it now.

On the morning of December 4th it was known that barricades were going up at most of the important street-corners in the district between the Hôtel de Ville and the boulevards, from the rue Montmartre on the west to the rue du Temple on the east. Their defenders perhaps numbered only 1200, but they were led by *revenants* of 1848 — Landrin, Marie, and others — who had hitherto held back: most of the inhabitants stayed at home and bolted their doors. Against this handful of poorly armed civilians Magnan had some 30,000 men; but, knowing the hard conditions of street-fighting, he was prepared for a long struggle, and served out sixty rounds of ammunition: Saint-Arnaud had advised him to provide four days' rations, and to make arrangements for resting part of his force behind the fighting-line. His plan — an Algerian plan which had already been successful in June 1848 — was to give the enemy time to concentrate in the quarter they had chosen (there were a few barricades on the south bank, but they could be ignored), and then to overwhelm them by a concentrated attack from all sides at once. 'All my troops (he wrote to Maupas on the evening of December 3rd) are returning to quarters for rest. I am abandoning Paris to the rebels: I am letting them make barricades. Tomorrow, if they are behind them, I am going to teach them a lesson. We must make an end of it (*Il faut en finir*) and restore safety to the city. Tomorrow every gathering will be broken up by force, and the barricades razed by artillery.'[27]

Magnan's advance did not begin till 3 in the afternoon, and within six hours the whole operation was over. The barricades were smashed by artillery, their defenders overwhelmed by musketry fire or bayonet charges. No quarter was given, and many who had been taken prisoner were shot out of hand.

But one incident did not go 'according to plan'. In the Boulevard des Italiens, on the northern edge of the fighting area, about 3 p.m., shots were fired at Canrobert's troops, apparently from shops or

private houses behind the 'front', where many civilians were at doors or windows watching the fight. The troops fired back, and for a few minutes there was a 'massacre', in which perhaps fifty non-combatants were killed, and two distinguished members of the Cercle du Commerce wounded. Such unhappy incidents are not uncommon in street-fighting, when the difference between combatants and spectators is often doubtful. That so much importance should have been attached, not merely by partisan writers at the time, but by later French historians, to a single incident in a day of violence and bloodshed illustrates chiefly the Parisian state of mind, which thought so much of the death of fifty middle-class citizens, and so little of the killing of at least four times as many workers — the official report gave the total of insurgents killed as 215, but this probably did not include an uncertain number of prisoners *passés sous les armes*: for these had come to be regarded since 1848 as 'public enemies' whom it was a patriotic duty to destroy.

This did not mean that Paris as a whole was less republican and socialistic than it had been three years before — in truth it was more so; but only that it was sick and tired alike of the theories of such men as Proudhon and Louis Blanc and of the threats of such *revenants* of 1848 as Landrin and Marie. It did not mean that Parisians approved of Louis' constitutional proposals, or welcomed the prospect of another Empire and another *grande armée*, but only that they condoned any stroke that secured them against the fear of another Red Terror.

And here Louis, who must have known this, made a mistake more serious than the affair of the Boulevard des Italiens. He had always claimed to be the representative of the French people, and had made it clear that by *le peuple* he meant above all the countryside and the provincial towns. He should have acted on that assumption now, when reports came in from various parts of the country of *émeutes* similar to and in sympathy with the Paris rising — a regular *jacquerie en province*, Maupas called it. These incidents were (as far as the evidence can be judged) of scattered occurrence — no great cities took part in them — and were easily suppressed. Louis would have been well advised to remember the experiences of his provincial tours, and to ignore them. He should have relied on the long-standing feud between the countryside and the towns, and between the provinces and Paris, to carry him over the crisis. Instead, he let himself be persuaded to allow the arrest of some 27,000 'republicans

and socialists' all over the country, and to set up (in addition to the courts-martial which condemned so many Parisians to death) departmental committees of three with power to determine, *in absentia*, without witnesses or appeal, the fate of thousands who might have nothing against them but a local reputation for 'dangerous' opinions.

In this arbitrary way, of the 26,884 prisoners (these are the official figures) more than 9500 were transported to Algeria, and 239 of the 'worst cases' to Cayenne; 3000 were 'interned' away from their homes, and more than 1500 expelled from the country. Too late to remedy the scandal, Louis had the sentences revised, and pardoned 3000–4000 victims of this national 'purge'. For they were of all classes: 5423 *cultivateurs*, 1850 *journaliers*, 1570 *rentiers*, 1107 *cordonniers*, 888 *menuisiers*, 733 *maçons*, 642 *tisserands*, 457 *forgerons*, 415 *boulangers*, 327 *médecins*, 251 *tailleurs de pierres*, etc. This brutal and indiscriminate proscription – indiscriminate because including so many innocent victims of local suspicion or dislike – was never forgotten or forgiven. Not even by Louis himself: for at the end of her life the Empress Eugénie told a friend: 'My husband and I often discussed this painful question. One day, seeing him plunged in gloomy thoughts, and guessing their cause, I could not avoid saying, "You wear the Second of December like a shirt of Nessus," and he replied, "Yes, it is always on my mind".'

He would not easily forget the approach made to him at the time by the most remarkable of the popular leaders, an old admirer too, who had written a letter full of flattery to Ham, and had since 1841 edited the *Révue Indépendante*, throwing herself into republicanism in the same headlong and muddle-headed fashion that she had thrown herself into free love – George Sand. She had asked him for an interview, and brought with her a long and eloquent appeal for an amnesty for the victims of December 2nd. Louis had pardoned some of her friends; but he had not altered his policy of repression.[28]

At the moment every other thought was outweighed by the result of the appeal to the people. In the *plébiscite* held on December 21st the question put was: 'Does the French people desire the maintenance of Louis Bonaparte's authority, and delegate to him the powers necessary to establish a constitution on the lines laid down in the proclamation?' Every Frenchman of age had a vote, which he expressed freely by word of mouth, though he knew that if he voted 'against the government' he would be black-listed. Out of

8 million voters, 7½ millions answered, YES, only 600,000 NO: but in Paris the numbers (out of 300,000) were 133,000 YES, and 80,000 NO; whilst another 80,000 failed to vote.

5

Whilst half Paris, and all but a twelfth part of France, approved of the *coup d'état*, it scandalized English opinion. Tennyson in some indifferent verse called it a 'public crime'. *The Times* of December 8th, after quoting the President's declaration of his intention to keep his oath of loyalty to the Constitution, said that 'these words must now strike their self-convicted author in the midst of his sanguinary triumph, and leave a stigma on his truth and honour which the Crown of an Empire cannot hide or efface...' Never was 'the fate of a great nation' more effectually disposed of 'by surprise and violence'; never were 'the principles of authority and morality' more audaciously invaded by force and dishonesty... 'Speaking within the limits of historical truth, we affirm that the bloody and treacherous deeds of December 4th will be remembered with horror in the annals even of that city which witnessed the massacre of St. Bartholomew and the Reign of Terror.' It made matters worse, the writer thought, that the *coup* had been carried out by the army, and that France was now to be under a military government, and at its head one who, 'if he possesses military talents, they are at present unknown, and his personal influence with the troops is confined to the prestige of his name, or the lavish prodigality of his means of corruption'.[29]

Louis may have smiled at this last phrase, when he remembered that all the capital he had left on the evening of December 1st was a few thousand pounds. But he must also have reflected how little, after all, his English friends understood France, if they let their whole judgment depend on a broken oath and a few hours' street-fighting: as though a country which had made and destroyed eight constitutions in sixty years would attach much importance to the loss of a ninth; or as though the Paris of February and June 1848 was likely to treat a republican *émeute* in the manner of a Chartist demonstration.

The editor of *The Times* was J. T. Delane; he had succeeded Thomas Barnes in 1841 at the age of twenty-three, and had staffed the paper with his Oxford friends. His policy from the first had been

to cultivate the society of those 'in the know', to publish important news sooner than any other paper, and to express the political opinions of the governing class. He had hitherto opposed Palmerston's foreign policy as endangering the peace of Europe and, with it, the prosperity of the British landlords and merchants — as in the 'Sicilian Arms' incident of 1848, and the reception of Kossuth in 1849; and he regarded Palmerston's approval of Louis Napoleon's *coup d'état* as another encouragement of a republican adventurer, nearer home, and far more dangerous. The Court agreed, Russell took the opportunity to get rid of an embarrassing colleague, and Palmerston's political career seemed to be over; but within a few years he was in power again, with Delane behind him, embodying the national policy during the Crimean War, and for ten years afterwards: a period during which *The Times*, with a circulation, immense for those days, of 40,000 to 60,000, could be described as *le quatrième pouvoir de l'état britannique*.

But there was in Paris in 1851 one of the cleverest Englishmen of his age, who sent to a rival paper, *The Inquirer*, under the name of AMICUS, a series of letters in which he tried to correct one insular point of view by another more pertinent to the issue. He pointed out that all Paris had for months past been living under the shadow of a great fear: fear of a repetition in May 1852 of the street-fighting of 1848 and even of the Terror of 1793-94, that anyone who delivered the Parisian shopkeeper and housewife from this danger earned their gratitude, whatever means he employed; that the events of December 4th proved the existence of at least 1250 real terrorists — 'for I saw them myself, men whose physiognomy and accoutrements exactly resembled the traditional *Montagnard*, sallow, stern, compressed, with much marked features, which expressed but resisted suffering, and brooding one-ideaed thought ... gloomy fanatics, *over*-principled ruffians'; that no one, except others of their own class, minded the imprisonment or exile of politicians and socialists; that Frenchmen did not care under what constitution they lived, so long as some strong ruler gave them repose and security under which to carry on their familiar way of life; and that, whatever his personal faults, Louis Napoleon had the name and the *audace* to qualify him as the current 'saviour of society'.

Walter Bagehot was too clear-headed to doubt that France would now be 'saved', not by any new-fangled constitution of Brumaire,

but by the institutions — 'the educational system, the banking system, the financial system, the municipal system, the administrative system, the civil legislation, the penal legislation, the commercial legislation' which 'all date from the time, and are more or less deeply inscribed with the genius, the firm will, and unresting energies of Napoleon'. These institutions could never be administered wholeheartedly by a Bourbon or an Orléans prince; but they could do their full work under the *Bas*-Empire (as it came to be called) of the nephew of Napoleon.[30]

Whilst the press attack on Louis was supported by members of the government such as Graham and Wood, Bagehot's opinion was shared by ministers who knew France better than they did. 'I thought (wrote Clarendon to Reeve of *The Times* on December 17th) that we should not measure his acts by an English standard, or ask ourselves how we should like to see our Parliament shut up, the press abolished, and everybody imprisoned at pleasure; for we must remember that the French are more or less accustomed to such proceedings, and that Louis Napoleon put an end to a system that everybody knew was a fraud and could not last.' And Malmesbury received from Persigny on December 26th a long letter which was evidently Louis' own apologia addressed to a sympathizer. He made the point that the parliamentary system worked well in England because the public interest was in the hands of an intelligent and responsible aristocracy; whereas in France the same class had none of the political virtues, and the parliamentary system was at the mercy of an undisciplined democracy. Louis' appeal to the army, which seemed so sinister to *The Times*, was in effect an appeal to the people against the politicians; and if there was any danger to England in the new regime, it did not lie in Louis' pacific government, but in the long-standing distrust of one nation for another.

Bagehot's view of the *coup d'état* was also that of a French critic of equal insight. Sainte-Beuve had discarded his youthful republicanism, and had refused a cross of the Legion of Honour from Louis-Philippe, to join the staff of the *Constitutionnel*. 'I am not a fanatical Bonapartist (he wrote in 1851), but I have good reasons for supporting the party. Louis has been elected by universal suffrage, and we need a strong and stable government.' It is good that the future of France should be in the grasp of one who 'has in his hands the power of a Louis XIV, and in his heart the democratic principles of the French Revolution'.[31]

What the character of the new regime was to be became clear enough from the moment when, on December 31st, the committee set up to receive the votes reported at the Elysée the result of the *plébiscite*, and its chairman reminded Louis of his phrase of December 2nd about 'France regenerated by the Revolution and organized by Napoleon'. It was certain when, on New Year's Day, 1852, Louis went in procession from the Elysée to Notre Dame and returned to the Tuileries, after a service whose grandeur recalled that of Whitsun Day, 1802: the declaration of the Second Empire was indeed to be delayed, as that of the First had been, but for less than a year. The publication of the new Constitution a fortnight later (January 14th) left no doubt in any mind that the President now had every attribute except the name of Emperor.

Like two other notable dictators of modern times, Louis had known and made known beforehand what he intended to do: like them he seized power at an age when he might hope for time and energy to do it; like them he fell before his life was fully run. Bonaparte in 1799 had published no political programme; but few could doubt, from his early writings 'in the Jacobin interest' or his letter to Sieyès in 1796 what his attitude was towards the principles of 1789, or on what conditions he would accept the Consulship of Brumaire. He became Consul for life at the age of 41: he was 46 at the time of Tilsit, which has often been taken as the climax of his career: he abdicated at 53. Hitler published when he was 37 the first volume of *Mein Kampf*, in which he explained what he intended to do and how he would do it: he achieved the Chancellorship at 44: he committed suicide at 56. Louis Napoleon's political ideas were explained in a number of publications, of which the *Rêveries politiques* (1832) and the *Idées Napoléoniennes* (1839) were the most explicit. He was 40 when he was elected President, 44 when he became Emperor: he fell at 62.

Louis' political aims never strayed far from what he had learnt from meditating on the career of Napoleon. He believed that the government France needed was that of an Empire inspired by the ideas of the Revolution; an autocracy sanctioned by and attentive to the will of the people; a republican monarchy which might equally well be called a monarchical republic: there was nothing paradoxical in such terms to the heirs of 1789. Thus in the *Rêveries* of 1832, taking his text from Montesquieu, he had written: 'The nature of the government of the Republic consisted in the desire to

establish the reign of equality and liberty: the passions by which it was actuated were a love of the fatherland and an impulse to exterminate all its enemies. The nature of the Empire was to consolidate a throne based on the principles of the Revolution, to heal all the wounds of France, to regenerate the people; the passions in that government were love of the fatherland, love of glory, love of honour.' 'The misfortune of the reign of the Emperor Napoleon', he admitted, 'was that he was not able to reap all that he had sown — that, having delivered France, he was not able to leave her free.' That misfortune he, Louis, intended to avoid: the *Acte additionel* of 1815 should be fused with the *Sénatus-consulte* of 1804; liberty should crown the edifice of the Empire.[32]

Seven years later, in the *Idées* of 1839, Louis had challenged France, with startling appropriateness to her situation a century later, to fulfil her providential mission in Europe. 'Whilst our old central Europe is like a volcano consuming itself in its own crater, two nations, Oriental and Occidental, proceed unhesitatingly towards perfection, the one at the will of one man, the other by liberty': the United States of America, by the principles of *laisser-faire, laisser-passer*; and Russia, by means of the Imperial dynasty, which 'for a century and a half past, has been rescuing that vast empire from barbarism'. 'But thou, France of Henry IV, of Louis XIV, of Carnot, of Napoleon, thou who wast ever for western Europe the source of progress, thou who possessest the two supports of empire — the genius of the arts of peace and the genius of war — hast thou no longer a mission to fulfil? Wilt thou exhaust thy strength and thy energy in an incessant struggle with thine own childern? No. Such cannot be thy destiny. Soon the day will come when they who govern thee must comprehend that it is thy part in every settlement to throw thy sword of Brennus into the scale of civilization.'[33]

6

In 1832 Louis had outlined the Constitution of this republican monarchy under which France was to undertake her mission. There were to be three authorities in the state: the people, the parliament, and the Emperor. The people would elect and sanction: the parliament would deliberate: the Emperor would be the sole executive power. How did he provide for this harmony of authorities in the Constitution of 1852? The part of the people, though it heads the

document (*Section I, Art. 1*), merely consists of the statement: 'The Constitution recognizes, confirms, and guarantees the great principles proclaimed in 1789, which form the bases of the public rights of the French people.' But it is added (*Section III, Art. 5*) that 'The President of the Republic is responsible to the French people, to whom he has always a right to appeal'; (*Section III, Art. 17*) that the President has the right to recommend his successor 'to the confidence of the people and to its suffrages'; and (*Section IV, Art. 32*) that changes in the Constitution must be 'adopted by the French people'.

With this empty gesture to the authority of the people, the Constitution of 1852 passed to *Section II: Forms of the government of the Republic*; and here it soon appeared that there was in effect only one such form, viz. 'Prince Louis Napoleon Bonaparte, elected President of the Republic for ten years, governing by means of the Ministers, the Council of State, the Senate, and the Legislative Body'; (i.e., Parliament is no longer a separate authority, for 'The legislative power is exercised collectively by the President, the Senate, and the Legislative Body'). This preponderance of the President is illustrated in no less than fourteen Articles in *Section III*. He is the Chief of the State. He commands the land and sea forces, declares war, concludes treaties of peace, and political and commercial alliances, and makes the rules and decrees for the execution of the laws. Justice is rendered in his name, and he has the right to pardon. He initiates, sanctions, and promulgates laws and *sénatus-consultes*; he can declare martial law (*état de siège*) in any part of the country. The Ministers are appointed and dismissed by him. They, as well as all members of the legislature, magistrates, and officers, take an oath of obedience to the Constitution and of loyalty to the President. Not only so; for in later Sections it is provided that the President nominates the President and Vice-Presidents of the Senate and Legislative Body, all unofficial members of the Senate, and all members of the State Council (these he may also dismiss), that he summons, prorogues, and dissolves both legislative bodies, that laws are drafted and matters of administration dealt with by the State Council under his chairmanship, and that the High Court of Justice, dealing without appeal with all crimes against the President or the safety of the state, is convened at his will. It would be difficult to imagine any constitution less republican, more monarchical, any which put the liberties of the people more at the mercy of a President whom a stroke of the pen would entitle 'Emperor'.

One sign of this which was not much to the taste of his old friends was the way in which, having used them to achieve his aim, Louis now dispensed with their services. D'Orsay, who claimed to have won him the support of *La Presse* and *Le Constitutionnel*, professed to want no reward, but hinted that none could be too great: yet how could he expect official employment in Paris, where he was as unpopular as Louis' other representative, 'Plon-Plon', was in London?[34] Morny, after several angry interviews, resigned on January 21st. 'His help was wanted to carry out the *coup d'état* (wrote his mistress, the Comtesse Le Hon to Flahaut the same day), but there it ended; and I may tell you that you also are wanted no longer. Such are the real feelings of this man (i.e. Louis), who has none of the finer qualities, and who, you may take it from me, is little worthy of your esteem. His sincerity and apparent courtesy serve to conceal all sorts of evil propensities.' Morny himself corroborated this account in a letter to Flahaut a few days later. 'I have occasionally in the past (he wrote) spoken to you very frankly on the subject of the President. Since the 2nd of December I have come to understand his character better still. In the first place, he has no real friendship for anyone, less perhaps for me than for others; and then my peculiar position is an annoyance to him, and yours makes the matter still worse ... He is mistrustful and ungrateful, and only likes those who obey him slavishly and flatter him... He could not find anyone else for the 2nd of December, so he made use of me. I risked my life; I accomplished my task: but what matter? I am in the way, I am neither a slave nor a sycophant, so I am cast off as useless!' It is easy to understand Morny's indignation. But it was not fair to accuse Louis of common ingratitude. He was no Prince Hal, dismissing the companions of his disorderly youth. Certainly he did not discard his mistress, Miss Howard, until the very eve of his marriage. But the 'peculiar position' of Flahaut, as the lover of Louis' mother, and of Morny as the son born of their liaison, made it excusable for a would-be Emperor, who hoped to be the founder of a legitimate dynasty, to renounce public relations with them. That this was in his mind appears from a letter he wrote to his cousin Prince Napoleon not many months later (November 6th). 'It is no longer a question merely of saving the situation, but of founding a dynasty ... When one bears such a name as ours and is at the head of the government, there are two things that must be done: One has to satisfy the interests of the masses and to conciliate the classes.' The Prince's part was to

watch his words. The Emperor's part was to be careful of his company, and to cultivate a royal detachment, even at the expense of his old friends.[35]

But the immediate cause or occasion of the break with both Morny and Flahaut was Louis' decision, embodied in a decree of January 14th, to compel the sale of the French estates of the Orléans family, and so the forfeiture of the grant made to Louis-Philippe on his accession, which he had alienated (illegally, it was maintained) to his sons. When Flahaut, who was now in London, heard of this proposal, he sent an indignant letter, evidently meant for Louis' eye, describing it as 'a deed of petty and shameful vengeance'; and Morny replied, 'I have done everything in the world, and gone so far as to risk loss of his confidence, in order to prevent it'. Flahaut, too, after consulting Palmerston, had a long but ineffectual interview with Louis (February 21st): 'Well, Monseigneur,' he ended, 'it will be for you what the condemnation of the Duc d'Enghien was for your uncle' — 'Oh! (said he) that was a very different affair' — 'Yes, Monseigneur, just as murder differs from robbery.'

The decree had a 'bad press'. Paris called it, by an untranslatable pun, *le premier vol de l'aigle*, and accused Louis of plain theft. 'He must be his own master (wrote the Comtesse Le Hon), and will brook no opposition ... Having made his *coup*, he intends to be supreme.' It was the the strong gesture of a weak man. But, again, it did not deserve Flahaut's epithets; for Louis was no common thief; he used the proceeds of his *vol* for purposes which might have been dictated by Louis Blanc: Mutual Benefit Societies, free burial, orphanages, asylums, workmen's dwellings, agricultural banks, baths and wash-houses, hospitals, pawn-shops, and Labour Exchanges: as though he agreed with Proudhon's famous dictum about property, and would make restitution to the working classes out of Louis-Philippe's own pocket for his eighteen years' neglect of their interests.[36]

Yet it was the benevolence of a despot. For Louis made full use of the three months which were allowed to intervene before the elections and the setting up of 'constitutional' government to institute an autocratic system which would be proof against any constitution. Till then the President's decrees had force of law (Tit. VIII, Art. 58), and he made full use of these powers. When the Republic came into being again, it would find the Empire already on its throne. Thus at the service of January 1st the prayer *Salvam*

fac Rempublicam had been followed, though not superseded, by *Salvum fac Ludovicum Napoleonem*. The imperial eagle had reappeared above the republican tricolour. The few remaining Trees of Liberty had been uprooted, and the fading inscriptions of *Liberté*, *Egalité*, *Fraternité* finally erased. Napoleon's birthday, August 15th, became a national festival.

More serious changes lay behind. The National Guard, once the safeguard of the *bourgeoisie* against the *canaille*, but by now an embarrassment to the army, was abolished. A new Press Law placed every kind of obstacle in the way of editors of political or economic journals, and put it in the power of any *Préfet*, after two warnings (*avertissements*), to suspend the publication of any paper — though this step was sometimes taken upon such frivolous grounds as to bring the censorship into contempt. All officials, from deputies to *professeurs*, had to take an oath of allegiance to the President and the Constitution; University teachers were even instructed to dress tidily and forbidden to grow 'anarchical' beards. The *maires* of the minutest towns were appointed by the government, and went into uniform; the *Préfets*, carefully chosen and highly paid, were responsible only to the central government. It was the Napoleonic administrative machine made more mechanical.[37]

But was not all this what German historians of the Early Church have called an *Interimsethik* — a way of life preparatory to the coming of the Kingdom? And was not the rule of Messiah, inaugurated by Universal (manhood) Franchise, to be the free expression of the Sovereign Will of the People? Certainly. But the more numerous the voters (eight million) and the fewer those eligible (the Chamber was to consist of only 261 members, a third of the old numbers), how could a bewildered People make its choice without help from the government? The *Préfets* were therefore instructed to post up the names of official candidates, and the *maires*, who also presided at the polls and had charge of the ballot-boxes, had to see that they were elected. Anyone ever convicted of a political crime was disfranchised; and members of the armed forces, who had a reputation for political independence, could vote only (where they were least likely to be) at their homes. If necessary, constituencies were split up or regrouped, to prevent a hostile vote. Only government papers could comment on the elections: others might publish the name of an unofficial candidate; no more. No political meetings were allowed. The result was as could be foretold. Of the 261 successful candidates

(elected for six years), three were Legitimists, three Republicans, and three Independents: but as all three Republicans (Cavaignac and Carnot for Paris, Hénon for Lyon) resigned rather than take the oath of allegiance to the President, the Chamber consisted almost to a man of Government nominees. In the Senate, the Guardian of the Constitution, there were not even three exceptions: all seventy-two members were nominated by the President: all that could be said was that, since they retained their offices for life, they might come to acquire an independence they did not yet possess.[38]

7

The newly elected Parliament was summoned to meet the President for the first time at the Tuileries on March 29th, 1852. Louis entered, to a salute of 101 guns, and took his seat, surrounded by generals, magistrates, and the diplomatic corps, with their ladies; the deputies sat on benches facing him, and listened to an Address almost 'from the throne'. 'I should not accept any alteration in the present state of things', he told them, 'unless forced to do so by plain necessity . . . If party spirit aimed at undermining the foundations of my government, then it would be reasonable to ask the people, in the name of national security, to grant me a new title that would crown me beyond recall with the power it has given me (*fixât irrévocablement sur ma tête le pouvoir dont il m'a revêtu*).' The next day the deputies met again in the old Palais Bourbon. But the form of the *salle des séances* had been once more changed. Instead of the lengthwise arrangement of seats which had given the revolution-ary *manège* a look of the House of Commons, instead of the semi-circle facing the speaker's desk which had turned the Convention in the *salle des machines* of the Tuileries into a single party assembly addressed by a Government spokesman, the deputies now sat in a block facing their President and the *Conseil d'état*: no desk was pro-vided for an orator: if any member of the audience (as they now seemed) had anything to say, he must speak from his seat. The Chamber had not elected its own President and Secretaries, or even those of its committees: no reporters were admitted to its debates. It could not originate legislation: it could only discuss proposals made by the President through the *Conseil d'état*. Its vote did not pass or reject a bill: it could not even amend one without leave of the Council.

Louis had in effect telescoped the procedure by which Napoleon had converted Republic into Empire fifty years before, and no one doubted that the formal change would soon follow. Nor did the country seem less likely to accept it now than then. But would the mood of subservience last? Were the alarms of 1848 and 1851 as pervasive and preventive as those of 1789-99? Would not the second Napoleon be tempted as the first was, and even sooner, to divert public attention from a repressive regime at home to exciting adventures abroad? Would not the army, which had placed him in power, want employment more distinguished and carrying more chance of promotion than garrison duty? Might not the programme of industrial expansion and prosperity to which Louis had committed himself lead to international rivalries? Might not the foundation of a new dynasty rouse dangerous jealousies in the old Courts? Might not the claims of nationality, which Louis was known to favour, reawaken the spirit of 1848, and lead to diplomatic quarrels, even to war?

When Lord Malmesbury took office as Foreign Secretary in Lord Derby's ministry in March 1852 he received from his predecessor, Lord Palmerston, 'a masterly sketch of the *status quo* in Europe, and some general hints' as to his procedure. The pith of them was 'to keep in well with France'. 'He said that the advent of Louis Napoleon to power was a good thing for France, and, from the extraordinary figures of the *plébiscite*, proved she was weary both of Bourbons and lawyers; but that, as it was quite possible that his tendencies might be to avenge his uncle's fate, we must turn all our attention to strengthening our national defences.' Afterwards Malmesbury visited Wellington: the old man's parting words were the same as Palmerston's: '*Mind you keep in well with France*, as that is a most important object for us; but (he went on) be careful as to this new change of dynasty. I don't believe Louis Napoleon will ever go to war with us if he can help it, but he must keep up his popularity, and then God knows what he may do.' Malmesbury's own impression (to Sir Hamilton Seymour, March 29th) was based on private knowledge. 'I have known him personally for many years, and I can answer for the most remarkable feature in his character being an obstinacy of intention, which, as it is maintained on all subjects with unruffled temper, is held to the last against all opposition . . . To be Emperor has been his *marotte* (hobby) since he was twenty years old, when I recollect his mother used to laugh at

him for indulging such a dream. Walewski tells me that the whole army is most eager to crown him. He is universally called *Altesse Impériale*, and there is good reason for supposing that his mantle is in the hands of the *brodeuses*.' But Malmesbury did not think a Second Empire would be taken very seriously in France, or become a source of danger to Europe.[39]

These questions were in many minds during the provincial tour upon which Louis set out once more in the autumn of 1852 — and in his own mind too. For he seems to have needed reassurance before he took the final step; and he sought it where he hoped it would be found, in the parts of France furthest away from Paris, in the traditional home of Resistance, since the days of the Albigensian heretics, the Huguenots, and the Girondins — since 1814, 1848, and even 1851. So he set out by the Napoleonic route of 1814 to Lyon, continued by Grenoble to Marseille, thence by Montpellier to Bordeaux, and returned to Paris by La Rochelle and Tours. The zealous Persigny had arranged wherever possible that he should be greeted with cries of *Vive l'Empereur! Vive Napoléon III!* But Louis professed to disown them. 'The cry *Vive l'Empereur!* (he said in a speech at Lyon) is a heart-touching reminder rather than a hope that flatters my pride ... If the modest title of President makes it easier for me to carry out the mission entrusted to me, then I am not the man to let personal interest exchange that title for the name of Emperor.' At Marseille the opportune discovery of a plot against his life spoke even more eloquently for Louis than his laying of the foundation-stone of the new cathedral. As the President travelled further west, in the still half-Latin Midi, he found himself addressed in terms of the Roman Empire: *Fiat Imperium! Vox Populi, vox Dei! Ave, Caesar Imperator!* At Bordeaux his doubts seem at last to have disappeared, and he was inspired to make a speech which echoed round Europe. 'France (he said) seems to want the return of the Empire. But there are people who say, The Empire means war. I say, The Empire means peace (*l'Empire, c'est la paix*).' And he went on to outline a policy of national regeneration and material expansion: 'That is what I mean by the Empire, if it is to be re-established; such are the only conquests I have in mind; and you — all of you round me here, who share my wish for the good of our nation — you are the only army I command (*vous êtes mes soldats*).'[40]

On November 9th, within three weeks of Louis' return to Paris, the Senate passed a *sénatus-consulte* constituting him Emperor, and

his heirs after him. There was only one dissentient, Vieillard, the man who had once been tutor to Louis' brother and was still his friend: perhaps he remembered that Carnot had voted alone against the hereditary Empire in 1804. The necessary *plébiscite* followed; and on November 20th to 21st ten million voters were urged to the poll. The question put to them was whether the French people wished for 'the re-establishment of the Imperial dignity in the person of Louis-Napoléon Bonaparte'. The votes were YES, 7,800,000; NO, 250,000; but with the large number of 2,000,000 abstentions (particularly in the west, and the big cities — Lyon, Marseille, Bordeaux). The year's experience of Louis' government since the *coup* of December 1851, had won him half a million new votes.[41]

He could hardly doubt that he was now Emperor by will of the People. On December 1st, seated on a throne in the royal palace of Saint-Cloud, he received from the *Corps législatif*, the *Sénat*, and the *Conseil d'État* the result of the *plébiscite* as the decision of the nation (*La France se livre à vous tout entière*); and replied with an address, in which he assumed the title of Napoleon III; for he did not wish to start a new dynasty, but to carry on that of his uncle and his uncle's son, whom Napoleon had named as his successor in 1815. Strictly speaking, as some critics pointed out, he should have recognized the succession of Joseph and Louis Bonaparte, and have called himself 'Napoleon V'. *The Times*, which remained bitterly hostile to the new Emperor, thought it necessary (December 3rd) to protest against this proclamation of 'a dynastic tradition unknown to history and to Europe'; for Napoleon's attempt to proclaim his son's accession at the time of his second abdication had been rejected both by the Allies and by the Assembly. Delane might have recognized that Louis did not date his accession from the death of the King of Rome, as Louis XVIII had done from the death of the Dauphin, 'Louis XVII', and that he wished to recognize the legitimacy both of the Bourbon and of the Orléans succession; for he argued that this would make it easier for foreign courts to recognize his own. Finally, in words which recalled the proudest boast of Napoleon, he said, 'My title does not date from 1815; it dates from this moment, at which you make known to me the suffrages of the nation'.[42]

The next day — it was once more the anniversary of Austerlitz — Napoleon III made his formal entry into the capital of the French Empire.

THE EMPEROR (1852-1856)

CAP. Truly to speak, and with no addition,
We go to gain a little patch of ground
That hath in it no profit but the name.
To pay five ducats, five, I would not farm it
Nor will it yield to Norway or the Pole
A ranker rate, should it be sold in fee.
HAM. Why, then the Polack never will defend it.
CAP. Yes, 'tis already garrison'd.   *Hamlet*, IV, iv

I

THE *coup d'état* of December 1851 was accepted outside France with philosophic shrugging of shoulders at the latest Parisian extravagance. The indignation of *The Times* over the bloodshed with which it was accompanied seemed a little absurd to countries accustomed to military rule and to sovereigns engaged in suppressing patriotic risings. Louis was known to be ambitious, but was not thought to be dangerous. If his countrymen preferred a dictator to a President, and did not grieve over the loss of their liberties, what matter? In any case, his regime probably would not last long. But when a year later the anonymous President proclaimed himself Emperor under the name of Napoleon III, Europe was suddenly alarmed. Had not the Powers assembled at the Congress of Vienna solemnly sworn that no Bonaparte should again sit upon the French throne? Was not Louis' choice of the number III (as the Tsar had warned him) a plain challenge to this decision, and a claim that the Bonaparte dynasty was as good as the Hapsburgs and the Hohenzollerns? Did it not reaffirm the Imperial claims of 1804 and 1805, and add another line to the epitaph of the Holy Roman Empire? Could the Tsar, the Emperor, the King of Prussia, and the Queen of England recognize the nephew of Napoleon as one of themselves?

Nicholas had on second thoughts given up the idea of an Anglo-Russian alliance against France, and had approved of December 2nd, 1851, but he hoped that Louis would not go further: 'Let him become President, or Consul if he likes, for ten years, or for life – nothing could be better: but I hope to God he is not thinking of making himself Emperor.' He felt so strongly that he wrote Louis a private letter (November 30th, 1852), and backed it up a fortnight later with an official dispatch. Louis did not reply to the letter: the

dispatch arrived after the Empire had been proclaimed. The Tsar had in fact decided, after consulting Austria and Prussia, to accredit his ambassador to the Emperor, but not to address Louis in the formula reserved for legitimate sovereigns, *Sire, mon Frère*. Louis sensibly refused to be insulted; and when Nicholas spoke of him as *nôtre très cher ami Napoléon, Empereur des Français*, he gracefully remarked: *On subit ses frères et on choisit ses amis* ('brothers' we put up with; we choose our 'friends'). Diplomacy has its uses. Austria and Prussia followed the Russian lead, but in the ordinary terms of royal courtesy. Yet both Frederick William of Prussia and Leopold of Belgium, his neighbours across the Rhine, were suspicious of Louis' territorial 'aspirations' in that quarter. Leopold as a boy had been present at Austerlitz, had fought on the Russian side at Bautzen and Leipzig, and had taken part in the occupation of Paris in 1814. 'My personal conviction (he wrote to Lord John Russell, April 20th, 1852) is that in the mind of Louis Napoleon there exists a programme inexorably fixed which contains the whole of the position of the Emperor Napoleon: i.e., the boundaries of the Empire as they were in 1811, the Protectorate over Germany, Italy, Poland, etc. This programme will appear to be put aside according to circumstances, but it will never be abandoned.' Perhaps only Victor Emmanuel of Sardinia and his new minister Cavour welcomed the Empire whole-heartedly, seeing in Louis a pledged friend of Italian liberty.[1]

In England Louis was best known as an occasional refugee, who came and went conspiratorially; a good sportsman, and a man of fashion, whom one met in London clubs, at race-meetings, and at country house parties; sometimes 'in funds', and able to keep an expensive mistress and his own carriage, sometimes borrowing and living on his 'expectations'; always nursing a strange ambition to become the ruler of France, and interviewing mysterious and rather sinister foreigners. During the summer of 1851 fashionable (and that meant, to a degree not possible nowadays, political) society was too much occupied with the Great Exhibition, the Ecclesiastical Titles Bill, and the difficulties between Victoria and Palmerston, to pay much attention to events in Paris. Yet the *coup d'état* of December came as a shock to the hopes of international peace and good will aroused by the Crystal Palace in Hyde Park. The indignation expressed by *The Times*, though it owed much to Tocqueville, Barrot, Faucher, and other French critics of the President, was backed by

the considered enmity of the proprietor, John Walter, and of the editor, John Delane, 'the best-informed man in Europe', who went on printing throughout 1852 attacks upon Louis' government by an anonymous 'Englishman in Paris'. The foreign correspondence and leaders in *The Times*, during the 'fifties, when its circulation was five or six times that of any other paper, were read in all the Chancelleries of Europe; and not least at the Elysée, whence Louis anxiously watched its championship of middle-class liberties and national defence, and tried through the official protests of Walewski and the unofficial influence of Flahaut (for he knew the paper was beyond bribery) to change its tone. But Walewski was disliked in England: hatred of him was said to be 'the strongest passion in Cowley's breast', and Greville described him as 'an adventurer, a needy speculator, without honour, conscience, or truth, and utterly unfit, both as to character and capacity for high office of any kind'. Persigny, too, called him *un sot*, and accused him before Louis (December 1855) of risking the English alliance 'by his *gaucheries*, his *mauvais foi*, and the *mauvaise rédaction* of his dispatches.[2] Such a reputation was no help to Louis' cause.

Towards the end of 1852 Delane was thinking of calling off his persecution of Louis in *The Times*; but the declaration of the Empire renewed his suspicions of French policy; and he took full opportunity of the 'War scares' of 1852 and 1853 to call for rearmament. His own visits to Paris had impressed him with the military preparedness of the country, and with the temptation to which Louis might be subjected at any moment to tighten his hold on public opinion by war.[3]

This view of Louis was not entirely shared at Windsor, where on the eve of the *coup d'état* of 1851 Victoria had written that 'in France there really ought to be a Monarchy before long, *qui que ce soit*'; and after it (to the King of the Belgians) 'Everybody says Louis Napoleon has behaved extremely well in the last crisis — full of courage and energy, and they say he is decidedly straight-forward'. Nor was she unduly surprised or disturbed by his assumption of Empire a year later. A month before the event (November 8th) she had written to Lord Malmesbury impressing upon him the importance of not joining in the refusal of other courts to recognize the title 'Napoleon III'. In December 1852 the British Government lost no time in accrediting Lord Cowley to the new regime in a letter from the Queen (December 4th) to 'My good Brother the Emperor of the

French'. Now that her bugbear Palmerston, 'Louis Napoleon's accomplice', had fallen into disgrace, it was possible to treat the chief criminal more dispassionately. Certainly, as Albert wrote, 'the violent seizure of the poor Orleans' entire property is a crime that cries to heaven', and 'the public is bothered by the idea of a possible French invasion': but Louis had shown a proper feeling in instructing Walewski (whom everybody knew was a son of Napoleon) to attend Wellington's funeral; and during a visit to Strasbourg he had conferred on Stockmar, the old friend of Victoria and Albert, the cross of the Legion of Honour. Such tactfulness, and his readiness, 'the moment despotism ceases to serve his aims, to employ democracy as a tool', might yet afford means for a Franco-British *entente*. Lord Derby recommended the Queen to read the *Idées napoléoniennes*: it would be interesting to know whether she did, and if so, what she thought of it.[4]

2

Prince Albert's remark that Louis was willing to 'employ democracy as a tool' was apparently a reference to the announcement which he had recently made to the Senate and the Assembly of his intention to marry a Spanish lady who was not of royal blood. It was a concession not only to democracy but also to domesticity; and this would perhaps win the sympathy of Victoria the wife and mother where diplomacy had alienated the favour of the Queen.

Solitary by nature, six years a prisoner, and with a mind full of secret hopes which he could only confide to a few friends, Louis was liable in his most social moments to fits of abstraction, of baffling silence and expressionless star-gazing. As Emperor he distrusted even his friends, and was most at his ease in the company of his secretary, his doctor, his valet — or of a succession of mistresses, whom he pursued with an appetite he admitted he could not control, and whom he kept, as many in his position have done, as a relaxation from the tedium of official life. As an exile in 1846-48 he had more than once thought of an English bride. As President he might have married his cousin Mathilde, would she have had him. Now as Emperor, with a dynasty to found, he was forced, as his uncle had been, to look for a royal or semi-royal bride.[5]

A royal bride was as difficult to find in 1852 as in 1810, and for the same reasons: the Emperor was a *parvenu* and a Catholic. Two princesses had been suggested: Caroline Stéphanie, the last of the

Swedish Vasa dynasty, and Adelaide of Hohenlohe, one of Victoria's many German nieces. Both were Protestants; but Louis hoped that the Queen might influence Adelaide's parents to consent to a match designed as a link of friendship with England (*de reserrer les liens de l'amitié entre Angleterre et la France*). Gossip said that Adelaide was 'dying to be an Empress', but that Victoria, who was against the idea, referred Louis to the girl's parents; anyhow nothing came of it. This was in December 1852. Louis was in fact already deeply committed to the love affair which ended in his marriage a month later to Eugenia de Montijo, a beautiful and spirited Spanish girl who was, except by birth, every inch an Empress.[6]

Her father, Don Cipriano, Comte de Teba and afterwards de Montijo, had fought and been wounded on the French side in the Peninsular War, and had taken part in the defence of Paris in 1814. Her mother, Maria Manuela, was by birth part French and part Scottish-American. They settled in Madrid, where (in 1830) the mother made the acquaintance of a French author whose books she admired, Prosper Mérimée; and it is through him that we know most about Eugénie's childhood and courtship. She was the younger of two sisters, whom their mother, when left a widow in 1839, carried into French and Spanish society with an eye to a rich or even royal marriage. Her sister Paca became Duchess of Alba in 1844. Eugénie, the more beautiful of the two, ambitious and romantic, seemed drawn by a sort of destiny towards the French throne. As a child of eight she had sat at Stendhal's knee and listened to his stories of the great Napoleon; for her he wrote the description of Waterloo at the opening of *La Chartreuse de Parme*; she treasured a picture he gave her of the battle of Austerlitz. As a girl she had seen Louis at Paris, after the failure of his attempt at Strasbourg. Four years later, at Pau, she met the singer Mrs. Gordon, who had been in the Strasbourg plot, told her about *mon prince* (as she called Louis), and offered to take her to see him in prison at Ham.

'Even as a girl', she said in her old age, 'I had a taste for politics'; not the party quarrels she heard so much of in her mother's drawing-room, in the time of Queen Christina, Narvaez, Espartero, Isturitz, and the 'Spanish Marriages' (though in 1848 she had interceded with Narvaez for some officers condemned to die), but 'the big questions in which national interests and prestige were at stake'. 'And that (she went on) was what first attracted me to my future husband, before I knew him personally. The chivalrous folly of his Strasbourg and

Boulogne adventures, his heroic attitude before the Cour des Pairs, the halo of suffering placed on his brow by his imprisonment at Ham, his proud proclamations in 1848, the noble patriotism of his language – it all roused my enthusiasm.'[7]

Nothing came of this hero-worship at the moment: but Eugénie's interest in Louis was revived when, in 1849, she met his cousin Jérôme as French ambassador at Madrid, and they talked about the new President. Eugénie declared that he ought to proceed, as Napoleon had done, from Consulate to Empire. There was no future for a French republic; failing a Bourbon, there should be a Bonaparte on the throne.

In the summer of 1850 Eugénie with her mother revisited Paris and Versailles. In September she was present at a review at Satory on horseback, when Louis noticed (as he would) her fine mount and good horsemanship. They met for the first time at a dinner at Princess Mathilde's some months later, and Louis was so taken with her that he invited her to the Elysée and to Saint-Cloud. On this second occasion – a summer evening in 1851 – they were alone, and Eugénie took alarm at the advances of a man who evidently thought of her not as a wife but as a mistress. But she was still attracted, not only by the charm which he always employed towards a pretty woman, but also, as she had long been, by the story of his career; for after she had left Paris she wrote a letter under cover to his Chamberlain, Count Baciocchi, offering all the money she had (it was not much) to help in the *coup d'état* of December 1851. Louis did not get the letter till the event was over. Remembering the financial help already given him by Miss Howard and Mrs. Gordon he would think of the Spanish girl as another victim of the Bonapartist romance . . . and perhaps as a future mistress.

The Montijos returned to Paris towards the end of 1852. Eugénie was now twenty-six, in the flower of her blue-eyed auburn-haired loveliness – a young woman who dressed almost too well, talked almost too confidently, and had rejected so many rich suitors that it might soon be too late for marriage. Yet she was proud, heart-whole, fastidious; with all the provenance of a Pompadour she would never consent to be a royal mistress. Louis invited her to Fontaine-bleau, made love to her, and asked leave to write: a discreet correspondence followed, in which her mother (now all ambitious for the marriage) and Mérimée (with some doubts) played their part. After the proclamation of the Empire he invited her again for the

hunting season at Compiègne, and the courtship ended, as it had begun, on horseback. The wives of the official guests, as might be expected, took offence at the attentions the Emperor paid to this 'foreign adventuress', and showed it: she complained to Louis, and said he must either declare himself or let her go. On January 12th, at a ball at the Tuileries, he asked her to be his wife. Ten days later he announced his decision to the senators, deputies, and counsellors of state. On the 30th they were married at Nôtre Dame, with every elaboration of Catholic ritual and of the florid taste of the 'fifties. 'Nothing could be more splendid (wrote Lady Augusta Bruce to the Duchess of Kent) than the decorations of the cathedral — velvet and ermine, gold and silver, flags and hangings of all colours were combined and harmonized with the splendid costumes of the clergy, the uniforms, civil and military, and the magnificent dresses of the ladies.' But Eugénie outshone them all. 'Her beautifully chiselled features and marble complexion, her nobly set-on head, her exquisitely proportioned figure and graceful carriage were most striking, and the whole was like a Poet's Vision!'[8]

In his speech on January 22nd Louis had said: 'The union that I am contracting does not follow the traditions of the old political system . . . The lady whom I have preferred is of lofty birth . . . A Catholic and a devout one, she will join in my prayers for the happiness of France. I have chosen a woman whom I love and respect rather than one unknown to me, or an alliance which would involve sacrifices as well as advantages. In a word, I put independence of mind, a warm heart, and domestic happiness above dynastic interests: I shall be the freer and therefore the stronger for it.' Louis knew he was acting against the advice of friends who were jealous of a new influence at the Tuileries, and of relations who had hoped for the Imperial succession. But he remembered how much more Napoleon owed to Joséphine than to Marie Louise; and he reckoned, as always, on the opinion of the People, which would understand a love match better than a dynastic alliance.[9]

'A love match'? Eugénie herself was old enough to have few illusions, either as to the character of her husband, or as to the difficulties of her new position. She did not love him, and she could not hope that he would love her long: she was too cool, he too sensuous; she too masculine, he too feminine, for a happy married life. But they were both in love with his career; and that might suffice. It was to Louis' credit that he had warned her what she might expect:

'You only talk to me, *ma chère enfant* (so she reported his words to an intimate friend) of the advantages of the position I am offering you. It is my duty to point out also its dangers, for they are great. I shall undoubtedly, whilst with you, be the object of more than one attempt at assassination. I must tell you too that serious plots are afoot in the army. I am keeping my eye on all this, and I reckon that by one means or another I can prevent any outbreak: perhaps by means of a war. But in that direction, too, there are plenty of chances of disaster.' If this warning was creditable to Louis' honesty, the way Eugénie took it was equally creditable to her courage. Her cult of Napoleon had only been equalled by her cult of Marie Antoinette: not merely as a leader of fashion (though it is said she always had by her the *Registre des toilettes de la reine*), but as one who proved her fortitude through her sufferings. If another revolution like 1848 came 'I should mount my horse (Eugénie said) and ride at the head of a regiment of cavalry: I should know how to save the crown for my son, and show what it means to be an Empress'.[10]

But as the state coach in which Louis and Eugénie drove to Nôtre Dame left the Tuileries — it was the same that had carried Napoleon with Joséphine to his coronation and with Marie-Louise to his second marriage — the gilt crown on its roof fell to the ground, as it had done in 1810.[11] Eugénie's son, born three years later, was to die, like the King of Rome, prematurely, and the second Bonapartist regime to end, like the first, without fulfilment. It was as though blind Destiny, which, for all we can see, acts as Viceroy for whatever Divinity rules our ends, were warning its devotees that Chance is a good servant, but a bad master.

Louis was as superstitious as his uncle; but he held to the greater omens. For the first four years of his reign everything that he touched turned to gold. By March 30th, 1856, which was as truly the climax of his career as April 18th, 1802, was of Napoleon's, he had avenged 1812, he had secured for France the leadership of Europe, he had won the alliance of England, and the friendship of her queen, he had established his Empire in France, and he had provided it with an heir. He was never again so successful or so secure.

3

The lever by which Louis raised himself to this eminence was the Crimean War. The 'best-informed man in Europe', walking the streets of Paris in January 1853, was 'more convinced than ever that

in order to retain his precarious hold upon the French people, and especially upon the army, Louis Napoleon was resolved upon a forward foreign policy'. And whilst Prince Albert, preoccupied with his Prussian sympathies, warned Prince William that 'once again in the West there appears a token of the old danger for Europe and of humiliation for Germany', Delane saw that Louis' real resentment was against Russia, whose Tsar was the one sovereign who had refused to recognize 'Napoleon III'.

Their quarrel, of course, went much deeper than personalities. Russia had defeated Napoleon in 1812, at the high tide of his ambition; and in 1815, at the moment when he was liberalizing the Empire, and intending (so the legend had it) to embody the national aspirations of the peoples in a free and federalized Europe, she had inspired the reactionary settlement of Vienna of which Metternich was the architect and Nicholas the patron. Louis belonged to the generation brought up under this repressive regime; and as a Bonaparte he had a double reason for dedicating himself to its destruction. It did not follow that he would be in any hurry to pick a quarrel with Nicholas, who at any rate preferred him to Louis-Philippe, or to risk embroilment with Austria and Prussia; but it did mean that, if he could so reverse the Napoleonic policy as to have England on his side, he would use any opportunity that might offer itself to challenge the continental predominance of Russia, and to restore French prestige and initiative to the place they had lost since Waterloo.[12]

One of the uses of diplomatists is to turn occasions into causes. Nicholas' refusal to call Louis *Mon Frère* was not such an occasion: every court in Europe was secretly pleased that a *parvenu* Emperor should be snubbed, and Louis was not in a strong enough position to take a personal affront as a national insult. But another occasion already presented itself, in a most unlikely quarter, and in the form of a fantastic controversy about rights granted three centuries ago, and the interpretation of a treaty eighty years old. For who would suppose that in the middle of the nineteenth century a quarrel about the protectorate of the Holy Places of Palestine would lead to a religious war between Catholic, Protestant, Orthodox, and Mohammedan powers more appropriate to the Age of the Crusades? Not that the motives were now, any more than then, wholly or even mainly religious. Religion was only an occasion that diplomacy transformed into a cause.

The Tsar, Nicholas I, was by choice and temperament a soldier: his strong sense of duty, when his elder brother refused to reign, had put 'a colonel on the throne' — a sovereign who set himself to order every detail of government and administration by rules better fitted for the barrack square; whose love of his country and belief in its traditional order made it impossible for him to forgive the Décabrist plotters of 1825 or the Polish rebels of 1830, whilst in his conscience he never forgave himself for the hanging of five conspirators or for the destruction of a Polish constitution which, though he detested it, he had sworn to uphold. A fierce champion of legitimacy, he refused to recognize the monarchy of Louis-Philippe, but accepted the empire of Louis Napoleon: a devoted husband and father, he deserted his German wife, after twenty years of marriage, for a Russian mistress: a great builder of palaces, a collector of pictures, a patron of literature, he lived austerely in one small room, sleeping (like Napoleon) on a camp-bed, and inspired the persecution of the intellectuals which ended in the death of Lermontov and Pushkin, and the exile of Dostoievsky to Siberia. Such inconsistencies were hardly thought strange in the last powerful champion of pre-revolutionary monarchy, and it was possible for President Routh of Magdalen in his 97th year (1852) to present Nicholas with a copy of his *Reliquiae Sacrae* inscribed 'to the most powerful King in the world' (*Regum Orbis Terrarum potentissimo*).

These clashes of principle and temperament reached a climax about 1853, when Nicholas was ill and overworked; and the Crimean crisis found him in an unstable condition of mind, unfit to deal with a very difficult situation. It was his tragedy that to his autocratic outlook the issue seemed so simple. He believed it his mission, as the father of his people, to insist on the protectorate of the Orthodox Christians in Turkey granted under the treaty of Kutchuk-Kainardji in 1774 and reasserted by that of Unkiar-Skelessi in 1833; and he believed that the Russian army could, if necessary (for he shrank from war) engage in a crusade to enforce this right. The Sultan, he constantly asserted — and all the more since his easy success in 1833 — was a 'sick man': Turkey was on the edge of dissolution: and he was confident — misinformed by his ambassadors — that Austria and Prussia would support him, whilst Catholic France would at any rate not intervene on the side of a Mohammedan state, and England could be held off by hope of compensation in the Levant. So arguments were found to excuse the megalomania of an aging autocrat.

The real issue was the old problem of the control of the contact-point of Europe and Asia, the Russian need of an outlet to the 'warm waters' of the Mediterranean, and the counter-claim, particularly by Austria (on the Danube) and England and France (in the Dardanelles) for free access to the trade-routes of the Black Sea. Such desires might only be met by a partition such as had befallen Poland at the end of the last century, and had been spared Turkey by the outbreak of the French Revolution. The dissolution of the country by decadence and misgovernment seemed every year more likely. Religion was still the most respectable cover for aggression. Nicholas might not set up, as his grandmother had done, arches marked 'To Byzantium'; but he too would hoist the cross above the crescent, and favour the religious minorities which supported Russian political interests in the Near East. 'The Greek and the Catholic church' were (as Palmerston put it with his usual lucidity) 'merely other names for Russian and French influence, and Russian and French influence are dissolving agents for the Turkish empire'. Yet these were aims that Nicholas hoped to accomplish without war. 'Although the Emperor walks about in a helmet (wrote the British ambassador from St. Petersburg in January 1853), and sleeps on a camp bed, and occasionally talks gunpowder, he is not more keen on war than his neighbours.'[12]

Louis' position was singularly like that of Nicholas, though more by calculation, and less by conviction. Nicholas' reading of history was that in 1812 and 1815 Providence had spoken the epilogue to the Napoleonic adventure. Louis' belief was that Providence had more to say; that the verdict of Moscow and Waterloo could be reversed; that the really liberal intentions of the First Empire would be carried out by the Second; and that the dynastic settlement of Vienna could still be reshaped into a federal union of European states. Again, Louis was in no sense a good Catholic; but he was the heir of the Second Republic, whose Catholic party had committed him to two ecclesiastical gestures: Oudinot's march on Rome, and Lavalette's successful demand for the restoration of the rights claimed by the Latin (Roman Catholic) monks in the Church of the Nativity at Bethlehem, and in the Church of the Holy Sepulchre at Jerusalem. It may have been true, as he told one of his ministers, that 'the idea of establishing Christianity where Infidelity now exists' had always appealed to him; for there was nothing in him to be attracted, as Napoleon had been, by the militarist monotheism of Islam: but the

necessity of holding the Catholic vote and the support of the Midi
— especially of the Levantine traders of Marseille — swayed him more.
And if the Turkish adventure could be carried through with England
and against Russia, what better proof could the world have of his
determination to reverse the pattern of Napoleonic diplomacy?

Louis was indeed as hopeful as Nicholas of a peaceful solution of
the Turkish question. Nothing could be less provocative than his
diplomacy at St. Petersburg or Vienna: no one took more trouble to
provide terms for an amicable settlement, or to convene a peace
conference at the earliest possible moment. 'The Emperor of the
French (said the Queen's Speech in August 1853) has united with
Her Majesty in earnest endeavours to reconcile differences the con-
tinuation of which would involve Europe in war.' He would not
be over-influenced by the taunts of his own republican minority, or
by Victor Hugo's vitriolic

Soldats! L'Empire, c'est la Peur!

He knew that war would be unpopular with the mass of his people.
But he would sooner fight than accept Russian dictation.

What interest had England in the problems of the Near East? As
regarded the ecclesiastical issue, the quarrel about the Holy Places,
none, except that it should be settled amicably, and without prejudice
to the newly established Protestant bishopric of Jerusalem: and so it
was, by the influence of our ambassador to the Sultan, Stratford de
Redcliffe, within three weeks of his return to Constantinople in the
spring of 1853. But that did not end the struggle for political influence over the Porte, and for economic advantages in the coast-lands
of European Turkey. British economic relations with Turkey were
as old as the Charter of the Levant Company in 1581 and the Capitu-
lations of 1675. In 1854 our imports from Turkey were worth £2
millions, and our exports much the same.

Yet the political, if not the economic interests of Britain might
well seem opposed to those of Turkey's continental neighbours. The
Sultan of Turkey might be a 'Sick man'; but there was nothing new
in that diagnosis: the Ottoman Empire had been 'breaking up' at
intervals ever since the sixteenth century, and the Sultan's life had
been prolonged by the rival prescriptions of his European doctors,
who agreed only in wishing to keep him alive until they were in a
position to divide up his possessions. To Britain, however, the
prospect of a share in such a partition, perhaps in Egypt, perhaps in

Crete, was outweighed by the menace of a Russian fleet in the Mediterranean close-based on the Black Sea and the Dardanelles; and it had become a recognized principle of our foreign policy to uphold the 'integrity of the Ottoman Empire' against another Polish Partition.

'The stability of the Ottoman Empire' (wrote Monkton Milnes to Sir Robert Peel from Smyrna in November 1842) 'is become such diplomatic slang that one can hardly write about it, yet after all it is the absorbing subject of one's reflections in Turkey. It is quite true that one feels at Constantinople that the Turks are only encamped in Europe, that it is to all intents and purposes a Greek town with mosques in it, and that the Turks are there to govern and to pray . . . But it is quite true that no part of the *élément chrétien* about which the French talk so much is fit or indeed has any inclination to assume the supremacy, and that so long as the Porte governs its Christian subjects with moderation . . . and is impressionable by the suggestions of Foreign Ministers on such points . . . they will prefer its authority to any other government.' And though Islam, 1200 years after its foundation, was no longer a missionary or militant religion, it was still capable, if attacked, of inspiring a fanatical defence of the Mohammedan way of life.[14]

In 1844, when the Tsar Nicholas visited England, he, Sir Robert Peel (then Prime Minister), the Duke of Wellington, and Lord Aberdeen (Foreign Secretary) had drawn up a Memorandum, the spirit and scope of which was to support Russia in her legitimate protectorship of the Greek religion and the Holy Shrines, and to do so without consulting France. Aberdeen was now Prime Minister; and though the enthronement of Louis Napoleon and the success of Lavalette's claim had altered the situation, Nicholas may well have supposed that Britain would not act with France against Russia.

In conversations with Sir Hamilton Seymour, the British ambassador, in January 1853, he re-opened negotiations for dealing with the break-up of Turkey. He would enforce his rights of protectorate under the treaties by a temporary occupation of Constantinople: the Principalities would become an independent state under Russian protection: so would Serbia and Bulgaria: England would receive Egypt and Crete. He added later, in a letter to Francis-Joseph, that Constantinople might be declared a free city under the guarantee of the Powers, and the forts in the Dardanelles and Bosphorus be destroyed. These proposals were rejected by the

British government. Meanwhile Prince Menschikoff — an envoy whose overbearing manner was expected to intimidate the Sultan, was dispatched to Constantinople with instructions to threaten him with the destruction of his capital and the occupation of the Dardanelles, if he did not admit the Russian claims. Nicholas evidently expected the Sultan to yield, as he had done twenty years before: instead, strengthened by the English ambassador, and by the proximity of the British fleet, he refused.[15] Thereupon Menschikoff was recalled, and Russian troops crossed the Pruth into territory (the Principalities) under Turkish suzerainty — a step which Nicholas described not as an act of war, or an acquisition of territory, but merely as a gesture to enforce acceptance of his claims.

In fact it led to a proposal for arbitration made by the Powers and accepted by Russia; the more willingly since Nicholas had been disappointed by the persistent neutrality of Prussia and Austria, whom he had relied upon for passive if not active support, and feared the approach of a Franco-British fleet to the Dardanelles. The conference held at Vienna in August should have prevented war:. Austrian objections to Russian occupation of the lower Danube (its one outlet to the Levant) were so strong; and it was so evident that England and France, though both anxious to keep the peace, would combine against any Russian attempt to coerce the Porte, that it seemed certain Nicholas would give way. And so he did, agreeing to the Vienna Note drawn up by the Powers, and undertaking to evacuate the Principalities as soon as the Porte had accepted it too.

But now, to the general consternation, the Sultan insisted on certain modifications — particularly a phrase denying the Russian claim to protect Christians in Turkey — which the Tsar refused to accept. Early in October, before a new Note was ready, the Porte demanded the withdrawal of Russian troops from the Principalities. On the 10th Nicholas refused. On the 22nd the Anglo-French fleet sailed through the Dardanelles. Early in November Turkish troops crossed the Danube and won a victory at Oltenitza. On the last day of the month a Turkish squadron, rashly adventuring into the Black Sea, was surprised at anchor off Sinope and annihilated by a superior Russian force. In England public opinion, forgetful of Copenhagen and Navarino, was so indignant at this 'unsportsmanlike' exploit that Malmesbury wrote, 'war has become inevitable'.[16]

Historians have naturally been puzzled to understand why Turkey lost the opportunity of peace by refusing to accept the Vienna Note:

the answer generally given is that it was due to the influence of Stratford de Redcliffe, and an old feud between himself and the Tsar. Twenty years before (in October 1832) Palmerston had tried to force Stratford on Nicholas as ambassador: the Tsar, remembering Stratford's pro-Greek and pro-Turkish sympathies at Constantinople in 1825-28 and 1831-32, had refused to accept him; and Stratford, still nominally accredited to Russia, but resident at Madrid, had nursed his grievance. The British Government must bear much of the responsibility for sending him back to Constantinople and retaining him there when it was pretty clear that, whilst publicly carrying out Aberdeen's peaceful instructions, he was privately using his influence over the Sultan to stiffen resistance to the Russian demands. It was an additional complication that he was (as Clarendon put it) 'born and bred in the old anti-Gallican school', and did his best to embarrass and thwart the French ambassador. Thouvenel's correspondence is full of complaints of his conduct: he supposed that Stratford was not recalled because he would have been more dangerous at the Foreign Office. At the time of the rejection of the Vienna Note Clarendon wrote to Cowley, 'I cannot, I am sorry to say, persuade myself that he is not at the bottom of the whole difficulty.'[17]

What Clarendon hinted privately Delane clearly implied in the rebuke he sent on September 5th to *The Times* correspondent at Constantinople, who had been backing Stratford's anti-Russian policy: 'You seem to imagine (he wrote) that England can desire nothing better than to sacrifice all its greatest interests and its most cherished objects to support barbarism against civilization, the Moslem against the Christian, slavery against liberty, to exchange peace for war — all to oblige the Turk. Pray undeceive yourself. For political purposes we connive at the existence of the Turk: he fills a blank in Europe, he is a barrier to a more aggressive Power. We had rather have the Straits in the hands of King Log than King Stork; but we have no love for the Turk. We suffer him, and will not permit the Russian to dispossess him; but we are not blind to the fact that he is rapidly decaying, and if we were slow to fight for him when he had more vitality, we are less than ever inclined to do so when he is visibly fading away, and when no amount of protection can preserve his boasted "independence and integrity".'[18]

But this reasonable view no longer ruled government policy so easily as it might have done a generation earlier. The Reform Bill

had given political power to a new middle class endowed by the industrial revolution; a 'public conscience' associated with Chartism, the Factory Acts, and the Co-operative Societies was voiced by the Evangelical and Christian Socialist movements; and the conviction that Britain had a mission to make its liberal and humanitarian opinion felt throughout the world – however oddly expressed in the provocative policy of Palmerston – gradually overruled the pacific intentions of the Aberdeen government. Already in October 1853 the Duke of Argyll was telling Lord John Russell, 'I am convinced that war may often be a duty as well as a necessity in support of Right, that the sword may be held in one hand and the Bible in the other as righteously now as in the days of the Covenant'; and Aberdeen himself said regretfully afterwards, 'It was not the Parliament or the public, but the Press that forced the Government into the war. The public mind was not at first in an uncontrollable state, but it was made so by the Press.'[19]

When war became inevitable, Delane, who had done nothing to provoke it, supported what he now recognized as the national policy, and *The Times* of March 13th, 1854, whilst pointing out that both combatants were using religion as a cover for political aims, declared that 'The zeal of the Czar for his "co-religionists" was neither more nor less than a desire to keep the Christianity of Turkey in a form subservient to his views', and that 'his success, had he been victorious, would have been followed by the extirpation of every form of Christian worship save that protected for purposes of his own, while the success of the allies, so far from operating to the damage of Christianity, will secure freedom of worship to all, and bring the true light of the Gospel into countries from which it has been long excluded'.[20] Thus what had begun as an ecclesiastical controversy was to end as a religious crusade; and Protestant Victoria stood side by side with Catholic Eugénie, who to the end of her life insisted that the issue was between Catholicism and Orthodoxy (*derrière ces chicanes des moines il y avait une grande question: l'antagonisme de la croix grecque et de la croix latine*).[21]

But Louis knew well that Eugénie's crusade represented a minority opinion in France, where the war was, from beginning to end, thoroughly unpopular. To the patriotic Bonapartism on which his rule rested, England, not Russia, was the enemy; 1812 was a disaster to be excused, but 1815 was a defeat to be avenged. Louis was asking France to forgive Waterloo and to avenge Moscow; it could

The desperate winter of 1854 rendered the war more than ever unpopular in France, and in England brought about the fall of Aberdeen's ministry, and the return of Palmerston to power. It brought about, too, at any rate in one mind sensitive to the social evils of the day — the underside of a prosperous peace — a mood which has recurred more than once at similar national crises, a mood that finds and welcomes a redemptive power in war. The hero of Tennyson's *Maud*, at which the poet was working during the last six months of 1854, decided that war was preferable to peace, and the poem ends with his determination to volunteer for service in the Crimea:

> We have proved we have hearts in a cause, we are noble still;
> It is better to fight for the good than to rail at the ill;
> I have felt with my native land, I am one with my kind,
> I embrace the purpose of God, and the doom assign'd.

5

Whilst British discontent with the conduct of the war rested mainly on letters and articles published in *The Times* by Delane, who had himself visited the battle-front, and whose war correspondents enjoyed a liberty never attempted before or allowed since, Louis, who would have tolerated no such public criticism, was in correspondence, during the early part of the campaign, with his temperamental but able cousin Prince Napoleon. Jérôme had landed at Gallipoli at the head of the 3rd division under Saint-Arnaud's command, and had written from Constantinople (May 20th, 1854) describing the incompetence of the Turks, the difficulties of a divided command, and the advisability of concentrating the attack on the Crimea. He fought at Alma, and was given the *médaille militaire*; but wrote home two months later (November 14th) saying that he was too ill to stay at the front, and wished to return to France. Louis did not believe in his illness, and put down his return to *défaut de persévérance* and *découragement*. 'He would not obey orders', said Tocqueville, and Canrobert gave him the choice of sick leave or a court-martial. Others believed his return was due to jealousy of his cousin 'Bo' Patterson, who was being favourably received at court. Paris remembered his childish nickname 'Plon-Plon', and applied it to the sound of the Russian bullets which had scared him home. But this did not prevent him from sending Louis

a long letter (April 1855) containing a considered criticism of the Sebastopol operations as too distant and difficult for success, and suggesting as more profitable an invasion of Poland.[24]

Louis paid less attention to his troublesome cousin than to the ablest of his military advisers, General Niel, who was now at the front, and with whom he agreed in believing that Sebastopol would never be carried by assault until it was completely invested, and deprived of the reinforcements it received overland. In this he was right, theoretically speaking; but he felt that he could only enforce his view upon the commanders in the field if he were himself at the front as their generalissimo; and he made no secret of his wish to take on the task. The alarm with which this prospect was viewed both in Paris and Constantinople was evident from the dispatches of Benedetti (the danger of some accident: the situation in France during Louis' absence: his misunderstanding of the position at the front — the fall of Sebastopol might not end the campaign) and the conversations of Persigny ('The Emperor in the Crimea would be fatal'): the only person gratified by the idea was the Sultan of Turkey, who at once set to work preparing palatial quarters for Louis and Eugénie — stables for his mounted guard, kiosques for his suite, lodgings for his domestics — and planning a royal reception: his only embarrassment was the prospect of the Empress visiting his harem.[25]

However in February, when Palmerston came into power, and took the opportunity to write a friendly letter to Louis suggesting that they should correspond privately (a 'novel and unconstitutional practice' which gave 'great uneasiness' to the Queen), the Emperor took advantage of the invitation (February 26th) to speak of his intention to visit the Crimea; and when he could not be dissuaded by the advice even of Clarendon or Granville, it seemed advisable to suggest a visit to England, where the whole position might be discussed at an Allied council of war. ('The English and French Governments', Malmesbury noted on March 31st, 'have prevailed upon Louis Napoleon to pay a visit to England, the main object being to prevent his going to the Crimea, which he was bent upon.')[26]

Accordingly the Emperor and Empress landed at Dover on April 16th, and travelled by train to Windsor: they were enthusiastically cheered as they drove across London, and the crowd in St. James' was pleased to see Louis point out to Eugénie, as they passed, the

house in King Street in which he had lived in 1847. At Windsor they attended a review and a ball: in London they lunched at the Guildhall, heard *Fidelio* at Her Majesty's theatre, and visited the Crystal Palace. *The Times* printed an extra verse for the National Anthem to be sung in the Emperor's honour. He was invested with the Order of the Garter. He told Walewski that his reception had gone far beyond anything he could have imagined. 'Everybody', wrote the grudging Greville, 'is struck by his mean and diminutive figure and vulgar appearance, but his manners are good and not undignified.'

Two War Councils were held, with the happy result that Louis on his return to Paris gave up the idea of visiting the battle-front. Perhaps what really decided him was the 'miracle' (as Thouvenel called it) of the death of the Tsar on March 2nd, which it was hoped would take all heart out of the enemy. But Louis' ministers were credited with having blocked his scheme by proposing that Prince Napoleon should act as Regent in his absence. And it may be that the attempt upon his life by the Italian Pianori on April 28th finally persuaded him (however unpleasantly) of the importance of his presence in Paris.[27]

But the most important fruit of the London visit was the friend-ship with Victoria which she reported challengingly (knowing how little he trusted Louis) to King Leopold. There can be no doubt from her letters that he impressed her no longer inexperienced but still intensely feminine mind with qualities which he would have wished more widely recognized. 'He is evidently possessed (she wrote in a long memorandum of May 2nd) of *indomitable courage, unflinching firmness of purpose, self-reliance, perseverance,* and *great secrecy*; to this should be added a great reliance on what he calls his *Star*, and a belief in omens and incidents as connected with his future destiny, which is almost romantic – and at the same time he is endowed with wonderful *self-control*, great *calmness*, even *gentle-ness*, and with a *power* of *fascination*, the effect of which upon all those who become more intimately acquainted with him is most *sensibly* felt.' Victoria in 1855 was no romantic girl, but a woman of the world who would not be taken in by a mere charlatan. He flattered her, but she knew it: he praised her husband and admired her family; she took it all for granted. She summed him up with a clear head. 'How far he is actuated by a strong moral sense of right and wrong is difficult (she thinks) to say.' He may have broken his

word: he may have been guilty of 'great severity' in his *coup d'état*. 'My impression is that in all these apparently inexcusable acts he has invariably been guided by the belief that he is *fulfilling a destiny* which God has *imposed* upon him, and that, though cruel or harsh in themselves, they were *necessary* to obtain the result which he considered *himself* as *chosen* to carry out, and *not* acts of *wanton* cruelty or injustice; for it is impossible to know him, and not to see that there is much that is truly amiable, kind, and honest in his character.' Victoria had not read Freud or Jung, but she knew that the Bible condemned 'double-minded men, unstable in all their ways', and praised men who were 'chosen by God' in spite of their crimes: hers was a simple-minded judgment, but not an absurd one. 'Another remarkable and important feature in his composition (she considered) is that everything he says or expresses is the *result* of deep reflection and of settled purpose, and not merely *des phrases de politesse* ... and therefore I would rely with confidence on his behaving honestly and faithfully towards us.' Perhaps: but what if the fulfilment of his destiny were to impose dishonesty or faithlessness? Her charity here would soon be put to a strain.

She ended by comparing her new friend favourably with her old friend Louis-Philippe; and that shrewdly enough. 'The poor King was *thoroughly French* in character, possessing all the liveliness and talkativeness of that people, whereas the Emperor is as *unlike* a *Frenchman* as possible, being much more German than French in character.' This was true; and so was the conclusion that 'He and the Empress are in a most isolated position, unable to trust the only relations who are near them in France, and surrounded by courtiers and servants who from fear or interest do not tell them the truth'; and they will therefore value the friendly and honest advice of another royal couple who, like Victoria and Albert, wish them well. Certainly: but again, would a Man of Destiny listen to any but his own 'voices'? Would he follow any guide but his own *Star*?

But for the moment all was confidence and even affection. 'There was immense embracing at the departure', reported that ironic observer Disraeli, 'and many tears. When the carriage door was at length closed, and all seemed over, the Emperor re-opened it himself, jumped out, pressed Victoria to his heart and kissed her on each cheek, with streaming eyes. What do you think of that?'[28]

The return visit of Victoria and Albert to Paris in August 1855 was as spectacular as Louis could make it; as intimate; as historical.

only be surmised for dynastic rather than national reasons. Even the clericals who had inspired the stand over the Holy Places had little liking for a war against the chief enemy of republicanism and champion of Legitimacy in Europe. It can hardly be doubted that in Louis' divided mind these arguments against war seriously over-shadowed the advantages that he had long seen in an adventure which, if successful, would set France once more on a Napoleonic path towards military renown and international prestige, but now — by a happy reversal of Napoleon's policy — in alliance with England, and with the approval of the Papacy. In this difficulty of choice he made a last-minute attempt to avoid hostilities — notably in a personal letter to the Tsar at the end of January 1854. Even Kinglake, whose thesis it is that Louis planned the war, admits that this letter offered Nicholas a dignified retreat, and that Louis was disappointed at its failure.

With the Allied fleet patrolling the Black Sea, and the Russian army still on the Danube, a precarious armistice might yet have been secured: but when Austria emerged from her neutrality far enough (but no further) to back the demand for evacuation of the Walla-chian territory, an Allied ultimatum was sent and rejected: and on March 27th-28th London and Paris declared war.

4

The war so inauspiciously begun was conducted with a lack of foresight and planning that was not unnatural after forty years of European peace, and with a courageous incompetence that might have been expected of officers and men, most of whom had never, or not for many years, been under fire. The British army was the only one in which all the officers were gentlemen and none of the rank and file conscripts: it was fitter for home than for foreign service. Lord Raglan, the British commander-in-chief, as well as his subordinates — Sir George Brown, Sir De Lacy Evans, Sir George Cathcart, Sir Colin Campbell, Sir John Burgoyne — were Peninsula and Waterloo veterans. The average age of the British generals and admirals was fifty-six, and eight were over sixty. The average age of the French generals was fifty, and only one was over sixty; their fighting experience had generally been won in Algeria, and was more recent than that of most of their British counterparts, except the few who had served in 'frontier campaigns' in Burma,

India, China, or South Africa. But, as Louis frankly said, 'the war they waged in Africa was of a peculiar character, and did not render them more capable of conducting great strategical operations in Europe': and much the same might have been said of our generals, who, if they had not, like Lord Raglan, vegetated at the Horse Guards, had no more experience than the French of manœuvring large forces or facing artillery in the open field; still less of the siege operations that would be necessary at Sebastopol. For such was the inevitable character of the campaign, once the Russian land forces had withdrawn from the lower Danube, and the 'soft-wood' Russian fleet, unable to face the oak and iron of the British navy, had retreated under cover of its port defences. 'The Black Sea', said Gladstone, 'is the true centre of the war, and Sebastopol the true centre of the Black Sea.' To England the Russian naval base was the real objective: to Louis, remembering Moscow, it seemed wiser to strike at an extremity rather than at the centre of the vast body of Russia.[22]

The Russian army, in which Nicholas took such pride, had for too many years lived upon the victories of 1812. Nothing had been done to lighten the severe discipline or to remedy the bad commissariat and the lack of hospitals which had made life in the ranks almost intolerable, and the death-rate, even in peace-time, higher than that of any other army in Europe. Its officers, from the seventy-two-year-old Paskévitch downwards, had no recent experience of war. To reach Sebastopol all reinforcements had to march 800 miles across country; for there was no railway south of Moscow.

Nevertheless the siege of Sebastopol was an operation of almost unprecedented difficulty. Imagine an 'amphibious' operation for the capture of the town and naval base of Plymouth conducted from the Black Sea. Suppose a naval expedition after voyaging round Europe to arrive off the Devon coast, and to find Plymouth Sound blocked by booms and sunken ships. It was a position which recurred at Port Arthur in 1904: there too a naval base had to be captured from the land; but with the important difference that Sebastopol was open to supply and reinforcement overland by a route which (though long and difficult) the Allies were too weak to close. Imagine, again, that everything needed for the siege of Plymouth has to be brought overseas, and landed under the protection of a fleet which has no satisfactory harbour; and that camps have to be established and maintained in a country almost trackless, tree-

less, and uninhabited; a country unmapped and unknown, save from travellers' tales, such as Oliphant's recent *Russian Shores of the Black Sea* (1853), a country which the Allied generals had been too careless or confident to reconnoitre.

After a voyage of 300 miles from Varna to the Crimean coast, and some days spent in looking for a landing-place (fortunately for our armada the Russian ships made no attempt to intervene), a landing-place was found at Eupatoria — corresponding to Fowey on the English map — on September 14th. The invading force consisted of 26,000 British infantry, 1000 cavalry, and 60 guns: 28,000 French and 7000 Turkish infantry, with 68 guns, but no cavalry. With only the lightest equipment, and no transport, this army proceeded to march overland forty-five miles to the northern side (Saltash) of Sebastopol (Plymouth) harbour. On the sixth day, on the little river Alma, they attacked and drove back a Russian line of defence with a loss of some 4000 men, mostly British. It has been said that if the pursuit had been pressed the defences of the northern side might have been stormed — their capture was in fact announced in the London papers. This would indeed have completed the investment of the fortress, but it would have been of little importance for the assault on the southern side of the harbour, where the town lay. One might as well hope to capture Portsmouth from Gosport, or Tynemouth from South Shields. Besides, it soon appeared that there was no place on this part of the coast where ships could lie, or a camp be pitched. There was nothing for it but to continue the march round Sebastopol, and to establish a base on its south side, where Balaclava (Bigbury Bay) and Kamiesh (Wembury Bay) provided anchorages for the fleet and camp-sites for the troops; the British, who were on the left, took Balaclava, and the French, who were on the right, Kamiesh.

The serious, and it might well have been the fatal defect of this plan was that it staked everything on the siege and assault of the southern town, whilst it ignored the fact that the northern town was open to reinforcement and supply overland from Kertch (on the Sea of Azov) and Simpheropol, by an upland route which the Allies were too weak to block. Not only so: the British, with the Turks on their right flank, were open to attack by any relieving force the Russians might bring up overland. The campaign accordingly took two forms: siege operations against the garrison of Sebastopol, and open operations against the Russian army in the field. But at first

every effort was concentrated on the assault. On October 9th the first entrenchments were begun; guns were landed and mounted; and by the 17th all was ready for the bombardment of the defences, to be followed by an infantry assault. By this time Todleben, the energetic engineer in charge of the defence, had strengthened his fortifications, and increased his garrison, with the help of Menschi-koff's land forces, to 25,000; and though the Allied fleet had con-tributed ships' guns and a naval brigade, they joined in the attack too late to have much effect.

At 6.30 on the morning of the 17th the bombardment began, on a scale hitherto unknown in such operations, and after four hours was seen to have failed: the French batteries were silenced, the Rus-sian still fired. The infantry assault could not be launched. The chance of a quick success was lost. It would be six months before another attempt could be made.

Within a week the Allies were in danger of being driven into the sea. An attack by Menschikoff on the right of the British position at Balaclava (October 25th) was repulsed by the aid of heroic cavalry charges, but with difficulty, and not far enough for security: and at Inkerman, ten days later (November 5th) on the Tchernaya, which in some degree protected the Allies' right flank, another costly victory gave the besieging force precarious safety during the winter which was now upon them. For on November 10th a furious storm crippled the fleet, destroyed part of the stores, and made the landing of the rest more difficult than ever. There followed four months of forced inaction, intensified by disease, lack of supplies, and bad communications: for everything required by the British forces, in particular, had to be landed on an open beach, and carried uphill over muddy tracks to the encampments.

It was not till January 1855, when the campaign was half over, that the first steps were taken towards building a railway from the beach-head at Balaclava to the British headquarters, four and a half miles inland, and thence to a point two and a half miles nearer the fighting-line, with a branch to the Sardinian camp to the north-east. All the materials and most of the workmen had to be brought from England. As an afterthought — for at first the wagons were horse-drawn except for a stationary engine at one incline — a few locomotives were sent out; and *The Alliance*, painted with the national flags of England, France, Turkey, and Sardinia, made history by being the first locomotive ever employed on military operations.[23]

Spectacular, because it was Louis' aim to impress upon his new allies and upon all Europe the magnificence of his capital, the strength of his armies (90,000 men, said Clarendon, lined the route from Paris to Saint-Cloud), and the splendour of his court. Intimate, because every detail of hospitality was attended to, and no opportunity missed of exploiting the good impression produced at Windsor. A special suite of rooms had been prepared for the royal guests, at vast expense, in the palace of Saint-Cloud, hung with choice pictures from the Louvre, and furnished with pieces that had belonged to Marie Antoinette. Because an antique table was judged too tall for Victoria's use, its legs were sawn down to suit her; and when she said that if only her pet dog were there she could imagine herself at home, Louis dispatched a special messenger to Osborne to fetch it for her. And historical; for visits to the monuments of past regimes — Neuilly, the Trianon, the Tuileries — alternated with the Exposition, the Opéra, and Napoleon's tomb at the Invalides: 'It was touching and pleasing in the extreme (wrote Victoria to Stockmar) to see the alliance sealed so completely, and without lowering *either* country's pride, and to see old enmities wiped out over the tomb of Napoleon I, before whose coffin I stood (by torchlight) at the arm of Napoleon III, now my nearest and dearest ally!'

'The Emperor, with perfect knowledge of women (as Clarendon rather cynically put it) had taken the surest way to ingratiate himself with her.' 'It is very odd (she confided to him), but the Emperor knows everything I have done, and where I have been ever since I was twelve years old: he even recollects how I was dressed, and a thousand little details it is extraordinary he should be acquainted with.'

Louis again took infinite trouble to be liked by Prince Albert, who sang German duets with him, and was impressed by the improvements in Paris, but did not lose his distrust of the Emperor; and by the royal children — for Vicky was allowed to go out shopping, and Louis took Bertie for a drive through the streets. 'The dear Empress, who was all kindness and goodness, whom we are all very fond of, we saw comparatively but little of, for *really* and *certainly very* good reasons she must take great care of herself.' (The Prince Imperial was born six months later.) As for the Queen's account of the Emperor, it would be tedious to quote all the underlined raptures in which she repeated his praises to Stockmar (September 11th). 'I shall always look back (she ended) on the time

passed not only in France, but with *him* personally, as *most* agreeable. The Prince, though less enthusiastic than I am, I can see well, shares this feeling, and I think it is very reciprocal on the Emperor's part; he is very fond of the Prince and truly appreciates him. With respect to the war, nothing can be more frank and fair and honest than he is about it, but it makes him unhappy and anxious.'[29]

Though Louis had now given up his plan to visit the battle-front, he still tried to impose his view of the situation upon the Allied generals. On the same day (April 25th) that he wrote to Victoria abandoning the projected visit he was for the first time in telegraphic communication with Constantinople. A fresh assault on Sebastopol had been planned for the 28th, when news came that Admiral Bruat had received orders from Paris to transport all the reserve troops to the Crimea. The attack was postponed until their arrival; and meanwhile (May 3rd) an expedition set out upon what might well have been regarded as the only practicable instalment of Louis' own plan — a naval attack upon Kertch, the starting-point of the supply line from the Sea of Azov to Simpheropol and Sebastopol. Next day an order came by telegraph that the reserve troops were to be used at once in operations against the Russian field army; and the expedition had to be recalled. Ten days later Canrobert, the French Commander-in-Chief, resigned, and was replaced by his understudy, Pélissier.

Telegraph or no, Pélissier was not the man to take his orders from the Tuileries. He believed — against Niel, but with Vaillant, the Minister of War — that if the siege were pressed with sufficient energy the town would fall. On the same day that he once more dispatched the expedition to Kertch (May 22nd) he delivered a fresh assault. The French lines were advanced, and in the Sea of Azov an immense amount of stores was destroyed. On June 7th another assault on the town captured an outlying fort, the Mamelon, and advanced the British trenches. But on June 18th what might have been the final attack was ruined by lack of artillery preparation, for which Pélissier was to blame, and this failure was followed ten days later by the death of Lord Raglan. On August 15th the Russians attempted to break the Allies' line on the Tchernaya, and failed. Two days later another bombardment began, now in overwhelming strength, so that the garrison was losing nearly 1000 men a day. Finally, after a continuous battering for three days, the Allies advanced to the decisive assault (September 8th). The British

attack on the Redan failed, but the French carried the Malakoff, and thus rendered the rest of the fortifications untenable. During the night the Russians sank their remaining ships, blew up their magazines, and retreated across the harbour. Sebastopol had fallen. Its capture had cost the Allies 115,000 casualties, and an expenditure which was reckoned at £2¾ millions a week: 'every shell costs £2, and 25,000 may easily be fired in a short morning'. The Russian losses were estimated at a quarter of a million men.[30]

Victoria's first thought, as a victory bonfire blazed on the hill above her new home at Balmoral, was for her brave troops: 'You know I am a soldier's daughter', she had said to Lord John Russell, 'and must take care of the army.' Her second thought was for the pleasure the news would give to her new and dear friend the Emperor of the French. Louis may well have thought the capture of the Tsar's fortress less important than that of the Queen's heart.

6

It is easier to begin a war than to end one: the danger-point for a victorious alliance is often the moment when its representatives meet at a peace conference. England, slowly moved into belligerency, was slow to change her mood, and demanded more security against Russian naval power both in the Baltic and the Black Sea. France, which always disliked a distant war without hope of territorial gain, was eager for a quick peace. Louis, though he was reported to have told Walewski, whose sympathies were Russian, 'If Great Britain chooses to carry on the war, I will continue it for the next twenty years', was placing all his hopes for his country and his dynasty in a peace conference at Paris which would crown the triumph of France over Russia, restore her leadership in Europe, and enable him to bring before the assembled Powers an international Agenda-paper hardly less impressive than that of the Congress of Vienna. For the defeat of Russia involved settling the future of the Principalities, and perhaps of Poland: the Turkish alliance carried some responsibility for the fate of Serbia, Bulgaria, and Greece: and the accession of Sardinia to the victorious side meant that the Congress would be asked to consider the liberation of Italy. The settlement of 1815 had been based upon dynastic claims and bargains made during war: that of 1856 should honour national rights and the principles vindicated by the revolutions of 1789 and 1848.

The Congress of Paris, meeting in the French capital under the chairmanship of Walewski, himself a son of Napoleon, became a personal triumph for the Emperor's nephew. The treaty it drew up (March 30th, 1856) carried clear marks of his policy for Europe: nationalism in the clauses that guaranteed the integrity of Turkey, now for the first time recognized as a member of the state-system of Europe; in the autonomy of Serbia; and in the right of the Principalities to choose their own government: internationalism in the provisions for the free navigation of the lower Danube, and in the Declaration respecting Maritime Law in time of war. And though nothing was put on paper concerning Greece or Poland, their national rights were discussed, and henceforth could not be entirely disregarded.

Poland, which never forgot the part it had played in the Napoleonic wars, and could always count on the sympathy of Paris, hoped much from the victory of another Bonaparte, who really believed in what his uncle had only professed — the rights of small nations. Again, Poland was almost a combatant: had not Polish contingents been set on foot in London and Constantinople, and appeared in the field in Silistria? Walewski, himself half a Pole, strongly supported Louis' desire to do something for his countrymen. But, since the death of Nicholas, Louis had been set on a reconciliation with his liberal-minded successor Alexander, and therefore accepted the Tsar's offer of a more tolerant policy in Poland — an amnesty for political prisoners, liberty of worship, and other reforms — which he promised privately to carry out.

Greece, a kingdom since 1832, had no representative at the Congress, and her aspirations were considered to have been met by the Sultan's *hatti humouin* of February 18th, 1856 — a measure which promised more liberties than it ever accorded in practice. Committed by his new allies to maintaining the integrity of Turkey, Louis had to agree to the exclusion of Greece from the Danube Commission; but he showed his new Russian sympathy by supporting Serbia and Montenegro in their declarations of independence in 1858.

The question of the Principalities was more complicated; but the clue to success lay in Louis' *entente* with Russia. For Britain was hostile to their union as Rumania, and Turkey rigged the elections arranged under the treaty of Paris so as to bring out an overwhelming vote against it. New elections were ordered; an international

commission reported to Paris; and by the Convention of August 19th, 1858, Wallachia and Moldavia were constituted as twin states, in permanent alliance, and with common laws and military organization – everything except the national unity they desired. But a year later the two states took matters into their own hands by electing the same *hospodar*, Prince Couza; the protests of Austria and Turkey were silenced by Russia and France; Louis sent arms and a military mission to Bucharest; and the French victory in Italy in 1859 made possible the creation of Rumania by the Turkish *firman* of December 2nd, 1861.

That he carried England with him in these negotiations – official and unofficial – was due to Louis' friendship with the Queen, and his understanding with Palmerston in Downing Street, Clarendon at the Foreign Office, and Cowley at the Paris Embassy. 'The fact is', as Palmerston put it in one of his sporting metaphors, 'that in our alliance with France we are riding a runaway horse, and must always be on our guard: but a runaway horse is best kept in by a light hand and an easy snaffle.' The terms of the peace of 1856 were not popular in London – indeed Derby talked of 'the Capitulation of Paris'; but at least it preserved the Anglo-French entente – for the moment.[31]

For the moment; no more. A belligerent speech to the Imperial Guard on the last day of the year started rumours that Louis intended another war – it might be against Prussia to extend the Rhine frontier and refound the Kingdom of Westphalia, it might be even an invasion of England. Clarendon, formerly his friend, now began to distrust all he did; and Louis had to look for a new friend in Disraeli, who, as editor of the *Press* since 1853, had supported the peace, and wanted to detach him from Palmerston, and to exploit the Anglo-French entente in the interests of his own party. Even Victoria grew distrustful, and it was not until the last day of 1856 that, with increasing doubts as to her new friend's honesty, she could at least congratulate him on the ingenious solution of the outstanding questions reached at a supplementary meeting of the Paris Congress. Fortunately Louis, realizing the change of atmosphere, invited himself to Osborne in August 1858; and that year ended in one more assertion of a dynastic friendship.[32]

Dynastic, not national. For the Crimean War had proved that in future negotiations foreign statesmen would have to deal not only with British ministers, but also with the British people. It was in

fact a shrewd Frenchman who (in an article on Peel in the *Revue des Deux Mondes*) quoted Talleyrand's remark that 'there is one person who has more wit than Napoleon or Voltaire – *tout le monde*'; and applied it to the British people. 'One can say the same today (he wrote) about England. There is one person who has more power there than the crown, and more than the aristocracy – the world at large, that is, the democracy.' No one could say where this democracy began or ended, or how it was distinguished from other elements of society: it included rich and poor, learned and ignorant, masters and workers, conservatives and liberals, friends of authority and fanatics for liberty. None the less 'the British democracy is no longer content merely to defend its liberties; it regards public affairs as its own, it keeps a strict watch on public men, and if it doesn't govern the state, at any rate it dominates those who do'. It was this development, the political influence of what Palmerston called 'the man with the umbrella on the top of the omnibus' – and Palmerston himself embodied it, as was shown by his triumph at the General Election of 1857 – which was to overrule British foreign relations in the new era opening with the Crimean War. Nor could there be any doubt that, whatever might be thought about Louis at Windsor or about Victoria at the Tuileries, this public opinion remained stubbornly anti-French.[33]

Nevertheless 1856 remained the climax of Louis' career. He had succeeded, where Napoleon himself had failed, in winning the alliance of England and in reversing the military verdict of 1812. By re-establishing an Imperial dynasty and inspiring an international treaty he had made himself the supplanter of Nicholas, and France once more the predominant power on the continent – a power which might well challenge the settlement of 1815. In 1853 Paris opinion had given the Second Empire another year of life – or perhaps a little more. Now no one would dare to set a limit to it. The danger was that Louis might be led by discontent at home, military strength abroad, and his own strange mixture of chivalry and careerism into adventures which, like Napoleon's, might change the map of Europe, but would no less certainly bring about the downfall of the Empire.

CHAPTER VI

THE LIBERATOR (1856-1859)

> Witness this army of such mass and charge
> Led by a delicate and tender prince,
> Whose spirit with divine ambition puff'd
> Makes mouths at the invisible event,
> Exposing what is mortal and unsure
> To all that fortune, death and danger dare,
> Even for an egg-shell. Rightly to be great
> Is not to stir without great argument,
> But greatly to find honour in a straw
> When honour's at the stake.
>
> *Hamlet*, IV, iv

I

NAPOLEON, though he ordered a palace there for his son, never entered Rome. His nephew never returned there after his expulsion by the Papal Government in 1831. But to them both it was a visionary place of adventure, and a lure to disaster. If Napoleon had lived there as a young man he might not have so fatally misunderstood the character of the Papacy and underestimated the expectation of life of the Temporal Power. Louis' weakness was that, having been brought up in 'the most corrupt spot in Europe' (it was Gregorovius, and none with closer knowledge, who called it so), he understood these things too well. Where Napoleon had imposed a bookish theory upon a protesting Curia, Louis read the Pope a lesson from the actual state of Italy: a lesson which he appreciated, but would not apply. Napoleon by persecuting Pius VII re-established the Temporal Power: Louis by protecting Pius IX destroyed it. As with England, so with Italy Louis took credit for reversing the Napoleonic pattern: but because he was not his own master, and because Europe had changed, the new policy was as fatal to the Second Empire as the old policy had been to the First.

Paléologue's *Cavour* opens with a story so *à propos* to the history of 1859 that it cannot be omitted. One day in the early years of the present century Victor Emmanuel III was driving a foreign prince round the sights of Rome when they passed a big building bearing the name *Caserna Cavour*. 'Why Cavour?' asked the prince; and then brightly added: 'I can guess; it must be the name of the architect.' 'You are right,' the king replied: 'He was an architect, and a celebrated one: *he built Italy*.'

Louis always thought of himself as a Man of Destiny; and if there was any one role he felt himself most fated to play, after making himself Emperor, it was that of Liberator of Italy. More than ten years ago, in December 1848, he had been asked by his old friend Mme Cornu, on behalf of Parisian Italians, what he intended to do for Italy. 'Tell them', he had replied, 'that my name is Bonaparte, and that I feel the responsibilities that name implies. Italy is dear to me, as dear almost as France; but my duties to France come first, and I must watch for an opportunity.' That opportunity had now come.[1]

But though a born plotter, he was not an organizer: he had never quite outgrown the crudity of Carbonarism. The *coup d'état* of 1851 succeeded because he let it be planned by Morny. The liberation and unification of Italy succeeded because he let himself be outmanœuvred by Cavour. Camillo, Conte di Cavour was two years his junior; a Piedmontese of mixed Italian-Swiss and Catholic-Protestant parentage; a vital voracious youth, with a Napoleonic turn for mathematics and geography, which won him a commission in the Engineers, and a part in the fortification of the Alpine frontier. Under the influence of a liberal-minded uncle, and of the reactionary regime of an Austrian government and Jesuitical church, he 'lost his faith', was suspected of Carbonarism, threw up his commission in the army, and devoted his gifts to scientific farming. This was in 1831, the year of Louis' enforced flight from Italy; and for the next seventeen years both were in effect exiles from their native country. But whereas Louis spent the time dreaming of a Bonapartist Empire, Cavour spent it preparing a plan to make his country and king the *point d'appui* without which Italy could never achieve liberty or unity. To do this, Sardinia must prove herself not only fit for political, military, and economic leadership (for the troubles out of which the Risorgimento arose were at bottom social discontents, and matters of food and wages), but also a modern and a model state, able to attract the sympathy and help of Liberal England and Revolutionary France — the only two Powers in Europe which might support her against Austria. For Cavour had studied the soil and climate of continental politics; in long conversations with d'Haussonville, the French ambassador at Turin; in the Parisian *salons* of 1835; and in England, where he had visited the chief industrial areas, and had investigated English political and social life at its most critical transition from pre- to post-Reform Bill conditions, when Bentham-

ism was fighting 'the battle against debt, pauperism, class-privilege, class-monopoly, abusive patronage, a monstrous criminal law, and all the host of sinister interests'. He came back from his five months' travels, as Mirabeau came back from Prussia or Louis from Ham, with a realistic view of the issue between the old monarchies and the new democracies, and of the economic foundations of national prosperity.[2]

He believed with the most distinguished pupil of Leopold and Stockmar that, whilst all government demands obedience, 'the obedience of the future must be founded on a conviction that the state system really satisfies the needs of the people . . . In these latter days of advance in education and civilization society knows fairly well what it needs and desires . . . Thus, if obedience is to be restored, the only way to it is to give society the means of making up its own mind about it . . . Nothing can effect all this except a representative Constitution with responsible ministers and unfettered expression of public opinion'.[3] But a system of government which Albert judged congenial to English tradition had proved itself utterly alien both to the Austrian and to the Papal regimes in Italy since 1815: if Italy were ever to be free and united, Austria and the Temporal Power must go. But how? Only Sardinia, in the whole of Italy, had a constitutional government, a patriotic king, a balanced economy, a cool-headed and independent people, and an army fit to lead a movement for liberation. Yet Sardinia had twice tried, and failed. The lesson of Custozza and Novara was clear. Italy could not save herself un-aided in the nineteenth any more than in the fifteenth century. France must intervene again, and help a reorganized Sardinia to shake off the Austro-Papal control of the Italian states.

Until that could be done, Cavour considered it a waste of time and a dissipation of energy to discuss the form that the new Italy should take. Gioberti would be a better statesman if he were a worse author, and Mazzini a better conspirator if he were a less angry moralist. Cavour was a journalist; but his *Il Risorgimento* (begun in December 1837) preached a middle course between reaction and revolution, Metternich and Mazzini — a constitution and a realistic reform programme to unite men of good will of all classes in working for the liberation of their country.

The year 1848 had brought both Louis and Cavour into sudden prominence as national deputies; in 1849 Louis was President, Cavour Minister of Commerce; and on the same day that the Senate

decreed the re-establishment of the French Empire (November 4th, 1852) Cavour was appointed President of the Council by the new King of Sardinia, Victor Emmanuel. During those three years, whilst Louis, carefully feeling his way to absolutism, was handicapped in any plans he might have for Italy by the French garrison in Rome, Cavour had been preparing Sardinia for the next move, by naval rearmament, by commercial treaties with France, Britain, and Belgium, by negotiating a loan in England, by Customs and Excise reform, and by the Siccardi Laws abolishing ecclesiastical courts — a first stroke against the power of the Church.

Recent historians of the Risorgimento have insisted upon a revaluation of what might be called the old-fashioned 'romantic' version of the birth of modern Italy. They admit that the liberation of Lombardy could not have been achieved without French military help, nor that of Sicily and Naples without British connivance: but they regard this foreign aid as superficial when compared with the national urge for freedom and better government. Similarly they minimize Cavour's diplomatic arrangements with Louis Napoleon by comparison with his adroit management of the *Connubio* (the coalition of Right and Left Centre parties in the Sardinian parliament); and they insist on Victor Emmanuel's important if not predominant role in an uneasy partnership of King and Minister — that coarse-fibred but courageous hero, who supported Cavour's economic and anticlerical reforms, in spite of public and domestic opposition, and the ill omen of four deaths in his family, for the sake of the one thing they had in common, the unity of Italy under the Sardinian crown; and who, when his minister resigned after Villafranca, stood firm, and saved the situation — a true leader and liberator of his people. In their ten years' partnership, at any rate, if Cavour supplied the impulse and ideas, Victor Emmanuel supplied the checks and actions; and it would be difficult to say which was the more indispensable — the imagination of the Minister or the common sense of the King.[4]

2

In a speech recommending his commercial treaty with France, Cavour had said that 'some European complication might find East and West in opposite camps — and how important it would then be to stand on good terms with France'. The outbreak of the Crimean War within two years of his appointment as Premier and

Louis' assumption of Empire confirmed a prophecy that was almost a prayer. In 1852, during a temporary retirement from office, he had re-visited England and France, had talked to Malmesbury, Palmerston, and Disraeli, and had dined with Louis Napoleon. He found the English, both Whigs and Tories, friendly to Italy, but unlikely to give her active support. 'It is upon France, above all (he wrote home) that our destiny depends. For good or ill we must be her partner in the great game that sooner or later must be played out in Europe.' On his return and his reappointment as Premier he initiated another series of measures — financial, commercial, and political — to strengthen the position of Sardinia in European opinion; and perhaps the success of his appeal to the Powers over the Lombard refugees question in 1853 was not better propaganda than the appearance of the Turin-Genoa railway in the issue of Bradshaw's *Continental Railway Guide* for August 1847.

When the Crimean War came, Cavour tried to find a way of turning it to the advantage of Italy. The obvious course would be to profit by Austrian alarm at Russia's advance on the Danube to resume hostilities in Lombardy. But Austria foresaw the danger, and made her support of the Allies dependent upon its being provided against; so that both England (through Clarendon) and France (by an official note in the *Moniteur*) warned Sardinia against such a step. Victor Emmanuel, a man of action, saw a better way. Why should not his country at once reassure Austria and earn the gratitude of the Allies by sending part of its army overseas to join in the siege of Sebastopol? Cavour would not have initiated such an adventure: but he was realist enough to support it. For six months the plan hung fire: the Cabinet opposed it as too expensive, or, if (as Cavour suggested) the cost were borne by England, as too undignified. The army disliked the idea of fighting abroad as mercenaries in a cause which did not concern their country; and the public, so far as there was one capable of expressing an opinion, agreed. Nor, so long as there was hope of Austria joining the Allies, could France encourage any movement for the liberation of Italy.

But at the end of the year 1854, when the need of reinforcements in the Crimea became so urgent that Palmerston talked of getting '6000 men from Portugal, 10,000 from Spain, and 10,000 from Piedmont', Louis was consulted and approved, and a definite request was made for a Sardinian contingent. Difficulties arose

about the conditions on which it should be sent. Cavour tried in vain to add to the proposed Convention a secret article to the effect that 'the high contracting parties will upon the establish-ment of peace take into consideration the state of Italy'. On January 10th, 1855, the Convention was signed, without this addition, and La Marmora and 15,000 Sardinians sailed for the Crimea. They arrived in time to play a gallant part in the victory of the Tchernaya (August 15th). A month later Sebastopol fell.[5]

The King had taken a terrible risk for his country and the Minister for his career. But Cavour never doubted that it was right, and defended his policy on grounds of national interest: 'We want to show Europe (he had said) that we have not forgotten how to fight, and that our military valour stands as high as it ever did. Believe me: the laurels that our men bring back from the East will do more for the future of Italy than all the speeches in the world.'[6]

The first sign that his plan would succeed was an invitation from Louis to Victor Emmanuel to visit Paris for the *Exposition Universelle* (November 1855). The King of Sardinia was a very different guest from the Queen of England, who had been there three months before. A strikingly ugly man – 'soldierlike and powerful' were the most complimentary epithets Clarendon could think of, whilst Lady Clarendon added that he had 'the most curious eyes', which, 'when excited, roll about, and look as if they were going to start from his head' – he had never before been abroad, and was quite at sea in civilized society. His camp manners and broad humour amused Paris and shocked London, which he visited a week later. But Victoria, determined to make the best of her new ally, decided that, in spite of his appearance (*eine ganz besondere abenteuer-liche Erscheinung*), 'he is more like a Knight or King of the Middle Ages than anything one knows nowadays', and even added *il faut l'aimer quand on le connait bien*.

For his part, Victor Emmanuel told Clarendon that 'he had no idea of finding such a woman. He knew all about her virtues; but her knowledge – her principles in politics and religion – the judicious advice she had given him – had perfectly astounded him'. And when, in a hurry to get home, he insisted on leaving Windsor at 4 a.m., she was up to see him off.[7]

Neither the King nor his Minister had made any secret, during their visit, that they expected a *quid pro quo* for the Italian interven-tion in Russia; and Cavour was hard at work, every minute he

could spare from court functions, talking to anyone who might help on his cause: Louis, Walewski, and Cowley in Paris, and in London Palmerston, Malmesbury, Clarendon, and others. Clarendon formed 'a very high opinion of him, and was especially struck with his knowledge of England and our constitution and constitutional history'. Palmerston told him 'that he might say to the French Emperor that for every step he might be ready to take in Italian affairs he would probably find us ready to take one and a half'.[8]

The Italians visited Paris again on their way home; and before they left, Louis said to Cavour: 'Write privately to Walewski what you think I can do for Piedmont and Italy.' How much did he mean by this? What was it worth? It was easy to be sure of the private sympathy of Louis and Clarendon, and of the friendliness of the British Cabinet. But would it be possible to secure their public support at the Peace Conference in face of the certain hostility of Austria?[9]

The plenipotentiaries met for the first time in Paris on February 25th, 1856: Walewski (as Chairman) and Bourqueney for France, Orloff and Brünnow for Russia, Buol and Hübner for Austria, Ali Pasha and Djemel Bey for Turkey, and Cavour and Villa-Marina for Sardinia. (Prussia was not a party to the Conference, but would be asked to accede to the results.) When he left Turin on February 13th Cavour had been uncertain whether he would be admitted to the Conference, for the 'Great Powers' disliked such a recognition of the small Italian state; but on his arrival Clarendon told him that it had been agreed he should be allowed to attend, without formal recognition; so his first point was won. He proceeded, with a cunning worthy of Talleyrand at Vienna, to prepare the way for bringing up the question of Italy: intervening seldom at the meetings, but always with effect, and impressing his colleagues with his knowledge and good sense; between the meetings (when, as usual on such occasions, the real work was done) losing no opportunity to indoctrinate the representatives of France and England.

Walewski and Bourqueney were, like Louis, almost pro-Russian in their desire for peace at any price; and they were against his wish to help Sardinia: yet they could not disobey his decision to bring up the Italian question. Cavour kept this alive through Prince Napoleon, Princess Mathilde, Mme Cornu, Bixio, Benedetti (the

secretary of the Conference), and Louis' old friend Dr. Conneau, who was specially commissioned to act as go-between. To these was soon added his niece, the lovely young Contessa di Castiglione, whom he instructed to spare no means to win the Emperor's ear, but whose indiscretion, after one night at Compiègne, lost it. On the English side too Cavour was in close touch with Clarendon, who was himself in Louis' confidence, and was prepared, as a plenipotentiary might more easily be a century ago, to act outside his instructions.

Cavour had two plans in his head. One was to bring about a rearrangement of territory in Italy which would allow Sardinia to be rewarded for her part in the war by the accession of Parma. The second was to get the question of Italy put on the Agenda of the Conference. It was soon clear that nothing could be done under the first head — Louis could not afford so to offend Austria — and it was not until the Conference was nearly over that Cavour succeeded under the second. Louis was so distracted by anxiety during the birth of the Prince Imperial (March 16th) that it was not till ten days before the signing of the Peace that Cavour got an interview with him. He took Clarendon with him to the Tuileries on the 19th. After discussion of various alternatives, it was agreed that Louis would instruct Walewski to add to the Agenda the questions of Greece and Italy (for Greece too was occupied by foreign troops), and that Clarendon would speak on the motion.

On April 8th, at a third supplementary meeting a week after the signing of the peace treaty (March 30th), Walewski, carrying out his instructions, but colouring them with his own views, proposed that the Conference should discuss, unofficially, matters which might lead to future complications: he specified the anarchy in Greece, the foreign occupation of Rome and the Romagna, and the revolutionary tone of the Belgian press, which had since 1853 been printing and distributing in France, especially in the French army, personal attacks on Louis and Eugénie. He dealt with the Italian question in such a way as to exculpate the French and Austrian protection of the Papacy. Clarendon, whose temper had been roused by two recent attempts of the Austrians to exclude the Sardinians from a position of equality at the Conference, and by Walewski's treatment of the Italian question, interposed with a speech roundly denouncing the Austrian regime in the Romagna, the government of the Papal States, and the political crimes of the King of Naples. Buol, taken

by surprise, did not attempt to meet Clarendon's charges, but made it clear that he considered such matters outside the scope of the Conference: he would refuse even to ask for instructions to deal with any questions raised about the Romagna. Hübner called attention to the French garrison in Rome and the Sardinian garrison at Monaco. Cavour contented himself with corroborating Clarendon's statements, condemning both the Austrian and the French occupations, and asking that the protest about the state of things in Italy should be entered on the protocol of the Conference. And this was done, but in terms as colourless as possible.[10]

Cavour had won his second point. The question of Italy was now before Europe. But as a question only. Victor Emmanuel had to go without the 'little piece of territory' he had hoped to win by his intervention in the war. Cavour had to be content with promises of help without the one thing needed, military action – 'sympathy without soldiers'. True, Clarendon, soon after the meeting of April 8th, had said to Cavour: 'If you are in a difficulty you can count on us, and you will see with what energy we will come to your aid'; but he was not speaking (as he should have been) for the British government; indeed in February 1862 he was challenged in the House of Lords, à propos of some recently published letters of Cavour, with having encouraged Italy to go to war, and made a poor defence. Nor was it at all likely that Louis, who was so anxious to free himself from one unpopular war, would, for some years at least, embark upon another. All he would say was: 'Austria will give way on nothing. She is ready to make war rather than consent to your obtaining Parma. At the moment I cannot present her with a casus belli: but make your mind easy; I have a presentiment that the present peace will not last long.' And to Louis a presentiment was often as near as he could get to a purpose.[11]

There, for the moment, the matter rested. The gambler in Cavour was bitterly disappointed: he seemed to have staked so much, and to have won so little. But the statesman in him could afford to wait. Sardinia was now certain, if attacked by Austria, of French support and English sympathy; and if such a situation did not arise naturally, then it might be possible to create it. Meanwhile he could go ahead with his plans for strengthening his own country, and preparing the other states of Italy for a united front against Austria. He rebuilt the fortifications of Alessandria, demolished by the Austrians; he made Spezia a naval base, and spent a great sum on

improving the port of Genoa; he pushed on the construction of the tunnel under the Alps at Mont Cenis, a plain hint of Franco-Italian co-operation. He had invited the help of Manin, the defender of Venice, whom he visited in Paris during the Conference: 'Make Italy, and I am with you,' had been the reply. He interviewed Garibaldi, the defender of Rome, and won him to the new plan. He persuaded la Farina to enlist the Società Nazionale under his leadership. The only one of the Old Republicans he could not and would not work with was Mazzini, whose futile attempt to raise revolt at Genoa and Naples in the summer of 1857 alienated French and British opinion from the Italian cause.

'The Italian cause'? There was by now little doubt what Louis wanted, and Victor Emmanuel, and Pio Nono, and Francis Joseph; but how could Cavour, a Sardinian rather than an Italian, or at best an Italian of the north who regarded Italy south of the Apennines almost as a foreign country, judge of the wishes of a people which had never been under a single government? Milan, Venice, Bologna, Florence, Rome, Naples, were centres of varied and conflicting loyalties. Those foreign residents who knew the country best were the least hopeful as to the results of intervention from outside. The clericals feared that reform would spell revolution. The anticlericals saw little beyond the abolition of the Temporal Power. The liberationists were agreed only that Austria must go. Even Cavour did not see clearly how Italy freed could become Italy united. D'Azeglio told Lord John Russell that 'he would be content if the Powers would shut the gates of the Alps and throw the keys into the sea, for out of disorder he thought order would at length arise'. But the only visible elements of order were the agencies of despotism. Gladstone's sensational letters to Lord Aberdeen and his painstaking translation of Farini were denunciations of Neapolitan and Papal misrule without reference to the possibility of Italian unity, or even of Italian liberty. Bourbon absolutism might be 'the negation of God erected into a system of government'; but it was part of the Vienna settlement, of the state-order which had kept Europe at peace for fifty years, and prevented the return of another 1848 revolution.[12]

3

Suddenly, all these calculations and illusions were shattered by one of those events which no philosophy of history can explain, and no statesmanship foretell. On the evening of January 14th, 1858,

Louis and Eugénie, accompanied by General Roguet, were attending a benefit performance at the Opéra. Just as their carriage, with its mounted escort, drew up outside the building, there was a triple explosion, which shattered the carriage, threw horses and men to the ground, and spread death and injury amongst the crowd. In the confusion and darkness the Emperor and Empress got out, practically unhurt, though Roguet was hit and bleeding. To prevent a panic in the theatre, where the noise of the explosion had been heard above the music of *William Tell*, they appeared in the royal box, and were rapturously cheered; and again on the drive home. Royalty had once more shown its courage in face of personal danger (who could forget Napoleon's escape almost on the same spot fifty-eight years before?) and had once more strengthened its hold on the nation.

But Louis was rightly indignant with the police, who, fully informed from London of Orsini's mission, had arrested one of the four conspirators, armed with a bomb, only half an hour before the Emperor was due, and had done no more. When the casualties were known (eight killed, a hundred and fifty injured), and when the names and origin of the assassins were published, there was a cry for vengeance on the two governments which Louis was least anxious to offend. Pieri, a Tuscan, Rudio, a Venetian, Gomez of Naples, and Orsini of the Romagna represented Italy: all had come from England, the plot had been hatched in London, the bombs made at Birmingham. Louis, wishing perhaps to divert attention from his new friends at Windsor and Turin, and remembering the precedent of 1800, concentrated on a measure aimed at his opponents at home, a *loi de sûreté générale*, creating and punishing new crimes, like the revolutionary *loi des suspects*, and rendered needlessly unpopular by its application to the departments, in each of which the *préfet* was set a quota of victims to be arrested, and was tempted to complete his list with names of notorious but at the moment innocent enemies of the government.[13]

Probably this proscription did the Empire more harm abroad, especially in England, than the ambassadorial protests and demands which soon arrived in London and Turin, Brussels and Berne. The Sardinian government was desired to suppress one paper and expel the editor of another, to get rid of all dangerous foreigners, and to strengthen the law dealing with crimes against sovereigns. The British government was assailed by the publication in the *Moniteur*

of insulting quotations from the congratulatory addresses of the French army, and was officially requested to take steps to prevent any further abuse of the right of asylum: for it was the general impression abroad, as King Leopold had warned Victoria five years ago (June 3rd, 1853) 'that in England a sort of menagerie of Kossuths, Mazzinis, Lagranges, Ledru Rollins, etc., is kept to be let occasionally loose on the continent to render its quiet and prosperity impossible'.[14]

The reactions to these demands were disconcerting in both London and Turin. In London Palmerston, instead of answering Walewski's dispatch of January 20th, introduced a Conspiracy Bill, making conspiracy to murder a felony instead of a misdemeanour (a distinction meaningless in Paris), and a Dr. Bernard was put on trial for complicity in Orsini's crime. The Bill was thrown out by a snap vote in Parliament, whose members chiefly resented the treatment of Walewski's dispatch, and Bernard was acquitted. This was not because Orsini was a romantic figure, who had escaped from an Austrian prison, and had friends in London society, but because members of Parliament and jurymen objected to being dictated to by a foreign government, and resented Palmerston's failure to answer the charges made by a dictator against a democracy. At Turin Cavour, who knew the Emperor well, and had behind him a king touchy upon any point of honour, bluntly refused Walewski's demands. Victor Emmanuel sent Della Rocca to the Tuileries, and, when he reported the Emperor to have used threatening language, wrote a stiff and proud reply, ending: 'Tell him that one does not treat a faithful ally so, that I have never tolerated compulsion from anyone, that my path is that of untarnished honour, and that I hold myself responsible to none but God and my people. For 850 years my race has held its head high, and no one shall make me lower it.' The King had chosen just the tone that Louis admired. 'Your King is a brave man,' he said to Della Rocca, 'and I like his answer'; his final message was: 'Assure him that in case of war with Austria I will come and fight beside my faithful ally.[15]

The fact was that the failure of Orsini's attempt to kill the Emperor had achieved what its success would have rendered impossible. Cowley, who knew Louis well, reported that his 'nerves were shaken to pieces by the *attentat*, and he was greatly changed', and Granville, dining with him on April 7th, said that 'he looked very low, and is evidently much preoccupied by the action of the secret societies and

the plots for assassination'. Nevertheless it was not physical fear which now determined Louis to proceed with the liberation of Italy. It was not because he was afraid of further acts of vengeance against a Carbonarist who had gone back on his oath, nor because the sudden shock reminded him of his brother's deathbed at Forli in 1831, of the flight from Ancona, and the refugee life in Paris and London. He had not forgotten his debt to Italy: it had never been out of his mind. It was not even because the situation at home and abroad was now favourable for a fresh adventure: on the contrary, an unpopular war was just over, and a challenge to Austria could not safely be made without the support of his still unreconciled enemy Russia and his growingly suspicious friend England. No: it was because to Louis' romantic soul he and Orsini had been fellow-conspirators and fellow-exiles in the same cause, and because, to his superstitious mind, the Opera plot seemed an omen, a sign from his Star that the moment had at last come for an adventure forecast thirty — nay, sixty — years ago; for would not 1859 be a recapitulation of the Napoleonic 'liberation' of Italy in 1796? The decision to intervene in Italy was taken with all the irresponsibility of a Man of Destiny: it would be carried out with all the cunning of a master of intrigue.[16]

The first and most surprising move was the use which Louis made of his would-be assassin. He too had the soul of an adventurer (said Cherbuliez): 'himself so long an outlaw, he kept a weakness for outlaws. Someone who knew him well said, Beneath the skin of the sovereign you will find the political refugee'. That the Emperor should feel some sympathy for the son of a soldier of the *grande armée* and a fellow-conspirator of 1831 was in any case understandable; understandable too that the romantic Empress should be moved to tears by so handsome a murderer, with his black beard and flashing eyes, his eloquence and dignified bearing, and should beg Louis to save him from the punishment he deserved. But pardon was not the Emperor's aim. He wanted to stage a trial which would do what the Peace Conference had failed to do, and make the Powers face as a practical issue the expulsion of Austria from Italy. Not content with a speech for defence by the most eloquent advocate of the day, Louis allowed Jules Favre to read in court a letter, purporting to be Orsini's, ending with the words: 'May your Majesty not reject the last prayer of a patriot on the steps of the scaffold! Let him liberate my country; and the blessings of its twenty-five million citizens will follow him through the ages!' Orsini had indeed written

this letter, and signed it: but the language was Favre's, and the sentiments had been dictated by Piétri, the Prefect of Police, who had orders from the Emperor to interview him in prison.[17]

That this was the explanation is made almost certain by the sequel: for there was one sentence in the letter which might have been misunderstood — 'Your Majesty must remember (Favre had dictated) that, until Italy regains her independence, there can be no certainty of peace for Your Majesty or for Europe'. Louis wanted to discourage further attempts on royal lives, but he did not wish it to be supposed that he was giving way to a threat. He therefore procured a second letter from Orsini, written two days before his execution, which made this double purpose clear. 'I declare with my last breath (the assassin wrote) that though by a fatal mistake I organized the attempt of January 14th, assassination, for whatever cause, is not part of my creed. Let my compatriots, instead of relying on this method, take it from me that the liberation of Italy can be achieved only by their restraint, their devotion, and their unity.'

Not content with the sensation caused by these proceedings in Paris and London, Louis specially asked that the Orsini letters should be printed in Turin. Cavour shrank from so open a challenge to Austria; but he did as he was told, adding a note which underlined Orsini's censure of assassination and the foolishness of his crime. Louis afterwards learnt to regard the risk of assassination more philosophically. In a speech made after an attempt on his life two years later he reflected that 'if one of the numerous attempts made against King Louis-Philippe had succeeded, the great probability is that the House of Orleans would still reign over the country. If tomorrow I were to fall, the people would rally round my son'.[18]

4

Now that Louis had published his aim, he set about the tortuous diplomacy which would turn intention into action. He explained to Clarendon 'that there had been two questions in which France was interested: one the regeneration of Poland, and the other the regeneration of Italy; that in the pursuit of the first France naturally became the ally of Austria against Russia, and in the pursuit of the second she became the ally of Russia and Sardinia against Austria; that the peace with Russia had put an end to anything being done about the first, and the second alone became possible'. He must

therefore do three things: cement the Sardinian alliance; secure the neutrality, if not the support, of England and Russia; and manœuvre Austria into a declaration of war. It took a year to do this, but it was cleverly and successfully done. Whether the immediate gain was worth the ultimate loss was fortunately hidden from Louis' fatalistic eyes.[19]

The traditional way to cement a royal alliance, Louis knew, was a royal marriage. Now, in January 1855, Victor Emmanuel had lost his wife, an Austrian princess, and was looking about for another bride. His emissary Marochetti had given him so pleasant an account of Princess Mary, sister of the Duke of Cambridge (and afterwards Duchess of Teck), that he was instructed, in September 1856, to sound the British court and government as to whether an offer of his hand would be accepted. Clarendon thought that it 'would be an excellent thing for Sardinia and not a bad one for England'; but the Queen and Prince Albert were against it, partly on the ground of religion — 'the painful position that Princess Mary (a Protestant) might feel herself in as the wife of a king of a religious, or rather a superstitious people, who might look upon her as a sort of Ann Boleyn, and make her life miserable' — and partly because her hand had already (in 1854) been refused to Prince Napoleon, upon religious grounds. (That both bridegrooms were notoriously loose in their relations with women was a minor consideration, where a royal marriage was concerned.) The decision was left to the Princess, and she had refused the chance of becoming the first Queen of Italy. Why should not Louis profit by this incident? He had no bride to offer to the King of Sardinia; but he had a husband for his daughter. Since his return under a cloud from the Crimea Jérôme Bonaparte had been more than usually embarrassing to his Imperial cousin. He had refused to be a member of the Council of Regency in November 1857: he had endangered Russian relations by trying to get up an official dinner on the anniversary of the battle of Alma: when appointed to a specially created Ministry of Algeria and the Colonies (June 1858) he resigned it after nine months, because his *amour propre* — that fatal touchiness which he took for self-respect — prevented his working with his colleagues. But he was a prince (the only one Louis could command, where his uncle had had so many), and a bachelor. Why should not Prince Napoleon marry Princess Clotilde?[20]

This idea was perhaps in the front of Louis' mind when he

arranged a secret conference with Cavour at Plombières on July 20th, 1858; though with a feminine touch he introduced it as a postscript to the main subjects under discussion. He had already told Conneau in an interview on May 15th that he could not help Sardinia in a purely Italian war based on the Lombard refugee question, or some Mazzinian revolution. He now raised with Cavour three important questions of procedure. How could a *casus belli* be found which would put the onus of war on Austria? How would the states of Italy be rearranged after the war? What reward might France expect for her services? These matters, which one might have thought serious enough for an International Conference, and which would certainly reduce the Assembly of the United Nations to impotent controversy, were settled between two intriguers — a dreamer and a planner — in four hours. Nothing was put on paper, except by Cavour for the King: but the later course of events shows that his account was substantially true. The plan was this. (1) Austria was to be manœuvred into declaring war by an appeal (not of course in Mazzinian terms) from the little Principality of Massa-Carrara for union with Sardinia, to be followed by the protests of its owner, the Duke of Modena, and its occupation by Victor Emmanuel. (2) The war with Austria would be localized in northern Italy, to avoid implicating the Pope and the King of Naples; but (3) when it was over, and Austria had been finally driven out, the country would be divided into a Sardinian Kingdom of Lombardy, Venetia, the Romagna, and the Duchies; a Kingdom of Central Italy, Tuscany, and the States of the Church under the Duchess of Parma: Rome with the Patriarchate (the Papal territory immediately round it) under the Pope; and the Kingdom of Naples under its old Bourbon misgovernment, unless freed by a fresh revolution. All four states (as Louis had outlined to la Marmora in January and to Mocquard in February 1856) were to form a Confederation under the nominal Presidency of the Pope. Finally Louis was to provide 200,000 men to Victor Emmanuel's 100,000; and in return for this help Sardinia would cede Savoy, and perhaps Nice, to France.[21]

After an hour's interval Louis took Cavour for a country drive, and broached the question of the royal marriage. What a subject for the cynic who looks over the shoulder of the historian! Two middle-aged *roués* planning to marry a devout girl of fifteen to an agnostic of thirty-six whose morals could only be defended on the ground of his fidelity to his successive mistresses: was not his good-

ness of heart proved by his deserting Paris, in Carnival time, to visit the deathbed of the actress Rachel, with whom he had had no relations for four years? Cavour had Victor Emmanuel's acceptance of this plan in his pocket, to use in case of necessity: but he judged that though Louis was set on the idea, he was not at present in a sticking mood; and the marriage was left over, like the cession of Nice, to be settled 'when the time came'.

Having thus committed their countries, without consultation, to a policy which would initiate a new era of wars in Europe, the two plotters went on their way: Louis to think how he could prevent England from interfering with his scheme; Cavour to tell the Russian and Prussian royalties who were enjoying the season at Baden what had been arranged, and to assure himself at least that Russia would be on his side. As for the timing of the plan, Cavour had none of Louis' doubts: in May 1856 he had told a friend, 'In three years we shall have war'; now, in December 1858, he told Lord Odo Russell in Rome that if Austria did not declare war he would force her to do so, and that it would be 'about the first fortnight in May'; actually it was on April 29th.[22]

Louis' first overture to England (in March 1858) had been the appointment of the Crimean general Pélissier, now Duc de Malakoff, as his ambassador to St. James' in succession to Persigny — 'which is *really* (Victoria thought) a compliment to the Army and the Alliance' — whilst all London admired the jewellery of his Spanish wife. In August Louis invited Victoria and Albert to visit Cherbourg, nominally to show them his new harbour works, but really to quieten their suspicions about Plombières. They found him '*boutonné* and silent', and the initials N.E.V.A. (Napoléon, Eugénie, Victoria, Albert) displayed in the streets were read as a reference to Russia; public opinion on both sides of the Channel remained hostile, especially in view of the naval rivalry embodied in the building of the French iron warship *La Guerre*. In fact Louis was just at this time arranging a fresh conference with Cavour's able and inconspicuous agent, Count Nigra. They met in Paris on August 4th. Louis was wondering, on second thoughts, whether the Massa-Carrara proposal at Plombières was not too Mazzinian after all: could not the Austrian proceedings in Lombardy provide a *casus belli*? What a pity it was that his friend Panizzi of the British Museum, who was travelling in Germany, could not be kidnapped by the Austrian police! what an admirable effect it would have on

British opinion! He was doubtful too whether he could be ready for war as soon as May 1859; perhaps not till the late summer, or even the following spring.[23]

When Cavour received the report of this interview from Nigra, he wrote to Louis pointing out the objections to delay — the discouragement it would cause in Italy, and the opportunity it would give for a hostile combination between the Powers. Louis at once (September 23rd) dispatched Prince Napoleon on a confidential mission to the Tsar, whose army was the most effective check on Austria and Prussia. This visit produced an undertaking by Alexander that, in consideration of a 'benevolent attitude' towards his 'aspirations' in Poland and the Black Sea, he would guarantee non-intervention, so far as concerned Germany (i.e. Prussia), if Louis would do the same on the side of England: he might even give military assistance. Roncière de Noury followed Prince Napoleon to hold the Tsar to his promise. At the end of September Nigra returned to Paris, and found Louis in a hopeful mood, prepared to accept Cavour's time-table, and to sign a treaty of military co-operation with Sardinia, provided it was combined with the marriage of Jérôme and Clotilde. The Princess was as unwilling as Marie Louise had been in 1810 to marry a Bonaparte she had never seen. But this scruple, Cavour thought, could be overcome.

Louis' next move was to invite the two British statesmen who were most friendly to him, Palmerston and Clarendon, to visit him at Compiègne (November 15th-20th); nominally for stag-hunting, which was conducted with all the traditional ceremony of the Bourbon court, with interludes of 'football in the gallery, and quadrilles on horseback in the *manège*, and the Emperor doing the lance exercise and other equestrian feats *à la Franconi* for the amusement of the court', but really to discuss the French occupation of Rome, which Louis wished to end, but did not know how, and his plan for the liberation of Italy. The two statesmen, who were out of office at the time, incurred some abuse from the press for flirting with the national enemy; but Louis rightly reckoned their complicity more valuable, should they return to power, than their temporary loss of prestige. Palmerston was unrepentant. 'I am very Austrian north of the Alps', he told Granville, 'but very anti-Austrian south of the Alps' (January 30th, 1859).[24]

There was one English friend whom Louis succeeded in hoodwinking, at any rate as to the imminence of his Italian adventure,

and who wrote to the Queen on December 10th: 'Lord Malmesbury thinks he can assure your Majesty that none (no war) is at present contemplated by the Emperor Napoleon (who has just contradicted the report officially), and Count Buol is of the same opinion. . . It appears impossible that Napoleon can make a *casus belli* against Austria. Besides this, your Majesty may be assured that no warlike preparations are making in France, such as must precede such a plan as an Italian war.' Yet on this very day Louis was drafting a *pacte de famille* with Victor Emmanuel (it was not known in London till the following March) under which the French and Sardinian armies were to co-operate to drive the Austrians out of Lombardy, Savoy and Nice would be ceded to France, and the states of northern Italy would be rearranged to form a new kingdom under Victor Emmanuel. True, Cavour disliked some of Louis' terms which did not square with the Plombières proposals, such as that Sardinia should pay for the French troops as well as their own, whilst Louis commanded them all: but he was not the man to risk so essential an alliance on a side issue; and if Louis half hoped for a respite, he was disappointed. He would be held to his promises by a more determined will than his own.[25]

The events of 1859 were heralded by two omens, one of which appealed to the superstitions and the other to the fears of Europe. Donati's comet, discovered in June 1858, was watched apprehensively all that autumn: it was the largest ever seen by the mid-Victorians, 'with a broad tail spread perpendicularly over the heavens'; and many people took it for an omen of war. On January 1st, 1859, at the usual reception of the diplomatic corps at the Tuileries, the Emperor, perhaps remembering a famous Napoleonic precedent, perhaps 'daring himself' to embark on a dangerous course which he was privately tempted to abandon, said to Hübner, the Austrian ambassador, 'I regret that our relations with your government are no longer so good as formerly; but I beg you to tell the Emperor that my personal sentiments for him have not changed'. According to Granville, 'Nobody heard this but Cowley and Chelsea, and it would probably not have been known if Chelsea had not announced it at the Club'; and he told the House of Commons that 'the words might have meant everything, or they might have meant nothing at all'. But in fact such words in diplomatic ears, and to the general public, meant war; and the sequel verified Louis' intention.[26]

The Empress was specially polite to Hübner the following day, and the *Moniteur* talked of peace. But the next word belonged to Louis' Italian ally, and Europe waited anxiously for the speech from the throne which Victor Emmanuel was due to make to his Parliament on January 10th. In order to be sure of his ground Cavour sent a draft to Louis beforehand. The last sentence spoke of Victor Emmanuel's determination to tread in the steps of his predecessor (Charles-Albert, who had twice fought against Austria), and to complete the mission (for the liberation of Italy) entrusted to him by Providence. Louis struck this out as 'too strong', and suggested instead a paragraph, which to Cavour seemed 'a hundred times stronger', saying that 'whilst we respect treaties (i.e., the treaty of peace with Austria) we cannot remain insensible to the *cri de douleur* (*grido di dolore*) that reaches us from so many parts of Italy'. Victor Emmanuel liked this amendment, but insisted, as a good Catholic, on restoring the reference to divine guidance. 'Strong in our unity (ran his peroration) and confident in the righteousness of our cause, we wait with prudence and resolution whatever Divine Providence may decree.'[27]

5

It may seem surprising that after such plain threats of war the peace was kept for another three months. But one did not open a campaign in mid-winter; Cavour had his time-table; England was working for a peaceful solution; and Louis had to pretend that he would prefer it that way — indeed, in view of the expected unpopularity of the war in France, and the intrigues of his ministers, it was sometimes more than a pretence.

Three days after Victor Emmanuel's speech from the throne Jérôme set out from Paris for Turin, with Louis' commission to exchange copies of the *pacte de famille* with Cavour and to marry the King of Sardinia's daughter. He took with him General Niel, to consult the chiefs of the Sardinian army. Ten days later he received a telegram from the Emperor which showed that he was alarmed at the hostile tone of the Powers, and especially of England. Prince Albert's letters at this period are full of denunciation of one who 'has been born and bred a conspirator, and at his present age will never get out of this turn of mind'. He had prevailed on Victoria to write privately to the Emperor (February 4th, 1859) urging peace: and had received a reply in which Louis undertook not

to support Sardinia unless Austria were the aggressor. 'Public
opinion' (Louis wired to his cousin) 'insists on connecting your
marriage with war. We must at all costs, if possible, in the interest
of both countries, allow more time for the war . . . I should like the
contract of marriage postponed at any rate till February 6th . . . I
am particularly anxious to know whether Piedmont *must* fight this
year.' Jérôme, now that he was at Turin, and found himself accepted
by the Princess and fêted at court, had become more Sardinian than
the Sardinians, and replied next day that he saw no need for delay.
'To put it off would be a great pity. The King and the Princess
would be disappointed: I should be charged with lack of seriousness,
and yourself with lack of decision.' On the 27th he heard again
from Louis: 'Public opinion in Europe is still rising against me, and
even more against you: it is thought that we want war.' However,
within twenty-four hours came another letter in a different tone,
congratulating the Prince on the signature of the *pacte*, and on the
reported beauty of his fiancée. But it is most important (Louis went
on) that the marriage contract should antedate the treaty, so that no
one can say it was made a condition of it. At the end of the letter
Louis returned to the old question of the best way of saddling Austria
with the declaration of war: he did not like the Massa-Carrara idea,
and still hoped a *casus belli* might be found in Lombardy.[28]

It would seem that by this time Louis had made up his mind for
war, and that all the world suspected it, but that, with his love of
intrigue, he still thought it worth while to blow hot and cold —
though there is evidence that this embarrassed his friends quite as
much as it misled his enemies. On February 4th there appeared in
the *Moniteur* an article entitled *L'Empereur Napoléon III et l'Italie*,
attacking the Italian governments under Austrian suzerainty,
praising Sardinia, and expounding a plan for Italian independence
based on that put forward by Napoleon at St. Helena — a Federation
of states under the presidency of the Pope. But whereas 'The Emperor Napoleon I thought it right to conquer peoples in order to
liberate them, Napoleon III wishes to liberate them without conquering them'. This article, it appeared, was not merely 'inspired';
Louis had himself dictated the substance of it, and corrected the
proofs. Three days later, in his speech at the opening of the *Corps
Législatif*, he elaborated the phrase about liberating without conquering by repeating the catchword of 1851, *l'Empire, c'est la paix*, and
asserting (as though it had been *l'épée*, not *la paix*) his intention to

rely on the strength of the French army, but not to be easily provoked. At the same time he was writing to Queen Victoria (February 14th) disclaiming any responsibility for the rumours of war, or any military preparations, and to Victor Emmanuel, underlining the difficulty and expense of preparing for hostilities.

The diplomatists might make what they could of all this: Cavour believed he knew Louis' real mind—that he was 'drifting into' a war not so much of purpose as of predestination, and that he would, when the time came, redeem his pledges.[29]

But the Emperor was in real difficulties. At home almost everyone was against him: 'Your ministers', wrote his 'remembrancer', Prince Napoleon (April 20th), 'serve yourself, but not your policy. Everyone feels it and knows it. The result is that there is no confidence or courage anywhere—neither amongst the friends of peace at any price, whom you don't sufficiently encourage, nor amongst those who are friendly to your cause, because they see you surrounded by unfriendly and hostile agents . . . Thus you incur the disadvantages of both policies.' And the Prince went on to denigrate each minister in turn: Fould as interested only in the Funds, Walewski as a Guizot-like reactionary, Vaillant as a sceptic, Delangle as an Orleanist, Hamelin as a fool, Magne as a mere Civil Servant, Baroche as an advocate of any cause that brings him profit: and all of them despised and detested by the general public. This opinion was shared in England; for Prince Albert had written (July 14th, 1858): 'If he could only manage to gather honest men around him as Ministers, it would do the Empire more good than any amount of repressive laws and army increases.'

Nor could Louis rely, as he used to do, on the 'men of 1851'. Persigny, fresh from the London embassy, took the English view of the Italian adventure. Morny, now President of the *Corps législatif*, and with a Russian wife, was newly conscious of both national and international dread of war. Even the Empress, though she welcomed the war, soon discovered that she could have no sympathy for a 'United Italy' which would rob the Pope of his estates.

Abroad there was constant risk of intervention by England, Russia, or Prussia: England pressing Francis-Joseph and Pio Nono to reform their regimes in Italy, and so deprive Louis of a *casus belli*; Prussia, if not backing this demand, threatening a counter-attack on the Rhine frontier; and Russia inclining towards a conference of the Powers to settle the whole question. This last course was now

(February 1859) adopted by Derby's government, and Cowley was instructed to sound Paris and Vienna as to their attitude towards it. Louis, anxious not so much for delay as for the appearance of it, consented. Besides, as he had written to Prince Napoleon (March 22nd), a Congress was the only means left him of dividing the Powers. 'In order to divide my enemies and win over part of Europe to neutrality, I must make loud profession of my moderation and of my desire for conciliation.' Cavour, at least, would not misunderstand.[30]

Did he, or did he not? Austria was making difficulties about entering on a conference, unless there were no question of territorial changes, and unless Sardinia (excluded from the conference) were disarmed beforehand. Cavour not unnaturally refused to be excluded or to disarm unless Austria did too. Finally, on April 19th, he agreed to a plan of disarmament on both sides: but on the 23rd he received an ultimatum from Vienna demanding unilateral disarmament (as we should call it), or war. The choice was war, and Austria was the aggressor.

6

On Easter Day (April 24th) the first French contingent marched through cheering and weeping crowds to the Gare de Lyon, and entrained in coaches which some enthusiast had chalked 'Excursion trains (*trains de plaisir*) for Italy and Vienna'. The Emperor himself followed them on May 10th, bound for Marseille, Genoa, and the battlefields where his uncle had first made himself famous sixty-three years ago. But Parisian opinion, always fickle, when the first enthusiasm had cooled, turned against a campaign which was not likely to bring the country any territorial advantages, according to Napoleonic precedent: no new departments, no new tax-payers, no new conscripts, no new posts for prefects or mayors, no new *débits de tabac*.[31]

Louis — was it by some scrap of inheritance from his uncle? — readily looked forward to military adventure: Eugénie was always a fighter; and both were fatalists. They laughed at Mérimée's suggestion that he should wear, for protection, a light cuirass. 'She expressed no alarm at all the dangers to which the campaign might expose him. I am happier, she said, than I have been for months. Our cause is good, our army is excellent, and *he* is full of confidence

and energy. The suspense of the last three months affected his health and spirits; now he is as happy as I am.'[32]

There were good reasons why he should hope to repeat the triumph of 1796. The Piedmontese army was not against him, but on his side. Under cover of peace talk he had become fully prepared. Though the Austrians were on the spot, and could be first in the field, they were not ready to fight, and would be outnumbered by three to two. Whereas Napoleon had been responsible for his every move to the Directory, Louis was in sole command at home and at the front — the most enviable position for any commander. His troops were well armed and disciplined regulars, many of whom had seen active service in the Crimea; not ill-equipped and undisciplined citizens-under-arms such as Napoleon had led down from the Alpine passes to liberate and to loot. Though they lacked the republican *élan* which had carried their fathers to victory, they had great memories in their knapsacks. What were Custozza and Novara to Marengo and the Malakoff? Louis intended to exploit these advantages to the full. He had been through the Swiss military course at Thun: he had held an Italian command under the rebel leaders of 1831: he had studied the Crimean battlefields, and had thought himself fit to assume command of the Allied armies there, and to carry out his plan for victory. He knew the people and country he had for so many years dreamed of delivering. For the rest, it was his destiny to defeat the Austrians, and that, like Napoleon's leadership, might be worth 40,000 men in the field.

A study of the campaign that opened in May 1859, suggests that, as in his other enterprises, Louis did in fact owe his success to destiny rather than to design; or, in other words, to luck rather than to skill. Giulai, the Austrian commander-in-chief, missed an opportunity of advancing at once from Milan on Turin: by the time he did so (May 9th), Canrobert was on his right flank, and he withdrew again, fancying the French to be stronger than they were; for it was not till the 18th that the Franco-Sardinian forces were ready to take the field. Then, remembering 1796, he supposed that Louis would repeat Napoleon's strategy, march down the right (southern) bank of the Po, and cross to the left bank at Piacenza, in order to outflank Milan. So he advanced up the Po valley, with one column on the south bank; and this was thrown back by the French at Montebello (May 20th) — a good omen for Louis, for it was there that Lannes in 1800 had won the action that preluded the victory of Marengo.

By this time he was throwing himself into the conduct of war with as much zest as though it were an Eglinton Tournament: he would be up before dawn, and at work in his tent or on horse back all day. More than once Guizot 'saw the Emperor in his shirt-sleeves, writing at his desk, sometimes smoking a cigar, but always at work; for he saw to almost everything himself, and did not spare either fatigue or trouble'. It was given out in Paris that his generals had full confidence in his leadership. But we have it on the authority of his *premier écuyer*, General Fleury, that he had only the vaguest idea as to the disposition of his army, and that he could not read a map intelligently, master the movements of troops in the field, or grasp the course of events. So confused and incoherent were his orders that he had the records of them destroyed at the end of campaign. Nevertheless he was determined not to be a mere imitator of Napoleon, and he succeeded in one stroke which perhaps by its sheer unorthodoxy, disconcerted the enemy. Whilst Giulai waited for a further attack on the south bank of the Po, Louis transported a large force by rail from south to north, and threatened to outflank the Austrian right. The capture of Palestro (May 30th) was Giulai's first warning of this move: he fell back behind the Ticino (the frontier of Lombardy), hoping still to cover and save Milan. But soon (June 3rd) the French were across the Ticino at Turbigo and San Martino; and his only hope was to defend the Naviglio Grande, a canal a few miles further east. Here, round the bridgehead of Magenta, was fought the first important action of the campaign (May 4th): a battle without plan or co-ordination of forces on either side: almost an Austrian victory in the middle of the afternoon, barely a French one by the evening. But next day Giulai retired, uncovering Milan, and on the 8th Louis and Victor Emmanuel entered the capital of Lombardy, as Napoleon had done after the similar bridgehead action of Lodi, and proclaimed once more its liberation from the tyranny of Austria.[33]

But what next? Louis had already realized, as he rode over the battlefield of Magenta, and heard that 700 Frenchmen had been killed, that, if he had an amateur's flair for strategy, he lacked the professional soldier's reckoning of casualties; and he knew that the very enthusiasm for liberty which his victory evoked in Tuscany, at Parma, at Modena, and in the Romagna alarmed all those of his own supporters who were enemies of republicanism or friends of the Pope. He had promised to throw the Austrians out of Italy, and he

was as yet scarcely on the edge of Lombardy: he must pursue them to their new positions on the Mincio (the frontier of Venetia) and the Quadrilateral of fortresses, where they were preparing to give battle under the command of the Emperor Francis-Joseph himself.

A fortnight later the two armies blundered into the decisive battle of Solferino (June 24th) — a confusion of colourful and murderous *mêlées* which showed how little military art had advanced since the Middle Ages. It was accounted another victory. But the losses were more than twice as heavy as at Magenta (1600 Frenchmen killed and 700 Piedmontese), and all the villages round were filled with wounded men. A further slow advance came up with the enemy on the Adige, twenty miles inside Venetia. But on July 7th, when they were preparing for another battle, the welcome news was given out that the two Emperors had agreed to an armistice.

There were many reasons why Louis had decided to break off the campaign. The casualties at Solferino had distressed him no less than at Magenta. He had lost twice as many men by disease, and had now only 100,000 in line to the Austrians' 150,000, and those were discouraged by bad leadership. He stood beyond the limits of Lombardy, and could go no further without leaving forces to contain the garrisons of the Quadrilateral. He had no siege-train to reduce the fortresses. He had almost rivalled Napoleon's great advance of 1796, marching a hundred miles in six weeks, fighting five actions, and clearing the enemy out of Lombardy. He might say, with little more exaggeration than Napoleon did when he reached Peschiera in 1796, that the Austrians had been 'utterly expelled from Italy', and that his outposts were 'on the mountains of Germany'. Meanwhile his Sardinian allies were exploiting the victory in further schemes for the unification of Italy — the annexation of Tuscany, the Duchies, and the Legations — which may have been part of Cavour's interpretation of the conversations at Plombières, but were certainly not of his own: and he was forced to face the danger to France of a rival power in the Mediterranean — a risk which Napoleon had never underrated until his irresponsible after-thoughts at St. Helena.

But there was another and a more urgent danger. What if Prussia, jealous of Louis' success, even at the expense of Austria, should seize the opportunity, whilst the Emperor was absent at the head of his army, to attack the Rhine frontier? Prince Napoleon, at the outset of the campaign, had warned Louis of this risk (May 1st, 1859) in

one of those long, clever, and tiresome Notes in which it was his habit from time to time to lecture his elder cousin. In a few weeks' time, he said, Germany would have 400,000 men under arms. A Prussian army of 200,000 could within a fortnight be carried by rail to the north-west frontier, which was open to attack from more than one direction. It would be called a defensive move; but at any moment it might become an invasion, against which France would have no more defences than against the Duke of Brunswick in 1792. Louis had made light of this risk in his first interview with Kossuth on May 5th, but had changed his mind about it by the time of their second meeting on July 3rd: if the Prussian threat materialized there could be no question of his extending his war of liberation from Italy to Hungary.[34]

And now this fear struck home: for the Empress, acting as Regent, and warned by the Russian Schuvaloff, had passed on to the Emperor — it reached him on the morning of Solferino — warning of a Prussian concentration on the Rhine. This Louis showed to Victor Emmanuel, with the remark that he was disposed to make peace (he had also recalled Pélissier from London to organize the defence of Lorraine). Cavour, hearing the news, went at once to see the King. It was the day after Solferino; and he seems to have thought that Louis, in view of this second victory, might again change his mind, and, if he could get reinforcements, carry on the campaign. Louis kept the negotiations to himself; and when Cavour returned on July 10th, it was too late to do anything: the two Emperors met at Villafranca the next day.[35]

Louis found Francis-Joseph (like Alexander at Tilsit) ready to yield to the charm and experience of an older man with a victorious army at his back. Provided he were allowed to hand over Lombardy nominally to France, not to Sardinia, and to keep Venetia (with the usual promises of reform), he would agree to the latter being included in a federation of Italian states under the nominal presidency of the Pope (who also would be asked to reform his regime), rather as Luxembourg, though under Dutch rule, was a member of the German Confederation. As an afterthought, Austria was allowed to retain the fortresses of Mantua and Peschiera which she still held; the Ducal governments of Tuscany and Modena were to be returned to their legitimate holders, but not by force; the future of Parma and Piacenza was left undetermined. The upshot of the two Emperors' unrecorded conversation was embodied in the armistice of Villa-

franca (July 11th): a draft of it was entrusted by Louis to Prince Napoleon, for final agreement and signature by Francis-Joseph. His assent was given at Verona the same day. The terms were ratified four months later by the Treaty of Zürich.[36]

Louis had extricated himself cleverly enough from a dangerous position, as Napoleon had done in 1797; and Villafranca resembled Leoben in winning Lombardy by the sacrifice of Venetia. But then there had been no third party to the undertaking to rid Italy of its traditional tyrant: now, when Louis' victorious army was within sight of Verona, and only a week's march short of Venice, the armistice seemed to Victor Emmanuel and Cavour a betrayal of their common cause. Two months ago Louis had proclaimed his intention to liberate Italy 'up to the Adriatic': now all Venetia, guarded by two frontier fortresses, was to remain in Austrian hands. How could the King of Sardinia be content with the addition of Lombardy to his dominions, if everything else that he dreamed of was to be thwarted by the continued presence of Austrian garrisons south of the Alps, Austrian police in Parma, Florence, and Modena, Papal police in Bologna and Ferrara, and more than half the work of liberation still unaccomplished? Cavour was so angry that he resigned. A King had not that remedy; but as he rode through Turin on July 15th at Louis' side Victor Emmanuel must have been aware that the cheers were all for himself, and may have noticed that the portraits of the French Emperor in the shop windows had been replaced by those of his would-be murderer, Orsini.[37]

That evening, after a state banquet which he refused to attend, Cavour was summoned to an interview with the Emperor. Louis explained why he had signed the armistice — 'it would have needed 300,000 men to carry on, and I hadn't got them' — and tried to reassure him as to the future of the Italian states still under Austrian control. 'I will plead their case', he said, 'before the coming Congress.' And he pledged himself, since he had not carried out to the full his promise to liberate the whole of northern Italy, to forego the annexation of Nice and Savoy which had been its promised reward. He was undertaking more than he would perform.[38]

Hurrying back to Paris, Louis received the congratulations of the Senate, the Legislative Body, and the State Council. In reply he claimed that by the annexation of Lombardy to Sardinia the cause of national liberty and reform had been brought home to all Italy; and he explained frankly that 'as soon as the destiny of his own

country seemed to be imperilled, he had made peace' — he could not fight both on the Adige and on the Rhine. France was satisfied; the *rentes* showed a rise; and on August 14th, the official birthday of Napoleon, his nephew reviewed a 'victory march' through the streets of Paris, 'mounted on a magnificent charger which he bought for 500 guineas off a fashionable horsedealer in Piccadilly', and with the infant Prince Imperial, dressed in the red and blue of the Guard, sitting on his saddle-bow. It was perhaps the most triumphant moment of his life.

But when he feasted his generals at the Louvre that evening Louis hinted that there were still imperfections in the organization of the army. He knew even better than they did how near victory had been to defeat; how two wars had been ended by a fortunate peace that could not have been secured by further fighting. He painfully realized that, though born a Bonaparte, he was not by character a Napoleon. At the age at which the uncle's energy had worn itself out at St. Helena it was unlikely that the nephew could be successful in fresh adventures. Nor would France, half a century older and more sophisticated, submit to the sacrifices that had carried the tricolour across Europe. But would either he or his generals remember this moment of self-reckoning when the temptation came of another war?[39]

THE ADVENTURER (1859-1869)

Our indiscretion sometimes serves us well
When our deep plots do pall; and that should teach us
There's a divinity that shapes our ends,
Rough-hew them how we will.   *Hamlet*, V, ii

I

THE Italian question was by no means settled by the terms of Zürich. It was to drag on for another ten years, embarrassing alike all the participants in the struggle of 1859; and leading to two more European wars, which set the stage for the world war of 1914. The liberation of Italy could not be complete until Austria was entirely excluded from the peninsula; nor its unification until the Papal regime in Rome was replaced by that of Piedmont, and it became, as no other place could be, by geography, history, or sentiment, the capital of the Kingdom of Italy. But Victor Emmanuel was in no position to expel Austria by his own efforts; and the intransigence of Pio Nono was reinforced by the presence at Rome of a French garrison, which Louis was prevented from withdrawing by his dependence on the Catholics and by his apprehension of a (not merely liberated, but) united Italy, a new power in the Mediterranean – a prospect as welcome to his European rivals as it was unwelcome to himself.

So now, from 1859 onwards, Louis' course was to be as tossed and twisted as an upland stream that plunges into a rocky gorge. His purpose in life, though still sometimes hearing the original voices, and recovering the old poise, was losing its unity, its initiative, its idealism. The biographer may rightly suspect that this change was natural enough, once the two master-impulses were satisfied – when Lombardy was liberated, and France restored to predominance in Europe – in a character too easily the victim of flattery, indolence, and easy living. But it was also due to Louis' un-kingly kindness, which allowed too much licence to old friends and to his ministers of the moment; to his love of popularity – it is all up with a sovereign, Napoleon had said, when he is called a Good Fellow; and to his confidence in his intuitions, his 'little ideas', and his astuteness. Napoleon had designed – and that with immense attention to detail – the first moves in a campaign, and had left the later steps

to 'the chances of war'. Louis seemed too often to be planning cunningly enough the consequential policies of an undertaking entered into by hazard, or in a mood of unreasoning optimism.

A bad master generally has bad servants. Greville's verdict was no less true of Louis' government in 1859 than it had been in 1855. 'His own position (he had written) is very strange, insisting upon being his own Minister, and directing everything, and at the same time from indolence and ignorance incapable of directing affairs himself, yet having no confidence in those he employs. The consequence is that a great deal is ill done, much not done at all, and a good deal done that he knows nothing about; and he is surrounded with quarrels, jealousies, and struggles for influence and power both between his own Ministers and between them and the foreign diplomatists at his court.' Clarendon agreed. 'Our friend is an odd little fellow (he wrote to Cowley, November 11th, 1857). It is impossible not to like him, and not to feel that he has qualities which could make him a most reliable friend, if he had good advisers about him. But a man who is so ignorant and indolent as the Emperor, and has so much unavoidable business to do, must depend upon others, and should have a Nestor for a Foreign Minister, instead of a man with an empty head and an abundant abdomen like Walewski, who leads him into quagmires from which others have to pull him out all covered with mud.'

Here was an adventurer living upon the memory of a successful *coup d'état*; a people regretting lost liberties; an army priding itself on deeds it could no longer accomplish; a church discredited by state favour; an aristocracy saying masses for a royal restoration; and a middle class governed and governing by corruption and intrigue. As external wealth and prosperity increased, as Paris became more gay and glamorous, and dinners and balls at the Tuileries alternated with hunting-parties and theatrical performances at Compiègne, some of the best virtues and faculties of the nation atrophied and dried up. The despotism of the First Empire, though it denied liberty to the people, had given something in its place: initiative, adventure, imagination, a new zest for living. The despotism of the Second Empire dulled the senses and drugged the will of the nation— it fell ill, as and when the Emperor did, and its illness too contributed to the final disaster.

But not yet. In August 1859, Louis might congratulate himself on having achieved, as far as circumstances allowed, the second

great aim of his life, and France could breathe again at escaping from another unpopular war with increased military power and international prestige. Only Louis and his ministers knew how great a risk had been run, and what difficulties lay ahead.

First, in Italy, and at Rome. This was a problem that beset the whole history of the Second Empire. Ancient Rome had been the capital of a Mediterranean Empire, not of an Italian state. The inheritance of the Caesars had passed to the Popes, and their Temporal Power — the political and military control of the Papal States — was the symbol of a super-national government incompatible with a secular Kingdom of Italy. Of this Pio Nono and his Secretary of State, Antonelli, were convinced beyond argument of reason or force. Equally Victor Emmanuel and Cavour were certain that there could be no united Italy unless and until its capital were Rome.

France had sent troops to Rome in 1849 less from love of the Papacy than from hatred of Austria. 'To know that the Austrian flag was flying on the castle of St. Angelo (said Thiers) is a humiliation under which no Frenchman could bear to exist ... It was not for the sake of the Roman people, or the Pope, or Catholicism that we went to Rome; it was for the sake of France ... to maintain our right to have one half of Italy if Austria seized the other.' But now, under the Empire, French policy was subservient to the Catholic vote. It followed that, so long as Louis' liberation of Italy still left Venice in Austrian hands and a French garrison remained in Rome, the foreign policy of Pius IX would be influenced by the prejudices of the French Ultramontane clergy. The Pope, thought Manin, had become even more a French subject than during the Captivity of Avignon: the French 'protect him against his subjects, they enable him to collect his revenue, he depends on them for his sovereignty, he is their puppet'. It would have been better for the Papacy, perhaps, if the political centre of its spiritual authority had been elsewhere — in Elba, some suggested; better, certainly, for Italy. Louis himself is said to have thought so. 'Italy has outgrown the Papacy,' wrote Lord John Russell; 'the Pope would be a saint at Madrid, Valencia, or Majorca. In Italy he is only an anachronism.'

But, unable to alter the policy of 1849, Louis could do no more than express, in Guéronnière's pamphlet, *Le Pape et le Congrès* (December 22nd, 1859) the view that, since there was no likelihood that Pius' control would be maintained in the Papal States, he had better reconcile himself to remaining master of Rome: 'the less

territory he has, the greater will be his sovereignty' (*plus le territoire des Etats pontificaux sera petit, plus leur souverain sera grand*): what he loses in material power he will gain in spiritual prestige.[1]

This pamphlet, as can be imagined, 'fell like a thunderbolt' in Italy. The Papacy was horrified, the anti-clericals jubilant, only the liberals satisfied. On January 1st, after receiving the New Year's wishes of the commander of the French garrison, Pius bestowed the customary blessing on their country, but followed it up by saying 'We also pray the Most High to let His light descend upon the Chief of this nation, so that he may recognize the falsity of certain principles recently expressed in a work which must be denounced as *un insigne monument d'hypocrisie et un ignoble tissu de paradoxes.*' 'The Emperor Napoleon', he declared, 'is *un menteur et un fourbe.* I don't trust his word...The hour of vengeance has struck. The sword of God is ready to strike him in the hands of men!'

But in England the pamphlet had the opposite effect: coming after Villafranca, it did much to restore Louis to popularity. 'He has wellnigh recovered in this country (wrote Greville) the confidence and the popularity which had become exchanged for distrust, suspicion, and alarm . . . He certainly has exhibited great courage and above all boundless confidence in his own power and authority in his own country.' Lord John Russell, who was well informed on Italian affairs through his private as well as official correspondence with Sir James Hudson at Turin, an ambassador 'more Italian than the Italians', followed up the pamphlet with a dispatch which Cavour was said to have declared 'worth a dozen victories in the field'.[2]

If this was a solution of the Roman question which Pius would never accept, it was also one which Louis could never enforce. But it was to the credit of his insight if not of his statesmanship that the view which he outlined in 1859 was accepted by Cavour in 1861 ('a free church in a free state'), and that the Law of Guarantees (1870) became the basis of a settlement which lasted till 1929.

2

The history of the political unification of Italy in its three stages — the proclamation of the Kingdom in January 1861, the inclusion of Venice in 1866, and the occupation of Rome in 1870 — admits of clear statement; but nothing could be more obscure than the wavering course of French policy during this period. Louis' aim was the

same throughout, but the means he adopted to reach it varied according to the circumstances of the moment, and considerations alien to the interests of either Italy or Rome. What those interests demanded, Louis knew very well: the political and economic organization of the whole peninsula on the lines laid down by Cavour in Piedmont, and under Piedmont's king; and the shifting of the capital from provincial Turin to metropolitan Rome.

'To you who have been born in Italy,' Mazzini had declared, God has allotted the best-defined country in Europe ... God has stretched round you sublime and indisputable boundaries; on one side the highest mountains in Europe, the Alps; on the other the sea, the immeasurable sea. Take a map of Europe and place one point of a pair of compasses in the north of Italy on Parma; point the other to the mouth of the Var, and describe a semi-circle with it in the direction of the Alps; this point, which will fall, when the semi-circle is completed, upon the mouth of the Isonzo, will have marked the frontier which God has given you. As far as this frontier your language is spoken and understood; beyond this you have no rights.' He went on to insist that, important as political, social, and economic reforms might be, the country must be conquered first. 'Where there is no Country there is no common agreement to which you can appeal ... Your emancipation can have no practical beginning until a National Government, seated in Rome, shall formulate a Declaration of Principles to be the guide for Italian progress.' Cavour, who disagreed with almost everything Mazzini did, would have accepted this programme; but with a corollary which Mazzini rejected to the very end of his life: that a country divided into rival communities, a country without resources or communications, a country burdened with a poor, illiterate, superstitious peasantry, must accept the central control of its one progressive state.[3]

But what of Rome? Was it ready or fit to become the capital of Italy? Louis had doubtless read the confidential report furnished by Mgr. Lavigerie to M. Thouvenel on December 4th, 1861. 'The city of Rome (he had written), and what remains of the Papal states are at the moment enjoying profound quiet. This is doubtless due to the presence of an army of occupation of 20,000 men; but the great majority of the population show no signs of constraint or fear. Indeed most people are either devoted to the Pope, or attached by interest to the present regime, or at least indifferent as to how they are governed.

'Some of the Romans — their numbers and courage might increase — are sincere adherents of the Pope. It was this party which during the last few months, and again only a week ago, greeted Pio Nono with such public ovations as had been forgotten since 1847. The Borghese family are the leaders of this genuinely devoted section.

'Interest ranks next to loyalty; and here must be placed the numberless legion of parasites living on the ecclesiastical establishment — agents, clerks, officials, chamberlains, domestics, and (last but not least) beggars. It is no exaggeration to say that thirty or forty thousand people make a living out of the ecclesiastical business of briefs, indulgence, relics, or the pickings of bishops and convents. Innumerable families view with terror the possibility of the Pope's departure, which would mean the loss of their livelihood; and so they cling to his regime. Besides, Rome has no industries, no commerce: it lives entirely on the exploitation of foreign visitors. Landlords, tradesmen, lodging-house keepers in a still larger number, know that the revenue drawn from their yearly clients depends absolutely on the presence of the Head of the Church; so they support the authority of the Holy See.

'I need not mention the indifferent or undecided elements, which form here, as elsewhere, a floating mass at the mercy of any momentary impulse or passion—cheering the Pope at the church doors in the morning and abusing him at the cafés in the evening.

'Finally, to complete the count, the most active, influential, and, it must be admitted, the most intelligent part of the population is radically opposed to the Temporal Power, and, since the two things get mixed up in their minds, are declared enemies also of the religious and spiritual power of the Holy Father. This party is much less numerous: two or three thousand, commoners for the most part, with a few nobles, but principally barristers and lawyers, its real leaders. This is understandable in a country which offers them next to no legal careers, since the higher judicial posts (in the *Rota* for instance and even the civil courts), are in the hands of ecclesiastics. Were there a change at the head of the state, these lawyers would be the natural heirs of the episcopate, as the Roman princes would be of the Cardinals. But these are not the only reasons why this class joins the movement. Personal interest combines in various degrees with patriotism, anticlericalism, and love of progress to give this party close cohesion and real power.

'I have not the least doubt that, if the French army left Rome, and

Piedmont were definitely prevented from crossing the frontier, the party of action *would overthrow the temporal power in twenty-four hours*'.[4]

This was Louis' difficulty. Another, hardly less serious, would soon face Victor Emmanuel. As Gregorovius, the historian of Rome, walked its streets, and found everywhere 'nothing but memorials and monuments of the Popes – churches, convents, museums, fountains, palaces . . . thousands of monuments to popes and saints, thousands of tombstones to bishops and abbots – an atmosphere penetrated by the spirit of the ruins, of the catacombs, and of religion', he thought it inconceivable that 'Rome, which had been for 1500 years the cosmopolitan city, the moral centre of the world', should 'be reduced to the head of an Italian kingdom'. 'The air of Rome (he felt) is not suited to a young aspiring kingdom, which requires for its capital a plastic material that can easily receive an impression, such as that of Berlin, Paris, or St. Petersburg . . . Rome will lose everything – her republican atmosphere, her cosmopolitan breadth, her tragic repose.' In a similar mood, when Florence in 1864 became for a time the capital of the new kingdom, Lord John Russell remarked: 'I am glad Florence is thought of as a permanent capital. It does not seem to me that the recollections of Nero, Caligula, Caesar Borgia, Alexander VI, and various other Emperors and Popes ancient and modern do much to consecrate Rome. A clean capital like Florence is required for a new Kingdom which is not the Republic, the Empire, or the Papacy.'[5]

3

Difficulties about the settlement of Italy had begun before Villafranca. At the outbreak of war Prince Napoleon had been sent to Florence with a French corps, and instructions to keep the peace there, whilst Ricasoli carried through his policy of union with Piedmont against a minority which was still for an Austrian regime. Louis' correspondence with his cousin during this time is reminiscent of Napoleon's letters to Jérôme during the Moscow campaign of 1812: he rewrites his proclamations, he dictates his strategy, he rebukes his disobedience to orders; and though he ends by praising the 'zeal and intelligence' with which he carried out his mission, he cannot but blame the misguided *amour-propre* which made him refuse to let his wife, the Princess Clotilde, take part in the Victory

March in Paris on August 15th, because his own corps was not re-presented at it. It was said by those who always suspected Louis' purposes that he intended to set up Prince Napoleon as a successor to the Grand Duke of Tuscany, and to make that state the nucleus of a Kingdom of Central Italy: but there is no hint of this in the cor-respondence; and Louis would not allow his troops to take any part in the occupation of Papal territory, which would have been part of the plan. Indeed, when Perugia rose against the Papal regime, and Pius allowed its brutal suppression by Schmidt's Swiss troops, he concurred in the occupation of the Romagna by Piedmontese forces — a first step towards its incorporation in the Kingdom of Italy.[6]

Least of all did Villafranca determine the Roman question. To the friends of Italian unity the settlement did not go far enough; to the friends of the Papacy it went too far. Louis' pamphlet pleased Liberals of all colours; but it did nothing to satisfy the mass of the French people, who had hated the war, and could only be reconciled to the peace if it brought some *quid pro quo*, financial or territorial. Cavour, who returned to power in January 1860, reflecting that after all Villafranca might prove a blessing in disguise, saw a way in which both France and Italy might benefit by it. At Turin, under the first impact of Italian disappointment, Louis had undertaken not to ask for the *pourboire* provided for in the *pacte de famille* — the annexation of Nice and Savoy: but Cavour knew how flimsy such a promise might become in retrospect. What if the cession of this territory were made conditional upon France, not Sardinia, paying the expenses of the campaign? Would not both countries think it a good bargain if one gained a population which by sentiment and interest was more than half French, and the other escaped paying a bill of £30 millions? Add that Louis would agree to overlook the incor-poration of Tuscany and Emilia into the Kingdom of Sardinia — would in fact represent this aggrandisement as justifying his own — provided that both transfers of population were, to save appearances, approved by *plébiscites*, showing that the sympathies of both districts were in favour of annexation. This transaction was put through without delay, by an exchange of signatures on March 22nd and 24th, and ratified by the Italian Parliament on the 26th.[7]

France and Italy might applaud; but to Europe, and especially to England, such a cynical transaction — for it had been arranged before consulting the population, and would probably have been carried through anyhow — shocked Louis' new friends, and finally

confirmed the suspicion that behind his crusades for liberation and national unity he was really seeking French aggrandisement. That he should have conspired and co-operated with Sardinia in bringing about the first European war since 1815 was bad enough, and had caused a war scare such as England had not experienced for half a century. But that he should, behind the back of a peace conference, and contrary to the settlement of 1815, bargain for a large extension of French territory was a threat to public security which caused consternation in all the chancelleries of Europe. Not least in England, where even Palmerston approved of the speech in the Commons (March 26th) in which Lord John Russell denounced Louis' action, in such terms that Persigny, who was in the House, 'was in a dreadful state, exclaiming: *Quel langage! Faut-il entendre de pareilles choses contre mon maître? C'est à ne pas y tenir!*' Palmerston had in fact been changing his mind about the Emperor for some months past. 'Till lately (he wrote to Russell, November 4th, 1859) I had strong confidence in the fair intentions of Napoleon towards England, but of late I have begun to feel great distrust, and to suspect that his formerly expressed intention of avenging Waterloo has only lain dormant, and has not died away. He seems to have thought to lay his foundation by beating, with our aid or with our concurrence or neutrality, first Russia, and then Austria, and by dealing with them generously to make them his friends in any subsequent quarrel with us.' A few months later Palmerston would be making to Cowley the often quoted remark (no one was so fond of sporting metaphors): 'The Emperor's mind seems as full of schemes as a warren is full of rabbits, and, like rabbits, his schemes go to ground for the moment to avoid notice or antagonism.'

The Queen too had changed her mind about her Dear Friend of 1855. 'Really it is too bad! (she wrote to Leopold on May 6th, 1860) *No* country, no human being would ever dream of *disturbing* or *attacking* France; everyone would be glad to see her prosperous; but *she* must needs disturb every quarter of the Globe and try to make mischief and set everyone by the ears; and of course it will end some day in a *regular crusade* against the *universal disturber* of the *world*. It is really monstrous!'[8]

Louis was well aware of these suspicions, and on July 25th wrote a letter to Persigny to be passed on to Palmerston, 'who (he said) knows me well, and will believe what I say'. 'Since Villafranca (he declared) I have only had one thought and one aim — to inaugurate

a new era of peace, and to live on good terms with all my neighbours, especially England. I had given up the claim of Savoy and Nice, and it was only the extraordinary enlargement of Piedmontese territory which made me reassert the right to restore to France provinces essentially French.' As to the charge of military and naval armament, he had done nothing since Villafranca that was not justified by the position in Syria or Algeria. His essential policy was peace. 'I have great conquests to make, but they are in France. I have still to organize this country on moral and social lines; I have to develop its internal resources, which are all in a backward state; and this aim opens a field big enough to satisfy all my ambitions.' As for Italy: 'I want to see Italy pacified, no matter how, provided that I can get out of Rome, and that there is no foreign intervention.'

To Earle, who saw him in Paris in April, he protested that England had no cause to object to 'annexations insignificant in themselves, and made with the consent of the Sovereign who loses them and of the people whose nationality is changed': he would not oppose similar English action, if occasion arose.[9]

This sounded well enough. But it did not destroy the suspicions that followed Louis' agents all over Europe: at Geneva, where he was said to be intriguing with the Catholic party with a view to annexation; at Baden, where he was thought to be bargaining with the Prince Regent of Prussia for the cession to France of the lower Rhine frontier; or at Turin, where he was supposed to be secretly supporting a Sardinian invasion of the Papal States; whilst all the time he was held to be plotting an invasion of England.[10]

4

Italy, after all, throughout the critical year 1860, was the decisive test of Louis' policy; and nothing showed so clearly how powerless he was to control the process he had started the year before. This is not the place to describe in detail the revolt in Sicily against the rule of Naples which broke out in April 1860, the diversion of Garibaldi from attacking the cession of Savoy in the Turin parliament to heading the expedition of the Ten Thousand, the landing at Marsala, the victory of Calatafimi, the surrender of Palermo, the defeat of the Neapolitans at Milazzo, the crossing of the Straits of Messina, and the capture of Naples. Garibaldi, it was reported, had said 'he would breakfast at Naples, and dine at Rome,

but he had not yet made up his mind whether he would sleep at Nice or Venice'.[11]

What did Louis do in face of these stirring events? When the fall of Palermo was reported at Naples early in June, the King's first thought was to appeal to the Pope for his blessing — and he did so five times within twenty-four hours. His second thought was the usual expedient of his house when in trouble — to grant a constitution, and to entrust the government, until the constitution could be safely recalled, to someone who could control the city crowds. So the constitution of 1848 was re-enacted, the tricolour was run up, and the keeping of order was entrusted to Liborio Romano, the Prefect of Police. But no one outside Naples supposed that these measures would meet the danger of Garibaldi's advance, supposing he once crossed the Straits of Messina, or that the Neapolitans would fight against one who was already a national hero, and whose defeat would mean a re-imposition of the Bourbon tyranny. Francis must have allies. Here Louis stepped in, and urged him as another head of his programme to accept the offer of alliance made two months before by Victor Emmanuel. This, he calculated, would prevent the overthrow of Francis, and the inclusion of Naples in a united Italy: equally it would embarrass Cavour, who was ready to employ any means to bring about just this result, by secretly helping Garibaldi, and planning to incite the Neapolitans to revolution, whilst compelled officially to pretend to be supporting the alliance. It was in this connection that he made the famous admission to d'Azeglio, 'If we had done for ourselves the things we are doing for Italy, we should be great rascals'. Louis might have made the same confession, if he had seen as clearly the distinction between public and private morality, or between the interests of his country and of his dynasty.[12]

Before the end of the month in which Garibaldi had seized Palermo Cavour was forced to look even further ahead. What if the Sicilian patriots or rebels (whichever they might be) crossed the straits into Italy, occupied Naples, and marched on Rome? Would it be possible to accept this crowning mercy at the hands of a guerilla leader in face of the disapproval, and perhaps the armed intervention, of France or Austria? How could Victor Emmanuel at the same time use Garibaldi, and restrain him; exploit the national enthusiasm to annex Naples without threatening Rome; even incorporate the Papal States in the Kingdom of Italy, and leave the

Pope untouched in Rome itself — perhaps, as Prince Napoleon suggested in a speech to the Senate on March 1st, 1861, with no more than the Vatican and Transtevare? Indeed it was Prince Napoleon who, knowing Louis' real mind, or, it would be truer to say, the ultimate balance of his fears, advised Cavour (June 30th) to take the Emperor into his confidence, and go boldly ahead with the annexation of 'Sicily, Naples, and Rome'.[13]

A month later Garibaldi, now almost at Messina, received two letters from Victor Emmanuel, the first ordering him not to cross the straits, the second leaving him 'full freedom of action' — in other words encouraging him to march on Naples. There could be little doubt of his answer: 'Sire (he wrote) allow me this time to disobey you; . . . as soon as I have fulfilled what I have undertaken I will lay down my sword at your feet, and obey you for the rest of my life.' But now a fresh difficulty arose. Louis was urging the British Government to join with France in a naval demonstration which would prevent Garibaldi from crossing the straits. This proposal, made through Persigny, was to be put before the Cabinet by Lord John Russell on July 25th. On the 24th, when he was closeted with Persigny, Russell received an urgent demand for an interview from Sir James Lacaita, a distinguished Italian now naturalized and living in London, to whom Cavour had appealed, on Hudson's advice, through the Sardinian ambassador. Lacaita put the case against intervention so strongly, and Russell himself was so well disposed towards the Italian cause, that next day Louis' proposal was turned down: he dared not act alone, and Garibaldi crossed the straits unopposed.

When Garibaldi entered Naples, and Francis fled to Gaeta, Louis made one more ineffectual gesture by using the French navy first to obstruct the blockade of the port, and then (February 1861) to rescue the royal refugees. But already he had secretly acquiesced in the policy he was publicly opposing. Whilst on a holiday at Chambéry in August 1860 he had been informed by Farini of Cavour's intention to carry out 'Jérôme's plan', in other words, to occupy Umbria and invade the Papal States before Garibaldi could advance from Naples, but to leave the Pope undisturbed in possession of Rome and the Patrimony of St. Peter; and to this plan Louis had agreed, only stipulating that his approval should not be published, and that there should be no delay. 'Do it quickly(*faites vite*)' were his parting words to Cavour's envoy. As to this he need have

had no qualms: for Cavour's only fear was lest Austria might intervene before the invasion was finished. But to prevent any second thoughts Farini's mission was kept alive in Louis' mind by his old friends Arese and Conneau.[14]

In September Sardinian troops invaded the Papal States: at the end of October Victor Emmanuel and Garibaldi met at Teano, and the union of Italy, save for Rome and Venice, was signed by the generous greeting of King and Liberator. A revolutionary was turned into a royal victory. On January 27th, 1861, a national parliament at Turin proclaimed Victor Emmanuel the first King of Italy.

Throughout the events of 1860, though 600-700 Irish volunteers were fighting in the Papal army, British naval support at Marsala, Palermo, and Messina had shown the national approval of a gallant if piratical adventure, and British diplomacy had superficially disguised our pleasure at the discomfiture of Louis' designs. When it was all over, and the other Powers showed their disapproval of the new Kingdom of Italy by withdrawing their ministers from Turin, Britain alone refused to do so, and Russell wrote a dispatch (October 17th) in which he said 'Her Majesty's Government can see no sufficient ground for the severe censure with which Austria, France, Prussia, and Russia have visited the act of the King of Sardinia. They will turn their eyes rather to the gratifying prospect of a people building up the edifice of their liberties, and consolidating the work of their independence amid the sympathies and good wishes of Europe.' Cavour was so delighted when he read this that 'he shouted, rubbed his hands, jumped up, sat down again, then began to think, and then he looked up tears were standing in his eyes. Behind your dispatch (Hudson wrote to Russell) he saw the Italy of his dreams, the Italy of his hopes, the Italy of his policy'. He could now deal without fear with the ineffective protests of the other Powers.[15]

It was the last service he did for his country. When he died on June 6th, 1861, Italy was a Kingdom, though Venice was still under Austrian rule, and in Rome the Papal regime was still protected by French arms. 'The despised, divided, and down-trodden race' — so *The Times* put it (February 25th, 1861) — 'are once more a people. The geographical expression has become a mighty kingdom, and the language of Dante and Petrarch is no longer destined to be the vehicle of ceaseless and unavailing complaints, but will henceforth

convey the thoughts of the statesman, and record the history of free men determining their own destiny by their own will and energy.'

But the richest rhetoric of *The Times* was reserved to denounce the Emperor of the French, who had vainly opposed the completion of the plan that he had inaugurated at Magenta and Solferino (the interview at Chambéry was either ignored or unknown). 'Has not the time arrived when even the Emperor of the French must perceive that the ungenerous policy by which he has half cancelled the boundless gratitude of Italy has been from beginning to end a failure, and has not altered the course of events, but only reacted on the reputation of its author? The last act but one of the great Italian drama is about to open. There is nothing now but the French garrison which intervenes between a settlement of the quarrel of United Italy and the Pope. It is impossible to doubt of the manner in which that quarrel must be settled . . . The Pope really has no choice. If he is to remain in Italy at all, he must make the best terms he can with the Italian nation, and by deferring this necessary result the Emperor of the French only makes the terms harder and the fall of the ecclesiastical power more complete and crushing . . . If the year we are commencing is to terminate in the peace which the Emperor assures us he is so anxious to obtain, no time should be lost in suppressing the most threatening cause of war by withdrawing the French garrison from Rome.'[16]

In principle there was nothing Louis would more willingly do: but in practice he knew, and the writer in *The Times* knew, that the withdrawal of the French garrison would mean the overthrow of Papal rule, and would be followed by the intervention of Piedmont, whose troops were already established within a few miles of the city, and only waited for just such an opportunity to make it the capital of the new Kingdom of Italy. Such an event would defeat both Louis' aims – his guardianship of the Pope and his prevention of Italian unity; it would ruin his reputation both as a good Catholic and as a good Frenchman; and it would destroy the domestic truce at the Tuileries. For, as Mérimée, staying with Louis and Eugénie at Biarritz in the autumn of 1861, reported, the Emperor was really no friend of the Pope, but was embarrassed by the Empress's Catholic sympathies: *en ce qui touche au spirituel* (he wrote) *il y a toujours de graves dissidences qui compliquent la situation.*[17]

Only two solutions were still possible. If Piedmont promised not

to intervene, it might be feasible to withdraw the French troops: or, if the Pope consented to the sacrifice of his temporal claims, some arrangement might be come to on the lines — already suggested by both Louis and Cavour — of 'a free church in a free state'. Cavour was working for this solution during the last months of his life. His death made it certain that nothing more could be done until there was a radical change in the conditions of the problem — such a change as, in this unaccommodating world, could only be looked for from Death or War.

5

Two wars had now been fought in Europe within five years, after forty years of peace. It was unlikely that their effects would be localized. Already, as though by a kind of international telepathy, there were 'rumours of war' in Syria, in China, in Algeria, in Mexico: already Louis was suspected of neo-Napoleonic plans to popularize his despotism and secure his succession by a re-partition of Europe: had not the firm of Stanford in 1860 published a map showing where the new frontiers would run?[18] Soon almost his only friend amongst the crowned heads and their advisers was the Queen of Holland, who passed on to Clarendon (August 17th, 1861) his answer to an appeal for peaceful policies. In this letter he protested that his only endeavour was to put the French army and navy on a footing worthy of the country (*sur un pied respectable*): he considered a peace establishment of 400,000 men indispensable, considering that he must keep 70,000 in Algeria, 30,000 in Rome, China and Cochin-China, not to mention 65,000 non-combatants in various subsidiary services: that only left 235,000 on active service in France. Meanwhile England had four ships of the line to France's one, and Prussia (with a population of only 18 millions) an army of 300,000 men. He could not help it, if his aims were distrusted: he would pursue his duty as a sovereign, and endeavour to keep the peace. 'These are facts, not words. I feel them to be true', was the Queen's comment. And no doubt they were — at the moment, and in Louis' present mood. But could one trust a sovereign so inconsistent in his policies, and so ill-advised? A *parvenu*, whose government had begun and might end in a revolution? A despot, who must distract attention from internal loss of liberties by external aggrandisement? A Bonaparte, whose scripture was the Gospel of St. Helena —

and he its only interpreter? *Les idées napoléoniennes* never had a tithe of the circulation of *Mein Kampf*: but there was no need to read it: the mere title was a programme; the name was warning enough.

The establishment of the Second Empire carried with it a reaction against what might be called the colonial republicanism of the years 1848-51. The abolition of slavery was maintained, in spite of its unpopularity amongst the West Indian planters; and the free trade measures of 1861 were extended to the French possessions overseas. But their political independence and parliamentary representation were withdrawn, and they were ruled from Paris. To employ the army, to please the Church party, and to enrich the merchants and settlers, fresh encouragement was given to conquest, missionary work, colonization, and commercial exploitation.

It would be rash to credit Louis himself with a consistent or consecutive colonial policy. But he was influenced by the Saint-Simonian Enfantin's book, *La colonisation de l'Algérie*, and by a Belgian carbonarist, Cusson, as well as by his regard for the Arab troops in the French army, to favour a regime that encouraged the education of the natives, and even a degree of self-government, against their exploitation by the French colonists. He may also have known the scheme for colonial free trade and parliamentary representation put forward by Disraeli in 1851 — a scheme which was closely followed by the plan for an Anglo-French commercial treaty which Louis was already believed to favour, and which he firmly supported a few years later.

However this may be, in 1858 he determined to remove the control of Algeria from the War Office, and to create a special department for its administration. His original idea was that Prince Napoleon, whom he designated as head of the new Ministry, should reside in Algeria as Prefect or Viceroy; but when the Prince insisted upon spending at least four months of the year in Paris, he acquiesced in a Ministry directed from the capital. This regime did not last. In 1860 there was a return to military control under General Pélissier, in 1863 Louis laid down a new policy, which enabled the Arabs to acquire landed proprietorship; and two years later declared his intention to make Algeria 'an Arab kingdom, a European colony, and a French factory (*comptoir*)'. This was after a visit which, remembering St. Louis and Napoleon, he himself paid to North Africa in June 1865. 'His Majesty', as Mérimée picturesquely put it,

went into the Great Desert with a score of Frenchmen as escort, and remained for forty-eight hours surrounded with between fifteen and twenty thousand Saharians, who fired their rifles in his ears (their manner of saluting), and cleaned his boots with their beards ... They gave him oxen roasted whole, they made him eat ostriches and other impossible animals; but everywhere he was received as a beloved sovereign. He is very proud and very pleased.'[19]

Under the new regime Algeria became less a training-ground for the army than a laboratory for experiments in the colonial policy which a later age misnamed Imperialism. It was an attempt to combine Arab autonomy with French officialdom and immigration – an early example of that national method which (helped by the absence of a 'colour bar' prejudice) has since built up a great Empire in northern Africa. 'The day will come (Louis prophesied) when the Arab race, regenerated and mixed with the French race, will recover a strong individuality', and be given the self-government it deserves.

In Senegal, following a period of native risings and military 'liberation', Faidherbe, an administrator of genius, appointed Governor in 1854, began by organizing the protection of a handful of French traders, and ended ten years later by conquering a country already as large as France, and destined to expand before long into the immense territories of French West Africa. Immense, and enlightened. He started schools, especially one for the sons of local chieftains, formed a native army, favoured Mohammedanism, and encouraged French officers and officials to learn the language and study the customs of the people.

In the Pacific New Caledonia was occupied in 1853, and colonized by transported criminals: it became the centre of the Loyalty Islands, still a French possession. The Wallis Islands, and Tahiti, the centre of the Society Islands, remained French. Madagascar, after wavering between French and British 'protection', might be reckoned a French possession from 1868; and a footing was obtained about the same time in what became French Somaliland.

During the same years French military enterprise, following the cross and the tricolour, founded an eastern empire in Cambodia and Cochin-China. Saigon was captured in 1859. An experiment of native rule under French control failed; the King of Annam was forced to cede Cochin-China (1862), and the King of Cambodia accepted a French protectorate. Within five years another colony

the size of France had been added to the Second Empire, conquered and administered by the initiative of the French navy. In July 1861 a Siamese delegation was entertained at Fontainebleau.[20]

The Chinese affair of 1856-60 was the first international adventure in the Far East. For ten years and more French missionaries had been baptizing, and French merchants making money, at Canton, Shanghai, and other ports thrown open by the Treaty of Nanking, which ended the 'first Opium War' (1842). In 1856, to enforce these 'rights', an Anglo-French fleet bombarded Canton and threatened Taku. The Chinese government promised concessions, to be embodied in a treaty signed at Peking; but in 1859 the allied fleet was fired on at Taku, and retired with loss. Next year a 'punitive expedition' landed, carried the forts, advanced to within a few miles of Peking, and seized, sacked and burnt the 'Summer Palace', looting or destroying two million pounds' worth of property. It then occupied the capital, and dictated terms under which the country was for half a century open to Western diplomacy, religion, and culture; whilst the museums and private collections of Europe were enriched by the paintings and porcelain of an older and no less artistic civilization.[21]

If in the Far East there was less cause of offence in exploits in which England was an accomplice before the fact, the French proceedings in Syria during the same years too closely affected British interests in the Levant, and too clearly recalled the events of 1798, to escape hostile criticism. The Sultan's undertaking (1856) to protect Christian privileges in his dominions caused much resentment amongst the Mohammedan majorities. In May 1860, in the remote Lebanon, Moslem Druses massacred their hereditary enemies of the Christian Maronite villages. Thanks to the activity of the consuls at Beyrout this local trouble was soon dealt with on the spot. But the Powers were quickly on the alert, as protectors of their various Churches, and as rivals for concessions in the trading ports of the Levant. French and British warships were already at Beyrout when news came of a three-days' massacre at Damascus, in which some five thousand Christians had perished. This brought into play an international Commission, which acquiesced in the landing of French troops at Beyrout, and in the rather half-hearted steps of the Sultan's representative to punish the Turkish officials responsible for the massacre. It was more difficult to agree on a regime which would prevent further trouble; and the settlement was probably less en-

dangered by the presence of French troops four months after the time limit set by the Commission than by the British demand for their withdrawal a month before it. But Louis complied; it was too soon after the annexation of Savoy to risk a charge of colonial expansion so near home (June 1861).[22]

6

So much for colonial adventure in the Old World. What of the New? There was in the southernmost part of North America a country once conquered for Spain and the Catholic Church by Cortes, but now sharing with the states of South America the privileges of liberty and anarchy; an area until the middle of the nineteenth century four times that of Indo-China, and still twice its size when it became the scene of Napoleonic adventure in 1861. Mexico and its neighbour states had attracted Louis' roving and ingenious mind when, a prisoner at Ham, he tried to barter his bondage for the direction of a scheme for a canal from the Atlantic to the Pacific Ocean — a scheme which he recommended to the City of London after his escape in a pamphlet named *Canal of Nicaragua; or a project to connect the Atlantic and Pacific Oceans by means of a Canal. By N. L. B.* (1846), which held the field of speculation until supplanted by the Panama route thirty years later.

But within fifteen years of Louis' first thought of central America the affairs of Mexico suddenly concerned Europe. In 1859 the Presidency of the republic was disputed between the Liberal and anti-clerical Juárez and the Conservative and Catholic Miramón. Juárez, representing the business interests of the southern ports, derived a considerable revenue from commerce with Europe: Miramón, supported by the land-owners of the interior, had to borrow money, where his rival earned it, from foreign sources, on the security of Mexican Government bonds. But in 1860, defeated by Juárez, he fled the country, and left his rival to deal with his debts, which by this time amounted to two years of the national income. Juárez declared a moratorium on the interest due on the bonds to Spanish, French, and British creditors. The Three Powers agreed by the Treaty of London (October 1861) to 'protect the interests' of their nationals by joint action; and soon their ships and troops (6000 Spaniards, 2500 French, and 700 British marines) appeared off Vera Cruz. This was common practice on the part of the Powers, and

the terms of the treaty disclaimed any threat to the right of the Mexican Republic to govern itself as it pleased.

But already the enemies of Juárez and the friends of the Church were inspiring bigger schemes. It had been suggested by the Mexican statesman Calderón Collantes (September 1861) that Spain should not merely ask for payment of a debt, but make sure of it by putting the government of the country in order. Louis, in a letter to the French ambassador in London (October 1861), had approved and improved this plan: Mexico should be enabled to develop its natural resources, and to prevent the loss of further territory by secession, as in the manner of Texas, California, and New Mexico, to the United States. Only England was set against any political interference. The result of these differences of opinion, and of quarrels between the rival commanders, was that Spain and England withdrew from the expedition (April 1862), and left France to carry on alone.

Louis might have withdrawn too, but for an unfortunate incident on May 5th — doubly unfortunate on the anniversary of the death of Napoleon — when a French column, now six thousand strong, under General Lorencez, which was marching up country, was defeated by Juárez's men outside Puebla with heavy losses. Now, as at Rome in 1849, an insult to national honour must be avenged; a *parvenu* dynasty must prove its mettle. At once minor but attractive motives came into account. The Conservative leaders who had inspired Louis' letter to Flahaut — Gutiérrez, Almonte, and Hidalgo — reminded him that Mexico had not always been a Republic; before Iturbide made himself Emperor in 1821 he had offered the crown to the Archduke Charles of Austria (Gutiérrez himself had been one of the deputation); there was a strong royalist-clerical party in the country ready to support a new sovereign; under no other government would the people settle down to peace and prosperity; without a king they would be unable to resist the aggression of the United States. Gutiérrez's arguments were backed by wealth, orthodoxy, and diplomatic experience. His lieutenant Hidalgo added social gifts which won the sympathy of Eugénie for the idea of a Spanish Catholic state blocking the southward expansion of Anglo-Saxon Protestantism.

A less reputable motive was suspected. Amongst the debts claimed by France was a sum of three and three-quarter million pounds owing to the creditors of a Swiss banker, since bankrupt, named Jecker;

and this man entered into an agreement with Louis' half-brother Morny to pay him thirty per cent of whatever might be recovered. After Morny's death Jecker wrote to Louis' secretary (December 8th, 1869), saying that Morny 'had undertaken to see that the debt was acknowledged and paid by the Mexican government', and lamenting that his death ended 'the privileged priority (*protection éclatante*) hitherto afforded him by the French government'. This is proof enough of Morny's intrigue, but not of Louis' part in it. The real importance of the affair is that the inclusion of the Jecker debt in the French claim for repayment, together with the landing of a formidable French force, contributed to the decision of Britain and Spain to retire from the adventure. That Louis was seriously affected by it was always denied by Eugénie, who insisted that the Mexican adventure was undertaken for the highest motives as *l'accomplissement d'une très haute pensée politique et civilisatrice*, and that the final impulse was given by herself at Biarritz in 1861.[23]

Not that Louis needed much persuasion or inducement. As long ago as 1857 he had mentioned to Disraeli 'his wish and willingness to assist in establishing a European dynasty in Mexico', and had said that 'for his part he would make no opposition to the accession of the Duc d'Aumale to such a throne. He looked upon its establishment as of high European importance'. Now the moment seemed to have come. They told him that the Mexicans were at heart Catholic (which was true) and monarchical (which was not); and his own experiences in France predisposed him to believe it. Since his intervention in Rumania and Lombardy he saw himself as a Nation-maker; and he was attracted by the idea of perfecting in the political vacuum of Central America a creation which had been hampered in Italy by the impediments of the Balance of Power. He was perhaps still haunted by the memory of Napoleon's unachieved oriental ambitions, and speculated on the industrial and commercial exploitation of a new India in the West.

There was, of course, the danger of American opposition; had not President Buchanan as recently as 1859 reasserted the Monroe doctrine, warning off European interference in America? But Lincoln, he believed, was too much occupied with the threat of southern secession (the Civil War had broken out in April 1861), his State Secretary Seward too busy beating up hostile feeling against England over the *Trent* case in 1861, and his minister Adams over the *Alabama* incident in 1862, to pay much attention to what might

happen in Mexico. Meanwhile, he might divert attention by offering to mediate in company with England between the North and South.

But this attempt was countered by the British ambassador. Lyons was aware that English opinion was divided between those who sympathized with the Federal case against slavery and those who held that the Confederates had as much right to secede from the Union as Italy had from Austria; whilst commercialists were chiefly concerned (as in France too) with the effect of the war upon cotton exports from the southern states. 'Intervention' and 'Conference' were too well known by this time as pass-words to international complications, and instruments of French policy ('traps', Palmerston called them, 'laid by Louis for the silly birds he was trying to lure into his decoy'), to have any attraction for British statesmen.[24]

Perhaps, after all, Louis would have shrunk from so big an adventure if he had not remembered an ideal candidate for the throne of Mexico. Of the four grandsons of the much-married Emperor Francis II the eldest, Francis-Joseph, was now Emperor of Austria: a dull, dour, conscientious prince, ambitious above all for the honour of the Habsburgs, and not unwilling to see his younger brother removed from courtly unemployment to a monarchy overseas. There was a spice of jealousy in this, for Ferdinand Maximilian, two years his junior, had tastes and qualities missing from the conventional Habsburg make-up: he loved the sea, he enjoyed foreign travel, and he had adopted Liberal opinions shocking in a pupil of Metternich. For he had seen at first hand something of the French regime in Algeria; he had visited the Portuguese court and had hoped to marry the Princess Maria Amelia; he had carried out a mission to Albania; he had borne a cross in a religious procession at Jerusalem, and described his experiences in the Holy Land to Pio Nono at the Vatican; he had studied the weaknesses of Louis and Eugénie at Paris in 1856, and listened to the good advice which was so freely dispensed by Leopold of Belgium.

It was at Brussels that he met and became engaged to Leopold's daughter Charlotte, married her (July 1857), and took her off to Vienna, Venice, and Milan. They were a handsome and should have been a happy pair, had they not been doomed to tragedy by the ambitions of others. In February 1857 Francis-Joseph tried to ease the burden of his unpopularity in northern Italy by appointing Maximilian Governor of Lombardy and Venetia, where for two

years he attempted to mitigate a policy of repression which only grew worse as Louis and Cavour plotted their campaign of 'liberation'. 'If it were not for my religious duties (he wrote to his mother Sophia in the autumn of 1858) I should long since have left this land of misery, where one is doubly depressed by having to act as the representative of an inactive government with no ideas, which one's judgment tries in vain to defend . . . Only one voice is heard now — that of indignation and disapproval: it pervades the whole country, and I stand impotent and alone before it. I am not afraid, for that is not the way of the Habsburgs, but I am silent and ashamed.' An impossible situation ended when, on the day before the Austrian ultimatum to Piedmont (April 19th, 1859) Francis-Joseph relieved his brother of his Governorship, to concentrate political and military control in the hands of General Giulai.[25]

Max and Carlotta (as she was generally called) consoled themselves by building a fantastic castle at Miramar on the Gulf of Trieste and restoring a ruined monastery on a lovely island near Ragusa. But before the end of the year they were off on their travels again, to Gibraltar, Tangier, Madeira, and Brazil. They then settled down to an outwardly untroubled existence at Miramar; but it was known that the marriage was already endangered by Carlotta's childlessness and Max's infidelities; so that it was perhaps a relief when in October 1861 an invitation came to them from Vienna to accept the throne of Mexico. It was an opportunity to make a fresh start in a new world.

If Maximilian was the dupe of Habsburg pride and Napoleonic ambition, he did not go to Mexico unwillingly or unwarned. He sincerely accepted an opportunity to recreate for the Habsburgs a Holy Roman Empire in the New World. But he was Liberal enough to listen to the advice of his father-in-law Leopold, who had himself refused two kingdoms (one of them this very Mexico), and to insist that the invitation to rule must come from the Mexican people: 'nothing (he said) but the clear and distinctly expressed will of the country itself can make me determine upon it'. But how could the Mexican people, exploited by rival parties and distracted by civil war, express any will of its own?[26]

The difficulty was arbitrarily solved by the French general Forey, who, replacing Lorencez in the spring of 1863, and with forces raised to 27,000 men, occupied Puebla and Mexico City (June 10th), set up a conservative Junta and a Provisional Regency, and summoned

an Assembly of Notables. This body proclaimed a monarchy, and offered the crown to Maximilian in the name of a nation which remained unconsulted and unconcerned. Louis suppressed reproachful memories of 1799 and 1848: Maximilian, always an optimist, hoped that he would be able to win what was still so evidently lacking of popular support. Perhaps the deciding voice was that of Rome, which spoke both from Paris and Vienna, denouncing Juárez' 'attacks on the Church', and turning a dynastic and commercial adventure (not for the first time in Papal history) into a Catholic crusade. So on April 10th, 1864, Maximilian accepted the crown, and two months later entered the capital of his new Empire. 'The undertaking is a perilous one', wrote King Leopold to Queen Victoria, 'but if it succeeds it will be one of the greatest and most useful of our time. He (Max) has a great wish to distinguish himself, and to get out of his present *dolce far niente*; Charlotte is not opposed to it; she is very venturesome, and would go with Max to the end of the world: she will be of the greatest use to him; and if success there is to be, much will be owing to her.'[27]

Louis was thus fully committed to an enterprise in which he only half believed, and which became more embarrassing every day. Bazaine, France's best general, now superseded Forey, and with 34,000 men under his command 'pacified' a great part of the country: his victories were celebrated in the Paris press, and his troops received the last military medal issued under the Empire. Mexico, like Egypt in 1798, received a scientific Mission. Maximilian and Carlotta, whether from the noisy and uncomfortable National Palace in Mexico City or from the almost Italian beauty of Chapultepec Castle, did their best to popularize their regime and to spread enlightenment and liberal institutions in a country accustomed to tyranny and superstition. 'We trust in God and are well content', Maximilian wrote home: 'We are helped on all sides with touching affection . . . There is deep joy in the thought that one is serving humanity, and that I can contribute a few drops of oil to the great lamp of enlightenment . . . I am living in a free country, where principles prevail undreamt of by you at home.' But Carlotta, who was not her father's daughter for nothing, wrote to Eugénie: 'There is room for a monarchy in this country; . . . none the less it remains a gigantic experiment; for one has to struggle against deserts and distances, lack of roads and utter chaos . . . Things will go well if Your Majesties stand by us; . . . but it is an appalling task; for when

a country has spent forty years of its existence destroying all it possessed of resources and government, it cannot be put right in a day.'[28]

But would their Majesties stand by them? It was possible, perhaps, in the strangeness of a foreign country and the daily business of government, to forget how precarious was the Imperial regime, and how dependent on French support. In Paris every difficulty that Maximilian had to face was magnified by distance, by doubts as to the wisdom of the undertaking, and by rival demands upon Louis' interests and resources. The army, for instance. How long could France afford the sacrifice and expense of 34,000 men squandered overseas? In March 1864, when Bazaine boasted that the 'pacification' of Mexico was complete, Maximilian had been induced to sign the Treaty of Miramar, by which Louis undertook to maintain a force of 20,000 men in Mexico until 1867, and a Foreign Legion until 1873, whilst Maximilian promised to pay the whole cost of the expedition, and to be responsible for the recovery of the debts for which it had been undertaken. This would mean sacrificing the whole revenue of the country – even supposing it could be collected – for several years; and already the Mexican budget showed an annual deficit of over two million pounds. Mexican loans launched by the Bank of France could never fill this gulf. Rome was bitterly disappointed at the failure, indeed the refusal, of Maximilian to recover the Church lands and revenues alienated under Juárez's regime; and Louis was once more distracted between his Liberalism and his obligations to the Catholics. Quarrels which had broken out between Bazaine and his generals, and between the army and the government, were reflected at the Tuileries. Meanwhile the settlement of Mexico was hampered by frontier incidents: to the south, encouraged by the prospect of a neighbouring Catholic empire under French protection, the states of Guatemala and Nicaragua started a sanguinary war with Salvador and Honduras: to the north, refugees from the Confederate territories were helping the 'rebels' with arms and ammunition, till it became increasingly plain that Louis could no longer count upon American indifference to the creation of a new power in the south. He remembered his own attempts to prevent the unification of Italy, and was afraid.[29]

The situation at home, too, what with the Polish insurrection in 1863 and the Schleswig-Holstein crisis of 1864, was by now growing so dangerous that when the politicians and the press clamoured for

the evacuation of Mexico Louis made the non-payment of the debts under the treaty of 1864 an excuse, and ordered the withdrawal of the French forces in 1866-67. Maximilian could have abdicated and come home: but he was a Habsburg and had, on Francis-Joseph's insistence, abandoned all claim to the family succession. Carlotta, as a last resort, hurried back to Europe (July 1866), and appealed to Louis, to Victor Emmanuel, and to the Pope, driven almost out of her mind by anxiety and the disappointment of all her hopes. For three days before she sailed the battle of Sadowa had begun the last stage in the fall of the Second Empire; and no one cared what might be happening in Mexico.

The news, when it came, was as tragic as could be. In February 1867 Bazaine finally left the country. Maximilian, struggling on alone with a few followers, was besieged in Querétaro, captured and shot (June 19th), gallant and optimistic to the last. Louis heard of it whilst he was distributing prizes awarded at the grand *Exposition* of 1867. Maximilian's body was brought back to Vienna, and laid by the side of that of the Duc de Reichstadt. Carlotta survived on the edge of insanity until, outliving both Louis and Eugénie, she died in 1927 at the age of eighty-six.[30]

7

Whatever the verdict on other foreign adventures of the Second Empire, Louis cannot be denied an important part in one scheme of lasting international importance — the construction of the Suez Canal. Though the idea of joining the Mediterranean and the Red Sea 'suggested itself to all the great men who have ruled over or passed through Egypt, including Sesostris, Alexander, Caesar, and the Arab conqueror Amrou', it was Bonaparte in 1798 who first seriously surveyed the ground, and believed that the work could be done; and it was through reading the report of Bonaparte's engineer Lepère that in 1832 Ferdinand de Lesseps, a young man of twenty attached to the French Consulate at Cairo, was fired by ambition to carry out the undertaking. But it was not till more than fifty years after the French retreat from Egypt (1801) that the accession of a new Viceroy, Abbas Pasha, and the enterprise of Linant and Mougel, the local directors of canal and barrage works, encouraged him to bring the project before the governments and financiers of Europe. Armed with a concession from the Viceroy (November

30th, 1854) he spent five years in persistent appeals for support: it was not till April 1859 that work on the canal was begun.[31]

There were sufficient reasons why these five years, more than others, should be unfavourable to de Lesseps' design. From March 1854 till March 1856 Britain and France were engaged with Turkey against Russia in the Crimean War. The Peace of Paris in 1856 was followed by the French annexation of Savoy and Nice, and an outbreak of suspicion and hostility against Louis, especially in England, which made him unwilling to oppose British policy in the Near East. But in January 1858 Orsini's attempt on Louis' life led to the declaration of his intention to liberate Italy, and a month later Palmerston, whose unique influence had been thrown against the Canal scheme, resigned; in the same year Stratford de Redcliffe's equally hostile control over the Turkish Government came to an end. It was not surprising that de Lesseps seized the opportunity. By this time, too, the foolishness of the Palmerston-Stratford opposition to the Canal — attacked in Parliament by Gladstone on economic grounds — had been demonstrated by the difficulty of transporting British troops across Egypt (by rail from Alexandria to Cairo and Suez) during the Indian Mutiny (1857).[32]

If, in spite of interviews with Clarendon and Palmerston, a communication to *The Times*, letters to Cobden, and a circular to Members of Parliament, de Lesseps had got little support in England (the list of twenty-four 'friends and supporters' that he circulated in 1856 included only six English names) he had much more success in Paris, where such important people as Walewski, Thiers, and Rothschild were on his side. More than this: Louis himself, as the author of the Nicaraguan Canal project, could not fail to be interested: Benedetti had told de Lesseps so in 1855; and on the day that peace was signed in 1856 he had an interview with the Emperor. All the plenipotentiaries, he reported afterwards to Thouvenel, the French ambassador to the Porte (April 6th, 1856), had declared in favour of the Canal, 'with the exception, of course, of the English'; 'now, therefore, the Emperor holds the key of the position, and he will know the right moment to act'. Three years later, when the 400,000 shares forming the capital of the Suez Canal Company were allotted (January 1st, 1859), more than half were taken up by France, and none by England.

Equally important, perhaps, was the interest that Eugénie took in the scheme. She advised de Lesseps when in London to approach

the East India Company; and he wrote to her (August 17th, 1855) saying that he had done so, apparently with results favourable enough to be reported to the Emperor.[33] Writing to the Empress' private secretary on October 7th, de Lesseps said that 'the intervention of the Emperor will increase his popularity at home and his influence abroad'; and added, 'I said at the last meeting of our Board that the Empress had been our guardian angel, and that she would be for the union of the two seas what Isabella the Catholic was for the discovery of America. We have therefore chosen November 15th, the feast of St. Eugénie, for our first general meeting of shareholders.' It was Louis who, in 1865, secured from the Porte the *firman* without which the work could not proceed; and at the opening ceremony on November 17th, 1869, after a ceremonial blessing of the canal locks by Mohammedan, Greek, Coptic, and Catholic clergy, and a grand illumination of Port Said, the Empress Eugénie in the Imperial yacht *l'Aigle*, a modern Cleopatra, led a procession of forty ships through the canal. At Cairo the opening was celebrated by the first production of Verdi's opera *Aida*. So another Napoleonic idea became a fact of history.[34]

In a leading article on the day of the opening *The Times*, without mentioning Louis' name, and doing its best to excuse British opposition to the scheme, hailed the Canal as 'a great achievement', and said that, whatever its future might be, its completion ought 'to call forth unqualified admiration, and to make us look upon this day as one of the most memorable dates of this wonder-working nineteenth century'.

Louis was an adventurer, too, in a land of ideas unexplored by his uncle's eighteenth-century mind. As a result of his experiences on the Italian battlefields he patronized the work of Henri Dunant, and promoted the Geneva Convention of 1864 which set up the international Red Cross Society; and when, at the *Exposition Universelle* of 1867 he granted a site to the English Evangelical Society, and accepted a Bible from the Society of Friends (and for the Empress the *Life and Philanthropic Labours of Elizabeth Fry*), he proved himself an unexpected pioneer of religious toleration.[35]

THE LIBERAL (1860-1869)

HAM. Why, look you now, how unworthy a thing you make of me. You would play upon me; you would seem to know my stops; you would pluck out the heart of my mystery; you would sound me from my lowest note to the top of my compass; and there is much music, excellent voice, in this little organ, yet cannot you make it speak.

Hamlet, III, ii

I

FROM the *dahabieh* on which she voyaged up the Nile in November 1869 Eugénie wrote long letters home. 'My dearest Louis (says one), I am writing on my way up the Nile . . . I get news of you and Louis (the Prince Imperial) every day by telegraph. It is a wonderful happiness for me to be in touch with a friendly shore by this thread which binds me to all I love . . . I was worried all yesterday by knowing that you were in Paris without me; but I see from your message that all went off well. I think that there is no reason for discouragement. Of course I am too far away and too ignorant of the business to speak so; but I am deeply convinced that a consistent policy is the only real strength. I have no fondness for impulsive acts (*à-coups*), and I am convinced that one cannot have two *coups d'état* in one reign . . . One must keep one's mental character in repair (*refaire un moral*) as one does an enfeebled constitution: a fixed idea ends by impoverishing the best organized brain. I have experienced this myself; and I would wish to put out of my memory everything in my life which has tarnished the bright colours of my illusions. My life is over, but I can live again in my son, and I think the truest joys are those which come through his heart into my own. . . .'

All the tragedy of Eugénie's disappointed hopes is in this letter, and more than one would have expected, perhaps, of the strength which she supplied, during the last years of the Empire, to Louis' enfeebled body and will. She has come to put his *idée constante* on a par with her own *illusions*. The Bonapartist plan of *coups d'état*, the reliance upon inspired *à-coups*, has proved a failure. The only safe course is *la suite dans les idées*, that is, the gradual introduction of liberal and constitutional changes which will preserve the Empire for their son.[1]

Historians like to divide their subject into definite periods by significant dates. The Empire which began in December 1852 is commonly held to have reached a first peak of success at the Peace of Paris in March 1856, and a second at the Treaty of Zürich in November 1859, then to have entered into a decline, leading to the crisis of Sadowa in July 1866, and the catastrophe of Sedan in September 1870. These divisions may be accepted. But how do they link up with the internal development of the Empire? This is commonly divided into two periods – the Authoritarian Empire, 1852-1859, and the Liberal Empire, 1860-69. This partition is justified by the Liberal concessions made in November 1860, November 1861, and January 1867; but it gives too little significance to the elections in June 1857, May 1863, and May 1869 – political barometer readings of the state of the national atmosphere – and it does not bring out the influence of such events as the Orsini plot (January 1858), the Anglo-French commercial treaty (January 1860), the Polish insurrection (January 1863), or the death of Morny (March 1865) upon the political situation. In fact the character of the Empire was changing all the time: there was no one moment at which authoritarianism ended and liberalism began: Louis himself had always intended his regime to conform throughout to a prefixed pattern – *la suite dans les idées napoléoniennes*. That it failed to do so was his tragedy. Why it failed to do so – how far through his own failings, how far from circumstances outside his control – has to be inquired.

The pattern which Louis imagined himself to be imposing upon the country was a misinterpretation of the First Empire in the light of 1815 – the year whose experiences had, even in his mother's mind, nearly effaced all that went before. He supposed, as Napoleon himself had almost come to believe at St. Helena, that the *acte additionnel* was not a temporary concession to win the support of the Liberals for an attempt to renew the dictatorship, but a step in the natural development of that dictatorship into a constitutional monarchy. Authoritarianism was to give way to Liberalism. Liberty was to crown the edifice of the Empire. This misreading of Napoleon's real mind was conscious and deliberate; for Louis well knew that little more would have been heard of the *acte additionnel* if Napoleon had won at Waterloo. He now found himself faced by much the same dilemma. The unpopularity of the July Monarchy, the Parisian fear of Red Revolution, and the power of the name

Napoleon amongst the mass of the people all pointed towards a Second Empire rather than another constitutional monarchy. It would have required a clearer conviction and a stronger will than Louis ever possessed to initiate at once in 1852 the transition from despotism to liberalism, from force to freedom, which he professed as part of the Napoleonic idea. He found that the authoritarian Empire *worked*; and he set about devising ways of making its authority acceptable, putting off the difficult day when, whether acceptable or not, it was *ex hypothesi* to be liberalized. This interim policy would satisfy the army with foreign adventures, placate the Church by garrisoning Rome, win bourgeois support by an industrial drive and a reduction of tariffs, conciliate Parisian opposition by 'clearing the slums' and creating new building sites, and raise the whole public morale by showy fêtes, expensive court functions, and international *expositions*.

But the weakness of an interim policy is that it deals with the surface symptoms of disease, not with its root causes. It was impossible to indulge the army in military adventures without rousing the hostility of the European powers. Louis' Italian policy after 1859 was no longer acceptable to his Catholic supporters, who knew that he would take the first opportunity to leave the Pope to his fate. It was difficult to favour 'big business' and the factory-owners without ignoring the claims of the workers, and playing into the hands of socialist agitators. The 'Haussmannizing' of Paris created those housing difficulties and financial scandals with which Zola's *La Curée* shocked the next generation – the generation that had to pay for the rebuilding of the capital. Fêtes and festivities were patronized by foreigners or *nouveaux riches*, whilst the old aristocracy stood aloof: court extravagance reminded people more of the Bourbon Monarchy than of the Napoleonic Empire. The *Exposition* of 1855 compared poorly with the Great Exhibition of 1851; that of 1867 was overshadowed by the ill omens of Sadowa and Querétaro.

During all these years Louis was gradually losing the vision which had inspired him in 1836, in 1840, and in 1848. His natural lethargy, whipped into action by a conspiracy or a crusade, wilted under safety and success. Accustomed to hear advice from many different quarters before making up his mind on a course of action, he now found his mind being made up for him by the Empress, or by the counsellor of the moment; he discovered that, instead of the enthusiasm of his old associates, he now had to reckon on the disloyal or

divergent policies of independent ministers. And with the fading of his vision the will inspired by it was weakening, till only the instinct for intrigue remained — intrigue more and more in the cause of the dynasty than of the country; intrigue to preserve the shadow of autocracy by liberal measures which under stronger control might have passed as an advance, not a retreat; whilst every concession encouraged the Opposition to demand more, and made the 'Liberal Empire' a theft, not a gift. So the imperial pattern was reversed, and appeared, like a tapestry turned back to front, a meaningless jumble of knots and colours to which the pattern-maker himself had lost the clue.

Already, in the early years of the Second Empire, its weaknesses began to appear, and opposition to be organized. There were things which even a 'Man of Destiny' could not do; persons whom even Louis' charm and kindness — weapons so unlike those of his great predecessor — could not conciliate. The cloak of despotism had never fitted the shoulders of a visionary humanitarian, a friend of the outlawed and the oppressed. Louis' policy, like his mind, was divided between his mission and his career, his schemes for the betterment of France and Europe and the security of the position which would enable him to carry them out. The Empire, he thought, must be at once repressive and progressive. It must use all the powers that the panic and proscription of 1848-51 had put into his hands to maintain order; and it must exploit all the opportunities offered by an expanding world-market to the most thrifty and hard-working people in Western Europe. By one way or another every class in the community must be kept contented and co-operative. This was indeed a Bourbon idea: Louis XIV would have understood it, Colbert would have exploited it. It was also a Napoleonic idea: this part of the *Idées napoléoniennes* was not legendary, but true to fact. Unhappily Louis was neither a *Grand Monarque* nor a *Napoléon le Grand*; France had grown fifty years older since Brumaire; and the Second Empire could only be, like most sequels, something of an anti-climax. Louis' 'enlightened despotism' came a century too late in European history.

Yet it could all be looked at in another way. Louis was a man of vision, surrounded by commonplace minds: a man with a mission amongst compromisers and careerists; a man of mystery whom no one rightly understood. His visions were distorted into programmes, his mission faded away into diplomatic agreements, his

mystery was made the excuse for hesitations and mistakes. Yet something in him remained unspoilt, unpublicized — an integrity of mind, a generous purpose of well-doing, which put to shame the policy he was driven to by circumstances and associates. He was a man to be pitied more than to be blamed.

2

The army, the force behind the name that put Louis in power, had good cause to congratulate itself. The Bourbon regime, restored by sufferance of the Allies, and reacting against the militarism of the First Empire, had dismissed the officers and disbanded the men of the *grande armée*. Louis-Philippe's economical and unadventurous policy had not ventured on more than a colonial campaign. Now that a Bonaparte was once more at the head of the state the army had recovered its ascendancy. In two European campaigns, fought under its old colours, it had re-established a great part of its renown. Promotion for a time became more rapid, and retirement more profitable under a law of 1853. Under a law of 1855 *remplacement* (the avoidance of conscription by payment of substitutes) was standardized at a fixed sum, and the proceeds went to bettering the pay and pensions of old soldiers. A new code, two years later, secured a fairer trial and lighter penalties for military offences. The *médaille militaire* rewarded courage in the field. Though his generals thought poorly of Louis' military accomplishments, the rank and file were proud to be once more under the command of an Emperor, and one who, unlike his Bourbon and Orléans predecessors, knew how to sit a horse.

The army of the Second Empire, however magnificent externally, was still the 'old army' of the Bourbon restoration and the *lois Gouvion-Saint-Cyr* of 1818, recruited either by volunteers or by partial conscription (*tirage au sort*); there was no full conscription till 1872. It was a closed corporation of poor men, with an increasingly professional spirit; most of its officers risen from the ranks, with a minority of those who could afford to purchase commissions, and a few aristocrats who entered it no longer as a calling but as a career. Owing to the expenses of a Military College training the highest commands were barred to those without means, and the majority of the lower commands were filled by men of the N.C.O. type, without education, initiative or ideas. The dullness and dissipation of

garrison duty in provincial towns increased the inner degeneration of the service.

These faults were to be dangerous in 1859 and fatal in 1870. But already the Crimean campaign had shown up weaknesses which no one had the courage to remedy. Marshal Vaillant, when Minister of War in 1855, made no secret of his inability to carry out reforms which he knew to be necessary. 'There is not a single man', he told an English friend, 'who dare tell the nation that its army is rotten to the core, that there is not a general who knows as much as a mere captain in the Austrian and Prussian armies; and if he had the courage to tell the nation, he would be hounded out of the country, his life would be made a burden to him.'

Nevertheless the army enjoyed immense prestige, from the moment when, in 1848, it saved Paris and France from 'Red Revolution', and became the guardian of public order, of national safety: not, be it noted, of Jacobinism, nor of the Republic — that had been the role of the now discredited and disbanded National Guard. And this prestige was perforce identified with the Empire, which Louis had founded on the appeal to the party of Order in 1848, and which rested upon the national fear of another resurgence of Jacobinism. Meanwhile the anti-militarism which had been popular under the Restoration became the heresy of the Opposition, and the fad of a literary clique — to disappear when in 1870 the army became the champion of national *revanche*, or again, in the years after 1870, when it once more saved the country from the Commune, and became the symbol of national regeneration.[2]

3

The eighteen years of the Second Empire were for the French Church a period of official favour and outward prosperity between the lean years of Louis-Philippe and of the Third Republic. For a number of reasons the Church had backed the revolution of 1848: because the movement was led by men who admired Pius IX, or shared Chateaubriand's romantic version of Christianity, and could cry in one breath *Vive le Christ! Vive la liberté! Vive Pie IX!*; because it hoped for liberties of association and education which had been denied it since 1830; because the mass of the country clergy, peasant-born and peasant-minded, hoped for a social as well as a political Utopia. The Republic of 1848 was supported by the

journalism of the Papalist Montalembert (*Le Correspondant*), the Ultramontane Veuillot (*L'Univers*), the Christian Socialist Buchez (*L'Atelier*), and by the pulpit eloquence of Lacordaire. When the elections came on, country *curés* might be seen heading processions of their parishioners to the poll.

But the very success of the revolution of 1848, and particularly the mass demonstrations and democratic harangues to which it gave rise in the capital, led to a reaction. Not amongst the Catholic rank and file in Paris, who remembered 1793 and hoped, as always, for higher wages, more food, and better housing; nor in the provinces, where any new government in the capital, the centre of authority, was expected to be better than any old one; but amongst the bourgeois-born episcopate, and bourgeois-thinking politicians. To them a political revolution, calculated to favour Church interests, was acceptable: a social revolution, trailing clouds of Jacobinism, with threats of confiscation of Church property, persecution of priests, and secular control, was an abomination. The popular demonstrations of March 17th, April 16th, and May 15th were alarming enough to timid republicans. The June days, with their street-fighting and bloodshed, in which the democratic Archbishop of Paris lost his life, led to an almost unanimous reaction of the Church party (as distinct from the Catholic masses) towards any authority which could restore order and safeguard the Church as an institution. And as trustee for The Faith, which was put forward — as it has been more than once in later days — as the panacea for social ills. 'I only know of one means of making the poor respect property,' declared Montalembert: 'they must be made to believe in God': and Veuillot, 'Poverty is the rule for a section of society; they must submit to a divine law.'

Consequently when Louis Napoleon put forward a candidature based both on the promise of Order and on the appeal of his name to the people, he secured an overwhelming majority — a success made the more sure by the pledge he gave to Montalembert that he would allow 'freedom of education' and defend the Temporal Power of the Papacy. And when he became Emperor, both sides to the bargain — an ominous one, as always, between State and Church — stood to gain and to lose. The Church, by its alliance with the bourgeois party of order, the rich propertied and business community, gained endowments and local patronage; by the support of the administration, fresh facilities for schools and monastic establishments; and by

the Loi Falloux, freedom to set up secondary as well as primary schools. Once again, as in Spain before the Civil War, government troops took part in religious processions. Diocesan bishops became as important as prefects of departments, and often more powerful. *Cabarets* were closed by government order during mass, and no anti-clerical literature might be sold in the streets.

But though the passing of the Constitution had been celebrated by an open-air mass in the Place de la Concorde, no clerical pressure could secure the abolition of civil marriage, or of the educational monopoly of the *Université*, or of the disciplinary clauses of the Organic Articles, even though compliance with this demand might have brought the Pope to Paris for Louis' coronation. The Napoleonic tradition was still too strong. The Catholic leaders themselves fell apart on this issue, and their political influence was compromised. It was weakened too by the indifference of the vast majority of the faithful, particularly in the countryside, to political and ecclesiastical controversies. To them a priest was a priest, and the mass was the mass. A little extra education, or a small rise in social consideration, might give their conformity an anti-clerical twist; but parish life went on undisturbed, much as it did in England at that time, with the difference that the French parson was not a resident gentleman but an ordained peasant in every parish. There was, during the Second Empire, a curious coincidence between a decline in popular religion and a flourishing of local saintship and visionary appearances: witness the miracles of the Curé d'Ars (d. 1859) and the vision that originated the cult of Lourdes (1858). Superstition was exploited in the name of Catholicism. Outwardly the Church was never so rich or so powerful: inwardly it was losing its hold on the real life of the people.

Louis was an eighteenth-century sceptic, as his uncle had been, and was no less willing to use the Church for his own ends. He knew that its bishops and journalists, though divided on some issues, had great political influence, and would unite against any attack on Church privileges. He knew that the parish clergy controlled the country voters. He was therefore ready to interpret the law liberally where religion was concerned, and to listen to ecclesiastical promptings in foreign as well as home affairs: asserting French rights in the Holy Places of Palestine, protecting the Maronites in Syria, revenging persecuted missionaries in China, or founding a Catholic Empire in Mexico. But in 1860 he was sufficiently angry with the

intransigent attitude of the clericals on the Roman question to risk a policy of retaliation, appointing less ultramontane bishops, limiting the increase of religious orders, stressing secular education, and for six years suppressing Veuillot's extravagant *L'Univers*: yet again three years later, when the elections of 1863 showed a republican recovery, he reversed this policy, making use of the see-saw principle (*politique de bascule*) which had once enabled the Directory to remain in power; so that — in spite of yet another *volte-face* in the educational reforms of Duruy (1865) — the Second Empire ended as it had begun by courting the clerical vote against parliamentarian and especially republican opposition.[3]

4

Louis was not the first French ruler to award economic prosperity as a consolation prize for loss of political liberty. Napoleon had only half succeeded in doing so because his plans for helping French industry and commerce were ruined by the Continental Blockade. Guizot had attempted it, to distract attention from the failure of Louis-Philippe's foreign policy and the suppression of parliamentary privileges; and some of his lieutenants — Fould, Magne, Billaud, Morny himself — were now free to make money out of the new regime: indeed Louis was only too willing that they should employ their dangerous talents 'in the city' rather than 'in Parliament'.

His opportunity and theirs was provided by the establishment of the Empire in 1852. The eighteen years of Louis-Philippe's reign have commonly and not unfairly been described as a period in which the middle classes were encouraged to enrich themselves at the expense of the poor. But the means and methods of enrichment were still elementary. When the revolution came in 1848 there were few big concentrations either of labour or capital: the economic situation was still what it had been in England fifty years earlier, with private banks, family businesses, and local industries, ruled by a bourgeois individualism which only wanted to make enough money for comfortable retirement.

The shock which this system suffered from the events of 1848 was more than offset by the feeling of fresh confidence inspired by the *coup d'état* of 1851. French economy, like French religion and French culture, always thrived upon political centralization, and an orderly administration: it needed discipline and direction. It was this aspect of the Napoleonic Idea that Louis had most clearly understood and

most firmly grasped. He was determined to use the whole power of government in the cause of national — not sectional, not class — prosperity.

Louis himself believed it was one of the duties of government to finance public works. 'It is better', he had written in *L'extinction du pauperisme*, 'to invest 300 millions in organizing employment than 120 in building new prisons'; and in *Les idées napoléoniennes*, 'Government exists in order to help society to overcome the obstacles to its progress . . . It is the beneficent mainspring of every social organism'. But how would the necessary capital be provided for such operations on a national scale? It would need a financial revolution. The government loans of the old regime had been taken up, right down to 1847, by private banking firms, of which the Rothschilds were the most famous, and the use to which the money might be put was limited by their interests — those of an international plutocracy in close touch with the old dynasties of Europe. A new dynasty and a new national development required larger resources and a freer hand in using them. It was for this purpose that in 1852 the Brothers Péreira — a name not unknown in the financial affairs of the Revolution — founded the first *Crédit mobilier*, which did not limit itself to state loans, but laid itself out to finance industrial societies; and, in order to extend its influence beyond anything attainable by the old-fashioned family banks, offered its shares to the general public. The only danger was of over-expansion; and when the expected crisis came in 1867 the Rothschilds said, 'We told you so'. But for fifteen crucial years the *Crédit mobilier* and its partner, the *Crédit foncier*, supplemented by the *Comptoir d'Escompte* and many *Sociétés de Dépôt*, and backed by the *Banque de France*, encouraged and financed industry and agriculture, and made Paris the financial centre of Europe.

Meanwhile the Rothschilds were not missing the opportunity for financial expansion. Their *Réunion financière* challenged Péreira's group of banks. Their protégé Talabot operated on a big scale in railways and iron-works. Their international connections enabled them to take over mines in Austria, railways in Switzerland, north Italy, and eastern Spain, and to form a company for the exploitation of Algeria. The industrial recovery under the Second Empire was not merely of domestic importance: it was becoming imperial.[4]

Though special war loans were raised to meet the expenses of the Crimea, Italy, Mexico and the rearmament of 1868, the wealth of

the country increased in greater proportion than its taxation; moreover there was a growing disposition to 'trust the government' — a government based on the 'party of Order' — with savings which under previous regimes would have been hoarded; as was shown later by the public subscription to the war loan of 1870, and the speedy payment of the war indemnity of 1871. There were no doubt world causes of this prosperity, such as the application of new discoveries and techniques to industry and agriculture; but that so much progress was made in face of middle-class individualism and the conservatism of employers and workers was chiefly due (after fifty years' freedom from invasion) to the impulse given by the Emperor and his agents.

Once the capital was found — and found in the pockets of the people — there need be no limit to national prosperity. The railways in particular benefited by this policy. In 1848 there were only a little over 2000 miles laid down in all France, and those had been constructed at haphazard, according to financial opportunity or local demand, and were running at a loss. Now the amalgamation of the existing lines provided the beginnings of a railway system resembling the road-system which Louis XIV imposed upon the old Roman roads, with Paris the heart of communications as it was of government, and the centre of exchange between the Rhineland, the Channel coast, and the Mediterranean. Most of the present main routes were laid down in the 'fifties, taking the place of the old devious canal and coastal traffic. Not that the state itself contributed much directly to the cost of these works; the whole expenditure on *travaux extraordinaires* in the ten years 1851-60 did not exceed £30 millions; but state patronage and guarantee were invaluable. And the railways were, as so often, the key to economic development. The improvement of communications increased trade, helped industry, and provided employment. The economic recovery which had begun in 1851-52 persisted, based upon an increasingly wide public investment and the 'easy money' provided by the new banks. Even the military expenses of two wars did not seriously compromise the economic prosperity of the Empire — a prosperity marked by bigger banks, bigger businesses, increased organization of industry, and international commitments — of which the two Paris *Expositions* were the symbol and the advertisement.[5]

The Emperor himself took great personal interest in all this. Though he had a certain weakness for charlatans and showy schemes,

he was genuinely concerned when the progress of the railways was held up by a shortage in the supply of rails, or by delays in the improvement of the ports; he intervened at a crisis in the affairs of the *Grand Central* in 1855; and when the agricultural interests in the country seemed to have been overlooked by comparison with the industrial interests he initiated a policy for the countryside which included agricultural committees, agricultural shows, improvement in the breed of horses, cattle, and sheep (with new strains imported from England), preservation of forests, reclamation of waste lands, model farms, and increased production of corn and wine.[6]

But the matter which he took most to heart — for it belonged to the essence of the Napoleonic idea, and affected the capital of the Empire and the international prestige of the country — was the improvement and embellishment of Paris. In spite of some betterment in the lighting and policing of the city made under the Revolution, in spite of Napoleon's fine new buildings and monuments, the capital was still in the 'fifties a medieval city of narrow streets and crowded tenements which British visitors contrasted unfavourably even with Edinburgh, and which, time after time, had shown itself better adapted to the building of barricades than to the preservation of public order and safety. The programme entrusted to the masterful Haussmann when he was brought from Bordeaux to be *préfet* of the Seine department in 1853 has indeed been too often represented as intended to safeguard Paris against another 1848 by driving wide boulevards for the passage of troops and the deployment of artillery through the slums. This was no doubt in Louis' mind; but, he was thinking also of the centre of his new national railway system; and, as Persigny said, 'his main aim throughout was to carry out big works in Paris, to improve the living conditions of the working classes, to destroy unhealthy districts, and to make the capital the most beautiful city in the world'. Nothing was to stand in the way of a grandiose and long-term reconstruction: neither the immense expense involved, nor the rising scale of compensation paid to owners dispossessed of their property, nor a displacement of the poorer classes which so checked the recent tendency to crowd into the capital that the population of Paris at the end of the Second Empire was nearer that of the eighteenth than that of the twentieth century. In five years new streets, new gardens, new bridges, and new drains transformed the centre of

Paris into something like its present stateliness of buildings and open spaces. Soon (1858) it became a question of the suburbs, and Haussmann's 'Greater Paris' (*deuxième réseau*) was to cost so much that without the Emperor's support it would never have been carried through. In his *L'An deux mille quatre cent quarante* (1775) Mercier had imagined what Paris could be in 700 years' time. Louis might well boast that he had made it so in eighty.

Such achievements of enlightened despotism might well rouse envy in democratic countries. 'The Galignani of yesterday', wrote the great philanthropist Shaftesbury to the perfect civil servant Chadwick on July 18th, 1853, 'contained a programme of improvements which makes my hair stand on end. Every working man that lives will on seeing these results shout *Vive la Despotisme! A bas les gouvernements libres!*'[7]

Haussmannisme was still in its early stages when the *Exposition* of 1855 brought to Paris visitors from all Europe, and particularly from England. But there was already much to admire. 'Paris is signally beautified', Prince Albert reported to King Leopold (August 29th) 'by the Rue de Rivoli, the Boulevard de Strasbourg, the completion of the Louvre, the great open square in front of the Hôtel de Ville, the clearing away of all the small houses which surrounded Nôtre Dame, by the fine Napoleonic barracks, the completion of the Palais de Justice, and restoration of the Sainte Chapelle, and especially by the laying out of the ornamental grounds in the Bois de Boulogne, which really may be said to vie with the finest English parks. How all this could have been done in so short a time no one comprehends.' Such praise carries special weight from one who distrusted Louis personally, but would himself have enjoyed reconstructing London, and could appreciate the problems faced and overcome by a fellow-planner.

Jerrold, the first English biographer of Louis Napoleon, pointed out with some glee thirty years later that 'Victor Hugo (the sworn enemy of the Second Empire) dwells in a fashionable quarter of his beloved city which had no existence when he went into exile. He tells every foreign visitor who calls upon him that there have been three cities in the world – Athens, Rome, Paris; when he says Paris he forgets the sovereign who made her what she is, and laid the foundations of that matchless city of the future . . . He spurns the genius to whose glory the Arc de Triomphe was raised, and the nephew of the great Captain who drew a new Paris around it.'[8]

Thus the army, the Church, the financiers, the Paris landlords, the foreign visitors — all had good words for the new regime. What of the common people, on whose instinctive loyalty Louis, in the long run, most relied? They were no more anxious than before to be conscripted for the army. It mattered little to them whether the priest to whom they went for confession or mass agreed with what was being done at Rome. Their concern, as always, was for food, health, wages, and a roof over their heads. It so happened that the years of Louis' greatest success abroad — those of the Crimean War and the Peace of Paris — were also years of food shortage, floods, and cholera. A succession of bad harvests in 1853-56 brought a return of troubles which had beset every French government, whether monarchical, republican, or imperial, since the population outpaced the production of the countryside. Some of the old false remedies were avoided: there was now no bar on imports of grain, no attempt to enact a *maximum* of food-prices: supplies were rushed in, obstacles to distribution removed, bread subsidized, the crisis gradually overcome. The floods in the Garonne, Rhône, and Loire valleys in 1855-56 roused Louis to special energy: he visited the flooded districts, distributed charity, headed subscriptions to make good the losses of cattle and crops, and insisted on steps being taken to prevent similar disasters in the future. As though these troubles were not enough, a cholera epidemic between 1853 and 1855 caused nearly 150,000 deaths in various parts of France, and 11,000 in Paris alone in 1854. Again, there could be no doubt of Louis' or Eugénie's personal concern for the victims.

5

But no expedients to meet special crises, no personal charities or sympathetic speeches are substitutes for a consistent policy and an efficient administration. Louis' original idea, which he never gave up, was that under a strong government the old antagonism of social class and economic status could be reconciled; the bourgeois wolf would dwell with the working-class lamb, the capitalist leopard lie down with the wage-earning kid. How was the working class to become confident enough to enter such a partnership? It must, Louis said, form associations, educate itself, and learn self-discipline. 'Nowadays (he had written) the day of class-rule is over, the day of mass-rule has begun. The masses must be organized so that they can

formulate their will, and disciplined so that they can be instructed and enlightened as to their own interests.'

But in practice, and because in Paris, which had put him into power, the workers were suspected of revolutionary republicanism, it was inevitable that the knowledge and capital required by any scheme for economic development should come from the bourgeoisie, and that the national prosperity that Louis foreshadowed should be mortgaged to capitalism. Academic Liberals such as Morny and Prince Napoleon could 'prove logically and sensibly to the unfortunate that the rich were not the cause of their sufferings; teach them to understand the working of the social machine; prove to them that social inequality is a law of nature, that there will always be workers and shirkers, strong and weak, governors and governed; that a regime of order is what suits them best, and that there was never an age in which the rich were more preoccupied with the poor'. But the prophets of the working class regarded the Emperor as the head of a political system which persecuted republicanism, and as the patron of an economic system which victimized the poor.[8]

Such certainly was the opinion of the ablest and most independent socialist of the day. 'People are never tired of saying', wrote Proudhon, 'that the success of Napoleon III is due to the memory of his uncle: what they too seldom see is that his failure also comes from his respect for this tradition. The whole analogy between the two Emperors was that the one had the duty of consummating and protecting an old revolution, and the other the duty of inaugurating and forwarding a new one. The one purpose of the counter-revolutionaries has therefore been to cry havoc on the republican party, and to proclaim Louis the saviour of society, because, with the ready connivance of bourgeoisie, nobles, clergy, etc., he crushed and scattered Socialism . . . The First Consul reopened the churches and re-established public worship. But after fifty years of philosophy and rationalism I make bold to say that to exalt the Church is a mere anachronism, as factitious and immoral as the enterprise of Julian the Apostate . . . During the Consulate and Empire the first Napoleon brought about conciliation and concord. In his Councils high dignitaries and royal officials sat side by side with Conventionals and Regicides. But today there is no rallying round the Emperor: instead they allot themselves railways, canals, and mines, banks and privileges; they crowd into the administration, the courts,

the higher commands; they all make themselves master, and leave the Emperor nothing but his entourage (*livrée*) – if one can use such a term of the spies and assassins who surround him.'

It is easy to see that Louis could never hope to please Proudhon, with whom he had had a famous interview in September 1848, nor Louis Blanc, with whom he had exchanged ideas at Ham, nor any other thoroughgoing republican; nor Paris itself, whose capricious and inexorable temper could sometimes be flattered but never cajoled by a Benthamite dictator. Yet there was found amongst his papers at the Tuileries in 1870 the project of a novel in which a Frenchman who had left his country in 1847 returned in 1868 to realize the immense benefits conferred upon France by the Empire. This was Louis' ruling idea. He never ceased to clutch the inviolable shade of social equality and justice which still eludes a less corrupt and prejudiced age. Yet, as so often happens, the end might be betrayed by the means. Paris might be handed over to prosperous builders and land-owning profiteers, its poorer citizens be driven out into the suburbs, and its centre become a place of show and entertainment. It might at last come to be thought too precious to defend against a foreign invader. Workers' associations and meetings might be prohibited in the name of public order, strikes broken to protect the labour market, wages kept down to stimulate production and public works. The Empire might become the victim of its own *élan vital*, the Emperor the prisoner of his dreams of prosperity and progress.

Louis was well aware of what was happening, and would make a fresh effort to right the economic balance in favour of the masses; to make their livelihood cheaper and more abundant; to assimilate their lot to that of their fellow-workers across the Channel. His plans took many forms, not all of them complete or effective: provident societies, old age pensions, accident insurance, co-operative mining, poor men's lawyers and priests (free litigation, free burial), the abolition of the workman's *livret* (identity card), equality of employer and employee before the law, and even a scheme (for which the preliminary work was entrusted to the energetic Mme Cornu) for compulsory State insurance. Meanwhile the Empress patronized hospitals and orphanages, and presided over meetings of a lifeboat league and a society which advanced loans to the workers.[10]

6

But Louis' socialism, always of a Saint-Simonian type, assumed that the prosperity of Labour ultimately depended upon that of Capital; that the lot of the worker could be improved only if trade as a whole prospered. When he came back victorious from Italy in 1859, and reflected how close he had been to war in the Channel or on the Rhine, he announced in a letter printed in the *Moniteur* (January 15th, 1860) a programme of peace abroad and prosperity at home: 'the development of national wealth by a system of good political economy' – a 'New Deal' it would be called nowadays. Its two main heads were to be a tariff treaty with Britain and a drive for agricultural reform.

It was not the first time that the suggestion of an Anglo-French commercial treaty had come from England, and had been seriously considered by the Emperor. In August 1852 Disraeli had hoped to include such a measure in his Budget, with the approval of Malmesbury, and with an assurance from Cowley and Drouyn de Lluys that the French Government would give it favourable consideration; and Sir Thomas Fremantle, Chairman of the Board of Customs, visited Paris for the purpose. But the plan broke down over the difficulty of making reductions of duty to France without doing the same for other countries. Again in December 1858 Disraeli had sent his secretary Earle to Paris to propose a commercial agreement; but Louis had been too absorbed in his Italian designs to do more than promise to make a public statement of his good intentions towards Britain.

As soon as the Italian affair was off his hands, Louis returned to Disraeli's suggestion. He had met Cobden in London just after his escape from Ham, and must have been aware not merely of his Anti-Corn Law campaign (the repeal of the Corn Laws had been carried through Parliament four days before he arrived in London in 1836), but also of the ruling motive behind it – a new impulse towards international and especially Anglo-French peace and friendship. 'They wanted', as John Bright had said, 'not that the Channel should separate this country from France: they hoped and wished that Frenchmen and Englishmen should no longer consider each other as naturally hostile nations.' Free trade, Cobden told his French collaborator Chevalier, 'is God's own method of producing an *entente cordiale* (Cobden was the first to use the phrase in this

context) and no other plan is worth a farthing' (*C'est la méthode de Dieu lui-même pour produire une entente cordiale, et tout autre système ne vaut pas un liard*).[11]

Cobden's visit to France in 1859 was undertaken at the suggestion of his friend Michel Chevalier, the author of *Lettres sur l'organisation du travail*, and with the approval of Gladstone, then Chancellor of the Exchequer, Rouher, Louis' Minister of Commerce, Prince Napoleon, and a few more. It was hoped that Louis would be an easy convert to a plan which appealed to business interests in both countries, and might counteract the suspicion due to the war in Italy and the annexation of Savoy. 'He is an excellent listener (reported Cobden), and seemed to be favourable to Free Trade.' But he was afraid of the Protectionist opposition in the *corps législatif* and Senate, and must therefore make use of his constitutional powers to draw up or revise commercial treaties, and present the Assembly with a *fait accompli*. And so he did (January 23rd, 1860) in a treaty which, when ultimately worked out in detail, reduced tariffs sufficiently to afford a ready and reciprocal market for British 'heavy' and French 'light' goods on opposite sides of the Channel, and in the long run led to improvements in French manufacture which had been held up by the abolition of the Eden Treaty in 1793, and by the Napoleonic wars. But Cobden always believed, and no doubt rightly, that Louis' reasons for agreeing to the treaty were 'nine-tenths political rather than politico-economical, with a view to cement the alliance with this country'. And with this view Disraeli agreed in an important judgment of Louis' intentions which he sent to Lord Derby on January 7th, 1859.[12]

In France the measure had the support of industrialists only so far as it cheapened the supply of raw materials; but it pleased Liberals of every school, and encouraged the workers to push on their programme of 'organization, education, and self-discipline'. The forthcoming London Exhibition of 1862 offered an opportunity of contact with British Trades Unionism which Louis himself encouraged by appointing Prince Napoleon, known to be a friend of Socialists and free traders, as President of the French Section. At any other moment the workers would have accepted royal patronage and expected to have their expenses met by the Government. Now – and it was a significant change of spirit – they elected their 183 representatives and maintained their independence. The discoveries they made as to the better status and wages of British workers issued

in a programme drawn up the same year which was a foundation-deed not only of the French Labour movement, but also of the First International. This, no doubt, went beyond anything that Louis had intended, and threatened the happy alliance of bourgeois and worker, capitalist and wage-earner, that he envisaged as the supporters of the Bonapartist coat of arms. It was not the way in which he had hoped to bring about the extinction of pauperism. But if progress were limited to the original ideas of its planners, the world would see little of it. The greatest advances have been due to the unplanned and unforeseen results of wars, revolutions, and social changes. And in this one Louis played a not unimportant part.[18]

7

That this act of emancipation should have been so long delayed signified two things: on the one hand the success of Louis' combined repressive and progressive policy, and on the other the failure of those who had launched the 'Labour Movement' of 1848 (if it may so be called) to control its course during the ten years that followed. Most of them were, in fact, in exile; some in Belgium, where they could do little more than inspire attacks on Louis in a press which was beyond his censorship; others in England, where Louis himself had so recently been a refugee. They complained and quarrelled, as only political exiles can: Louis Blanc shut himself up in the British Museum to write his history of the Revolution: Victor Hugo from his rock in the Channel Islands hurled insults in prose and verse against *Napoléon le Petit*.

Of those literary Liberals who remained, Lamartine lived in poverty and retirement, and accepted a pension from the Empire before he died in 1859. Michelet, dismissed from his professorship in 1851, abandoned political for natural history, and hymned the beauties of sea and mountain in place of the virtues of the French people. Tocqueville reported to his friend Senior, with the accuracy of a thermometer, every change in the imperial temperature. George Sand, who had corresponded with Louis in prison, and played such a fiery part in 1848, went back to romances of the country-side and the exploitation of her love affairs. Flaubert was prosecuted for publishing *Madame Bovary* (1857). Renan's *Vie de Jésus* led to his dismissal under clerical pressure from the chair of Hebrew at the Collège de France (1863). Not these, but Mérimée, the admirer of Stendhal, the childhood friend of Eugénie, the literary link

between Balzac and Flaubert, was the favourite of the Tuileries. Louis and Eugénie might have poor taste in literature, as they had in music and art; but they were patriots, and a reader of the de Goncourts' *Journal* cannot blame them for disliking literary men who were at heart 'not Frenchmen, but foreigners, full of nostalgia for other lands, other ages', who lost no chance of sneering at the Court and Government, and who lived in an idealistic dream like a character in Dostoievsky's *The Possessed*. Even Renan could exclaim in 1870 *Périsse la France, périsse la Patrie! Il y a au-dessus le royaume de Devoir, de la Raison.*

Zola's indictment of the Second Empire in *La Fortune des Rougon* (1869) and its many sequels was historically documented (especially from Delord's anti-Napoleonic *Histoire du Second Empire*), but antedated: he wrote under the experiences of the *débâcle* of 1870, and used figures of the Empire to symbolize faults and vices which belonged just as truly to the Third Republic: so too in *La Terre* he transferred the agricultural crisis of the 1880's to the 1860's, when things had not been so bad, and exploited the bitter *Pensées* of the abbé Roux (1886). His realism was journalistic; he was at heart a romantic, a moralist, a humanitarian. It was one of the penalties Louis had to pay for his amateurish Socialism and easy-going dictatorship that his government was blamed for failure to reform customs many centuries old, and the millennial vices of mankind.[14]

Though Louis might fail to patronize literature, he did not persecute it. The repressive regime of his first Minister of Education, Fortoul (1851-56) was soon relaxed; the Censorship objected only to attacks on the Government or the Church; and Sainte-Beuve, who accepted the regime of 1852, when he left the *Constitutionnel* to join the staff of the official *Moniteur*, was not the only literary man to feel gratitude to the Second Empire for safety and toleration. 'I owe it to the Emperor (he wrote in 1865) that I have been able to work for 15 years in peace and security under a regime which allows everyone to exercise his talents and to spend his leisure on whatever work he finds useful or congenial: Is that nothing?'[15]

With the scientists Louis was more at his ease: Claude Bernard, Bertrand, Berthelot, and especially Louis Pasteur, whom he interviewed in 1863, and with whom he collaborated between 1865 and 1868 in a scheme for a laboratory for the study of infectious diseases. Pasteur, in his turn, was a fervent Bonapartist, and hung in his room portraits of Napoleon and the King of Rome. Though

Louis was meant by nature, as Hortense Cornu said, to be a poet, his tastes in later life were not artistic, still less musical, but historical, scientific. His cousins deputized for him in a world which was becoming more and more alien to his political ambitions and the business of government.[16]

As for 'Society' — the Court had never been so formal or magnificent since the time of Louis XV, or so frivolous since that of Marie Antoinette. But it was shunned by the old aristocracy, and frequented by those who owed their titles to the First Empire, or their emoluments to the Second, as well as by the wealthy bankers and men of business. The 'tone' of Parisian society was no longer set by the *salons*, but by the *cafés* and the theatres: foreigners were everywhere. But in the provinces the old respectable conservative ideas still flourished. The rich were still rich, the poor were still poor. When it came to election time the countryman would remember that, though food was more expensive than it had been, there was no fear of local famine (*disette*), that though hours were long and wages small, yet work was plentiful and labour free; and he would vote for the Government candidate. So the Empire went on.

8

But what then were Louis' relations with the politicians? How was the government carried on, and what part did the Emperor play in it? In theory it was a dictatorship as centralized and simple as Napoleon's: all initiative in legislation in the hands of a council of personally chosen ministers and advisers, inspired by and contributing to the Imperial mind; an impotent and submissive Chamber, representing the consent of the people; a dignified Senate of 'elder statesmen' who could be trusted to underwrite the risks of Empire; all executive and administrative power in the hands of prefects and mayors appointed by the Government, and backed by army and police. In the hierarchy of law-makers the Council of State was supreme; everything depended upon its initiative. Its members were chosen, as they had been under the First Empire, not for partisanship, but for expertness and efficiency: lawyers, administrators, scientific men, economists, and speakers able to explain their proposals to the Chamber: at their head Baroche, an experienced lawyer, deputy, and minister, a man without strong character or convictions, but a good parliamentarian, a skilful advocate, a tactful

intermediary between despotism and freedom – resembling, like Louis himself, the impartial piece of metal which had borne on one side *Napoléon Empereur* and on the other *République Française*.

This body of experienced men who owed their position to the Empire did their best to deserve it by a programme of legislation only less distinguished than that of Napoleon's Council: the one thing lacking was a Napoleonic will. But even if Louis had been less visionary and lethargic, his Council, like the Legislative Assembly of 1791 following the Constituent Assembly of 1789, was saddled with a ready-made constitution, and represented a people already disillusioned as to the externals of the New Order. The flesh and blood of the French state was there, in the codes and institutions provided by Napoleon to perpetuate the Revolution. All they had to do was to clothe this body in the fashions of the moment, to make it presentable in a more humanitarian and democratic age: not an easy task, but a transitory one, and perhaps irrelevant to the real needs of a growing people.

The deputies of the *Corps législatif* were people of such varied interests – merchants and landlords, lawyers and literary men, semi-monarchists and semi-republicans – that their only common bond was jealousy of the power of the Council, and a desire to exploit any small liberty of criticism allowed them by the constitution; particularly in proposals affecting provincial privileges, the Church, or finance: for, beneath the skin of politics ran the blood of the regionalism, the Catholicism, and the innate thrift of the countryside. These resentments and prejudices were not always easy to control; and it needed all that their Presidents – Billault and (from 1854) Morny – could do to make them think that they were taking a line of their own when they were in reality countersigning the Emperor's decisions.

The Senate, the third link in the chain of legislation, was apparently the most important, but in fact the most impotent. Ex-ministers, ex-generals, or ex-officials for the most part, elderly and irremovable, they discussed eloquently and knowledgeably bills which they could not alter, and projects which they could not enforce: they once exercised their veto upon a proposal of small importance on the ground that it was unconstitutional. But as no one heard their debates, and they were not reported in the Press, their proceedings were utterly ineffective. The Senate was what our House of Lords might be under a Communist dictatorship.

9

In a government which left so little initiative or discretion to its constitutional bodies, it becomes of special importance to inquire into the relations between the Emperor and those who were his immediate associates: the Empress, his Bonaparte relations, the friends of his youth, his ministers and ambassadors. There is a penalty that every tyrant must pay, if he is not one of a legitimate line. He is surrounded by people who owe their position to his favour, who will almost certainly flatter him as he rises and desert him when he falls. What their relations are with him meanwhile will vary as widely as, for instance, those of Carnot, Fouché, and Talleyrand to Napoleon, or those of Goering, Goebbels, and Ribbentrop to Hitler. Obviously much will depend upon his continuing successful enough to command their confidence; more upon the character of his personal ascendancy. Is it due to a superiority of mind, a consistent policy, a concentrated energy, a wide grasp of affairs; or to an intuition, a flair for intrigue, a gambler's belief in his luck, which leads to occasional triumphs, perhaps cumulatively as effective?

Louis' hold over his associates was more of the second than the first type. It has been suggested before that there was something feminine in his temperament; certainly his mind showed less of the rational than of the intuitive capacity, and there was an irrelevance in some of his favourite designs of a kind to suggest that he did not know where he was going. He might have called himself, as Hitler did, a 'sleep-walker'. His associates might be forgiven for working sometimes behind his back, as he did behind theirs. But he was so easy-going, so free of malice, so little a bully, that he held by habit, and even by affection, people who had lost belief in his capacity, or in his luck, and he could work for twenty years with a man so different in origin and outlook as Baroche.

Nothing had more often complicated and embarrassed Napoleon's plans than the misbehaviour of his relations. Louis might think himself fortunate in this: that when he came into power in 1851 only one of his uncles was still alive, and that one the least likely to take a part in politics. Jérôme Bonaparte had played many parts in his youth; but the ex-King of Westphalia was now sixty-seven — an amiable irresponsible spendthrift, and as ready to recognize his nephew in 1851 as he had been to disown him in 1836 and 1840 and to make his peace with Louis-Philippe in 1847; provided he could be subsidized to live at ease in the Palais-Royal and preside over a

decorative Senate. He was dead when, in 1861, his first wife returned from America to claim the family succession for their 'illegitimate' son Jérôme Napoléon. The only other Bonaparte of the second generation who might give trouble was Lucien Bonaparte's youngest son by his second marriage, Pierre, whose colourful and disreputable career had already crossed Louis' path in Italy, the United States, and London, and was to do so again in Paris at a critical moment in 1870.

There remained, however, two of Jérôme's children by his second, his 'legitimate' and royal marriage, with Catherine of Wurttemberg. Jérôme, Prince Napoleon, prided himself on his likeness to Napoleon, and presumed on his elder cousin Louis' constant forbearance to criticize and embarrass him at every turn. This he did in two roles: as unacknowledged heir to the throne, and as the Emperor's unofficial 'remembrancer'. As the first he carried on a life-feud against Eugénie and the Prince Imperial: as the second he was for ever reminding Louis of the Liberal and anti-clerical ideas in which they both believed, but which it was easier for a free-lance to profess than for a prince to apply. Their correspondence often reads like a dialogue between Louis' reason and his conscience, and illustrates better than anything else how difficult he found it to live up to his ideas. 'The world's juggernauts are not men without conscience, but something much more dangerous – men with consciences they can square.'[17]

In a letter written to Jérôme in March 1863 Louis summed up his causes of complaint against his cousin. 'From the very day of my election as President of the Republic – during the Presidency, on December 2nd, and since the founding of the Empire – you have never failed to be hostile to my policy in speech and act. How have I retaliated? By seeking every opportunity to advance your career, to find you positions worthy of your rank, and to open up a field for your conspicuous qualities. The command you held in the Crimea, your marriage and marriage settlement, your Algerian Ministry, your generalship in Italy, your membership of the Senate and State Council – all are proofs of my friendship. Need I remind you how you have recompensed it? In the East you became discouraged, and lost the fruit of a campaign well begun. Your marriage nearly ruined my own policy by making M. Cavour believe what was the exact opposite of my intention, that your alliance with the King of Sardinia's daughter was a condition *sine qua non* of our treaty. Your

Ministry in Algeria? You took it into your head to resign it because of an article in the *Moniteur*. Your speeches in the Senate have always been a serious embarrassment to my government. You complain of my treatment of you; but the fact is, people are astonished at my continued toleration, in a member of my family, of an opposition which alarms and discourages supporters of my cause ... I do not, of course, demand that your words should be a mere echo of my intentions and thoughts: but what I have a right to ask of a prince of my blood is that in speaking before the first body in the State he should at least clothe a difference of opinion, if such exists, in conventional language.'[18]

Prince Napoleon's indiscretions were frequent and provocative, and the company he kept made him a spokesman of the critical and discontented intelligentsia. His sister Princess Mathilde, who had nearly married Louis in 1836, had since then earned his gratitude by supporting his candidacy in 1848, acting as his hostess at the Elysée, and introducing him to Eugénie. Now, since her separation from Davidoff, a wealthy woman with a Paris residence and a house in the country, she too entertained the literary world, and was not over-particular as to the political opinions expressed by her guests. Sharing her brother's Napoleonic profile, she had more than his share of the Napoleonic character, and remained to the end of her long life (she survived till 1904) a fervid supporter and monument of Bonapartism. But, unlike her brother, she was neither in Louis' confidence nor on his conscience, and had little direct influence upon his mind.[19]

One naturally asks, how far were the old friends and supporters of Louis' 'Pretender' period still in his confidence? Four certainly: Dr. Conneau and the valet Thélin, who had shared his imprisonment at Ham, Mocquard, his secretary, and Mme Cornu, his childhood companion and literary helper. A republican in 1848, Hortense did not write to Louis again till 1860. The most significant sentence in their later correspondence is in a letter in the third person dated May 10th of that year: 'The Emperor thanks Mme Cornu for all the trouble she is taking (she was once more helping him to write his *Life of Caesar*). It reminds him of her constant eagerness to be of service to the prisoner of Ham. Extremes meet, after all: the Tuileries is a prison too.' It was indeed a prison into which his old friends could not easily penetrate, and from which he could never escape. But Hortense was admitted there in 1862; Louis reproached

her for having held him at arm's length for twelve years; but they were reconciled; and there were several moments during the last eight years of the Empire when her influence was felt: in the appointment of a tutor for the Prince Imperial, in Duruy's education policy, and in the candidature of Charles of Hohenzollern for the throne of Rumania.[20]

Of the other intimates it is impossible not to repeat the Emperor's traditional dictum: 'How could you expect the Empire to work smoothly? The Empress is a Legitimist; Morny is an Orleanist; my cousin Napoleon is a Republican; I am a Socialist; only Persigny is a Bonapartist, and he is crazy.' Morny, the illegitimate son of Hortense Beauharnais, and Louis' half-brother, a leader of sport and fashion, would have been an important figure in any event; but in fact his abilities as the organizer of the *coup d'état* of December 1851, as President of the Chamber from 1854, and as Ambassador to Russia in 1856 were as remarkable as the business acumen which won him a fortune on the Bourse and the suspicion of being behind the Jecker scandal in the Mexican affair.[21]

Whatever Morny's moral reputation, his judgment was at any rate a counterpoise to the notorious rashness of a still older intimate, Persigny, who, as Minister of the Interior in 1852 and ambassador to England in 1854, could always be counted on for uncalculating loyalty to the man he had adventured with at Strasbourg and Boulogne. A third might be added to this group, if only because, like Morny, he was almost royal — Alexandre Walewski, Napoleon's son by Marie Walewska. Louis employed him, for his Napoleonic good looks and habit of high society, as ambassador in Florence, Naples, Madrid, and London: his great moment was as Minister of Foreign Affairs at the Paris Conference in 1856. No one trusted him; but he had not Talleyrand's qualities of a great intriguer.

What was the relationship between the Emperor and his official advisers? 'Your ministers,' Prince Napoleon wrote on April 20th, 1859, 'are loyal to yourself, but not to your policy. Everyone feels it and knows it. The result is a general lack of confidence and courage. Every party is distrustful and discontented: those who want peace at any price, because you do not give them enough encouragement; and the friends of your chosen cause, because they see you surrounded by those who are hostile to it and working against it ... Thus you reap the disadvantages of two policies. Your Majesty is too disposed to undervalue people; you think there is little

difference between the services obtainable from a clever man and an imbecile, a patriot and a reactionary, a gentleman and a Jew; and you use indiscriminately any instrument that comes to hand. Believe me, Sire, that is very dangerous. You cannot do everything for yourself; and your intentions are constantly being betrayed by those who implement them.'

Louis' answer was characteristic: 'The situation is too serious for us to put personal likes and dislikes before the interests of the country. The men you mention are not perfect, but what others are available? Will your friends Girardin and Bixio lift a finger to save France? If only everyone would be busy about his own business, and not worry about other things, all would be well.' He knew that much of what his cousin said was true; but he had not the energy to enforce respect and obedience amongst his ministers, and he persisted in the belief that, after taking their advice, he adopted a policy of his own choosing. So he did sometimes, when his ordinary lethargy was stirred by a political intuition or by some challenge from his liberal conscience. But such initiatives were becoming rarer year by year, and the field for their exercise more and more restricted by external suspicions and internal discontents.[22]

10

On January 1st, 1860, Louis and Eugénie danced in the New Year at the Tuileries to Viennese waltzes played on the piano by Metternich, the Austrian ambassador: a dramatist might make it a defiant gesture against the fate that was closing in on the Second Empire. Three weeks later the commercial treaty with England roused the bourgeois and parliamentary opposition which, on Morny's advice, was met by the decree of November 24th, generally regarded as the first step towards the 'Liberal Empire'. The concessions might not seem large to countries accustomed to free speech in Parliament and press: merely permission to the Chamber to hold a 'debate on the Address', in the course of which the government might be interpellated on its policy, and be obliged to explain its projects of law — any member of the Council of Ministers might be called before the House: and a detailed daily report of the Chamber's proceedings to be issued to the press. But in a country and capital accustomed for nearly ten years to being told no more than a dictatorial government thought fit, even this was like the miraculous restoration of speech and hearing to one born deaf and dumb.

Such a cure needs faith on the part of the patient to match the power of the healer. Would Louis' appeal to the nation be justified? Could the Empire re-establish itself upon the popular basis of 1848 and 1852? Would the throne be safe for the young Prince Imperial, who, as Louis grew old and ill, seemed to embody all the hopes of Bonapartism? Yes, perhaps, if it had really been an appeal to the masses who had put and kept Louis in power. But in fact the appeal was not to France, but to Paris, not to the people, but to the politicians and the press. Instead of a lead from strength, an act of trust, a call for co-operation, it was a concession made under pressure to opponents who would take it as a sign of weakness, and ask for more. 'I wish it were mere talk,' wrote Mérimée; 'but in France talking leads to revolutions.' And in fact within a year, fearing Catholic opposition to his Italian policy, Liberal opposition in the Chamber, and exploitation by the press of the Government's economic difficulties, Louis made another concession. By the *sénatus-consulte* of December 31st, 1861 (this method was necessary for an alteration in the constitution), the *corps législatif* was given power to discuss and vote the budget, clause by clause; yet in practice this right was emptied of meaning by a subsequent decree which enabled the Government to 'rectify' the budget; and the old system returned in a new guise.

It will be asked, how was Louis at the same time forced into concessions and free to nullify them? Two explanations are possible. At best he was attempting, and attempting honestly, the most difficult operation that ever faces an autocratic government — that of gradually introducing constitutional liberties. Napoleon in 1815 could risk the *acte additionnel* because he knew that he was going to fight the battle of Waterloo; and if he won, as he expected to do, he could return to autocracy. But Louis, having begun a retreat, must carry it on to the end. Liberty, once admitted, must, as he had boasted, 'crown the edifice'.

At the same time there must have been in his two-way mind the thought of the general election due in May 1863. That would be in a sense his Waterloo. Not that he would, if successful, withdraw the concessions just made; but if Bonapartism once more swept the country he might so administer a new Liberal constitution as to make it in practice as autocratic as the old. The decree about the budget was an experiment in this technique. He was already feeling confident that he would win at the polls. True, the Opposition

would be more serious than in 1857. The irreconcilables of 1848 were mostly in exile, and their printed attacks on the Empire flew over the heads of the electorate; but 'The Five', whom they never forgave for remaining at home, pursued their vendetta in the Chamber, criticizing Louis' concessions, and asking for more. Thiers in 1864 would still be demanding five 'necessary liberties'. The younger Republicans tried to organize the party vote in the country constituencies, and to nominate republican candidates: they were confident that Paris would vote for them, as it had done before. On the extreme Right of the Opposition the Legitimists were under orders to abstain; but the Ultramontanes tried to work up feeling against the Church policy of the Government; the academic Liberals and Orleanists appealed to the intelligentsia.

Against such divided forces the Government had the immense advantage of centralization and force. Persigny, now Minister of the Interior, and as single-minded as ever, was in charge of the arrangements for rigging the elections, by rearranging the constituencies so that 'dangerous' districts, in town or country, were split up, by prohibiting meetings, muzzling the press, and backing the 'official' candidates with promises of local benefits. When the election results were known it was found that in Paris (where not much more than 50 per cent went to the poll) only 22,000 votes were cast for the Government, and 175,000 against; but in the country only 32 seats went to the Opposition (17 of the Left and 15 of the Right) against 250 to the Government. It might look like a victory for the Empire: but Louis remembered that in 1857 only 665,000 votes had been cast for the Opposition, and now they numbered two millions; and he was disturbed.

There was no possibility now of reversing the policy of the last two years. The Liberal programme must be extended. The elections, as Morny told Louis, had brought the Empire face to face with Democracy; and the challenge could be met only by fresh concessions: more freedom of speech, more publicity of government policy, more social reform. The Emperor accepted Morny's guidance (for the last two years of his life) as some Enlightened Despot might have done a hundred years before, dismissed the 'die-hards' Persigny and Walewski, and put the advocacy and administration of the 'New Deal' into the competent and unimaginative control of Eugène Rouher — the man who had drafted and still believed in the Constitution of 1852, and who for the last ten years, as unofficial head of what

he called the Ministry of Hard Labour (*ministère des travaux forcés*) had been behind every economic measure of the Empire, from banks and railways to the commercial treaty with England.[22]

For a time the crisis seemed to have passed, and the transition from an authoritative to a liberal Empire to be proceeding according to plan. A far-reaching scheme of educational reform carried through by Duruy in 1865-66 pleased the Liberals, and was made less offensive to the Catholics by the dismissal of Renan from his professorship. The workers' representatives who came back from the London Exhibition with demands for trades unions and the right to strike found in Emile Ollivier a parliamentary champion of unrivalled eloquence, who carried a measure legalizing both liberties; but with the proviso that they could not be used to the serious detriment of free labour – in other words, so long as they remained ineffective. Louis was so evidently placing his stakes on black and red at the same time that it needed the single-track mind of Pio Nono (all the more so since he had once played the Liberal himself) to see beneath all these half-measures the plain heresies of rationalism and liberalism. The Encyclical *Quanta Cura* (December 8th, 1864) and the death of Morny (March 10th, 1865) were ill omens for a gambler's mind.

In 1865 Walter Bagehot revisited France, and contributed to the *Economist* an article in which he resumed, and in some particulars revised, the view he had expressed of Louis Napoleon's regime fourteen years earlier. Louis had just published his *Life of Julius Caesar*; and how appropriately! For 'Julius Caesar was the first who tried on an imperial scale the characteristic principles of the French Empire – as the first Napoleon revived them, as the third Napoleon has consolidated them': he was 'the first instance of a democratic despot'. And Louis' despotism is quite unlike 'the despotisms of feudal origin and legitimate pretensions'. He is a Benthamite despot. He is for 'the greatest happiness of the greatest number'. He says: 'I am where I am, because I know better than any one else what is good for the French people, and they know that I know better. He is not the Lord's anointed; he is the people's agent.'

Bagehot still maintains that 'the French Empire is really the *best finished* democracy which the world has ever seen', meaning that 'an absolute government with a popular instinct has the unimpeded command of a people renowned for orderly dexterity. A Frenchman (he thinks) will have arranged an administrative organization

really and effectually, while an Englishman is still bungling and a German still reflecting'. And 'the French Emperor knows well how to use these powers. His bureaucracy is not only endurable, but pleasant . . . The welfare of the masses (in particular) is felt to be the object of the Government and the law of the polity'. Mainly, of course, in material affairs. 'No former French Government has done as much for free-trade as this Government. No Government has striven to promote railways, and roads, and industry, like this Government.'

'But', Bagehot goes on, 'if, not the present happiness of the greatest number, but their *future elevation* be, as it is, the true aim and end of government, our estimate of the Empire will be strangely altered. It is an admirable Government for present and coarse purposes, but a detestable Government for future and refined purposes.' For, first, 'it stops the *teaching apparatus*'; thought is free, but publication is not: there is no popular press, no public speech. 'The daily play of the higher mind upon the lower mind is arrested.' 'A democratic despotism is like a theocracy': it professes a creed, it imposes orthodoxy. Secondly, where the Government does everything, too great a strain is placed upon its agents. 'The system requires angels to work it'; and France has not found men honest enough to be above 'the two temptations of civilization, money and women'. Above all, Bagehot thinks, France cannot command credit, because she does not trust her own future. 'If you propose the simplest operations of credit to a French banker, he says: "You do not remember 1848; I do."' In other words, social prosperity and public order depend on 'the permanent occupation of the Tuileries by an extraordinary man', and 'the present happiness of France is happiness on a short life-lease; it may end with the life of a man who is not young, who has not spared himself, who has always thought, who has always *lived*'.[24]

Perhaps Bagehot exaggerated the personal contribution of the Emperor to the Imperial regime: he did not speak with the intimate knowledge of Cowley or Clarendon; but he was not wrong in identifying the security and credit of that regime with the life of the man who had originated it: no one believed that it could continue under a Regency of the Empress for the Prince Imperial, still less under Prince Napoleon, however he might fancy himself as a rival claimant.

So France moved on into 1870.

THE GAMBLER (1863-1869)

> That we would do
> We should do when we would, for this 'would' changes,
> And hath abatements and delays as many
> As there are tongues, are hands, are accidents:
> And then this 'should' is like a spendthrift sigh,
> That hurts by easing.
> *Hamlet*, IV, vii

I

THE change in the home policy of the Empire marked by the elections of 1863 was already complicated by the first of a series of crises in European affairs which were to lead inexorably from Sebastopol to Sedan. The death of Cavour in June 1861 and of the Prince Consort at the end of the same year removed the two men whose suspicions of Louis' policy might have kept his adventures within bounds; but the problem of Rome was as perplexing as ever, and the friendship of England as precarious. Meanwhile the accession of William I as King of Prussia and his appointment of Bismarck as Minister-President was a warning — a warning which the Powers were too slow to appreciate — that a new centre of energy and initiative had to be reckoned with in European affairs. The king was a soldier, set on strengthening the army: Bismarck was a patriot, determined to federate Germany, apart from Austria, under Prussian political, military, and economic predominance. The refusal of the Prussian Diet to sanction army reform made the crisis in which Bismarck was recalled from his ambassadorship in Paris, and began weaving a spider's web of diplomacy which, stretching from Poland in 1863 to Denmark in 1864, Austria in 1866, Luxembourg in 1867, and Spain in 1868, finally entangled and destroyed the French Empire.

Born a few weeks before Waterloo, Otto, Count von Bismarck, spent his youth on his father's country estate, at a Berlin school, and at Göttingen University, under the authoritarian and nationalist influences common at that period, sharing both the barbarous taste for duelling and the aspirations for liberal reform which were so strangely combined in University life in the 'thirties; then took a Doctor's degree in Law, served in the army, and settled down in the

'forties, as Cavour did, as an agriculturalist of the old 'feudal farmer' (*Junker*) type – a married man, a devout Lutheran, but determined (again like Cavour) upon a political career for the glorification of his country. Ten years before coming into power he had experienced at the Frankfurt *Bundestag*, and at the Embassies in St. Petersburg and Paris, the antagonisms of the German small-state system, the futile talk of Liberals and Nationalists, the corruption of the Press, and the intrigues of foreign diplomats. At Paris, visiting the *Exposition* of 1855, he had a conversation with Prince Albert, full of suspicion on both sides, and anticipating Bismarck's lasting feud against the Princess Royal (the Empress Frederick). Louis spoke to him about his hopes for a Franco-Prussian partnership in European predominance. 'I have the impression', he reported to the King when he got home, 'that the Emperor Napoleon is a judicious (*gescheiter*) and amiable man, but not so shrewd (*klug*) as the world thinks him' – an opinion which he still held with fifteen years' experience behind him: 'He is very good-tempered', he said in 1870, 'as is generally believed, but much less of a shrewd fellow (*kluge Kopf*) than he is taken to be.'

As for French impressions of Bismarck, Mérimée, who met him in Paris in October 1865, was much taken with him. '*C'est un grand Allemand, très-poli, qui n'est point naif* (civil, but disingenuous). *Il a l'air absolument dépourvu de gemüth, mais plein d'esprit* (with no soul, but plenty of intelligence). *Il a fait ma conquête.*' He too did not change this first opinion. '*Il est bien évident que M. Bismark est un grand homme,*' he wrote again in 1866; and in 1867 (comparing him with Ollivier and other French statesmen) '*Il n'y a que M. de Bismark qui soit un vrai grand homme.*'[1]

Louis would assuredly need all the shrewdness Bismarck denied him to deal with the international problems which now faced France. It was no consolation to realize that they were the result of two wars for which he was largely responsible, into which he had been led by idealistic impulses and dynastic ambitions, and which had in all appearance been justified by their results. His intervention in the Crimea, which had reversed the verdict of 1812 and restored to France the leadership of the continent, had led to nationalist movements in the Balkan states. His 'liberation' of Italy had extended unrest nearer home: Prussia was hoping to exploit the old separatism and new nationalism of the German states in her own interests; whilst Austria was beginning to feel the centrifugal forces which

would still take sixty years to destroy her unity. Would Louis'
sympathy with nationalism lead him to support Sardinia against the
Pope, the Balkan states against the Sultan, Hungary against the
Emperor, Poland against the Tsar?

These questions first became acute when in 1863 the Poles rose
against the Russian government, which had destroyed their constitution in 1831, and had done its best, during the last thirty years, to
stamp out their national traditions and culture. Polish refugees of
the 'thirties with their headquarters at Czartoryski's house in Paris,
and organized in a *Société démocratique des Polonais parisiens*, kept up
a constant agitation. Their cause appealed to republicans, to liberals,
and to Catholics alike. France had historical relations with Poland
going back to the sixteenth century; she had failed to stop its partition in the eighteenth; she had done nothing to help the rising of
1831, or to prevent the suppression of liberties that followed. Could
she afford to fail again?

On February 20th Prince Napoleon sent his cousin a *Note sur les
affaires de Pologne* in which he not only stressed these obvious considerations, but went on, in his usual manner, to outline a policy
and a procedure out of all relation to political common sense. The
re-establishment of Poland being 'an axiom of our policy', a war
for such a purpose would be a national as well as a religious crusade;
and France (he said) is in a position to impose her will on Europe,
and to reorganize its state-system. Poland, with all its ancient
possessions, to be independent; Venetia ceded to Italy; the Balkan
states freed and federated; Constantinople made a free city; Greece
to acquire Epirus, Macedonia, and Thessaly; Austria to be compen-
sated in Germany for the loss of Venetia and Galicia; France to
receive Bavaria, Hesse, and Prussian territory on the left bank of the
Rhine; Finland, and perhaps Denmark, to be added to Sweden . . .
and England 'will have to be persuaded to regard these territorial
rearrangements as favourable to her interests'. To carry out this
policy Louis must at once send a private letter to Francis-Joseph to
find out his reactions to it, and publish a manifesto assuring Poland
of French support. If the Austrian reply is favourable, diplomatic
action will be followed by an ultimatum to Prussia demanding that
she shall break with Russia and cease helping in the repression of the
Poles. If it is not, the French army will advance to the Rhine; its
first objective Berlin, and its second Warsaw: whilst another will

be transported from Cherbourg to the Baltic, and cut the Russian line of communications at Vilna . . . So his imagination goes running on.

Louis' reply to this 'dream' (*rêve*) was easy. 'I have to deal (he wrote) with Powers full of scruples (*très méticuleuses*), and if they once credited me with such ambitious views they would refuse any alliance with me.' But it was not so easy to know what to do. His facile sympathy went all the way to Warsaw. But how could it be followed up by action? He could not afford to offend Russia, of which he had been all but an open ally since the Crimean War, and which under its new Tsar, Alexander II, whilst repressing rebellion in Poland, was attempting at home a programme of reform not unlike his own; nor England, which no doubt sympathized with the Poles, but not to the length of collaborating with France against their persecutors. Could any policy be devised to deal with so difficult a situation which would not endanger his peaceful professions, or his social and economic programme? Were his military commitments in China, in Syria, and in Mexico (as Jérôme had reminded him) consistent with the necessity which might arise of backing his intervention by force of arms?

Compelled by public opinion to do something, Louis first (in April) joined England, Austria, and Italy in Notes to the Tsar reminding him of national rights, of the Treaty of Vienna, and of the claims of common humanity; then again (in June) with British and Austrian concurrence he proposed an amnesty for the rebels, and the granting of national rights under six heads; and finally (in November) he suggested, as he so often did, the calling of a European Congress, not only to regulate the Polish question, but also to review the settlement of 1815, and, as Jérôme had suggested, to reconstruct the map of Europe.

This last move roused fresh suspicions of Louis' territorial ambitions, and was even less successful than the first two. Palmerston, who in March had warned Leopold of Belgium that Louis schemed to invade the Rhenish provinces as a means of detaching Prussia from Russia, now (November 15th) sent him unanswerable arguments against a congress, and told Russell (December 2nd) that Louis would use it to secure an international guarantee of the Papal States which would enable him to withdraw his garrison from Rome. But more: to Louis himself he declared: 'It is the conviction of H.M.'s government that the main provisions of the treaty of 1815 are in full force . . .

and that on those foundations rests the balance of power in Europe
. . . H.M.'s government would feel more apprehension than confidence for the meeting of a Congress of Sovereigns and Ministers
without fixed objects, ranging over the map of Europe, and exciting
hopes and aspirations which they might find themselves unable
either to gratify or to quiet.' Though the Queen of Holland, writing
to Clarendon (January 13th, 1864) called this reply 'deplorable',
and 'the death-blow of an alliance which ought to have dominated
the world, managed the affairs of the continent, and assured us an
era of peace', yet there could be no doubt that it reflected the general
distrust of the Second Empire, whose *raison d'être* was believed to
be to revise the settlement of 1815 in the interests of France.[2]

The centre of suspicion was of course the Rhine valley, which
ever since the times of Caesar and Charlemagne had been a meeting-
place of rival national habits and imperial policies, and remained so
in the mind of the biographer of Caesar and the nephew of the self-
appointed successor of Charlemagne. But Louis' thought, even on so
vital an issue, was neither consecutive nor clear; and it would be an
exaggeration to suppose that his whole foreign outlook was
dominated by a *Rheinpolitik*. Sometimes, as in 1860 and 1866, he
talked of annexing Belgium, sometimes the Palatinate; sometimes
(in 1857 or 1866) he would be content with a few miles on the
Lorraine frontier, sometimes he would claim the whole right bank
of the Moselle; sometimes he would think of the Palatinate as
annexed to France, sometimes as a buffer state. And always there was
in the background the question of Luxembourg and Belgium.

A clear and consistent policy of aggression would really have been
less alarming to Louis' contemporaries than the uncertainty as to
what he wanted or where he might strike. Their suspicion would
not have been less if the views expressed by Eugénie to Metternich
in February and by Louis himself through Gramont in November
had been generally known. Poland was to be reconstituted, Austria
to give up Venetia in exchange for Rumania, Prussia to receive
Hanover and other territory in North Germany, and to give up
the left bank of the Rhine — not to France, but as a reconstituted
Rhineland or Burgundy under the King of Belgium; whilst Belgium
itself would be partitioned between France and Holland. It is
arguable that some such re-drawing of the map of Europe on
nationalist lines was overdue and, if carried through, might have
anticipated by peaceful means the settlement of 1918. But the sum

of Louis' intuitions never amounted to a fixed purpose; he had not the will to persist in one plan; Europe had not the wish and France had not the power to enforce it.[3]

2

Having abandoned Poland in 1863, Louis abandoned Denmark in 1864. The question at issue was fifty years old and infinitely complicated. Between Denmark and Germany, occupying the southern half of the Jutland peninsula, lay two territories, Schleswig in the north, Holstein (with Lauenburg) in the south. Both were held, and held together, as Dukedoms, under the rule of the King of Denmark; such anomalies were not uncommon in Germany, where, for instance, the last three Sovereigns of England had been Dukes of Hanover. But since the break-up of the Holy Roman Empire in 1815 Holstein-Lauenburg had also been part of the German Confederation (*Bund*). The Holsteiners were mainly German, the Schleswigers mainly Danish; but there were enough Germans in Schleswig to make it what would have been called a century later a *Sudetenland*, and to encourage German nationalist claims for its separation from Denmark under the rule of the Duke of Augustenburg. In 1848 its formal relationship to the King of Denmark was changed into territorial incorporation in the Danish Kingdom: the Duchies rebelled, and appealed to the *Bund*, which intervened: after two years of inconclusive fighting the London settlement of 1852 guaranteeed the continued union of the two Duchies under the Danish crown.

However by the time a new King, Christian IX, came to the throne in 1863 the Danish parliament had made (1858) a fresh constitution which he signed unwillingly and unwisely annexing and 'Danicizing' Schleswig, whilst excluding Holstein. Both Duchies appealed against their separation, and the Duke of Augustenburg claimed the sovereignty of them both. Prussian and Austrian troops, acting for the *Bund*, invaded Schleswig, nominally to reassert the settlement of 1815, but really to detach that territory too from Denmark. The campaign was one-sided and successful: by the terms of peace (October 1864) Christian gave up both Duchies to Prussia and Austria. A year later, by the Convention of Gastein (August 1865), Austria ruled Holstein, Prussia Schleswig and (for a consideration) Lauenburg: Prussia thus gained Kiel and the site of the Kiel Canal.[4]

English sympathies were excited but divided. The friends of

Denmark thought it an opportunity to 'enter upon the most popular, the easiest, and the cheapest war of the century'. But Victoria, faithful to Albert's German background, and more devoted to her 'Vicky', now Crown Princess of Prussia, than to the Prince of Wales' Danish bride 'Alix', believed that, 'unreasonable though the Germans may be, the Danes are far more so', and was anxious above all to avoid another war in alliance with France. But when her government proposed a Congress of the signatories of 1852, Louis remembered Palmerston's rejection of his similar proposal a year ago, and refused to take part in a plan which would ordinarily have appealed to him. Clarendon, who saw him in Paris in April, reported that, though uncommonly friendly, he 'made out a case for doing nothing *in re* Denmark'; 'he was frank enough on the subject with me, and said that in the present peaceful mood of the French people and the *corps législatif* he could not go to war for a question that did not touch the dignity or the interests of France, unless there was a prospect of compensation held out; and as Europe in general and England in particular would be averse to any such compensation, he must be specially cautious not to be accused of provoking a war that might lead to it'.[5]

The Duke of Saxe-Coburg, to whom he made much the same protestations of indifference, commented: 'he is watching like a cat for the first false move of either Prussia or Austria; and then his opportunity and interest will appear'. It was clear enough to such observers as Delane, who was aware of the secret communications Louis had been making to *The Times* during Palmerston's ministry, that what he hoped for was Bismarck's consent to his annexing the left bank of the Rhine, and so outflanking Belgium, the prey France really coveted. But it was a mistake not to co-operate with England, however non-committally; for at the end of the summer he had sacrificed nationalist principles which he could not enforce without risk to France and his throne, only to find that he had lost the friendship of Russia, Prussia, Austria, and England, and had territorially gained nothing.[6]

Certainly the whole episode left an unpleasant impression on Palmerston's mind. 'Europe (he wrote to the Queen on February 2nd, 1864) is full of combustible materials like the town of Kagosima (in Japan, destroyed by a British fleet in 1862), and the typhoon of political passions is ready to blow from one end of Europe to the other the flames of war which have been lit up in Denmark.' Louis

Napoleon, he thought, was only waiting for 'the moment best adapted to promote the ambitious projects of France, and he feels quite sure that when the proper moment for action arrives he will have a military force sufficient for any purpose, and that he will be backed up by the general approval of the French nation'. But Victoria was not so Francophobe as her minister, and said that in her view (August 1865: a year's experience of Bismarck had had its effect) 'In Germany things look rather critical and threatening. Prussia seems inclined to behave as atrociously as possible, and as she *always has done!* Odious people the Prussians are, that I *must say*.'[7]

It was none the easier to acquiesce in the methods of Prussian progress if one were convinced that the thing itself was inevitable. One could only hope that the worst mistakes would be avoided. 'It is clear', wrote Russell to Clarendon as early as September 1861, 'that the course for Prussia, though not easy, is grand and glorious. As Austria declines, the star of Prussia must rise. But she must avoid on the one hand the delusions of *Nationalverein*, and on the other the feudal dreams of his late Prussian Majesty . . . She must comply with the demand for a free government in Prussia, but not assume stiffly, harshly, pedantically, and prematurely the supremacy in Germany. The pear will fall when it is ripe.'

But Bismarck was not the man to wait for the pear to fall: he would make sure of it by shaking the tree. From his first coming into power — he admitted it in later years — he worked for the annexation of the Danish Duchies, because their seaboard was necessary for Prussian naval expansion. Every step in the Schleswig-Holstein affair was designed. And it was itself a stage towards another and more important undertaking. 'I shall seize the first good pretext (he told Disraeli in 1862) to declare war against Austria, dissolve the German Diet, subdue the minor states, and give national unity to Germany under Prussian leadership.' And, commented Disraeli, 'he means what he says'.[8]

3

Indeed Russell and Disraeli were not deceived, for from this moment the European situation, which to Bismarck was becoming crystal clear — a war with Austria, to exclude her from the new Germany, of which not Vienna but Berlin was to be the political and economic capital, and a war with France, to consolidate the northern and southern states into a German Empire — found France struggling

blindly to recover her lost initiative and her lost allies, to reassert her championship of national rights, or, in the last resort, to extort payment (as she had done in Savoy and Nice) for services rendered or promises of friendly neutrality.

Louis' first move, when the treaty of Vienna (October 30th, 1864) had closed the Danish war, was towards friendship with Prussia: he transformed his Legation at Berlin into an Embassy, and arranged an interview with Bismarck, who for his part was anxious not to proceed against Austria without some assurance of French neutrality. The two men — the positive and negative poles of European diplomacy, the man who made situations and the man who accepted them — met at Biarritz in October 1864, and again a year later; the one plain, plausible, persuasive, the other silent and secretive. Bismarck explained as fully as he thought advisable his ambitions for Prussia; the rectification of her unnatural frontiers, and her claim to the headship of a German confederation; if France would remain neutral during the coming struggle with Austria, Bismarck might support her designs on the Rhineland and Belgium.

Louis had no anti-Prussian prejudices. He had met and liked the new king at Baden and entertained him at Compiègne: General Roon this same year (1864) visited Châlons and Cherbourg, and was invested by the young Prince Imperial with the *grand cordon* of the Legion of Honour. Bismarck himself had been a popular ambassador in Paris, and his successor de Goltz was in high favour at the Tuileries. There was no fear at this time that a new Germany under Prussian leadership would be more dangerous to France than the old.

Yet Austria too had to be considered; for without her consent, willing or unwilling, to the cession of Venetia there could be no solution of the Italian question. For the moment, Francis-Joseph, by signing the Convention of Gastein, had shown himself more aware of danger in the south than in the north, refusing another French offer to buy out his interests in Venetia, whilst allowing Prussia to obtain an overwhelming advantage in the Danish Duchies. The second conversation at Biarritz was perhaps Louis' last opportunity of striking a bargain with Bismarck which might at least have postponed the war of 1870. That he did not take it seems to have been due partly to his obsession by the Austro-Venetian problem ('If Italy had not existed', said Bismarck when he came back, 'it would have had to be invented'), and partly to a sick and tired man's fatalistic mood — he would 'wait and see'.[9]

But when, in February 1866, the Rumanians deposed Prince Couza, and were looking about for a new King, Louis seized the opportunity urged on him by his old friend Mme Cornu, who was in close touch with the Catholic branch of the Hohenzollern family, to satisfy the national will and at the same time do Prussia a favour by carrying through the candidature of Charles of Hohenzollern. He thus earned for the second time the title of Founder of Rumania; and it was the last stroke that he made in the name of his almost forgotten creed of nationalism. But it was a dangerous triumph; for it antagonized Austria, with whom he was hoping to patch up an alliance against Prussia; and it suggested to Bismarck the counter-stroke by which Charles' brother became, three years later, a candidate for the throne of Spain.[10]

By this time it was generally agreed that an Austro-Prussian war was inevitable. Thus at the end of March 1866 Victoria received a letter from the Duchess of Coburg which left no doubt in her mind as to its imminence, or as to who would be responsible for it. 'Ernest, the Duke,' she wrote, 'entreats you not to indulge in ANY *hopes of peace*, as the sad probability becomes ever more evident and inevitable, and is as dexterously and as surely prepared. In Berlin NO ONE wishes for war, neither the King nor the Princes, but singly and solely Count Bismarck.' Victoria, acting on this warning, wrote on April 10th to the King of Prussia, appealing for peace.[11]

Not so Louis. He had little doubt about the issue of the coming war, or of his ability to profit by it. He had confided to Walewski that 'war between Austria and Prussia is one of those unhoped-for happenings that never seemed likely to occur; and it is not for us to oppose warlike intentions which contain so many advantages for our policy'. He was so sure that Austria would win that he encouraged Italy to ally herself with Prussia (April 1866), whilst offering his neutrality to the Emperor, in return for a promise to cede Venetia (June 9th-12th): he was thus making doubly certain of a solution of the Italian question, which worried him more than any other. At the same time he hoped to obtain his compensations on the Rhine: if Prussia were beaten he could take what he wanted without difficulty, if she were victorious he counted on it as the reward of his neutrality. Here he made his greatest blunder; for, expecting the first eventuality, he had made no preparations for dealing with the second. Though the King of Prussia, to strengthen his armies, withdrew practically all his garrisons from Trèves, Luxembourg, and

Saarlouis — it was almost an invitation to France to take compensation as a gift — Louis had no troops ready to occupy them.[12]

On June 15th the King of Prussia summoned the chief north German states — Saxony, Hanover, and Hesse — to keep out of the war: when they refused, they were invaded and disarmed. Most of the smaller states conformed; the southern states officially stood with Austria, but in fact gave her little or no assistance. On June 24th the Italians were worsted at Custozza by the southern Austrian army under the Archduke Albrecht; but on July 3rd the main Austrian army under Benedek was overwhelmed at Sadowa.

Francis-Joseph immediately appealed to Louis as his ally to intervene; and on the night of July 4th–5th Louis telegraphed to the Kings of Prussia and Sardinia urging them to make an armistice. Both resented his interference: William because he was hoping to crown his victory in the field by a triumphal entry into Vienna; Victor Emmanuel because he disliked receiving Venetia as a gift instead of a conquest. William gave way only because Bismarck insisted on the danger of a French attack on the Rhine, which might put Prussia in the position that France had been in at Villafranca, and because it was important for the unification of Germany that Austria should be given easy terms. Victor Emmanuel refused to stop hostilities until Louis threatened a naval demonstration against Venice. Neither monarch forgave Louis for his intervention: Bismarck in particular added it to the reckoning against his next victim.

He would have been even less grateful for Louis' unbenevolent neutrality if he had known how hollow was the threat of an advance on the Rhine. A meeting of the Council was hurriedly called at Saint-Cloud on the morning of July 5th. The Emperor presided, and the Empress was by his side. It was known that Francis-Joseph had already surrendered Venetia, and accepted French mediation. What attitude should France adopt towards the victor, Prussia? Drouyn de Lhuys proposed a military demonstration on the Rhine. The Empress asked the Minister of War, Marshal Randon, whether the army was ready. He replied 'Yes; we can concentrate 80,000 men immediately on the Rhine, and 250,000 in about three weeks'. The Empress seconded Drouyn de Lhuys' proposal. La Valette argued on the other side that to attack Prussia was to back Austria, break with Italy, and lose all the fruits of the Italian policy; there was no need to threaten Prussia, he thought; Bismarck could be trusted to give the compensations he had promised. Eugénie retorted that

Bismarck, once free from a French threat, would forget his promises. In 1859 the Prussian threat on the Rhine had forced Louis to halt his advance at Solferino: now was the moment for a French threat on the Rhine to stop the Prussian advance at Sadowa. The Council finally adopted this view, and resolved to ask the Legislature for credit for a general mobilization of the army; to demonstrate at once with 50,000 men on the Rhine; and to send a Note to Berlin saying that France would not allow any territorial changes in Europe that had not her consent. These decisions were to have been published in next day's official *Moniteur*. But they never appeared. During the night the Emperor at last made up his wavering mind against war, and on his own authority countermanded the decisions of the Council.[13]

Was he right or wrong? There is more than enough evidence that a French advance on the Rhine would have been effective — though much more so, if it had been made before, not after, Sadowa. Bismarck himself admitted before the Reichstag in 1874, and in private conversation, that the appearance of 15,000 *pantalons rouges* upon the Rhine would have led to an anti-Prussian rising in South Germany, the reinforcement of Benedek's Austrian army in Bohemia by that of the Archduke Albrecht from Italy, and a Prussian withdrawal to cover Berlin. Louis himself, according to Eugénie, admitted his mistake a few days later: the realization of it contributed to the illness which forced him to retire to Vichy for a cure towards the end of the month. But *was* it a mistake, on a longer view? Everything would have depended upon the readiness of the army. Is there good reason to suppose that Randon was any more right in 1866 than Lebœuf in 1870? Louis may be supposed to have been better informed than his generals. In any case his diplomacy had secured Venetia for Italy — though Italy was anything but grateful to him — and might still give France the Rhineland. All Europe, and especially England, suspected him of warlike intentions: he would prove them wrong. And even if war were only postponed there might at least be time for the reorganization of the French army.[14]

4

What was to be done meanwhile? Louis, with his ministers at sixes and sevens, his army unready to move, and himself suffering from one of his periodical attacks of pain, came wearily back to the

idea of territorial compensation. For the moment he accepted almost without question the Prussian terms dictated to Austria by the Peace Conference at Nikolsburg, where Benedetti spent a fortnight pressing Bismarck in vain for a definite answer to Louis' demands. Three weeks after Sadowa (July 23rd) he suggested that Prussia should cede to France the frontier of 1814, and Luxembourg; and again, on July 29th, all the German territory on the left bank of the Rhine. Bismarck refused (August 6th) what he called a tip (*pourboire*), or an inn-keeper's account (*note d'aubergiste*), and passed on the suggestion to the correspondent of the Paris *Siècle*. Its publication (August 11th) had the worst possible effect on European opinion, reviving all the old fears of French aggression, and consolidating the southern states of Germany behind their new champion, Prussia. The British government instructed Cowley to ask for Louis' denial of the report, which, if true, 'would cause a very painful impression in this country, and which it would be impossible to justify in the eyes of Europe'.[15]

Bismarck, surer than ever of his prey, would not even consider a compromise that Louis still thought it worth while to propose — the setting up of a neutral buffer state under a Hohenzollern ruler on the left bank of the Rhine. Finally, in an attempt to persuade himself that France still held the diplomatic initiative, Louis instructed Benedetti to ask again for the cession of the Rhine frontier of 1814, and for a promise to allow the annexation of Luxembourg, to be followed eventually by that of Belgium. This time Bismarck agreed to a secret treaty, by which Louis recognized the recent enlargement of Prussia, and the confederation of the northern and southern states under her leadership, whilst he undertook to facilitate the French acquisition of Luxembourg, and to come to the aid of France 'in the event of her being led by circumstances to march into Belgium or to conquer the country'. Bismarck had this bargain in Benedetti's writing, and kept the document: he was to make fatal use of it four years later.

There already hung over this transaction the shadow of things to come. 'I have no doubt', wrote Lord Stanley to General Grey (January 10th, 1867) 'that Bismarck (and probably the King of Prussia) would be glad to see Belgium sacrificed, if that act would avert the jealousy so generally felt in France of the increase of German power, and thus save Germany from being involved in war, which, as matters stand, seems a very possible event.' But he went

on to repeat 'possible' rather than 'probable'. 'I should say the chances were considerably against it: the French are growing every year a more peace-loving and commercial people: not one of the wars of the Second Empire has been popular in France, and the Emperor himself is neither young nor in good health; and the proposed increase in the army is unpopular in all quarters.' These were good reasons against war: but how few wars are reasonable![16]

5

Of one problem Sadowa might seem to have made a happy solution possible. By a convention of September 1864 Louis had undertaken to withdraw his troops from Rome in two years' time, and Victor Emmanuel, whilst shifting the capital of Italy to Florence, had promised to leave the Papal States for the time untouched. But no Italian, let alone Garibaldi, gave up the hope of making Rome the capital; whilst Louis, backed by the French Catholics, was still stubbornly opposed to letting this key-stone be set in the arch of Italian unity. He would in fact support any arrangement by which Prussia might buy Italian help against Austria with the promise of Venetia: it would at least distract attention from Rome. Then (July 3rd, 1866) came Sadowa. 'Venetia has been ceded, Italy is made, a great fact in history!' wrote Odo Russell to his uncle (August 27th). 'All foreign questions cease for Italy from now . . . The Pope will have to bend before public opinion, when his French bayonets are gone, and the *inexorable logic of facts* will assimilate and absorb Rome, without the interference of men. Everybody one meets has some ingenious or fantastic solution of the Roman question. My humble opinion would be to *do nothing* and *let the question settle itself.*'[17]

But things did not turn out so. Italian patriots who would have been proud to win Venetia as a reward of a national victory at Custozza felt ashamed to receive it as a consolation prize after a foreign triumph at Sadowa. And the country was still without its capital. True, the French troops left Rome in December 1866; but they went no further than Toulon, and a volunteer *légion d'Antibes* was ready to take their place. Garibaldi reappeared at Genoa, and once more marched on Rome. When he arrived there, Louis' garrison had returned (October 30th), and Victor Emmanuel's troops were only 'maintaining order' in the Papal States. On

November 3rd the Pope's own forces (which had been organized to replace the French garrison) attacked and defeated Garibaldi at Mentana. They were supported by 200 French, whose new *chassepots* (it was reported in the Paris press) had done marvels (*ont fait merveille*). The unhappy phrase offended the Italians as much as Rouher's declaration in the *corps législatif*, that Italy should never have Rome (*Jamais l'Italie ne s'emparera de Rome*), offended the Liberals. Louis was unfairly blamed for both indiscretions; yet it was a penalty perhaps deserved by nearly twenty years' ambiguous policy. The final unification of Italy was once more postponed, and did not come about until the disaster of 1870 forced the withdrawal of the French garrison and the liquidation of all Louis' hopes.[18]

Louis tried to hide the disastrous events of 1866 by dismissing the minister, Drouyn de Lhuys, who had been nominally responsible for them, and by circulating an optimistic memorandum to all his representatives in Europe (September 16th), whose main thesis was that, as a result of the war, the Treaty of Vienna no longer existed, and the anti-French Coalition of 1815 had been destroyed. France, with a population (including Algeria) of forty millions, could confidently face Germany with thirty-seven, Austria with thirty-five, or Italy with twenty-six: in any case she could count on Italian friendship. The Emperor had, by his wise policy, avoided war; but it would be necessary to 'perfect the military organization' of the country, and to rearm the infantry with M. Chassepot's 'marvellous' new breech-loading rifle, an improvement on the 'needle-gun' with which the Prussians had just beaten the Austrians. This was singing to keep one's courage up, with the highwayman standing by. Nothing could be less realistic than to regard the Germany of 1866, divided for the moment into three fragments (*tronçons*: it was Rouher's word), of which two were already being welded together, as less dangerous than the artificial *Bund* of 1815. No historical judgment is more sound than that war between France and Prussia was by now inevitable, or that it was precipitated by the failure of French diplomacy in 1864-66.

Nevertheless there followed an interlude during which a dangerous situation was settled amicably, and war once more postponed. Louis remembered that, whilst Bismarck had, in their various negotiations, refused any cession of German territory, he had been un-

expectedly helpful with regard to the Duchy of Luxembourg, whose 200,000 inhabitants, nominally a Dukedom under the rule of the King of the Netherlands, had since 1815 formed part of the German Confederation, and enjoyed virtual independence. The Confederation was now (by the terms of Prague, 1866) dissolved; but the Prussian garrison placed in Luxembourg in 1815 had not been withdrawn. Louis was too conscious of the analogy of the Danish Duchies affair of 1863 to propose plain annexation; but he sounded the Powers as to whether there would be any objection to his acquiring the territory by purchase from Holland. Encouraged by Bismarck (who undertook to withdraw the garrison) and with the acquiescence of Britain and Russia, Louis persuaded the King of the Netherlands to consent to the sale. But at the last minute there was an outcry in the German Diet, which Bismarck was suspected of having contrived, and which he certainly could have prevented; and Louis was forced to withdraw.

All he could do now was to win over the Powers to the idea that Prussia should evacuate the fortress, as being an unnecessary threat to France, and that a Congress should decide the future of the state. This solution was adopted in London on May 11th, 1867. The capital was evacuated, and the state declared neutral by the 'scrap of paper' which Bethmann-Hollweg 'tore up' in 1914. French diplomatic prestige was restored for the moment; war was at least postponed; and Paris settled down to exploit the crowd of English visitors who (encouraged by the abolition of passports) crossed the Channel to enjoy the *Exposition* of 1867 — if not the actual exhibits, most of which were as dully utilitarian as the 'Test House' building in the British section, 'showing every form of patent or experimental chimney, cowl, ornamental tile, drain-pipe, and other convenience', yet at least the Festival Fair to which natives of every land contributed their exotic dress and food, dances and entertainments.

But even so black care rode at the horseman's back. On June 6th, as the Tsar, the most honoured of such a crowd of royal guests as had not been gathered in one place since Erfurt or Dresden, was driving back with Louis from a review at Longchamp, he was shot at by a Polish malcontent; and on June 30th came the news, not wholly unexpected since Carlotta's lamentable visit a year ago, of the capture and execution of Maximilian, the Emperor of Mexico. This was not merely a personal or dynastic loss, but a national tragedy: the Mexican adventure had cost France 6000 men killed and £45

millions of money spent at a time when the military situation on the continent was never more insecure.[19]

Perhaps good might still come out of evil if the two sovereigns most to blame for the Mexican disaster and most afflicted by it could meet and condole with one another? In August Louis travelled to Salzburg, and in October Francis-Joseph repaid the visit in Paris. They had not met since Villafranca — the beginning of all their misfortunes. Their talk, it could be assumed, was less about Mexico than Germany, where both Louis and Francis-Joseph were watching with apprehension the gradual unfolding of Bismarck's plans for a new Confederation — economic, political, and if need be military — from which Austria was, by the treaty of Prague, excluded, and by which the safety of the French Rhine frontier, depending upon the disunity of the west German states, was increasingly threatened. It was no longer possible to belittle the Prussian menace, and it was significant that, though there was no promise of a Franco-Austrian alliance, Bismarck, in his newly confident mood, should take offence at their inevitable conversations about the European situation, and warn them that no foreign power (for such was Austria as well as France now, in his reckoning) would be allowed to interfere with the affairs of Germany.

Louis had to admit publicly that there were 'clouds on the horizon' (*des points noirs sont venus assombrir notre horizon*). Nor were they only in the northern sky; for the visit of Francis-Joseph to the Paris *Exposition* coincided (October 30th) with the arrival of the second French expeditionary force in Rome — a reminder that Louis was as truly as Pius himself an enemy of Italian unity, and a fellow-prisoner of the Vatican.[20]

Delane of *The Times*, visiting Paris at this turn of affairs, brought back two impressions, which may be placed as a footnote to 1867. 'The bitterest enemies of Louis Napoleon here (he wrote on October 25th, thinking of the internal situation) admit that he has redressed his position *d'une manière éclatante*, and he seems to me now better off than he has been for years . . . Even Thiers could only console himself by the reflection that all was not yet over.' But when Delane lunched with the Rothschilds — 'people whose fortunes depend on peace and the funds' — he found them indignant with an 'intolerable situation: the honour of France at stake: Louis Napoleon only tolerated because he had upheld it *v*. Russia and Austria: France had not given him an army and fleet for nothing'. Delane suggested that

a war with Germany would be long, and perhaps unsuccessful. 'Never mind,' was the reply: 'let us rather have the Prussians on the boulevards again than be disgraced.'[21]

It would seem that the warlike temper of Paris which carried the Empire to its catastrophe in 1870 was at least of three years' standing, and was not confined to the politicians or the *canaille*. Certainly it had its roots in the diplomatic disillusionments of 1866.

6

No reckoning of Louis' position at the end of 1867 would be complete without the 'constitutional reforms' which he had announced as his New Year's gift to the people, and which twelve months' experience had proved to be as empty of real content as those of November 1860. In a letter to Rouher on January 14th, 1867, he had said that he wished 'to give to the institutions of the Empire their fullest possible development, and a fresh extension of public liberties, without compromising the power entrusted to him by the nation'. Any of the ministers might now be summoned before the *corps législatif* or the Senate. The *droit d'interpellation* would take the place of the *adresse* of 1860. The Press would no longer be answerable to the *préfets*, but only to the courts. The law on public meetings (*réunions*) would be made more liberal.

Prince Napoleon, for whom Louis thought he had at last found an occupation which would keep him out of mischief — the editing of Napoleon's *Correspondance* — at once wrote (January 20th) to congratulate him on an *acte additionnel en faveur de la liberté*; but complained that he had spoilt the measure by reappointing, to carry it out, ministers committed to the old regime, especially Rouher as *ministre d'état et des finances*. New measures (he said) require new men. 'What confidence can one have in the words of a minister who praises today a policy which a year ago he condemned as seditious? . . . Our present trouble is due to instability and weakness of character, softening of conscience, and the sight of ministers supporting from one day to another a policy they previously opposed, or staying in office to intrigue against it, and bring it to nothing.' Louis' answer (January 28th) was that Rouher had made himself indispensable, as the only minister capable of dealing with such questions before the House. Evidently Louis was determined that no concession to parliamentary government should impugn the personal dictatorship conferred on him by the vote of the nation and the constitution of the

Empire. The liberty that was to crown the edifice would be another laurel leaf on the brow of the Emperor.[22]

Rouher, who for nearly four years became what his enemies called 'Vice-Emperor', had all a lawyer's talent for defending a weak case, and more than a lawyer's indifference to principles. To a Persigny his Bonapartism was a creed rehearsed without conscience or conviction. But in fact he accepted half its clauses. His political life, he once said, dated from 1848; twenty years later he still believed that repression was the only safeguard against a fresh outbreak of anarchy, and that Louis had been entrusted by the nation with precisely that task. The other clauses of his creed – those dealing with political progress – equally depended on the will of the people, to be expressed by such a *plébiscite* as that of 1852. The Empire was a democratic and representative institution springing from the heart of the nation. To the end of his life Rouher maintained that his sole aim had been to preserve the constitution of 1852, so long as Louis wished it so. The Liberal Empire meant no more to him than minor constitutional changes made by the Legislature, without appeal to the nation; and he would do his best to see that they did not impugn the Emperor's prerogatives. Louis' answer to Prince Napoleon, then, did not give the true reason for his retaining Rouher under the 'new dispensation' of January 1867. He was not a great orator, and he never commanded the confidence of the genuine Liberals, represented since the death of Morny by Prince Napoleon and Emile Ollivier. His supreme merit, in Louis' eyes – and perhaps his only recommendation to Eugénie – was that he believed in maintaining the prerogatives of 1852, to be handed on intact to the Prince Imperial.[23]

It was an additional merit that Rouher showed himself willing to collaborate in Louis' tortuous foreign policy during the years before and after Sadowa. There was a *Sécret du Roi*, as there had been under Louis XV, and Rouher played the part of a de Broglie. But more: a lover of the countryside and of country people, he believed that free trade would bring cheaper food and clothing; free trade required peaceful relations between state and state; and that could only be when national aspirations were satisfied. 'When we recognize', he said in 1867, 'that a nation has a vigorous constitution, and has achieved real unity and homogeneity, we have no wish to attack it or destroy it.' And then, prophetically, 'A day will come when the vast domains of Russia carry a larger population, and when America,

whose development increases every day, will cover the distance of 3000 leagues which now separates her from us ... The day will come when it will no longer be a question of the balance of power (*l'équilibre*) in Europe, but of the balance of power in the world – a day when perhaps the great powers will try to dominate it; and then a natural common feeling will bring together the peoples of the West, and unite them to resist the threat of invasion.'[24]

Feeling thus, Rouher lent himself to a foreign policy whose ideals had been from the first, and still were in Louis' intermittent mind, nationalistic, peace-loving, and patriotic. In the Polish affair of 1863 he was for a peaceful settlement by a Congress. He was against the Mexican adventure, or merely excused it as a commercial enterprise. He devised and defended the plan of 1864 for the evacuation of the French garrison in Rome. He was in favour of settling the Danish dispute by a Congress. He shared Louis' indifference to the formation of a north German confederation, and his fears of the inclusion in it of the southern states – Bismarck claimed later to have discovered in his papers evidence of anti-Prussian intrigues there before 1866. In the critical days after Sadowa he was against any military move on the Rhine; and the Empress spoke so bitterly of his influence over the Emperor at this time – he was, she told Metternich, 'completely at the mercy of the man he had made First Minister ... the man who is the cause of our moral abdication (*déchéance*), and would have been willing, if allowed, to see us dethroned' – that one suspects he was one of those *autres influences* which changed Louis' mind during the night of July 5th, 1866, and cancelled the resolutions of the Council which might have antedated the Franco-Prussian war by three years.[25] Rouher too had been behind the scenes during all the tragi-comedy of compensations during the summer of 1866. He had made himself the indispensable counsel (or his enemies would say, accomplice) of the Emperor both in home and foreign policy. It was unthinkable, then, that he should not remain in office to carry through the 'reforms' promised in the letter of January 19th. And it was equally unthinkable that, unless he were ordered to do so, he would go out of his way to make them effective.

Such certainly was the firm conviction of Emile Ollivier, the disciple of Morny, and the most eloquent champion of Liberalism in the *corps législatif*, where he had for two years now carried on a duel with Rouher. He would have said he was opposing Rouher in the

name of a Liberal Emperor; for in 1865 he had been twice invited to the Tuileries for talks with Louis and Eugénie, and had come back as charmed by them as they were impressed by his honesty and idealism. He had declared in the House (March 27th, 1865) that if Louis XVI had listened to Mirabeau, the Revolution might have been avoided; if Robespierre to Vergniaud, the Terror; if Napoleon had introduced the *acte additionnel* in 1814, there would have been no Waterloo or St. Helena; if Charles X had taken Guizot's advice instead of Polignac's, or Louis-Philippe that of Odilon Barrot, the monarchy would have been saved; and for the Second Empire 'it is not too soon to make reforms; it is not too late; it is the very moment'. He was of course accused of personal ambition; but he always maintained that any Liberal minister would suffice. In 1865 he and a few friends formed a Third Party in the House, which could muster some 60 votes out of 270. When, after Sadowa, Louis was moved to make further concessions to 'reform', Ollivier was offered the Ministry of Education, and refused it; but he was persuaded by the Emperor against his better judgment to consult with Rouher as to carrying out the programme of January 19th, 1867. He found himself treated with friendly indifference by the 'Vice-Emperor', and attacked in the House both by those who said that he was betraying the Liberal cause, and by those who accused him of trying to displace Rouher, and impose his Liberalism upon the Emperor.[26]

When it was clear that the 'reforms' of January 19th were so whittled down by exceptions and restrictions as to be of little value, and when Louis refused to consider his advice as to new ministers and a general election, Ollivier openly attacked Rouher (July 12th), calling him a 'Grand Vizier', a 'Mayor of the Palace'. Louis replied by sending Rouher the grand cross of the Legion of Honour, and Ollivier accepted no more invitations to the Tuileries. Eighteen months later (March 1869) he published *Le 19 janvier*, an apologia in the form of a *compte rendu* to his constitutents: Louis saw it in proof, and allowed its truthfulness, however compromising it might be to his support of Rouher's policy.[27]

7

Almost at the moment when Ollivier was breaking with Rouher, and the Liberal Empire was once more found to be a mirage, a new witness appeared on the Paris scene, a man of judgment and in-

dependence, whose evidence is of uncommon value. Lord Lyons, who had first made his name as Secretary of Legation at Florence in 1857, and had since distinguished himself as Ambassador at Washington and Constantinople, arrived at the Paris embassy in October 1867, to remain there some twenty years. He was a man of immense diligence: during one year at Washington he had received 6490 dispatches and letters, and sent out 8326. He disliked public functions, and boasted that during his five years in the States he had never 'taken a drink or made a speech'; but he thought all the more, and acted with consistent tact and firmness.

Two of Lyons' early dispatches to his Foreign Secretary, Lord Stanley, describe interviews with the Empress Eugénie (who 'spoke with much grace both of manner and of expression, and I think with very great ability'), and Prince Napoleon ('He spoke with great animation and remarkably well') about the eternal question of Rome, which had just paused at another stage with Mentana and the proposal of a Paris conference. They of course took opposite sides: and when Lyons questioned Louis himself about the object of a conference, his reply was vague and unpractical. It might well be: for he was trying to find a diplomatic way out of an inescapable trap set by his own Catholic supporters. 'A permanent French occupation' was, as Odo Russell, the British representative at Rome, believed, 'the only possible machinery by which the Temporal Power can be imposed on Italy'; and the Pope was using all the levers of Catholic influence in France to preserve it.[28]

But Lyons was too shrewd a man to suppose that the questions about which speeches were made in the Chamber were more important than those which were discussed in the *cafés* and at the street-corners. 'The real danger to Europe', he wrote on January 16th, 1868, 'appears to be in the difficulties of the Emperor Napoleon at home. The discontent is great and the distress amongst the working classes severe. The great measure of the session, the new Conscription Act, is very unpopular. There is no glitter at home or abroad to divert public attention, and the French have been a good many years without the excitement of a change.' A week later he reported a conversation with Louis about a supposed plot to assassinate sovereigns, including a fresh attempt upon himself inspired by Mazzini. Lord Cowley, after visiting Fontainebleau that summer, reported that he found the Emperor 'aged, and much depressed'. 'His Majesty said little of foreign politics, but spoke gloomily of his

own position in France.' He had perhaps been reading Prévost-Paradol's *La nouvelle France* (1868), a warning of national danger which could be compared with Demosthenes' *Philippics*. He had found, touring the provinces, that 'the country districts were still for him, but that all the towns were against him'. Louis was even thinking of abdication. 'I hear from other persons besides Lord Cowley (Lyons went on) that the Emperor is very much out of spirits. It is even asserted that he is weary of the whole thing, disappointed at the contrast between the brilliancy at the beginning of his reign and the present gloom — and inclined, if it were possible, to retire into private life. This is no doubt a great exaggeration, but if he is really feeling unequal to governing with energy, the dynasty and the country are in great danger.'[29]

Was it an 'exaggeration' to speak of abdication? When questioned many years afterwards, Eugénie asserted that, though she strenuously opposed the 'reforms' of 1867, it was only because they were premature. 'I entirely agreed', she said, 'that the constitution of 1852 could not last for ever, and that sooner or later it would have to be modified in a democratic direction. The Emperor had often spoken to me about this. But his intention was to leave to our son the task of re-establishing in France the regime (*fonctionnement*) of public liberties. This great reform the Emperor did not think he could carry through himself, because he was the very embodiment of the authoritarian principle: it was his *raison d'être*. Nevertheless, so as not to postpone it too long, he had made the resolve, which he confided to no one but myself, to abdicate about the year 1874, when the Prince Imperial would be old enough to ascend the throne.' Louis had even planned the places of his retirement — Pau in the winter, Biarritz in the summer. The publication of the letter of January 19th (about which Eugénie had not been consulted) was due to the Emperor's growing concern about his health, and the feeling that he could not bear the burden of Empire another seven years. His illness was not mortal, but the attacks of pain were more frequent and disabling.

'God is my witness', the Empress said on another occasion, 'that in my mind I never separated France from the Empire; I never thought of the grandeur and prosperity of France apart from the Imperial rule. Since the state of my husband's health had become so disquieting, my supreme duty was to hand on to our son an undiminished prerogative (*une puissance intacte*): it was for him to

bring about the rejuvenation of the Napoleonic institutions.' Such was the spirit which rejected reform in 1867, and three years later plunged France into a suicidal war.[30]

The pity of it was that whilst Louis grew weaker in body and mind Eugénie grew more wilful and resolute. She was fond of quoting from *Hamlet*:

> This above all: to thine own self be true,
> And it must follow, as the night the day,
> Thou canst not then be false to any man.

'These fine lines (she would say) I have for a long time made my motto (*je les ai pris depuis longtemps pour devise*).' 'True', no doubt, she would be, like her heroine Marie Antoinette, to her foreign pride, 'true' to her husband's Bonapartism, 'true' to the hope of her son's succession: but in what sense true to France?[31]

8

Two general elections had been held in France since that of 1852: in 1857 and 1863. A third was due in May 1869; and every political party was on tip-toe to increase its representation. But this did not at all mean what it would in a country accustomed to party government. Where the legislature is divided into a majority which provides a ministry and controls legislation, and a minority which criticizes its policy and tries to throw out its bills, an election is a vote of censure on one possible party regime and a vote of confidence in another: whatever its result, the government of the country will go on. But where the legislature does not provide ministers or control legislation an election becomes a request for a vote of confidence in the only possible government — that of the sovereign or political party controlling the state; and every negative vote is a vote, not for a change in the government, but for the destruction of it; for a revolution, which might end in a new constitution, or in sheer anarchy. The dictatorial regime of the Second Empire — none the less dictatorial because it claimed to be based on the will of the people — had survived without much loss of power the elections of 1857 and 1863: but Louis had been forced by the dwindling majority for his government and the growing minority against it to make seeming concessions to democracy — the Liberal decrees of November 1860, May 1864, and January 1867; and now in

1868 fresh reforms were promised in respect of Trade Unionism, press censorship, and civic equality.

Yet nothing of this sort seriously affected the plain issue for or against the Empire. Such is the inevitable weakness of a dictatorship, which no elaboration of 'official candidature', a silenced press, government propaganda, or police intimidation can permanently conceal. Napoleon had ruled without question for fourteen years because his elections were meaningless, and his legislature without power even to question or to criticize. Louis had reigned (not unquestioned) for sixteen years, with surprising skill and unexpected success: but now it seemed that the gambler was at his last throw. If next year's vote went against him, there would be no space even for voluntary abdication.

At this moment occurred one of those *affaires* which are so congenial to the French character and the temper of Paris. Eugène Tenot, who had already published a work on the state of the French provinces in 1851 – a book still quoted by historians – followed it up with another entitled *Paris en décembre 1851: étude historique sur le Coup d'Etat*. London would not easily excite itself about events, however serious, sixteen years old: but to Paris, which still argued about August 10th and January 21st, still danced in the streets on July 14th, still spoke familiarly of the 13th *vendémaire*, the 18th *brumaire*, or the days of July, December 2nd was an indelible date – that of the death of Republicanism, and of the birth of the Second Empire; a reminder (if any reminder were needed in a people of such long memories) of the hateful origin of a once popular regime of which (again, as good Parisians) they were growing heartily tired. Tenot's passionless narrative revived old hatreds and old enthusiasms. It was recalled that one Baudin, a deputy, had been the first martyr for republicanism. His supposed grave was fêted, inflammatory speeches made, and the most violent of the orators, Delescluze, found himself put on trial by the Government. He was defended by the eloquent Gambetta, who compared Louis to Catiline, and said that the people would celebrate every December 2nd 'as the anniversary of our dead, until the day when the country becomes its own master again, and charges you with a great act of national expiation in the name of liberty, equality, and fraternity'.[32]

Few countries provide an edifying spectacle during the months preceding a general election. But perhaps even France never so closely as in the autumn and winter of 1869 resembled a people in

disintegration. At its head was a man prematurely aged, painfully ill, and hopelessly bewildered by events at home and abroad. By his side was a woman whom he had dishonoured as a wife and indulged as an Empress; a woman who had said that if another revolution came she would mount her horse and ride at the head of a regiment of cavalry; she would know how to save the crown for her son, and show what it meant to be an Empress; a woman of courage and intelligence, but wilful, impatient, domineering. For advisers there were still Persigny, Maupas, and Fleury of Louis' original followers; but they had been ousted from influence by Rouher and his friends, the political executors of Strasbourg, Boulogne, and December 2nd; these men too were growing old in office, and (as is the fate of dictatorial governments) had found no successors in the younger generation of statesmen. Their policies wavered like the Emperor's: their only common interest was to win the elections, and remain in power. This they had good hope of doing by the tactics which had served so well in 1857 and 1863, and through the mass vote of the countryside, which was still swayed by the name Napoleon and the fear of Parisian republicanism.

But if the supporters of the Empire were leaderless and divided, the Opposition suffered from too many parties and from leaders too ready to assert that only they could save the country: Orleanists, legitimists, moderate republicans, thorough-going democrats; Jules Ferry, with his attack on *Les comptes fantastiques d'Haussmann*, Rochefort, the workers' candidate, Raspail, the prophet of universal suffrage, or Gambetta, fresh from his defence of Delescluze, with his Belleville programme. 'I am passionately devoted', he declared, 'to the principles of Liberty and Fraternity: my political method is to revive and establish, in opposition to Caesarian Democracy, the creed, the claims, the demands, and even the inconsistencies (*incompatibilités*) of Loyal Democracy'; but would this be more than a rehash of the Jacobin constitution of 1893? These controversies were carried into every *café* and *salon de lecture* by the popular press: Hugo's *Le Rappel*, Delescluze's *Le Réveil*, de Rochefort's *La Marseillaise*, and — most abusive of all, recalling the worst publication of 1793 — Maroteau's *Le Père Duchesne*.

One might expect that the Emperor himself would stand aloof from such a contest. Not at all. In the Seine-et-Marne department there were three candidates: Jeaucourt, the official nominee, Jouvencel, one of the republicans proscribed after December 2nd, and

Ernest Renan, the distinguished ex-clerical and anti-clerical writer, whom Prince Napoleon numbered amongst his literary friends. Louis heard that the Prince had urged Renan to retire in favour of Jouvencel, and wrote to him: 'I hope it is not true, for it is very important to collaborate against the common enemy.' Renan did not retire; he split the government vote with Jeaucourt, and Jouvencel, 'the common enemy', was elected.[33]

When the results of the elections were known (May 23rd-24th), the figures could be read in two ways. The Government had a safe majority in the *corps législatif*; but the government vote in the country had sunk by 900,000 in the six years since the last election, whilst the opposition vote had risen by 1,400,000. This swing of opinion would have been normal and of little significance in an election between rival political parties: but when it showed a serious and growing defection on the part of the People itself which had put and kept Louis is power, it could not be taken lightly. What would the Emperor do?

The alternatives were put to him clearly enough in one of Prince Napoleon's admirable and irritating memoranda (May 28th). The name Napoleon (he agreed) had once more carried the polls. But (he asserted) 'the addresses, circulars, and speeches of the successful candidates, indeed the whole tone of the election, make it strikingly evident that the great majority of the electors hold liberal views. The personal government is generally condemned: the reactionary Empire numbers a very small number of adherents – perhaps less than thirty – in the new Chamber. The Emperor is therefore once more in a position to decide the destiny of France . . . If, by a change of policy and personnel, he enters on a course of constitutionalism and liberalism, if he agrees to sacrifice a part of his powers which is more apparent than real, there can be no doubt that he will be followed by the Chamber, and that his popularity in the country will be increased. Past mistakes will be excused; the Opposition, without being disarmed, will lose its influence over the masses; the Empire will strike its roots deeper than ever. If on the other hand the Emperor uses his influence to favour a reactionary clerical policy, if he continues to employ discredited and unpopular men like the present ministry, he may secure a passing success, he may dominate the country for a time, but he will be strengthening the republican, socialist, and revolutionary Opposition of the future; and this new power given to it will be terribly dangerous when any crisis

occurs at home or abroad.' Louis had therefore to choose one of three courses: reaction, conciliation, or compromise – what Prince Napoleon called *la politique d'indécision*. The Prince of course pressed for conciliation, and ended his memorandum with an outline programme for political and social reform, together with a foreign policy of partial disarmament, peaceful relations with Germany, and the evacuation of Rome.[34]

There was nothing new in all this: Louis had chased the alternatives to and fro in his mind for fifteen years. He came back once more, as a sick and disillusioned man would do, with the shrug of a fatalist, to the old familiar policy of compromise.

Malmesbury dined at the Tuileries on May 19th, 1869, and had a private talk with the Emperor. He found him disappointed with the result of the *plébiscite*, because some 50,000 hostile votes had been cast by the army; but, he explained, it was only in certain barracks where the officers were unpopular and the recruits numerous; the mass, 300,000, had voted for him. Malmesbury expressed surprise at this figure, imagining the French army to be twice as large. Louis 'looked suddenly very grave and absent'; but he evidently had no suspicions of the approach of war. He believed that Italy would be grateful to him for what he had done towards her liberation. He thought (Malmesbury guessed) that the liberal reforms which weakened his own hold on the Empire were likely to strengthen that of his son.[35]

This summer of 1869 Louis was increasingly incapacitated by illness. Indeed early in September Delane of *The Times* had his obituary notice ready: 'I do not think he will die this bout (he wrote); but if he does, Tom Mozley will have written the article upon him.' Another invalid might have appeared to be *in articulo mortis* – the French state.

For six months Louis tried to apply the old prescription of 1852 – repression and progress – to a sickness which was nearly twenty years past curing. On June 16th in an open letter he declared that 'It is always useless to meet popular movements by conceding principles or sacrificing persons: a self-respecting government cannot give way to pressure, inducement, or violence'; and he nominated a supporter of Rouher as Vice-President of the *corps législatif*. But a month later (July 12th), faced by a letter of resignation from the President and an interpellation backed by over a hundred deputies, he anounced a new programme of parliamentary concessions. The

corps législatif would in future have the right to nominate its own officials, initiate legislation, propose amendments, put down subjects for discussion (*motiver l'ordre du jour*), and vote the budget clause by clause. The senate could interpellate the government and amend or veto legislation proposed by the *corps législatif*: its sessions would be held in public. The Ministers could be deputies, and had the right to attend debates: but they were still to be appointed by and responsible to the Emperor. Thus Louis seemed to concede the forms of parliamentary government, whilst really retaining his superiority to it. Rouher was at last dismissed — there would now be no *ministre d'état* — but his understudies remained in office, and his policy went on, during the three months' grace before the meeting of the newly elected parliament at the end of October.[36]

9

By that time, warned by press attacks, by strikes, by provocative proceedings at the International at Bâle and a Congress of Peace and Liberty at Lausanne, and by the return of socialist candidates at the supplementary elections in Paris, Louis at last faced the inevitable, sent for Ollivier, and empowered him to form a Ministry of deputies 'representing the majority in the *corps législatif*, and pledged to implement in spirit and letter the *sénatus-consulte* of September 8th'. The Emperor presided over this Cabinet, and had a casting vote; but Ollivier was in effect Premier. The Empress was excluded.

None but extreme republicans could fail to welcome this regime. But the general feeling was that the concessions came too late, and would only encourage the extremists to ask for more. 'Ollivier's task', wrote that most intimate observer, Lord Clarendon, 'requires tact, experience, knowledge of men, and a few other qualities in which he seems singularly deficient, and I cannot think his ministry will last. La Valette thinks that the object of the implacables is to discredit the Chamber collectively and individually, so as to make its dissolution appear a necessity; then to pass a new electoral law; then to have a General Election with which the Government would be prohibited from interfering; and then to have a Chamber of Rocheforts and Raspails, which would be more than the *commencement de la fin.*' Indeed it was on January 10th that Gambetta, the most eloquent of the 'implacables', warned Ollivier in the Chamber: 'Your government is only a bridge between the Republic of 1848

and the Republic of the future; and it is a bridge that we intend to cross.'[37]

It was sheer bad luck that at this moment Louis' good-for-nothing cousin, Pierre Bonaparte, Lucien's son, who had twice before embarrassed him by his presence in America and England, became involved in a Paris brawl, and shot his opponent, Victor Noir. The *affaire* blazed up in the best Parisian tradition into newspaper articles, speeches, and rioting, and a crowd of 100,000 conveyed the latest victim of 'Bonapartist tyranny' to the cemetery at Neuilly. The Government found itself forced to take repressive measures which harmonized ill with Ollivier's conciliatory programme.

But good came out of evil when the Senate protested that its position under the revised constitution was inconsistent with the settlement of 1852, and Rouher, now its President, demanded an appeal to the electorate. Louis, with both Rouher and Ollivier behind him, seized the opportunity for a *plébiscite* on the whole issue of the Liberal Empire. On May 8th every Frenchman was invited to say 'Yes' or 'No' to the proposition; 'The People approves of the Liberal reforms brought about in the Constitution since 1860 by the Emperor in agreement with the great *corps de l'état*, and ratifies the *sénatus-consulte* of April 20th, 1870.' It was a clever move; for those who voted for Liberalism must vote for the personal Empire, and those who voted against the personal Empire must pass for anti-Liberals. The result was as might have been expected. Paris, Lyon, Marseille, Bordeaux, and Toulouse voted 'No'; but the countryside polled an overwhelming 'Yes': in all, 7,359,000 votes were cast for the Liberal Empire, not many less than the 7,800,000 cast for the Illiberal Empire of 1852. It was one more triumph for Louis and Bonapartism. He could not know that it was the last. The Empire seemed, even to its enemies, stronger than ever. 'The country (Louis declared) has been challenged to choose between revolution and the Empire, and it has made its choice. My government shall not deviate from the liberal course that it has chosen. Better than ever before we can face the future without fear.'[38]

'We can face the future without fear.' Louis was thinking first of his own position: of the Empire, once more nationalized by *plébiscite*, liberalized by 'consent of parliament', and so made ready for handing on to his son; of the Napoleonic dynasty, ranking henceforth alongside those of England, Prussia, Austria, Russia, Italy, and Spain; of the memory of 1815 wiped out, and France once more, as

Napoleon had made her, the leader of Europe in civilization, diplo-macy, and military power. This was a curious transformation of Louis' youthful dreams, but one which was sure to happen if once he gained mastery over the French state, and then found himself mastered in turn by national forces and traditions which were older than the Napoleonic Empire, older than the Revolution, older even than the Bourbon monarchy.

But Louis was also thinking of France's international situation. A dynasty among dynasties could not stand alone: it must have friends — in diplomatic terms, allies. And a *parvenu* dynasty, without family relationship with other royal families (towards which Prince Napoleon's marriage was a tentative beginning), must hold its allies by favour or fear. This had been Louis' most constant and anxious concern ever since he came into power; and it would not be too much to say that, after twenty years of advances and with-drawals, compliments and coolnesses, royal visits and ambassadorial conversations, nobody trusted him. The veiled eyes and expression-less face which had been schooled to hide dreaminess and indecision were suspected of masking a deep duplicity. The less he said, the more ominous the meaning read into his silences. When, as on occasion, he talked freely, his indiscretions were taken to reveal his true mind. In reality his true mind was star-gazing, and each problem was dealt with as it arose by a calculation of the interests and chances of the moment.

Just now, as an antidote against fear, he was thinking of the allies on whom he counted to help him against the obvious hostility of Prussia (none the less obvious when masked by talk of 'good relations') — a hostility which had good cause in the events of 1866, and in the unfortunate proposals for territorial compensation which had been used by Bismarck to win the support of the German states south of the Main, and would be used again to alienate Louis' possible allies; whilst Bismarck made no secret of his feeling (and one Bismarckian feeling was worth a dozen Bonapartist dreams) that war with France was inevitable and expedient (*Dass ein franzö-sischer Krieg auf den östreichischen folgen werde, lag in der historischen Konsequenz ... Ich nahm als sicher an, dass der Krieg mit Frankreich auf dem Wege zu unsrer weitern nationalen Entwicklung notwendig werde geführt werden müssen.*)[39]

Louis still seems to have believed that he could count on the support of Austria and Italy. He had during the last year (March

1869), working with the officially discarded but still indispensable Rouher, proposed a triple alliance with these two countries, including a secret promise of help in case of war. True, Austria would do no more than remain neutral, if France were the aggressor against Prussia; and Italy would go with Austria only on condition that France withdrew her garrison from Rome. The whole project was unofficial, unwritten, inconclusive; and it would be easy for the parties to it to evade any obligations Louis might think them to have incurred. Yet he seems really to have counted it, along with Marshal Niel's equally ineffective scheme of army reform, as good ground for 'facing the future without fear'.[40] As for the Papacy, Pius IX's determination to carry through the decree *De Infallibilitate Pontificis* gave Louis an excuse to withdraw his garrison from Rome; for, as he told Cardinal Antonelli (February 14th, 1870), 'he could not afford to have a schism in France, where all the employé class, all the literary class, and even the Faubourg St. Germain are against the infallibility of the Pope'. But his political embarrassments first made it impossible for him to carry out the implied threat, and then forced him to do so unconditionally.[41]

CHAPTER X

THE FATALIST (1869-1870)

HAM. I shall win at the odds. But thou would'st not think how ill all's here about my heart;
but it is no matter.

HOR. Nay, good my lord, —

HAM. It is but foolery; but it is such a kind of gain-giving as would perhaps trouble a
woman.

HOR. If your mind dislike anything, obey it; I will forestal their repair hither, and say you
are not fit.

HAM. Not a whit, we defy augury; there's a special providence in the fall of a sparrow. If
it be now, 'tis not to come; if it be not to come, it will be now; if it be not now, yet it will
come: the readiness is all. Since no man has aught of what he leaves, what is't to leave betimes?
Let be.

Hamlet, V, ii

I

THE 'future without fear' that Louis dreamed of in 1869 was in one
respect a mere delusion. For three years now it had become impossible to look eastwards from the Tuileries without visualizing a
Prussian army on the far bank of the Rhine; and it was plain to all in
Louis' confidence that the feeling inspired by the sight of it was not
confidence, but fear. It had already taken shape in two policies: a demand for compensation, and a counter-alliance. It was doubly
unfortunate for French prestige that the failure of both these policies
should be followed so closely by putting forward a third: that of
disarmament.

Within six months of the settlement of the Luxembourg affair Prince
Napoleon went on what was represented to be a private mission
from Louis to the Prussian court. He returned convinced of three
things: First, it would be useless to talk to the King of Prussia about
disarmament: he was a soldier, immensely proud of his army, and
could fairly claim that with only 200,000 men under arms he could
not safely reduce his forces: still less would he consider changing the
system which would enable him to put twice or thrice that number
of men in the field within ten days of a declaration of war. Secondly,
the consolidation of north and south Germany was going on rapidly;
so that, if France wished to attack Prussia, the sooner the better.
But, thirdly, such an attack would only hasten that consolidation,
instead of retarding it.

'Prince Napoleon', reported Lord Lyons (March 31st, 1868), 'is
himself opposed to war. He considers that an unsuccessful war

would overthrow the Emperor and his dynasty and send the whole Bonaparte family to the right-about. A war only partially successful would, he thinks, rather weaken than strengthen the Emperor at home, while a thoroughly successful war would simply give His Majesty a fresh lease of "Caesarism" and adjourn indefinitely the liberal institutions which he considers essential to the durability of the dynasty. At the same time the Prince is not without apprehension as to war being made this season. He fears weak men, and he looks upon the Emperor as a weak man. He fears the people who surround His Majesty — the Generals, the Chamberlains, the ladies of the Palace.'[1]

Six months later (October 20th, 1868) Lyons obtained from Clarendon, who had also visited the Prussian court, the other side of the picture. He had conversations with the King and Queen of Prussia, and with Count Moltke. 'The sum of what was said by all three is that Prussia earnestly desires to keep at peace with France; that she will be very careful not to give offence, and very slow to take offence: that if a war is brought on she will act so as to make it manifest to Germany and to Europe that France is the unprovoked aggressor: and that a war brought on evidently by France would infallibly unite all Germany . . . In short, Lord Clarendon is sure that the Emperor Napoleon may be confident that he has nothing to fear from Prussia if he does not give her just provocation: but on the other hand that Prussia does not fear a war if she can show Germany and the world that she is really forced into it.' This opinion Clarendon passed on to Louis at Saint-Cloud a week later. 'The Emperor heard the pacific assurances with evident satisfaction, and spoke very strongly himself in the same sense . . . At the same time His Majesty declared that if anything like a challenge came from Prussia it would be impossible for him to oppose the feeling of the army and the nation, and that he must in such a case for the sake of his own safety make war.' Louis might not admit that he was afraid of Prussia: he could not deny that he was afraid of France.[2]

So matters remained for a year. In January 1870, when it became known that Prussian ambition aimed at crossing the Main, and declaring an Empire of all Germany, Clarendon was asked by Ollivier through La Valette, the French ambassador, to raise once more the question of disarmament. He knew — they all knew — that it was playing with fire; for the King of Prussia would certainly resent any attempt to interfere with his military arrangements

('his army is his idol', Clarendon told the Queen), and in France a public rebuff would be fatal — '*un échec*', said Ollivier, '*c'est la guerre!*' But he had the sanction of Victoria and Gladstone to make the attempt; and on February 2nd he sent to Bismarck, through the British ambassador, a 'private and confidential letter', which 'invited his attention to the enormous standing armies that now afflict Europe . . . a state of things that no thoughtful man can contemplate without sorrow and alarm, for this system is cruel, it is out of harmony with the civilization of our age, and it is pregnant with danger'. He went on to emphasize Louis' wish for peace, and to say that 'there would be no opposition on the part of the French Government to a reduction of the army *pari passu* with Prussia'; and since neither government might wish to make the first move, he suggested sounding opinion at Paris himself confidentially.[3]

Bismarck's answer to this *démarche* was, as Clarendon and Lyons had expected, entirely unhelpful. 'You,' he said to the British ambassador, 'live in a happy island, and have not to fear an invasion. For 250 years Germany has been exposed to and suffered French invasion; no one can accuse us of being aggressive; Germany as now constituted has all that she wants, and there is no object of conquest for her. But our position is an exceptional one. We are surrounded by three Empires with armies as large as our own, any two of whom might coalesce against us.' He then recalled a conversation with Louis in 1867, when 'he had discussed with him the causes which had led to the overthrow of Louis XVI, Charles X, and Louis-Philippe — that their fall was due to want of energy and decision . . . Bismarck said that the Emperor had had but two courses to pursue: either to grant more internal liberty, or war; and the Emperor had told him very clearly that if the one failed there could be no alternative' (i.e., no other alternative but war). The written answer with which Bismarck followed up this conversation (Bismarck to Bernstorff, February 9th) added nothing to these arguments; 'Your Majesty (wrote Clarendon to the Queen on February 9th) will regret to hear that the proposal has proved a total failure' — but he still pursued the attempt to bring the two sides together, and on March 11th the British ambassador again interviewed Bismarck, with the request that he would submit Clarendon's letters to the King, whom he had previously said he was afraid to approach on the subject. This he did, and reported that William would not consider any sort of disarmament. Clarendon at last admitted 'that it was useless to

pursue the question further'. It was his last effort for European peace: he died on June 27th the same year. But when the war was over, Bismarck, meeting one of his daughters, 'opened the conversation with the singular remark that never in the whole course of his life had he been so relieved as when her father died; and then proceeded to explain that had Lord Clarendon lived there would never have been a Franco-German war'.[4]

Can Bismarck really have thought so? Had he not been firmly convinced that the 'logic of history' would lead from Solferino to Sadowa, and from Sadowa to Sedan? Had he not been doing his best to make that proposition come true, with the aid of a single-minded diplomacy and a centralized authority which outmatched at every turn the vacillating policy and disintegration of power at the Tuileries? What could the Clarendon correspondence have meant to him but a proof that Louis, who evidently inspired it, was trying to secure another Conference of the Powers, or was hoping to gain more time for military preparations?

He must have guessed, too, how half-hearted these would be. The easy successes of French arms in Italy and the Crimea had confirmed belief in the old system by which a small standing army of veterans was recruited by lot from those who were unlucky enough to draw a *mauvais numéro*, or too poor to pay for a substitute; whilst half the poor and all the rich escaped any kind of military training. Even the shock of discovering in 1866 that Prussia had a formidable army based on universal conscription, even the set-back to French military prestige in Mexico, even General Trochu's damaging pamphlet, *L'armée française en 1867*, even the *Moniteur's* demand for an army of 800,000 men, even the appointment of Marshal Niel, with his reform programme, as Minister of War, achieved nothing more than a provision that those who drew a *bon numéro* and could not afford to pay a substitute should form a kind of *garde mobile*, and do a fortnight's training a year, but not in camp or barracks, and not under military discipline — a very different affair from the Prussian *Landwehr*, whose members had all been through three years' service in the standing army and a period in the reserve. Nevertheless there was great appearance of activity upon the surface of this fundamentally unsound system. The new *chassepot* was being mass-produced, and the newer *mitrailleuse* tried out. Railway transport was being organized, and maps were being printed — but only of the country on the German side of the Rhine. It was proudly announced that in

case of war France could put in the field, within a week, an army of three-quarters of a million men. But the death of Niel in August 1869, and his replacement by Lebœuf, slowed down every improvement; as did the refusal or reduction of war credits by the *corps législatif*. The country was in that dangerous state when the feeling that war may break out at any moment finds relief in a credulous pacifism.[5]

2

Yet there was never a time, perhaps, when the foreign observer would have been less likely to suspect the hidden weaknesses of a regime which made such a public show of confidence and prosperity. Englishmen, in particular, contrasted the dullness of London and the seclusion of Windsor with the constant shows and festivities that enlivened Paris and the Tuileries. 'In France there seemed to be bands and banners or military display almost every day . . . congresses of *Orphéonistes* with gorgeous lyres on their standards, or of *Pompiers* with magnificent brass helmets . . . religious processions with choirs and hundreds of little girls in blue sashes, and statues of the Virgin Mary, or other saints, borne aloft . . . local fairs — *Kermesses* or *Foires* — with gilt gingerbread, dancing, and performing apes . . . and military shows by far the most frequent attractions — ranging from the evening march of the buglers of the garrison of a small town down the Grande Rue, sounding the well-known air of the *réveillé*, up to spectacular parades on the Champ de Mars at Paris, and occasional imperial reviews . . . Under the Second Empire the soldier was everywhere, very conspicuous because of his various multicoloured and sometimes fantastic uniform . . . the trooper of the Cent Gardes — the hundred horsemen — in the brightest sky-blue, with cuirass and steel helmet . . . the bear-skins of the grenadiers of the Imperial Guard . . . the white breeches and black gaiters of the original *grognards* of Napoleon I . . . the Zouaves of the Guard with their floppy tasselled headgear and immense baggy breeches, with yellow lace upon their absurdly small cut-away jackets.'

The intelligent small boy who noticed all this — he grew up to be the historian Sir Charles Oman — was present at a ceremony in the Tuileries gardens which might well serve as an ominous interlude between the life and death of the Second Empire. 'The Prince Imperial, then a boy of twelve, was a cadet, and was to drill a com-

pany of other cadets of his own age on the gravel in front of the Palace' — that part of the building which was burnt down by the Commune less than two years later. 'On a bench overlooking the gravel sat a very tired old gentleman, rather hunched together, and looking decidedly ill. I do not think I should have recognized him but for his spiky moustache. He was anything but terrifying in a tall hat and a rather loosely-fitting frock coat . . . Behind him stood the Empress Eugénie, a splendid figure, straight as a dart, and to my young eyes the most beautiful thing that I had ever seen . . . wearing a zebra-striped black and white silk dress, with very full skirts, and a black and white bonnet. But it was the way that she wore her clothes, and not the silks themselves, that impressed the beholder, young or old . . . The Empress was a commanding figure, and dominated the whole group on the terrace — the Emperor, huddled in his seat, was a very minor show. She appeared extremely satisfied and self-confident as she watched the little manœuvres below. Her son, the Prince Imperial, a slight nice-looking boy of twelve in his cadet uniform, drilled his little flock with complete success and not a single hitch or hesitation. His mother beamed down upon him. The boys marched off, and the spectators broke up after indulging in a little *Vive l'Empereur!*'[6]

3

Whilst every eye was fixed apprehensively on the Ardennes, a storm was blowing up over the Pyrenees. It arose, as so often, out of a disputed throne. After the deposition of Couza, in 1868, the crown of Rumania had been offered to the Count of Flanders, and, on his refusal, to Charles, son of Prince Antony of Hohenzollern-Sigmaringen. This proposal, as Bismarck was quick to see, was obviously in the interests of Prussia. That it also had the support of France was due not so much to any wish on Louis' part to conciliate Prussia as to the pressing influence of his old friend Mme Cornu, who had long been intimate with this Catholic branch of the Hohenzollerns. Prince Charles' acceptance set the pattern in Bismarck's mind for the trap into which Louis fell two years later.

For in May 1869 the throne of Spain, vacant since the revolution of September 1868, had been offered by the Minister-President, Marshal Prim, to Charles' younger brother, Prince Leopold. It had already been refused by more than one royal family, and Leopold's

candidature had been discussed for some six months past: in March it had been reported by Benedetti from Berlin to Louis, and he was instructed to ask for assurances that Prussia would not support a suggestion so objectionable to France. This at once raised the question to international status; and any part that Bismarck took in the later negotiations must have been with full knowledge of what might happen if the candidature were persisted in. In February 1870, it was renewed in the form of an official letter from Prim to William and Bismarck. William was no doubt the head of the Hohenzollern family, but he was also King of Prussia: in other words the invitation was no longer a private affair; and, though William might be unwilling to admit it, Bismarck at least was well aware of the capital that his country might make out of it. Spain would be grateful to Prussia if she provided a king to put an end to a period of anarchy. The presence of a pro-German power on the Pyrenees would divert French attention and troops from the Rhine frontier, and be a guarantee that France would keep the peace. There would be an increase of trade between Germany and Spain. It would strengthen the prestige of the Hohenzollerns. France might well prefer it to a Spanish republic or to an Orleanist on the Spanish throne.[7]

William himself wished to keep the matter on a family level, and refused to see Prim's emissary, whilst the Crown Prince asked his wife to write to Windsor, and to get the advice of her mother, Queen Victoria. But it was agreed that a conference should be held on the subject (March 15th) at which Prince Antony and his two sons were present, as well as Bismarck, Moltke, and Roon. These three, a significant triumvirate in view of what was to follow, were in favour of Leopold's acceptance; but he again refused, and so did his younger brother Frederick whom Bismarck proposed in his place. Three months later a third invitation arrived in the hands of the Spaniard Salazar, accompanied now by the Prussian Foreign Office agent Bucher, whom Bismarck had sent to Spain after the abortive conference. This time (June 21st) William gave way to pressure (*nach schweren Kampfe*), and Leopold accepted the crown.[8]

The whole affair had been conducted in secrecy: neither the French ambassador at Madrid nor the Spanish ambassador in Paris knew of it till it was all over. The French government was so unapprehensive that on June 30th Ollivier declared in the *corps législatif*: 'There was never a time at which peace in Europe seemed to me more assured.

In whatever direction I look, I see no critical question being raised: all the cabinets realize that the respect for treaties is a common duty.' In London Granville had just succeeded Clarendon at the Foreign Office, and was being congratulated by his Assistant Secretary Hammond on 'the greatest lull he ever remembered' in diplomatic questions.[9]

In view of what had happened in Rumania in 1866, and of Clarendon's and Benedetti's warnings, it is difficult to accept the view of Bismarck's apologists that he never anticipated war in 1870, that his revival of the Hohenzollern candidature in the spring of that year was designed only to raise Prussian prestige in Germany, that the secrecy with which the negotiations were conducted was not expected to offend France, and that no one could have foreseen that the French would make the candidature a *casus belli*. It is true that even Bismarck could not have foreseen exactly what would happen. But, being the man he was, and knowing France as he did, he must have had two thoughts in his mind when he encouraged the candidature, and at the same time kept it so dark: either the sudden and secret enthronement of a Hohenzollern at Madrid would keep France quiet, or it would excite her to violence. And, knowing as he well did the temper of Paris, the foolishness of Gramont, and the weakness of Louis, there can be little doubt that he ranked the second possibility at least as high as the first. Nothing could have been better calculated to cause just such an outbreak of national resentment as followed. In London, where the trouble due to the 'Spanish Marriages' of 1846 was not forgotten, Granville condemned the secrecy of the whole affair as 'certainly offensive to France, and not courteous to other Powers'; and the only reason why Bismarck risked this bad impression was because he knew that it would have been impossible to carry out the plan openly.[10]

In Paris the thunderbolt fell from a clear sky. On Saturday July 2nd the *Gazette de France* announced that the throne of Spain had been offered to and accepted by a prince of the hated house of Hohenzollern: the official dispatch from the French ambassador in Madrid reached the Quai d'Orsay the next day. A Hohenzollern at Madrid was a very different thing from a Hohenzollern at Bucharest. Frenchmen remembered Wellington's Pyrenees invasion of 1814, and had not forgotten the threat of German encirclement a century — or, for that matter, two and a half centuries — earlier. After Prince Leopold's refusal of the Spanish crown a year ago his

fresh acceptance of it must have had the consent of the King of Prussia, and could hardly be anything but a plot of Bismarck's, a challenge to French pride. The Duc de Gramont, whom Louis had recently (in May) recalled from Vienna to be Foreign Minister, was just the man to fall into the 'trap' – a proud, hot-headed, anti-Prussian patriot, who believed in the French army as he believed in the Pope, and would not shrink from pitting his wits against Bismarck's, or hurrying a sick Emperor and an inexperienced Premier into war. Indeed Gramont, as soon as he heard the news, assumed the worst, and lost no time in informing the foreign powers – Lord Lyons, Metternich, and the French ambassador at St. Petersburg – that 'France would go to war sooner than allow a Hohenzollern to rule at Madrid'.[11]

There followed a week of anxious uncertainty. At Saint-Cloud on the 6th the Council discussed the diplomatic and military situation, and authorized Gramont to make a declaration in the *corps législatif* which was moderate enough in its terms (as even King William recognized), but was delivered in such a tone of defiance as to be interpreted by the excited deputies as little less than an ultimatum: the whole house rose to their feet, waved their hats in the air, and cried *Vive la France! Vive l'armée! Vive l'Empereur! A Berlin!* Most of the Paris papers took up the cry.[12]

The next day Gramont, in the course of an unauthorized correspondence with Benedetti, who had been sent on a special mission to the Prussian court, wrote that the only hope of peace lay in his securing a personal undertaking from King William disowning and forbidding Prince Leopold's acceptance of the throne. 'I insist (he said) upon your not allowing any time to be wasted by evasive answers. We must know whether it is to be peace, or whether a refusal is to mean war. If you get the King to recall the Prince's acceptance, it will be an immense sucess, and a great service. The King will, of his own accord, have assured the peace of Europe. If not, it is war.' On the 10th he wrote again: 'You must absolutely insist upon having the King's answer – Yes or No. We must have it tomorrow: the day after will be too late.' He wrote again in the same terms on the 11th. 'If the Prince of Hohenzollern's renunciation is announced in 24 or 48 hours', Lyons reported on the 10th, 'there will be peace for the moment. If not, there will be an immediate declaration of war against Prussia.'[13]

4

The only sensible steps towards preserving peace at this critical moment were taken by Louis himself. The French ambassador in London was instructed to ask the British Government to use its influence in Berlin and Madrid against the Hohenzollern candidature; and Granville made representations accordingly — as indeed he continued to do until the declaration of war. But Louis relied even more upon private pressure. He wrote to the young King of Belgium (Leopold II had succeeded his father in 1865) urgently requesting him (*demande pressante mais très secrète*) to write to Prince Leopold and tell him that the peace of the world depended upon his renouncing the Spanish throne. The King did so on the evening of July 9th; and he passed on the message to Queen Victoria, who also wrote on the 11th to Philip Count of Flanders, whose wife was Prince Leopold's sister, in the same sense. Louis also sent Strat, a Rumanian agent, to Sigmaringen, to interview Prince Antony, Leopold's father: he was to emphasize the difficulties Leopold might expect to face in Spain, and the danger of Rumanian plots in Paris against his brother Charles — plots against which only Louis, to whom he owed his throne, could protect him.[14]

On the morning of July 12th, impressed by all this good advice, Prince Antony telegraphed to Prim at Madrid that he had persuaded his son to withdraw his acceptance of the Spanish crown. Louis heard of the success of his appeal the same day; but for some reason he kept the news to himself, as Gramont had kept to himself his private letters to Benedetti; and it was left to Ollivier, who received a copy of the telegram from the *cabinet noir* of the Paris Post Office that evening, to announce the news to the *corps législatif*. Queen Victoria heard of it in a letter from the Crown Prince of Prussia on the 13th: 'all pretext of war (he wrote) on the part of France is removed . . . my Father has acted in an upright and honourable manner, and has shown his decided love of peace'.[15]

But what would Paris say? Not unnaturally, in view of the growing excitement during the last nine days, the deputies, balked of their *revanche*, threw doubt upon the Spanish communiqué. It was only a private undertaking by the Prince and his father; it contained no mention of France or Prussia. What guarantees were there that it carried the consent of the Prussian King or government? Might not the decision be again reversed? The word *garanties* quickly became the slogan of the war party, and the cry of the Paris crowd:

soon it obsessed the mind of the Foreign Minister. The bare with-drawal of the candidature (he argued) was not enough. Prussia must publicly and officially dissociate herself from the whole affair. There must be a guarantee that the question would not be raised again. By this time (it is charitable to suppose) private ambition and public duty, his fear of public opinion and his desire to humiliate Bismarck, were so confused in Gramont's mind that he hardly knew what he was doing.

It was understood that the whole question would be discussed at a meeting of the Council the next day, the 13th. But that same even-ing, July 12th, at five o'clock, the Emperor, the Empress, and Gramont met at Saint-Cloud, without summoning even Ollivier, and decided the fate of France outright. After two hours' talk Gramont telegraphed to Benedetti: 'In order that this withdrawal by Prince Antony may have its full effect, it appears necessary that the King of Prussia should associate himself with it, and assure us that he will not authorize the candidacy afresh. You are to have an audience with the king at once, and to ask him for this declaration, which he can hardly refuse if his intentions are really honest. Although the renunciation is now public, tempers are so high that it is not certain whether we shall succeed in controlling them.'

The essential words of this instruction — *Veuillez vous rendre im-médiatement auprès du roi pour lui demander cette déclaration qu'il ne saurait refuser, s'il n'est véritablement animé d'aucune arrière-pensée* — could hardly have been more tactless and provocative. When Ollivier heard of it he sent Benedetti, too late, a postscript: 'Be sure you say that we are not seeking an excuse for war.'[16]

In after years the Empress admitted that she had backed Gramont's action, believing, as he did, that French opinion would not be satis-fied with anything less than the King of Prussia's guarantee. 'Unless we obtained it, France would be humiliated and insulted in the face of all Europe; there would be an outbreak of anger in every French heart against the Emperor; it would be all up with the Empire . . . No: after Sadowa and Mexico we could not subject the national pride to a fresh trial. We must have our revenge (*Il nous fallait une revanche*). To the objection that war might still have been avoided by exposing the trick of the Ems telegram — 'No, no! (she replied); it was too late to avoid war. You cannot imagine what an outburst of patriotism carried all France away at that moment. Even Paris, hitherto so hostile to the Empire, showed wonderful enthusiasm,

confidence, and resolution. Frantic crowds in the boulevards cried incessantly, *A Berlin! A Berlin!* No, I can assure you, it was beyond human power to prevent war any longer.' Eugénie, then, never really supposed that Benedetti's *démarche* was expected to put an end to Bismarck's *machinations* without undue risk of war? She was in truth too single-minded to care; and if war came, she believed — as everyone did except perhaps the Emperor — the French army to be invincible.[17]

So, on the 13th, in the Kurgarten at Ems, Benedetti had his last and decisive interview with the King of Prussia. William, who had been delighted to hear of Prince Leopold's withdrawal, and hoped the whole matter was now settled, had answered his request for an interview by making an appointment late in the morning, 'after his promenade'; but the ambassador, encouraged by an exchange of polite messages, put himself in his way while he was still in the park, delivered Gramont's tactless demand not too tactfully, and, thinking to carry his point, ended: 'Well, Sire, I can then write to my government that Your Majesty has consented to declare that you will never permit Prince Leopold to renew the candidature in question?' 'At these words (the King wrote later) I stepped back a few paces and said in a very earnest tone: It seems to me, Mr. Ambassador, that I have so clearly and plainly expressed myself to the effect that I could never make such a declaration that I have nothing more to add. Thereupon I lifted my hat and went on.' Later in the day the King cancelled the original appointment, and authorized Abeken to send a telegram to Bismarck describing the whole incident.[18]

Bismarck had been afraid that William might weaken in face of French persistence, and had started for Ems on the 12th to prevent his meeting Benedetti; but when he heard of Leopold's withdrawal he assumed that the affair was ended ('He regards peace as assured', wrote the Crown Prince in his diary on the 13th), and returned to Berlin. He was at dinner with Roon and Moltke on the evening of the 13th when Abeken's telegram arrived. He at once saw that it could be communicated to the press in a shortened form which would imply that the King had felt insulted by Benedetti's request, and had refused to have anything more to do with him — *Se. Majestät der König hat es darauf abgelehnt, den französischen Bothschafter nochmals zu empfangen, und demselben durch den Adjutanten vom Dienst sagen lassen, dass Se. Majestät dem Bothschafter nichts weiter mitzutheilen habe.* This version appeared in a special supplement of

the *Norddeutsche Allgemeine Zeitung* next morning, and caused almost as much public indignation in Berlin as the news of July 3rd had caused in Paris.[19]

The 'Ems telegram', as Bismarck's *communiqué* to the press came to be called, had exactly the effect that he had counted on when it was known in Paris on the 14th. 'It is a blow in the face of France', said Gramont to Ollivier, 'and (still confusing his personal and public feelings) I would sooner resign than put up with such an outrage.'

The Council met three times on the 14th. Louis knew, in spite of his Minister of War's assurances, that the army was not ready; in spite of his Foreign Minister's confidence, that he had no allies. But he was ill – so ill that his doctors had already recommended an operation – and at the end of his tether. His last attempt to keep the peace had been destroyed by public suspicion and excitement. At 6 p.m. the party for peace still prevailed. But the Empress, Gramont, Ollivier, and Lebœuf were set on war. At the final meeting, at 10 p.m., Eugénie herself was present – for the first time at a full Council meeting since Ollivier's appointment – and declared that the honour of France demanded war. It was decided that the army reserves should be called up, and that a message announcing this and other war measures should be read in the Assembly the next day. The wording of this message was unanimously approved at another Council meeting the next morning. At 1 o'clock Gramont carried it to the Senate, and Ollivier to the *corps législatif*. It reported Benedetti's interview with the King, and the Ems telegram. It announced that the reserves had been called up, and ended: 'With your consent we shall take immediate steps to safeguard the interests, the security, and the honour of France'. The Senate received this declaration of war – for what else could it be? – with unanimous enthusiasm. The *corps législatif*, where there was still a peace party, debated it for eleven hours, and asked awkward questions about the diplomatic negotiations and the state of the army – Benedetti had returned and was present, but was not questioned. At last, after midnight, the war credits asked for by the government were voted almost unanimously against a minority that sank, after the first division, from 10 to 1. Four days later (July 19th) war was officially declared.[20]

There was no question in 1870, as there had been at so many earlier crises, of Paris dictating to France what course the country should follow. The war fever was not confined to the capital. From Per-

pignan the *préfet* reported: 'The idea of war with Prussia is warmly received by the bulk of the population . . . No one for a moment doubts the results of the war. Everywhere, in town and village, the same confidence is shown.' Whilst a Paris bookseller advertised *Dictionnaire Français-Allemand à l'usage des Français à Berlin*, at Marseille there was a torchlight procession of over ten thousand people singing the *Marseillaise* and crying *A bas la Prusse!* and *A Berlin!* English visitors, of whom there were many in France that summer, may have been struck by the confusion by which the mobilization of the army was accompanied; but few of them doubted that the 'red-breeches' would get the better of the 'sauerkrauts'.[21]

It was overlooked that Bismarck had succeeded in making France the aggressor, and that the southern states of Germany would now join the north in resisting a foreign invasion of their common fatherland. It was not reckoned that Carlyle would soon be expressing in *The Times* the opinion of most neutral observers: 'That noble, patient, deep, pious, and solid Germany should at length be welded into a nation, and become Queen of the Continent, instead of vapouring, vainglorious, gesticulating, quarrelsome, restless and over-sensitive France seems to me the hopefullest public fact that has occurred in my time.' When Ollivier declared, 'It is a great responsibility that we are undertaking, but we accept it with a light heart (*nous l'acceptons d'un cœur léger*)', it was the end of his political career: but it was also the epitaph of the Second Empire.[22]

France had plunged into war without allies, and without friends. Bismarck had seen to it that Russia, since the Polish revolt, would not intervene, unless it were to check any movement by Austria. Austria, in any case, could not easily forgive Louis' failure to help her in 1866, or the presence of French troops in Italy. Victor Emmanuel was not as grateful as Louis thought he should be for the 'liberation' of Italy and the gift of Venetia, and demanded Rome as the price of intervention. Any lingering sympathy that these or other courts might have with the Tuileries was effectively stifled by the publication in *The Times* on July 25th of a document communicated by the Prussian embassy (Bismarck had shown it to Leopold's minister at Berlin on the 24th, as he wrote to Victoria the same day): it was nothing less than the project of treaty between France and Prussia drawn up in 1866, of which Article 5 stated that Prussia would not oppose the French conquest and annexation of Belgium. The existence of this document — it was in the handwriting of Bene-

detti – had been disclosed to Greville and Gladstone by Bernstorff, the Prussian ambassador, a few days before: they could not doubt, as many did, its authenticity, but they had kept it to themselves; Gladstone was not exaggerating when he wrote to the Queen, after its publication: 'Your Majesty will, in common with the world, have been shocked and startled' by it.[23]

Nevertheless Louis made a last bid for Italian help when on August 19th he sent Prince Napoleon to see his father-in-law, Victor Emmanuel, at Florence. Two days later Jérôme telegraphed that he had seen the King and his ministers: they were friendly, and would do what they could diplomatically, but could take no immediate military action (*Italie bien disposée mais impuissante militairement avant un mois*). His later telegrams (August 23rd, 25th, 27th) told the same tale: Italy would talk, but not act . . . unless there were a French victory (*Si notre armée avait succes cela pourrait changer*). And what hope was there of that?[24]

5

Although it would be six months before Paris fell, and nearly ten before peace was made, the Franco-German war was over, as far as effective fighting went, within six weeks. During that time the dramatic tension between the Empress and the Emperor, between the positive and negative, the optimistic and pessimistic outlooks, extended from the Tuileries to the army headquarters on the north-east frontier. But it made little difference to either result of the struggle – the defeat of the French armies and the destruction of the Empire. What bravery could do was done. But bravery was not enough where diplomacy was outmatched, forces outnumbered, and generals outwitted.

Nine days after the declaration of war (July 28th) Eugénie drove the invalid Emperor and the young Prince Imperial in her pony-carriage to the private station at Saint-Cloud, and saw them off by train to Metz. There Louis found himself in nominal command of eight *corps d'armée*, some 220,000 men in all, posted along a salient front of 150 miles behind the Saar and the upper Rhine from Thionville on the Luxembourg frontier to Belfort on the border of Switzerland. They had planned to invade Germany, and the enemy expected them to do so. Louis' proclamation to the army had said, 'Whatever road we may take beyond our frontiers, we shall find glorious traces of our fathers. We will prove ourselves worthy of them.'

But already the French army was undermanned, short of equipment, and unprepared to advance. Louis' own account of the situation is sufficiently revealing. 'Instead of having, as we had a right to expect, 385,000 men in line to oppose the 430,000 of North Germany and the southern states, the army, when the Emperor arrived at Metz, numbered only 220,000 men; and even so, not only were there gaps in the ranks, but there was a shortage of indispensable equipment. The army of the Moselle had only 110,000 men in place of 220,000: that of Marshal MacMahon only 40,000 instead of 107,000. There were great difficulties in making up General Douay's corps at Belfort; and that of Marshal Canrobert was not yet complete.'[25]

The reservists who were to have filled the depleted ranks were posting up and down France looking for uniforms and arms: the railways were blocked with supplies still lacking at the front: officers could not find the units they were to command: generals at the front telegraphed to say that they had plenty of maps of the German side of the frontier, but none of the French; that they had no canteens, ambulances, or baggage-carts: 'there is an utter lack of everything'. Louis himself was almost too ill to travel: nominally in supreme command, he was no soldier, and his generals knew it. Only the young Prince Imperial thought it a brave adventure, and behaved with admirable coolness when he came under fire at Saarbrücken on August 2nd. (*Une fois même*, his proud father telegraphed home, *il a tranquillement ramassé une balle qui venait de tomber à ses pieds. Des soldats de la Garde ont pleuré en le voyant si calme*). But when Ollivier published the gallant incident, Paris only laughed.[26]

With the easy capture of Saarbrücken, two miles inside Germany (August 2nd), the French offensive, upon which all the plans and hopes had been based, came to an end. On the German side everything was ready; and it was they who, unexpectedly the aggressors owing to French dilatoriness (as the Crown Prince wrote from Spires on August 1st), now advanced across the frontier. They had never counted on taking the offensive, and entered upon the campaign with more anxiety than confidence. 'The odds are fearfully against us', wrote the Crown Princess to her mother, Queen Victoria, on July 18th; 'in the awful struggle which is about to commence, and which we are forced into against our will, *knowing* that our existence is at stake.'[27]

The French stake was a dynasty, the German stake was a nation. It might well seem that the chances of war were on the side of a

dynasty which had such a wave of national enthusiasm behind it, and such a tradition of military glory; that the success of the Prussian army in 1866 against an enemy accustomed to failure could not be repeated against one which had not known defeat since 1815; and that the precarious alliance between the northern and southern states would break down under the pressure of invasion.

But at the first clash it was apparent that the southern army, which the Crown Prince (entrusted, as in 1866, with the most difficult and dubious command) had feared might fail him, was united by hatred of the French invader. Mobilization was so quick and complete that Lord Houghton could write on August 1st, 'I was going in the middle September to Ammergau to see the Miracle Play; but the chief person is taken off to serve in the artillery, with Judas Iscariot as his superior officer.' At Wissembourg on August 4th and Fröschwiller or Wörth on August 6th — both at the salient angle of the French line — considerable parts of MacMahon's army were overrun by superior German forces, and driven back into Lorraine. Strasbourg was invested; and further north, near Saarbrücken, another force was defeated at Forbach or Spicheren the same day.[28]

On the evening of this ominous August 6th rumours of victory reached Paris, and crowds paraded the streets singing the *Marseillaise*. But at midnight at Saint-Cloud the Empress was roused to receive a telegram from the Emperor giving the news of Fröschwiller and Forbach, and ending (as though he saw in the first set-back the certainty of final defeat) with instructions to proclaim Martial Law and prepare to defend Paris (*Il faut déclarer l'état de siège et de se préparer à la défense de la capitale*). The crisis fired all Eugénie's Castilian courage. Like her heroine Marie Antoinette on another fatal 6th (of October, 1789), she set out for Paris and the deserted Tuileries. 'The dynasty is doomed', she said. 'now our only thought must be for France.' She summoned the Council to meet her at the Tuileries at 2 a.m. Next morning she telegraphed confidently to Louis that the invaders would soon be driven back to the frontier and that she could answer for Paris. (*Je suis persuadée que nous mènerons les Prussiens l'épée dans les reins jusqu'à la frontière. Courage donc; avec l'énergie nous dominerons la situation. Je réponds de Paris.*) At midday she had posted in the streets a placard acknowledging a defeat and calling for a united effort to save the national honour. (*Qu'il n'y ait parmi vous qu'un seul parti, celui de la France, un seul drapeau, celui de l'honneur national.*)[29]

The Assembly, summoned to meet on the 8th, instead of taking

this brave message to heart, echoed the public panic, and demanded a change of ministers and generals: Ollivier and Gramont to go, Palikao to replace Lebœuf at the Ministry of War, Trochu to command at the front. As Regent, Eugénie had no power to appoint ministers; but she was not one to shirk responsibility. She told her old friend Mérimée, who saw her at the Tuileries on the 9th, that Paris was being garrisoned and provisioned for a siege, and that she would stay there, whilst a second government at Tours would organize the defence of the south. 'We shall dispute every foot of ground. The Prussians don't know what they are in for. Rather than accept humiliating terms, we will keep up the fight for ten years.'[30]

But Mérimée wrote to a friend the same day, advising her not to come to Paris. 'There is nothing to be seen here but drunken or despondent crowds singing the *Marseillaise*. Chaos everywhere! The army has been and still is admirable; but it seems that we have no generals. All may still be put right: but it would need something like a miracle.' Even victory, he reflected three weeks later, would not be the end of the trouble. 'It would end, no less surely than defeat, in a revolution. Every drop of blood shed or to be shed is an argument for a revolution, that is to say for organized chaos.'[31]

The double defeat of August 6th threw the French commanders back upon a defensive campaign for which they were utterly unprepared. In the north, Bazaine, after fighting a delaying action at Borny or Colombey, fell back behind Metz, with the intention of retreating towards Verdun; in the south the broken armies on the Saar retreated to the line of the Moselle. By the middle of the month the Emperor and MacMahon were at Châlons, attempting to reorganize their disordered and disillusioned troops, and to fuse them with the reinforcements sent from Paris.

On the 21st there arrived from the capital no accredited agent of the Regency, but Louis' faithful friend Rouher, who alone, perhaps, thought that salvation lay in his resuming control of the government, if not of the army. A conference was held. The issue was: should Louis fall back with MacMahon's army on Paris, and head the defence of the capital; or should he march with it to meet and rescue Bazaine? If the first, there might still be hope for the dynasty: if the second, France might still have two armies in the field. Rouher himself was for the second, believing that time was on

the French side: the ultimate resources of the country were so much greater than those of Prussia. Louis was persuaded, and Rouher drafted orders nominating MacMahon commander-in-chief at Châlons and Paris, and announcing a retreat on the capital.[32]

But at this moment there arrived not only a dispatch from Palikao carrying the Empress's orders against the retreat, and for an attempt to join up with Bazaine, but also a telegram from Bazaine himself to the effect that he was marching west, and hoped to be on the Aisne by the 24th. This altered everything, and the march was resumed from Reims towards Verdun. But in fact it was the enemy who now dictated the French tactics. At Vionville south-west of Metz on the 16th and at Saint-Privat or Gravelotte north-east of it on the 17th the Germans won two costly but decisive victories, which finally cut off the eastern group of French forces centred at Metz from the western group centred at Châlons.

Gravelotte was one of the last European battles to be described in the romantic style of the old war correspondence. 'All day long,' wrote Archibald Forbes (who had outmanœuvred Russell of *The Times* in getting to the front), 'from noon until nearly the going down of the sun, the roar of the cannon and the roll of musketry has been incessant. The deep ravine of the Mance between Gravelotte and St. Hubert was a horrible pandemonium wherein seethed masses of German soldiery, torn by the shell-fire of the French batteries, writhing under the stings of the *mitrailleuses*, bewildered between inevitable death in front and no less inevitable disgrace behind. Again and again frantic efforts were being made to force up out of the hell of the ravine and gain foothold on the edge of the plateau beyond; and ever the cruel sheet of lead beat them back and crushed them down. The long summer day was waning into dusk, and the fortunes of the battle still trembled in the balance, when the last reserve of the Germans — the second army corps — came hurrying up towards the brink of the abyss. In the lurid glare of the blazing village the German king stood by the wayside and welcomed his stalwart Pomeranians as they passed him. High over the roll of the drums, the blare of the bugles, and the crash of the cannons rose the eager burst of cheering as the soldiers answered their sovereign's greeting, and then followed their chiefs down into the fell depths of the terrible chasm. The strain of the crisis was sickening as we waited for the issue in a sort of rapt spasm of sombre silence. The old King sat with his back against a wall on a ladder, one end of

which rested on a broken gun-carriage and the other on a dead horse. Bismarck, with an elaborate assumption of coolness which his rest-lessness belied, made a pretence to be reading letters. The roar of the close battle swelled and deepened, till the very ground trembled beneath us. The night fell like a pall, but the blaze of an adjacent conflagration lit up the anxious group here by the churchyard wall. From out the medley of broken troops littering the slope in front rose suddenly a great shout that grew in volume as it rolled nearer. The hoofs of a galloping horse rattled on the causeway. A moment later Moltke, his face for once quivering with excitement, sprang from the saddle, and running towards the King cried out: "It is good for us; we have restored the position, and the victory is with Your Majesty!" The King sprang to his feet with a fervent "God be thanked!" and then burst into tears. Bismarck with a great sigh of relief crushed his letters in the hollow of his hand; and a simultaneous *Hurrah!* welcomed the glad tidings.'[33]

Twenty years later Emile Zola in *La Débâcle* showed the hollowness of all this romanticism. The failure of the French army on the battlefields of 1870 was not merely the end of the Empire: it was the end of an age of unrealism, of incomprehension: the democratic armies of the twentieth century would fight unfanatically, unromantically, as men who could find no less hateful way out of an *impasse* and were almost ashamed if they found violence enjoyable.

There was at least one leader on the German side in whom realism and romanticism were strangely combined. The Crown Prince of Prussia, afterwards Frederick III, was in command of the 3rd Army, and led it successfully in the early victories of Wissembourg and Wörth. No one could have been more sure of the justice of the German cause, or more imbued with Protestant piety: his *War Diary* notes with what enthusiasm his soldiers sang the old Lutheran hymns, *Ein feste Burg* and *In allen meiner Thaten*, how tears of pride sprang to their eyes when they were presented with the Iron Cross. But he was as much shocked by the sight of the battlefield of Wörth as Louis had been by that of Solferino, and would confess: 'I ask myself every day how the present mangling of each other like wild beasts, contrary to all Christian precepts of virtue and morality, can still be possible'; or again, on Christmas Day: 'It sounds almost like irony, amidst the miseries of war and in days that speak only of death and destruction to the foe to listen to the Christian message of salvation: *On earth peace and good will toward men.* Christendom is still far from

acting in the spirit of those words. The clergy have a difficult task set them to explain the contradiction involved in the strife of Christians against Christians, where each side invokes God for its own as the only just cause.'[34]

6

Gravelotte really ended the war. Bazaine's army was now invested at Metz, and it was useless for him to talk of forcing his way out either to Châlons by St. Menehould or by Sedan to Mezières. Nevertheless MacMahon was under orders from Paris to move towards Verdun, and join up with Bazaine. On August 21st he marched towards Reims – a compromise which might still enable him to carry out his original plan of a retirement on Paris; but, warned by Palikao of the fatal political effects of such a move, he redirected his march on the 23rd towards Metz, and by the 25th stood half way between Reims and Sedan. No move could have been more dangerous; for the Germans were closing in from the south, and driving him away from Paris towards the Belgian frontier. But he pressed on, and by the 30th stood on the right bank of the Meuse, where, if Bazaine had been able to escape from Metz, they might have met. Instead, he was in a trap, isolated, his communications cut, and with no line of escape except over the Belgian frontier. A series of local actions on the 30th and 31st closed even this exit, and on September 1st the remnants of MacMahon's army, and the Emperor with them, were penned like sheep into the little town of Sedan, within the narrow circle of hills which afforded its only rampart.

The last stand began at 5 a.m. on September 1st, when Bavarian troops attacked the comparatively open south-east side of the French position at Bazeilles and La Moncelle. Here fighting went on all the morning, and the German line was gradually extended northwards until, early in the afternoon, it met another extension from the west, and the whole position was encircled. The French infantry now began to retreat into the town. Desperate cavalry charges could not break through the enemy line. MacMahon had been wounded early in the day: Ducrot, who succeeded him, planned a break-out northwards, before the last gap was closed. But when Wimpffen arrived, with orders from Paris to take command, he determined to stand his ground. Louis himself repeatedly risked his life in the fighting at Bazeilles. About 2 o'clock (it would seem) he became convinced that it was useless to prolong the defence, and humane,

or rather humanitarian at this crisis, as he had been all his life, hoised a white flag. But Wimpffen would have none of it, and ordered it to be cut down before it was seen by the enemy: he would now attempt to repeat Ducrot's break-out; but southwards, and too late. At 4 o'clock the Prussians determined to give the *coup de grace* to the defence by bombarding the town, which was by now crowded with troops, from the hill of Frénois, close to the west side; and before long a white flag was seen to be flying on the citadel.

Two German officers, Bronsart and Winterfeld, went in under a flag of truce, and found themselves, unexpectedly, in the presence of the Emperor: they had not known he was there. They asked him to appoint an officer to negotiate: he referred them to Wimpffen, but said that he would send a letter to the King of Prussia. The German officers rode back with this message, and Bronsart, in his excitement, spurred his horse up the hill at Frénois, and, flinging his arm behind him, shouted *Der Kaiser ist da!* A little later (it was now about 6 p.m.) a French officer, Reille, rode out with Louis' letter. He had written, not as Emperor or Commander-in-Chief, but as man to man, vanquished to victor, saying that, as he had not been able to die on the battlefield, he would surrender his sword in token of defeat:

Monsieur mon frère, n'ayant pas pu mourir au milieu de mes troupes, il ne me reste qu'à remettre mon épée entre les mains de Votre Majesté. Je suis de Votre Majesté le bon frère Napoléon.

The King, after reading this, told Reille that he could only negotiate if the whole French army laid down its arms. But he wrote, then and there, a courteous reply, accepting Louis' sword, but insisting on the surrender of the French army: *Monsieur mon frère, En regrettant les circonstances dans lesquelles nous nous rencontrons, j'accepte l'épée de Votre Majesté, et je prie de bien vouloir un de Ses officiers muni de Ses pleins pouvoirs pour traiter des conditions de la capitulation de l'armée qui s'est si bravement battue sous Vos ordres. De mon côté j'ai désigné le Général de Moltke à cet effet. Je suis de Votre Majesté le bon frère Guillaume.* Whilst this letter was being written, the Crown Prince, with the gentlemanly tact that marked his character, walked over to Reille, whom he had known in Paris in 1867, and spoke kindly to him. He asked after the Prince Imperial, and was told that he was no longer with the Emperor.[35]

Reille rode back with the King's answer, whilst the Prussian staff dispersed — William to his headquarters at Vendresse, Bismarck to Donchéry, where he had arranged to discuss the terms of surrender.

There, in the *salle-à-manger* of the little Hôtel de Commerce, he read out Louis' letter, led the cheers that greeted it, and gave the toasts of 'King' and 'Fatherland'. About midnight Wimpffen arrived, with Faure and Castelnau, for the conference, and asked for the Prussian terms. Moltke, with Bismarck and Blumenthal behind him, said that the whole French army, officers and men, must lay down arms and become prisoners of war. Wimpffen protested; refused to accept such terms; threatened to resume fighting. Moltke said the armistice expired at 4 a.m., and he would then re-open the bombardment. In the end it was agreed to extend the armistice to 9 a.m., so that Wimpffen might consult the Emperor.

Late as it was, Louis said that he would start from Sedan at five in the morning to ask for better terms. He left the town, perhaps expecting to return, in a shabby open carriage, with three officers: he was wearing a general's uniform and decorations under a blue cloak with scarlet lining, and was smoking his usual cigarette. The Zouaves at the town gate shouted *Vive l'Empereur!* for the last time. Within an hour he met Bismarck, who had been told by Reille of his coming, and had ridden to meet him. Bismarck dismounted, uncovered, and bowed. Louis asked to be allowed to rest at a wayside cottage outside Donchéry; and there, in a small room upstairs, or sitting in chairs at the door, they had a preliminary talk. In after years the owner of the cottage, Mme Fournaise, used to take visitors over it, sell them copies of the chair the Emperor had sat in, and tell them how, when he left, he had with his habitual kindness given her four gold *louis*: three (*louis-philippes*) were kept to pay for her funeral, and the fourth (a *napoléon*) was buried with her.[36]

Meanwhile Wimpffen had submitted the terms of capitulation to a Council of War at Sedan. At nine they still hesitated to accept them; but an assurance that the bombardment would begin at ten clinched the argument; Wimpffen rode out again to the Château de Bellevue, on the river-bank on the right of the road to Donchéry, and there, with Moltke, signed the surrender. As soon as this was reported to King William at Frénois, he rode down to Bellevue, and there met Louis on the steps of the porch. They went in, and talked for some twenty minutes: about the responsibility for the war, the political situation (Louis could not negotiate for the Government, which was, he said, at Paris), the Emperor's place of detention (Wilhelmshöhe near Cassel was agreed upon), the bravery of the French army, and the fate of the Empress and Prince Imperial. The rest of

the day Louis remained at the château; in the afternoon preparations were made for the journey next day (it was the last appearance of the imperial equipages): that night he read himself to sleep with a copy of Bulwer Lytton's *The Last of the Barons*, which he found in his bedroom bookcase.[37]

7

At the time of his surrender, and almost in the words of his letter to the King of Prussia, Louis had sent a telegram to Eugénie telling her that the army was defeated and himself a prisoner: *L'armée est défaite et captive; n'ayant pu me faire tuer au milieu de mes soldats, j'ai dû me constituer prisonnier pour sauver l'armée. Napoléon.*

The same night he wrote to the Empress, heading the letter *Quartier impérial, 2 septembre 1870.* My dear Eugénie, I cannot tell you what I have suffered and am suffering. We made a march contrary to all the rules and to common sense: it was bound to lead to a catastrophe, and that is complete. I would rather have died than have witnessed such a disastrous capitulation; and yet, things being as they are, it was the only way of avoiding the slaughter of 60,000 men.

Then again, if only all my torments were concentrated here! I think of you, of our son, of our unfortunate country. May God protect you! What is going to happen at Paris?

I have just seen the King. There were tears in his eyes when he spoke of the sorrow I must be feeling. He has put at my disposal one of his *châteaux* near Hesse-Cassel. But what does it matter where I go? I am in despair. Adieu; I embrace you tenderly.

NAPOLÉON.[38]

Perhaps Eugénie was not unprepared for such a disaster. Two days before, whilst Louis, with the bulk of MacMahon's army, was being encircled at Sedan, Lord Lyons saw her 'for the first time since the war'. 'She was calm and natural, well aware, I think, of the real state of things, but courageous without boasting or affectation ... She did not invite, nor did I offer any advice or assurances or conjectures as to what England or any other Power was likely to do.'[39]

In the cruelly heroic mood in which she had sent the Emperor and the Prince Imperial to the front she had refused to let them return to the capital. For a moment on August 9th she had given way to the pressure of her Council, and drafted a telegram recalling Louis to Paris; but within a few hours she cancelled it. As wife and

NAPOLEON III

from a photograph taken on his fiftieth birthday

LOUIS NAPOLEON IN ENGLAND, 1840

from a drawing by John Doyle

LOUIS NAPOLEON AS DEPUTY AND PRESIDENT, 1848

from a contemporary print

THE EMPRESS EUGÉNIE

from a painting by Winterhalter

JÉRÔME, PRINCE NAPOLEON

from a painting by Flandrin

THE DYNASTY

from a photograph, about 1860

A GERMAN CARICATURE, 1870

LOUIS' LETTER OF SURRENDER AT SEDAN, SEPT. 1ST, 1870

mother she was distracted for their safety: as Empress she knew that their place was with the army. It would not, she thought, be safe in the present state of public opinion for Louis to reappear in his capital; and she felt she could play a better part as Regent. 'That he, a Napoleon, should abandon his troops on the eve of battle! . . . He would be shamed for ever in the eye of history! I would rather (she cried) that he had killed himself.' He had indeed run every risk of death at Sedan — risks which the great Napoleon had been re-proached for shirking in 1814. He — and she — had nothing to be ashamed of. The Empire was dead; but the Napoleonic legend was still alive.[40]

As for her son: the boy had faced the same dangers until, just before Sedan, Louis insisted on his being taken by his aide-de-camp Duperré into comparative safety at Amiens. When Eugénie heard it, she wrote to Duperré: 'You have one duty more pressing than safety: it is honour, and I consider this retreat to Amiens unworthy of the Prince and his parents (nous). My heart is torn, but resolute. I have had no news of my husband or of you since yesterday. I am suffering terribly; but, before anything else, I want both of you to do your duty. Be sure of one thing: I can weep for my son if he is dead or wounded, but if he flies . . . I shall never forgive you. Do what is best, but act as a soldier. We shall hold out in Paris, if we are besieged, and if away from Paris we shall hold out — just the same. Peace is impossible!'[41]

But already since the middle of August she must have known that Paris was in no mood to accept her sacrifice. Not in the capital only, but all over the country, those who had cried A bas la Prusse! were now crying A bas l'Empire! 'There are ups and downs (wrote Lyons on the 16th) in the spirits of the French about the war, but the Emperor and the dynasty seem to sink lower and lower. La Tour d'Auvergne (the Foreign Minister) speaks still as a loyal sub-ject, but I know of no one else who does. The Empress shows pluck, but not hope. No party wishes to come into office, with the risk of having to sign a disadvantageous peace.' This was on the day of Gravelotte. Afterwards, for a fortnight, Paris was almost without news. On September 3rd Palikao announced to the Assembly the surrender of Sedan. The official publication of the news was post-poned till Sunday the 4th. Within a few hours there were public demonstrations in the streets and outside the Palais Bourbon demand-ing the deposition (déchéance) of the Emperor.[42]

In the Assembly an attempt was made to save, not the dynasty, but the constitution, by setting up a provisional government and summoning a national convention. Even the Empress unwillingly agreed. But this was to reckon without the people of Paris, who had never forgotten 1848 or forgiven 1851. When Gambetta declared that it was now the moment 'to set up an order of government (*pouvoir régulier*) based upon free and universal suffrage', everyone knew the answer — 'The Republic!' and set off to the Town Hall to proclaim it once more from the building which had, ever since 1789, symbolized Parisian opposition to the Tuileries.

Eugénie, warned by Piétri, the prefect of police, that if she remained in the palace the crowds which were already at the gates would force her to abdicate the Regency, at last consented to leave. It was impossible to do so from the Tuileries itself, but a way was found through the Louvre, and she drove off with one companion, Mme Lebreton, in a passing *fiacre*. First to the house of a friendly member of the Council, M. Besson. But he was not at home, and after waiting a quarter of an hour outside his door they walked on, found another cab, and drove to M. de Peinnes' *appartement*; but he too was out. They thought of trying the American Legation, but did not know where it was. At last the Empress remembered her American dentist, Dr. Evans; and there, in the Avenue Malakoff, they found a night's lodging, and a good friend. Early next morning they drove away in Dr. Evans' carriage, with passports provided by Piétri representing Eugénie as an English invalid lady being taken to London by her doctor (Crane, a friend of Evans), accompanied by her brother (Evans) and her nurse (Mme Lebreton). They drove all day, with a series of relays, by Saint-Germain, Poissy, and Meulan to Mantes; then on, in a hired carriage, to Pacy, and in another again to Evreux and Serquigny; then by train to Lisieux, and the last stage by road to Deauville, where at 3 a.m. the next morning, after travelling nearly twenty-four hours, they found Dr. Evans' wife staying at the Casino Hotel.[48]

The rest of the story can be read in the letter which Sir John Burgoyne wrote to Colonel Ponsonby ten days later. Sir John had taken his yacht *Gazelle* to Trouville (the port for Deauville) to bring back his wife on August 24th from a holiday abroad, but was delayed there by bad weather. 'On Tuesday the 6th September at about 2 p.m. two strangers came on board and asked to be allowed to see an English yacht. I happened to be on board, and myself showed

them over the yacht; one of them suddenly asked to be allowed to say a few words in private; he then informed me that the Empress was concealed in Deauville, wishing to be conveyed to England, and asked me if I would undertake to take her over in the yacht. After consulting with Lady Burgoyne, considering the scanty accommodation on board, I at once agreed to her request.' Later it was settled that the Empress should come aboard just after midnight . . . and so she did. 'The Empress was very much agitated and sobbed bitterly, and on my saying to her, *N'ayez pas peur, Madame*, she replied in English, I am safe with an English gentleman. I then introduced her to my wife, who told her the last three days' news, and read the papers to her.' After a rough passage they landed at Ryde a little before seven on September 8th. Eugénie left the same day for Portsmouth, Brighton, and Hastings, where at the Marine Hotel the Prince Imperial was waiting for her.[44]

8

Meanwhile Louis, crossing neutral Belgian territory under parole, found himself hospitably interned in Jérôme Bonaparte's old palace at Wilhemshöhe, near Cassel. Achille Murat was with him, and Corvisart, and Conneau. He was soon in better health, and made himself accessible and popular. He talked almost as freely as Napoleon at St. Helena. He followed events in France, but intervened only to urge moderation on the German government, and to protest against his deposition by any authority short of a *plébiscite*: he was still, like his uncle, Emperor by will of the French nation. But when an old friend, Col. Cohausen, called to see him, and his daughter (as the fashion was), asked him to add a motto to her fan, he wrote these lines from the *Inferno*:

> Nessun maggior dolore
> Che ricordarsi del tempo felice
> Nella miseria.

> ('No greater grief than to remember days
> Of joy, when misery is at hand').[45]

EPILOGUE

O God! Horatio, what a wounded name,
Things standing thus unknown, shall live behind me.
If thou didst ever hold me in thy heart,
Absent thee from felicity awhile,
And in this harsh world draw thy breath in pain,
To tell my story.   *Hamlet*, V, ii

I

IT was Louis' choice that made England his last home. Like Napoleon he wished to end his life in an English country house. Dr. Evans, who had devoted himself to Eugénie's service, found the ideal retreat: in the country, but near London, a fine house with good grounds, but not too big, and with a Catholic church close by. Camden Place, Chislehurst, belonged to a Mr. Strode, who had acted as trustee for Louis' ex-mistress Miss Howard, and let it to him at a rent he could afford. It was a three-floored Georgian mansion furnished in 'Empire' style, standing in an ornamental garden with fine trees, and had over its porch the Latin motto *Malo mori quam foedari* (Death before Dishonour) which might have been put there for the fallen sovereigns. Here Eugénie arrived on September 20th, and soon settled in, with Filon, her secretary, Mme Lebreton, her reader, Ullmann, the Prince Imperial's valet, Dr. Conneau and his son, and others, with seven or eight servants. By degrees more adherents settled down within close reach; till the little court lacked only its Emperor.

For Louis remained six months more a prisoner at Wilhelmshöhe, and Eugénie, refusing to recognize the revolution of September 4th, still regarded herself as Regent. It was as Regent that she quarrelled with Prince Napoleon, who had settled down with his mistress, Cora Pearl, in London, and that she refused to have anything to do with the regime he planned with Walewski and Changarnier at Brussels. It was as Regent that she sounded Bismarck as to his peace terms, and as Regent that she snubbed the incompetent negotiations of Regnier and Bourbaki with Bazaine, until his surrender at Metz (October 28th) deprived her of her last argument. But it was as wife, rather than Regent, that on October 30th she paid a short visit to Wilhelmshöhe. She found Louis outwardly impassive, but inwardly as moved as she was by their misfortunes, as ready to make up their differences, as anxious to start their broken life over again.

314

It was soon after this journey that Queen Victoria, who could always put personalities above policy, visited Chislehurst, and afterwards wrote in her Journal:

November 30th, 1870.

At the door (of Camden Place) stood the poor Empress, in black, the Prince Imperial, and, a little behind, the Ladies and Gentlemen... She looks very thin and pale, but still very handsome. There is an expression of deep sadness in her face, and she frequently had tears in her eyes. She was dressed in the plainest possible way, without any jewels or ornaments, and her hair simply done, in a net, at the back. She showed the greatest tact in avoiding everything which might be awkward, and asked if I had any news, saying '*Oh! si seulement l'on pouvait avoir la paix!*'[1]

A week later Victoria received Eugénie at Windsor, and wrote again:

December 5th, 1870.

After an early luncheon, went down to the door at half past two to receive the poor Empress. She was very nervous when she arrived, and as she walked upstairs said crying: *Cela m'a fait une telle émotion,* and quite sobbed. I pressed her poor little hand ... When I asked her about her visit to Wilhelmshöhe, where she went about five weeks ago, she said she had intended staying two days, but *Quand j'ai appris que les Maréchaux arrivaient, je suis partie!* ... In driving she again said how she prayed for Peace, and I answered I hoped it might be soon. *Croyez-vous? Mais quelle paix peut-on faire? Il n'y a pas de Gouvernement,* in which I quite agreed and said what a misfortune the Revolution had been. *S'il n'y avait pas eu la Révolution, la paix se serait faite le lendemain, parce que nous ne pouvions plus résister* ... What a fearful contrast to her visit here in '55! Then all was state and pomp, wild excitement and enthusiasm — and now? How strange that I should have seen those two Revolutions, in '48 and '70! The poor Empress looked so lovely in her simple black, and so touching in her gentleness and submission.[2]

On March 19th Louis, a free man again, left Wilhelmshöhe; and next day he found Eugénie and her son waiting for him on the Admiralty Pier at Dover, which has seen so many famous comings and goings, but few more moving than this. Did it surprise him — it would not have surprised Napoleon in 1815 — to be received with

cheers by a crowd which forgot its suspicions of the Emperor in its sympathy for the man? At Camden Place Eugénie had decorated his bed-hangings with Napoleonic bees and initials, and had hung on the wall portraits of the Tsar whom he had conquered and of the son of Napoleon whose rights he had vindicated. Close by was the kind of study he best liked – small, intimate, stuffy. Davillier his equerry, Piétri his secretary, Corvisart his doctor, and Gamble his groom were close at hand. He soon settled down to a domestic routine, reading his papers, entertaining his friends, playing patience, listening to the piano, walking in the grounds or through the village, sometimes attending a local bazaar, or a cricket match on the neighbouring West Kent ground; always kindly, friendly, accessible. Occasionally he would take the train to London, stroll down Bond Street, and spend an hour or two at the Army and Navy or Junior United Services Club, chatting with the friends of thirty years ago.[3]

A week after his arrival at Chislehurst he was invited to Windsor. Let the Queen again describe her impressions:

March 27th, 1871.
At a little before three went down to receive the Emperor Napoleon. I went to the door and embraced the Emperor *comme de rigueur*. It was a moving moment, when I thought of the last time he came here in '55, in perfect triumph, dearest Albert bringing him from Dover, the whole country mad to receive him, and now! He seemed much depressed and had tears in his eyes, but he controlled himself, and said *Il y a bien longtemps que je n'ai vu votre Majesté.* He is grown very stout and grey and his moustaches are no longer curled or waxed as formerly, but otherwise there was the same pleasing, gentle, and gracious manner.[4]

Malmesbury's account may be added:
'On March 20th, 1871 (he wrote), Louis Napoleon landed at Dover after his captivity at Wilhelmshöhe, and on the 21st I went down to Chislehurst to see him. After a few minutes he came into the room alone, and with that remarkable smile which could light up his dark countenance he shook me heartily by the hand. I confess that I never was more moved. His quiet and calm dignity and absence of all nervousness and irritability were the grandest examples of human moral courage that the severest Stoic could have imagined.' Malmesbury thought of Louis' romantic career, at so many points of

which their paths had crossed – in Rome, at Ham, in London, in Paris, both as President and Emperor, an event 'which had realized all his early dreams': he thought of 'the glory of his reign of twenty years over France, which he had enriched beyond belief (as was proved by the ease with which the war indemnity was paid), and adorned beyond all other countries and capitals': 'all these memories crowded upon me as the man stood before me whose race had been so successful and romantic, now without a crown, without an army, without a country or an inch of ground which he could call his own, except the house he hired in an English village. I must have shown what I felt, as, again shaking my hand, he said: *A la guerre, comme à la guerre. C'est bien bon de venir me voir* . . . During half an hour he conversed with me as calmly as in the best days of his life, with a dignity and resignation which might be that of a fatalist, but could hardly be obtained from any other creed; and when I left him that was, not for the first time, my impression.'[5]

2

There followed eighteen months during which Louis' health seemed so much improved that he moved about the country in his old way – visiting friends, inspecting factories (which always interested him) at Woolwich or Chatham, seeing schools; in the autumn of 1871, whilst Eugénie was with her relations in Spain, he went with the Prince Imperial to Torquay and Bath; and in the summer of 1872 they all stayed at Brighton, and then at Cowes, where they rented two villas on the parade, and the Prince Imperial enjoyed, as his father had at Rome in the 'twenties, a free and easy life with young people of his own age. But as winter came on Louis had a return of the pains which had prostrated him before: he could not walk far; it hurt him to drive; he had to refuse invitations. It became increasingly uncertain whether he would be able to play any part in the fantastic plan which was now being secretly discussed for another military attempt, on the old Strasbourg-Boulogne model – or was it rather another Return from Elba? – and for the restoration of the Empire.

But on the day after one of Prince Napoleon's visits to Chislehurst to talk about this project Louis at last allowed two surgeons to be called in – Sir William Gull and Sir Henry Thompson – and consented to be operated on for stone in the bladder. Two operations

were performed, on January 2nd and 6th, 1873; a third, perhaps the last, was to have followed three days later; but on the evening of the 8th he was taken worse, and died at 10.45 on the morning of January 9th. It would seem that his dying thoughts had gone back to the doubt which beset the most tragic memory of his life: for his last words, as his old friend bent over him, were: *N'est-ce pas, Conneau, que nous n'avons pas été des lâches à Sedan?*[6]

Victoria was at Osborne.

'January 7th, 1873.

'At luncheon received a letter from Bertie (the Prince of Wales) with two enclosures from Sir H. Thompson, stating that he had performed the operation on the poor Emperor, and that though there were no very untoward symptoms, still he considered the case very serious, and that he was not sure whether he would be able to pull the Emperor through! This alarmed me.'

'9th Jan. – Had inquired but was surprised at getting no news from Chislehurst, and soon after I came home, Janie E. came into my room with a telegram in her hand, saying, It is all over, which I could not believe, so impossible it seemed. The telegram was from M. Piétri, the Emperor's Secretary (nephew of the former Minister of Police), begging her to communicate to me the sad news that *l'Empereur a cessé de souffrir à 11 heures moins ¼. L'Impératrice est dans les larmes.* Was quite upset. Had a great regard for the Emperor, who was so amiable and kind, and had borne his terrible misfortunes with such meekness, dignity, and patience. He had been such a faithful ally to England . . . And now to die like this from the results of an operation, though it may have been inevitable, seems too tragic and sad!'[7]

When the Empress and the Prince Imperial returned from the funeral, a crowd followed them bareheaded to the door of Camden Place. As the Prince passed inside they cried *Vive l'Empereur! Vive Napoléon IV!* The boy turned, and called for silence. 'Don't cry *Vive l'Empereur!*' he said; 'Cry *Vive la France!*'

A fortnight after Louis' death Eugénie sent Victoria a souvenir of the Emperor: a small clock which had stood beside his bed: 'it has recorded the happy hours of the old days and the long hours of moral and physical suffering; years of joy, and years of sorrow – and Oh! how long these last have been!'[8]

3

Louis' Bonapartism outlived the Second Empire by half a century: some would say it is still alive. The Prince Imperial was killed in South Africa in 1879, a military adventurer as his father had once been, and fighting for the country whose friendship he had always prized. Prince Napoleon died in 1891, his eldest son, Victor Napoleon, in 1926, his sister Princess Mathilde in 1904. Eugénie herself lived on through the first World War, to die in her ninety-fifth year on July 11th, 1920. Victor Emmanuel's life ended, by a curious coincidence which Victoria noted in her journal, on January 9th, 1878, the anniversary of Louis' death. Poor mad Carlotta of Mexico survived them all, and did not die till January 1927.

In the will he drew up in 1865 Louis had written of his son: 'Let him never forget the motto of the head of our family, Everything for the French people (*tout pour le Peuple français*). Let him fix his mind on the writings of the prisoner of St. Helena: let him study the Emperor's deeds and correspondence: finally let him remember, when circumstances so permit, that the cause of the people is the cause of France.' Then, thinking of that saving clause, he went on: 'Power is a heavy burden, because one cannot always do all the good one could wish, and because your contemporaries seldom render you justice; so that, in order to fulfil one's mission, one must have faith in and consciousness of one's duty. It is necessary to consider that from heaven on high (*du haut des cieux*) those whom you have loved regard and protect you: it is the spirit of my illustrious uncle (*l'âme de mon grand oncle*) that has always inspired and sustained me.'

When the young Prince came to make his own will he passed on that message. 'I have no need to recommend my mother (he wrote) to leave nothing undone to defend the memory of my great-uncle and of my father. I beg her to remember that so long as there are Bonapartes there will be representatives of the Imperial cause. The duties of our House towards the country do not end with my life; when I am dead the task of continuing the work of Napoleon I and Napoleon III rests on the eldest son of Prince Napoleon.'[9]

The Queen herself was by now almost a Bonapartist.
Queen Victoria to Mr. Theodore Martin, Osborne, January 19th, 1873.
'... The Queen does *not* (think) the Bonapartist cause will lose by the poor Emperor's death, on the contrary *she* thinks the reverse.

For the peace of Europe SHE thinks though the Orleans Princes are her dear friends and connections, and — some — relations, and she would not for the world have it *said* as coming from her, that it would be best if the Prince Imperial was *ultimately* to succeed.'[10]

It was not to be so; but how much depended on the aim of a Zulu assegai!

In a speech soon after the death of the Prince Imperial the Prince of Wales (afterwards Edward VII) said: 'If it had been the will of Providence that he should have been called to succeed his father as the sovereign of that great country our neighbour, I believe he would have proved an admirable sovereign, and that he, like his father, would have been a true and great ally of this country.'[11]

4

Eugénie spent her last years in building at Farnborough the flamboyant mausoleum in which the bodies of the Emperor and Prince — and her own — now lie, and in foreign travel. Whenever she visited Paris, she took rooms overlooking the Tuileries. 'Yes, I know (she would say), they think me insensitive because I stay at this hotel, in constant sight of the Tuileries. But, you see, nothing matters any more ... I have suffered too much to care ... What is a choice of outlook compared with the memories at the back of my mind?' ... Then she would point to the portrait of the Emperor, which stood by her, and would say: 'I want to tell you how fine he was, how unselfish, how generous. In our happy times I always found him simple and good, kindly and compassionate: he would put up with opposition and misrepresentation with wonderful complaisance ... When we were overwhelmed with misfortune his stoicism and gentleness were sublime. You should have seen him during those last years at Chislehurst: never a word of complaint, or blame, or abuse.' When urged to answer his accusers, he would say: 'No, I shall not defend myself ... Sometimes a disaster falls upon a nation of such a kind that it is justified in blaming it all, even unfairly, upon its ruler ... A sovereign can offer no excuses, he can plead no extenuating circumstances. It is his highest prerogative to shoulder all the responsibilities incurred by those who have served him ... or those who have betrayed him.'[12]

An indefatigable wanderer, Eugénie came back at last to die (1920) at Madrid, in the country of her birth. Seven months before, the old

lady of ninety-three had said to Paléologue (it was the last talk he had with her) how grateful she was that she had lived to see the reunion of Alsace to France. 'I have had the supreme consolation of seeing France restored to her national wholeness: I have had the consolation of being able to tell myself that our men who died in 1870, the heroes of Wissembourg and Forbach, of Fröschwiller and Reichshoffen, of Rezonville and Gravelotte, are at last reconpensed for their sacrifice.'[13]

5

POSTSCRIPT

Now that I have come to the end of the life, I am not sure how to sum it up. To write a man's life is not to make a list of all he did, year by year, from his birth to his death, as though each act had the same worth. It is to paint a work of art, in which the light and shade fall where they should, if the man is to look as God and the world made him. His mind was his own before birth; what he has done is still marked on his face when he is dead. Who can say past doubt that while he lived he was to be blamed, or that when he died he had failed?

This was a life ruled from first to last by a great name; a life hitched to a star; a life in which fate — now kind, now hard — seemed to hold the strings and to guide the moves. What can I say of it all, but that here he took the right turn, and there the wrong; that this thought of his seems to have been true to his best self, and this not; that he had his eyes fixed on a goal, but could not find the way to reach it? For I think that at the back of all his twists and turns, all his ups and downs, he held close in his mind and warm in his heart the will to be great and the wish to do good; and that he must be judged, if at all, by the ends he tried to win more than by the means he took to win them: by the France of *l'ordre* and *la gloire* which he hoped to build up out of the heap of stones fate put at his feet; by all he risked and dared so that he might set free the land of his first fame; by the new Rome that he thought — but not as the Pope thought — might rise out of the old; by the seeds of fresh life he would have sown in the far east and west and south; by the rights of race and tongue that he wished to make safe for all the world; yes, and — since he won more trust as a man than as a prince — by the love of his friends, the faith he shared with the crowd, and the care he

showed for the poor. By these he should be judged, not by the wrong ways in which, now and then, he tried to win his ends.

Yet he was a man too small for the great things he set out to do; too prone to be led by weak or bad friends; too quick to take dreams for facts; one who walked in his sleep, and woke too late to save a fall. And so I have been led to put at the head of each scene of his life some lines from the play in which a brave and wise young prince, called to mend a deep wrong done to his house, and born to set right a world that is out of joint, finds that the task is too much for him, and that he has not the strength to make his dreams come true.

NOTES

CHAPTER I: THE HEIR

[1] NAPOLEON's *Correspondance*, April 4th, 1807.

[2] NABONNE, *La reine Hortense* (1951), p. 95.

[3] NABONNE, p. 76.

[4] NABONNE, Ch. 5; DE LA FUYE, *Louis Napoléon Bonaparte avant l'Empire* (1951), Ch. 1; on the question of Louis' legitimacy, SIMPSON, *The rise of Louis Napoleon* (ed. 1925), p. 358.

[5] NABONNE; DE LA FUYE.

[6] *Lettres de Napoléon III à Madame Cornu* (ed. Emerit, 1937), I, 7.

[7] DE LA FUYE, 24; *Souvenirs de ma vie*, in PROUDHON, *Napoléon III* (1900).

[8] SENIOR, *Conversations with M. Thiers* (1878), II, 335; I, 220.

[9] PROUDHON, p. 329.

[10] *The reminiscences and reflections of Captain Gronow* (1892), II, 249.

[11] DE LA FUYE, p. 39; SIMPSON, *The Rise*, p. 32 (according to another version it was Soult, not Berthier).

[12] NABONNE; TURQUAN, *La reine Hortense* (1927), II, Ch. 8. *Souvenirs et correspondance de Madame Récamier* (ed. 1860), I, III.

[13] E. T. of *Idées napoléoniennes* in *Life and Works of Louis Napoleon Bonaparte* (1852), I, 250.

[14] *Lettres de Napoléon III*, II, 8.

[15] *Napoléon III et le Prince Napoléon* (ed. D'Hauterive, 1925), p. 268.

[16] DE LA FUYE, p. 54.

[17] *Lettres de Napoléon III*, II, 22; for Florenton, *The secret of the Coup d'état*, ed. Earl of Kerry (1924), p. 99.

[18] *Lettres de Napoléon III*, I, 11; II, 31, 60.

[19] STÉFANE-POL, *La jeunesse de Napoléon III*, letters of July 19th, August 10th, 1820; for Mme Cornu, *Œuvres de Ernest Renan*, II, 1113.

[20] STÉFANE-POL, August 14th, 1827.

[21] STÉFANE-POL, December 4th, 1820.

[22] STÉFANE-POL, February 21st, 1821; November 13th, 1820.

[23] *Lettres de Napoléon III*, I, 181.

[24] STÉFANE-POL.

[25] STÉFANE-POL; MME RÉCAMIER, II, 72; GRABINSKI, *Le Comte Arese* (1897), p. 27.

[26] GOURGAUD, *Sainte-Hélène* (3rd ed.), I, 287.

[27] They are reproduced in STÉFANE-POL.

[28] *Lettres de Napoléon III*, I, 183.

[29] WHYTE, *The Evolution of Modern Italy* (1950); GENTILE, *Profeti del Risorgimento* (1913).

[30] LEFLON, *Histoire de l'Eglise: La crise révolutionnaire* (1949).

[31] CHARLES-ROUX, *Rome asile des Bonapartes* (1952); cp. letters of Las Cases to Bertrand (February 15th, April 15th, 1818) in *Mémorial de Sainte-Hélène*, ed. Dunan, II, 796, 807; MME RÉCAMIER, II, 47.

[32] DAYET in *Annales historiques de la Révolution française*, January 1953.

[33] CHARLES-ROUX, p. 141f. The date of Louis' departure from Florence disproves Orsi's 'recollection' of his presence at a Carbonari meeting there on February 26th (FORBES, *Life of Napoleon III* (1898), p. 30; cp. throughout *Mémoires de Valérie Masuyer* (1937), Ch. II.)

[34] SIMPSON, *The Rise*, pp. 333, 362; TURQUAN, p. 170f (the story that Napoléon-Louis was killed in action or assassinated can be disregarded). It is worth noting that Stendhal was at this same time journeying from Venice to Civita Vecchia (MARTINEAU, *Le cœur de Stendhal*, 1953, II, 209.

[35] VALÉRIE MASUYER; SIMPSON, *The Rise*; DE LA FUYE; TURQUAN.

[36] E. T. in *Life and Works*.

[37] PROUDHON, p. 360.

[38] DE LA FUYE; PROUDHON, p. 361; JERROLD, *Life of Napoleon III* (1874-1882), I, 193; VALÉRIE MASUYER, Ch. 4; MAXIME DU CAMP, *Souvenirs d'un demi-siècle* (1949), I, 26.

[39] SIMPSON, *The Rise*, p. 83.

[40] GUEST, *Napoleon III in England* (1952); ILCHESTER, *Chronicles of Holland House* (1937), p. 136; VALÉRIE MASUYER, Ch. 5.

[41] The question whether Louis was ever a Carbonaro was put in later years by Queen Victoria to Lord Malmesbury; and his reply was (March 7th, 1858), 'In attending to the idea referred to by Your Majesty that the Emperor took the oath of the Assassins' Society, Lord Malmesbury can almost assure your Majesty that such is not the case. Lord Malmesbury first made His Majesty's acquaintance in Italy when they were both very young men (twenty years of age). They were *both* under the influence of those romantic feelings which the former history and the present degradation of Italy may naturally inspire even at a more advanced time of life — and the Prince Louis Napoleon, to the knowledge of Lord Malmesbury, certainly engaged himself in the conspiracies of the time — but it was with the higher class of the Carbonari, men like General Sercognani and General Pépé. The Prince used to talk to Lord Malmesbury upon these men and their ideas and plans with all the openness that exists between two youths, and Lord Malmesbury has many times heard him condemn with disgust the societies of villains which hung on the flank of the conspirators, and which deterred many of the best families and ablest gentlemen in Romagna from joining them. Lord Malmesbury believes the report therefore to be a fable' (*Queen Victoria*, Letters, 2nd Series, I, 346). One wonders whether the Queen had similar doubts about Lord Tennyson, who at the same time (1830) had set off with Arthur Hallam to join the revolutionaries in Spain (TENNYSON, *Alfred Tennyson*, p. 94).

CHAPTER II: THE PRETENDER

[1] SIMPSON, *The Rise*, pp. 27, 85, 94; PROUDHON, p. 363.

[2] E. T. in *Life and Works*, I, 163.

[3] SIMPSON, *The Rise*, Ch. 5.

[4] JERROLD, I, 236.

[5] JERROLD, I, 248.

[6] DE LA FUYE, Ch. 8; MME RÉCAMIER, II, 413.

[7] JERROLD, I, 244.

[8] DE LA FUYE, Ch. 8.

[9] DE LA FAYE, *La princesse Mathilde* (1928), p. 42; VALÉRIE MASUYER, Ch. 7.

[10] PROUDHON, p. 372; ROTHAN, *L'Europe et l'avènement du second Empire* (1890), p. 161; *Mémoires du Duc de Persigny* (ed. 1896).

[11] Letter in SIMPSON, *The Rise*, p. 335.

[12] NABONNE, *Joseph Bonaparte* (1949), Ch. 14.

[13] SENIOR, *Correspondence and Conversations with de Tocqueville* (1872), January 27th, 1836; August 25th, 1847; May 14th, August 22nd, 1850. cp. DESSEL, *Charles Delescluze* (1952), a detailed biography of an unrepentant, irrepressible Jacobin who was involved in every anti-government movement from 1830 to 1871, and died on the barricades of the Paris Commune.

[14] REUSS, *Histoire de Strasbourg* (1922), Ch. 4; PONTEIL, *L'opposition politique à Strasbourg*; VALÉRIE MASUYER, Ch. 8.

[15] PROUDHON, p. 377.

[16] AUBRY, *L'Impératrice Eugénie* (1933), I, 38. According to another account (PAILLERON, *George Sand et les hommes de '48*) they saw him drive up in the *voiture* from Strasbourg.

[17] DIDIER, *The life and letters of Madame Bonaparte* (ed. 1879); ODDIE, *The Bonapartes in the New World* (mostly from Didier, 1932).

[18] PROUDHON, p. 390; for Joseph in America, v. DUNAN, *Sainte-Hélène*, I, 641.

[19] DE LA FUYE, Ch. 9; JERROLD, II, Bk. IV, Ch. 1; HASWELL, *The Story of the life of Napoleon III* (1871), Chs. 4-5. For Arese, PALÉOLOGUE, *Cavour* (6th ed.), p. 80, and GRAVINSKI, p. 61; for American authorities, SIMPSON, *The Rise*, p. 365; for the Murats, MME RÉCAMIER, II, 145.

[20] NABONNE, *Joseph Bonaparte*, p. 238; for Hortense's illness, VALÉRIE MASUYER, Ch. 9; cp. MME RÉCAMIER, II, 474.

[21] GUEST, p. 28.

[22] NABONNE, *La reine Hortense*, p. 227; *Mémoires de la reine Hortense* (ed. Hanotaux, 1927).

[23] SIMPSON, *The Rise*, Ch. 7; *Procès de Armand Laity* (1838).

[24] DE LA FUYE, p. 121; CHEETHAM, *Louis Napoleon and the Genesis of the Second Empire* (1909), p. 232.

[25] GUEST, p. 43f; MALMESBURY, *Memoirs of an Ex-minister* (1884), I, 105.

[26] GUEST, p. 40; SADLEIR, *Blessington d'Orsay* (ed. 1947), p. 245.

[27] GUEST, p. 48f; MALMESBURY, I, 112; PERSIGNY, p. 202.

[28] HASWELL, p. 88.

[29] GUEST, p. 34.

[30] SENCOURT, *Louis Napoleon* (1933), p. 73.

[31] JERROLD, II, 87.

[32] DE LA FUYE, p. 141; SADLEIR, p. 303.

[33] HASWELL, p. 92; for Hüber v. DESSEL, *Charles Delescluze*, p. 115n.

[34] GAUBERT, *Le retour des cendres* (1952).

[35] GUEST, p. 53.

[36] SIMPSON, *The Rise*; DE LA FUYE.

[37] HASWELL, pp. 104, 112; for Rémusat, v. *Chronicles of Holland House*, p. 295; for the Conciergerie, v. MME RÉCAMIER, II, 500.

[38] SIMPSON, *The Rise*; DE LA FUYE.

[39] HASWELL, p. 108.

CHAPTER III: THE OUTLAW

[1] *Lettres de Napoléon III*, I, 14f.

[2] E. T. in *Life and Works*.

[3] *Lettres de Napoléon III*, II, August 8th, 1828; February 11th, November 15th, 1841; CHEETHAM, p. 207; for Demidoff, BAC, *La Princesse Mathilde* (1928), p. 62.

[4] JERROLD, II, 465.

[5] *Lettres de Napoléon III*, II, 31.

[6] *Lettres de Napoléon III*, II, 34.

[7] *Life and Works*, I, 65.

[8] *Lettres de Napoléon III*, February 2nd, 15th, August 26th, 1843; *Napoléon III et le Prince Napoléon*, p. 26.

[9] JERROLD, II, 284; *Life and Works*, II, 93; George Sand's long letter is in PAILLERON, p. 219, with Louis' reply.

[10] SIMPSON, *The Rise*, p. 219; JERROLD, II, 186, 198.

[11] *Lettres de Napoléon III*, II, 127.

[12] *Napoléon III et le Prince Napoléon*, p. 16.

[13] MALMESBURY, I, 158.

[14] *Lettres de Napoléon III*, I, 26-7; *Life and Works*, I, 69f; SIMPSON, *The Rise*, p. 225f.

[15] *Life and Works*, I, 76f; *Lettres de Napoléon III*, I, 28f.

[16] MALMESBURY, I, 173.

[17] GUEST, p. 91n.

[18] *Napoléon III et le Prince Napoléon*, p. 34.

[19] GUEST, p. 85.

[20] GUEST, pp. 70, 72; JERROLD, II, 376; *Lettres de Napoléon III*, II, 209.

[21] SIMPSON, *The Rise*, p. 261.

[22] GUEST, p. 78; CHEETHAM, p. 235.

[23] SIMPSON, *The Rise*, p. 237.

[24] SIMPSON, *The Rise*, p. 264.

[25] *Lettres de Napoléon III*, I, 167.

[26] *Napoléon et le Prince Napoléon*, p. 39; TURQUAN, II, 177n.

[27] NORMANBY, *A year of revolution in Paris* (1857), I, 6.

[28] DUVEAU, *La vie ouvrière en France sous le second Empire* (ed. 1946), pp. 195, 210; DOLLÉANS, *Histoire du mouvement ouvrier, 1830-71* (1948), Ch. 1.

[29] GAVIN, *Louis-Philippe* (1933), p. 96.

[30] DOLLÉANS, pp. 79, 174.

[31] PLAMENATZ, *The revolutionary movement in France, 1851-71* (1952).

[32] *Souvenirs de Alexis de Tocqueville;* E. T. (1893), p. 128.

[33] Juliette Adam in DANSETTE, *Deuxième République et Second Empire* (1942), p. 19.

[34] GUEST, p. 92.

[35] *Napoléon et le Prince Napoléon*, p. 36; for Lady Holland's story, *Chronicles of Holland House*, p. 360.

[36] PROUDHON, p. 412.

[37] TOCQUEVILLE, p. 12f; cp. FLAUBERT's *L'éducation sentimentale* (1869); for a modern analysis v. NAMIER, *1848: the Revolution of the Intellectuals* (1944).

[38] MALMESBURY, I, 217.

[39] PERSIGNY's account is in *An Englishman in Paris*, Ch. 11; for the death of Chateaubriand, MME RÉCAMIER, II, 564.

[40] DE LA FUYE, p. 203; VILLAT, *Clio, L'Epoque contemporaraine, I, Restaurations et Révolutions*, p. 109.

[41] SIMPSON, *The Rise*, p. 276; DE LA FUYE, p. 206; PROUDHON, p. 414.

[42] PROUDHON, p. 415; DE LA FUYE, p. 208.

[43] PROUDHON, p. 415.

[44] DE LA FUYE, p. 209.

[45] PROUDHON, pp. 416-17.

[46] PROUDHON, p. 418.

[47] *Napoléon et le Prince Napoléon*, pp. 46, 50.

[48] GUEST, p. 95.

[49] HASWELL, p. 207.

[50] DE LA FUYE, p. 217.

[51] DE LA FUYE, p. 218; PROUDHON, p. 420.

[52] *An Englishman in Paris*, I, 3.

[53] Thiers in SENIOR, *Conversations with M. Thiers, etc.* (1878), I, 31.

[54] SENIOR, *Conversations*, I, 363.

[55] SENIOR, *Conversations*, I, 220.

[56] SENIOR, *Conversations*, I, 256.

[57] *Revue des Deux Mondes* (1915), III, 867.

[58] cp. GUÉRARD, *Napoléon III* (1943), p. 89.

[59] DE LA FUYE, p. 218.

[60] PROUDHON, p. 421.

[61] DE MAUPAS, *Mémoires sous le second Empire* (1884), p. 35; *Lettres de Napoléon III*, II, 259 for Louis' corrections. In ZOLA's *La Fortune des Rougon*, the first of his long series of novels describing 'the natural and social history of a family under the Second Empire', there is a good account of the conversion of a provincial *petit bourgeois* to Bonapartism in 1851. For the peasantry cp. Marx's analysis in *The 18th Brumaire of Louis Bonaparte* (tr. Paul, ed. 1939), p. 132; but he exaggerates their lack of cohesion.

[62] TAINE, *Derniers essais de critique et d'histoire* (ed. 1903), p. 157.

CHAPTER IV: THE PRESIDENT

[1] DE LA FUYE, p. 232.

[2] cp. throughout KERRY, *The Secret of the Coup d'Etat*.

[3] *Mazzini's Letters* (ed. Jarvis, 1930), p. 129.

[4] *Wanderbuch* in JERROLD, IV, 121.

[5] *Napoléon III et le Prince Napoléon*, p. 53.

[6] DANSETTE, p. 66.

[7] DE LA FUYE, p. 245; DE MAUPAS, pp. 76, 83.

[8] HENRY, *Napoléon III et les peuples* (1943), p. 16f.

[9] TREVELYAN, *Life of Macaulay* (ed. 1932), I, 461.

[10] WHYTE; PALÉOLOGUE, *Cavour* (1926).

[11] AUBERT, *Le Pontificat de Pie IX* (1952); HALES, *Pio Nono* (1954); for Papal policy, DEMARCO, *Pio IX e la rivoluzione romana del 1848* (1947); for Ernani, TOYE, *Giuseppe Verdi* (1931), p. 38; for Monte Cassino, RENAN, *Œuvres*, II, 148.

[12] PALÉOLOGUE, *Cavour*, p. 81; DE LA FUYE, p. 290.

[13] DE LA FUYE, pp. 292, 295; HENRY, pp. 17, 19; ARNAUD, *La deuxième République et le second Empire* (1929), p. 38.

[14] DE MAUPAS, p. 87; DUVEAU, p. 47; ARNAUD, p. 39.

[15] DE MAUPAS, p. 103; PLAMENATZ, p. 92.

[16] MALMESBURY, I, 259.

[17] DE LA FUYE, p. 258; BILLY, Sainte-Beuve (1952), II, 26.

[18] DANSETTE, p. 86; for Changarnier, PERSIGNY, p. 126; MAXIME DU CAMP, *Souvenirs d'un demi-siècle* (1949), I, 105; MAURAIN, *Baroche* (1936), pp. 87-8.

[19] DE LA FUYE, p. 265.

[20] SENIOR, *Correspondence*, I, 93, 103, 189; BUCKLE, *Life of Disraeli* (1910), III, 404.

[21] DE LA FUYE p. 278.

[22] DANSETTE, p. 90; DE MAUPAS, pp. 241, 346.

[23] DANSETTE, p. 84; *Letters of Queen Victoria*, II, 248; ASHLEY, *Lord Palmerston* (1876), I, 287, 294.

[24] DE LA FUYE, Ch. 22; DE MAUPAS, p. 189f; for Morny, PALÉOLOGUE, *Les entretiens de l'Impératrice Eugénie* (1928), p. 84; KERRY, p. 105; MAXIME DU CAMP, I, 227; Ollivier in JERROLD, III, 208.

[25] *An Englishman in Paris*, II, 43.

[26] The latest and most detailed account is by GUILLEMIN, *Le coup du 2 décembre* (1951); the Proclamations are reproduced in facsimile in KERRY, p. 122.

[27] DE MAUPAS, p. 44; KERRY, p. 105f.

[28] DE MAUPAS, p. 528f; GUILLEMIN, p. 416; PALÉOLOGUE, *Entretiens*, p. 30; MAUROIS, *Lélia* (tr. Hopkins, 1953), p. 360; the official report of the casualties is in KERRY, p. 156.

[29] *History through The Times* (1937), p. 139.

[30] BAGEHOT, *Literary Studies* (ed. 1895), III, 1; COOK, *Delane of The Times* (1915).

[31] MALMESBURY, I, 294; BILLY, II, 52.

[32] *Life and Works*, I, 166, 168.

[33] *Life and Works*, I, 253-4.

[34] SADLEIR, p. 303.

[35] KERRY, p. 195. It appears that in October 1851, ex-King Jérôme was counting on 'the succession of himself and his son to the Empire' (*Chronicles of Holland House*, p. 395).

[36] KERRY, p. 192f; MAURAIN, *Baroche* (1936), p. 116.

[37] DE MAUPAS.

[38] ARNAUD, Ch. 2.

[39] MALMESBURY, I, 318, 324.

[40] ARNAUD, p. 68.

[41] ARNAUD, p. 71.

[42] *History through The Times*, p. 144; ROTHAN, p. 345; HASWELL, p. 282.

CHAPTER V: THE EMPEROR

[1] SIMPSON, *Louis Napoleon and the recovery of France* (ed. 1951), p. 198n; ROTHAN, p. 335f; *Later Correspondence of Lord John Russell* (ed. Gooch, 1952), II, 103. According to MAURAIN (p. 124) Louis originally proposed the title *Napoléon III, Empereur des Français, Roi d'Algérie*.

[2] GRANVILLE (*Life*, by Fitzmaurice, 1906), I, 57, 138, 218.

[3] DASENT, *John Delane* (1908), I, 136, 145.

[4] *Queen Victoria's Letters*, II, 243, 254, 482, 453.

[5] MALMESBURY, I, 395.

[6] GREVILLE, *Journal* (1837-52), III, 40, 160.

[7] DE LESSEPS, *Recollections of Forty Years* (1887), I, 125; PALÉOLOGUE, *Les entretiens*, p. 73; Martineau, *Le cœur de Stendhal* (1953), II, 332.

[8] *Queen Victoria's letters*, II, 528; AUBRY, I, 107.

[9] AUBRY, I, 109.

[10] GREVILLE, III, 38; *Queen Victoria's letters*, II, 530; MAXIME DU CAMP, I, 163.

[11] SIMPSON, *The Recovery*, p. 215.

[12] DASENT, I, 154; *Letters of the Prince Consort* (1938), p. 185.

[13] *Later Correspondence of Lord John Russell*, II, 145; HENRY, p. 28f; STOCKMAR (*Memoirs*, 1872), II, 208, 101, 108, 114; DE GRUNVALD, *La vie de Nicolas Ier* (1946). The clause of the treaty of Kutchuk that Nicholas relied on was in Article 7: 'La Sublime Porte promet une protection constante à la religion chrétienne et aux églises de cette religion. Elle permet au Ministre de la Cour Impériale de faire en toute occasion des représentations à la Porte, tant en faveur de l'église construite à Constantinople ... qu'en faveur de ceux qui la desservent, et elle promet de donner attention à ces observations comme venant d'une personne considérée....' For Routh, v. BURGON, *Lives of Twelve Good Men* (1888), I, 479.

[14] STRATFORD DE REDCLIFFE, *The Eastern Question*, p. 70; *The life, letters, and friendships of Richard Monkton Milnes* (ed. 1890), I, 287.

[15] HOBSON, *Richard Cobden, the international man* (1919), p. 26; MALMESBURY, I, 402; DE GRUNVALD, Ch. 12.

[16] MALMESBURY, I, 422.

[17] MAXWELL, *Life and letters of the fourth Earl of Clarendon* (1913), II, 38, 50; SIMPSON, *The Recovery*, pp. 232, 393; MALCOLM SMITH, *Life of Stratford Canning*; TEMPERLEY, *The Crimea*.

[18] DASENT, I, 159.

[19] GREVILLE, IV, 19; RUSSELL, II, 154; HOBSON, p. 167; SIMPSON, *The Recovery*, p. 237.

[20] CLARENDON, II, 38, 50; *History through The Times*, p. 159.

[21] PALÉOLOGUE, *Les entretiens*, p. 243; HOBSON, p. 167.

[22] SENIOR, I, 260; GREVILLE, III, 266.

[23] ROBBINS in *Journal of Transport History* (May 1953).

[24] SENIOR, II, 97; ODDIE, *The Bonapartes in the New World* (1932), pp. 206, 210; *Napoleon III et le Prince Napoléon*, p. 83. For Elizabeth Patterson's unsuccessful attempt, after ex-King Jérôme's death, to have the legitimacy of her son by him recognized, ibid., p. 199.

[25] GRANVILLE, I, 103; THOUVENEL, *Pages de l'histoire du Second Empire* (1903), p. 146.

[26] GRANVILLE, I, 102; MALMESBURY, II, 12.

[27] HASWELL, p. 287; RUSSELL, II, 206; GREVILLE, III, 257, 263; MAURAIN, p. 161.

[28] *Queen Victoria's letters*, BUCKLE, IV, 5.

[29] CLARENDON, III, 90; *Queen Victoria's letters*, III, 176, 178; GREVILLE, III, 253; SAUNDERS, *A distant summer* (1946).

[30] BUCKLE, IV, 17, 23; HAMLEY, *The war in the Crimea* (1891), p. 272.

[31] HENRY, p. 46f; CLARENDON, September 29th, 1857, II, 109, 120;

DAWSON, *The German Empire* (1919), I, Ch. 3; for the Congress of Paris, SETON WATSON, *Britain in Europe*.

[32] MORLEY, *Gladstone* (ed. 1911), II, 3.

[33] GREVILLE, IV, 67; MORLEY, I, 421; BUCKLE, IV, 56.

CHAPTER VI: THE LIBERATOR

[1] PALÉOLOGUE, *Cavour*, p. 2; SENIOR, II, 262.

[2] PALÉOLOGUE, *Cavour*, Ch. 1; MORLEY, I, 115.

[3] *Letters of the Prince Consort*, p. 188.

[4] WHYTE, *Early Life and Political Career of Cavour*; COGNASSO in *Questione di storia del Risorgimento e del unità d'Italia*; BIANCHI, *La politique de Cavour* (1885). The publication (not yet complete) of *Il carteggio Cavour-Nigra* suggests some revision of the accepted view of Cavour. v. MACK SMITH, *Cavour and Garibaldi* (1954).

[5] RUSSELL, II, 172, 181; GREVILLE, IV, 301.

[6] PALÉOLOGUE, *Cavour*, p. 61.

[7] CLARENDON, II, 106; *Queen Victoria's letters*, III, 168.

[8] GREVILLE, III, 301; BELL, *Palmerston*, II, 153.

[9] GRANVILLE, I, 163.

[10] GREVILLE, III, 102; MALMESBURY, II, 268; THOUVENEL, p. 280; DECAUX, *La Castiglione* (1953), p. 92; *Chronicles of Holland House*, p. 413; DE LA FAYE, p. 178; LOLIÉE, *Women of the Second Empire* (1907), pp. 10, 60.

[11] MALMESBURY, II, 268.

[12] RUSSELL, II, 219; MORLEY, I, 294.

[13] ARNAUD, p. 126f.

[14] *Queen Victoria's letters*, II, 545.

[15] SENCOURT, p. 188; *Cambridge History of British Foreign Policy*, p. 399; CLARENDON, II, 136, 294; PALÉOLOGUE, *Cavour*, p. 153.

[16] GREVILLE, IV, 189; GRANVILLE, I, 229.

[17] MÉRIMÉE, *Lettres à M. Panizzi* (1881); PALÉOLOGUE, *Entretiens*, p. 172.

[18] HASWELL, p. 289.

[19] GREVILLE, IV, 215.

[20] GREVILLE, III, 136; BELL, II, 93. For the proposed marriage of Princess Mary to 'Plon-Plon', *Chronicles of Holland House*, p. 398.

[21] PALÉOLOGUE, *Cavour*, Ch. v; HENRY, p. 61.

[22] WHYTE, *Political Career*, pp. 258, 269.

[23] *Queen Victoria's letters*, III, 350, 375; BELL, II, 194; *Cambridge History*, p. 399.

[24] CLARENDON, II, 168; GRANVILLE, I, 325.

[25] *Queen Victoria's letters*, III, 390; PALÉOLOGUE, *Cavour*, Ch. vi.

[26] GRANVILLE, I, 322; *Hansard*, cliii, 30; PALÉOLOGUE, *Cavour*, p. 198.

[27] WHYTE, *The political career*, p. 271.

[28] *Napoléon et le Prince Napoléon*, p. 122f; BUCKLE, IV, 227.

[29] ARNAUD, p. 143; JERROLD, IV, 545; HALES, *Pio Nono*, p. 192.

[30] *Napoléon III et le Prince Napoléon*, p. 161; *Letters of the Prince Consort*, p. 310; Rémusat in SENIOR, II, 39. But liberal opinion in England backed Louis: e.g. the Italian Committee formed by FREDERIC HARRISON (*Autobiographic Memoirs*, 1911) and Francis Newman; and MATTHEW ARNOLD'S *England and the Italian Question* (1859).

[31] MÉRIMÉE, April 29th, May 1st, 1859, in SENIOR, II, 244.

[32] JERROLD, IV, 215; MÉRIMÉE, June 30th, 1859.

[33] Chrzanowski in SENIOR, II, 358; THOMPSON, *Napoleon Bonaparte* (1952), p. 69; PALÉOLOGUE, *Cavour*, p. 238; for Eugénie's Regency, MAURAIN, p. 177.

[34] *Napoléon III et le Prince Napoléon*, p. 342; JERROLD, IV, 548.

[35] PALÉOLOGUE, *Entretiens*, pp. 76, 247; WHYTE, *Political Career*, p. 314; the imminence of a Prussian attack was confirmed by Bismarck in 1888 (HENRY, p. 68).

[36] *Napoléon III et le Prince Napoléon*, p. 186; *Revue des Deux Mondes*, August 1909.

[37] ARNAUD, p. 158.

[38] PALÉOLOGUE, *Cavour*, p. 247.

[39] DANSETTE, p. 222; BUCKLE, IV, 262.

CHAPTER VII: THE ADVENTURER

[1] GREVILLE, III, 314; SENIOR, I, 53, 61, 125; RUSSELL, II, 250; HALES, p. 198.

[2] PALÉOLOGUE, *Cavour*, p. 264; GREVILLE, IV, 282; GRANVILLE, I, 368; Hudson's obituary notice in *The Times* said that he disobeyed the instructions of two successive governments, and acted according to the wisdom of the people of England.

[3] MAZZINI, *The Duties of Man* (Everyman ed. 1907), p. 53.

[4] THOUVENEL, p. 329.

[5] THOUVENEL, p. 333; GREGOROVIUS, *Roman Journals* (tr. Hamilton, 1907), p. 132; RUSSELL, II, 293. Zola's *Rome* (clever journalism in the form of romance) sums up the argument for the Temporal Power in the popular cry *Evviva el papa re!*, and the saving pride of the common people in the old Garibaldian's remark, *Io son Romano di Roma*. His conclusion is that Rome can survive only as a secular capital.

[6] *Napoléon III et le Prince Napoléon*, pp. 167f, 188.

[7] PALÉOLOGUE, *Cavour*, p. 269.

[8] ARNAUD, p. 167; MALMESBURY, II, 223; Palmerston to Cowley, April 1860; *Queen Victoria's letters*, III.

[9] CLARENDON, II, 217; BUCKLE, IV, 320.

[10] MALMESBURY, II, 229.

[11] DELANE, II, 10.

[12] TREVELYAN, *Garibaldi and the making of Italy* (ed. 1911), p. 23; cp. throughout, MACK SMITH.

[13] TREVELYAN, *Garibaldi*, p. 25.

[14] TREVELYAN, *Garibaldi*, p. 211.

[15] RUSSELL, p. 222; TREVELYAN, *Garibaldi*, p. 253.

[16] *History through The Times*, p. 188.

[17] MÉRIMÉE, October 14th, 1861.

[18] SENCOURT, p. 250; *Napoléon III et le Prince Napoléon*, p. 101f; Mérimée to Panizzi, June 13th, 1865; Emerit in *Clio*, p. 459; HENRY, p. 84; BUCKLE, III, 333; ARNAUD, p. 206f.

[19] MÉRIMÉE, *Lettres à une inconnue*, II, 162.

[20] BLANCHARD, *Le second Empire* (1950), p. 172f.

[21] ARNAUD, p. 210f; MALMESBURY, II, 244.

[22] ARNAUD, p. 214f.

[23] PALÉOLOGUE, *Entretiens*, p. 101f; AUGUSTIN-THIERRY, *Le Duc de Morny* (1951), p. 207; SCHEFER, *La grande pensée de Napoléon III* (1939), Ch. 3; for Jecker cp. *Papiers secrets et Correspondance du Second Empire* (1873) p. 2.

[24] BUCKLE, IV, 348; MALMESBURY, II, 281; RUSSELL, II, 317; NEWTON, *Lord Lyons* (ed. Nelson), pp. 38, 54.

[25] HYDE, *Mexican Empire* (1946), pp. 75, 82.

[26] HYDE, Ch. 5.

[27] ARNAUD, p. 222; *Queen Victoria's letters*, September 30th, 1863.

[28] ARNAUD, p. 229; HYDE, pp. 145, 151. Readers of Conrad's *Nostromo* will be reminded of Mrs. Gould's experiences in Costaguana (Ch. 7).

[29] ARNAUD, p. 224; BLANCHARD, p. 186.

[30] HYDE, Chs. 8 and 10. A letter from Fould advising Louis to cut his losses in Mexico (Aug. 1866) is in *Papiers secrets*, p. 312.

[31] DE LESSEPS, *The Suez Canal* (1816), p. 14.

[32] MORLEY, I, 441.

[33] DE LESSEPS, *The Suez Canal*, pp. 222, 81, 246, 267.

[34] *Monckton Milnes*, II, 208; for Eugénie in Egypt, cp. *Papiers secrets*, pp. 126, 183, 294.

[35] GUÉRARD, p. 179; JERROLD, IV, 557.

CHAPTER VIII: THE LIBERAL

[1] AUBRY, II, 38.

[2] *An Englishman in Paris*, II, 160; GIRARDET, *La société militaire dans la France contemporaine* (1953).

[3] MAURAIN, *La politique ecclésiastique du Second Empire* (1930); AUBERT, *Le pontificat de Pie IX* (1952), pp. 40f, 108f; for Veuillot, GAUTIER, *Le génie satirique de Louis Veuillot*, p. 59.

[4] DANSETTE, p. 128f; for the *Crédit Mobilier*, BAGEHOT, III, p. 280.

[5] GIRARD, *La politique des travaux publics du second Empire* (1951), pp. 38n, 103; GILLE, *La concentration industrielle en France au debut du*

Second Empire, in Bulletin de la société d'histoire moderne, November-December 1952.

⁶ DANSETTE, p. 128f; JERROLD, IV, 368.

⁷ GIRARD, p. 116; DUVEAU, p. 204f; JERROLD, IV, 364f; LEWIS, *Edwin Chadwick* (1952); CHEVALIER, *La formation de la population parisienne au XIXᵉ siècle* (1950); LAROUZE, *Le Baron Haussmann* (1932); PERSIGNY, p. 253f.

⁸ *Letters of the Prince Consort*, p. 232; JERROLD, IV, 366; LAROUZE.

⁹ DUVEAU, pp. 50, 54.

¹⁰ JERROLD, IV, Ch. II. For the interview with Proudhon, v. DESSEL, *Charles Delescluze*, p. 87n. It is worth adding the tribute Anatole France paid to Louis through the mouth of Dechartre in *Le Lys Rouge* (Ch. 26). 'L'Empereur était bon, mais il n'avait pas d'influence ... Il m'est resté une vague sympathie pour cet homme qui manquait de génie, mais dont l'âme était affectueuse, qui portait dans les grandes aventures de la vie un courage simple et un doux fatalisme ... Et puis, ce qui me le rend sympathique, c'est qu'il fut combattu et injurié par des gens ... qui n'avaient pas même, comme lui, au fond de l'âme, l'amour du peuple.'

¹¹ *Monckton Milnes*, II, 388; HOBSON, pp. 37, 242f; BUCKLE, III, 395; IV, 220; MAURAIN, *Baroche*, p. 184f.

¹² HOBSON, p. 348; BUCKLE, IV, 221; TREVELYAN, *Life of John Bright* (ed. 1913), p. 285.

¹³ DOLLÉANS, p. 272.

¹⁴ KAHN, *Science and aesthetic judgement* (1953), p. 35; HEMMINGS, *Emile Zola* (1953); SPENCER, *Flaubert* (1952); ROBERT, *La Terre d'Emile Zola* (1952); VAN TIEGHEM, *Renan* (1948).

¹⁵ BILLY, II, pp. 26, 54; E. and J. GONCOURT, *Journal*.

¹⁶ VALLEY-RADOT, *Pasteur* (E. T.), pp. 104, 181. Louis would have liked RENAN's *Avenir de la science*, but though written in 1849 it was not published till 1890.

¹⁷ CANNAN, *Ithuriel's hour*, p. 276; for Baroche, MAURAIN, p. 506.

¹⁸ *Napoléon III et le Prince Napoléon*, p. 241.

¹⁹ DE LA FAYE, *La Princesse Mathilde* (1928). There are many accounts of Princess Mathilde's *salon*; one of the best in PROUST, *Chroniques*.

²⁰ *Lettres de Napoléon III*, I, 58. For the *Life of Caesar*, which did not go beyond the beginning of the Civil War, JERROLD, IV, 356f.

²¹ AUGUSTIN-THIERRY; CHRISTOPHE, *Le Duc de Morny* (1951).

²² *Napoléon III et le Prince Napoléon*, p. 161.

²³ SCHNERB, *Rouher et le Second Empire* (1949); for government electioneering, *Papiers secrets*, p. 10f.

²⁴ BAGEHOT, *Literary Studies*, III, 72f.

CHAPTER IX: THE GAMBLER

[1] BISMARCK, *Gedanken und Erinnerungen* (ed. Gibson, 1940), pp. 50, 60; MÉRIMÉE, *Lettres à une inconnue*, II, 275, 292, 301; PERSIGNY, p. 281f.

[2] *Napoléon III et le Prince Napoléon*, pp. 236, 351. BELL, II, 351.

[3] HENRY, pp. 87, 93, 97.

[4] BISMARCK, p. 93; RUSSELL, II, 295; OAKES and MOWAT, *The great European treaties of the nineteenth century.*

[5] BUCKLE, IV, 353; Clarendon to Delane, May 2nd, 1864; Torrington to Delane, May 10th, 1864.

[6] *Delane*, II, 152n.

[7] *Queen Victoria's letters*, III, 162, 187, 271.

[8] RUSSELL, II, 297; BUCKLE, IV, 341.

[9] HENRY, p. 103.

[10] *Lettres de Napoléon III*, I, 58f.

[11] *Queen Victoria's letters*, III, 313, 317.

[12] SOREL, *Essais d'histoire et de critique* (1883), pp. 243, 246.

[13] PALÉOLOGUE, *Entretiens*, p. 117.

[14] PALÉOLOGUE, *Entretiens*, p. 124.

[15] *Queen Victoria's letters*, III, 365.

[16] *Queen Victoria's letters*, III, 387; BISMARCK, p. 105.

[17] RUSSELL, II, 357.

[18] ARNAUD, p. 257.

[19] *Monckton Milnes*, II, 168f; ARNAUD, p. 250; one of the prizes went to an exhibit of Krupp guns from Essen; M. Krupp was made an Officer of the Legion of Honour (*Papiers secrets*, p. 324).

[20] ARNAUD, p. 255; DAWSON, pp. 273, 301.

[21] *Delane*, II, 209.

[22] ARNAUD, p. 267; *Napoléon III et le Prince Napoléon*, p. 280.

[23] SCHNERB, p. 159.

[24] SCHNERB, p. 178.

[25] PALÉOLOGUE, *Entretiens*, p. 120.

[26] SAINT-MARC, *Emile Ollivier* (1950), Ch. VI, p. 155.

[27] ARNAUD, p. 270f; SAINT-MARC, p. 186.

[28] NEWTON, *Lord Lyons*, p. 125f.

[29] *Lord Lyons*, p. 131; for Prévost-Paradol, DE LA GORCE, *Napoléon III et sa Politique* (ed. 1933).

[30] PALÉOLOGUE, *Entretiens*, p. 150.

[31] PALÉOLOGUE, *Entretiens*, p. 135; in *Papiers secrets* (p. 58) is a plan for a Regency in the event of Louis' death, submitted to the Senate in October 1869.

[32] ARNAUD, p. 278.

[33] ARNAUD, p. 286; *Napoléon III et le Prince Napoléon*, p. 296; REINACH, *La vie politique de Gambetta*, p. 10.

[34] *Napoléon III et le Prince Napoléon*, p. 386.

[35] MALMESBURY, II, 414.
[36] ARNAUD, Ch. IX; *Lord Lyons*, p. 165.
[37] *Lord Lyons*, p. 167; on the Empress in Council, PERSIGNY, p. 387f.
[38] ARNAUD, p. 290; GUÉRARD, p. 265.
[39] BISMARCK, pp. 106, 113.
[40] SCHNERB, p. 270; SEIGNOBOS, *Histoire politique de l'Europe contemporaine*, II, 1138.
[41] LORD ACTON's *Correspondence* (1917), I (to Gladstone); cp. HALES, Ch. VIII.

CHAPTER X: THE FATALIST

[1] *Lord Lyons*, p. 135. Already in October 1868 General Ducrot had warned General Frossard, the Prince Imperial's tutor, that Prussia intended war (*Papiers secrets*, p. 128).
[2] *Lord Lyons*, p. 142.
[3] *Queen Victoria's letters*, IV, 15.
[4] *Lord Lyons*, p. 176; *Queen Victoria's letters*, IV, 8; *Lord Lyons*, p. 196.
[5] ARNAUD, p. 300.
[6] OMAN, *Things I have seen* (1933), Ch. I.
[7] BISMARCK, p. 246f.
[8] *Queen Victoria's letters*, IV, 10; BISMARCK, p. 257.
[9] SAINT-MARC, p. 263; Granville to Russell, July 7th, 1870.
[10] TAYLOR, *Rumours of war* (1952), p. 64; RUSSELL, II, 371; DAWSON, Ch. 8.
[11] SAINT-MARC, p. 269.
[12] SAINT-MARC, p. 272.
[13] SAINT-MARC, pp. 276, 278.
[14] *Queen Victoria's letters*, IV, 25, 28.
[15] *Queen Victoria's letters*, IV, 29.
[16] SAINT-MARC, pp. 290n, 293.
[17] PALÉOLOGUE, *Entretiens*, pp. 149, 152.
[18] BISMARCK, p. 143.
[19] BISMARCK, p. 251 (the two versions printed side by side).
[20] SAINT-MARC, p. 325f. *C'est vrai, il (Louis) ne voulait pas la guerre, mais il est si bon, qu'il me l'accordé, quand il a vu que je la désirais* (Ollivier to du Camp, July 31st, 1870).
[21] LEGGE, *The comedy and tragedy of the Second Empire* (1911), p. 285; *An Englishman in Paris*, II, 185; OMAN, p. 16.
[22] GUÉRARD, p. 266; SAINT-MARC, p. 327.
[23] *Queen Victoria's letters*, IV, 45; COOK, *Delane of The Times*, p. 226
[24] *Napoléon III et le Prince Napoléon*, p. 307f.
[25] AUBRY, II, 43; *Œuvres posthumes de Louis Napoléon*, p. 214.
[26] PALÉOLOGUE, *Entretiens*, p. 159; *An Englishman in Paris*, II, 198.

[27] *War diary of Emperor Frederick III* (ed. Atkinson, 1929), p. 19; *Queen Victoria's letters*, IV, 42.

[28] *Monckton Milnes*, II, 232; FORBES, p. 284.

[29] AUBRY, II, 59.

[30] AUBRY, II, 69; MÉRIMÉE, *Lettres à une inconnue*, II, 370.

[31] MÉRIMÉE, *Lettres à une inconnue*, II, 372.

[32] SCHNERB, p. 280f.

[33] FORBES. For Forbes and Russell, v. COOK, *Delane*, p. 232.

[34] *Prince Frederick's war diaries*, pp. 110, 233; Tolstoy had expressed the same feelings in *Sevastopol*, Ch. 16.

[35] *Prince Frederick's war diaries*, p. 91f; FORBES, I, 107f. The comment on Louis' humanity is from DE LA GORCE, p. 178.

[36] FORBES, I, 146.

[37] LEGGE, p. 219; FORBES, I, 144.

[38] AUBRY, II, 81, 84.

[39] *Lord Lyons*, p. 220.

[40] SAINT-MARC, p. 350; PALÉOLOGUE, *Entretiens*, p. 209.

[41] AUBRY, II, 76.

[42] *Lord Lyons*, p. 218.

[43] AUBRY, II, 90f.

[44] *Queen Victoria's letters*, IV, 68.

[45] GREGOROVIUS, *Roman Journals*, p. 420.

EPILOGUE

[1] *Queen Victoria's letters*, IV, 89; two letters from Rouher to Baroche in MAURAIN, *Appendix*.

[2] *Queen Victoria's letters*, IV, 92.

[3] GUEST, Ch. 9.

[4] *Queen Victoria's letters*, IV, 124.

[5] MALMESBURY, II, 417.

[6] GUEST, p. 195.

[7] *Queen Victoria's letters*, IV, 236.

[8] AUBRY, II, 151.

[9] JERROLD, IV, App. XIII.

[10] *Queen Victoria's letters*, IV, 237.

[11] SIDNEY LEE, *Life of King Edward VIII*, I, 341.

[12] PALÉOLOGUE, *Entretiens*, p. 11.

[13] PALÉOLOGUE, *Entretiens*, p. 257.

INDEX

Date Due

"The episode where Archie gives the eulogy."

"I know."

"Where he comments that he never thought Stretch Cunningham was Jewish because of the 'ham' in his last name."

"I know the episode, Win."

"And you're willing to miss it for the sake of the Web?"

"You have it on tape."

"That's not the point."

The two men looked at each other, comfortable in the silence. After some time passed, Win said, "Tell me."

He barely hesitated. "Emily said I'm the boy's father."

Win nodded and said, "Ah."

"You don't sound surprised."

Win used the chopsticks to grab another shrimp. "You believe her?"

"Yes."

"Why?"

"For one thing, it's a hell of thing to lie about it."

"But Emily is good at lying, Myron. She's always lied to you. She lied to you in college. She lied to you when Greg disappeared. She lied in court about Greg's behavior with the children. She betrayed Greg the night before their wedding by sleeping with you. And, if you will, if she is telling the truth now, she lied to you for the better part of thirteen years."

Myron thought about it. "I think she's telling the truth about this."

"You *think*, Myron."

"I'm going to take a blood test."

Win shrugged. "If you must."

"What does that mean?"

"I'll let the statement speak for itself."

Myron made a face. "Didn't you just say I should find out for sure?"

"Not at all," Win said. "I was merely pointing out the obvious. I didn't say it made a difference."

Myron thought about it. "You're confusing me."

"Simply put," Win said, "so what if you are the boy's biological father? What difference does it make?"

"Come on, Win. Not even you can be that cold."

"Quite the opposite. As strange as this might sound, I am using my heart on this one."

"How do you figure?"

Win swirled the liquid again, studied the amber, took a sip. It colored his cheeks a bit. "Again I'll put it simply: No matter what a blood test might indicate, you are not Jeremy Downing's father. Greg is. You may be a sperm donor. You may be an accident of lust and biology. You may have provided a simple microscopic cell structure that combined with one slightly more complex. But you are not this boy's father."

"It's not that simple, Win."

"It is that simple, my friend. The fact that you insipidly choose to confuse the issue does not change the fact. I'll demonstrate, if you'd like."

"I'm listening."

"You love your father, correct?"

"You know the answer to that."

"I do," Win said. "But what makes him your father? The fact that he once grunted on top of Mommy after a few drinks—or the way he has cared for you and loved you for the past thirty-five years?"

Myron looked down at the can of Yoo-Hoo.

"You owe this boy nothing," Win continued, "and equally important, he owes you nothing. We will try to save his life, if that is what you wish, but that should be where it ends."

Myron thought about it. The only thing scarier than Win irrational was when Win made sense. "Maybe you're right."

"But you still don't think it's that simple."

"I don't know."

On the television, Archie approached the pulpit, a yarmulke on his head. "It's a start," Win said.

6

Myron mixed childlike Froot Loops and very adult All-Bran into a bowl and poured on skim milk. For those not reading the Cliffs Notes, this act denotes that there is still a great deal of boy in the man. Heavy symbolism. How poignant.

The Number 1 train took Myron to a platform on 168th Street so far below ground that commuters had to take a urine-encapsulated elevator to reach the surface. The elevator was big and dark and shaky and brought on images of a PBS documentary on coal mining.

Located in Washington Heights, a quick stone's toss from Harlem and directly across Broadway from the Audubon Ballroom where Malcolm X was gunned down, Columbia Presbyterian Medical Center's famed pediatric building was called Babies and Children's Hospital. It used to be called just Babies Hospital, but a committee of learned medical experts was formed and after hours of intense study, they decided to change the name from Babies Hospital to Babies and Children's Hospital. Moral of the story: Committees are really, really important.

But the name, while not exactly Madison Avenue, does adequately reflect the reality of the situation—the hospital is strictly pediatric and deliveries, a well-worn twelve-floor edifice with eleven of them devoted to sick children. There was something very wrong with that, but probably nothing beyond the theologically obvious.

Myron stopped before the entranceway and looked up at the pollution-brown brick. Lots of misery in the city and much of it ended up here. He ducked inside and checked in at the security desk. He gave his name to a guard. The guard tossed him a pass, almost glancing up from his *TV Guide* in the process. Myron waited a long time for the elevator, reading the Patient's Bill of Rights, which was printed in both English and Spanish. There was a sign for the Sol Goldman Heart Center right next to a sign for the hospital's Burger King. Mixed messages or assuring future business—Myron wasn't sure which.

The elevator opened on the tenth floor. Directly in front of him, there was a rainbow-hued "Save the Rain Forest" mural, painted, according to the sign, by the "pediatric patients" of the hospital. Save the Rain Forest. Oh, like these kids didn't have enough on their plate, right?

Myron asked a nurse where he might find Dr. Singh. The nurse pointed to a woman leading a dozen interns through the corridor. Myron was a little surprised to see that Dr. Singh was of the female persuasion, mostly because he had somehow imagined her being a man. Terribly sexist, but there you go.

Dr. Singh was, as her name strongly implied, Indian, from-India Indian as opposed to Native American Indian. Mid-thirties, he figured, her hair a lighter brown than what he was used to seeing on India Indians. She wore a white doctor coat, of course. So did all the interns, most of them appearing to be about fourteen years of age, their white coats more like smocks, like they were about to finger-paint or maybe dissect a frog in a junior high biology class. Some wore grave expressions that were almost laughable on their cherubic faces, but most emanated that medical-intern exhaustion from too many nights on call.

Only two of the interns were men—boys really—both sporting blue jeans, colorful ties, and white sneakers like waiters at Bennigan's. The women—to call them girls would use up Myron's anti-PC quota for the week—favored hospital scrubs. So young. Babies taking care of babies.

Myron followed the group at a semi-discreet distance. Every once in a while he glanced in a room and immediately regretted it. The corridor walls were festive and brightly painted, jammed with Disney/Nick Junior/PBS kiddie images and collages and mobiles, but Myron only saw black. A floor filled with dying children. Bald little boys and girls in pain, their veins blackened by toxins and poisons. Most of the children looked so calm and unafraid and unnaturally brave. If you wanted to see the stark terror, you had to look in the eyes of the parents, as though Mom and Dad were sucking the horror toward them, taking it on so that their child wouldn't have to.

"Mr. Bolitar?"

Dr. Singh met his eye and held out her hand. "I'm Karen Singh."

Myron almost asked her how she did this, how she stayed on this floor day in and day out, watching children die. But he didn't. They exchanged the usual pleasantries. Myron had expected an Indian accent, but the only thing he picked up was a little Bronx.

"We can talk in here," she said.

She pushed open one of the superheavy, superwide doors endemic to hospitals and nursing homes, and they stepped into an empty room with stripped beds. The barrenness ignited Myron's imagination. He could almost see a loved one rushing into the hospital, repeatedly pushing the elevator call button, diving inside, pushing more buttons, sprinting down the corridor into this silent room, the bed being stripped by a nurse, then the sudden cry of anguish. . . .

Myron shook his head. He watched too much TV.

Karen Singh sat on the corner of the mattress, and Myron studied her face for a moment. She had long sharp features. Everything pointed down—her nose, her chin, her eyebrows. Sort of harsh.

"You're staring," she said.

"I don't mean to."

She pointed to her forehead. "You were maybe expecting a dot?"

"Er, no."

"Very good, then let's get to it, shall we?"

"Okay."

"Mrs. Downing wants me to tell you whatever you want to know."

"I appreciate your taking the time."

"Are you a private investigator?" she asked.

"More like a family friend."

"Did you play basketball with Greg Downing?"

Myron was always surprised by the memory of the public. After all these years, people could still recall his big games, his big shots, sometimes with more clarity than Myron could. "You're a fan?"

"Nope," she said. "Can't stand sports actually."

"So how did you—"

"Just a deduction. You're tall and about the right age and you said you were a family friend. So . . ." She shrugged.

"Nice deduction."

"It's what we do here when you think about it. Deduce. Some diagnoses are easy. Others must be deduced from the evidence. You ever read Sherlock Holmes?"

"Sure."

"Sherlock said that you should never theorize before you have facts—because then you twist facts to suit theories rather than twisting theories to suit facts. If you see a misdiagnosis, nine times out of ten they ignored Sherlock's axiom."

"Did that happen with Jeremy Downing?"

"As a matter of fact," she said, "it did."

Somewhere down the hall, a machine started beeping. The sound hit the nerves like a police taser.

"So his first doctor screwed up?"

"I won't get into that. But Fanconi anemia isn't common. And because it looks like other things, it's often misdiagnosed."

"So tell me about Jeremy."

"What's to tell? He has it. Fanconi anemia, that is. In simple terms, his bone marrow is corrupted."

"Corrupted?"

"In layman's term, it's shit. It makes him susceptible to a host of infections and even cancers. It commonly turns into AML." She saw the puzzled look on his face and added, "That's acute myelogenous leukemia."

"But you can cure him?"

" 'Cure' is an optimistic word," she said. "But with a bone marrow transplant and treatments with a new fludarabine compound, yes, I believe his prognosis is excellent."

"Fluda-what?"

"Not important. We need a bone marrow donor that matches Jeremy. That's what counts here."

"And you don't have one."

Dr. Singh shifted on the mattress. "That's correct."

Myron felt the resistance. He decided to back off, test another flank. "Could you take me through the transplant process?"

"Step by step?"

"If it's not too much trouble."

She shrugged. "First step: find a donor."

"How do you go about that?"

"You try family members, of course. Siblings have the best chance of matching. Then parents. Then people of similar background."

"When you say people of similar background—"

"Blacks with blacks, Jews with Jews, Latino descent with Latino descent. You'll see that quite often in marrow drives. If the patient is, for example, a Hasidic Jew, the donation drives will take place within their shuls. Mixed blood is usually the hardest to match."

"And Jeremy's blood or whatever you need to match—it's fairly rare?"

"Yes."

Emily and Greg were both of Irish descent. Myron's family came from the usual potpourri of old Russia and Poland and even a little Palestine thrown in. Mixed blood. He thought about the paternity implications.

"So after you exhausted the family, how do you search for the match?"

"You go to the national registry."

"Where are they located?"

"In Washington. You listed?"

Myron nodded.

"They keep computer records there. We search for a preliminary match in their banks."

"Okay, now assuming you find a match in the computer—"

"A *preliminary* match," she corrected. "The local center calls the potential donor and asks them to come in. They run a battery of tests. But the odds of matching are still fairly slim."

Myron could see that Karen Singh was relaxing, comfortable with the familiar subject matter, which was exactly what he wanted. Interrogations are a funny thing. Sometimes you go for the full frontal attack, and sometimes you sidle up, friendly-like, and sneak in the back. Win put it simpler: Sometimes you get more ants with honey, but you should always pack a can of Raid.

"Let's suppose you find a full-fledged donor," Myron said. "What then?"

"The center acquires the donor's permission."

"When you say 'center,' do you mean the national registry in Washington?"

"No, I mean the local center. Do you have your donor card in your wallet?"

"Yes."

"Let me see it."

Myron took out his wallet, flipped through about a dozen supermarket discount cards, three video club memberships, a couple of those buy-a-hundred-coffees-get-ten-cents-off-the-hundredth coupon, that sort of thing. He found the donor card and handed it to her.

"See here," she said, pointing to the back. "Your local center is in East Orange, New Jersey."

"So if I was a preliminary match, the East Orange center would call me?"

"Yes."

"And if I ended up being a full match?"

"You'd sign some papers and donate marrow."

"Is that like donating blood?"

Karen Singh handed the card back to him and shifted again. "Harvesting bone marrow is a more invasive procedure."

Invasive. Every profession has its own buzzwords. "How so?"

"For one thing, you have to be put under."

"Anesthesia?"

"Yes."

"And then what do they do?"

"A doctor sticks a needle through the bone and sucks the marrow out with a syringe."

Myron said, "Eeuw."

"As I just explained, you're not awake during the procedure."

"Still," Myron said, "it sounds much more complicated than giving blood."

"It is," she said. "But the procedure is safe and relatively painless."

"But people must balk. I mean, most probably signed up the same way I did: They had a friend who was sick and ran a drive. For someone you know and care about, sure, you're willing to make a sacrifice. But for a stranger?"

Karen Singh's eyes found his and settled in hard. "You are saving a life, Mr. Bolitar. Think about that. How many opportunities do you get to save a fellow human being's life?"

He had hit a nerve. Good. "Are you saying people don't balk?"

"I'm not saying it never happens," she said, "but most people do the right thing."

"Does the donor get to meet the person he or she is saving?"

"No. It's totally anonymous. Confidentiality is very important here. Everything is held in the utmost secrecy."

They were getting to it now, and Myron could sense that her defenses were starting to slide back up like a car window. He decided to pull back again, let her resettle on comfy ground. "What's the patient going through during all this?" he asked.

"At what point?"

"While the marrow is being harvested. How do you prep the patient?" Prep. Myron had said "prep." Like a real doctor. Who said watching *St. Elsewhere* was a waste of time?

"It depends on what you're treating," Dr. Singh said. "But for most diseases, the recipient goes through about a week's worth of chemotherapy."

Chemotherapy. One of those words that hush a room like a nun's scowl. "They get chemo before the transplant?"

"Yes."

"I would think that would weaken them," Myron said.

"To some degree, yes."

"Why would you do it, then?"

"You have to. You're giving the recipient new bone marrow. Before you do that, you have to kill the old marrow. With leukemia, for example, the amount of chemo is high because you have to kill off all the living marrow. In the case of Fanconi anemia, you can be less aggressive because the marrow is already very weak."

"So you kill off all the bone marrow?"

"Yes."

"Isn't that dangerous?"

Dr. Singh gave him the steady eyes again. "This is a dangerous procedure, Mr. Bolitar. You are in effect replacing a person's bone marrow."

"And then?"

"And then the patient is infused with new marrow through an IV. He or she is kept isolated in a sterile environment for the first two weeks."

"Quarantined?"

"In effect. Do you remember the old TV movie *The Boy in the Plastic Bubble*?"

"Who doesn't?"

Dr. Singh smiled.

"Is that what the patient lives in?" Myron asked.

"A bubble chamber of sorts, yes."

"I had no idea," Myron said. "And this works?"

"Rejection is always a possibility, of course. But our success rate is quite high. In the case of Jeremy Downing, he can live a normal, active life with the transplant."

"And without it?"

"We can keep treating him with male hormones and growth factors, but his premature death is inevitable."

Silence. Except for that steady mechanical beep coming from down the hall.

Myron cleared his throat. "When you said that everything involving the donor is confidential—"

"I meant totally."

Enough wading. "How does that sit with you, Dr. Singh?"

"What do you mean?"

"The national registry located a donor who matched Jeremy, didn't they?"

"I believe so, yes."

"So what happened?"

She tapped her chin with her index finger. "May I speak candidly?"

"Please."

"I believe in the need for secrecy and confidentiality. Most people don't understand how easy, painless, and important it is to put their name in the registry. All they have to do is give a little blood. Just a little tube of the stuff, less than you would for any blood donation. Do that simple act—and you can save a life. Do you understand the significance of that?"

"I think so."

"We in the medical community must do all we can to encourage people to join the bone marrow registry. Education, of course, is important. So, too, is confidentiality. It has to be honored. The donors have to trust us."

She stopped, crossed her legs, leaned back on her hands. "But in this case, something of a quandary has developed. The importance of confidentiality is bumping up against the welfare of my patient. For me, the quandary is easy to resolve. The Hippocratic oath trumps all. I'm not a lawyer or a priest. My priority must be to save the life, not protect confidences. My guess is that I'm not the only doctor that feels that way. Perhaps that's why we have no contact with the donors. The blood center—in your case, the one in East Orange—does everything. They harvest the marrow and ship it to us."

"Are you saying that you don't know who the donor is?"

"That's right."

"Or if it's a he or she or where they live or anything?"

Karen Singh nodded. "I can only tell you that the national registry found a match. They called and told me so. I later received a call telling me that the donor was no longer available."

"What does that mean?"

"My question exactly."

"Did they give you an answer?"

"No," she said. "And while I see things on the micro level, the national registry has to remain macro. I respect that."

"You just gave up?"

She stiffened at his words. Her eyes went small and black. "No, Mr. Bolitar, I did not give up. I raged against the machine. But the people at the national registry are not ogres. They understand that this is a life-or-death situation. If a donor backs out, they try their best to bring them back into the fold. They do everything I would do to convince the donor to go through with it."

"But nothing worked here?"

"That seems to be the case."

"The donor would be told that he's sentencing a thirteen-year-old boy to death?"

She didn't hesitate. "Yes."

Myron threw up his hands. "So what do we conclude here, Doctor? That the donor is a selfish monster?"

Karen Singh chewed on that one for a moment. "Perhaps," she said. "Or perhaps the answer is simpler."

"For example?"

"For example," she said, "maybe the center can't find the donor."

Hello. Myron sat up a bit. "What do you mean, 'can't find'?"

"I don't know what happened here. The center won't tell me, and that's probably how it should be. I'm the patient's advocate. It's their job to deal with the donors. But I believe they were"—she stopped, searching for the right word—"perplexed."

"What makes you say that?"

"Nothing concrete. Just a feeling that this might be more than a donor with cold feet."

"How do we find out?"

"I don't know."

"How do we find the donor's name?"

"We can't."

"There has to be a way," Myron said. "Play pretend with me. How could I do it?"

She shrugged. "Break into the computer system. That's the only way I know."

"The computer in Washington?"

"They network with the local centers. But you'd have to know codes and passwords. Maybe a good hacker could get through, I don't know."

Hackers, Myron knew, worked better in the movies than in real life. A few years ago, maybe—but most computer systems nowadays were secure against such invasions.

"How long do we have here, Doctor?"

"There's no way of telling. Jeremy is reacting well to the hormones and growth factors. But it's only a question of time."

"So we have to find a donor."

"Yes." Karen Singh stopped, looked at Myron, looked away.

"Is there something else?" Myron asked.

She did not face him. "There is one other remote possibility," she said.

"What?" Myron asked.

"Keep in mind what I said before. I'm the patient's advocate. It's my job to explore every possible avenue to save him."

Her voice was funny now.

"I'm listening," Myron said.

Karen Singh rubbed her palms on her pant legs. "If Jeremy's biological parents were to conceive again, there is a twenty-five percent chance that the offspring would be a match."

She looked at Myron.

"I don't think that's a possiblity," he said.

"Even if it's the only way to save Jeremy's life?"

Myron had no reply. An orderly walked by, looked in the room, mumbled an apology, left. Myron stood and thanked her.

"I'll show you to the elevator," Dr. Singh said.

"Thank you."

"There's a lab on the first floor in the Harkness Pavilion." She handed him a slip of paper. Myron looked at it. It was an order form. "I understand you might want to take a certain confidential blood test."

Neither of them said anything else as they walked toward the elevators. There were several children being wheeled through the corridor. Dr. Singh smiled at them, the pointed features softening into something almost celestial. Again the children looked unafraid. Myron wondered if the calmness spawned from ignorance or acceptance. He wondered if the children did not understand the gravity of what was happening to them or if they possessed a quiet clarity their parents would never know. Such philosophical queries, Myron knew, were best left to those more learned. But maybe the answer was simpler than he imagined: The children's suffering would be relatively short; their parents' would be eternal.

When they reached the elevator, Myron said, "How do you do it?"

She knew what he meant. "I could say something fancy about finding solace in helping, but the truth is, I block and I compartmentalize. It's the only way."

The elevator door opened, but before Myron could move he heard a familiar voice say, "What the hell are you doing here?"

Greg Downing stepped toward him.

7

oo much history. Again.

The last time the two men had been in the same room, Myron was straddled over Greg's chest, trying to kill him, punching him repeatedly in the face until Win—Win of all people—pulled him off. Three years ago. Myron hadn't seen him since, except on highlight films during the evening news.

Greg Downing glared at Myron, then at Karen Singh, then back at Myron as though he expected him to have evaporated by then.

"What the hell are you doing here?" he asked again.

Greg was clad in a flannel shirt over some waffle knit you'd buy at Baby Gap, faded jeans, and preternaturally scuffed work boots. The Suburban Lumberjack.

Something sparked hot in Myron's chest, ignited, took flight.

From the day they first battled for a rebound in the sixth grade, Greg and Myron were the pure definition of cross-town rivals. In high school, where their competitive cup truly runneth over, Greg and Myron met up eight times, splitting the games evenly. Rumor had it that there was bad blood between the budding superstars, but that was just standard sports hyperbole. The truth was, Myron barely knew Greg off the court. They were killer competitors, sure, willing to do just about anything to win, but once the final buzzer sounded, the two boys shook hands and the rivalry hibernated until the next opening tap.

Or so Myron had always thought.

When he accepted a scholarship at Duke and Greg chose the University of North Carolina, basketball fans rejoiced. Their seemingly innocent rivalry was ready for ACC prime time. Myron and Greg did not disappoint. The Duke-UNC matchups drew fantastic television ratings, no game decided by more than three points. Both had spectacular college careers. Both were named first-team All-Americans. Both were on covers of *Sports Illustrated*, once even sharing it. But the rivalry stayed on the court. They would do battle until bloody, but the competition never overlapped into their personal arenas.

Until Emily.

Before the start of senior year, Myron broached the subject of marriage with Emily. The next day she came to him, held his hands, looked into his eyes, and said, "I'm not sure I love you." Bam, like that. He still wondered what happened. Too much too soon, he guessed. A need to spread the proverbial wings a bit, play the proverbial field, what have you. Time passed. Three months, by Myron's count. Then Emily took up with Greg. Myron publicly shrugged it off—even when Greg and Emily got engaged just before graduation. The NBA draft took place right about then too. Both went in the first round, though Greg was surprisingly picked before Myron.

That was when it all unraveled.

The end result?

Almost a decade and a half later, Greg Downing was winding down an All-Star pro basketball career. People cheered him. He made millions and was famous. He played the game he loved. For Myron, his lifelong dream had ended before it had begun. During his first preseason game with the Celtics, Big Burt Wesson had slammed into him, sandwiching Myron's knee between himself and another player. There was a snap, crackle, pop—and then a hot, ripping pain, as though metal talons were shredding his kneecap into thin strips.

His knee never recovered.

A freak accident. Or so everyone thought. Including Myron. For more than ten years, he'd believed that the injury was merely a fluke, the fickle work of the Fates. But now he knew better. Now he knew the man who stood in front of him had been the cause. Now he knew that their seemingly innocent childhood rivalry had grown monstrous, had feasted upon his dream, had slaughtered Greg and Emily's marriage, and had in all probability led to the birth of Jeremy Downing.

He felt his hands tighten into fists. "I was just leaving."

Greg put a hand on Myron's chest. "I asked you a question."

Myron stared at the hand. "One good thing," he said.

"What?"

"No transportation time," Myron said. "We're already at the hospital."

Greg sneered. "You sucker-punched me last time."

"You want to go again?"

"Pardon me," Karen Singh said. "But are you guys for real?"

Greg kept glaring at Myron.

"Stop it," Myron said, "or I'll wet myself."

"You're a son of a bitch."

"And you're not on my Christmas card list either, Greggy-poo."

Greggy-poo. Very mature.

Greg leaned closer. "You know what I'd like to do to you, Bolitar?"

"Kiss me on the lips? Buy me flowers?"

"Flowers for your grave maybe."

Myron nodded. "Good one, Greg. I mean, ouch, I'm wounded."

Karen Singh said, "Just because this is a children's floor doesn't mean you two have to act like ones."

Greg took a step back, his eyes never leaving Myron. "Emily," he spat suddenly. "She called you, right?"

"I have nothing to say to you, Greg."

"She asked you to find the donor. Like you found me."

"You always were a bright boy."

"I'm calling a press conference today. I'm going to make a direct appeal to the donor. Offer a reward."

"Good."

"So we don't need you, Bolitar."

Myron looked at Greg, and for a moment they were back on the court, faces drenched with sweat, the crowd cheering, the clock ticking down, the ball bouncing. Nirvana. Gone forever. Snatched away by Greg. And by Emily. And maybe most of all, when he looked at it honestly, by Myron's own stupidity.

"I've got to go," Myron said.

Greg took a step back. Myron moved past him and pressed the elevator button.

"Hey, Bolitar."

He faced Greg.

"I came here to talk to the doc about my son," Greg said, "not re-hash our past."

Myron said nothing. He turned back to the elevator.

"You think you can help save my boy?" Greg asked.

Myron's mouth went dry. "I don't know."

The elevator dinged and opened. There were no good-byes, no nods, no further communication of any sort. Myron stepped inside and let the doors close. When he reached the first level, he went to the lab. He rolled up his sleeve. A woman drew his blood, untied the tourniquet, and said, "Your doctor will be in touch with you about the results."

8

Win was bored, so he drove Myron to the airport to pick up Terese. His foot pushed down on the gas pedal as though it had offended him. The Jag flew. As was his custom when driving with Win, Myron kept his eyes averted.

"It would appear," Win began, "that our best option would be to locate a satellite marrow clinic in a somewhat remote area. Upstate maybe or in western Jersey. We would then break in at night with a computer expert."

"Won't work," Myron said.

"Por qua?"

"The Washington center shuts down the computer network at six o'clock. Even if we were to break in, we couldn't bring up the mainframe."

Win said, "Hmm."

"Don't fret," Myron said. "I have a plan."

"When you talk like that," Win said, "my nipples harden."

"I thought only the real thing aroused you."

"This isn't the real thing?"

They parked in JFK Airport's short-term parking and reached the Continental Airlines gate ten minutes before the flight touched down. When the passengers began to appear, Win said, "I'll stand over in the corner."

"Why?"

"I wouldn't want to cast a shadow on your greeting," he said. "And standing over there affords me a better view of Ms. Collins's derriere."

Ah, Win.

Two minutes later, Terese Collins—to use a purely transportational term—disembarked. She was casually decked out in a white blouse and green slacks. Her brown hair was up in a ponytail. People lightly elbowed one another, whispering and subtly gesturing, giving her that surreptitious glance, the one that says "I recognize you but don't want to appear fawning."

Terese approached Myron and offered up her breaking-to-commercial smile. It was small and tight, trying to be friendly but reminding viewers that she was telling them about war and pestilence and tragedy and that maybe a big happy smile would be somewhat obscene. They hugged a little too tightly, and Myron felt the familiar sadness overwhelm him. It happened to him every time they hugged—a sense that something inside of him was crumbling anew. He sensed that the same thing happened to her.

Win came over.

"Hello, Win," she said.

"Hello, Terese."

"Checking out my ass again?"

"I prefer the term 'derriere.' And yes."

"Still choice?" .

"Grade A."

"Ahem," Myron said. "Please wait for the meat inspector."

Win and Terese looked at each other and rolled their eyes.

Myron had been wrong before. Emily was not Win's favorite. Terese was—though it was strictly because she lived far away. "You are the pitiful, needy type who feels incomplete without a steady girl-friend," Win had told him. "Who better than a career woman who lives a thousand miles away?"

Win headed for his Jag while they waited for her luggage. Terese watched Win walk away.

Myron said, "Is his ass better than mine?"

"No ass is better than yours," she said.

"I know that. I was just testing you."

Terese kept looking. "Win is an interesting fellow," she said.

"Oh yeah," Myron agreed.

"On the outside, he's all cold and detached," she said. "But underneath that—way down deep inside—he's all cold and detached."

"You read people well, Terese."

Win dropped them off at the Dakota and returned to the office. When Myron and Terese got inside the apartment, she kissed him hard. Always an urgency with Terese. A desperation in their lovemaking. Pleasant, sure. Awesome even. But there was still the aura of sadness. The sadness didn't go away when they made love, but for a little while it lifted like cloud cover, hovering above instead of weighing them down.

They had hooked up at a charity function a few months back, both dragged there by well-meaning friends. It was their mutual misery that drew them, as though it were one of those psychic crowns only they could spot on each other. They met and ran away that very night to the Caribbean on a let's-just-flee dare. For the usually predictable Myron, the spontaneous act felt surprisingly right. They spent a numbingly blissful three weeks alone on a private island, trying to stave off the flow of pain. When Myron was finally forced to return home, they'd both assumed it was over. They'd assumed wrong. At least, it appeared that way.

Myron recognized that his own healing was finally under way. He wasn't back to full strength or normal or any of that. He doubted he ever would be. Or even wanted to be. Giant hands had twisted him and then let go, and while his world was slowly untwisting, he knew that it would never fully return to its original position.

Again with the poignant.

But whatever had happened to Terese—whatever had brought on the sadness and twisted her world, if you will—still held firm, refusing to let go.

Terese's head lay on his chest, her arms wrapped around him. He could not see her face. She never showed him her face when they finished.

"You want to talk about it?" he asked.

She still hadn't told him, and Myron rarely asked. Doing so, he knew, was breaking an unspoken though cardinal rule.

"No."

"I'm not pushing," he said. "I just wanted you to know that if you're ever ready, I'm here."

"I know," she said.

He wanted to say something more, but she was still at a place where words were either superfluous or they stung. He stayed quiet and stroked her hair.

"This relationship," Terese said. "It's bizarre."

"I guess."

"Someone told me you're dating Jessica Culver, the writer."

"We broke up," he said.

"Oh." She did not move, still holding him a little too tightly. "Can I ask when?"

"A month before we met."

"And how long were you two together?"

"Thirteen years, on and off."

"I see," she said. "Am I the recovery?"

"Am I yours?"

"Maybe," she said.

"Same answer."

She thought about that a little. "But Jessica Culver is not the reason you ran away with me."

He remembered the cemetery overlooking the school yard. "No," he said, "she's not the reason."

Terese finally turned to him. "We have no chance. You know that, right?"

Myron said nothing.

"That's not unusual," she went on. "Plenty of relationships have no chance. But people stay in them because it's fun. This isn't fun either."

"Speak for yourself."

"Don't get me wrong, Myron. You're a hell of a lay."

"Could you put that in a sworn affidavit?"

She smiled but there was still no joy. "So what do we have here?"

"Truth?"

"Preferably."

"I always overanalyze," Myron said. "It's my nature. I meet a woman, and I immediately picture the house in the burbs and the white picket fence and the two-point-five kids. But for once I'm not doing that. I'm just letting it happen. So, to answer your question, I don't know. And I'm not sure I care."

She lowered her head. "You realize that I'm pretty damaged."

"I guess."

"I have more baggage than most."

"We all have baggage," Myron said. "The question is, does your baggage go with mine?"

"Who said that?"

"I'm paraphrasing from a Broadway musical."

"Which one?"

"*Rent.*"

She frowned. "I don't like musicals."

"Sorry to hear that," Myron said.

"You do?"

"Oh yeah."

"You're in your mid-thirties, single, sensitive, and you like show tunes," she said. "If you were a better dresser, I'd say you were gay."

She pressed a hard, quick kiss to his lips, and then they held each other a little more. Once again he wanted to ask her what had happened to her, but he wouldn't. She would tell him one day. Or she wouldn't. He decided to change subjects.

"I need your help with something," Myron said.

She looked at him.

"I need to break into a bone marrow center's computer system," he said. "And I think you can help."

"Me?"

"Yup."

"You got the wrong technophobe," she said.

"I don't need a technophobe. I need a famous anchorwoman."

"I see. And you're asking for this favor postcoital?"

"Part of my plan," Myron said. "I've weakened your will. You cannot refuse me."

"Diabolical."

"Indeed."

"And if I refuse?"

Myron wiggled his eyebrows. "I'll once again use my brawny body and patented lovemaking technique to make you succumb."

" 'Succumb,' " she repeated, pulling him closer. "Is that one word or two?"

9

I t took a shockingly short time to set up.

Myron told Terese his plan. She listened without interruption. When he finished, she started placing calls. She
never asked why he was looking for the donor or how he and the
donor were connected. The unspoken rule again, he guessed.

Within the hour a news van complete with a handheld television
camera was delivered to the Dakota. The director of the Bergen
County Blood Center—a nearby New Jersey bone marrow center—
had agreed to drop everything for an immediate interview with Terese
Collins, anchorwoman extraordinaire. The power of the idiot box.

They took the Harlem River Drive up to the George Washington
Bridge, crossing the Hudson and exiting onto Jones Road in Englewood, New Jersey. After they parked, Myron hoisted up the camera.
Heavier than he thought. Terese showed him how to hold it, how to
lean it against his shoulder and aim. There was something bazooka-
like about the whole thing.

"Do you think I should wear a disguise?" Myron asked.

"Why?"

"People still recognize me from my playing days."

She made a face.

"I'm rather famous in certain circles."

"Get real, Myron. You're an ex-jock. If someone by some miracle recognizes you, they'll think you got lucky and didn't end up in a gutter like most ex-jocks."

He thought about it. "Fair enough."

"One other thing," she said. "And this will be nearly impossible for you."

"What?"

"You have to keep your big mouth shut," Terese said.

"Egads."

"You're just the cameraman here."

"We prefer to be called 'photographic artists.' "

"Just play your part. Trust me to handle him."

"Can I at least use a pseudonym?" He put the camera to his eye. "You can call me Lens. Or Scoop."

"How about Bozo? No, wait, that would be a synonym."

Everyone's a wise guy.

When they entered the clinic's lobby, people turned toward Terese and did that surreptitious stare again. Myron realized that today was the first time he had been with her in public. He had never quite thought about how famous she was.

"You get these stares wherever you go?" he whispered.

"Pretty much."

"Does it bother you?"

She shook her head. "That's horseshit."

"What is?"

"Celebrities who complain about people staring at them. Want to really piss off a celebrity? Let him go someplace and not be recognized."

Myron smiled. "You're so self-realized."

"That a new way of saying cynical?"

The receptionist said, "Mr. Englehardt will see you now."

She led them down a corridor with thin plaster walls and a bad paint job. Englehardt sat behind a plastic-wood desk. He was probably late twenties with a slight build and a chin weaker than machine-dispensed coffee.

Myron quickly noted the computer setup. Two of them. One on his desk. One on the credenza. Hmm.

Englehardt jumped up as though he'd just been passed a note that his chair had cooties. His eyes were wide and fixed on Terese. Myron was ignored and felt like, well, the cameraman. Terese smiled brightly at Englehardt, and he was lost.

"I'm Terese Collins," she said, extending her hand. Englehardt did everything but take a knee and kiss it. "This is my cameraman, Malachy Throne."

Myron sort of smiled. After the Broadway-musical debacle, he had worried. But Malachy Throne? Genius. Pure genius.

They all exchanged quick pleasantries. Englehardt kept touching his hair, trying very hard to look subtle about it and not like he was prepping for the camera. Not happening, bub. Finally Terese signaled that they were ready to begin.

"Where would you like me to sit?" Englehardt asked.

"Behind the desk would be nice," she said. "Don't you agree, Malachy?"

"Behind the desk," Myron said. "Yeah, that's the ticket."

The interview began. Terese kept her gaze on her subject; Englehardt, trapped in the beam, could look nowhere else. Myron put his eye to the camera. The consummate professional. Very Richard Avedon.

Terese asked Englehardt how he'd gotten started in this business, his background, general crap, relaxing him, putting him on that comfy ground, not all that different from the technique Myron had used with Dr. Singh. She was in on-air mode now. Her voice was different, her eyes steadier.

"So the national registry in Washington keeps track of all donors?" Terese asked.

"That's correct."

"But you can access the records?"

Englehardt tapped the computer on his desk. The screen faced him, the back of the monitor toward them. Okay, Myron thought, so it was the one on his desk. That would make it more difficult, but not impossible.

Terese looked at Myron. "Why don't you get a back shot, Malachy?" Then turning to Englehardt, "If that's okay with you."

"No problem at all," Englehardt said.

Myron started moving into position. The monitor was off. No surprise.

Terese continued to hold Englehardt's gaze. "Does everyone in the office have access to the national registry's computer?"

Englehardt shook his head firmly. "I'm the only one."

"Why's that?"

"The information is confidential. We don't breach the secrecy under any circumstance."

"I see," she said. Myron was in place now. "But what's to stop someone from coming in here when you're not around?"

"I always lock my office door," Englehardt said, up on his haunches and eager to please. "And you can only access the network with a password."

"You're the only one who knows the password?"

Englehardt tried not to preen, but he didn't try too hard. "That's correct."

Ever see those hidden-camera stories on *Dateline* or *20/20*? They always shoot from some strange angle and in black-and-white. Truth is, it's easy for any layperson to buy one and it's even easy to get one that films in color. There are stores that sell them right in Manhattan, or you can go online and search under "spy stores." You'll see hidden cameras in clocks, pens, briefcases and, most common of all, smoke detectors—available to anyone with the proper buckage. Myron had one that looked like a film case. He dropped it now on the window ledge with the lens pointing toward the computer monitor.

When it was in place, Myron tapped his nose with his finger, à la Redford in *The Sting*. Their signal. *Bolitar. Myron Bolitar. A Yoo-Hoo. Shaken not stirred.* Terese picked up her cue. The smile dropped off her face like an anvil.

Englehardt looked startled. "Ms. Collins? Are you okay?"

For a moment she could not bear to face him. Then: "Mr. Englehardt," Terese said, her voice Gulf War–grave, "I must confess something."

"I'm sorry?"

"I am here under somewhat false pretenses."

Englehardt looked confused. Terese was so good, Myron almost looked confused.

"I sincerely believe you are doing important work here," she continued. "But others are not so sure."

Englehardt's eyes were widening. "I don't understand."

"I need your help, Mr. Englehardt."

"Billy," he corrected.

Myron made a face. Billy?

Terese didn't miss a beat. "Someone is trying to disrupt your work, Billy."

"My work?"

"The national registry's work."

"I'm still not sure what you—"

"Are you familiar with the case of Jeremy Downing?"

Englehardt shook his head. "I never know the names of patients."

"He's the son of Greg Downing, the basketball star."

"Oh, wait, yes, I heard about this. His son has Fanconi anemia."

Terese nodded. "That's correct."

"Isn't Mr. Downing supposed to hold a press conference today? To track down a donor?"

"Exactly, Billy. And that's the problem."

"What is?"

"Mr. Downing has found the donor."

Still confused. "That's a problem?"

"No, of course not. If the person is the donor. And if the person is telling the truth."

Englehardt looked at Myron. Myron shrugged and moved back to the front of the desk. He left the film case on the windowsill.

"I'm not following you, Ms. Collins."

"Terese," she said. "A man has come forward. He claims that he is the matching donor."

"And you think he's lying?"

"Let me finish. He not only claims he's the donor, but he says that the reason he refused to donate his marrow was because of the terrible treatment he received from this center."

Englehardt nearly tipped back. "What?"

"He claims he was treated shabbily, that your staff was rude, and that he's even debating leveling a lawsuit."

"That's ridiculous."

"Probably."

"He's lying."

"Probably," she said again.

"And he'll be found out," Englehardt continued. "They'll test his blood and see he's a phony."

"But when, Billy?"

"What?"

"When will they do that? A day from now? A week from now? A month? But by then the damage is done. He's going to appear at the press conference today with Greg Downing. The media will be there in force. Even if it ends up being false, no one remembers the retraction. They just remember the allegation."

Englehardt sat back. "Jesus."

"Let me be frank, Billy. A number of my colleagues believe him. I don't. I smell a publicity hound. I'm having some of my best investigators dig into this man's past. So far they've come up with nothing, and time is running short."

"So what can I do?"

"I need to *know* it's not true. I can't stop it merely because I *believe* it's not true. I have to know for certain."

"How?"

Terese chewed on her lower lip. Deep thought. "Your computer network."

Englehardt shook his head. "The information in here is confidential. I explained that before. I can't tell you—"

"I don't need to know the name of the donor." She leaned forward. Myron moved as far away from the action as possible, trying to be no threat whatsoever. "I need to know what's *not* the name."

Englehardt looked hesistant.

"I'm sitting over here," she said. "I can't see the monitor. Malachy is by the door." She turned to Myron. "Your camera is off, Malachy?"

"Yes, Terese," Myron said. He put it down for emphasis.

"So here is what I suggest," Terese said. "You look up Jeremy Downing in your computer. It will list a donor. I give you a name. You tell me if the name matches. Simple?"

Englehardt still looked hesistant.

"You wouldn't be violating anyone's confidentiality," she said.

"We can't see your screen. We can even leave the room while you look it up, if you'd like."

Englehardt said nothing. Terese said nothing either. Waiting him out. The perfect interviewer. She finally turned to Myron. "Grab your stuff," she said to him.

"Wait." Englehardt's eyes slid left, then right, up then down. "Jeremy Downing, you say?"

"Yes."

He did another quick series of eye-slides. When he saw that the coast was clear, he hunched over the keyboard and typed quickly. A few seconds later, he asked, "What's the name of this supposed donor?"

"Victor Johnson."

Englehardt looked at the monitor and smiled. "That's not him."

"You're sure?"

"Absolutely."

Terese matched the smile. "That's all we needed to know."

"You'll stop him?"

"He won't even get to the press conference."

Myron grabbed the film case and camera, and they hurried down the corridor. Once outside he turned to her and said, "Malachy Throne?"

"You know who he is?"

"He played False Face on *Batman*."

Terese smiled and nodded. "Very good."

"Can I tell you something?"

"What?"

"It turns me on when you talk *Batman*," he said.

"And even when I don't."

"Are you trying to make a point?"

Five minutes later they were watching the tape in the van.

10

Mr. Davis Taylor
221 North End Ave
Waterbury, Connecticut

The social security and phone numbers were there too. Myron took out his cell phone and dialed. After two rings, a machine picked up and a robotic voice, the default greeting, asked him to leave a message at the tone. He left his name and mobile number and asked Mr. Taylor to return his call.

"So what are you going to do?" Terese asked.

"I guess I'll drive up and try to talk to Mr. Davis Taylor."

"Hasn't the clinic already tried that?"

"Probably."

"But you're more persuasive?"

"Questionable."

"I have to cover the Waldorf tonight," she said.

"I know. I'll go alone. Or maybe I'll bring Win."

She still would not face him. "This boy who needs the transplant," she said. "He's not a stranger, is he?"

Myron was not sure how to answer that. "I guess not."

Terese nodded in a way that told him not to say any more. He didn't. He picked up the phone and called Emily. She answered half-way through the first ring.

"Hello?"

"When is Greg doing the news conference?" he asked.

"In two hours," Emily said.

"I need to reach him."

He heard a hopeful gasp. "Did you find the donor for Jeremy?"

"Not yet."

"But you have something."

"We'll see."

"Don't patronize me, Myron."

"I'm not patronizing you."

"This is my son's life we're talking about here."

And mine? "I have a lead, Emily. That's all."

She gave him the number. "Myron, please call me if—"

"The moment I know something."

He hung up and called Greg.

"I need you to put off the press conference," Myron said.

"Why?" Greg asked.

"Just give me till tomorrow."

"You have something?"

"Maybe," Myron said.

"Maybe nothing," Greg said. "Do you have something or not?"

"I have a name and address. It might be our man. I want to check it out before you make a public plea."

"Where does he live?" Greg asked.

"Connecticut."

"You driving up?"

"Yes."

"Right now?"

"Pretty much."

"I want to go with you," Greg said.

"That's not a good idea."

"He's my kid, dammit."

Myron closed his eyes. "I understand that."

"So then you'll understand this: I'm not asking your permission.

I'm going. So stop dicking around and tell me where you want me to pick you up."

Greg drove. He had one of those fancy SUV four-by-fours that are all the rage with New Jersey suburbanites whose idea of "off-road" is a speed bump at the mall. Très truck chic. For a long while neither man spoke. The tension in the air was more than the cut-with-a-knife variety; it pressed against the car windows, weighed Myron down, made him tired and gloomy.

"How did you get this name?" Greg asked.

"It's not important."

Greg left it alone. They drove some more. On the radio, Jewel earnestly insisted that her hands were small, she knew, but they were hers and not someone else's. Myron frowned. Not exactly "Blowing in the Wind," was it?

"You broke my nose, you know," Greg said.

Myron kept quiet.

"And my vision hasn't been the same. I'm having trouble focusing on the basket."

Myron could not believe what he was hearing. "You blaming me for your crappy season, Greg?"

"I'm just saying—"

"You're getting old, Greg. You've played fourteen seasons, and sitting out the strike didn't help you."

Greg waved a hand. "You wouldn't understand."

"You're right." Myron's knob turned from Simmer to Boil. "I never got to play pro ball."

"Right, and I never fucked my friend's wife."

"She wasn't your wife," Myron said. "And we weren't friends."

They both stopped then. Greg kept his eyes on the road. Myron turned away and stared out the passenger window.

Waterbury is one of those cities you bypass to reach another city. Myron had probably taken this stretch of 84 a hundred times, always remarking that at a distance Waterbury was a butt-ugly city. But now that he had the opportunity to see the city up close, he realized that he had underestimated the city's offensiveness to the eyes, that indeed the city had a butt-ugly quality to it that you just couldn't appreciate from afar. He shook his head. And people make fun of New Jersey?

Myron had gotten directions from the MapQuest Web site. He read them off to Greg in a voice he barely recognized as his own. Greg followed them in silence. Five minutes later, they pulled up to a dilapidated clapboard house in the middle of a street of dilapidated clapboards. The houses were uneven and crammed so close together, they looked like a set of teeth needing extensive orthodontic work.

They got out of the car. Myron wanted to tell Greg to stay back, but that would be pointless. He knocked on the door and almost immediately a gruff voice said, "Daniel? That you, Daniel?"

Myron said, "I'm looking for Davis Taylor."

"Daniel?"

"No," Myron said, yelling through the door. "Davis Taylor. But maybe he calls himself Daniel."

"What are you talking about?" An old man opened the door, already in full-suspicious squint. He wore glasses too small for his face, so that the metal earpieces were embedded into the folds of skin beneath both temples, and a bad yellow wig, like something Carol Channing wore once too often, adorned his crown. He had on one slipper and one shoe, and his bathrobe looked as if it'd been trampled over during the Boer War.

"I thought you was Daniel," the old man said. He tried to readjust the glasses, but they wouldn't move. He squinted again. "You look like Daniel."

"Must be the clouds in your eyes," Myron said.

"What?"

"Never mind. Are you Davis Taylor?"

"What do you want?"

"We're looking for Davis Taylor."

"Don't know no Davis Taylor."

"This is 221 North End Drive?"

"That's right."

"And there's no Davis Taylor living here?"

"Just me and my boy Daniel. But he's been away. Overseas."

"Spain?" Myron asked. He pronounced it Spahhheeeeen. Elton would have been proud.

"What?"

"Never mind." The old man turned to Greg, tried again to re-adjust the glasses, gave another squint. "I know you. You play basketball, right?"

Greg gave the old man a gentle if not superior smile—Moses gazing down at a skeptic after the Red Sea parted. "That's right."

"You're Dolph Schayes."

"No."

"You look like Dolph. Helluva shooter. Saw him play in St. Louis last year. What a touch."

Myron and Greg exchanged a glance. Dolph Schayes had retired in 1964.

"I'm sorry," Myron said. "We didn't catch your name."

"You're not wearing uniforms," the old man said.

"No, sir, he only wears it on the court."

"Not that kind of uniform."

"Oh," Myron said, though he had no idea why.

"So you can't be here about Daniel. That's what I mean. I was afraid you were with the army and . . ." His voice drifted off then.

Myron saw where this was going. "Your son is stationed overseas?"

The old man nodded. "Nam."

Myron nodded, feeling bad now about the Elton John teasing. "We still didn't catch your name."

"Nathan. Nathan Mostoni."

"Mr. Mostoni, we're looking for someone named Davis Taylor. It's very important we find him."

"Don't know no Davis Taylor. He a friend of Daniel's?"

"Might be."

The old man thought about it. "Nope, don't know him."

"Who else lives here?"

"Just me and my boy."

"And it's just the two of you?"

"Yep. But my boy is overseas."

"So right now you live here alone?"

"How many different ways you gonna ask that question, boy?"

"It's just that it's a pretty big house," Myron said.

"So?"

"Ever take in any boarders?"

"Sure. Had a college girl just moved out of here."

"What was her name?"

"Stacy something. I don't remember."

"How long did she live here?"

"About six months."

"And before that?"

That one took some thought. Nathan Mostoni scratched his face like a dog going after his own belly. "A guy named Ken."

"Did you ever have a tenant named Davis Taylor?" Myron asked. "Or something like that?"

"Nope. Never."

"Did this Stacy have a boyfriend?"

"I don't think so."

"Do you know her last name?"

"My memory ain't so good. But she's at the college."

"Which college?"

"Waterbury State."

Myron turned to Greg and another thought hit him. "Mr. Mostoni, have you heard the name Davis Taylor before today?"

Another squint. "What do you mean?"

"Has anybody else visited you or called you and asked about Davis Taylor?"

"No, sir. Never heard the name before."

Myron looked at Greg again, then turned back to the old man. "So no one from the bone marrow center has been in touch with you?"

The old man cocked his head and put a hand to his ear. "The bone what?"

Myron asked a few more questions, but Nathan Mostoni started time-traveling again. There was nothing more to get here. Myron and Greg thanked him and headed back down the cracked pathway.

When they were back in the car, Greg asked, "Why didn't the bone marrow center contact this guy?"

"Maybe they did," Myron said. "Maybe he just forgot."

Greg didn't like it. Neither did Myron. "So what's next?" Greg asked.

"We run a background check on Davis Taylor. Find out everything we can about him."

"How?

"It's easy nowadays. Just a few keystrokes and my partner will know it all."

"Your partner? You mean that violent wacko you used to room with in college?"

"A, it is unhealthy to refer to Win as a violent wacko, even when he appears not to be in the vicinity. B, no, I mean my partner at MB SportsReps, Esperanza Diaz."

Greg looked back at the house. "What do I do?"

"Go home," Myron said.

"And?"

"And be with your son."

Greg shook his head. "I don't get to see him until the weekend."

"I'm sure Emily wouldn't mind."

"Yeah, right." Greg smirked, shook his head. "You don't know her too well anymore, do you, Myron?"

"I guess not, no."

"If she had her way, I'd never get to see Jeremy again."

"That's a bit harsh, Greg."

"No, Myron. If anything, it's being generous."

"Emily told me that you're a good father."

"Did she also tell you what she charged in our custody battle?"

Myron nodded. "That you abused the kids."

"Not just abused them, Myron. *Sexually* abused them."

"She wanted to win."

"And that's an excuse?"

"No," Myron said. "It's deplorable."

"More than that," Greg said. "It's sick. You have no idea what Emily's capable of doing to get her way."

"For example?"

But Greg just shook his head and started up the car. "I'll ask you again: What can I do to help?"

"Nothing, Greg."

"No good. I'm not sitting around while my kid is dying, you understand?"

"I do."

"You have anything besides this name and address?"

"Nope."

"Fine," Greg said. "I'll drop you off at the train station. I'm staying up here and watching the house."

"You think the old man is lying?"

Greg shrugged. "Maybe he's just confused and forgot. Or maybe I'm wasting my time. But I got to do something."

Myron said nothing. Greg continued to drive.

"You'll call me if you hear something?" Greg asked.

"Sure."

During the train ride back to Manhattan, Myron thought about what Greg had said. About Emily. And about what she'd done—and what she'd do—to save her son.

11

Myron and Terese started out the next morning showering together. Myron controlled the temperature and kept the water hot. Prevents, er, shrinkage.

When they stepped out of the steamy stall, he helped Terese towel off.

"Thorough," she said.

"We're a full-service operation, ma'am." He toweled her off some more.

"One thing I notice when I shower with a man," Terese said.

"What's that?"

"My breasts always end up squeaky clean."

Win had left several hours ago. Lately he liked to get to the office by six. Overseas markets or something. Terese toasted a bagel while Myron fixed himself a bowl of cereal. Quisp cereal. They didn't have it in New York anymore, but Win had it shipped in from a place called Woodsman's in Wisconsin. Myron downed an industrial-size spoonful; the sugar rush came at him so fast he nearly ducked.

Terese said, "I have to go back tomorrow morning."

"I know."

He took another spoonful, feeling her eyes on him.

"Run away with me again," Terese said.

He glanced up at her. She looked smaller, farther away.

"I can get us the same house on the island. We can just hop on a plane and—"

"I can't," he interrupted.

"Oh," she said. Then: "You need to find this Davis Taylor?"

"Yes."

"I see. And after that . . . ?"

Myron shook his head. They ate some more in silence.

"I'm sorry," Myron said.

She nodded.

"Running away isn't always the answer, Terese."

"Myron?"

"What?"

"Do I look in the mood for platitudes?"

"I'm sorry."

"Yeah, you said that already."

"I'm just trying to help."

"Sometimes you can't help," she said. "Sometimes all that's left is running away."

"Not for me," he said.

"No," she agreed. "Not for you."

She wasn't angry or upset, just flat and resigned, and that scared him all the more.

An hour later Esperanza came into Myron's office without knocking.

"Okay," she began, grabbing a seat, "here's what we've got on Davis Taylor."

Myron leaned back and put his hands behind his head.

"One, he's never filed a tax return with the IRS."

"Never?"

"Glad you're paying attention," Esperanza said.

"Are you saying he's never shown any income?"

"Will you let me finish?"

"Sorry."

"Two, he has virtually no paperwork. No driver's license. One credit card, a Visa recently issued by his bank. It has very little activity. Only one bank account, with a current balance of under two hundred dollars."

"Suspicious," Myron said.

"Yes."

"When did he open the account?"

"Three months ago."

"And before that?"

"Nada. At least nada that I've been able to come up with so far."

Myron stroked his chin. "No one flies that far below the radar screen," he said. "It has to be an alias."

"I thought the same thing," Esperanza said.

"And?"

"The answer is yes and no." Myron waited for the explanation. Esperanza tucked some loose tresses behind both ears. "It appears to be a name change."

Myron frowned. "But we got his social security number, right?"

"Right."

"And most records are kept by social security number, not name, right?"

"Another right."

"So I don't get it," Myron said. "You can't change your social security number. A name change might make you harder to find, but it wouldn't wipe out your past. You'd still have tax returns and stuff like that."

Esperanza turned both palms upward. "That's what I mean by yes and no."

"There's no paperwork under the social security number either?"

"That's correct," Esperanza said.

Myron tried to digest this. "So what's Davis Taylor's real name?"

"I don't have it yet."

"I would have thought it'd be easy to locate."

"It would," she said, "if he had any records at all. But he doesn't. The social security number has no hits. It's as though this person hasn't done a thing in his whole life."

Myron thought about it. "Only one explanation," he said.

"That being?"

"A fake ID."

Esperanza shook her head. "The social security number exists."

"I don't doubt that. But I think someone pulled the classic tombstone-fake-ID trick."

"That being?"

"You go to a graveyard and find the tombstone of a dead child," Myron said. "Someone who would be about your age if he'd lived. Then you write and request his birth certificate and paperwork and *voilà*, you've set up the perfect fake ID. Oldest trick in the book."

Esperanza gave him the look she saved for his most idiotic moments. "No," she said.

"No?"

"You think the police don't watch TV, Myron? That doesn't work anymore. Hasn't worked in years, except maybe on cop shows. But just to make sure, I double-checked."

"How?"

"Death records," she said. "There's a Web site that has the social security numbers of all the deceased."

"And the number isn't there."

"Ding, ding, ding," Esperanza said.

Myron leaned forward. "This makes absolutely no sense," he said. "Our phony Davis Taylor has gone to a great deal of trouble to create this phony ID—or at least to fly below the radar, right?"

"Right."

"He wants no records, no paperwork, nothing."

"Right again."

"Even changes his name."

"You go, boy."

Myron put his arms out. "Then why would he sign up to be a bone marrow donor?"

"Myron?"

"Yeah."

"I don't know what you're talking about," Esperanza said.

True enough. He'd called last night and asked her to check out Davis Taylor. He had not yet told her why.

"I guess I owe you an explanation," he said.

She shrugged.

"I sort of promised you I wouldn't be doing this anymore," he said.

"Investigating," she said.

"Right. And I meant it. I wanted this to be a straight agency from now on."

She didn't respond. Myron glanced at the wall behind her. The sparse Client Wall again reminded him of a hair transplant that hadn't taken. Maybe he should paint on a couple of coats of Rogaine.

"You remember Emily's call?" he said.

"It was yesterday, Myron. My memory can sometimes go back a whole week."

He explained it all. Some men—men Myron grudgingly admired—keep it all inside, bury their secrets, hide the pain, the whole cliché. Myron rarely did. He was not one to walk down the mean streets alone—he liked Win to be his backup. He didn't grab a bottle of whiskey and drown his sorrows—he discussed them with Esperanza. Not very macho, but there you have it.

Esperanza stayed silent as he spoke. When he got to the part about being Jeremy's father, she let out a small groan and closed her eyes and kept them shut for a very long time. When she finally opened them, she asked, "So what are you going to do?"

"I'm going to find the donor."

"That's not what I meant."

He knew that. "I don't know," he said.

She thought about it, shook her head in disbelief. "You have a son."

"Seems so."

"And you don't know what you're going to do about it?"

"That's right."

"But you're leaning," she said.

"Win made a pretty good case for not saying anything."

She made a sound. "Win would."

"Actually he claims to be using his heart."

"If only he had one."

"You don't agree?"

"No," she said. "I don't agree."

"You think I should tell Jeremy?"

"I think first and foremost you should put aside your Batman complex," she said.

"What the hell does that mean?"

"It means you always try a little too hard to be heroic."

"And that's bad?"

"Sometimes it clouds your thinking," she said. "The heroic thing is not always the right thing."

"Jeremy already has a family. He has a mother and a father—"

"He has," Esperanza interrupted, "a lie."

They sat there and stared at each other. The phone, usually so active, was silent, as it had been for too long now. Myron wondered how he could explain it so that she would understand. She stayed still, waiting.

"We were both lucky when it came to parents," Myron said.

"Mine are dead, Myron."

"That's not what I mean," he said. He took a deep breath. "How many days pass that you don't still miss them?"

"None," she said without hesitation.

He nodded. "We were both loved unconditionally and we both loved our parents the same way."

Esperanza's eyes started misting. "So?"

"So—and this was what Win said—isn't that what makes a mother or father? Isn't it about who raised us and loved us and not simply an accident of biology?"

Esperanza leaned back. "Win said that?"

Myron smiled. "He has his moments."

"That he does," she said.

"And think about your father—the one who raised and loved you. What happens to him?"

Her eyes were still misty. "My love for him is strong enough to survive the truth. Isn't yours?"

He tilted back as though the words were jabs at his chin. "Sure," he said. "But it would still hurt him."

"Your father would be hurt?"

"Of course."

"I see," Esperanza said. "So now you're worried about poor Greg Downing?"

"Hardly. You want to hear something awful?"

"Love to."

"When Greg constantly refers to Jeremy as 'my son,' I want to yell out the truth. Right in his smug face. Just to see his reaction. Just to watch his world crumble."

"So much for your Batman complex," Esperanza said.

Myron held out his hands. "I have my moments too," he said.

Esperanza stood and headed for the door.

"Where you going?"

"I don't want to talk about this anymore," she said.

He sat back.

"You're blocking," she said. "You know that?"

He nodded slowly.

"When you move past it—and you will—we'll talk about it again. Otherwise, we're wasting our time here, okay?"

"Okay."

"Just don't be stupid."

" 'Don't be stupid,' " he repeated. "Check."

Her departing smile was brief.

12

Myron spent the rest of the day working the phones. He strapped on his Ultra Slim headset and paced the office. He talked up college coaches, mining for potential free agents. He touched base with his clients and listened to their problems, both real and imagined, therapist-style, which was a large part of his job. He sifted through his Rolodex of companies, trying to conjure up a few endorsement deals.

One serious lead came a-knocking on its own:

"Mr. Bolitar? I'm Ronny Angle from Rack Enterprises. Are you familiar with us?"

"You run a bunch of topless bars, right?"

"We prefer they be called upscale exotic nightclubs."

"And I prefer to be called a well-endowed stallion," Myron said. "What can I do for you, Mr. Angle?"

"Ronny please. Can I call you Myron?"

"Myron please."

"Great, Myron. Rack Enterprises is entering a new venture."

"Uh-huh."

"You've probably read about it. A chain of coffeehouses called La, La, Latte."

"For real?"

"Pardon?"

"Well, I think I did see something about this, but I figured it was a joke."

"It's no joke, Mr. Bolitar."

"So you guys are really going to open up topless coffee bars?"

"We prefer they be called upscale erotic coffee experiences."

"I see. But you're, uh, *baristas* will be topless, correct?"

"Correct."

Myron thought about it. "Makes asking for milk something of a double entendre, don't you think?"

"That's very funny, Myron."

"Thanks, Ronny."

"We're going to open with a big splash."

"That another milk joke, Ronny?"

"No, Myron, but you're a pretty funny guy."

"Thanks, Ronny."

"Let me cut right to it, okay? We like Suzze T." Suzze T was Suzze Tamirino, a journeyman (or is it journeywoman?) on the pro tennis circuit. "We saw her picture in the *Sports Illustrated* swimsuit issue, and, well, we were very impressed. We'd like her to do a cameo for our grand opening."

Myron rubbed the bridge of his nose with his thumb and forefinger. "When you say cameo—"

"A brief performance."

"How brief?"

"No more than five minutes."

"I don't mean brief in terms of time. I mean in terms of clothing."

"We'd require full frontal nudity."

"Well, thanks for thinking of us, Ronny, but I don't think Suzze will be interested."

"We're offering two hundred thousand dollars."

Myron sat up. Easy to hang up, but with this kind of dough, he had a responsibility to follow up. "How about if she wears a small top?"

"No."

"A bikini?"

"No."

"An itsy-bitsy, teeny-weeny bikini?"

"Like in the song?"

"Exactly," Myron said. "Like in the song."

"I'm going to state this as plainly as I can," Ronny said. "There must be nipple visibility."

"Nipple visibility?"

"This point is nonnegotiable."

"So to speak."

Myron promised to call him back later in the week. The two men hung up. Negotiating nipple visibility. What a business.

Esperanza came in without knocking. Her eyes were wide and bright.

"Lamar Richardson is on line one," she said.

"Lamar himself?"

She nodded.

"No relative or personal manager or favorite astrologer?"

"Lamar himself," Esperanza repeated.

They both nodded. This was a good thing.

Myron picked up the phone. "Hello."

"Let's meet," Lamar said.

"Sure," Myron said.

"When?"

"You name it."

"When are you free?"

"You name it," Myron said.

"I'm in Detroit right now."

"I'll catch the next plane out."

"Just like that?" Lamar said.

"Yup."

"Shouldn't you pretend you're really busy?"

"We going to date, Lamar?"

Lamar chuckled. "No, I don't think so."

"Then I'll skip the playing-hard-to-get stage. Esperanza and I want you to sign up with MB SportsReps. We'll do a good job. We'll make you a priority. And we won't play mind games with you."

Myron smiled at Esperanza. Was he good or what?

Lamar said he was going to be in Manhattan later in the week and would like to meet then. They set up a time. Myron hung up. He and Esperanza sat there and smiled at each other.

"We have a chance," she said.

"Yep."

"So what's our strategy?"

"I thought I'd impress him with my nimble mind," he said.

"Hmm," Esperanza said. "Maybe I should wear something low cut."

"I was kinda counting on that."

"Hit him with brains and beauty."

"Yes," Myron said. "But which one of us is which?"

When Myron got back to the Dakota, Win was heading out with his leather gym bag and Terese was gone.

"She left a note," Win said, handing it to Myron.

Had to go back early. I'll call.
   Terese

Myron read the note again. It didn't change. He folded it up and put it away.

"You going to Master Kwon's?" Myron asked. Master Kwon was their martial arts instructor.

Win nodded. "He's been asking for you."

"What did you tell him?" Myron asked.

"That you wigged out."

"Thanks."

Win gave a slight bow and lifted his gym bag. "May I make a suggestion?"

"Shoot."

"You haven't been to the *dojang* in a long while."

"I know."

"You have a great deal of stress in your life," Win said. "You need an outlet. You need some focus. Some balance. Some structure."

"You're not going to make me snatch a pebble from your hand, are you?"

"Not today, no. But come with me."

Myron shrugged. "I'll grab my stuff."

They were halfway out the door when Esperanza called. He told her they were just on their way out.

"Where?" she asked.

"Master Kwon's."

"I'll meet you there."

"Why? What's up?"

"I got some information on Davis Taylor."

"And?"

"And it's more than a little strange. Is Win going with you?"

"Yes."

"Ask him if he knows anything about Raymond Lex's family."

Silence. "Raymond Lex is dead, Esperanza."

"Duh, Myron. I said *family*."

"This has something to do with Davis Taylor?"

"It'll be easier to explain in person. I'll see you down there in an hour."

She hung up.

One of the doormen had already fetched Win's Jag. It sat waiting for them on Central Park West. The rich. Myron settled into the lush leather. Win hit the accelerator pad. He was big with the accelerator pad; he had a bit more trouble when it came to the brake.

"Do you know Raymond Lex's family?"

"They used to be clients," Win said.

"You're kidding?"

"Oh yes, I'm a regular Red Buttons."

"Were you directly involved in this inheritance squabble?"

"Calling this a squabble would be similar to calling nuclear Armageddon a campfire."

"Hard to divide up billions, huh?"

"Indeed. So why are we discussing the Lex clan?"

"Esperanza is going to meet us down at the *dojang*. She has some information on Davis Taylor. Somehow the Lex family is connected."

Win arched his eyebrow. "The plot doth thicken."

"So tell me a little about them."

"Most of it was in the media. Raymond Lex writes a controversial bestseller called *Midnight Confessions*. Said bestseller becomes an

Oscar-winning blockbuster. Suddenly he goes from obscure junior-college instructor to millionaire. Unlike most of his artistic brethren, he understands business. He invests and amasses private holdings with a substantial yet confidential net worth."

"The papers place it in the billions."

"I won't argue."

"That's a lot of money."

"The way you word things," Win said. "It's like Proust."

"He never wrote another book?"

"No."

"Odd."

"Not really," Win said. "Harper Lee and Margaret Mitchell never wrote another book. And at least Lex kept busy. It's hard to build one of the largest privately held corporations and do book signings."

"So now that he's dead, his family is—how to say it?—nuclear Armageddoning?"

"Close enough."

Master Kwon had moved his headquarters and main *dojang* into the second floor of a building on Twenty-third Street near Broadway. Five rooms—studios really—with hardwood floors, mirrored walls, high-tech sound system, sleek and shiny Nautilus equipment—oh, and some of those rice-paper Oriental scroll-posters. Gave the place a real Old World Asia feel.

Myron and Win slipped into their *dobok*, a white uniform, and tied their black belts. Myron had been studying tae kwon do and *hapkido* since Win had first introduced him to them in college, but he hadn't been to a *dojang* more than five times in the past three years. Win, on the other hand, remained devoutly lethal. Don't tug on Superman's cape, don't spit in the wind, don't pull the mask off the ol' Lone Ranger, and you don't mess around with Win. Bah, bah, dee, dee, dee, dee, dee.

Master Kwon was in his mid-seventies but could easily pass for two decades younger. Win had met him during his Asian travels when he was fifteen. As near as Myron could tell, Master Kwon had been a high priest or some such thing at a small Buddhist monastery straight out of a Hong Kong revenge flick. When Master Kwon emigrated to the United States, he spoke very little English. Now, some twenty years later, he spoke almost none. As soon as the wise master hit our shores, he opened up a chain of state-of-the-art tae kwon do schools—with Win's financial backing, of course. Once he saw the *Karate Kid* movies, Master Kwon started playing the old wise man to the hilt. His English disappeared. He started dressing like the Dalai Lama and began every sentence with the words "Confucius say," ignoring the small fact that he was Korean and Confucius was Chinese.

Win and Myron headed to Master Kwon's office. At the entrance, both men bowed deeply.

"Please in," Master Kwon said.

The desk was fine oak, the chair rich leather and orthopedic looking. Master Kwon was standing near a corner. He held a putter in his hands and wore a splendidly tailored suit. His face brightened when he saw Myron, and the two men embraced.

When they broke apart, Master Kwon said, "You better?"

"Better," Myron agreed.

The old man smiled and grabbed his own lapel. "Armani," he said.

"I thought so," Myron said.

"You like?"

"Very nice."

Satisfied, Master Kwon said, "Go."

Win and Myron bowed deeply. Once in the *dojang*, they fell into their customary roles: Win led and Myron followed. They started with meditation. Win loved meditating, as we already graphically witnessed. He sat in the lotus position, palms tilted up, hands resting on knees, back straight, tongue folded against the upper teeth. He breathed in through his nose, forcing the air down, letting his abdomen do all the work. Myron tried to duplicate—had been trying for years—but he had never quite gotten the hang of it. His mind, even during less chaotic times, wandered. His bad knee tightened. He got fidgety.

They cut down the stretching to only ten minutes. Again Win was effortless, executing splits and toe touches and deep bends with ease, his bones and joints as flexible as a politician's voting record. Myron had never been a naturally limber guy. When he was training seriously, he could touch his toes and complete a hurdle stretch with little problem. But just then, that felt like a long time ago.

"I'm already sore," Myron said through a grunt.

Win tilted his head. "Odd."

"What?"

"That's precisely what my date said last night."

"You weren't kidding before," Myron said. "You really are another Red Buttons."

They did a little sparring, and Myron immediately realized how out of shape he was. Sparring is the most tiring activity in the world. Don't believe it? Find a punching bag and pretend-box with it for one three-minute round. Just a bag that can't fight back. Try it, just one round. You'll see.

When Esperanza came in, the sparring mercifully ceased and Myron grabbed his knees, sucking wind. He bowed to Win, threw a towel over his shoulder, grabbed some Evian. Esperanza folded her arms and waited. A group of students walked past the door, saw Esperanza, did a double take.

Esperanza handed Myron a sheet of paper. "The birth certificate of Davis Taylor né Dennis Lex."

"Lex," Myron repeated. "As in . . . ?"

"Yep."

Myron scanned the photocopy. According to the document, Dennis Lex would be thirty-seven years old. His father was listed as one Raymond Lex, his mother as Maureen Lehman Lex. Born in East Hampton, New York.

Myron handed it to Win.

"They had another child?"

"Apparently so," Esperanza said.

Myron looked at Win. Win shrugged.

"He must have died young," Win said.

"If he did," Esperanza said, "I can't find it anywhere. There's no death certificate."

"No one in the family ever mentioned another child?" Myron asked Win.

"No one," Win said.

He turned back to Esperanza. "What else you got?"

"Not much. Dennis Lex changed his name to Davis Taylor eight months ago. I also found this." She handed him a photocopy of a news clipping. A small birth announcement from the *Hampton Gazette* dated thirty-seven years ago:

Raymond and Maureen Lex of Wister Drive in East Hampton are delighted to announce the birth of their son, Dennis, six pounds eight ounces on June 18th. Dennis joins his sister Susan and his brother Bronwyn.

Myron shook his head. "How could no one know about this?"

"It's not all that surprising," Win said.

"How do you figure?"

"None of the Lex family holdings are public. They are fiercely protective of their privacy. Security around them is around-the-clock and the best money can buy. Everyone who works with them must sign confidentiality agreements."

"Even you?"

"I don't do confidentiality agreements," Win said. "No matter how much money is involved."

"So they never asked you to sign one?"

"They asked. I refused. We parted ways."

"You gave them up as clients?"

"Yes."

"Why? I mean, what would have been the big deal? You keep everything confidential anyway."

"Exactly. Clients hire me not only because of my brilliance in the ways of finance but because I am the very model of discretion."

"Don't overlook your startling modesty," Myron added.

"I don't need to sign a contract saying I won't reveal anything. It should be a given. It's the equivalent of signing a document saying that I won't burn down their house."

Myron nodded. "Nice analogy," he said.

"Yes, thank you, but I'm trying to illustrate how far this family will go to maintain their privacy. Until this inheritance feud erupted, the media had no idea how extensive Raymond Lex's holdings were."

"But come on, Win. This is Raymond Lex's son. You'd know about a son."

Win pointed to the top of the clipping. "Notice when the child was born—*before* Raymond Lex's book came out, when Lex was just a typical small-town professor. It wouldn't make news."

"You really buy that?"

"Do you have a better explanation?"

"So where is the kid now? How can the son of one of America's wealthiest families have no paperwork? No credit cards, no driver's license, no IRS filings, no trail at all? Why did he change his name?"

"The last one is easy," Win said.

"Oh?"

"He's hiding."

"From?"

"His siblings perhaps," Win said. "As I said before, this inheritance battle is rather nasty."

"That might make sense—and I stress the word 'might'—if he'd been around before. But how can there be no paperwork on him? What is he hiding from? And why on earth would he put his name in the bone marrow registry?"

"Good questions," Win said.

"Very good," Esperanza added.

Myron reread the article and looked at his two friends. "Nice to have a consensus," he said.

13

The mobile phone blew him out of his sleep like a shotgun blast. Myron's hand reached up blindly, his fingers bouncing along the night table until they located the phone.

"Hello?" he croaked.

"Is this Myron Bolitar?"

The voice was a whisper.

"Who is this?" Myron asked.

"You called me."

Still whispering, the sound like leaves skittering across pavement.

Myron sat upright, his heartbeat picking up a little steam. "Davis Taylor?"

"Sow the seeds. Keep sowing. And open the shades. Let the truth come in. Let the secrets finally wither in the daylight."

Ooookay. "I need your help, Mr. Taylor."

"Sow the seeds."

"Yes, of course, we'll sow away." Myron flicked on the light. 2:17 A.M. He checked the LCD display on the phone. The Caller ID was blocked. Damn. "But we have to meet."

"Sow the seeds. It's the only way."

"I understand, Mr. Taylor. Can we meet?"

"Someone must sow the seeds. And someone must unlock the chains."

"I'll bring a key. Just tell me where you are."

"Why do you wish to see me?"

What to say? "It's a matter of life and death."

"Whenever you sow the seeds, it's a matter of life and death."

"You donated blood for a bone marrow drive. You're a match. A young boy will die if you don't help."

Silence.

"Mr. Taylor?"

"Technology cannot help him. I thought you were one of us." Still whispering but sad now.

"I am. Or at least I want to be—"

"I'm hanging up now."

"No, wait—"

"Good-bye."

"Dennis Lex," Myron said.

Silence, except for the sound of breathing. Myron wasn't sure if the sound was coming from him or the caller.

"Please," Myron said. "I'll do whatever you ask. But we have to meet."

"Will you remember to sow the seeds?"

Small chunks of ice dropped down his back.

"Yes," Myron said, "I'll remember."

"Good. Then you know what you must do."

Myron gripped the receiver. "No," he said. "What must I do?"

"The boy," the voice whispered. "Say one last good-bye to the boy."

14

S ow the seeds?" Esperanza said.

They were in Myron's office. The morning sun striped the floor with Venetian slits, two cutting across Esperanza's face. She didn't seem to mind.

"Right," Myron said. "And something about that phrase keeps gnawing at me."

"It was a Tears for Fears song," Esperanza said.

" 'Sowing the Seeds of Love.' I remember."

"Wasn't that the name of the tour too? We saw them at the Meadowlands in, what, 1988?"

"Eighty-nine."

"What happened to those guys?"

"They broke up," Myron said.

"Why do they all do that?"

"Got me."

"Supertramp, Steely Dan, the Doobie Brothers—"

"Not to mention Wham."

"They break up and then they never make anything decent on their own. They flounder around and end up a segment of VH-1's *Where Are They Now?*"

"We're getting off the subject."

Esperanza handed him a slip of paper. "Here's the office number for Susan Lex, Dennis's older sister."

Myron read the number like it was in code and might mean something. "I had another thought."

"What's that?"

"If Dennis Lex exists, then he had to have gone to school, right?"

"Maybe."

"So let's see if we can find out where the Children Lex schooled—public, private, whatever."

Esperanza frowned. "You mean like college?"

"Start there, yes. Not that siblings go to the same school, but maybe they did. Or maybe they all went to Ivy League schools. Something like that. You might want to start with high school. It's more likely that they all went to the same one."

"And if I don't find any record of him in high school?"

"Go back even further."

She crossed her legs, folded her arms. "How far?"

"As far as you can."

"And what good will this exercise in futility do us?"

"I want to know when Dennis Lex fell off the radar screen. Did people know him in high school? In college? In grad school?"

She did not look impressed. "And assuming I somehow manage to find, say, his elementary school, what exactly is that going to do for us?"

"Damn if I know. I'm grasping at straws here."

"No, you're asking *me* to grasp at straws."

"Then don't do it, Esperanza, okay? It was just a thought."

"Nah," she said with a wave of her hand. "You may be right."

Myron put his palms on his desk, arched his back, looked left, looked right, looked up, looked down.

"What?" she said.

"You said I may be right. I'm waiting for the world as we know it to end."

"Good one," Esperanza said, standing. "I'll see what I can dig up."

She left the room. Myron picked up the telephone and dialed Susan Lex's number. The receptionist transferred the call, and a woman identifying herself as Ms. Lex's secretary picked it up. She had a voice like a steel-wool tire over gravel.

"Ms. Lex does not see people she doesn't know."

"It's a matter of grave importance," Myron said.

"Perhaps you did not hear me the first time." Classic Battle-ax. "Ms. Lex does not see people she doesn't know."

"Tell her it's about Dennis."

"Excuse me?"

"Just tell her that."

Battle-ax put Myron on hold without another word. Myron listened to a Muzak version of Al Stewart's "Time Passages." Myron had thought the original was Muzak-y enough, thank you very much.

The battle-ax came back with a snap. "Ms. Lex does not see people she doesn't know."

"I've been thinking about that, but it doesn't really make sense."

"Excuse me?"

"I mean, at some time she must see people she doesn't know—otherwise she'd never meet anybody new. And if we follow my logic, how did you ever get to see her for the first time? She was willing to see you before she knew you, right?"

"I'm hanging up now, Mr. Bolitar."

"Tell her I know about Dennis."

"I just—"

"Tell her if she doesn't agree to see me, I'll go to the press."

Silence. "Hold." A click and then the Muzak came back on. Time passed. So, mercifully, did "Time Passages," replaced by the Alan Parsons Project's "Time." Myron nearly slipped into a coma.

Battle-ax returned. "Mr. Bolitar?"

"Yes?"

"Ms. Lex will give you five minutes of her time. I have an opening on the fifteenth of next month."

"No good," Myron said. "It has to be today."

"Ms. Lex is a very busy woman."

"Today," Myron said.

"That simply will not be possible."

"At eleven. If I'm not let in, I go immediately to the press."

"You're being terribly rude, Mr. Bolitar."

"To the press," Myron repeated. "Do you understand?"

"Yes."

"Will you be there?"

"What possible difference could that make?"

"All this sexual tension is driving me batty. Maybe afterward we could get together for a nice cool latte."

He heard the phone go click and smiled. The charm, he thought. It's baaaaack.

Esperanza buzzed in. "Topless tennis, anyone?"

"What?"

"I got Suzze T on line one."

He hit a button. "Hey, Suzze."

"Hey, Myron, what's shaking?"

"I got an offer for you to refuse."

"You mean you're going to hit on me?"

The charm suffers a setback. "Where are you going to be this afternoon?"

"Same place as now," she said. "The Morning Mosh. You know it?"

"No."

She gave him the address, and Myron agreed to meet her there in a few hours. He hung up the phone and leaned back.

" 'Sow the seeds,' " he said out loud.

He stared at the wall. An hour to kill before he headed over to the Lex Building on Fifth Avenue. He could sit here and think about life and maybe contemplate his navel. No, too much of that already. He swiveled his seat to the computer, double-clicked the proper icon, connected to the Net. He tried Yahoo first and typed *sow the seeds* into the search field. Only one hit: a Web site for the San Francisco League of Urban Gardeners. They went by the acronym SLUG. Tough guys probably. A gang. Probably wore green bandannas and engaged in drive-by waterings.

He tried AltaVista's search engine next, but they listed 2,501 Web pages. It was kinda like Goldilocks and the Three Bears. Yahoo's search was toooo small. AltaVista's was toooo big. They didn't have

LEXIS–NEXIS at the office, but Myron tried a less powerful media engine. He typed in the same three words and pressed the return key, and bammo.

http://www.nyherald.com/archives/9800322

Myron hit the link and the article came up:

New York Herald
THE MIND OF TERROR—YOUR DARKEST FEAR
by Stan Gibbs

Whoa, hold the phone. Myron knew the name. Stan Gibbs had been a big-time newspaper columnist, the kind of guy who regularly pontificated (read: pimped) on the cable news talk shows, though he'd been less annoying than most, which is like saying syphilis is less annoying than gonorrhea. But that had all been before the scandal gutted him like Ted Nugent over a fallen moose. Myron read:

> The phone call comes out of the blue.
> "What is your darkest fear?" the voice whispers. "Close your eyes now and picture it. Can you see it? Do you have it yet? The very worst agony you can imagine?"
> After a long pause, I say, "Yes."
> "Good. Now imagine something worse, something far, far worse . . ."

Myron took a deep breath. He remembered the series of articles. Stan Gibbs had broken a story about a bizarre kidnapper. He'd told the heart-wrenching tale of three abductions that the police had supposedly wanted to keep quiet, out of, Stan Gibbs claimed, embarrassment. No names were mentioned. He had spoken with the families under the condition of anonymity. And, the coup de grâce, the kidnapper had granted Gibbs access:

> I ask the kidnapper why he does it. Is it for the ransom?
> "I never pick up the ransom money," he says. "I usually leave explosives

at the spot and burn it. But sometimes money helps me sow the seeds. That is what I'm trying to do. Sow the seeds."

Myron felt his blood stop.

"You all think you're safe," he continues, "in your technological co-coon. But you're not. Technology has made us expect easy answers and happy endings. But with me, there is no answer and there is no end."

He has kidnapped at least four people: the father of two young children, age 41; a female college student, age 20; and a young couple, newly-weds ages 28 and 27. All were abducted while in the New York City area.

"The idea," he says, "is to keep the terror going. Let it grow, not with gore or obvious bloodletting, but with your own imagination. Technology is trying to destroy our ability to imagine. But when someone you love is taken away, your mind can conjure up horrors darker than any machine— than anything even I can do. Some minds won't go that far. Some minds stop and put up a barrier. My job is to push them through that barrier."

I ask him how he does that.

"Sow the seeds," he repeats. "You sow the seeds over time."

He explains that sowing the seeds means giving hope and taking it away over a sustained period of time. His first call to the victim's family is naturally devastating, but merely the beginning of a long and torturous ordeal.

He begins the call, he claims, with a normal hello and asks the family member to please hold. After a pause, the family member hears their loved one give a blood-curdling shriek. "Just one," he says, "and it's very short. I cut them off in mid-scream.

"This is the last they'll ever hear from their loved one," he continues. "Imagine how that scream echoes."

But for the victim's family, it does not end there. He demands a ransom that he has no intention of claiming. He calls after midnight and asks the family to imagine their darkest fear. He convinces them that this time, he will really let their loved one go, but he is only extending hope to those who no longer have it, rekindling their agony.

"Time and hope," he says, "sow the seeds of despair."

The father of two has been missing for three years. The young pre-med college student has been missing for twenty-seven months. The newlyweds were married almost two years ago this weekend. To date, not a trace of any of them has been found. Rarely does a week pass when the families don't get a call from their tormentor.

When I ask him if his victims are alive or dead, he is coy. "Death is closure," he explains, "and closure stops the sowing."

He wants to talk about society, how computers and technology are doing our thinking for us, how what he does lets us see the power of the human brain.

"That is where God exists," he says. "That is where all things valuable exist. True bliss can only be found inside of you. The meaning of life is not in your new home entertainment system or sports car. People must see their limitless potential. How do you make them see? Right now imagine what these families are going through."

His voice soft, he invites me to try.

"Technology could never conjure up the horrors you are now imagining. Sow the seeds. Sowing the seeds shows us the potential."

Myron's heart pounded in big thuds. He sat back, shook his head, started reading again. The crazed kidnapper ranted on, his theories feverishly demented, sort of Symbionese Liberation Army by way of Ted Kaczynski. Stan Gibbs's column continued into the next day's paper. Myron hit the link and read on. During the second day, Gibbs opened with some heartbreaking quotes from the family of the victims. Then he questioned the kidnapper some more:

I ask him how he has managed to keep these kidnappings out of the media.

"By sowing the seeds," he repeats yet again.

I ask for an example.

"I tell his wife to go to the garage and open the red Stanley toolbox on the third shelf. I tell her to pick out the black pliers with the bubble grip. Then I send her to the basement. I tell her to stand in front of the Mission chair they bought the previous summer at that tag sale on the Cape. Imagine, I say, your husband tied naked to that chair. Imagine those pliers in my hand. And finally, imagine what I'll do if I see anything about him in the newspaper."

But he does not stop there.

"I ask her about the children. I mention their names. I mention their schools and their teachers and their favorite breakfast cereal."

I ask him how he knows these things.

His answer is simple. "Daddy tells me."

Myron fell back. "Jesus," he uttered.

Deep breaths, he told himself again. In and out. That's it. Think it through. Slowly now. Carefully. Okay, first off: Horrible as this is, what does it have to do with Davis Taylor né Dennis Lex? Probably nothing. The worst sort of long shot. And again, horrible as this is, Myron knew that there was more to the story. More—and in a sense, less.

The Gibbs columns drew weeks' worth of nationwide attention and criticism—until, Myron remembered, it all blew up in the most public way possible. What had happened exactly? Myron hit some keys and clicked the mouse. He started a search of articles where Stan Gibbs was the subject. They came up in date order:

FEDS DEMAND GIBBS'S SOURCE

The Federal Bureau of Investigation, which in recent weeks has been denying the allegations listed in Stan Gibbs's columns, took a new tack today. They demanded his notes and information.

Dan Conway, a spokesman for the FBI, began by saying, "We know nothing about these crimes," then added, "But if Mr. Gibbs is being truthful, he has important information on a possible serial kidnapper and killer, perhaps even harboring or aiding him. We have a right to that information."

Stan Gibbs, a popular columnist and television journalist, has refused to reveal his sources. "I'm not protecting a killer here," Mr. Gibbs said. "The families of the victims as well as the perpetrator of the crimes spoke to me under the strict condition of confidentiality. It's a cry as old as our country: I will not reveal my sources."

The *New York Herald* and American Civil Liberties Union have already denounced the FBI and plan on backing Mr. Gibbs. The judge has ordered the case sealed from the public.

Myron read on. The arguments on both sides were pretty standard. Gibbs's attorneys naturally wrapped themselves in the First Amendment, while the feds equally naturally countered that the First Amendment was not an absolute, that you can't yell "Fire!" in a crowded theater, and that freedom of expression does not include protecting possible criminals. The country also argued the issue. It played well on CNBC and MSNBC and CNN and a bunch of other cable letters, lighting up the phone lines like a radio giveaway. The judge was about to render a verdict when the whole story exploded in a way no one expected.

Myron hit the link:

GIBBS FIBS?
Reporter accused of plagiarism

Myron read the endgame shocker: Someone had found a mystery novel published by a tiny press with a minuscule print run in 1978. The novel, *Whisper to a Scream,* by F. K. Armstrong, closely mirrored Gibbs's story. Too closely. Certain snippets of dialogue were pretty much copied verbatim. The crimes in the novel—kidnappings with no resolution—were too similar to what Gibbs had written to be dismissed as coincidence.

The plagiaristic spectres of Mike Barnicle and Patricia Smith and the like rose from the grave and would not disperse. Heads rolled. There were resignations and hand-wringing. For his part, Stan Gibbs refused to comment, which didn't look good. Gibbs ended up "taking a leave of absence," a modern-day euphemism for *getting fired.* The ACLU issued an ambiguous statement and retreated. The *New York Herald* quietly retracted the story, saying that the matter "was under internal review."

After some time passed, Myron reached for the phone and dialed.

"News desk. Bruce Taylor speaking."

"How about meeting me for a drink?"

"I know this is out nowadays, Myron, but I'm strictly hetero."

"I have the ability to change you."

"I don't think so, pal."

"Several women I've dated started out hetero," Myron said. "But one date with me and whammo, they switched teams."

"I love it when you're self-deprecating, Myron. It's just so real."

"So what do you say?"

"I'm on deadline."

"You're always on deadline."

"You buying?"

"To quote my brethren during Passover seders, why should this night be different from any other night?"

"I buy sometimes."

"Do you even own a wallet?"

"Hey, I'm not the one asking for favors," Bruce said. "Four o'clock. The Rusty Umbrella."

15

The Lex Building's wrought-iron gates lined a Fifth Avenue façade with vegetation so dense you wouldn't see light through it if a supernova burst on the other side. The famed edifice was a converted Manhattan mansion with a European courtyard and a regal art deco exterior and enough security to handle a Tyson boxing match. The building had wonderful old lines and detailed Venetian touches, except that for the sake of privacy, the windows had been converted into the smoky-limo variety. It made for a distracting and unnatural mix.

Four blue-blazered, gray-slacked guards stood at the entrance—real guards, Myron noted, with cop eyes and KGB facial tics, not the rent-a-uniforms you saw at department stores or airports. The four of them stood silently, eyeing Myron like he was wearing a tube top in the Vatican.

One of the guards stepped forward. "May I see some ID please?"

Myron took out his wallet and showed him a credit card and driver's license.

"There's no photo on the driver's license," the guard said.

"New Jersey doesn't require them."

"I need a photo ID."

"I have my picture on my health club membership card."

Cop-patient sigh. "That won't do, sir. Do you have a passport?"

"In midtown Manhattan?"

"Yes, sir. For the purposes of ID."

"No," Myron said. "Besides, it's a terrible picture. Doesn't fully capture the radiant blue in my eyes." Myron batted them for emphasis.

"Wait here, sir."

He waited. The other three guards frowned, crossed their arms, studied him as though he might start drinking from a toilet. Myron heard a whirring noise and looked up. A security camera was on him now, focusing in. Myron waved, smiled into the lens, performed a few flexes he had picked up from watching he-man events on ESPN 2. He ended with a pretty dramatic back lat spread and waved to the appreciative crowd. The blue-blazers looked unimpressed.

"All natural," Myron said. "I've never taken steroids."

No replies.

The first guard came back. "Follow me, please."

Stepping into the courtyard was like stepping into C. S. Lewis's wardrobe, another world, the other side of the shrubbery, so to speak. Here in the middle of Manhattan, the street noises were suddenly very far away, muted. The garden was lush, the tile walkways forming a pattern not unlike an Oriental carpet. There was a sprouting fountain in the middle with a statue of a horse rearing back its head.

A new set of blue-blazers greeted him by the ornate front door. This place, Myron thought, must rack up a hell of a dry-cleaning bill. They made him empty his pockets, confiscated his cell phone, frisked him by hand, ran a metal wand over his person so thoroughly he almost asked for a condom, walked him through a metal detector twice, again frisked him with a little too much gusto.

"If you touch my wee-wee one more time," Myron said, "I'm telling my mommy."

More no replies. Maybe the Lexes demanded not only confidentiality but a discriminating sense of humor.

"Follow me, sir," the talking blue-blazer said.

The stillness of the place—a building in the middle of Manhattan, for chrissake—was unnerving, the only sound now the steady echo of their footsteps against the cool marble. It was like walking through an old museum at night, the whole experience like something out of *From the Mixed-up Files of Mrs. Basil E. Frankweiler*. The guards formed a poor man's presidential motorcade—the talking blue-blazer and a buddy three paces in front of him, two other blue-blazers three paces back. Just for fun, Myron would slow down or speed up and watch the guards do likewise. Like a really bad line dance, which was something of a redundancy. At one point he almost did a moonwalk, à la Michael Jackson, but these guys were already viewing him as a potential pedophile.

The mahogany staircase was wide and smelled a bit like lemon Pledge. There were enormous tapestries on the wall, the kind with swords and horses and hedonistic feasts of suckling pig. There were two more blue-blazers on the second floor. Now it was their turn to inspect Myron as though they'd never seen a man before. Myron twirled for their benefit. They too seemed unimpressed.

"You should have seen me flex before," Myron said.

The double doors opened and Myron entered a room slightly larger than a sports arena. Two guards followed him and took up positions in the back corners. There was a big man sitting to the right in a wing chair. At least he looked big in the chair. Or maybe the chair was tiny. The man was probably in his mid-forties. His head and neck formed a near-perfect trapezoid, the top buzzed into a military crew cut. He had a flat nose and ham-hock hands and knockwurst fingers. Ex-boxer or ex-marine or probably both. A man of ninety-degree angles and granite blocks.

Granite Man gave Myron more hard eyes, though his were more relaxed, as though Myron amused him in the way a little kitty nipping at his pant leg might. He didn't stand, choosing instead to stare at Myron and crack his knuckles one at a time.

Myron looked at Granite Man. Granite Man cracked another knuckle.

"Shiver," Myron said.

No one asked him to take a seat. Hell, no one spoke. Myron stood there and waited with the three sets of eyes weighing on him.

"Okay," Myron said. "I'm intimidated. Can we get past this, please?"

Granite Man nodded at the two blazers. They both left. Almost simultaneously, a door on the other side of the room opened and two women appeared. They were pretty far away, but Myron guessed that the first one was Susan Lex. Her hair was done up in an impossibly neat, semi-shellacked bun, and her lips were pursed as if she'd just swallowed a live beetle. The other woman—she looked no more than eighteen or nineteen—had to be her daughter, a carbon copy with the same pursed lips and twenty-five years less wear and tear, not to mention better hair.

Myron started to cross the room with his hand extended, but Susan Lex held up her palm in a stop gesture. Granite Man sat forward, nearly leaning into Myron's path. He gave Myron a small shake of the head, which was no easy task when you have no neck. Myron stayed where he was.

"I don't like being threatened," Susan Lex called from across the room.

"I apologize for that. But I had to see you."

"And that makes it right to threaten and blackmail me?"

Myron had no quick answer to that. "I need to talk to you about your brother Dennis."

"So you said on the phone."

"Where is he?"

Susan Lex looked at Granite Man. Granite Man frowned and cracked his knuckles again. "Just like that, Mr. Bolitar?" Susan Lex said. "You call my office. You threaten me. You insist I alter my schedule to accommodate you. And then you come in here and make demands?"

"I don't mean to be abrupt," Myron said. "But this is a matter of life and death."

Whenever he said "a matter of life and death," he expected to hear that melodramatic *dum-dum-duuuummm* music.

"That's hardly an explanation," Susan Lex said.

"Your brother registered with the national bone marrow center," Myron said. "His marrow matched a sick child's." After the creepy say-good-bye-to-the-boy conversation last night, Myron had decided to stop being gender specific. "Without that transplant, the child will die."

Susan Lex arched an eyebrow. The rich are really good at that, at arching eyebrows without altering anything else on their face. Myron wondered if they learned it at rich-people summer camp. Susan Lex looked at Granite Man again. Granite Man was trying to smile now. "You're mistaken, Mr. Bolitar," she said.

Myron waited for her to say more. When she didn't, he said, "Mistaken how?"

"If you're telling the truth, you've made a mistake. I will say no more."

"With all due deference," Myron said, "that's not good enough."

"It will have to be."

"Where is your brother, Ms. Lex?"

"Please leave, Mr. Bolitar."

"I can still go to the press."

Granite Man crossed his legs and started cracking his knuckles again.

Myron turned to him. "Yes, but can you do this?" Myron patted his head with one hand and rubbed his belly with the other.

Granite Man didn't like that one.

"Look," Myron said, "I don't want to cause any trouble here. You're private people. I understand that. But I need to find this donor."

"It's not my brother," Susan Lex said.

"Then where is he?"

"He's not your donor. More than that is none of your concern."

"Does the name Davis Taylor mean anything to you?"

Susan Lex repursed the lips as though a fresh beetle had sneaked through. She turned and walked out. Her daughter did likewise. Again on cue, the door behind Myron opened and the two blue-blazers filled it. More glares. They stepped fully into the room. Granite Man finally stood, which took some time. He was indeed big. Very big.

The men approached Myron.

"Let's go to the judges," Myron said. "Charles Nelson Reilly, your score?"

Granite Man stepped in front of him, shoulders square, eyes calm.

"The not introducing yourself," Myron said, doing his best Charles Nelson Reilly lisp, which was not very good. "I thought that was really very macho. And that whole silent persona combined with the amused glare. Very nicely done, really. Professional. But—and here's where you kinda lost me—the knuckle cracking, well, Gene, that was overkill, don't you think? Overall score: an 8. Comment: stick with the subtle."

Granite Man said, "You finished?"

"Yes."

"Myron Bolitar. Born in Livingston, New Jersey. Mother Ellen, father Al—"

"They like to be called El-Al," Myron interjected. "Like the Israeli airline."

"Basketball All-American at Duke University. Picked eighth in the NBA draft by the Boston Celtics. Blew out your knee in your first preseason game, ending your career. Currently owns MB SportsReps, a sports representation firm. Dated the novelist Jessica Culver since you graduated college, but you two recently parted ways. Should I go on?"

"You left off the part about my being a snazzy dancer. I can demonstrate if you like."

Granite Man smirked. "You want my score on you now?"

"Suit yourself."

"You wisecrack too much," Granite Man said. "I know you do it to look confident, but you're trying too hard. And since you raised the issue of subtlety, your story about a dying kid needing a bone marrow transplant was touching. The only thing missing was the string quartet."

"You don't believe me?"

"No, I don't believe you."

"So why am I here, then?"

Granite Man spread his satellite-dishes excuse for hands. "That's what I'd like to know."

The three men formed a triangle, Granite in front, the two blue-blazers in back. Granite made a small nod. One of the blazers produced a gun and aimed at Myron's head.

This was not good.

There are ways of disarming a man with a gun, but there's an inherent problem: It might not work. If you miscalculate or if your opponent is better than you think—something not unlikely in an opponent who knows how to handle a gun—you could get shot. That's a serious drawback. And in this particular situation there were two other opponents, both of whom looked good and were probably armed. There is a word expert fighters use for a sudden move at this juncture: *suicide.*

"Whoever did your research on me left something out," Myron said.

"What might that be?"

"My relationship with Win."

Granite Man didn't flinch. "You mean Windsor Horne Lockwood the Third? Family owns Lock-Horne Security and Investments on Park Avenue. Your college roommate from Duke. Since moving out of the Spring Street loft you shared with Jessica Culver, you've been living at his apartment in the Dakota. You have close business and personal ties, might even be called best friends. That relationship?"

"That would be the one," Myron said.

"I am aware of it. I am also aware of Mr. Lockwood's"—he paused, searching for the word—"talents."

"Then you know that if that bozo gets itchy"—Myron head-gestured toward the blazer with the gun—"you die."

Granite Man wrestled with his facial muscles and this time he achieved a smile, though not without effort. Heart's song "Barracuda" played in Myron's head. "I am not without my own, uh, talents, Mr. Bolitar."

"If you really believe that," Myron said, "then you don't know enough about Win's, uh, talents."

"I won't debate the point. But I will point out that he doesn't have an army like this at his disposal. Now, are you going to tell me why you're asking about Dennis Lex?"

"I told you," Myron said.

"You're really going to stick with the dying-child story?"

"It's the truth."

"And how did you get Dennis Lex's name?"

"From the bone marrow center."

"They just gave it to you?"

Myron's turn. "I too am not without my own, uh, talents." It somehow didn't sound right when he said it about himself.

"So you're saying that the bone marrow center told you that Dennis Lex was a donor—that about right?"

"I'm not saying anything," Myron said. "Look, this is a two-way street here. I want some information."

"Wrong," Granite Man said. "It's a one-way street. I'm a Mack truck. You're like an egg in the road."

Myron nodded. "Cutting," he said. "But if you're not going to give me anything, I'm not giving you anything."

The guy with the gun stepped closer.

Myron felt a quiver in his legs, but he didn't blink. Maybe he did overplay the wisecracks, but you don't show fear. Ever. "And let's not pretend you're going to shoot me over this. We both know you won't. You're not that stupid."

Granite Man smiled. "I might beat on you a bit."

"You don't want trouble, I don't want trouble. I don't care about this family or its fortune or any of that. I'm just trying to save a kid's life."

Granite Man played air violin for a moment. Then he said, "Dennis Lex is not your salvation."

"And I'm just supposed to believe you?"

"He's not your donor. That much I personally guarantee."

"Is he dead?"

Granite Man folded his arms across his paddleball-court chest. "If you're telling the truth, the bone marrow people either lied to you or made a mistake."

"Or you're lying to me," Myron said. Then added, "Or you're making a mistake."

"The guards will show you out."

"I can still go to the press."

Granite Man walked away then. "We both know you won't," he said. "You're not that stupid either."

16

Bruce Taylor was in print-journalist garb—like he'd gone to his laundry hamper and dug out whatever was on the bottom. He sat at the bar, scooped up the free pretzels, and pushed them into his mouth as though he were trying to swallow his palm.

"Hate these things," he said to Myron.

"Yeah, I can see that."

"I'm at a bar, for crying out loud. I gotta eat something. But nobody serves peanuts anymore. Too fattening or some such crap. Pretzels instead. And not real pretzels. Little tiny buggers." He held one up for Myron to see. "I mean, what's up with that?"

"And the politicians," Myron said. "They spend all that time on gun control."

"So what do you want to drink? And don't ask for that Yoo-Hoo crap here. It's embarrassing."

"What are you having?"

"The same thing I always have when you pay. Twelve-year-old Scotch."

"I'll just have a club soda with lime."

"Wuss." He ordered it. "What do you want?"

"You know Stan Gibbs?"

Bruce said, "Whoa."

"What whoa?"

"I mean, whoa, you get involved in some hairy-ass shit, Myron. But Stan Gibbs? What the hell could you possibly have to do with him?"

"Probably nothing."

"Uh-huh."

"Just tell me about him, okay?"

Bruce shrugged, took a sip of Scotch. "Ambitious s.o.b. who went too far. What else do you need to know?"

"The whole story."

"Starting with?"

"What exactly did he do?"

"He plagiarized a story, the dumbass. That's not unusual. But to be so stupid about it."

"Too stupid?" Myron asked.

"What do you mean?"

"I mean we both agree that stealing from a published novel is not only unethical but idiotic."

"So?"

"So I'm asking if it's *too* idiotic."

"You think he's innocent, Myron?"

"Do you?"

He chucked down a few more pretzels. "Hell no. Stan Gibbs is guilty as sin. And as stupid as he was, I know plenty stupider. How about Mike Barnicle? The guy steals jokes from a George Carlin book. George Carlin, for chrissake."

"Does seem pretty stupid," Myron agreed.

"And he's not the only one. Look, Myron, every profession's got their dirty laundry, right? The stuff they want swept under the rug. Cops got their blue line when one of them pounds a suspect into the earth. Doctors cover each other's asses when they take out the wrong gallbladder or whatever. Lawyers . . . well, don't even get me started on their dirty little secrets."

"And plagiarism is yours?"

"Not just plagiarism," Bruce said. "Wholesale fabrication. I know reporters who make up sources. I know guys who make up dialogue. I know guys who make up whole conversations. They run stories about crack mothers and inner-city gang leaders who never existed. Ever read those columns? Ever wonder why so many drug addicts, say, sound so friggin' poignant when they can't even watch *Teletubbies* without a tutor?"

"And you're saying this happens a lot?"

"Truth?"

"Preferably."

"It's epidemic," Bruce said. "Some guys are lazy. Some are too ambitious. Some are just pathological liars. You know the type. They'll lie to you about what they had for breakfast just because it comes so naturally."

The drinks came. Bruce pointed at the empty pretzel bowl. The bartender replaced it.

"So if it's so epidemic," Myron said, "how come so few get caught?"

"First off, it's hard to catch. People hide behind anonymous sources and claim people moved, stuff like that. Second, it's like I said before. It's our dirty little secret. We keep it buried."

"I'd think you'd want to clean house."

"Oh, right. Like cops want to. Like doctors want to."

"You're not the same thing, Bruce."

"Let me give you a scenario, Myron, okay?" Bruce finished up his drink, and now he pointed to his glass for a refill. "You're an editor with, say, *The New York Times*. A story is written for you. You print it. Now it's brought to your attention that the story was fabricated or plagiarized or maybe just totally inaccurate, whatever. What do you do?"

"Retract it," Myron said.

"But you're the editor. You're the dumbass responsible for its publication. You're probably the dumbass who hired the writer in the first place. Who do you think the higher-ups are going to blame? And do you think the higher-ups are going to be happy to hear that their paper printed something false? You think the *Times* wants to lose business to the *Herald* or the *Post* or whatever? And hell, the other papers don't even want to hear about it. The public already doesn't trust us as an institution, right? If the truth gets out, who gets hurt? Answer: everyone."

"So you quietly fire the guy," Myron said.

"Maybe. But, again, you're this editor for *The New York Times*. You fire, say, a columnist. Don't you think a higher-up is going to want to know why?"

"So you just let it go?"

"We're like the church used to be with pedophiles. We try to control the problem without hurting ourselves. We transfer the guy to another department. We pass the problem to someone else. Maybe we team him up with another writer. Harder to make shit up with someone looking over your shoulder."

Myron took a sip of his club soda. Flat. "Okay, let me ask the obvious question then. How did Stan Gibbs get caught?"

"He was dumb, dumber and dumbest. It was too high profile a piece to plagiarize like that. Not only that, but Stan rubbed the feds' face in a public crapper and flushed. You don't do that if you don't have the facts, especially to the feds. My guess is he thought he was safe because the novel had a negligible print run from some shitass vanity press in Oregon. I don't think they published more than five hundred copies of the thing, and that was more than twenty years ago. And the author was long dead."

"But someone dug it up."

"Yup."

Myron thought about it. "Strange, don't you think?"

"Most of the time I'd say yes, but not when it's this high-profile. And once the truth was uncovered, boom, Stan was done. Every media outlet got an anonymous press release about it. The feds held a press conference. I mean, there was almost a campaign against him. Someone—probably the feds—were out for their pound of flesh. And they got it."

"So maybe the feds were so pissed they set him up."

"How do you figure?" Bruce countered. "The novel exists. The passages Stan copied exist. There is no way around that."

Myron mulled that one over, looking for a way around it. Nothing came to him. "Did Stan Gibbs ever defend himself?"

"He never commented."

"Why not?"

"The guy's a reporter. He knew better. Look, stories like these become the worst kind of brushfire. Only way to get the fire out is to stop feeding the flame. No matter how bad, if there's nothing new to report—nothing new to feed the flame—it dies out. People always make the mistake of thinking they can douse the flame with their words, that they're so smart, their explanations will work like water or something. It's always a mistake to talk to the press. Everything— even wonderfully worded denials—feed the flames and keep it stoked."

"But doesn't silence make you look guilty?"

"He *is* guilty, Myron. Stan could only get himself in more trouble by talking. And if he hung around and tried to defend himself, someone would dig into his past too. Mainly his old columns. All of them. Every fact, every quote, everything. And if you've plagiarized one story, you've plagiarized others. You don't do it for the first time when you're Stan's age."

"So you think he was trying to minimize the damage?"

Bruce smiled, took a sip. "That Duke education," he said. "It wasn't wasted on you." He grabbed more pretzels. "Mind if I order a sandwich?"

"Suit yourself."

"It'll be worth it," Bruce said with a suddenly big smile. "Because I haven't yet mentioned the last little tidbit that convinced him to keep quiet."

"What's that?"

"It's big, Myron." The smile slid off his face. "Very big."

"Fine, order fries too."

"I don't want this to become public knowledge, you understand?"

"Come on, Bruce. What?"

Bruce turned back to the bar. He picked up a cocktail napkin and tore it in half. "You know the feds took Stan to court to find his sources."

"Yes."

"The court documents were kept sealed, but there was a bit of nastiness. See, they wanted Stan to provide some sort of corroboration. Something to show he didn't totally make the story up. He wouldn't offer any. For a while he claimed that only the families could back him and he wouldn't give them up. But the judge pressed. He finally admitted that there was one other person who could back his story."

"Back up his made-up story?"

"Yes."

"Who?"

"His mistress," Bruce said.

"Stan was married?"

"Guess the word 'mistress' gave it away," Bruce said. "Anyway, he was. Still is, technically, but now they're separated. Naturally Stan was hesitant about naming her—he loved his wife, had two kids, the backyard, whatever—but in the end he gave the judge her name under the condition that it stay sealed."

"Did the mistress back him?"

"Yes. This mistress—one Melina Garston—claimed to have been with him when he met the Sow the Seeds psycho."

Myron's brow creased. "Why does that name ring a bell?"

"Because Melina Garston is dead now. Tied and tortured and you don't want to know what."

"When?"

"Three months ago. Right after the shit hit Stan's fan. Worse, the police think Stan did it."

"To keep her from telling the truth?"

"Again that Duke education."

"But that makes no sense. She was killed after the plagiarism was discovered, right?"

"Right after, yeah."

"So it was too late by then. Everyone thinks he's guilty already. He's lost his job. He's disgraced. If his mistress now comes out and says 'Yeah, I lied,' it wouldn't really change a thing. What would Stan have gained by killing her?"

Bruce shrugged. "Maybe her retraction would have removed any doubt."

"But there's not much doubt there anyway."

The bartender came over. Bruce ordered a sandwich. Myron shook him off. "Can you find out where Stan Gibbs is hiding?"

Bruce waved down the bartender again. "I already know."

"How?"

"He was my friend."

"Was or is?"

"Is, I guess."

"You like him?"

"Yeah," Bruce said. "I like him."

"Yet, you still think he did it."

"Murder, probably not. Plagiarize . . ." He shrugged. "I'm a cynical guy. And just because a guy is a friend of mine doesn't mean he can't do dumb things."

"Will you give me his address?"

"Will you tell me why?"

Myron sipped his flat club soda. "Okay, this is the part where you say you want to know what I have. Then I say I have nothing and when I do, you'll be the first to know. Then you get kinda huffy and say I owe you and that's not good enough, but in the end you take the deal. So why don't we skip all that and just give me the address?"

"Will I still get my sandwich?"

"Sure."

"Fine, then," Bruce said. "Doesn't matter. Stan hasn't talked to anyone since he resigned—not even his close friends. What makes you think he'll talk to you?"

"Because I'm a witty dinner companion and natty dresser?"

"Yeah, that." He turned to Myron and looked at him heavily. "Now, this is the part where I tell you that if you find anything, anything, that suggests that Stan Gibbs is being set up, you tell me because I'm his friend and I'm a reporter hungry for a big story."

"Not to mention a sandwich."

No smile. "You got me?"

"Got you."

"Anything you want to tell me now?"

"Bruce, I got less than nothing. It's just a thread I need to snip away."

"You know Cross River in Englewood?"

"A mid-eighties condo development that looks like something out of *Poltergeist*."

"Twenty-four Acre Drive. Stan just came back to the area. He's renting there."

17

The Morning Mosh was not really the establishment's name. Located in a converted warehouse downtown on the West Side, the Mosh had a neon sign that changed as the day went on. The word *Mosh* stayed lit all the time, but in the morning it blinked *Morning Mosh*, then *Mid-Day Mosh* (as it now read) and later on, *Midnight Mosh*. And that's *Mosh*, not *Nosh*. Myron had expected a bagel store. But the letter was *M*, not *N*, and this place was *Mosh*. As in *Mosh Pit*. As in some retro heavy-metal band minus the talent blaring sounds that could strip paint while kids danced—and we're using that term in its loosest form here—in a pit, careening off one another like a thousand pinballs released into the machine at the same time.

A sign by the front door read FOUR BODY PIERCE MINIMUM TO ENTER (EARS DON'T COUNT).

Myron stayed on the sidewalk and used his cell phone. He called the Mosh's number. A voice answered, "Go for it, dude."

"Suzze T please."

"Dig."

Dig?

Suzze came on two minutes later. "Hello?"

"It's Myron. I'm out on the curb."

"Come in. No one bites. Well, except for that guy who bit the legs off a live frog last night. Man, that was so cool."

"Suzze, please meet me out here, okay?"

"What-ev-er."

Myron hung up, feeling old. Suzze came out less than a minute later. She wore bell-bottom jeans with a gravity-defying waist that stayed up south of her hips. Her top was pink and much too small, revealing not only a flat stomach but a bottom-side hint of what interested the fine folks at Rack Enterprises. Suzze sported only one tattoo (a tennis racket with a snake's head grip) and no piercings, not even her ears.

Myron pointed to the sign. "You don't meet the minimum piercing requirement."

"Yeah, Myron, I do."

Silence. Then Myron said, "Oh."

They started walking down the street. Another strange Manhattan neighborhood. Kids and the homeless hung out together. There were bars and nightclubs alongside daycare centers. The modern city. Myron passed a storefront with a sign: TATTOOS WHILE U WAIT. He reread the sign and frowned. Like how else would you do it?

"We got a weird endorsement offer," Myron said. "You know the Rack Bars?"

Suzze said, "Like, upscale topless, right?"

"Well, topless anyway."

"What about them?"

"They're opening up a chain of topless coffee bars."

Suzze nodded. "Cool," she said. "I mean, taking the popularity of Starbucks and mixing it with Scores and Goldfingers, well, it's totally wise."

"Uh, right. Anyway, they're having this big grand opening and they're trying to generate excitement and media attention and all that. So they want you to make a, uh, guest appearance."

"Topless?"

"Like I said on the phone, I had an offer I wanted you to refuse."

"Totally topless?"

Myron nodded. "They insist on nipple visibility."

"How much they willing to pay?"

"Two hundred thousand dollars."

She stopped. "Are you shitting me?"

"I shit you not."

She whistled. "Lots of cha-ching."

"Yes, but I still think—"

"This was, like, their first offer?"

"Yes."

"Do you think you could get them up?"

"No, that would be your job."

She stopped and looked at him. Myron shrugged his apology.

"Tell them yes," she said.

"Suzze . . ."

"Two hundred grand for flashing a bit of booby? Christ, last night I think I did it in there for free."

"That isn't the same thing."

"Did you see what I wore in *Sports Illustrated*? I might as well have been naked."

"That isn't the same thing either."

"This is Rack, Myron, not some sleazoid place like Buddy's. It's upscale topless."

"Saying 'upscale topless' is like saying 'good toupee,' " Myron said.

"Huh?"

"It might be good," he said, "but it's still a toupee."

She cocked her head. "Myron, I'm twenty-four years old."

"I know that."

"That's like 107 in women-tennis years. I'm ranked thirty-one in the world right now. I haven't made two hundred grand over the past two years on tour. This is a big score, Myron. And man, will it change my image."

"Exactly my point."

"No, listen up, tennis is looking for draws. I'll be controversial. I'll get tons of attention. I'll suddenly be a big name. Admit it, my appearance fees will quadruple."

Appearance fees are the money paid to the big names just to show up, win or lose. Most name players make far more in appearance fees than prize money. It's where the potential major *dinero* is, especially for a player ranked thirty-first.

"Probably," Myron said.

She stopped and grabbed his arm. "I love playing tennis."

"I know that," he said softly.

"Doing this will extend my career. That means a lot to me, okay?"

Christ, she looked so young.

"All of what you're saying may be true," Myron said. "But at the end of the day, you're still appearing at a topless bar. And once it's done, it's done. You will always be remembered as the tennis player who appeared topless."

"There are worse things."

"Yes. But I didn't become an agent to get in the stripping business. I'll do what you want. You're my client. I want what's best for you."

"But you don't think this is best for me?"

"I have trouble advising a young woman to appear topless."

"Even if it makes sense?"

"Even if it makes sense."

She smiled at him. "You know something, Myron? You're cute when you're being a prude."

"Yeah, adorable."

"Tell them yes."

"Think about it for a few days, okay?"

"It's a no-brainer, Myron. Just do what you do best."

"What's that?"

"Get the number up. And tell them yes."

18

Cross River Condos was one of those complexes that looked like a movie façade, like whole buildings might topple over if you pushed against any one wall. The development was sprawlingly cramped, with every building looking exactly the same. Walking through it was like something out of *Alice in Wonderland*, all avenues mirroring the others, until you got dizzy. Have too much drink and you're bound to stick your key in the wrong lock.

Myron parked near the complex pool. The place was nice but too close to Route 80, the major artery that ran from, well, here in New Jersey to California. The traffic sounds sloshed over the fence. Myron located the door to 24 Acre Drive and then tried to figure out which windows belonged to it. If he had it right, the lights were on. So was the television. He knocked on the door. Myron saw a face peer through the window next to the door. The face did not speak.

"Mr. Gibbs?"

Through the glass, the face said, "Who are you?"

"My name is Myron Bolitar."

A brief pause. "The basketball player?"

"At one time, yes."

The face looked through the window for a few more seconds before opening the door. The odor of too many cigarettes wafted through the opening and happily nested inside Myron's nostrils. Not surprisingly, Stan Gibbs had a cigarette in his mouth. He had a gray stubble-to-beard going, too far gone for retro *Miami Vice*. He wore a yellow Bart Simpson sweatshirt, dark green sweatpants, socks, sneakers, and a Colorado Rockies baseball cap—the standard fashion fare shared with equal fervor by joggers and couch potatoes. Myron suspected the latter here.

"How did you find me?" Stan Gibbs asked.

"It wasn't difficult."

"That's not an answer."

Myron shrugged.

"It doesn't matter," Stan said. "I have no comment."

"I'm not a reporter."

"So what are you?"

"A sports agent."

Stan took a puff of the cigarette, didn't remove it from his mouth. "Sorry to disappoint you, but I haven't played competitive football since high school."

"May I come in?"

"No, I don't think so. What do you want?"

"I need to find the kidnapper you wrote about in your article," Myron said.

Stan smiled with very white teeth, especially when you considered the smoking. His skin was sort of clumpy and winter-colorless, his hair thin and tired, but he had those bright eyes, superbright eyes, the kind that look like supernatural beacons are shining out from within. "Don't you read the papers?" he asked. "I made the whole thing up."

"Made it up or copied it from a book?"

"I stand corrected."

"Or maybe you were telling the truth. In fact, maybe the subject of your articles called me on the phone last night."

Stan shook his head, the growing ash on the cigarette holding on like a kid on an amusement park ride. "This is not something I want to revisit."

"Did you plagiarize the story?"

"I already said I wouldn't comment—"

"This isn't for public consumption. If you did—if the story was a fake—just tell me now and I'll go away. I don't have time to waste on false leads."

"Nothing personal," Stan said, "but you're not making a whole lot of sense here."

"Does the name Davis Taylor mean anything to you?"

"No comment."

"How about Dennis Lex?"

That threw him. The dangling cigarette started to slip from Stan's lips, but he caught it with his right hand. He dropped it on the walkway and watched it sizzle for a moment.

"Maybe you better come in."

The condo was a duplex centered with that staple of new American contruction, the cathedral ceiling. Plenty of light came in from the big windows, splashing down on a decor straight out of a Sunday circular. A blond-wood entertainment center took up one wall, a matching coffee table not far from it. There was also a white-and-blue-striped couch—Myron would bet his lunch money it was a Serta Sleeper—and matching love seat. The carpeting was the same neutral as the exterior, a sort of inoffensive tan, and the place was clean yet disorderly in a divorcé way, newspapers and magazines and books piled here and there, nothing really put in a specific place.

He had Myron sit on the couch. "Want something to drink?"

"Sure, whatever," Myron said. The coffee table had one photograph on it. A man had his arms around two boys. All three were smiling too hard, like they'd just come in second place and didn't want to appear disappointed. They were standing in a garden of some sort. Behind them loomed a marble statue of a woman with a bow and arrow over her shoulder. Myron picked up the frame and studied it. "This you?"

Gibbs lifted his head while scooping a handful of ice into a glass. "I'm on the right," he said. "With my brother and my father."

"Who's that a statue of?"

"Diana the Huntress. You familiar with her?"

"Didn't she turn into Wonder Woman?"

Stan chuckled. "Sprite okay?"

Myron put the photograph down. "Sure."

Stan Gibbs poured the drink, brought it out to Myron, handed it to him. "What do you know about Dennis Lex?"

"Just that he exists," Myron said.

"So why mention his name to me?"

Myron shrugged. "Why did you react so strongly to hearing it?"

Gibbs took out another cigarette, lit it. "You're the one who came to me."

"True."

"Why?"

No secret. "I'm looking for a man named Davis Taylor. He's a bone marrow donor who matched a kid and then vanished. I traced him to an address in Connecticut, but he's not there. So I dug a little more and found out that Davis Taylor is a name change. His real name is Dennis Lex."

"I still don't see what this has to do with me."

"This might sound a little nutty," Myron said. "But I left a voice mail message for Davis Taylor né Dennis Lex. When he called back, he made little sense. But he kept telling me to 'sow the seeds.' "

A small quake ran through Stan Gibbs. It passed quickly. "What else did he say?"

"That was pretty much it. I should sow the seeds. I should say good-bye to the child. Stuff like that."

"It's probably nothing," Gibbs said. "He probably just read my article and decided to have a little fun at your expense."

"Probably," Myron said. "Except that wouldn't really explain your reaction to Dennis Lex's name."

Stan shrugged, but there wasn't much behind it. "The family is famous."

"If I said Ivana Trump, would you have reacted the same?"

Gibbs stood. "I need some time to think about this."

"Think out loud," Myron said.

Stan just shook his head.

"Did you make up the story, Stan?"

"Another time."

"Not good enough," Myron said. "You owe me something here. Did you plagiarize the story?"

"How do you expect me to answer that?"

"Stan?"

"What?"

"I don't care about your situation. I'm not here to judge you or tell on you. I don't give a rat's ass if you made up the story or not. All I care about is finding the bone marrow donor. Period. End of story. *El Fin.*"

Stan's eyes started to well up. He took another puff of the cigarette. "No," he said. "I never plagiarized. I never saw that book in my life."

It was like the room had been holding its breath and finally let go.

"How do you explain the similarities between your article and that novel?"

He opened his mouth, stopped, shook his head.

"Your silence makes you look guilty."

"I don't have to explain anything to you."

"Yeah, you do. I'm trying to save a kid's life here. You're not that wrapped up in your problems, are you, Stan?"

Stan moved back into the kitchen. Myron stood and followed him. "Talk to me," Myron said. "Maybe I can help."

"No," he said. "You can't."

"How do you explain the similarities, Stan? Just tell me that, okay? You must have thought about it."

"I don't need to think about it."

"Meaning?"

He opened the refrigerator and grabbed another can of Sprite. "Do you think all psychotics are original?"

"I'm not following you."

"You received a call from a guy who told you about sowing the seeds."

"Right."

"There are two possibilities that explain why he did that," Stan said. "One, he is the same killer I wrote about. Or two?" Stan looked at Myron.

"He just repeated what he'd read in the article," Myron said.

Stan snapped and pointed at Myron.

"So you're saying that the kidnapper you interviewed read this novel and it, what, influenced him somehow? That he copied it?"

Stan took a swig from the can. "That's a theory," he said.

And a damn good one, Myron thought. "So why didn't you say that to the press? Why didn't you defend yourself?"

"None of your goddamn business."

"Some people say it's because you were afraid they'd look closer at your work. That they'd find other fabrications."

"And some people are morons," he finished.

"So why didn't you fight?"

"I spent my whole life being a journalist," Stan said. "Do you know what it means for a journalist to be called a plagiarist? It's like a daycare worker being called a child molester. I'm done. No words can change that. I've lost everything to this scandal. My wife, my kids, my job, my reputation—"

"Your mistress?"

He shut his eyes suddenly, tightly, like a child trying to make the bogeyman go away.

"The police think you killed Melina," Myron said.

"I'm well aware of that."

"Tell me what's going on here, Stan."

He opened his eyes and shook his head. "I have to make some calls, check out some leads."

"You can't just cut me loose."

"I have to," he said.

"Let me help."

"I don't need your help."

"But I need yours."

"Not right now," Stan said. "You'll have to trust me on this."

"I'm not big on trust," Myron said.

Stan smiled. "Neither am I," he said. "Neither am I."

19

Myron pulled out. So, too, he noticed, did two men in a black Oldsmobile Ciera. Hmm.

The cell phone rang.

"Have you learned anything?" It was Emily.

"Not really," Myron said.

"Where are you?"

"Englewood."

"Do you have any plans for dinner?" Emily asked.

Myron hesitated. "No."

"I'm a good cook, you know. We dated in college, so I didn't have much chance to demonstrate my culinary skills."

"I remember you cooking for me once," Myron said.

"I did?"

"In my wok."

Emily chuckled. "That's right, you had an electric wok in your dorm, right?"

"Yep."

"I almost forgot about that," Emily said. "Why did you have one, anyway?"

"To impress chicks."

"Really?"

"Sure. I thought I'd invite a girl up to my room, slice up some vegetables, add a little soy sauce—"

"To the vegetables?" she asked.

"For starters."

"So how come you never pulled that one on me?"

"Didn't have to."

"You calling me easy, Myron?"

"How exactly does one answer that," Myron asked, "and maintain possession of both testicles?"

"Come on over," Emily said. "I'll make us some dinner. No soy sauce."

Another hesitation.

"Please don't make me ask again," Emily said.

He wanted very much to say no. "Okay."

"Just take Route 4—"

"I know the way, Emily."

He hung up then and checked the rearview mirror. The black Oldsmobile Ciera was still following. Better safe than sorry. Myron hit the preprogrammed number on his cell phone. After one ring, Win answered.

"Articulate," Win said.

"Got a tail, methinks."

"License plate?"

Myron read it off to him.

"Where should we coordinate?"

"Garden State Plaza mall," Myron said.

"On my way, fair maiden."

Myron stayed on Route 4 until he saw a sign for the Garden State Plaza. He took a rather complicated cloverleaf overpass and veered into the mall's lot. The black Olds followed, dropping back a bit. Stall time. Myron circled a few times before finding a parking space. The Olds kept its distance. He turned off the car and headed for the "Northeast Entrance."

The Garden State Plaza had all the artificial elements endemic in malls—the mall ear-pop when you enter, the stale mall air, the mall hollow acoustics, as though all sound were traveling through a high-volume distorter—the audial equivalent of a shower door, voices somehow rendered both loud and incomprehensible. Too much with the high ceilings and faux marble, nothing soft to cushion the sound.

He strolled through the nouveau riche section of the Garden State Plaza, past several barren shoe stores, the kind that display maybe three pairs of shoes on the ends of what look like deer antlers. He reached a store called Aveda, which sold wildly overpriced cosmetics and lotions. The Aveda saleswoman, a starving young thang in tourniquet-tight black, informed Myron that they were having a sale on face moisturizers. Myron refrained from crying out "Yippee!" and went on his way. Victoria's Secret was next, and Myron did that male surreptitious glance at the lingerie window displays. Most of your more sophisticated heterosexual males are well versed in this art, awarding the racily clad supermodels the most casual of once-overs, feigning a lack of interest in the blown-up, blown-clear images of Stephanie and Frederique in Miracle Bras. Myron, of course, did the same thing—and then he thought, why pretend? He stopped short, squared his shoulders, ogled in earnest. Honesty. Shouldn't a woman respect that in a man too?

He checked his watch. Not yet. More stall. The plan, as it were, was fairly simple. Win drives to the Garden State Plaza. When he arrives, he calls Myron on the cell phone. Myron then goes back to his car. Win looks for the black Olds and follows the followee. Super clever, no?

Myron hit Sharper Image, one of the few places in the world where people use the words *shiatsu* and *ionic* and nobody laughs. He tried out a massage chair (setting: Knead) and debated purchasing a $5,500 life-size statue of a *Star Wars* star-trooper that had been reduced to a mere $3,499. Talk about redefining nouveau riche. Here's a little tip for you: If you've purchased a Sharper Image life-size *Star Wars* star-trooper, take out your platinum-est charge card, hand it to the nearest cashier, and buy a life.

The cell phone rang. Myron picked it up.

"They're feds," Win said.

"Yikes."

"Yes."

"No reason to follow them, then."

"No."

Myron spotted two men in suits and sunglasses behind him. They were studying the fruit-flavored shampoos in the Garden Botanica store window a little too closely. Two men in suits and sunglasses. Oh, like that happens. "I think they're following me in here too."

"If they arrest you with lingerie," Win said, "tell them it's for your wife."

"That what you do?"

"Keep the phone on," Win said.

Myron did as he asked. An old trick of theirs. Myron kept his cell phone on, thereby freeing Win to listen in. Okay, fine, now what? He kept strolling. Two more men in business suits were window-shopping up ahead. They turned as Myron approached, both staring him down. Some tail. Myron glanced behind him. The first two feds were right there.

The two feds in front of him stepped directly into his path. The other two came up behind him, boxing him in.

Myron stopped, looked at all four feds. "Did you guys check out the facial moisturizer sale at Aveda?"

"Mr. Bolitar?"

"Yes."

One of them, a short guy with a severe haircut, flashed a badge. "I'm Special Agent Fleischer with the Federal Bureau of Investigation. We'd like a word with you, sir."

"What about?"

"Would you mind coming with us?"

They had the standard-issue stone expressions; Myron would get nothing out of them. Probably didn't even know anything themselves. Probably just delivery boys. Myron shrugged and followed them out. Two got into a white Olds Ciera. The other two stayed with Myron. One opened the back door of the black Ciera and head-gestured for Myron to get in. He did so. The interior was very clean. Nice, smooth seats. Myron ran his hand over it.

"Corinthian leather?" he asked.

Special Agent Fleischer turned around. "No, sir, that would be the Ford Granada."

Touché.

No one spoke. No radio played. Myron settled back. He debated calling Emily and postponing their soy-sauce-less encounter, but he didn't want the feds to hear him. He sat tight and kept his mouth shut. He didn't do that often. It felt odd and somehow right.

Thirty minutes later, he was in the basement of a modest high-rise in Newark. He sat at a table with his hands on a semi-sticky table. The room had one barred window and cement walls the color and texture of dried oatmeal. The feds excused themselves and left Myron alone. Myron sighed and sat back. He'd figured that this was the old soften-him-up-by-making-him-wait bit, when the door flew open.

The woman was first. She wore a pumpkin-orange blazer, blue jeans, sneakers, and ball-and-chain earrings. The word that came to mind was *husky*. Not big really. Husky. Everything was husky—even her hair, a sort of canned-corn yellow. The guy riding in on her fumes was geeky thin with a pointy head and a small, greased shock of black hair. He looked like an upside-down pencil. He spoke first.

"Good afternoon, Mr. Bolitar," Pencil said.

"Good afternoon."

"I'm Special Agent Rick Peck," he said. "This is Special Agent Kimberly Green."

The orange-blazered Green did a caged-lion pace. Myron nodded at her. She nodded back but grudgingly, like her teacher had just told her to apologize for something she didn't do.

Pencil Peck continued. "Mr. Bolitar, we'd like to ask you a few questions."

"What about?"

Peck kept his eyes on his notes and spoke like he was reading. "Today you visited one Stan Gibbs at 24 Acre Drive. Is that correct?"

"How do you know I didn't visit two Stan Gibbs?"

Peck and Green exchanged a glance. Then Peck said, "Please, Mr. Bolitar, we'd appreciate your cooperation. Did you visit Mr. Gibbs?"

"You know I did," Myron said.

"Fine, thank you." Peck wrote something down slowly. Then he looked up. "We'd very much like to know the nature of your visit."

"Why?"

"You are the first visitor Mr. Gibbs has had since moving to his current residence."

"No, I mean, why do you want to know?"

Green crossed her arms. She and Peck looked at each other again. Peck said, "Mr. Gibbs is part of an ongoing investigation."

Myron waited. No one said anything. "Well, that pretty much clears it up."

"That's all I can say for the moment."

"Same here."

"Pardon?"

"If you can't say any more, I can't say any more."

Kimberly Green put her hands on the table, gave a toothy grimace—husky teeth?—and leaned down like she might take a bite out of him. The canned-corn hair smelled like Pert Plus. She eyeballed him—must have read a memo on intimidating glares—and then spoke for the first time. "Here's how we're going to play it, asshole. We're going to ask you questions. You're going to listen to them and then you're going to answer them. You got it?"

Myron nodded. "I want to make sure I got this straight," he said to her. "You're playing bad cop, right?"

Peck picked up the ball. "Mr. Bolitar, no one is interested in making trouble here. But we'd very much like your cooperation in this matter."

"Am I under arrest?" Myron asked.

"No."

"Bye then."

He started to stand. Kimberly Green gave him a shove mid-rise and he fell back into the chair. "Sit down, asshole." She looked over at Peck. "Maybe he's part of it."

"You think so?"

"Why else would he be so reluctant to answer questions?"

Peck nodded. "Makes sense. An accomplice."

"We can probably arrest him now," Green said. "Lock him up for the night, maybe leak it to the press."

Myron looked up at her. "Gasp," he said. "Now. I. Am. Really. Scared. Second gasp."

She narrowed her eyes. "What did you say?"

"Don't tell me," Myron said. "Maybe I'm guilty of aiding and abetting. That's my personal favorite. Does anyone actually get prosecuted for that?"

"You think we're playing games here?"

"I do. And by the way, how come you're all called 'special' agent? Doesn't that sound like something someone made up one day? Like a kid's game to raise self-esteem. 'We're promoting you from agent to special agent, Barney,' and then what, super-special agent?"

Green grabbed his lapels and leaned his chair back. "You're not funny."

Myron looked at her hands gripping him. "Are you for real?"

"You want to try me?" she said.

Peck said, "Kim."

She ignored him and kept her glare on Myron. "This is serious," she said.

Her tone aimed for angry but came out more like a frightened plea. Two more agents entered. With the four delivery boys, that made eight. This was something big. What, Myron had no idea. The murder of Melina Garston maybe. But that was doubtful. The locals usually handled murders. You don't call in the feds.

The new guys came at Myron in different ways, but there were only so many routes to travel and Myron knew them all. Threatening, friendly, flattering, insulting, building up, belittling, hard, soft, every sell. They denied him the bathroom, they made excuses to keep him longer, all the while they're working him and he's working them and neither one is giving. Sweat started flowing, mostly from them, the stains and stench filling the air, metastasizing into something Myron could swear was genuine fear.

Kimberly Green came in and out and she kept shaking her head at him. Myron wanted to cooperate, but here's the pertinent cliché: Once the genie is out of the bottle, you can't put it back in. He didn't know what they were investigating. He didn't know if it would benefit Jeremy to talk or hurt him. But once he spoke, once his words were in the public domain, he couldn't take them back. Any leverage he might later be able to apply would be gone. So, for now, even if he might want to help, he wouldn't. Not until he learned more. He had the contacts. He could find out quickly enough, make an informed decision.

Sometimes, negotiating meant shutting up.

When things wound down, Myron got up to leave. Kimberly Green blocked his path. "I'm going to make your life hell," she said.

"That your way of asking me out?"

She leaned back as if he'd slapped her. When she recovered, she shook her head slowly. "You have no idea, do you?"

Shutting up, he reminded himself. Myron pushed past her and headed outside.

20

He called Emily from the car.

"I thought I was being stood up," she said.

Myron checked out the rearview mirror and spotted what might be another fed tail. No matter. "Sorry," he said. "Something came up."

"Involving the donor?"

"I don't think so."

"You still in Jersey?" Emily asked.

"Yes."

"Come on over. I'll reheat dinner."

He wanted to say no. "Okay."

Franklin Lakes was about sprawling. Everything sprawled. The houses were mostly new construction, big brick mansions on eternal cul-de-sacs, little gates at the front of the driveways that opened with push-button or intercom, like that would really protect the owners from what lay outside the lush lawns and pedicure-clipped hedges. The interiors were sprawling too, dining rooms big enough to house helicopters, remote-controlled blinds, Sub-Zero/Viking Stove kitchens with marble islands that overlooked family rooms the size of movie theaters, always with complicated state-of-the-art entertainment centers.

Myron rang the bell and the door opened and for the first time in his life, Myron was face-to-face with his son.

Jeremy smiled at him. "Hi."

Strong, totally alien surges ricocheted haphazardly through Myron, his nervous system melting down and in overdrive all at once. His diaphragm contracted and his lungs stopped. So, he was sure, did his heart. His mouth weakly opened and closed like a dying fish on a boat deck. Tears headed up and pushed toward the eyes.

"You're Myron Bolitar, right?" Jeremy said.

An ocean-shell rushing filled Myron's ears. He managed a nod.

"You played ball against my dad," Jeremy said, still with the smile that ripped at the corners of Myron's heart. "In college, right?"

Myron found his voice. "Yes."

The kid nodded back. "Cool."

"Yeah."

A horn honked. Jeremy leaned to the right and looked behind Myron. "That's my ride. Later."

Jeremy leaped past Myron. Myron numbly turned and watched the boy jog down the driveway. Imagination maybe, but that gait was oh-so-familiar. From Myron's old game films. More surges. *Oh Christ . . .*

Myron felt a hand on his shoulder, but he ignored it and watched the boy. The car door opened and swallowed Jeremy into the darkness. The driver's window slid down and a pretty woman called out, "Sorry I'm late, Em."

From behind him, Emily said, "No problem."

"I'll take them to school in the morning."

"Great."

A wave and the pretty woman's window slid back into place. The car started on its way. Myron watched it disappear down the road. He felt Emily's eyes on him. He slowly turned to her.

"Why did you do that?"

"I thought he'd be gone by now," Emily said.

"Do I really look that stupid?"

She stepped back into the house. "I want to show you something."

Trying to get his legs back, his head wobbly and his internal referee still giving him the eight count, Myron followed her silently up the stairway. She led him down a darkened corridor lined with modern lithographs. She stopped, opened a door, and flipped on the lights. The room was teenage-cluttered, as if someone had put all the belongings in the center of the room and dropped a hand grenade on them. The posters on the walls—Michael Jordan, Keith Van Horn, Greg Downing, Austin Powers, the words *YEAH, BABY!* across his middle in pink tie-dye lettering—had been hung askew, all tattered corners and missing pushpins. There was a Nerf basketball hoop on the closet door. There was a computer on the desk and a baseball cap dangling from a desk lamp. The corkboard had a mix of family snapshots and construction-paper crayons signed by Jeremy's sister, all held up by oversized pushpins. There were footballs and autographed baseballs and cheap trophies and a couple of blue ribbons and three basketballs, one with no air in it. There were stacks of computergame CD-ROMs and a Game Boy on the unmade bed and a surprising amount of books, several opened and facedown. Clothes littered the floor like war wounded; the drawers were half open, shirts and underwear hanging out like they'd been shot mid-escape. The room had the slight, oddly comforting smell of kids' socks.

"He's a slob," she said. Leaving off the obvious "like you."

Myron stayed still.

"He keeps Oxy 10 in his desk drawer," Emily said. "He thinks I don't know. He's at that age where crushes keep him up all night, but he's never even kissed a girl." She walked over to the corkboard and snatched up a photograph of Jeremy. "He's beautiful, don't you think?"

"This isn't helping, Emily."

"I want you to understand."

"Understand what?"

"He's never been kissed. He is going to die and he's never even kissed a girl."

Myron held up his hands. "I don't know what you want me to say here."

"Try to understand, okay?"

"I don't need melodrama. I understand."

"No, Myron, you don't. You look back at the night and see it as some sort of Gothic blunder. We did something sinful and for that we all paid a heavy price. If we could just go back and erase that tragic mistake, well, it's all so *Hamlet* and *Macbeth*, isn't it? Your ruined basketball career, Greg's future, our marriage—all laid to waste in that one moment of lust."

"It wasn't lust."

"Let's not go through that argument again. I don't care what it was. Lust, stupidity, fear, fate. Call it whatever the hell you want to—but I would never want to go back. That 'mistake' was the best thing that ever happened to me. Jeremy, our son, came out of that mess. Do you hear what I'm saying? I'd destroy a million careers and marriages for him."

She looked at him, challenging. He said nothing.

"I'm not religious and I don't believe in fate or destiny or any of that," she went on. "But maybe, just maybe, there had to be a balance. Maybe the only way to produce something so wonderful was to surround the event with so much destruction."

Myron started backing out of the room. "This isn't helping," he said again.

"Yes," she said, "it is."

"You want me to find the donor. I'm trying to do that. But this kind of distraction doesn't help. I need to stay detached."

"No, Myron, you need attachment. You need to get emotional. You have to understand the stakes—your son, that beautiful boy who opened the door—is going to die before he's even kissed a girl." She moved closer to him and looked into his eyes and Myron thought that her eyes had never looked so clear before.

"I watched you play every game at Duke," she said. "I fell in love with you on that court—not because you were the team star or because you were graceful or athletic. You were so open out there, so raw and emotional. And the more emotional you got, the more pressure there was, the better you played. If the game was a blowout, you lost interest. You needed it to matter. You needed to be double-teamed with only a few seconds on the clock. You needed to lose control a little."

"This isn't a game, Emily."

"Right," she said. "The stakes are higher. The emotion should be higher. I want you desperate, Myron. That's when you're at your best."

He looked at the photograph of Jeremy, and he knew that he was feeling something that he had never felt before. He blinked, caught the expression on his face in the closet-door mirror, and for a moment he saw his own father staring back.

Emily hugged him then. She buried her face in his shoulder and started to cry. Myron held on tight. They stood that way for several minutes before making their way downstairs. Over dinner, Emily told him about Jeremy, and he soaked in every story. They moved to the couch and broke out the photo albums. Emily tucked her legs under her, her elbow on the top of the couch, her head leaning on the heel of her hand, and told him more. It was nearly two in the morning when she walked him to the door. They were holding hands.

"I know you spoke to Dr. Singh," she said in the open door.

"Yes."

She let loose a deep breath. "I'm just going to say this, okay?"

"Okay."

"I've been keeping track. I bought one of those home tests. The, uh, optimum conception day will be Thursday."

He opened his mouth but she stopped him with her hand.

"I know all the arguments against this, but it might be Jeremy's only chance. Don't say anything. Just think about it."

She closed the door. Myron stared at it for a few moments. He tried to conjure up the moment Jeremy had opened it, the crooked smile on the boy's face, but already the image was hazy and fading fast.

21

First thing in the morning, Myron called Terese. Still no answer. He frowned at the phone. "Am I getting the big kiss-off?" he asked Win.

"Doubtful," Win said. He was reading the newspaper and wearing silk pajamas with a matching bathrobe and slippers. Give him a pipe and he could have been something Noël Coward created on an off day.

"What makes you say that?"

"Our Ms. Collins appears to be rather direct," Win said. "If you were being tossed into the dung heap, you'd know the smell."

"And then there's the part about my being irresistible to women," Myron said.

Win turned the page.

"So what's she up to?"

Win tapped his chin with his index finger. "What's the term you relationship people use? Oh, yes. Space. Perhaps she needs some space."

" 'Needing space' is usually a code phrase for the big kiss-off."

"Yes, well, whatever." Win crossed his legs. "You want me to look into it?"

"Into what?"

"What Ms. Collins might be up to."

"No."

"Fine," Win said. "Let's move on, shall we? Tell me about your encounter with the Federal Bureau of Investigation."

Myron recapped the interrogation.

"So we don't know what they wanted," Win said.

"Correct."

"Not a clue?"

"Nothing. Except that they were scared."

"Curious."

Myron nodded.

Win took a sip of tea, pinky up. Oh, the horrors that pinky had witnessed, partaken in, even. They sat in Win's formal dining room and used a silver tea set. Victorian mahogany table with lion-paw feet, silver tea set, silver milk pitcher, boxes of Cap'n Crunch and some new cereal called Oreo, which is exactly what you would imagine. "Theorizing at this juncture is a waste of time. I'll make some calls, see what I can find out."

"Thanks."

"I'm still not sure I see a connection between Stan Gibbs and our blood donor."

"It's a long shot," Myron agreed.

"More than that. A newspaper columnist makes up a story about a serial kidnapper and now—what?—we think the fictional character is the donor?"

"Stan Gibbs claims the story is real."

"Does he now?"

"Yes."

Win rubbed his chin. "Pray tell, why does he not defend himself?"

"No clue."

"Presumably because he is guilty," Win said. "Man is, above all, selfish. He's into self-preservation. It's instinctive. He does not martyr himself. He cares about one thing above all else: saving his hide."

"Assuming I agree with your sunny view of human nature, wouldn't you agree that man would lie to save himself?"

"Of course," Win said.

"So armed with this pretty decent defense—the idea that the serial kidnapper copycatted the novel—why wouldn't Stan use it to defend himself, even if he was guilty of plagiarism?"

Win nodded. "I like the way you're thinking."

"Cynically, yes."

The intercom buzzed. Win pressed the button, and the doorman announced Esperanza. A minute later, she swept into the room, grabbed a chair, and poured herself a bowl of Oreo cereal.

"Why do they always say it's 'part of this complete breakfast'?" Esperanza asked. "Every single time, every single cereal. What's all that about?"

Nobody replied.

Esperanza took a spoonful, looked at Win, head-gestured toward Myron. "I hate it when he's right," she said to Win.

"A bad omen," Win agreed.

Myron said, "I was right?"

She turned her gaze to Myron. "I did that school check on Dennis Lex. I tracked down any and all educational institutions any of his siblings or parents had gone to. Nothing. College, high school, middle school—even grammar school. No trace of Dennis Lex."

"But?" Myron said.

"Preschool."

"You're kidding me."

"Nope."

"You found his preschool?"

"I'm more than just a great piece of ass," Esperanza said.

Win said, "Not to me, my dear."

"You're sweet, Win."

Win bowed his head slightly.

"Miss Peggy Joyce," Esperanza said. "She still teaches and runs the Shady Wells Montessori School for Children in East Hampton."

"And she remembers Dennis Lex?" Myron said. "From thirty years ago?"

"Apparently." Esperanza shoved in another spoonful and tossed Myron a sheet of paper. "This is her address. She's expecting you this morning. Drive safely now, ya hear?"

22

The car phone rang.

"The old man is a lying sack of shit." It was Greg Downing.

"What?"

"The geezer is lying."

"You mean Nathan Mostoni?"

"Jesus Christ, what other old man have I been watching?"

Myron switched ears. "What makes you think he's lying, Greg?"

"Lots of things."

"Like?"

"Like starting with Mostoni never hearing from the bone marrow center. Does that sound logical to you?"

He thought of Karen Singh and her dedication and the stakes. "No," Myron said, "but it's like we said before—he might be confused."

"I don't think so."

"Why not?"

"Nathan Mostoni goes out plenty on his own, for one thing. Sometimes he acts loony, but other times, he seems just fine. He shops himself. He talks to people. He dresses like a normal person."

"That doesn't mean anything," Myron said.

"No? An hour ago he went out, right? So I got close to the house, right up against the back window, and I dialed that number, the one you got for the donor."

"And?"

"And I hear a phone inside the house ringing."

That made Myron pause.

"So what do you think we should do?" Greg asked.

"I'm not sure. Have you seen anybody else at the house?"

"Nobody. Mostoni goes out but nobody's been here. And I tell you something else. He looks younger now. I don't know how else to explain it. It's weird. You making any headway on your end?"

"I'm not sure."

"That's some answer, Myron."

"The only one I got."

"So what do you think we should do about Mostoni?"

"I'll have Esperanza do a background check. In the meantime, stay on him."

"Time's a-ticking away here, Myron."

"I know that. I'll be in touch."

He disconnected the call and flipped on the radio. Chaka Khan was singing "Ain't Nobody Love You Better." If you can listen to that one without moving your feet, you got some serious rhythm issues. He took the Long Island Expressway east, which was shockingly clear today. Usually the road was more or less a parking lot that swayed forward every couple of minutes.

People always tell you that the Hamptons, the swanky Long Island summer spot where Manhattanites get away from it all by being with other Manhattanites, is best in the off season. You always here that about vacation spots. People, mostly vacationers themselves, whine through the high-season months, waiting to reach this apex of a theoretically swarmless nirvana. But—and this was the part Myron never understood—no one is ever in the Hamptons in the off months. No one. Downtown is dead to the point of craving tumbleweeds. Shop owners sigh and discount nothing. The restaurants are less crowded, sure, but they're also closed. And hey, let's be honest here, the weather and beaches and even the people-watching are big draws here. Who goes to a Long Island beach in the winter?

The school was in a residential neighborhood with older, more modest homes—a place where the true Long Island regulars, none of whom hang out with Alec and Kim at Nick and Toni's, resided. Myron parked in a church lot and followed the signs down the steps into the rectory's basement. A young woman, a hall monitor of sorts, greeted Myron at the landing. He gave her his name and said he was here to see Ms. Joyce. The young woman nodded and told him to follow her.

The corridor was silent. Strange when one considered that this was a preschool. *Preschool.* Another new term. In Myron's day, they had called them nursery schools. Myron wondered when the name had changed and what group had considered the term *nursery school* somehow discriminatory. Professional RNs? Breast-feeding mothers? Bottle-fed infants maybe?

Still silent. Perhaps it was vacation or naptime. Myron was about to ask the young hall monitor when she opened a door. He looked in. Wrong-a-mundo. The room was chock full of small children, probably twenty give or take, and they were all working independently and in total silence. The older teacher smiled at Myron. She whispered to the little boy she was working with—he was doing something with blocks and letters—and stood.

"Hello," she said to Myron, speaking softly.

"Hi," Myron whispered back.

She leaned toward the young monitor. "Miss Simmons, will you help Mrs. McLaughlin?"

"Of course."

Peggy Joyce wore an open yellow sweater over a buttoned-at-the-neck blouse. The collar was frilly. She had half-moon glasses dangling from a chain around her neck. "We can chat in my office."

"Okay." He followed her. The place was silent as, well, a place without children. Myron asked, "Do you give those kids Valium?"

She smiled. "Just a little Montessori."

"A little what?"

"You don't have children, do you?"

The question caused a pang, but he answered in the negative.

"It's a teaching philosophy created by Dr. Maria Montessori, Italy's first female physician."

"It seems to work."

"I suppose."

"Do the children act like this at home?"

"Good Lord, no. Truth be told, it doesn't translate into the real world. But few things do."

They moved into the office, which consisted of a wooden desk, three chairs, one file cabinet.

"How long have you taught here?" Myron asked.

"I'm in my forty-third year."

"Wow."

"Yes."

"I guess you've seen lots of changes?"

"In kids? Almost none. Children don't change, Mr. Bolitar. A five-year-old is still a five-year-old."

"Still innocent."

She cocked her head. " 'Innocent' isn't the word I would use. Children are total id. They are perhaps the most naturally vicious creatures on God's green earth."

"Strange outlook for a preschool teacher."

"Just an honest one."

"So what word would you use?"

She thought about it. "If pressed, I'd say 'unformed.' Or maybe 'undeveloped.' Like a picture you've already taken but haven't processed yet."

Myron nodded, though he had no idea what she meant. There was something about Peggy Joyce that was a little, well, scary.

"Do you remember that book *All I Really Need to Know I Learned in Kindergarten*?" she asked him.

"Yes."

"It's true, but not in the way you think. School removes children from their warm parental cocoon. School teaches them to bully or be bullied. School teaches them how to be cruel to one another. School teaches them that Mommy and Daddy lied to them when they told them that they were special and unique."

Myron said nothing.

"You don't agree?"

"I don't teach preschool."

"That's sidestepping, Mr. Bolitar."

Myron shrugged. "They learn socialization. That's a hard lesson. And like every hard lesson, you have to get it wrong before you can get it right."

"They learn boundaries, in other words?"

"Yes."

"Interesting. And perhaps true. But you remember when I was giving the film-processing example earlier?"

"Yes."

"School only processes the picture. It doesn't snap it."

"Okay," Myron said, not wanting to follow her train of thought.

"What I mean is, everything is pretty much decided by the time these children leave here and enter kindergarten. I can tell who will be successful and who will fail, who will end up happy and who will end up in prison, and ninety percent of the time I'm right. Maybe Hollywood and video games have an influence, I don't know. But I can usually tell which kid will be watching too many violent movies or playing too many violent games."

"You can tell all this by the time they're five years old?"

"Pretty much, yes."

"And you feel that's it? That they don't have the ability to change?"

"The ability? Oh, probably. But they're already on a path, and while they may still be able to change it, the majority do not. Staying on the path is easier."

"So let me ask you the eternal question: Is it nature or nurture?"

She smiled. "I get asked that all the time."

"And?"

"I answer nurture. Know why?"

Myron shook his head.

"Believing in nurture is like believing in God. You might be wrong, but you might as well cover your bases." She folded her hands and leaned forward. "Now, what can I do for you, Mr. Bolitar?"

"Do you remember a student named Dennis Lex?"

"I remember all my students. Does that surprise you?"

Myron didn't want her going off on another tangent. "Did you teach the other Lex children?"

"I taught them all. Their father made a lot of changes after his book became a bestseller. But he kept them here."

"So what can you tell me about Dennis Lex?"

She sat back and regarded him as though seeing him for the first time. "I don't want to be rude, but I'm wondering when you're going to tell me what this is all about. I'm talking to you, Mr. Bolitar—and breaching confidences, I suspect—because I think you're here for a very specific reason."

"What reason is that, Ms. Joyce?"

Her eyes had a steely glint. "Don't play games with me, Mr. Bolitar."

She was right. "I'm trying to find Dennis Lex."

Peggy Joyce kept still.

"I know this sounds weird," he went on. "But as far as I can tell, he fell off the earth after preschool."

She stared straight ahead, though Myron had no idea at what. There were no photographs on the walls, no diplomas, no drawings by little hands. Just cold wall. "Not after," she said finally. "During."

There was a knock on the door. Peggy Joyce said, "Come in." The young hall monitor, Miss Simmons, entered with a little boy. His head was down and he'd been crying. "James needs a little time," Miss Simmons said.

Peggy Joyce nodded. "Let him lie on the mat."

James eyed Myron and left with Miss Simmons.

Myron turned to Peggy Joyce. "What happened to Dennis Lex?"

"It's a question I've been waiting for someone to ask for more than thirty years," she said.

"What's the answer?"

"First, tell me why you're looking for him."

"I'm trying to find a bone marrow donor. I think it might be Dennis Lex." He gave her as few details as he could. When he finished, she put a bony hand to her face.

"I don't think I can help you," she said. "It was so long ago."

"Please, Ms. Joyce. A child will die if I don't find him. You're my only lead."

"You spoke to his family?"

"Only his sister Susan."

"What did she tell you?"

"Nothing."

"I'm not sure what I can add."

"You could start by telling me what Dennis was like."

She sighed and neatly arranged her hands on her thighs. "He was like the other Lex children—very bright, thoughtful, contemplative, perhaps a bit too much so for so young a child. With most students, I try to get them to grow up a bit. With the Lex children, that was never an issue."

Myron nodded, trying to encourage.

"Dennis was the youngest. You probably know that. He was here the same time as his brother Bronwyn. Susan was older." She stopped, looked lost.

"What happened to him?"

"One day he and Bronwyn didn't come to school. I got a call from their father saying that he was taking them on an unplanned vacation."

"Where?"

"He didn't say. He wasn't being very specific."

"Okay, go on."

"That's pretty much it, Mr. Bolitar. Two weeks later, Bronwyn came back to school. I never saw Dennis again."

"You called his father?"

"Of course."

"What did he say?"

"He told me that Dennis wouldn't be coming back."

"Did you ask him why?"

"Of course. But . . . did you ever meet Raymond Lex?"

"No."

"You didn't question a man like that. He mentioned something about home schooling. When I pressed, he made it clear it was none of my concern. Over the years, I've tried to keep track of the family, even when they moved out of the area. But like you, I never heard anything about Dennis."

"What did you think happened?"

She looked at him. "I assumed he was dead."

Her words, though not all that surprising, worked like a vacuum, sucking the room dry, forcing out the air.

"Why?" Myron asked.

"I figured that he was ill, and that was why he was pulled out of school."

"Why would Mr. Lex try to hide something like that?"

"I don't know. After his novel became a bestseller, he became private to the point of paranoia. Are you sure this donor you're looking for is Dennis Lex?"

"Not sure, no."

Peggy Joyce snapped her fingers. "Oh, wait, I have something you may find interesting." She stood and opened a file drawer. She sifted through it, pulled something out, studied it for a moment. Her elbow smacked the drawer closed. "This was taken two months before Dennis left us."

She handed him an old class photograph, the color not so much fading as greening from age. Fifteen kids flanked by two teachers, one a far younger Peggy Joyce. The years had not been unkind to her, but they'd passed anyway. A small black sign with the white lettering read SHADY WELLS MONTESSORI SCHOOL and the year.

"Which one is Dennis?"

She pointed to a boy sitting in the front row. He had a Prince Valiant cut and a face-splitting smile that never quite hit his eyes. "Can I have this?"

"If you think it will help."

"It might."

She nodded. "I better get back to my students."

"Thank you."

"Do you remember your preschool, Mr. Bolitar?"

Myron nodded. "Parkview Nursery School in Livingston, New Jersey."

"How about your teachers? Do you remember them at all?"

Myron thought about it. "No."

She nodded as though he'd answered correctly. "Good luck," she said.

23

AgeComp. Or age-progression software, if you prefer.

Myron had learned a bit about it when searching for a missing woman named Lucy Mayor. The key was in the digital imaging. All Myron had to do—or in the case of their office, all Esperanza had to do—was take the class photograph and scan it into the computer. Then, using common software programs like Photoshop or Picture Publisher, you blow up the face of young Dennis Lex. AgeComp, a software program constantly being retooled and perfected by missing-children organizations, does the rest. Using advanced mathematical algorithms, AgeComp stretches, merges, and blends digital photographs of missing children and produces a color image of what they might look like today.

Naturally, a lot is left to chance. Scarring, facial fractures, facial hair, cosmetic surgery, hairstyle or, in the case of some of the older ones, male pattern baldness. Still, the class photo could be a serious lead.

When he was back in Manhattan, the cell phone rang.

"I spoke to the feds," Win said.

"And?"

"Your impression is correct."

"What impression?"

"They are indeed frightened."

"Did you speak to PT?"

"I did. He put me onto the right person. They requested a face-to-face."

"When?"

"Pretty pronto. We are, in fact, waiting in your office."

"The feds are in my office right now?"

"Affirmative."

"Be there in five."

More like ten. When the elevator opened, Esperanza was sitting at Big Cyndi's desk.

"How many?" he asked.

"Three," Esperanza said. "One blond woman, one extra-strength dork, one nice suit."

"Win's with them?"

"Yep."

He handed her the photograph and pointed to Dennis Lex's face. "How long before we could get an age progression on this?"

"Jesus, when was this taken?"

"Thirty years ago."

Esperanza frowned. "You know anything about age progression?"

"Some."

"It's mostly used to find missing kids," she said. "And it's usually used to age them five, maybe ten years."

"But we can get something, right?"

"Something very rough, yeah maybe." She flicked on the scanner and placed the photo facedown. "If they're in the lab, we'll probably have it by the end of the day. I'll crop it and e-mail it over."

"Do it later," he said, gesturing toward the door. "Mustn't keep the feds waiting. Our tax dollars and all that."

"You want me in there?"

"You're a part of everything that goes on here, Esperanza. Of course I want you in there."

"I see," she said. Then: "Is this the part where I blink back tears because you're making me feel oh-so-special?"

Wiseass.

Myron opened his office door. Esperanza followed. Win sat behind Myron's desk, probably so that none of the feds would. Win could be territorial—just one of the ways he was like a Doberman. Kimberly Green and Rick Peck rose with lack-of-sleep-luggage eyes and squared-off smiles. The third fed stayed in his seat, not moving, not even turning to see who'd entered. Myron saw his face and felt a jolt.

Whoa.

Win watched Myron, an amused smile curling the ends of his mouth. Eric Ford, deputy director of the Federal Bureau of Investigation, was the man in the suit. His presence meant one thing: This was serious big-time.

Kimberly Green pointed at Esperanza. "What's she doing in here?"

"She's my partner," Myron said. "And it's not polite to point."

"Your partner? You think this is a business transaction?"

"She stays," Myron said.

"No," Kimberly Green said. She was still wearing the ball-and-chain earrings, still the jeans and black turtleneck, but the jacket now was spearmint green. "We're not exactly thrilled talking to you and Cheekbones boy over there"—she gestured toward Win—"but at least you have some clearance. We don't know her. She goes."

Win's smile spread and his eyebrows did a quick up-and-down. Cheekbones. He liked that.

"She goes," Green said again.

Esperanza shrugged. "No biggie," she said.

Myron was about to say something, but Win shook his head. He was right. Save it for the important battles.

Esperanza left. Win got up and gave Myron the chair. He stood on Myron's right, arms crossed, totally at ease. Green and Peck fidgeted. Myron turned to Eric Ford. "I don't think we've met."

"But you know who I am," Ford said. He had one of those smooth soft-rock-DJ voices.

"Yes."

"And I know who you are," he said. "So what would be the point?"

Oookay. Myron glanced back at Win. Win shrugged.

Ford nodded at Kimberly Green. She cleared her throat. "For the record," she said, "we don't think we should have to go through this."

"Through what?"

"Telling you about our investigation. Debriefing you. As a good citizen, you should be willing to cooperate with our investigation because it's the right thing to do."

Myron looked at Win and said, "Oh boy."

"Some aspects of an investigation need to be contained," she continued. "You and Mr. Lockwood should understand that better than most. You should be anxious to cooperate with any federal investigation. You should respect what we're trying to do here."

"Right, okay, we respect. Can we skip ahead, please? You looked us up. You know we'll keep our mouths shut. Otherwise none of us would be here."

She folded her hands and put them in her lap. Peck kept his head down and scribbled notes, Lord knew on what. Myron's decor maybe. "What we say here cannot leave this room. It is classified to the highest—"

"Skipping," Myron said with an impatient hand roll. "Skipping."

Green slid her eyes toward Ford. He nodded again. She took a deep breath and said, "We have Stan Gibbs under surveillance."

She stopped, settled back. Myron waited a few seconds and then said, "Label me surprised."

"That information is classified," she said.

"Then I'll leave it out of my diary."

"He isn't supposed to know."

"Well, that's usually implied with words like 'classified' and 'surveillance.' "

"But Gibbs does know. He loses us whenever he really wants. Because when he's out in public, we can't get too close."

"Why can't you get too close?"

"He'll see us."

"But he already knows you're there?"

"Yes."

Myron looked up at Win. "Wasn't there an Abbott and Costello skit that went like this?"

"Marx Brothers," Win said.

"If we were out in the open about tailing him," Green said, "the fact that he's a target could become public knowledge."

"And you're trying to contain that?"

"Yes."

"How long has he been under surveillance?"

"Well, it's not that simple. He's been out of range a lot—"

"How long?"

Again Green looked at Ford. Again Ford nodded. She balled her hands into fists. "Since the first article on the kidnappings appeared."

Myron sat back, feeling something akin to a head rush. He shouldn't have been surprised, but damned if he wasn't. The article came flooding back to him—the sudden disappearances, the awful phone calls, the constant, eternal anguish, the picket-fenced lives suddenly bulldozed over by inexplicable evil.

"My God," Myron said. "Stan Gibbs was telling the truth."

"We never said that," Kimberly Green said.

"I see. So you've been tailing him because you don't like his syntax?"

Silence.

"The articles were true," Myron said. "And you've known it all along."

"What we did or did not know is not your concern."

Myron shook his head. "Unbelievable," he said. "So let me see if I got this straight. You have a serial psycho out there who snatches people out of the blue and torments their families. You want to keep a lid on it because if word got out to the public, you'd have a panic situation. Then the psycho goes directly to Stan Gibbs and suddenly the story is in the public domain . . ." Myron's voice died off, seeing that his logic trail had hit a major pothole. He frowned and forged ahead. "I don't know how that old novel or the plagiarism charges tie in. But either way, you decided to ride it. You let Gibbs get fired and disgraced, probably in part because you were pissed off that he upset your investigation. But mostly"—he spotted what he thought was a clearing—"but mostly you did it so

you could watch him. If the psycho contacted him once, you figured, he'd probably do it again—especially if the articles had been
discredited."

Kimberly Green said, "Wrong."

"But close."

"No."

"The kidnappings Gibbs wrote about took place, right?"

She hesitated, gave Ford an eye check. "We can't verify all of his
facts."

"Jesus, I'm not taking a deposition here," Myron said. "Was his
column true, yes or no?"

"We've told you enough," she said. "It's your turn."

"You haven't told me squat."

"And you've told us less."

Negotiating. Life is being a sports agent—constant negotiating.
He had learned the importance of leverage, of doling out, of being
fair. People forget that last one, and it always costs you in the end.
The best negotiator isn't the one who gets the whole pie while leaving
scant crumbs behind. The best negotiator is the one who gets what
he wants while keeping the other side happy. So normally, Myron
would dole out a little something here. Classic give-and-take. But not
this time. He knew better. Once he told them the reason for his visit
to Stan Gibbs, his leverage would be zippo.

The best negotiator, like the best species, also knows how to adapt.

"First answer my question," Myron said. "Yes or no, was the story
Stan Gibbs wrote true?"

"There is no yes-or-no answer to that," she said. "Parts were true.
Parts were not true."

"For example?"

"The young couple was from Iowa, not Minnesota. The missing
father had three children, not two." She stopped, folded her hands.

"But there have been kidnappings?"

"We knew about those two," she said. "We had no information
about the missing college student."

"Probably because the psycho got to her parents. They probably
never reported it."

"That's our theory," Kimberly Green said. "But we don't know
for sure. Still, there are major discrepancies. The families swear they

never spoke to him, for example. Many of the phone calls and events don't match what we know to be true."

Myron saw more clearing. "So you asked Gibbs about it? About his sources?"

"Yes."

"And he refused to tell you anything."

"That's right."

"So you destroyed him."

"No."

"The one part I don't get is the plagiarism," Myron said. "I mean, did you guys somehow set that up? I can't see how. Unless you made up a book and . . . no, that's too far-fetched. So what's the deal with that?"

Kimberly Green leaned forward. "Tell us why you went to his apartment."

"Not until—"

"For several months we couldn't find Stan Gibbs," she interrupted. "We think maybe he left the country. But since he's moved into that condo, he's always alone. As I said before, he loses us sometimes. But he never accepts visitors. Several people have tracked him down. Old friends even. They come to his door or they call on the phone. And you know what always happens, Myron?"

Myron didn't like her tone of voice.

"He sends them away. Every single time. Stan Gibbs sees no one. Except you."

Myron looked up at Win. Win nodded very slowly. Myron took a look at Eric Ford before going back to Kimberly Green. "You think I'm the kidnapper?"

She leaned back with a partial shrug, looking satiated. Turning the tables and all that. "You tell us," she said.

Win started for the door. Myron rose and followed.

"Where the hell are you two going?" Green asked.

Win grabbed the knob. Myron headed around the desk and said, "I'm a suspect. I'm not talking until I have an attorney present. If you'll excuse me."

"Hey, we're just talking here," Kimberly Green said. "I never said I thought you were the kidnapper."

"Sounded that way to me," Myron said. "Win?"

"He snatches hearts," Win told her, "not people."

"You got something to hide?" Green said.

"Just his fondness for cyber pornography," Win said. Then: "Oops."

Kimberly Green stood and blocked Myron's path. "We think we know about the missing college student," she said, her eyes locked hard on his. "Do you want to know how we found out about it?"

Myron kept still.

"Through her father. He got a call from the kidnapper. I don't know what was said. He hasn't said a word since. He's catatonic. Whatever that psycho said to that girl's father put him in a padded room."

Myron felt the room shrink, the walls closing in.

"We haven't found any bodies yet, but we're pretty sure he kills them," she went on. "He kidnaps them, does Lord knows what, and makes the families suffer interminably. And you know he won't stop."

Myron kept his eyes steady. "What's your point?"

"This isn't funny."

"No," he said. "It's not. So stop playing stupid games."

She said nothing.

"I want to hear it from your mouth," Myron said. "Do you think I'm involved in this, yes or no?"

Eric Ford took this one. "No."

Kimberly Green slid back into her chair, her eyes never leaving Myron's. Eric Ford made a big hand gesture. "Please sit down."

Myron and Win moved back to their original positions.

Eric Ford said, "The novel exists. So do the passages Stan Gibbs plagiarized. The book was sent to our office anonymously—more specifically, to Special Agent Green here. We admit that we found that issue confusing at first. On the one hand, Gibbs knows about the kidnappings. On the other hand, he doesn't know everything and he clearly copied excerpts from an old, out-of-print mystery novel."

"There's an explanation," Myron said. "The kidnapper might have read the book. He might have identified with the character, become a copycat of sorts."

"We considered that possibility," Eric Ford said, "but we don't believe that's the case here."

"Why not?"

"It's complicated."

"Does it involve trigonometry?"

"You still think this is a joking manner?"

"You still think it's smart to play games?"

Ford closed his eyes. Green looked on edge. Peck continued scribbling notes. When Ford opened his eyes, he said, "We don't believe Stan Gibbs made up the crimes," he said. "We believe he perpetrated them."

Myron felt a pow. He looked up at Win. Nothing.

"You have some background in the criminal mind, do you not?" Ford asked.

Myron might have nodded.

"Well, here we have an old pattern with a new twist. Arsonists love to watch firemen put out the blaze. Ofttimes they're even the ones who report the fire. They play the good Samaritan. Murderers love to attend the funerals of their victims. We videotape funerals. I'm sure you know this."

Myron nodded again.

"Sometimes killers make themselves part of the story." Eric Ford was gesturing a lot now, his knotted hands rising and falling as though this were a press conference in too big a room. "They claim to be witnesses. They become the innocent bystanders who happened to find the body in the brush. You're familiar with this moth-near-the-flame phenomenon, are you not?"

"Yes."

"So what could be more enticing than being the only columnist to report the story? Can you imagine the high? How mind-bogglingly close to the investigation you'd be. The brilliance of your deception—for a psychotic, it's almost too delicious. And if you are perpetrating these crimes to get attention, then here you get a double dose. Attention as the serial kidnapper, one. Attention as the brilliant reporter with the scoop and possible Pulitzer, two. You even get the bonus attention of a man bravely defending the First Amendment."

Myron was holding his breath. "That's a hell of a theory," he said.

"You want more?"

"Yes."

"Why won't he answer any of our questions?"

"You said it yourself. First Amendment."

"He's not a lawyer or psychiatrist."

"But he is a reporter," Myron said.

"What kind of monster would continue to protect his source in this situation?"

"I know plenty."

"We spoke to the victims' families. They swore they never spoke to him."

"They could be lying. Maybe the kidnapper told them to say that."

"Okay, then why hasn't Gibbs done more to defend himself against the charges of plagiarism? He could have fought them. He could have even provided some detail that would have proved he was telling the truth. But no, instead he goes silent. Why?"

"You think it's because he's the kidnapper? The moth flew too close to the flame and is licking his wounds in darkness?"

"Do you have a better explanation?"

Myron said nothing.

"Lastly, there's the murder of his mistress, Melina Garston."

"What about it?"

"Think it through, Myron. We put the screws to him. Maybe he expected that, maybe he didn't. Either way, the courts don't see everything his way. You don't know about the court findings, do you?"

"Not really, no."

"That's because they were sealed. In part, the judge demanded that Gibbs show some proof he had been in contact with the killer. He finally said that Melina Garston would back him."

"And she did, right?"

"Yes. She claimed to have met the subject of his story."

"I still don't understand. If she backed him up, why would he kill her?"

"The day before Melina Garston died, she called her father. She told him that she lied."

Myron sat back, tried to take it all in.

Eric Ford said, "He's back now, Myron. Stan Gibbs has finally surfaced. While he was gone, the Sow the Seeds kidnapper was gone too. But this brand of psycho never stops on his own. He's going to strike again and soon. So before that happens, you better talk to us. Why were you at his condominium?"

Myron thought about it but not for long. "I was looking for someone."

"Who?"

"A missing bone marrow donor. He could save a child's life."

Ford looked at him steadily. "I assume that Jeremy Downing is the child in question."

So much for being vague, but Myron was not surprised. Phone records probably. Or maybe there had indeed been a tail when he visited Emily's. "Yes. And before I go on, I want your word that you will keep me in the loop."

Kimberly Green said, "You're not a part of this investigation."

"I'm not interested in your kidnapper. I'm interested in my donor. You help me find him, I'll tell you what I know."

"We agree," Ford said, waving Kimberly Green silent. "So how does Stan Gibbs fit in with your donor?"

Myron reviewed it for them. He started with Davis Taylor and then moved on to Dennis Lex and then the cryptic phone call. They kept their faces steady, Green and Peck scratching on their pads, but there was a definite jolt when he mentioned the Lex family.

They asked a few follow-up questions, like why he got involved in the first place. He said that Emily was an old friend. He wasn't about to go into the patrimony issue. Myron could see Green getting antsy. He had served his purpose. She was anxious to get out and start tracking things down.

A few minutes later, the feds snapped their pads closed and rose. "We're on it," Ford said. He looked straight at Myron. "And we'll find your donor. You stay out."

Myron nodded and wondered if he could. After they left, Win took a seat in front of Myron's desk.

"Why do I feel like I was picked up at a bar and now it's the next morning and the guy just handed me the 'I'll call you' line?" Myron asked.

"Because that's precisely what you are," Win said. "Slut."

"Think they're holding something back?"

"Without question."

"Something big?"

"Gargantuan," Win said.

"Not much we can do about it now."

"Nope," Win said. "Nothing at all."

24

Myron's mom met him at the front door.

"I'm picking up the takeout," Mom said.

"You?"

She put her hands on her hips and shot him her best wither. "There a problem with that?"

"No, it's just . . ." He decided to drop it. "Nothing."

Mom kissed his cheek and fished through her purse for the car keys. "I'll be back in a half hour. Your father is in the back." She gave him the imploring eyes. "Alone."

"Okay," he said.

"No one else is here."

"Uh-huh."

"If you catch my drift."

"It's caught."

"You'll be alone."

"Caught, Mom. Caught."

"It'll be an opportunity—"

"Mom."

She put her hands up. "Okay, okay, I'm going."

He walked around the side of the house, past the garbage cans and recycling bins, and found Dad on the deck. The deck was sanded redwood with built-in benches and resin furniture and a Weber 500 barbecue, all brought to being during the famed Kitchen Expansion of 1994. Dad was bent over a railing with a screwdriver in his hand. For a moment, Myron fell back to those "weekend projects" with Dad, some of which lasted almost an entire hour. They would go out with toolbox in tow, Dad bent over like he was now, muttering obscenities under his breath. Myron's sole task consisted of handing Dad tools like a scrub nurse in the operating room, the whole exercise boring as hell, shuffling his feet in the sun, sighing heavily, finding new angles from which to stand.

"Hey," Myron said.

Dad looked up, smiled, put down the tool. "Screw loose," he said. "But let's not talk about your mother."

Myron laughed. They found molded-resin chairs around a table impaled by a blue umbrella. In front of them lay Bolitar Stadium, a small patch of green-to-brown grass that had hosted countless, oft-solo football games, baseball games, soccer games, Wiffle ball games (probably the most popular sport at Bolitar Stadium), rugby scrums, badminton, kickball, and that favorite pastime for the future sadist, bombardment. Myron spotted Mom's former vegetable garden—the word *vegetable* here being used to describe three annual soggy tomatoes and two flaccid zucchinis; it was now slightly more overgrown than a Cambodian rice paddy. To their right were the rusted remnants of their old tetherball pole. Tetherball. Now, there was a really dumb game.

Myron cleared his throat and put his hands on the table. "How you feeling?"

Dad gave a big nod. "Good. You?"

"Good."

The silence floated down, puffy and relaxed. Silence with a father can be like that. You drift back and you're young and you're safe, safe in that all-encompassing way only a child can be with his father. You still see him hovering in your darkened doorway, the silent sentinel to your adolescence, and you sleep the sleep of the naive, the innocent, the unformed. When you get older, you realize that this safety was just an illusion, another child's perception, like the size of your backyard.

Or maybe, if you're lucky, you don't.

Dad looked older today, the flesh on his face more sagged, the once-knotted biceps spongy under the T-shirt, starting to waste. Myron wondered how to start. Dad closed his eyes for a three count, opened them, and said, "Don't."

"What?"

"Your mother is about as subtle as a White House press release," Dad said. "I mean, when was the last time she picked up the takeout instead of me?"

"Has she ever?"

"Once," Dad said. "When I had a fever of a hundred and four. And even then she whined about it."

"Where's she going?"

"She has me on a special diet now, you know. Because of the chest pains." *Chest pains.* Euphemism for *heart attack.*

"Yeah, I figured that."

"She's even tried cooking a little. She told you?"

Myron nodded. "She baked something for me yesterday."

Dad's body went stiff. "By God," he said. "Her own son?"

"It was pretty scary."

"The woman has many, many talents, but they could airdrop that stuff into starving African nations and no one would eat it."

"So where's she going?"

"Your mother is high on some crazy Middle Eastern health food place. Just opened in West Orange. Get this, it's called Ayatollah Granola."

Myron gave him flat eyes.

"Hand to God, that's the name. Food is almost as dry as that Thanksgiving turkey your mother made when you were eight. You remember that?"

"At night," Myron said. "It still haunts my sleep."

Dad looked off again. "She left us alone so we could talk, right?"

"Right."

He made a face. "I hate when she does stuff like that. She means well, your mother. We both know that. But let's not do it, okay?"

Myron shrugged. "You say so."

"She thinks I don't like growing old. News flash: No one does. My friend Herschel Diamond—you remember Heshy?"

"Sure."

"Big guy, right? Played semipro football when we were young. So Heshy, he calls me and he says now that I'm retired, I can do tai chi with him. I mean, tai chi? What the hell is that anyway? If I want to move slowly, I have to drive down to the Y to do it with a bunch of old yentas? I mean, what's that about? I tell him no. So then Heshy, this great athlete, Myron, he could hit a softball a country mile, this marvelous big ox, he tells me we can walk together. Walk. At the mall. Speedwalk, he calls it. At the mall, for chrissake. Heshy always hated the place—now he wants us to trot around like a bunch of jackasses in matching sweatsuits and expensive walking shoes. Pump our arms with these little *faigelah* barbells. Walking shoes, he calls them. What the hell is that anyway? I never had a pair of shoes I couldn't walk in, am I right?"

He waited for an answer. Myron said, "As rain."

Dad stood up. He grabbed a screwdriver and feigned working. "So now, because I don't want to move like an old Chinaman or walk around a godforsaken mall in overpriced sneakers, your mother thinks I'm not adjusting. You hear what I'm saying?"

"Yes."

Dad stayed bent, fiddling a little more with the railing. In the distance, Myron heard children playing. A bike bell rang. Someone laughed. A lawn mower purred. Dad's voice, when he finally spoke again, was surprisingly soft. "You know what your mother really wants us to do?" he said.

"What?"

"She wants you and I to reverse roles." Dad finally looked up through his heavy-lidded eyes. "I don't want to reverse roles, Myron. I'm the father. I like being the father. Let me stay that, okay?"

Myron found it hard to speak. "Sure, Dad."

His father put his head back down, the gray wisps upright in the humidity, his breathing tool-work heavy, and Myron again felt something open up his chest and grab hold of his heart. He looked at this man he'd loved for so long, who'd gone without complaint to that damn muggy warehouse in Newark for more than thirty years, and

Myron realized that he didn't know him. He didn't know what his father dreamed about, what he wanted to be when he was a kid, what he thought about his own life.

Dad kept working on the screw. Myron watched him.

Promise me you won't die, okay? Just promise me that.

He almost said it out loud.

Dad straightened himself out and studied his handiwork. Satisfied, he sat back down. They started talking about the Knicks and the recent Kevin Costner movie and the new Nelson DeMille book. They put away the toolbox. They had some iced tea. They lounged side by side in matching molded-resin chaises. An hour passed. They fell into a comfortable silence. Myron fingered the condensation on his glass. He could hear his father's breathing, moderately wheezy. Dusk had settled in, bruising the sky purple, the trees going a burnt orange.

Myron closed his eyes and said, "I got a hypothetical for you."

"Oh?"

"What would you do if you found out you weren't my real father?"

Dad's eyebrows went skyward. "You trying to tell me something?"

"Just a hypothetical. Suppose you found out right now that I wasn't your biological son. How would you react?"

"Depends," Dad said.

"On?"

"How you reacted."

"It wouldn't make a difference to me," Myron said.

Dad smiled.

"What?" Myron said.

"Easy for both of us to say it wouldn't matter. But news like that is a bombshell. You can't predict what someone will do when a bomb lands. When I was in Korea—" Dad stopped, Myron sat up. "Well, you never knew how someone would react . . ." His voice tailed off. He coughed into his fist and then started up again. "Guys you were sure would be heroes completely lost it—and vice versa. That's why you can't ask stuff like this as a hypothetical."

Myron looked at his father. His father kept his eyes on the grass, taking another deep sip. "You never talk about Korea," Myron said.

"I do," Dad said.

"Not with me."

"No, not with you."

"Why not?"

"It's what I fought for. So we wouldn't have to talk about it."

It didn't make sense and Myron understood.

"There a reason you raised this particular hypothetical?" Dad asked.

"No."

Dad nodded. He knew it was a lie, but he wouldn't push it. They settled back and watched the familiar surroundings.

"Tai chi isn't so bad," Myron said. "It's a martial art. Like tae kwon do. I've been thinking of taking it up myself."

Dad took another sip. Myron sneaked a glance. Something on his father's face began to quiver. Was Dad indeed getting smaller, more fragile—or was it like the backyard and safety, again the shifting perception of a child turned adult?

"Dad . . . ?"

"Let's go inside," his father said, standing. "We stay out much longer, one of us is going to get misty and say, 'Wanna play catch?' "

Myron bit off a laugh and followed him inside. Mom came home not long after that, lugging two bags of food as though they were stone tablets. "Everybody hungry?" she called out.

"Starving," Dad said. "I'm so hungry I could eat a vegetarian."

"Very funny, Al."

"Or even your cooking . . ."

"Ha-ha," Mom said.

". . . though I'd prefer the vegetarian."

"Stop it, Al, I'm going to phlegm up, you keep making me laugh like this." Mom dropped the bags onto the kitchen counter. "See, Myron? It's a good thing your mother is shallow."

"Shallow?" Myron asked.

"If I judged a man on brains or sense of humor," Mom continued, "you'd have never been born."

"Right-o," Dad said with a hearty smile. "But one look at your old man in a bathing suit and whammo—all mine."

"Oh please," Mom said.

"Yes," Myron said. "Please."

They both looked at him. Mom cleared her throat. "So did you two, uh, have a nice talk?"

"We talked," Dad said. "It was very life-affirming. I see the errors of my ways."

"I'm being serious."

"So am I. I see everything differently now."

She put her arms around his waist and nuzzled him. "So you'll call Heshy?"

"I'll call Heshy," he said.

"Promise."

"Yes, Ellen, I promise."

"You'll go to the Y and do jai alai with him?"

"Tai chi," Dad corrected.

"What?"

"It's called tai chi, not jai alai."

"I thought it was jai alai."

"Tai chi. Jai alai is the game with the curved rackets down in Florida."

"That's shuffleboard, Al."

"Not shuffleboard. The other thing with the sticks. And the gambling."

"Tai chi?" Mom said, testing it for sound. "Are you sure?"

"I think so."

"But you're not positive?"

"No, I'm not positive," Dad said. "Maybe you're right. Maybe it is called jai alai."

The name debate continued for a while. Myron didn't bother correcting them. Never cut in on that strange dance known as marital discourse. They ate the health food. It was indeed nasty. They laughed a lot. His parents must have said "You don't know what you're talking about" to each other fifty times; maybe it was a euphemism for "I love you."

Eventually Myron said good night. Mom kissed his cheek and made herself scarce. Dad walked him to the car. The night was silent save a lone dribbling basketball somewhere on Darby Road or maybe Coddington Terrace. A nice sound. When he hugged his father good-bye, Myron again noticed that his father felt smaller, less substantial. Myron held on a little longer than usual. For the first time he felt like the bigger man, the stronger man, and he suddenly remembered what Dad had said about reversing roles. So he held on in the dark. Time passed. Dad patted his back. Myron kept his eyes closed and held on tighter. Dad stroked his hair and shushed him. Just for a little while. Just until the roles reversed themselves again, returning both of them to where they belonged.

25

Granite Man was waiting outside the Dakota.

Myron spotted him from his car. He picked up the cell phone and called Win. "I have company."

"A rather large gentleman, yes," Win said. "Two cohorts are parked across the street in a corporate vehicle owned by the Lex family."

"I'll leave the cell phone on."

"They confiscated it last time," Win said.

"Yes."

"Likely they'll do the same."

"We'll improvise."

"Your funeral," Win said, and hung up.

Myron parked in the lot and approached Granite Man.

"Mrs. Lex would like to see you," Granite Man said.

"Do you know what she wants?" Myron asked.

Granite Man ignored the question.

"Maybe she saw me flexing on the security tape," Myron said. "Wanted to get to know me better."

Granite Man did not laugh. "You ever think about doing this comedy thing professionally?"

"There have been offers."

"I bet. Get in the car."

"Okay, but I have a curfew, you know. And I never French-kiss on the first date. Just so we understand each other."

Granite Man shook his head. "Man, I'd like to waste you."

They got in the car. Two blue-blazers sat in front. The car ride was silent except for Granite Man and His Magic Cracking Knuckles. The Lex building emerged grudgingly through the dark. Myron traveled through the security travail again. As Win predicted, they confiscated his phone. Granite Man and the two blazers turned left this time instead of right. They escorted him into an elevator. It opened into what appeared to be living quarters.

Susan Lex's office had been done sort of Renaissance palatial, but the apartment up here—it looked like an apartment anyway—did a one-eighty. Modern and minimalism were the major themes. The walls were painted stark white and had nothing on them. The floors were a pigeon-gray wood. There were black and white bookshelves made of fiberglass, most empty, some with indistinct figurines. The couch was red and shaped like two lips. There was a well-stocked see-through bar constructed out of Lucite. Two metallic swivel stools were painted red on the base, looking about as inviting as rectal thermometers. A fire danced lazily in the fireplace, fake logs casting an unnatural glow over the black mantel. The whole place had a feel and aura about as warm as a cold sore.

Myron strolled, feigning interest. He stopped at a crystal statue with a marble base. Something modern or cubist or what-have-you. Symmetrical Bowel Movement maybe. Myron put his hand on it. Substantial. He looked out the one-way glass. Too low for much of a view beyond the hedges lining the front gate. Hmm.

The two blue-blazers did the Buckingham Palace Guard thing on either side of the door. Granite Man followed Myron, his hands clasped behind his lower back. A door on the other side of the room opened. Myron was not surprised to see Susan Lex enter, again keeping her distance. There was a man with her this time. Myron did not bother approaching.

"And you are?" he called out.

Susan Lex answered this one. "This is my brother Bronwyn."

"Not the brother I'm interested in," Myron said.

"Yes, I know. Please sit down."

Granite Man gestured toward the lips-couch. Myron sat on the lower lip, waiting to be swallowed. Granite Man sat right next to him. Cozy.

"Bronwyn and I would like you to answer some questions, Mr. Bolitar," Susan Lex said.

"Could you move a little closer?"

She smiled. "I think not."

"I showered."

She ignored the remark. "I understand that you occasionally do some investigative work," Susan Lex said.

Myron did not reply.

"Is that correct?"

"Depends on what you mean by investigative work."

"I'll take that as a yes," Susan Lex said.

Myron gave her a suit-yourself shrug.

"Is that why you're searching for our brother?" she asked.

"I already told you why I was searching for him."

"That bit about him being a bone marrow donor?"

"It's not a bit."

"Please, Mr. Bolitar," Susan Lex said with that rich-people air. "We both know that's a lie."

Myron started to rise. Granite Man put a hand on Myron's knee. It felt like a cinder block. Granite Man shook his head. Myron stayed where he was. "It's not a lie," he said.

"We're wasting time," Susan Lex said. She flicked her eyes at Granite Man. "Show him the pictures, Grover."

Myron turned to him. "Grover is the name of my very favorite *Sesame Street* character. I want you to know that."

"We've been following you, *Myron*." Granite Man handed him a pile of photographs. Myron looked at them. They were eight-by-tens of him at the condo with Stan Gibbs. The first one showed him knocking on the door. The second one showed Stan sticking his head out. The third one showed them both heading inside the condo.

"Well?"

Myron frowned. "I have no knack for accessorizing."

"We know that you're working for Stan Gibbs," Susan Lex said.

"Doing what exactly?" Myron asked.

"Investigating. As I stated earlier. So now that we understand your true motive, tell me how much it will cost for you to go away."

"I don't know what you're talking about."

"Simply put, how much will it cost to have you cease and desist?" Susan Lex asked. "Or are you going to force us to destroy you too?"

Too?

Brain click.

Myron turned his attention to the silent brother. "Let me ask you something, Bronwyn," he said. "You and Dennis were both going to nursery school. You both disappeared. Two weeks later, only you came back. How come? What happened to your brother?"

Bronwyn's mouth opened and closed, marionette style. He looked to his sister for help.

"It's like he disappeared off the face of the earth after that," Myron went on. "For thirty years, he's totally off the radar. But now, well, it's like he's come back for some reason. He changed his name, opened a small checking account, donated blood to a bone marrow center. So what gives, Bron? You got a clue?"

Bronwyn said, "That simply cannot be!"

His sister silenced him with a look. But Myron felt something in the air. He mulled the feeling over and another thought hit him: Maybe the Lex siblings didn't know the answer themselves. Maybe they were looking for Dennis too.

It was while he was lost in that thought that Granite Man punched him deep in the stomach. The fist followed through to the point where it seemed the knuckles must have reached the fabric of the couch. Myron snapped closed at the waist. He dropped to the floor, struggled to regain a breath, suffocating from within. He lowered his head to his knees, consumed with one thought: air. He needed air.

Susan Lex's voice boomed in his ears. "Stan Gibbs knows the truth. His father is a disgusting liar. His accusations are totally without merit. But I'll defend my family, Mr. Bolitar. You tell Mr. Gibbs he has not yet begun to suffer. What has happened to him so far is nothing compared to what I will do to him—and you—if he doesn't stop. Do you understand?"

Air. Gulps of air. Myron managed not to throw up. He took his time, looked up, met her eye. "Not even a little," he said.

Susan Lex looked at Grover. "Then make him."

With that, she left the room. Her brother took one last look and followed.

Myron gathered his breath a hitch at a time. "Nice sucker punch, Grover," he said.

Grover shrugged. "I went easy on you."

"Next time, go easy when I'm looking, tough guy."

"Won't change the outcome."

"We'll see." Myron sat up. "So what the hell is she talking about?"

"I thought Ms. Lex made herself very clear," he said. "But because you appear to be a little vacant between the ears, I'll restate her position. She doesn't like people interfering with her affairs. Stan Gibbs, for example, interfered. You can see what happened to him. You interfered. You're about to see what's going to happen to you."

Myron struggled to his feet. The blue-blazers stayed by the door. Granite Man started cracking his knuckles again. "Listen closely, please," he said. "I'm going to break your leg. Then you're going to limp your sorry ass out of here and tell Gibbs that if he sniffs around again, I will exterminate you both. Any questions?"

"Just one," Myron said. "Don't you think leg breaking is a tad cliché?"

Grover smiled. "Not the way I do it."

Myron looked around the room.

"Nowhere to run, my friend."

"Who wants to run?" Myron countered.

Without warning, he grabbed the heavy bowel-movement statue. The blue-blazers drew their guns. Granite Man ducked. But Myron wasn't going for them. He heaved the statue, straightened his arms, spun around like a discus thrower, and hurled it marble-base-forward at the plate-glass window. The window exploded.

And that was when the gunfire began.

"Hit the deck!" Myron shouted.

The blue-blazers obeyed. Myron dove. The bullets continued. Sniper fire. One took out the overhead light. One hit the lamp.

Gotta love that Win.

"You want to live," Myron shouted, "stay down."

The bullets stopped. One of the blue-blazers started rising. A bullet sang out, nearly parting the man's hair. The blazer dropped back down, flattening himself into a bearskin rug.

"I'm getting up now," Myron said. "And I'm leaving. I'd advise you guys to stay down. And, Grover?"

"What?"

"Radio downstairs. Tell them not to stop me. I can't be certain but I'm pretty sure my friend will lob in grenades if I'm unduly delayed."

Granite Man made the call. No one moved. Myron stood up. He almost whistled as he walked out.

26

It was midnight when Myron knocked on the door of Stan Gibbs's condo.

"Let's take a walk," Myron said to him.

Stan threw down his cigarette, smothered it with his toe. "A drive might be better," he countered. "The feds use long-range amplifiers."

They got into Myron's Ford Taurus, aka the Chick Trawler. Stan Gibbs flicked on the radio and started playing with the stations. Commercial for Heineken. Does anyone really care that it's imported by Van Munchin and Company?

"Are you wearing a wire, Myron?"

"No."

"But the FBI spoke to you," Stan said. "After you left."

"How did you know?"

"They're watching me," he said with a shrug. "It would only be logical to assume they questioned you."

"Tell me about your connection with Dennis Lex," Myron said.

"I already told you. I don't have one."

"A big guy named Grover picked me up tonight. He and Susan

Lex gave me a very stern warning not to play with you anymore. Bronwyn was there too."

Stan Gibbs closed his eyes and rubbed them. "They knew about your visit here."

"Had eight-by-ten glossies."

"And they concluded that you're working for me."

"Bingo."

Stan shook his head. "Get out of this, Myron. You don't want to mess with these people."

"Is that advice you wished someone had given you earlier?"

His smile had nothing behind it. Exhaustion came off him like heat squiggles on a hot sidewalk. "You have no idea," he said.

"Tell me about it."

"No."

"I can help," Myron said.

"Against the Lexes? They're too powerful."

"And being powerful, you wanted to do a story on them, right?"

He said nothing.

"And they didn't like that. In fact, they took exception."

More nothing.

"You started digging where they didn't want you to. You learned that there was another brother named Dennis."

"Yes."

"And that really pissed them off."

Stan started biting a hangnail.

"Come on, Stan. Don't make me drag this out of you."

"You've pretty much got it."

"Then tell me."

"I wanted to do a story on them. An exposé, really. I even had a publisher all lined up for a book deal. But then the Lexes got wind of it. They warned me to stay away. A big man came to my apartment. I didn't catch his name. Looked like Sergeant Rock."

"That would be Grover."

"He told me that I could stop or I could be destroyed."

"And that only made you more curious."

"I guess."

"So you found out about Dennis Lex."

"Just that he existed. And that he vanished into thin air when he was a young child." Stan turned to him. Myron slowed the car and felt something creep along the top of his scalp.

"Like the Sow the Seeds victims," Myron finished.

"No."

"Why not?"

"It's different."

"How?" Myron asked.

"This is going to sound silly," Stan said, "but the family doesn't have that same sense of terror that the other families have."

"The rich are good with façades."

"It's more than that," Stan said. "I can't put my finger on it exactly. But I'm sure Susan and Bronwyn Lex know what happened to their brother."

"But they want to keep it a secret."

"Yes."

"Do you have a guess why?"

"No," Stan said.

Myron glanced back. The feds were following at a discreet enough distance.

"Do you think Susan Lex is responsible for that novel surfacing?"

"The thought has crossed my mind."

"But you never looked into it?"

"I started to. After the scandal hit. But I got a call from the big guy. He told me that it was just the beginning. That he was just flicking his finger and next time he would crush me between both palms."

"He can be a poetic fellow," Myron said.

"Yes."

"But I still don't get something."

"What?"

"You don't scare easily. When they warned you away the first time, you ignored it. After what they did to you, I'd have thought you'd fight back even harder."

"You're forgetting something," Stan said.

"What?"

"Melina Garston."

Silence.

"Think about it," Stan said. "My mistress, the only person who can back up my meeting with the Sow the Seeds kidnapper, ends up dead."

"Her father claims she retracted that."

"Oh, right. In some bizarre before-death confession."

"You think the Lexes arranged that too?"

"Why not? Look at what happened here. Who's the lead suspect in Melina's murder? I am, right? That's what the feds told you. They think I killed her. We know that the Lexes have enough juice to dig up this novel I supposedly plagiarized. Who knows what else they can do?"

"You think they could frame you for the murder?"

"At the very least."

"Are you saying they killed Melina Garston?"

"Maybe. Or it could have been the Sow the Seeds kidnapper. I don't know."

"But you think Melina was a warning."

"She was definitely a warning," Stan Gibbs said. "I just don't know who sent it."

On the radio, Stevie sang out about a landslide coming down. Oh yeah.

"You're leaving something out, Stan."

Stan kept his eyes forward. "What's that?"

"There's a personal connection here," Myron said.

"What do you mean?"

"Susan Lex mentioned your father. She said he was a liar."

Stan shrugged. "She might be right."

"What does he have to do with this?"

"Take me back."

"Don't hold back on me now."

"What do you really want here, Myron?"

"Excuse me?"

"What's your interest here?"

"I told you."

"That boy who needs a bone marrow transplant?"

"He's thirteen years old, Stan. He'll die without it."

"And what if I don't believe you? I did a little research of my own. You used to do government work."

"A long time ago."

"And maybe now you're helping the FBI. Or even the Lex family."

"No."

"I can't take that chance."

"Why not? You're telling me the truth, right? The truth can't hurt you."

He snorted. "You really believe that?"

"Why did Susan Lex mention your father?"

Nothing.

"Where is your father?" Myron said.

"That's just it."

"What?"

Stan looked at him. "He vanished. Eight years ago."

Vanished. That word again.

"I know what you're thinking and you're wrong. My father wasn't a well man. He had been in and out of institutions all his life. We've always assumed he ran off."

"But you never heard from him."

"That's right."

"Dennis Lex vanishes. Your father vanishes—"

"More than twenty years apart," Stan interjected. "It's not connected."

"So I still don't get it," Myron said. "What does your father or his disappearance have to do with the Lexes?"

"They think he's the reason I wanted to do the story. But they're wrong."

"Why would they think that?"

"My father was a student of Raymond Lex's. Before *Midnight Confessions* came out."

"So?"

"So my father claimed the novel was his. He said that Raymond Lex stole it from him."

"Jesus Christ."

"No one believed him," Stan added quickly. "Like I said, he wasn't right in the head."

"Yet you suddenly decided to investigate the family?"

"Yes."

"And you're telling me that's just a coincidence? That your own investigation had nothing to do with your father's accusations?"

Stan leaned his head against the car window like a little kid longing for home. "No one believed my father. That includes me. He was a sick man. Delusional even."

"So?"

"So at the end of the day, he was still my father," Stan said. "Maybe I owed it to him to at least give him the benefit of the doubt."

"Do you think Raymond Lex plagiarized your father?"

"No."

"Do you think your father is still alive?"

"I don't know."

"There has to be a connection here," Myron said. "Your story, the Lex family, your father's accusations—"

Stan closed his eyes. "No more."

Myron switched tracks. "How did the Sow the Seeds kidnapper get in touch with you?"

"I never reveal sources."

"Come on, Stan."

"No," he said firmly. "I may have lost a lot. But not that part of me. You know I can't say anything about my sources."

"You know who it is, don't you?"

"Take me home, Myron."

"Is it Dennis Lex—or did the same kidnapper take Dennis Lex?"

Stan crossed his arms. "Home," he said.

His face closed down. Myron saw it. There would be no more give tonight. He took a right and started heading back. Neither man spoke again until Myron stopped the car in the front of the condominium.

"Are you telling the truth, Myron? About the bone marrow donor?"

"Yes."

"This boy is someone close to you?"

Myron kept both hands on the wheel. "Yes."

"So there's no way you'll walk away from this?"

"None."

Stan nodded, mostly to himself. "I'll do what I can. But you have to trust me."

"What do you mean?"

"Give me a few days."

"To do what?"

"You won't hear from me for a little while. Don't let that shake your faith."

"What are you talking about?"

"You do what you have to," he said. "I'll do the same."

Stan Gibbs stepped out of the car and disappeared into the night.

27

Greg Downing woke Myron early the next morning with a phone call. "Nathan Mostoni left town," he said. "So I came back to New York. I get to pick up my son this afternoon."

Goody-goody for you, Myron thought. But he kept his tongue still.

"I'm going to the Ninety-second Street Y to shoot around," Greg said. "You want to come?"

"No," Myron said.

"Come anyway. Ten o'clock."

"I'll be late." Myron hung up and rolled out of bed. He checked his e-mail and found a JPEG image from Esperanza's contact at AgeComp. He clicked the file and an image slowly appeared on the screen. The possible face of Dennis Lex as a man in his mid to late thirties. Weird. Myron looked at the picture. Not familiar. Not familiar at all. Remarkable work, these age-enhanced images. So lifelike. Except in the eyes. The eyes always looked like the eyes of the dead.

He clicked on the print icon and heard his Hewlett-Packard go to work. Myron checked the clock on the bottom right-hand corner of the screen. Still early in the morning, but he didn't want to wait.

He called Melina Garston's father.

George Garston agreed to meet Myron at his penthouse at Fifth Avenue and Seventy-eighth Street, overlooking Central Park. A dark-haired woman answered the door. She introduced herself as Sandra and led him silently down the corridor. Myron looked out a window. He could see the Gothic outline of the Dakota all the way across the park. He remembered reading somewhere how Woody and Mia would wave towels from their respective apartments on either side of Central Park. Happier days, no doubt.

"I don't understand what you have to do with my daughter," George Garston said to him. Garston wore a collared blue shirt nicely offset by a shock of white neck-to-chest hairs sprouting out like a troll doll's. His bald head was an almost perfect sphere jammed between two boulder-excuses for shoulders. He had the proud, burly build of a successful immigrant, but you could see that he'd taken a hit. There was a slump there now, the stoop of the eternally grieving. Myron had seen it before. Grief like his breaks your back. You go on, but you always stoop. You smile, but it never really reaches the eyes.

"Probably nothing," Myron said. "I'm trying to find someone. He may be connected to your daughter's murder. I don't know."

The study was too-dark cherry-wood with drawn curtains and one lamp giving off a faint yellow glow. George Garston turned to the side, staring at the rich paisley wallpaper, showing Myron his profile. "We've worked together once," he said. "Not us personally. Our companies. Did you know that?"

"Yes," Myron said.

George Garston had made his fortune with a chain of Greek quasi-restaurants, the kind that work best as mall stands in crowded food courts. The chain was called Achilles Meals. For real. Myron had a Greek hockey player who endorsed the chain regionally, in the upper Midwest.

"So a sports agent is interested in my daughter's murder," Garston said.

"It's a long story."

"The police aren't talking. But they think it's her boyfriend. This reporter. Do you agree?"

"I don't know. What do you think?"

He made a scoffing noise. Myron could barely see his face anymore. "What do I think?" he said. "You sound like one of those grief counselors."

"Didn't mean to."

"Spewing all that sensitivity garbage. They're just trying to distract you from reality. They say they want you to face it. But really, it's the opposite. They want you to dig so far into yourself you won't be able to see how terrible your life is now." He grunted and shifted in his chair. "I don't have an opinion on Stan Gibbs. I never met him."

"Did you know he and your daughter were dating?"

In the dark, Myron saw the big head silently go back and forth. "She told me she had a boyfriend," he said. "She didn't tell me his name. Or that he was married."

"You wouldn't have approved?"

"Of course I wouldn't have approved," he said, trying to sound snappish, but he was beyond petty indignation. "Would you approve if it was your daughter?"

"I guess not. So you knew nothing about her relationship with Stan Gibbs?"

"Nothing."

"I understand that you spoke to her not long before she died."

"Four days before."

"Can you tell me about the conversation?"

"Melina had been drinking," he said in that pure monotone you get when the words have been ricocheting around your brain too long. "A lot. She drank too much, my daughter. Got that from her papa— who got it from his papa. The Garston family legacy." He made a chuckling sound that sounded far closer to a sob than anything in the neighborhood of a laugh.

"Melina talked to you about her testimony?"

"Yes."

"Could you tell me what she said exactly?"

" 'I made a mistake, Papa.' That's what she said. She said that she lied."

"What did you say?"

"I didn't even know what she was talking about. It's as I told you before—I didn't know about this boyfriend."

"Did you ask her to explain?"

"Yes."

"And?"

"And she didn't. She said to forget about it. She said she'd take care of it. Then she told me she loved me and hung up."

Silence.

"I had two children, Mr. Bolitar. Did you know that?"

Myron shook his head.

"A plane crash killed my Michael three years ago. Now an animal has tortured and killed my girl. My wife, her name was Melina too, passed away fifteen years ago. There is no one. Forty-eight years ago, I thought I came to this country with nothing. I made a lot of money. And now I truly have nothing. You understand?"

"Yes," Myron said.

"Is that all, then?"

"Your daughter had an apartment on Broadway."

"Yes."

"Are her personal belongings still there?"

"Sandra—that's my daughter-in-law—she's been packing her things. But it's all still there. Why?"

"I'd like to go through them, if it's okay with you."

"The police already did that."

"I know."

"You think you might find something they didn't?"

"I'm almost positive I won't."

"But?"

"But I'm attacking this thing from a different perspective. It gives me a fresh set of eyes."

George Garston flicked on his desk lamp. The yellow from the bulb painted his face a dark jaundice. Myron could see that his eyes were too dry, brittle like fallen acorns in the sun. "If you find whoever killed my Melina, you will tell me first."

"No," Myron said.

"Do you know what he did to her?"

"Yes. And I know what you want to do. But it won't make you feel any better."

"You say this like you know it for a fact."

Myron kept silent.

George Garston flicked off the light and turned away. "Sandra will take you over now."

"He sits in that study all day," Sandra Garston told him, pressing the elevator button. "He won't go out anymore."

"It's still new," Myron said.

She shook her head. Her blue-black hair fell in a big, loose curls, like thermal fax paper fresh out of the machine. But despite the hair color, her overall effect was almost Icelandic, the face and build of a world-class speed skater. Her features were sharp and ended rather abruptly. Her skin had the red of raw cold.

"He thinks he has no one," she said.

"He has you."

"I'm a daughter-in-law. He sees me and it's like a tether to Michael. I don't have the heart to tell him I finally started dating."

When they reached the street, Myron asked, "Were you and Melina close?"

"I think so, yes."

"Did you know about her relationship with Stan Gibbs?"

"Yes."

"But she never told her father."

"Oh, she would never. Papa didn't approve of most men. A married one would have sent him off the ledge."

They crossed the street and into the mid-city wonder known as Central Park. The park was packed on this rather spectacular day. Asian sketch artists hustled business. Men jogged by in those shorts that look suspiciously like diapers. Sunbathers lazed around on the grass, crowded together yet totally alone. New York City is like that. E. B. White once said that New York bestows the gift of loneliness and the gift of privacy. Damn straight. It was like everyone was plugged into their own internal Walkman, each playing a different tune, bopping obliviously to his or her own beat.

A yah-dude with a bandanna around his head tossed a Frisbee and yelled "Fetch," but he had no dog. Hard-bodied women skated by in black jogging bras. Lots of men with various builds had their shirts off. Examples: A guy thick with flab that looked like wet Play-Doh jiggled past him. Behind him, a well-built guy skidded to a stop and arrogantly flexed a bicep. Actually flexed. In public. Myron frowned. He didn't know which was worse: guys who shouldn't take their shirts off and do, or guys who should take their shirts off and do.

When they reached Central Park West, Myron asked, "Did you have a problem with her dating a married man?"

Sandra shrugged. "I worried, of course. But he told Melina he would leave his wife."

"Don't they all?"

"Melina believed it. She seemed happy."

"Did you ever meet Stan Gibbs?"

"No. Their relationship was supposed to be a secret."

"Did she ever tell you about lying in court?"

"No," she said. "Never."

Sandra used her key and swung the door open. Myron stepped inside. Colors. Lots of them. Happy colors. The apartment looked like the Magical Mystery Tour meets the Teletubbies, all bright hues, especially greens, with hazy psychedelic splashes. The walls were covered with vivid watercolors of distant lands and ocean voyages. Some surreal stuff too. The effect was like an Enya video.

"I started throwing her stuff in boxes," Sandra said. "But it's hard to pack up a life."

Myron nodded. He started walking around the small apartment, hoping for a psychic revelation or something. None came. He ran his eyes over the artwork.

"She was supposed to have her first show in the Village next month," Sandra said.

Myron studied a painting with white domes and crystal blue water. He recognized the spot in Mykonos. It was wonderfully done. Myron could almost smell the salt of the Mediterranean, taste the grilled fish along the beach, feel the night sand clinging to a lover's skin. No clue here, but he stared another minute or two before turning away.

He started going through the boxes. He found a high school year-

book, class of 1986, and flipped through it until he found Melina's
picture. She'd like to paint, it said. He glanced again at the walls. So
bright and optimistic, her work. Death, Myron knew, was always
ironic. Young death most ironic of all.

He turned his attention back to her photograph. Melina was looking off to the side with the hesitant, unsure smile of high school. Myron knew it well. Don't we all. He closed the book and headed to her
closets. Her clothes were neatly arranged, lots of sweaters folded on
the top shelf, shoes lined like up like tiny soldiers. He moved back to
the boxes and found her photographs in a shoebox. A shoebox of
all things. Myron shook his head and started going through them.
Sandra sat on the floor next to him. "That's her mother," she said.

Myron looked at the photograph of two women, clearly mother
and daughter, embracing. There was no sign of the unsure smile this
time. This smile—the smile in her mother's arms—soared like an angel's song. Myron stared at the angel-song smile and imagined that
celestial mouth crying out in hopeless agony. He thought about George
Garston alone in that jaundice-lit study. And he understood.

Myron checked his watch. Time to pick up the pace. He thumbed
through pictures of her father, her brother, Sandra, family outings,
the norm. No pictures of Stan Gibbs. Nothing helpful.

He found makeup and perfume in another box. In another, he
stumbled across a diary, but Melina hadn't written anything in it for
two years. He paged through it, but it felt like too much an unnecessary violation. He found a love letter from an old boyfriend. He found
some receipts.

He found copies of Stan's columns.

Hmm.

In her address book. All the columns. There were no markings on
them. Just the clippings themselves, held together by a paper clip. So
what did that mean? He checked them again. Just clippings. He put
them aside and did some more flipping. Something fell out near the
back. Myron picked up a piece of cream-colored or aged-white paper
torn along the left edge, more a card really, folded in half. The outside was totally blank. He opened it. On the upper half, the words
With Love, Dad had been written in script. Myron thought again
about George Garston sitting alone in that room and felt a deep burn
flush his skin.

He sat on the couch now and tried again to conjure up something. That might sound weird—sitting in this too empty room, the sweet smell of a dead woman still hovering, feeling not unlike that tiny old lady in the *Poltergeist* movies—but you never knew. The victims didn't speak to him or anything like that. But sometimes he could imagine what they'd been thinking and feeling and some spark would hit the edges and start to flame. So he tried it again.

Nothing.

He let his eyes wander across the canvases and the burn under his skin started up again. He scanned the bright colors, let them assault him. The brightness should have protected her. Nonsense, but there you have it. She'd had a life. Melina worked and she painted and she loved bright colors and had too many sweaters and stored her precious memories in a shoebox and someone had snuffed that life away because none of that meant anything to him. None of that was important. It made Myron mad.

He closed his eyes and tried to turn the anger down a notch. Anger wasn't good. It clouded reason. He'd let that side of him out before—his Batman complex, as Esperanza had called it—but being a hero seeking justice or vengeance (if they weren't the same thing) was unwise, unhealthy. Eventually you saw things you didn't want to. You learned truths you never should have. It stings and then it deadens. Better to stay away.

But the heat in his blood would not leave him. So he stopped fighting it, let the heat soothe him, relax his muscles, settle gently over him. Maybe the heat wasn't such a bad thing. Maybe the horrors he'd seen and the truths he'd learned hadn't changed him, hadn't deadened him, after all.

Myron closed the boxes, took one last, lingering look at the sun-kissed isle of Mykonos, and made a silent vow.

28

reg and Myron met up on the court. Myron strapped on his knee brace. Greg averted his eyes. The two men shot for half an hour, barely speaking, lost in the pure strokes. People ducked in and pointed at Greg. Several kids came up to him and asked him for autographs. Greg acquiesced, glancing at Myron as he took pen in hand, clearly uncomfortable getting all this attention in front of the man whose career he had ended.

Myron stared back at him, offering no solace.

After some time, Myron said, "There a reason you wanted me here, Greg?"

Greg kept shooting.

"Because I have to get back to the office," Myron said.

Greg grabbed the ball, dribbled twice, took a turn-around jumper. "I saw you and Emily that night. You know that?"

"I know that," Myron said.

Greg grabbed the rebound, took a lazy hook, let the ball hit the floor and slowly bounce toward Myron. "We were getting married the next day. You know that?"

"Know that too."

"And there you were," Greg said, "her old boyfriend, screwing her brains out."

Myron picked up the ball.

"I'm trying to explain here," Greg said.

"I slept with Emily," Myron said. "You saw us. You wanted revenge. You told Big Burt Wesson to hurt me during a preseason game. He did. End of story."

"I wanted him to hurt you, yes. I didn't mean for him to end your career."

"You say tomato, I say tomahto."

"It wasn't intentional."

"Don't take this the wrong way," Myron said in a voice that sounded awfully calm in his own ears, "but I don't give two shits about your intentions. You fired a weapon at me. You might have aimed for a flesh wound, but that didn't happen. You think that makes you blameless?"

"You fucked my fiancée."

"And she fucked me. I didn't owe you anything. She did."

"Are you telling me you don't understand?"

"I understand. It just doesn't absolve you."

"I'm not looking for absolution."

"Then what do you want, Greg? You want us to clasp hands and sing 'Kumbaya'? Do you know what you did to me? Do you know what the one moment cost me?"

"I think maybe I do," Greg said. He swallowed, put out a pleading hand as though he wanted to explain more, and then he let the hand drop to the side. "I'm so sorry."

Myron started shooting but he felt his throat swell.

"You don't know how sorry I am."

Myron said nothing. Greg tried to wait him out. It didn't work.

"What else do you want me to say here, Myron?"

Myron kept shooting.

"How do I tell you I'm sorry?"

"You've already done it," Myron said.

"But you won't accept it."

"No, Greg. I won't. I live without playing pro ball. You live without my accepting your apology. Pretty good deal for you, you ask me."

Myron's cell phone rang. He ran over, picked it up, said hello.

A whisper asked, "Did you do as I instructed?"

His bones turned to solid ice. He swallowed away something thick and said, "As you instructed?"

"The boy," the voice whispered.

The stale air pressed against him, weighed down his lungs. "What about him?"

"Did you say one last good-bye?"

Something inside of Myron withered up and blew away. His knees buckled as the realization seeped into his chest. And the voice came on again:

"Did you say one last good-bye to the boy?"

29

Myron snapped his head toward Greg. "Where's Jeremy?"

"What?"

"Where is he?"

Greg saw whatever it was on Myron's face and dropped the basketball. "He's with Emily, I guess. I don't get him until noon."

"Got a cell phone?"

"Yes."

"Call her."

Greg was already heading toward his gym bag, the athlete with the wonderful reflexes. "What's going on?"

"Probably nothing."

Myron explained about the call. Greg did not slow down to listen. He dialed. Myron started running toward his car. Greg followed, the phone pressed against his ear.

"No answer," Greg said. He left a message on the machine.

"Does she have a cell phone?"

"If she does, I don't have the number."

Myron hit a stored number as they walked. Esperanza picked up.

"I need Emily's cell phone number."

"Give me five," Esperanza said.

Myron hit another stored number. Win answered and said, "Articulate."

"Possible trouble."

"I'm here."

They reached the car. Greg was calm. That surprised Myron. On the court, when the pressure mounted, Greg's modus operandi was to get freaky, start screaming, psych himself into a frenzy. But of course, this was not a game. As his father had recently told him, when real bombs drop, you never know how someone will react.

Myron's phone rang. Esperanza gave him Emily's cell phone number. Myron dialed it. After six rings, Emily's voice mail picked up. Damn. Myron left a message. He turned to Greg.

"Any clue where Jeremy might be?" Myron asked.

"No," Greg said.

"How about a neighbor we can call? Or a friend?"

"When Emily and I were married, we lived in Ridgewood. I don't know the neighbors in Franklin Lakes."

Myron gripped the steering wheel. He hit the accelerator. "Jeremy's probably safe," Myron said, trying to believe it. "I don't even know how this guy would know his name. It's probably a bluff."

Greg started shaking.

"He'll be all right."

"Jesus, Myron, I read those articles. If that guy has my kid . . ."

"We should call the FBI," Myron said. "Just in case."

"You think that's the way to go?" Greg asked.

Myron looked at him. "Why? You don't?"

"I just want to pay the ransom and get my boy back. I don't want anybody screwing it up."

"I think we should call," Myron said. "But it's your decision."

"There's something else we have to consider," Greg said.

"What?"

"There's a good chance this wacko is our donor, right?"

"Yes."

"If the FBI kills him, it's over for Jeremy."

"First things first," Myron said. "We have to find Jeremy. And we have to find this kidnapper."

Greg kept shaking.

"What do you want to do, Greg?"

"You think we should call?"

"Yes."

Greg nodded slowly. "Call," he said.

Myron dialed Kimberly Green's number. He felt waves pounding in his head, the blood flowing to his ears. He tried not to think about Jeremy's face, what his smile had looked like when he opened that door.

Did you say one last good-bye to the boy?

A voice said, "Federal Bureau of Investigation."

"Myron Bolitar calling Kimberly Green."

"Special Agent Green is unavailable."

"The Sow the Seeds kidnapper may have taken somebody else. Put her on."

The hold was longer than Myron expected.

Kimberly Green started with a bark. "What the hell are you ranting about?"

"He just called me." Myron filled her in.

"We're on our way," she said.

They hit a patch of traffic where Route 4 met Route 17, but Myron went up on the grass and knocked over several orange construction buckets. He broke off at Route 208 and exited near the synagogue. Two miles later, they made the final turn onto Emily's street. Myron could see two FBI cars making the turn at the same time.

Greg, who had gone into something of a trance, woke up and pointed. "There she is."

Emily was putting her key in the front door. Myron started honking madly. She looked back confused. He turned the car and skidded. The FBI car followed. Myron and Greg were both out the door almost before the car had stopped.

"Where's Jeremy?" they both said in unison.

Emily had her head tilted to the side. "What?" she called back. "What's going on here?"

Greg took it. "Where is he, Emily?"

"He's with a friend—"

From inside the house, the phone started ringing. Everyone froze. Emily snapped out of it first. She ran inside and picked up the phone. She put the phone to her ear, cleared her throat, and said, "Hello."

Through the receiver, they could all hear Jeremy's scream.

30

There were six federal agents in all. Kimberly Green was the task force leader. They set up with quiet efficiency. Myron sat on one couch, Greg the other. Emily paced between them. There was probably something symbolic in that, but Myron was not sure what. He tried to push himself past the numb so he could get to a place where he could do some good.

The phone call had been brief. After the scream, the whispery voice had said, "We'll call back." That was it. No warnings not to contact the authorities. No telling them to prepare funds. No setting up another time to call. Nothing.

They all sat there, the boy's scream still echoing, mauling, shredding, conjuring up images of what could have made a thirteen-year-old boy scream like that. Myron shut his eyes and pushed hard. That was what the bastard wanted. Unwise to play into that.

Greg had contacted his bank. He was not a risky investor, and so most of his assets were liquid. If ransom money was needed, he'd be ready. The various feds, all male except for Kimberly Green, put traces on all the possible phones, including Myron's. She and her men were doing a lot of sotto voce. Myron hadn't pressed them yet. But that wasn't going to last.

Kimberly caught his eyes and waved him over. He stood and excused himself. Greg and Emily paid no attention, still lost in the vortex of that scream.

"We need to talk," she said.

"Okay," Myron said. "Start by telling me what happened when you checked out Dennis Lex."

"You're not family," she said. "I could throw you out."

"This isn't your house," he said. "What happened with Dennis Lex?"

She put her hands on her hips. "It's a dead end."

"How so?"

"We traced it down. He's not involved in any of this."

"How do you know that?"

"Myron, come on. We're not stupid."

"So where is Dennis Lex?"

"It's not relevant," she said.

"The hell it's not. Even if he's not the kidnapper, we still have him as the bone marrow donor."

"No," she said. "Your donor is Davis Taylor."

"Who changed his name from Dennis Lex."

"We don't know that."

Myron made a face. "What are you talking about?"

"Davis Taylor was an employee in the Lex conglomerate."

"What?"

"You heard me."

"So why did he donate blood for a bone marrow drive?"

"It was a work thing," she said. "The plant boss had a sick nephew. Everyone at the plant gave."

Myron nodded. Something finally made sense. "So if he didn't give a blood sample," he said, "it would have been conspicuous."

"Right."

"You got a description on him?"

"He worked on his own, kept to himself. All anyone remembers is a man with a full beard, glasses, and long blond hair."

"A disguise," Myron said. "And we know Davis Taylor's original name was Dennis Lex. What else?"

Kimberly Green raised her hand. "Enough." She sort of hitched herself up, trying to alter momentum. "Stan Gibbs is still our top suspect here. What did you two talk about last night?"

"Dennis Lex," Myron said. "Don't you get it?"

"Get what?"

"Dennis Lex is connected into all this. He's either the kidnapper, or maybe he was the first victim."

"Neither," she said.

"Then where is he?"

She shook it off. "What else did you two talk about?"

"Stan's father."

"Edwin Gibbs?" That got her attention. "What about him?"

"That he vanished eight years ago. But you already know about that, don't you?"

She nodded a little too firmly. "We do," she said.

"So what do you think happened to him?" Myron asked.

She hesitated. "You believe that Dennis Lex may be Sow the Seeds' first victim, correct?"

"I think it's something to look into, yes."

"Our theory," she went on, "is that the first victim may have been Edwin Gibbs."

Myron made a face. "You think Stan kidnapped his own father?"

"Killed him. And the others. We don't believe any of them are still alive."

Myron tried not to let that sink in. "You have any evidence or motive?"

"Sometimes the apple doesn't fall far from the tree."

"Oh, that'll go over big with a jury. Ladies and gentlemen, the apple doesn't fall far from the tree. And you should never put the cart before the horse. Plus every dog has his day." He shook his head. "Are you listening to yourself?"

"On its own, I admit it doesn't make sense. But put it all together. Eight years ago, Stan was starting out on his own. He was twenty-four, his father forty-six. By all accounts, the two men did not get along. Suddenly Edwin Gibbs vanishes. Stan never reports it."

"This is silly."

"Maybe. But then add back everything else we already know.

The only columnist to get this scoop. The plagiarism. Melina Garston. Everything that Eric Ford discussed with you yesterday."

"It still doesn't add up."

"Then tell me where Stan Gibbs is."

Myron looked at her. "Isn't he at the condo?"

"Last night, after you two talked, Stan Gibbs slipped surveillance. He's done that before. We usually pick him up a few hours later. But that hasn't happened this time. He's suddenly out of sight—and by coincidence, Jeremy Downing has been snatched by the Sow the Seeds kidnapper. You want to explain that one to me?"

Myron's mouth felt dry. "You're searching for him?"

"We got an APB. But we know he's good at hiding. You got any clue where he went?"

"None."

"He said nothing to you about it?"

"He mentioned that he might go away for a few days. But that I should trust him."

"Bad advice," she said. "Anything else?"

Myron shook his head. "Where is Dennis Lex?" he tried again. "Did you see him?"

"I didn't have to," she said. But her voice had a funny monotone to it. "He's not involved in this."

"You keep saying that," Myron said. "But how do you know?"

She slowed down. "The family."

"You mean Susan and Bronwyn Lex?"

"Yes."

"What about them?"

"They gave us reassurances."

Myron almost stepped back. "You just took their word for it?"

"I didn't say that." She glanced around, let loose a sigh. "And it's not my call."

"What?"

She looked straight through him. "Eric Ford handled it personally."

Myron could not believe what he was hearing.

"He told me to stay away," she said, "that he had it covered."

"Or covered up," Myron said.

"Nothing I can do about it." She looked at him. She had stressed the word *I*. Then she walked away without another word. Myron dialed his cell phone.

"Articulate," Win said.

"We're going to need help," Myron said. "Is Zorra still working freelance?"

"I'll call her."

"Maybe Big Cyndi too."

"Do you have a plan?"

"No time for a plan," Myron said.

"Ooo," Win said. "Then we're going to get nasty."

"Yes."

"And here I thought you weren't going to break the rules anymore."

"Just this once," Myron said.

"Ah," Win countered. "That's what they all say."

31

Win, Esperanza, Big Cyndi, and Zorra were all in his office.

Zorra wore a yellow monogrammed sweater (the monogram being one letter: Z), large white pearls à la Wilma Flintstone, a plaid skirt, and white bobby socks. Her—or if you want to be anatomically correct, his—wig looked like early Bette Midler or maybe Little Orphan Annie on methadone. Shiny red high-heel shoes like something stolen from a trampy Dorothy in Oz adorned the men's-size-twelve feet.

Zorra smiled at Myron. "Zorra is happy to see you."

"Yeah," Myron said. "And Myron is happy to see you too."

"This time, we're on the same side, yes?"

"Yes."

"Zorra pleased."

Zorra's real name was Shlomo Avrahaim, and she was a former Israeli Mossad agent. The two had had a nasty run-in not long ago. Myron still carried the wound near his rib cage—a scar-shaped Z made by a blade Zorra hid in her heel.

Win said, "The Lex Building is too well guarded."

"So we go with Plan B," Myron said.

"Already in motion," Win said.

Myron looked at Zorra. "You armed?"

Zorra pulled a weapon out from under her skirt. "The Uzi," Zorra said. "Zorra likes the Uzi."

Myron nodded. "Patriotic."

"Question," Esperanza said.

"What?"

Esperanza settled her eyes on his. "What if this guy doesn't cooperate?"

"We don't have time to worry about it," Myron said.

"Meaning?"

"This psycho has Jeremy," Myron said. "You understand that? Jeremy has to be the priority here."

Esperanza shook her head.

"Then stay behind," he said.

"You need me," she said.

"Right. And Jeremy needs *me*." He stood. "Okay, let's go."

Esperanza shook her head again, but she went along. The group— a sort of cut-rate Dirty (One-Third of a) Dozen—broke off when they reached the street. Esperanza and Zorra would walk. Win, Myron, and Big Cyndi headed into a garage three blocks away. Win had a car there. Chevy Nova. Totally untraceable. Win had a bunch of them. He referred to them as disposable vehicles. Like paper cups or something. The rich. You don't want to know what he does with them.

Win drove, Myron took the front passenger seat, and Big Cyndi squeezed into the back, which was a little like watching a film of childbirth on rewind. Then they were off.

The Stokes, Layton and Grace law firm was one of the most prestigious in New York. Big Cyndi stayed in reception. The receptionist, a skinny skirt-suit of gray, tried not to stare. So Big Cyndi stared at her, daring her not to look. Sometimes Big Cyndi would growl. Like a lion. No reason. She just liked to do it.

Myron and Win were ushered into a conference room that looked like a million other big Manhattan law firm conference rooms. Myron doodled on a yellow legal that looked like a million other big Manhattan law firm legal pads, watched through the window the smug, pink, fresh-scrubbed Harvard grads stroll by, again all looking exactly the same as the ones at a million other big Manhattan law firms. Reverse discrimination maybe, but all young white male lawyers looked the same to him.

Then again, Myron was a white Harvard law school graduate. Hmm.

Chase Layton trollied in with his rolly build and well-fed face and chubby hands and gray comb-over, looking like, well, a name partner at a big Manhattan law firm. He wore a gold wedding band on one hand and a Harvard ring on the other. He greeted Win warmly—most wealthy people do—and then gave a firm, I'm-your-guy handshake to Myron.

"We're in a rush," Win said.

Chase Layton shoved the big smile out of the room and strapped on his best battle-ready face. Everyone sat. Chase Layton folded his hands in front of him. He leaned forward, putting a bit of a belly push on the vest buttons. "What can I do for you, Windsor?"

Rich people always called him Windsor.

"You've been after my business for a long time," Win said.

"Well, I wouldn't say—"

"I'm here to give it to you. In exchange for a favor."

Chase Layton was too smart to snap-bite at that. He looked at Myron. An underling. Maybe there'd be a clue how to play on this plebeian's face. Myron kept up the neutral. He was getting better at it. Must be from hanging around Win so much.

"We need to see Susan Lex," Win said. "You are her attorney. We'd like you to get her to come here immediately."

"Here?"

"Yes," Win said. "At your office. Immediately."

Chase opened his mouth, closed it, checked on the underling again. Still no clue. "Are you serious, Windsor?"

"You do that, you get the Lock-Horne business. You know how much income that would generate?"

"A great deal," Chase Layton said. "And yet not even a third of what we receive from the Lex family."

Win smiled. "Talk about having your cake and eating it too."

"I don't understand this," Chase said.

"It's pretty straightfoward, Chase."

"Why do you want to see Ms. Lex?"

"We can't divulge that."

"I see." Chase Layton scratched a ham-red cheek with a manicured finger. "Ms. Lex is a very private person."

"Yes, we know."

"She and I are friends."

"I'm sure," Win said.

"Perhaps I can set up an introduction."

"No good. It has to be now."

"Well, she and I usually conduct business at her office—"

"Again no good. It has to be here."

Chase rolled his neck a bit, stalling for time, trying to sort through this, find an angle to play. "She's a very busy woman. I wouldn't even know what to say to get her here."

"You're a good attorney, Chase," Win said, steepling his fingers. "I'm sure you'll come up with something."

Chase nodded, looked down, studied his manicure. "No," he said. He looked back up slowly. "I don't sell out clients, Windsor."

"Even if it meant landing a client as big as Lock-Horne?"

"Even then."

"And you're not doing this just to impress me with your discretion?"

Chase smiled, relieved, as though he finally got the joke. "No," he said. "But wouldn't that be having my cake and eating it too?" He tried to laugh it off. Win didn't join him.

"This isn't a test, Chase. I need you to get her here. I guarantee that she won't find out you helped me."

"Do you think that's all that concerns me here—how it would look?"

Win said nothing.

"If that's the case, you've misread me. The answer is still no, I'm afraid."

"Think about it," Win said.

"Nothing to think about," Chase said. He leaned back, crossing one leg over the other, making sure the crease sat right. "You didn't really think I'd go along with this, did you, Windsor?"

"I hoped."

Chase again looked at Myron, then back at Win. "I'm afraid I can't help you, gentlemen."

"Oh, you'll help us," Win said.

"Pardon me?"

"It's just a matter of what we need to do to get your cooperation."

Chase frowned. "Are you trying to bribe me?"

"No," Win said. "I already did that. By offering you our business."

"Then I don't understand—"

Myron spoke for the first time. "I'm going to make you," he said.

Chase Layton looked at Myron and smiled. Again he said, "Pardon me?"

Myron rose. He kept his expression flat, remembering what he'd learned from Win about intimidation. "I don't want to hurt you," Myron said. "But you will call Susan Lex and get her to come here. And you'll do it now."

Chase folded his arms and sat them atop his belly. "If you wish to discuss this further—"

"I don't," Myron said.

Myron walked around the table. Chase did not back away. "I will not call her," he said firmly. "Windsor, would you tell your friend to sit down?"

Win feigned a helpless shrug.

Myron stood directly over Chase. He looked back at Win. Win said, "Let me handle it."

Myron shook his head. He loomed over Chase and let his gaze fall. "One last chance."

Chase Layton's face was calm, almost amused. He probably saw this as a bizarre put-on—or perhaps he was just certain that Myron would back down. That was how it was with men like Chase Layton. Physical violence was not a part of the Layton equation. Oh, sure, those uneducated animals on the street might engage in it. They might knock him on the head for his wallet. Other people—lesser people, really—yes, they solved problems with physical violence. But that was another planet—one filled with a more primitive species. In Chase

Layton's world, a world of status and position and lofty manners, you were untouchable. Men threatened. Men sued. Men cursed. Men schemed behind one another's backs. Men never engaged in face-to-face violence.

That was why Myron knew that no bluff would work here. Men like Chase Layton believed that anything remotely physical was a bluff. Myron could probably point a gun at him, and he wouldn't budge. And in that scenario, Chase Layton would be right.

But not this one.

Myron boxed Chase Layton's ears hard with his palms.

Chase's eyes widened in a way they probably never had before. Myron put his hand over the lawyer's mouth, muffling the scream. He cupped the back of the man's skull and pulled him back, knocking him off his chair and onto the floor.

Chase lay on his back. Myron looked him straight in the eye and saw a tear roll down the man's cheek. Myron felt ill. He thought about Jeremy and that helped keep his face neutral. Myron said, "Call her."

He slowly released his hand.

Chase's breathing was labored. Myron glanced at Win. Win shook his head.

"You," Chase said, spitting out the word, "are going to jail."

Myron closed his eyes, made a fist, and punched the lawyer up and under the ribs, toward the liver. The lawyer's face fell into itself. Myron held the man's mouth again, but this time there was no scream to smother.

Win eased back in his chair. "For the record, I am the sole witness to this event. I'll swear under oath that it was self-defense."

Chase looked lost.

"Call her," Myron said. He tried to keep the pleading out of his voice. He looked down at Chase Layton. Chase's shirttail was out of his pants, his tie askew, his comb-over unraveling, and Myron realized that nothing would ever be the same for this man. Chase Layton had been physically assaulted. He would always walk a little more warily now. He would sleep a little less deeply. He would always be a little different inside.

Maybe so too would Myron.

Myron punched him again. Chase made an *oof* noise. Win stood by the door. Keep your face even, Myron told himself. A man at work. A man who won't stop no matter what. Myron cocked his fist again.

Five minutes later, Chase Layton called Susan Lex.

32

Would have been better," Win said, "if you let me hurt him."

Myron kept walking. "It would have been the same," he said.

Win shrugged. They had an hour to set up. Big Cyndi was now in the conference room with Chase Layton, supposedly going over her new professional-wrestling contract. When she entered the room, all six-six, three hundred pounds of her wearing her Big Chief Mama costume, Chase Layton barely looked up. The pain from the punches, Myron was sure, was ebbing. He had not struck the man in any place that would do lasting damage, except maybe to the obvious.

Esperanza was set up in the lobby. Myron and Win met Zorra two levels down, on the seventh floor. Zorra had staked out the lower floors and decided that this would be the quietest and easiest to contain. The office suites on the northern side were empty, Zorra noted. Anyone entering or leaving had to do so from the west. Zorra was stationed there with one cell phone. Esperanza had the other one downstairs. Win held the third. They were on a three-way line with one another. Myron and Win were in position. In the last twenty minutes, the elevator had stopped at their floor only twice. Good. Both times the door opened, Myron and Win feigned conversation, just two guys waiting for an elevator heading in the opposite direction. Real undercover commandos.

Myron hoped like hell no one happened upon the scene when it all went down. Zorra would warn them, of course, but once the operation was under way, it couldn't be stopped. They'd have to come up with some excuse, say it was a drill maybe, but Myron was not sure he could stomach hurting any more innocents today. He closed his eyes. Can't back down now. Too far gone.

Win smiled at him. "Wondering yet again if the ends justify the means?"

"Not wondering," Myron said.

"Oh?"

"I know they don't."

"And yet?"

"I'm not in the mood for introspection right now."

"But you're so good at it," Win said.

"Thanks."

"And knowing you as well as I do, you'll save it for later—for when you have more time. You'll gnash your teeth over what you just did. You'll feel ashamed, remorseful, guilty—though you'll also be oddly proud that you didn't have *moi* do your dirty work. You'll end up making a clear declaration that it will never happen again. And perhaps it won't—not, at least, until the stakes are this high."

"So I'm a hypocrite," Myron said. "Happy?"

"But that is my point," Win said.

"What?"

"You're not a hypocrite. You aim toward lofty heights. The fact that your arrow cannot always reach them does not make you a hypocrite."

"So in conclusion," Myron said, "the ends do not justify the means. Except sometimes."

Win spread his hands. "See? I just saved you hours of soul-searching. Perhaps I should consider penning one of those how-to-manage-your-time manuals."

Esperanza broke in through the phone. "They're here," she said.

Win put the phone to his ear. "How many?"

"Three coming in. Susan Lex. That granite guy Myron keeps talking about. Another bodyguard. Two more staying parked outside."

"Zorra," Win said into the phone. "Please keep an eye on the two gentlemen outside."

Zorra said, "And if they move?"

"Detain them."

"With pleasure." Zorra giggled. Win smiled. Welcome to the Psycho Hotline. Only $3.99 per minute. First call is free.

Myron and Win waited now. Two minutes past. Esperanza said, "Middle elevator. All three are inside."

"Anyone else with them?"

"No . . . wait. Damn, two businessmen are going in."

Myron closed his eyes and cursed.

Win looked at him. "Your call."

Panic squeezed Myron's chest. Innocent people in the elevator. There was sure to be violence. Witnesses now.

"Well?"

"Hold the phone." It was Esperanza. "The granite guy blocked their path. Looks like he told them to wait for another elevator."

"Top-notch security," Win said. "Good to see we're not dealing with amateurs."

"Okay," Esperanza said. "Just the three of them are inside now."

The relief in Myron's face was palpable.

Esperanza said, "Elevator closing . . . now."

Myron pressed the Up button. Win took out his forty-four. Myron pulled out a Glock. They waited. Myron kept the gun by his thigh. It felt heavy in a terrible, comforting way. Myron kept glancing down the corridor. No one. He hoped their luck would hold. He felt his pulse start to race. His mouth was dry. The room suddenly felt warmer.

A minute later, the light above the middle elevator dinged.

Win's face was in the zone, semi-euphoric. He wriggled his eyebrows and said, "Showtime."

Myron tensed his muscles, leaned in a bit. The elevator's whirring noise stopped. There was a delay and then the doors started sliding open. Win didn't wait. He was inside before the opening had reached a foot. He found Grover and stuck the gun in the big man's ear. Myron did the same with the other guard.

"Waxy ear buildup a problem, Grover?" Win said in his best voice-over. "Smith and Wesson has the solution!"

Susan Lex started to open her mouth. Win cut her off with a finger against her lip and a gentle "Shh."

Win frisked and disarmed Grover. Myron followed his lead with the second guard. Grover glared daggers at Win. Win took them on and said, "Please—no, pretty please—make a sudden move."

Grover didn't budge.

Win stepped back. The elevator door started closing. Myron stopped it with his foot. He pointed the weapon at Susan Lex. "You're coming with me," Myron said.

"Don't you want revenge first?" Grover said.

Myron looked at him.

"Go ahead." Grover spread his hands. "Hit me in the gut. Go ahead, give it your best shot."

"Pardon *moi*," Win said. "But does that offer apply to me too?"

Grover looked at the smaller man like a tasty leftover. "I heard you're not bad," he said.

Win looked back at Myron. " 'Not bad,' " he repeated. "Monsieur Grover heard I was 'not bad.' "

"Win," Myron said.

Win snapped his knee deep into Grover's groin. He followed through, driving the man's testicles all the way into his stomach. Grover did not make a sound. He simply folded like a bad hand of poker.

"Oh, wait, you said 'gut,' didn't you?" Win looked down at him, frowned. "Must work on my aim. Perhaps you're right. Perhaps I am merely 'not bad.' "

Grover was on his knees, his hands between his legs. Win kicked him in the head with his instep. Grover toppled over like a bowling pin. Win looked over at the other guard, who was putting his hands up and backing quickly into a corner.

"Will you tell your friends I was 'not bad?' " Win asked him.

The guard shook his head.

"Enough," Myron said.

Win picked up the cell phone. "Zorra, report."

"They are not moving, handsome."

"Come back up then. You can help me clean up."

"Clean up? Ooo, Zorra will hurry."

Win laughed.

"No more," Myron said. Win did not reply, but Myron hadn't really expected him to. Myron grabbed Susan Lex's arm. "Let's go."

He pulled her into the stairwell. Zorra bounded into view—on high heels no less. Leaving two unarmed men alone with Win and Zorra. Talk about scary. But he had no choice here. Myron turned to Susan Lex, keeping tight hold of her elbow.

"I need your help," he said to her.

Susan Lex looked at him, head high, not backing off.

"I promise not to say anything," he went on. "I have no interest in hurting you or your family. But you're going to take me to see Dennis."

"And if I say no?"

Myron just looked at her.

"You'd hurt me?" she said.

"I just beat up an innocent man," Myron said.

"And you'd do the same to a woman?"

"I wouldn't want to be accused of sexism."

Her expression remained defiant, but unlike Chase Layton, she seemed to understand how the real world worked. "You know what sort of power I have."

"I do."

"Then you know what I'll do to you when this is all over?"

"I don't much care. A thirteen-year-old boy has been kidnapped."

She almost smiled. "I thought you said he needed a bone marrow transplant."

"I don't have time to explain."

"My brother isn't involved in this."

"I keep hearing that."

"Because it's true."

"Then prove it to me."

Something in her face shifted then, changing her features, relaxing them into something strangely approaching tranquility. "Come," she said. "Let's go."

33

Susan Lex directed him north on the FDR to the Harlem River Drive and then north again to 684. Once they were in Connecticut, the roads grew quieter. Woods thickened. Buildings grew scarce. Traffic was pretty much nonexistent.

"We're almost there," Susan Lex said. "I'd like the truth now."

"I'm telling you the truth."

"Fine," she said. Then: "How do you plan on getting away with this?"

"With what?"

"Are you going to kill me when this is all over?"

"No."

"Then I'll come back after you. I'll press charges, if nothing else."

"I told you before. I don't much care. But I've thought of something."

"Oh?"

"Dennis will save me."

"How?"

"If he is the Sow the Seeds kidnapper—"

"He's not."

"—or somehow involved with him, then what I'm doing here will be small potatoes by comparison."

"And if he's not?"

Myron shrugged. "Either way, I'm going to learn whatever it is you want to hide. We make a deal. I never tell what I saw. In exchange, you leave me alone."

"Or I can simply kill you."

"I don't believe you'd do that."

"No?"

"You're not a killer. And even if you were, it would be too complicated. I'd leave evidence behind. I have Win covering my back. It would be too messy."

"We'll see," she said, but there was no starch there. She pointed up ahead. "Turn off up here."

She pointed to a dirt road that seemed to materialize from nowhere. There was a guardhouse fifty yards down and to the left. Myron pulled up. Susan Lex leaned over and smiled. The guard waved her through. There were no signs, no identification marks, nothing. The whole setup looked like some sort of militia compound.

After the gatehouse, the dirt road stopped and a paved one began. New pavement from the looks of it colored the dark black-gray of heavy rain. Trees crowded the sides like parade watchers. Up ahead, the road narrowed. The trees closed in too. Myron veered the car to the left and passed through wrought-iron gates guarded by two stone falcons.

"What is this?" Myron asked.

Susan Lex did not reply.

A mansion seemed to push out of the green, elbowing its way forward. The exterior was classic off-white Georgian but on an oversized scale. Palladian windows, pilasters, fancy pediments, curved balconies, brick cornering and what looked like real stone masonry were all garnished with hints of green ivy. A set of oversized double doors were dead center, the entire edifice perfectly symmetrical.

"Park in the lot over there," Susan Lex said.

Myron followed her finger. There was indeed a paved lot. Myron figured it contained close to twenty cars. Various makes. A BMW, a couple of Honda Accords, three Mercedes of different lineage, Fords,

SUVs, one station wagon. Your basic American melting pot. Myron glanced back at the oversize manor. He noticed ramps now. Lots of them. He checked the cars. Several had MD license plates.

"A hospital," he said.

Susan Lex smiled. "Come along."

They headed up the brick path. Gloved gardeners were on their knees, working on the flower beds. A woman walked by in the opposite direction. She smiled politely but said nothing. They passed through an arched entranceway and into a two-story foyer. A woman seated behind the desk stood, slightly startled.

"We weren't expecting you, ma'am," she said.

"That's fine."

"I don't have security set up."

"That's fine too."

"Yes, ma'am."

Susan Lex barely broke stride. She took the sweeping staircase on her left, staying in the middle, not touching a handrail. Myron followed.

"What did she mean about security?" Myron asked.

"When I visit, they make sure the hallways are kept clear and that no one else is present."

"To keep your secret?"

"Yes," she said. She did not stop moving. "Perhaps you noticed that she called me 'ma'am.' That's part of the discretion here. They never use names."

When they reached the top level, Susan turned to the left. The corridor had raised wallpaper in a classic floral design and nothing else. No small tables, no chairs, no pictures in frames, no Oriental runners. They passed by maybe a dozen rooms, only two with doors open. Myron noticed that the doors were extra wide and he remembered his visit to Babies and Children's Hospital. Extra wide doors there too. For wheelchairs and stretchers and the like.

When they reached the end of the corridor, Susan stopped, took a deep breath, looked back at Myron. "Are you ready?"

He nodded.

She opened the door and stepped inside. Myron followed. A four-poster antique bed, like something you'd see on a tour of Jefferson's Monticello, overwhelmed the room. The walls were warm green with woodwork trim. There was a small crystal chandelier, a burgundy Victorian couch, a Persian rug with deep scarlets. A Mozart violin concerto was playing a bit too loudly on the stereo. A woman sat in the corner reading a book. She too started upright when she saw who it was.

"It's okay," Susan Lex said. "Would you mind leaving us for a few moments?"

"Yes, ma'am," the woman said. "If you need anything—"

"I'll ring, thank you."

The woman did a semi-curtsy/semi-bow and hurried out. Myron looked at the man in the bed. The resemblance to the computer rendering was uncanny, almost perfect. Even, strangely enough, the dead eyes. Myron moved closer. Dennis Lex followed him with the dead eyes, unfocused, empty, like windows over a vacant lot.

"Mr. Lex?"

Dennis Lex just stared at him.

"He can't talk," she said.

Myron turned to her. "I don't understand," he said.

"You were right before. It's a hospital. Of sorts. In another era, I suppose one would have called it a private sanitarium."

"How long has your brother been here?"

"Thirty years," she said. She moved toward the bed, and for the first time, she looked down at her brother. "You see, Mr. Bolitar, this is where the wealthy store unpleasantness." She reached down and stroked her brother's cheek. Dennis Lex did not respond. "We're too cultured not to give our loved ones the best. All very humane and practical, don't you know."

Myron waited for her to say more. She kept stroking her brother's cheek. He tried to see her face, but she kept it lowered and away from him.

"Why is he here?" Myron asked.

"I shot him," she said.

Myron opened his mouth, closed it, did the math. "But you were only a child when he disappeared."

"Fourteen years old," she said. "Bronwyn was six." She stopped stroking the cheek. "It's an old story, Mr. Bolitar. You've probably heard it a thousand times. We were playing with a loaded gun. Bronwyn wanted to hold it, I said no, he reached for it, it went off." She said it all in one breath, staring down at her brother, still stroking the cheek. "This is the end result."

Myron looked at the still eyes in the bed. "He's been here since?"

She nodded. "For a while I kept waiting for him to die. So I could officially be a murderer."

"You were a child," Myron said. "It was an accident."

She looked at him and smiled. "My, that means so much coming from you, thank you."

Myron said nothing.

"No matter," she said. "Daddy took care of it. He arranged for my brother to have the best care. He was a very private person, my father. It was his gun. He'd left it where his children could play with it. His business and reputation were both growing. He had political aspirations at the time. He just wanted it all to go away."

"And it did."

She tilted her head back and forth. "Yes."

"What about your mother?"

"What about her?"

"What did she say?"

"My mother hated unpleasantness, Mr. Bolitar. After the incident, she never saw her son again."

Dennis Lex made a sound, a guttural scrape, nothing remotely human. Susan gently shushed him.

"Did you and Bronwyn ever get help?" Myron asked.

She cocked an eyebrow. "Help?"

"Counseling. To help you through it."

She made a face. "Oh please," she said.

Myron stood there, his mind circling nowhere over nothing.

"So now you know the truth, Mr. Bolitar."

"I guess," he said.

"Meaning?"

"I wonder why you told me all this. You could have just shown Dennis to me."

"Because you won't talk."

"How can you be so sure?"

She smiled. "After you shoot your own brother, shooting strangers becomes so easy."

"You don't really believe that."

"No, I suppose not." Susan Lex turned and faced him. "The fact is, you really don't have much to tell. As you said earlier, we both have reasons to keep our mouths shut. You'll be arrested for kidnapping and Lord knows what. The evidence of my crime—if indeed it was a crime—is nonexistent. You'd be worse off than I."

Myron nodded, but his mind still whirred. Her story might be true or just something she told him to gain sympathy, to contain the damage. Still, there was the ring of truth in her words. Maybe her reason for talking was simpler. Maybe, after all this time, she just needed someone who'd listen to her confession. Didn't matter. None of it mattered. There was nothing here. Dennis Lex was truly a dead end.

Myron looked out the window. The sun was starting to dip away. He checked his watch. Jeremy had been missing five hours now—five hours alone with a madman—and Myron's best lead, his *only* lead, was lying brain-damaged in a hospital room.

The sun was still strong, bathing the expansive garden in white. Myron saw what looked like a maze made of shrubbery. He spotted several patients in wheelchairs, legs covered with blankets, sitting by a fountain. Serene. The rays reflected off a pool of water and a statue in the middle of—

He stopped. The statue.

Myron felt the blood in his veins turn to crystal. He shaded his eyes with his hand and squinted again.

"Oh Christ," he said.

Then he sprinted toward the stairs.

34

Susan Lex's helicopter was starting to descend toward the sanitarium's landing pad when Kimberly Green called him on the cell phone.

"We've caught Stan Gibbs," she said. "But the boy wasn't with him."

"That's because he isn't the kidnapper."

"You know something I don't?"

Myron ignored the question. "Has Stan told you anything?"

"Nope. He lawyered up already. Says he won't talk to anyone but you. You, Myron. Why don't I find that particularly surprising?"

Had Myron responded, the helicopter's propeller would have drowned it out. He backed off a few steps. The copter touched down. The pilot stuck his head out and waved to him.

"I'm on my way," Myron shouted into the phone. He switched it off and turned to Susan Lex. "Thank you."

She nodded.

He ducked and ran toward the helicopter. As they rose, Myron looked back down. Susan Lex's chin was tilted up, her eyes still on him. He waved. And she waved back.

• • •

Stan was not in a holding cell because they had nothing to hold him on. He sat in a waiting room with his eyes on the table and let his attorney, Clara Steinberg, do the talking. Myron had known Clara—he called her Aunt Clara though there was no familial relationship—since he was too young to remember. Aunt Clara and Uncle Sidney were Mom and Dad's closest friends. Dad had gone to elementary school with Clara. Mom had roomed with her in law school. Aunt Clara, in fact, had set up Mom and Dad on their first date. She liked to remind Myron with a wink that "you wouldn't be here if it weren't for your aunt Clara." Then she'd wink again. Subtle, that Clara. During the holidays, she always pinched Myron's cheeks in admiration of his *punim*.

"Let me set up the ground rules, *bubbe*," she said to him. Clara had gray hair and a pair of oversized glasses that magnified her eyes to Ant-Man size. She looked up at him and the giant eyes seemed to reel in everything all at once. She wore a white blouse with a gray vest, matching skirt, a kerchief around her neck, and teardrop pearl earrings. Think Shtetl Barbara Bush.

"One," she said, "I am Mr. Gibbs's attorney of record. I have requested that this conversation not be overheard. I have changed rooms four times to make sure the authorities don't listen in. But I don't trust them. They think your aunt Clara is an old dodo bird. They think we're going to chat right here."

"We're not?" Myron said.

"We're not," she repeated. There was little hint of the cheek pincher here; if she were an athlete, you'd say that she'd strapped on her game face. "What we're going to do first is stand up. Got me?"

"Stand up," Myron repeated.

"Right. Then I'm going to lead you and Stan outside, across the street. I'm going to remain on the other side of the street with all those friendly agents. We do this right now, quickly, so they won't have a chance to set up surveillance. Understood?"

Myron nodded. Stan kept his eyes on the Formica.

"Good, just so we're all on the same page here." She knocked on the door. Kimberly Green opened it. Clara walked past her without speaking. Myron and Stan followed. Kimberly rushed up behind them.

"Where do you think you're going?"

"Change of plans, doll."

"You can't do that."

"Sure I can. I'm a sweet little old lady."

"I don't care if you're the Queen Mother," Kimberly said. "You're not going anywhere."

"You married, hon?"

"What?"

"Never mind," Clara said. "Try this on for size. See how it fits. My client demands privacy."

"We already promised—"

"Shh, you're talking when you should be listening. My client demands privacy. So he and Mr. Bolitar are going to take a little walk somewhere. You and I will watch from a distance. We will not listen in."

"I already told you—"

"Shh, you're giving me a headache." Aunt Clara rolled her eyes and kept walking. Myron and Stan followed. They reached the doorway. Clara pointed to a bus depot across the street. "Sit over there," she said to them. "On the bench."

Myron said okay. Clara put a hand on his elbow.

"Cross at the corner," she said. "And wait for the light."

The two men walked to the corner and waited for the light before crossing the street. Kimberly Green and her fellow agents fumed. Clara took them by the hand and led them back toward the building's entrance. Stan and Myron sat on the bench. Stan watched a New Jersey Transit bus go by like it carried the secret to life.

"We don't have time to enjoy the scenery, Stan."

Stan leaned forward, put his elbows on his knees. "This is difficult for me."

"If it makes it any easier," Myron said, "I know that the Sow the Seeds kidnapper is your father."

Stan's head fell into his hands.

"Stan?"

"How did you find out?"

"Through Dennis Lex. I found him in a private sanitarium in Connecticut. He's been there for thirty years. But you already knew that, didn't you?"

Gibbs said nothing.

"At the sanitarium, there's a big garden in the back. With this statue of Diana the Huntress. There's a picture in your condo of you and your father standing in front of that same statue. He was a patient there. You don't have to confirm or deny it. I was just there. Susan Lex has pull. An administrator told us Edwin Gibbs had been in and out of there for fifteen years. The rest is fairly obvious. Your father was there a long time. It'd be easy to learn who else was there, no matter how strict the so-called security. So he knew about Dennis Lex. And he stole his identity. It's a hell of a twist, I'll give him that. Fake IDs used to be somewhat pretty easy to come by. You'd visit a graveyard, find a child who died, request his social security card, bingo. But that doesn't work anymore. Computers closed down that loophole. Nowadays when you die, your social security number dies with you. So your father took the identity of someone still alive, someone who has no use for it, someone committed permanently. In other words, he used the ID of a living person who has no life. And to go deeper undercover, he changed the person's name. Dennis Lex became Davis Taylor. Untraceable."

"Except you traced it."

"I got lucky."

"Go on," Stan said. "Tell me what else you know."

"We don't have time for this, Stan."

"You don't understand," he said.

"What?"

"If you're the one who says it—if you figure it out on your own—it's not as much a betrayal. You see?"

No time to argue. And maybe Myron did see. "Let's start with the question every reporter wanted to know: why you? Why did the Sow the Seeds kidnapper choose you? The answer: because the kidnapper was your father. He knew you wouldn't turn him in. Maybe part of you hoped someone would figure it out. I don't know. I also don't know if you found him or he found you."

"He found me," Stan said. "He came to me as a reporter. Not as a son. He made that clear."

"Sure," Myron said, "double protection. He gets you with the fact that you'd be turning in your own father—plus he gives you an ethical foundation for remaining silent. The beloved First Amendment. You couldn't name a source. It gave you a very neat out—you could be both moralistic and the good son."

Stan looked up. "So you see that I had no choice."

"Oh, I wouldn't be so easy on myself," Myron said. "You weren't being totally altruistic. Everyone says you were ambitious. That played a part here. You got fame out of this. You were handed a monster story—the kind that propels careers into the stratosphere. You were on TV and got your own cable show. You got a big raise and invited to fancy parties. You want to tell me that wasn't a part of it?"

"It was a by-product," Stan said. "It wasn't a factor."

"You say so."

"It's like you said—I couldn't turn him in, even if I wanted to. There was a constitutional principle here. Even if he wasn't my father, I had an obligation—"

"Save it for your minister," Myron said. "Where is he?"

Stan did not reply. Myron looked across the street. Lots of traffic. The cars started blurring and through them, standing on the other side of the street with Kimberly Green, he saw Greg Downing.

"That man over there," Myron said, pointing with his chin. "That's the boy's father."

Stan looked, but his face didn't change.

"There's a kid in danger," Myron said. "That trumps your constitutional cover."

"He's still my father."

"And he's kidnapped a thirteen-year-old boy," Myron said.

Stan looked up. "What would *you* do?"

"What?"

"Would you give up your father? Just like that?"

"If he was kidnapping children? Yeah, I would."

"Do you really think it's that easy?"

"Who said anything about easy?" Myron said.

Stan put his head back in his hands. "He's sick and he needs help."

"And there's also an innocent boy out there."

"So?"

Myron looked at him.

"I don't mean to sound callous, but I don't know this boy. He has no connection to me. My father does. That's what matters here. You hear about a plane crash, right? You hear about how two hundred people die and you sigh and you go on with your life and you thank God it wasn't your loved one in the plane. Don't you do that?"

"What's your point?"

"You do that because the people on the plane are strangers. Like this boy. We don't care about strangers. They don't count."

"Speak for yourself," Myron said.

"Are you close to your father, Myron?"

"Yes."

"And in your heart of hearts, in your deepest, most honest moments, if you could sacrifice his life to save those two hundred people on the airplane, would you do it? Think about it. If God came down to you and said, 'Okay, that plane never crashed. Those people all arrive safely. In exchange, your father will die.' Would you make that trade?"

"I'm not into playing God."

"But you're asking me to," Stan said. "I turn my father in, they'll kill him. He'll get the lethal injection. If that's not playing God, I don't know what is. So I'm asking you. Would you trade those two hundred lives for your father's?"

"We don't have time—"

"Would you?"

"Okay, if it was my father shooting down the plane," Myron said, "yes, Stan, I would make that trade."

"And suppose your father wasn't culpable? If he was sick or deranged?"

"Stan, we don't have time for this."

Something in Stan's face dropped. He closed his eyes.

"There's a boy out there," Myron said. "We can't let him die."

"And if he's already dead?"

"I don't know."

"You'll want my father dead."

"Not by my hand," Myron said.

Stan took a deep breath and looked over at Greg Downing. Greg stared back, stared right through him. "Okay," he said at last. "But we go alone."

"Alone?"

"Just you and me."

Kimberly Green had a major conniption. "Are you insane?"

They were back inside, sitting around the Formica table. Kimberly Green, Rick Peck, and two other faceless feds were hunched together as one. Clara Steinberg sat with her client. Greg sat next to Myron. Jeremy's kidnapping had siphoned all the blood from Greg's face. His hands looked sucked dry, his skin almost crisp, his eyes too solid and unblinking. Myron put a hand on his shoulder. Greg didn't seem to notice.

"You want my client to cooperate or not?" Clara asked.

"I'm supposed to let my number one suspect go?"

"I'm not running away," Stan said.

"How am I supposed to know that?" Kimberly countered.

"It's the only way," Stan said, his voice a plea. "You'll go in with guns blazing. Someone is going to get hurt."

"We're professionals," Green countered. "We don't go in with guns blazing."

"My father is unstable. If he sees a lot of cops, I can guarantee there will be bloodshed."

"Doesn't have to be that way," she said. "It's up to him."

"Exactly," Stan said. "I'm not taking that chance with my father's life. You let us go. You don't follow us. I'll have him surrender to you. Myron will be with me the whole time. He's armed and he has a cell phone."

"Come on," Myron said. "We're wasting time here."

Kimberly Green chewed on her lower lip. "I don't have the authorization—"

"Forget it," Clara Steinberg said.

"Excuse me?"

Clara pointed a meaty finger at Kimberly Green. "Listen up, missy, you haven't arrested Mr. Gibbs, correct?"

Green hesitated. "That's correct."

Clara turned to Stan and Myron and waved the backs of both hands at them. "So shoo, go, good-bye. We're talking nonsense here. Hurry along. Shoo."

Stan and Myron slowly rose.

"Shoo."

Stan looked down at Kimberly. "If I spot a tail, I'm calling this off. You got me?"

She stewed in silence.

"You've been trailing me for three weeks now. I know what one of your tails looks like."

"She won't tail you."

It was Greg Downing. He and Stan locked eyes again. Greg stood. "I want to go with you too," Greg said. "And I probably have the strongest interest in keeping your father alive."

"How do you figure?"

"Your father's bone marrow can save my son's life. If he dies, so does my son. And if Jeremy has been hurt . . . well, I'd like to be there for him."

Stan didn't waste a lot of time thinking about it. "Let's hurry."

35

Stan drove. Greg sat in the front passenger seat, Myron in the back.

"Where are we going?" Myron asked.

"Bernardsville," Stan said. "It's in Morris County."

Myron knew the town.

"My grandmother died three years ago," Stan said. "We haven't sold the house yet. My father sometimes stays there."

"Where else does he stay?"

"Waterbury, Connecticut."

Greg looked back at Myron. The old man, the blond wig. It clicked for both of them at the same time.

"He's Nathan Mostoni?"

Stan nodded. "That's his main alias. The real Nathan Mostoni is another patient at Pine Hills—that's what we call that fancy loony bin, Pine Hills. Mostoni was the one who came up with the idea of using the identification of the committed, mostly for scams. He and my father became close friends. When Nathan slipped into total delirium, my father took his identity."

Greg shook his head, made two fists. "You should have turned the crazy bastard in."

"You love your son, don't you, Mr. Downing?"

Greg gave Stan a look that could have bored holes through titanium. "What the hell does that have to do with anything?"

"Would you want your son to turn you in one day?"

"Don't hand me that. If I'm a raving psychopathic maniac, yeah, my son can turn me in. Or better, he can put a bullet in my head. You knew your old man was sick, right? The least you could have done was get him help."

"We tried," Stan said. "He was in institutions most of his adult life. It didn't do any good. Then he ran off. When he finally called me, I hadn't seen him in eight years. Imagine that. Eight years. He calls me and tells me he needs to talk to me as a reporter. He made that clear. As a reporter. No matter what he told me, I couldn't reveal the source. He made me promise. I was confused as all hell. But I agreed. And then he told me his story. What he'd been doing. I could barely breathe. I wanted to die. I wanted to just dry up and die."

Greg put his fingers to his mouth. Stan concentrated on the road. Myron stared out the window. He thought about the father of three young children, age forty-one; the female college student, age twenty; and the young newlyweds, ages twenty-eight and twenty-seven. He thought about Jeremy's scream over the phone. He thought about Emily waiting at the house, her mind sowing the seeds, sick and blackening.

They got off Route 78 and took 287 north. They exited onto winding streets with no straightaways. Bernardsville was about old money and rustic wealth, a town of converted mills and stone houses and waterwheels. There were fields of long brown grass swaying in death, everything a little too old and too neatly overgrown.

"It's on this road," Stan said.

Myron looked out. His mouth was dry. He felt a tingle deep in his belly. The car traveled down another corkscrew of a street, the loose gravel crunching under the tires. There were deeply wooded lots commingling with your standard suburban front lawns. Plenty of center-hall colonials and those mid-seventies ranches that aged like milk left out on the counter. A yellow sign warned about children at play, but Myron saw none.

They pulled into a cake-dried driveway with weeds poking up through the cracks. Myron lowered his window. There was plenty of burnt-out grass, but the sweet summer smell of lillies still loomed and even cloyed. Crickets droned. Wildflowers blossomed. Not a hint of menace.

Up ahead Myron spotted what looked like a farmhouse. Black shutters stood out against the white clapboards. There were lights coming from inside, giving the house a glow that was big and soft and oddly welcoming. The front porch was the type that craved a swinging settee and a pitcher of lemonade.

When the car reached the front of the house, Stan shifted into park and turned off the ignition. The crickets eased up. Myron almost waited for someone to note that it was "Quiet" and for someone else to add, "Yeah, too quiet."

Stan turned to them. "I think I should go in first," he said.

Neither man argued. Greg stared out the window at the house, probably conjuring up unspeakable horrors. Myron's left leg started jackhammering. It often did when he was tense. Stan reached for the door handle.

That was when the first bullet smashed through the front passenger-side window.

The glass exploded, and Myron saw Greg's head fly back at a rate it was never supposed to achieve. A thick gob of crimson smacked Myron in the cheek.

"Greg!"

No time. Instincts took over. Myron grabbed Greg, pushed him down, trying to keep his own head down too. Blood. Lots of it. From Greg. He was bleeding, bleeding heavily, but Myron couldn't tell from where. Another bullet rang out. Another window shattered, raining shards of glass down on Myron's head. He kept his hand on top of Greg, tried to cover him, protect him. Greg's own hand fumbled absently on his chest and face, calmly searching for the bullet hole. Blood kept flowing. From the neck. Greg's neck. Or collarbone. Whatever. He couldn't see through the blood. Myron tried to stop the flow with his bare hand, pushing the sticky liquid away, finding the wound with his finger, applying pressure with his palm. But the blood slipped through the cracks between his fingers. Greg looked up at him with big eyes.

Stan Gibbs put his hands over his head and ducked into a quasi-emergency-landing position. "Stop!" he yelled, almost childlike. "Dad!"

Another bullet. More glass shards. Myron reached into his pocket and pulled out his gun. Greg grabbed his hand and pulled it down. Myron looked at him.

"Can't kill him," Greg said to Myron. There was blood in his mouth now. "If he dies . . . Jeremy's only hope."

Myron nodded, but he didn't put the gun away. He looked over at Stan. In the distance, they heard a helicopter. Then sirens. The feds were on their way. No surprise. There was no way they weren't going to follow. By air, at the very least.

Greg's breathing was short spurts. His eyes were going hazy-gray.

"We got to do something here, Stan," Myron said.

"Just stay down," Stan said. Then he opened the car door and shouted, "Dad!"

No reply.

Stan got out of the car. He raised his hands and stood. "Please," he shouted. "They'll be here soon. They'll kill you."

Nothing. The air was so motionless that Myron thought he could still hear the echoes from the gun blasts.

"Dad?"

Myron lifted his head a little and risked a glance. A man stepped out from behind the side of the house. Edwin Gibbs wore full army fatigues with combat boots. He had an ammunition belt hanging off his shoulder. His rifle was pointed toward the ground. Myron could see it was Nathan Mostoni, though he looked twenty years younger. His head was high, chin up. His back was straight.

Greg made a gurgling sound. Myron ripped off his shirt and pushed it against the wound. But Greg's eyes were closing. "Stay with me," Myron urged. "Come on, Greg. Stay here."

Greg did not reply. His eyes fluttered and closed. Myron felt his heart slam into his throat. "Greg?"

He felt for a pulse. It was there. Myron was no doctor, but it didn't feel strong. Oh damn. Oh come on.

Outside the car, Stan moved closer to his father. "Please," Stan said. "Put down the rifle, Dad."

The fed cars poured into the driveway. Brakes squealed. Feds jumped out of their vehicles, took position using the open doors as shields, aimed their weapons. Edwin Gibbs looked confused, panicked, Frankenstein's monster suddenly surrounded by angry villagers. Stan hurried toward him.

The air seemed to thicken, molasses-like. It was hard to move, hard to breathe. Myron could almost feel the officers tense up, fingers itchy, tips touching the cold metal of the trigger. He let go of Greg for a moment and shouted, "You can't shoot him!"

A fed had a megaphone. "Put down the rifle! Now!"

"Don't shoot!" Myron shouted.

For a moment nothing happened. Time did that in-and-out motion where everything rushes and freezes all at one time. Another fed car skidded up the driveway. A news van followed, screeching when it hit the brakes. Stan kept walking toward his father.

"You are surrounded," the megaphone said. "Drop the rifle and put your hands behind your head. Drop to your knees."

Edwin Gibbs looked left, looked right. Then he smiled. Myron felt the dread rise up in his chest. Gibbs lifted his rifle.

Myron rolled out of the car. "No!"

Stan Gibbs broke into a sprint. His father spotted him, his face calm. He aimed the rifle at his approaching son. Stan kept running. Time did stop this time, waiting for the blast of gunfire. But it didn't come. Stan had gained on him too fast. Edwin Gibbs closed his eyes and let his son tackle him. The two men fell to the ground. Stan stayed on top of his father, blanketing him, leaving no space open.

"Don't shoot him," Stan yelled. His voice sounded hurt, again so childlike. "Please don't shoot him."

Edwin Gibbs lay on his back. He let go of the rifle. It dropped into the grass. Stan pushed it away, still on top of his father, still shielding him from harm. They stayed there until the officers took over. They gently removed Stan and then rolled Edwin Gibbs onto his stomach, cuffing his hands behind his back. The news camera caught it all.

Myron turned back to the car. Greg's eyes were still closed. He wasn't moving. Two of the officers ran toward the car, calling into their radios for an ambulance. Nothing Myron could do for Greg now. He looked back at the farmhouse, his heart still lodged in his throat. He ran toward the house and grabbed the knob. The door was locked. He used his shoulder. The door came down. Myron stepped into the foyer.

"Jeremy?" he called out.

But there was no reply.

36

They didn't find Jeremy Downing.

Myron checked every room, every closet, the basement, the garage. Nothing. The feds streamed in with him. They started knocking down walls. They used a heat sensor to check for underground caves or hidden places. Nothing. In the garage, they found a white van. In the back of it, they found one of Jeremy's red sneakers.

But that was it.

News vans, lots of them, gathered at the end of the driveway. What with the kidnapped boy, his famous father shot and in critical condition, a potential serial killer in custody, the connection to Stan Gibbs and the famed plagiarism charges—the story was getting the full, round-the-clock, give-it-a-banner-and-theme-music, death-of-Diana coverage. Stiffly coiffed correspondents flashed their best grim-news teeth and led with phrases like "the vigil continues" or "the search is reaching its xth hour" or "behind me lurks the lair" or "we'll be here until."

A recent photograph of Jeremy, the one Emily had on the Web, ran continuously on all the stations. Brokaw, Jennings and Rather interrupted their programming. Viewers called in tips, but so far none amounted to anything.

And the hours passed.

Emily drove to the scene. It played on all the usual outlets, her head lowered, hurrying toward a waiting car like an arrested felon, the flashbulbs creating a grotesque strobe effect. Cameramen elbowed each other out of the way to capture a glimpse of the stricken mother collapsing in the back of the car. They even got a shot of her through the passenger seat crying. Great TV.

Nightfall brought out searchlights. Volunteers and law officials scoured the nearby grounds for signs of recent graves or digging. Nothing. They brought in dogs. Nothing. They spoke to neighbors, some of whom "never trusted that family" but most gave the standard "seemed like nice folk, real quiet neighbors" spiel.

Edwin Gibbs had been taken into custody. They tried to question him at the Bernardsville Police Station, but he wasn't talking. Clara Steinberg became his attorney. She stayed with him. So did Stan. They pleaded with Edwin, Myron guessed, but so far, he hadn't talked.

Back at the farmhouse, the wind picked up. Myron's bad knee ached, each step giving him a fresh jolt of pain. The pain was unpredictable, arriving whenever it damn well pleased, staying on like the most unwelcome houseguest. There was no side benefit to the knee pain, no weather forecasting or anything like that. Some days it just ached. Nothing he could do about it. He approached Emily and put his arm around her.

"He's still out there," Emily said to the dark.

Myron said nothing.

"He's all alone. And it's night. And he's probably scared."

"We'll find him, Em."

"Myron?"

"Hmm."

"Is this more payback for that night?"

Another search party returned, their shoulders slumped in resignation, if not defeat. Odd thing, these search parties. You wanted to find something, yet you didn't want to find something.

"No," Myron said. "I think you were right. I think our mistake was the best thing that could have happened. And maybe there's a price to pay to have something so good."

She closed her eyes, but she did not cry. Myron stayed next to her. The wind howled, scattering the surrounding voices like dead leaves, whipping branches, and whispering in your ear like the most frightening lover.

37

Myron and Win looked through the one-way glass at Clara Steinberg's back and the faces of Stan and Edwin Gibbs. Kimberly Green stood with them. So did Eric Ford. Emily had gone to the hospital to sit vigil while Greg was in surgery. No one seemed to know if he'd make it.

"Why aren't you listening in?" Myron asked.

"Can't," Ford replied. "Attorney-client."

"How long they been at it?"

"On and off since we took him into custody."

Myron checked the clock behind his head. Nearly three in the morning. Evidence collection teams had leveled the house, but still no clue where Jeremy was. Fatigue lined everyone's face, except maybe Win's. Fatigue never registered on his face. Win must internalize it. Or maybe it had something to do with having little to no conscience.

"We don't have time for this," Myron said.

"I know," Eric Ford said. "It's been a long night for all of us."

"Do something."

"Like what?" Ford snapped. "What exactly would you like me to do?"

Win picked up that one. "Perhaps you could speak to Ms. Steinberg in private."

That hooked Ford's attention. "What?"

"Take her into another room," Win said, "and leave me alone with your suspect."

Eric Ford looked at him. "You shouldn't even be here. He"—a gesture toward Myron—"represents the Downing family, as much as I don't like it. But you got no reason to be here."

"Make a reason," Win said.

Eric Ford waved his hand as if this wasn't worth his time.

Win kept the voice at a low, soothing level. "You don't have to be a part of it," he said. "Simply talk to his attorney. Leave Gibbs alone in the room. That's all. Nothing unethical about that."

Ford shook his head. "You're crazy."

"We need answers," Win said.

"And you want to beat them out of him."

"Beating leaves marks," Win said. "I never leave marks."

"That's not how it works, pal. Ever heard of the U.S. Constitution?"

"It's a document," Win said, "not a trump card. You have a choice. The obscure rights of that subhuman"—Win gestured through the glass—"or a young boy's right to live."

Ford leaned his forehead against the glass.

"If the boy dies while we're standing here," Win said, "how will you feel then?"

Ford shut his eyes. In the holding room, Clara Steinberg rose from her chair. She turned, and for the first time, Myron saw her face. He knew that she had represented bad people before—very, very bad people—but whatever horrors she was now hearing had washed away her skin tone and etched in something that would probably never leave. She approached the one-way mirror and knocked. Ford hit the sound switch.

"We need to talk," she said. "Let me out."

Eric Ford met Clara and Stan by the door. "Let's head down this way," he said.

"No," Clara said.

"Pardon me?"

"We'll talk in here," she said, "where I can watch my client. Wouldn't want an accident, now, would we?"

There were no chairs so they all stood by the one-way window—Kimberly Green, Eric Ford, Clara Steinberg, Stan Gibbs, Myron and Win. Stan kept his head down and plucked at his lower lip with his fingers. Myron tried to meet his eyes. Stan never gave him the chance.

"Okay," Clara said. "First off, we need a D.A."

"What for?" Eric Ford asked.

"Because we want a deal."

Ford tried to snicker. "Are you out of your mind?"

"No. My client is the only one who can tell you where Jeremy Downing is. He'll only do so under specific conditions."

"What conditions?"

"That's why we need a D.A."

"A D.A. will back whatever I agree to," Eric Ford said.

"I'll still want it in writing."

"And I want to hear what you're looking for here."

"Okay," Clara said, "here's the deal. We help you find Jeremy Downing. In exchange, you guarantee not to seek the death penalty for Edwin Gibbs. You also agree to psychiatric tests. You then recommend he be placed in a proper mental health facility, not a prison."

"You have to be kidding me."

"There's more," Clara said.

"More?"

"Mr. Edwin Gibbs will also agree to donate bone marrow to Jeremy Downing if the need arises. I understand that Mr. Bolitar is representing the family here. For the record, we should note that he is present as a witness to this agreement."

No one said anything.

"So we clear?" Clara said.

"No," Ford said, "we're not."

Clara adjusted her eyeglasses. "This deal is nonnegotiable." She turned to leave, her gaze snagging on Myron's. Myron just shook his head.

"I'm his attorney," she said to him.

"And you'll let a boy die for him?" Myron said.

"Don't start," Clara said, but her voice was soft.

Myron studied her face again, saw no give. He turned to Ford. "Agree," he said.

"Are you nuts?"

"The family cares about retribution. But they care more about finding their son. Agree to her terms."

"You think I'm taking orders from you?"

Myron's voice was soft. "Come on, Eric."

Ford frowned. He rubbed his face with his hands and then dropped them back to his side. "This agreement assumes, of course, that the boy is still alive."

"No," Clara Steinberg said.

"What?"

"Alive or dead does not change the state of Edwin Gibbs's mental health."

"So you don't know if he's alive or—"

"If we did, it would be an attorney-client communication and thus confidential."

Myron looked at her in stark horror. She met his eyes and would not blink. Myron tried Stan, but his head was still lowered. Even Win's face, usually the model of neutrality, was on edge. Win wanted to hurt somebody. He wanted to hurt somebody badly.

"We can't agree to that," Ford said.

"Then there's no deal," Clara said.

"You have to be reasonable—"

"Do we have a deal or not?"

Eric Ford shook his head. "No."

"See you in court, then."

Myron moved into her path.

"Step aside, Myron," Clara said.

He just looked down at her. She raised her eyes.

"You think your mother wouldn't be doing the same thing?" Clara said.

"Leave my mother out of this."

"Step aside," she said again. Aunt Clara was sixty-six. For the first time since he'd known her, she looked older than her age.

Myron turned back to Eric Ford. "Agree," he said.

He shook his head. "The boy is probably dead."

"Probably," Myron repeated. "Not definitely."

Win spoke up this time. "Agree," he said.

Ford looked at him.

"He won't get off easily," Win said.

Stan's head finally rose at that one. "What the hell is that sup-posed to mean?"

Win gave him flat eyes. "Absolutely nothing."

"I want this man kept away from my father."

Win smiled at him.

"You don't get it, do you?" Stan said. "None of you get it. My fa-ther is sick. He's not responsible. We're not making this up. Any competent psychiatrist in the world will agree. He needs help."

"He should die," Win said.

"He's a sick man."

"Sick men die all the time," Win said.

"That's not what I mean. He's like someone who has a heart con-dition. Or cancer. He needs help."

"He kidnaps and probably kills people," Win said.

"And it doesn't matter why he does it?"

"Of course it doesn't matter," Win said. "He does it. That's enough. He should not be put in a comfortable mental hospital. He should not be allowed to enjoy a wonderful film or read a great book or laugh again. He should not be able to see a beautiful woman or listen to Beethoven or know kindness or love—because his victims never will. What part of that don't you understand, Mr. Gibbs?"

Stan was shaking. "You agree," he said to Ford. "Or we don't help."

"If the boy dies because of this negotiation," Win said to Stan, "you will die."

Clara stepped into Win's face. "You threatening my client?" she shouted.

Win smiled at her. "I never threaten."

"There are witnesses."

"Worried about collecting your fee, Counselor?" Win asked.

"That's enough." It was Eric Ford. He looked at Myron. Myron nodded. "Okay," Ford said slowly. "We agree. Now, where is he?"

"I'll have to take you," Stan said.

"Again?"

"I wouldn't be able to give you directions. I'm not even sure I can find it after all these years."

"But we come along," Kimberly Green said.

"Yes."

There was an empty space, a sudden stillness that Myron didn't like.

"Is Jeremy alive or dead?" Myron asked.

"Truth?" Stan said. "I don't know."

38

E ric Ford drove with Kimberly Green riding shotgun and Myron and Stan in the backseat. Several cars' worth of agents followed them. So too did the press. Nothing they could do about that.

"My mother died in 1977," Stan said. "Cancer. My father was already unwell. The one thing in his life that mattered to him—the one good thing—was my mother. He loved her very much."

The time on the car clock read nearly 4:03 A.M. Stan told them where to turn off Route 15. A sign read DINGSMAN BRIDGE. They were heading into Pennsylvania.

"Whatever sanity was still there, my mother's death stripped away. He watched her suffer. Doctors tried everything—used all their technological advances—but it only made her suffer more. That's when my father started with the strength of the mind. If only my mother hadn't relied on technology, he thought. If only she used her mind instead. If only she'd seen its limitless potential. Technology killed her, he said. It gave her false hope. It stopped her from using the one thing that could save her—the limitless human brain."

No one had a comment.

"We had a summerhouse out here. It was beautiful. Fifteen acres of land, walking distance to a lake. My father used to take me hunting and fishing. But I haven't been out here in years. Haven't even thought about the place. He took my mother out here to die. Then he buried her in the woods. See, it's where her suffering finally ended."

The obvious question hung in the air, unasked: *And who else's?*

Myron would later remember nothing about the drive. No buildings, no landmarks, no trees. Outside his window was total night, the black folding over black, eyes squeezed shut in the darkest of rooms. He sat back and waited.

Stan told them to stop at the foot of a wooded area. More crickets sounded. The other cars pulled up alongside them. Feds got out and started combing the area. Beams from powerful flashlights revealed uneven earth. Myron ignored them. He swallowed and ran. Stan ran with him.

Before morning broke, the federal officers would find graves. They'd find the father of three children, the female college student, and the young newlyweds.

But for now, Myron and Stan kept running. Branches whipped Myron's face. He tripped over a root, curled into a roll, stood back up, kept running. They spotted the small house, barely visible in the faint moonlight. There were no lights on inside, no hint of life. Myron did not bother trying the knob this time. He took it full on, crashing the door down. More darkness. He heard a cry, turned, fumbled for the light switch, flipped it up.

Jeremy was there.

He was chained to a wall—dirty and terrified and still very much alive.

Myron felt his knees buckle, but he fought them and stayed upright. He ran to the boy. The boy stretched out his arms. Myron embraced him and felt his heart fall and shatter. Jeremy was crying. Myron lifted his hand and stroked the boy's hair and shushed him. Like his father. Like his father had done to him countless times. A sudden, beautiful warmth streamed through his veins, tingling his fingers and toes, and for a moment, Myron thought that maybe he understood what his father felt. Myron had always cherished being on the son side of the hug, but now, for just the most fleeting of moments, he experienced something so much stronger—the intensity and overwhelming depth of being on the other side—that it shook every part of him.

"You're okay," Myron said to him, cupping the boy's head. "It's over now."

But it wasn't.

An ambulance came. Jeremy was put inside. Myron called Dr. Karen Singh. She didn't mind being woken at five in the morning. He told her everything.

"Wow," Karen Singh said when he finished.

"Yes."

"We'll get someone to harvest the marrow right away. I'll start prepping Jeremy in the afternoon."

"You mean with chemo."

"Yes," she said. "You done good, Myron. Either way, you should be proud."

"Either way?"

"Come by my office tomorrow afternoon."

Myron felt a thumping in his chest. "What's up?"

"The paternity test," she said. "The results should be in by then."

Jeremy was on his way to the hospital. Myron wandered back outside. The feds were digging. The news vans were there. Stan Gibbs watched the mounds of earth grow, his face now beyond emotion. No sound, not even the crickets now, except for shovel hitting dirt. Myron's knee was acting up. He felt bone-weary. He wanted to find Emily. He wanted to go to the hospital. He wanted to know the results of that test and then he wanted to know what he was going to do with them.

He climbed back up the hill toward the car. More media. Someone called out to him. He ignored them. There were more federal officers working in silence. Myron walked past them. He didn't have the heart to hear what they'd found. Not just yet.

When he reached the top of the landing—when he saw Kimberly Green and the lifeless expression on her face—his heart took one more plummet.

He took another step. "Greg?" he said.

She shook her head, her eyes hazy and unfocused. "They shouldn't have left him alone," she said. "They should have watched him. Even after a careful search. You can never search too carefully."

"Search who?"

"Edwin Gibbs."

Myron was sure he'd heard wrong. "What about him?"

"They just found him," she said, having trouble with the words. "He committed suicide in his cell."

39

Karen Singh summed it up for them: You can't get bone marrow from a dead man.

Emily did not collapse when she heard the news. She took the blow without blinking and immediately segued to the next step. She was on a calmer plane now, somewhere just outside panic.

"We have incredible access to the media right now," Emily said. They were sitting in Karen Singh's hospital office. "We'll make pleas. We'll set up bone marrow drives. The NBA will help. We'll get players to make appearances."

Myron nodded, but the enthusiasm wasn't there. Dr. Singh mimicked his motion.

"When will you have the paternity results?" Emily asked.

"I was just about to call for them," Dr. Singh said.

"I'll leave you two alone, then," Emily said. "I have a press conference downstairs."

Myron looked at her. "You don't want to wait for the results?"

"I already know the results."

Emily left without a backward glance. Karen Singh looked at Myron. Myron folded his hands and put them in his lap.

"You ready?" she asked.

He nodded.

Karen Singh picked up the phone and dialed. Someone on the other end answered. Karen read off a reference number. She waited, tapping a pencil on the desk. Someone on the other end said something. Karen said, "Thank you," hung up, focused her eyes on Myron.

"You're the father."

Myron found Emily in the hospital lobby, giving the press conference. The hospital had set up a podium with their logo perfectly positioned behind it, sure to be picked up by any and all television cameras. Hospital logo. Like they were McDonald's or Toyota, trying to sleaze some free advertising. Emily's statement was direct and heartfelt. Her son was dying. He needed new bone marrow. Everyone who wanted to help should give blood and get registered. She plucked the strings of societal grieving, making sure it rang personal in the same way that Princess Diana's and John Kennedy Jr.'s deaths rang personal, wanting the public to mourn as if they actually knew him. The power of celebrity.

When she finished her statement, Emily hurried off without answering questions. Myron caught up to her in the closed-off area near the elevators. She glanced at him. He nodded, and she smiled.

"So now what are you going to do?" she asked him.

"We have to save him," Myron said.

"Yes."

Behind them the press were still yelling out questions. The sound trickled and then faded into the background. Someone ran by with an empty gurney.

"You said Thursday was the optimum day," Myron said.

Hope lit her eyes. "Yes."

"Okay, then," he said. "We try it on Thursday."

The bullet that had struck Greg had entered in the lower part of his neck and traversed toward his chest. It had stopped short of the heart. But it had done plenty of damage anyway. He survived surgery but remained unconscious in "critical" and "guarded" condition.

Myron looked in on him. Greg had tubes in his nose and a frightening assortment of machinery Myron hoped never to understand. He looked like a corpse, waxen and gray-white and sucked dry. Myron sat with him for a few minutes. But not very long.

He returned to the offices of MB SportsReps the next day.

"Lamar Richardson is coming in this afternoon," Esperanza said.

"I know."

"You okay?"

"Dandy."

"Life goes on, huh?"

"Guess so."

Special Agent Kimberly Green came semi-bouncing by a few minutes later. "It's all wrapping up," she told him, and for the first time he saw her smile.

Myron sat back. "I'm listening."

"Edwin Gibbs, under his Dennis Lex/Davis Taylor identity, still had a locker at work. We found the wallets of two of his victims, Robert and Patricia Wilson, in there."

"They were the honeymoon couple?"

"Yes."

They both took a moment, out of respect for the dead, Myron guessed. He pictured a healthy young couple beginning their life, coming to the Big Apple to see some shows and do a little shopping, walking the bustling streets hand in hand, a little scared about the future but ready to give it a go. *El fin.*

Kimberly cleared her throat. "Gibbs also rented a white Ford Windstar using the Davis Taylor credit card. It was one of those automatic reservations. You just make a call, walk straight to the rental, and drive off. No one sees you."

"Where did he pick up the van?"

"Newark Airport."

"I assume that's the van we found in Bernardsville," Myron said.

"The very."

"Tidy," he said, using a Win word. "What else?"

"Preliminary autopsies reveal that all the victims were killed with a thirty-eight. Two shots to the head. No other signs of trauma. We don't think he tortured them or any of that. His modus operandus seemed to involve the early scream and then he just killed them."

"He ends the seed sowing for them," Myron said, "but not the families."

"Right."

"Because for his victims, the terror would be real. He wanted it all in the mind." Myron shook his head. "What did Jeremy tell you about his ordeal?"

"You didn't talk to him about it?"

Myron shifted in his chair. "No."

"Edwin Gibbs wore the same disguise he used at work—the blond wig and beard and glasses. He blindfolded Jeremy as soon as he had him in the van and drove straight to that cabin. Edwin told him to scream into the phone—even made him practice first to make sure he had it right. After the call, Edwin chained him up and left him alone. You know the rest."

Myron nodded. He did.

"What about the plagiarism charge and the novel?"

She shrugged. "It was like you and Stan said. Edwin read it, probably right after his wife was dying of cancer. It influenced him."

Myron stared at her for a moment.

"What?" she said.

"You guys figured that part out when you first got the novel," Myron said. "That Stan hadn't plagiarized. That the book influenced the killer."

She shook her head. "No."

"Come on. You knew that the kidnappings had taken place. You just wanted to put pressure on Stan so he'd talk. And maybe you wanted to embarrass him a little."

"That's not true," Kimberly Green said. "I'm not saying some of our agents didn't take it personally, but we believed that he was the Sow the Seeds kidnapper. I already told you some of the reasons why. Now we know that a lot of the same evidence pointed to his father."

"What same evidence?"

She shook her head. "It's not important anymore. We knew Stan was more here than just a reporter. And we were right. We even thought he was getting stuff wrong on purpose—that he was using the book rather than what he'd really done just to throw us off."

Her words didn't resonate the way the truth does, but Myron didn't argue the point. He scanned his Client Wall and tried to bring his focus around to Lamar Richardson's visit. "So the case is closed."

She smiled. "Like legs in a nunnery."

"You make that one up?"

"Yup."

"Good thing you carry a gun," Myron said. "So are you going to get a big promotion?"

She rose. "I think I get to be a super-secret-special agent now."

Myron smiled. They shook hands. Kimberly left then. Myron sat alone for a while. He rubbed his eyes and thought about what she'd said and what she hadn't said and realized that something was still very wrong.

Lamar Richardson, shortstop extraordinaire, showed up on time and by himself. Positively shocking. The meeting went well. Myron gave his standard spiel, but the standard spiel was pretty good. Damn good, actually. All businesspeople need a spiel. Spiel is good. Esperanza spoke up too. She had started developing her own spiel. Well honed. The perfect complement to Myron's. Quite the partnership, this was becoming.

Win stopped by briefly as planned. If recruitment was a baseball game, Win was the big closer. People knew his name. They checked out his reputation—er, his business reputation, that is. When prospective clients learned that Windsor Horne Lockwood III himself would handle their finances, that Win and Myron further insisted that clients meet with Win at least five times a year, they started smiling. Score one for the small agency.

Lamar Richardson played it close to the vest. He nodded a lot. He asked questions but not too many. Two hours after arriving, he shook their hands and said he'd be in touch. Myron and Esperanza walked him to the elevator and bade him good-bye.

Esperanza turned to Myron. "Well?"

"Got him."

"How can you be so sure?"

"I'm all-seeing," Myron said. "All-knowing."

They moved back into Myron's office and sat down. "If Lamar chooses us over IMG and TruPro"—she stopped, smiled—"we're baaaaack."

"Pretty much."

"And that means Big Cyndi will come back."

"That's supposed to be a good thing, right?"

"You're starting to love her, you know."

"Yeah, don't rub it in."

Esperanza studied his face. She did that a lot. Myron didn't much believe in reading faces. Esperanza did. Especially his. "What happened in that law office?" she asked. "With Chase Layton?"

"I boxed his ears once and punched him seven times."

Her eyes stayed on his face.

"You're supposed to say, 'But you saved Jeremy's life,' " Myron added.

"No, that's Win's line." She adjusted herself and faced him full. She wore an aquamarine business suit, cut low with no blouse, and it was a wonder Lamar had been able to concentrate on anything. Myron was used to her, but the effect was still there, still dazzling. He just saw the dazzle from a different angle.

"Speaking of Jeremy," she said.

"Yes."

"You still blocking?"

Myron thought about it, remembered the embrace in that cabin, stopped. "More than ever," he said.

"So what now?"

"The blood test came back. I'm the father."

Something popped onto her face—regret maybe—but it didn't stay long. "You should tell him the truth."

"Right now I just want to save his life."

She kept studying the face. "Maybe soon," she said.

"Maybe soon what?"

"You'll stop blocking," Esperanza said.

"Yeah, maybe."

"We'll chat then. In the meantime . . ."

"Don't be stupid," he finished for her.

The health club was located in a chi-chi hotel in midtown. The walls were fully mirrored. The ceiling and the trim and the front desk were whole-milk white. Same with the clothes worn by the personal trainers. The weights and exercise machines were sleek and chrome and so beautiful you didn't want to touch them. Everything about the place gleamed; you were almost tempted to work out in sunglasses.

Myron found him on a bench press, struggling without a spotter. Myron waited, watching him wage war on gravity and the barbell. Chase Layton's face was pure red, his teeth gritted, veins in his forehead doing their pop-up video. It took some time, but the attorney achieved victory. He dropped the weight onto the stand. His arms fell to his sides like he'd missed a brain synapse.

"You shouldn't hold your breath," Myron said.

Chase looked over at him. He didn't seem surprised or upset. He sat up, breathing heavily. He wiped his face with a towel.

"I won't take up much of your time," Myron said.

Chase put the towel down and looked at him.

"I just wanted to say that if you want to press charges, Win and I won't get in your way."

Chase did not reply.

"And I'm very sorry for what I did," Myron said.

"I watched the news," Chase said. "You did it to save that boy's life."

"Doesn't excuse it."

"Maybe not." He stood and added a dumbbell to both sides of the bar. "Frankly, Mr. Bolitar, I'm not sure what to think."

"If you want to press charges—"

"I don't."

Myron was not sure what to say, so he settled for "Thank you."

Chase Layton nodded and sat back on the bench. Then he looked at Myron. "Do you want to know what the worst part of it is?"

No, Myron thought. "If you want to tell me."

"The shame," Chase said.

Myron started to open his mouth, but Chase waved him quiet.

"It's not the beating or the pain. It's the feeling of total helplessness. We were primitive. We were man to man. And there was nothing I could do but take it. You made me feel like"—he looked up, found the words, looked straight at Myron—"like I wasn't a real man."

The words made Myron cringe.

"I went to these great schools and joined all the right clubs and made a fortune in my chosen profession. I fathered three kids and raised them and loved them the best I could. Then one day you punch me—and I realize that I'm not a real man."

"You're wrong," Myron said.

"You're going to say that violence is no measure of a man. On some level you're right. But on some level, the base level that makes us men, we both know you're wrong. Don't pretend you don't know what I'm talking about. It'd just be a further insult."

Myron swallowed down the clichés. Chase took deep breaths and reached for the bar.

"Need a spotter?" Myron said.

Chase Layton gripped it and jerked it off the stand. "I don't need anybody," he said.

Thursday came. Karen Singh introduced him to a fertility expert named Dr. Barbara Dittrick. Dr. Dittrick handed Myron a small cup and told him to masturbate into it. There were more surreal and embarrassing experiences in life, Myron guessed, but being led to a small room to masturbate into a cup while everyone waited for you in the next room had to be right up there with the best of them.

"Step in here, please," Dr. Dittrick said.

Myron frowned at the cup. "I usually insist on flowers and a movie."

"Well, at least you got the movie," she said, pointing at the television. "The TV has X-rated videos." She left the room and closed the door behind her.

Myron checked the titles. *On Golden Blonde. Father Knows Breast* (starring Robert Hung). *Field of Wet Dreams* ("If you watch it, they will come"). He frowned and passed. So to speak. He stared at the swivel leather chair, one of those lean-back kind, where probably hundreds of other men had sat and . . . He covered it with paper towels and did his bit, though it took some time. His imagination was spinning in the wrong direction, generating an aura about as erotic as mole hair on an old man's buttock. When he was, uh, finished, he opened the door and handed the cup to Dr. Dittrick and tried to smile. He felt like the world's biggest doofus. She wore rubber gloves, even though the, uh, specimen was in a cup. Like it might scald her. She brought it to a lab where they "washed" (their expression, not his) the semen. The semen was declared "serviceable but slow." Like it was falling behind in algebra.

"Funny," Emily said. "I usually found Myron to be serviceable but quick."

"Ha-ha," Myron said.

A few hours later Emily was in a hospital bed. Barbara Dittrick smiled while inserting what looked suspiciously like a turkey baster into her and pressed the plunger. Myron took her hand. Emily smiled.

"Romantic," she said.

Myron made a face.

"What?"

"Serviceable?" he said.

She laughed. "But quick."

Dr. Dittrick finished her part. Emily stayed prone for another hour. Myron sat with her. They were doing this to save Jeremy's life. That was all. He didn't let the future enter the equation. He didn't consider the long-term effects or what this might one day mean. Irresponsible, sure. But first things first.

They had to save Jeremy. The hell with the rest.

Terese Collins called him from Atlanta that afternoon. "Can I come up and visit?" she asked.

"The station will give you more time off?"

"Actually, my producer encouraged me."

"Oh?"

"You, my studly friend, are part of a huge story," Terese said.

"You used the words 'studly' and 'huge' in the same sentence."

"That turn you on?"

"Well, it might a lesser man."

"And you are that lesser man."

"I thank you," he said.

"You're also the only one in this story who won't talk to the press."

"So you just want me for my mind," Myron said. "I feel so used."

"Dream on, hot buns. I want your bod. It's my producer who wants your brain."

"Your producer cute?"

"No."

"Terese?"

"Yes."

"I don't want to talk about what happened."

"Good," she said. "Because I don't want to hear it."

There was a brief silence.

"Yeah," Myron said. "I'd like it very much if you came up."

Ten days later, Karen Singh called him at home.

"The pregnancy didn't take."

Myron closed his eyes.

"We can try again next month," she said.

"Thanks for calling, Karen."

"Sure."

There was empty space. "Anything else?" Myron asked.

"There's been a lot of marrow drives," she said.

"I know."

"One donor looks like a match for an AML patient in Maryland. A young mother. She would have probably died if it weren't for these drives."

"Good news," Myron said.

"But no matches for Jeremy."

"Yeah."

"Myron?"

"What?"

"I don't think we have much time here."

• • •

Terese returned to Atlanta later that day. Win invited Esperanza to his place for a night of mindless television. The three of them sat in their customary spots. Fritos and Indian takeout were on the night's menu. Myron had the remote. He paused when he saw a familiar image on CNN. A basketball superstar simply known as "TC," one of the NBA's most controversial players and a teammate of Greg's, was on *Larry King Live*. His hair was razor-carved to spell out *Jeremy*, and both gold earrings had Jeremy's name on them. He wore a ripped T-shirt that simply read HELP OR JEREMY DIES. Myron smiled. TC was something else, but he'd get the people out in droves.

More flipping. Stan Gibbs was on some talking-head show on MSNBC. Nothing new. The only thing the press loves as much as tearing somebody down is a story of redemption. Bruce Taylor had gotten the exclusive, as promised, and he'd set the tone. The public was mixed on what Stan had done, but for the most part, they sympathized with him. In the end, Stan had risked his own life to catch a killer, saved Jeremy Downing from certain death, and been wrongly accused by a too-eager-to-convict media. The fact that Stan had been confused about turning in his own father played for him, especially since the media was anxious to wipe away the awful mar of plagiarism they'd so quickly tattooed on him. Stan got his column back. Rumor had it his show was coming back too but in a better time slot. Myron wasn't sure what to think. Stan was no hero to him. But so few people were.

Stan, too, was pounding the bone-marrow-drive drum. "This boy needs our help," he said directly into the camera. "Please come down. We'll be here all night."

A blond talking head asked Stan about his own part in this drama, about tackling his father, about racing to the cabin. Stan played the modesty card. Wise. The man knew the media.

"Boring," Esperanza said.

"Agreed," Win said.

"Isn't there a *Partridge Family* marathon on TV Land?"

Myron suddenly stopped.

"Myron?" Win said.

He did not reply.

"Hello, world." Esperanza snapped her fingers in Myron's face. "There's a song that we're singing. Come on, get happy."

Myron switched off the television. He looked at Win, then at Esperanza. "Say one last good-bye to the boy."

Esperanza and Win exchanged a glance.

"You were right, Win."

"About what?"

"Human nature," Myron said.

40

Myron called Kimberly Green at her office. She answered the line and said, "Green."

"I need a favor," Myron said.

"Shit, I thought you were out of my life."

"But never your fantasies. You want to help me or not?"

"Not."

"I need two things."

"Not. I said 'not.'"

"Eric Ford said that the supposedly plagiarized novel was sent directly to you."

"So?"

"Who sent it?"

"You heard him, Myron. It was sent anonymously."

"You have no idea."

"None."

"Where is it now?"

"The book?"

"Yes."

"In an evidence locker."

"Ever do anything with it?"

"Like what?"

Myron waited.

"Myron?"

"I knew you guys were holding something back," he said.

"Listen to me a second—"

"The author of that novel. It was Edwin Gibbs. He wrote it under a pseudonym after his wife died. It makes perfect sense now. You were searching for him right from the get-go. You knew, dammit. You knew the whole time."

"We suspected," she said. "We didn't know."

"All that crap about thinking he was Stan's first victim—"

"It wasn't total crap. We knew it was one of them. We just didn't know which one. We couldn't find Edwin Gibbs until you told us about the Waterbury address. By the time we got there, he was already on his way to kidnap Jeremy Downing. Maybe if you had been more forthcoming—"

"You guys lied to me."

"We didn't lie. We just didn't tell you everything."

"Jesus, you ever listen to yourself?"

"We owed you nothing here, Myron. You weren't a federal agent on this. You were just a pain in the ass."

"A pain in the ass who helped you solve the case."

"And for that I thank you."

Myron's thoughts entered the maze, turned left, turned right, circled back.

"Why doesn't the press know about Gibbs being the author?" Myron asked.

"They will. Ford wants all his ducks in a row first. Then he'll hold yet another big press conference and present it as something new."

"He could do that today," Myron said.

"He could."

"But then the story dies down. Right now the rumors keep it going. Ford gets more time in the limelight."

"He's a politician at heart," she said. "So what?"

Myron took another few turns, hit a few more walls, kept feeling for the way out. "Forget it," he said.

"Good. Can I go now?"

"First I need you to call the national bone marrow registry."

"Why?"

"I need to find out about a donor."

"This case is closed, Myron."

"I know," he said. "But I think a new one might be opening."

Stan Gibbs was at the anchor chair when Myron and Win arrived. His new cable show, *Glib with Gibbs,* was filming in Fort Lee, New Jersey, and the studio, like every television studio Myron had ever seen, looked like a room with the roof ripped off. Wires and lights hung in no discernible pattern. Studios, especially newsrooms, were always much smaller in person than on television. The desks, the chairs, the world map in the background. All smaller. The power of television. A room on a nineteen-inch screen somehow looks smaller in real life.

Stan wore a blue blazer, white shirt, red tie, jeans and sneakers. The jeans would stay under the desk and never get camera time. Classic anchorman-wear. Stan waved to them when they entered. Myron waved back. Win did not.

"We need to talk," Myron said to him.

Stan nodded. He sent away the producers and motioned Myron and Win to the guest chairs. "Sit."

Stan stayed in the anchor chair. Win and Myron sat in guest chairs, which felt pretty strange, as though a home audience were watching. Win checked his reflection in a camera glass and smiled. He liked what he saw.

"Any word on a donor?" Stan asked.

"None."

"Something will come through."

"Yeah," Myron said. "Look, Stan, I need your help."

Stan intertwined his fingers and rested both hands on the anchor desk. "Whatever you need."

"There's a lot of things that don't add up with Jeremy's kidnapping."

"For example?"

"Why do you think your father took a child this time? He never did that before, right? Always adults. Why this time a child?"

Stan mulled it over, chose his words one at a time. "I don't know. I'm not sure taking adults was a pattern or anything. His victims seemed pretty random."

"But this wasn't random," Myron said. "His choosing Jeremy Downing couldn't have been just a coincidence."

Stan thought about that one too. "I agree with you there."

"So he picked him because he was somehow connected with my investigation."

"Seems logical."

"But how would your father have known about Jeremy?"

"I don't know," Stan said. "He might have followed you."

"I don't think so. You see, Greg Downing stayed up in Waterbury after our visit. He kept his eye on Nathan Mostoni. We know he didn't travel out of town until the day before the kidnapping."

Win looked into the camera again. He smiled and waved. Just in case it was on.

"It's strange," Stan said.

"And there's more," Myron said. "Like the call where Jeremy screamed. With the others, your father told the family not to contact the cops. But he didn't this time. Why? And are you aware that he wore a disguise when he kidnapped Jeremy?"

"I heard that, yes."

"Why? If he planned on killing him, why go to the trouble of donning a disguise?"

"He kidnapped Jeremy off the streets," Stan said. "Someone might have been able to identify him."

"Yeah, okay, that makes sense. But then why blindfold Jeremy once he was in the van? He killed all the others. He would have killed Jeremy. So why worry about him seeing his face?"

"I'm not sure," Stan said. "He might have always done it that way, for all we know."

"I guess," Myron said. "But something about it all just rings wrong, don't you think?"

Stan thought about it. "It rings funny," he said slowly. "I'm not sure it rings wrong."

"That's why I came to you. All these questions have been swirling in my head. And then I remembered Win's credo."

Stan Gibbs looked over at Win. Win blinked his eyes and lowered them modestly. "What credo is that?"

"Man is into self-preservation," Myron said. "He is, above all, selfish." He paused a moment. "You agree with that, Stan?"

"To some degree, of course. We're all selfish."

Myron nodded. "You even."

"Yes, of course. And you too, I'm sure."

"The media is making you out to be this noble guy," Myron said. "Torn between family and duty and ultimately doing the right thing. But maybe you're not."

"Not what?"

"Noble."

"I'm not," Stan said. "I did wrong. I never claimed to be a saint."

Myron looked at Win. "He's good."

"Damn good," Win agreed.

Stan Gibbs frowned. "What are you talking about, Myron?"

"Follow me here, Stan. And remember Win's credo. Let's start at the beginning. When your father first contacted you. You talked to him and you decided to write the Sow the Seeds story. What was your motive at first? Were you trying to find an outlet for your fear and guilt? Was it simply to be a good reporter? Or—and here's where we're using the Win credo—did you write it because you knew it would make you a big star?"

Myron looked at him and waited.

"Am I supposed to answer that?"

"Please."

Stan looked in the air and rubbed his fingertips with his thumb. "All of the above, I guess. Yes, I was excited by the story. I thought it could very well be a big deal. If that's selfishness, okay, I'm guilty."

Myron glanced at Win again. "Good."

"Damn good."

"Let's keep following this track, Stan, okay? The story did indeed become a big deal. So did you. You became a celebrity—"

"We covered this already, Myron."

"Right. You're absolutely right. Let's skip to the part where the feds sued you. They demanded to know your source. You refused. Now again there might be several reasons for this. The First Amendment, of course. That could be it. Protecting your father would be another. The combination of the two. But—and again Win's credo—what would be the selfish choice?"

"What do you mean?"

"Think selfishly and you really have only one option."

"That being?"

"If you caved in to the feds—if you said, Okay, now that I'm in legal trouble, my source is my father—well, how would that have looked?"

"Bad," Win said.

"Damn bad. I doubt you'd have been much of a hero if you sold out your father—not to mention the First Amendment—just to save your hide from vague legal threats." Myron smiled. "See what I mean about Win's credo?"

"So you think I acted selfishly by not telling the feds," Stan said.

"It's possible."

"It's also possible that the selfish thing was also the right thing."

"Possible too," Myron agreed.

"I never claimed to be a hero in all this."

"Never denied it either."

Stan smiled this time. "Maybe I didn't deny it because I'm using Win's credo."

"How's that?"

"Denying it would harm me," Stan said. "As would boasting about it."

Myron didn't have a chance to look before he heard Win say, "Damn good."

"I still don't see the relevance of any of this," Stan said.

"Stick with me, I think you will."

Stan shrugged.

"Where were we?" Myron asked.

"The feds take him to court," Win said.

"Right, thanks, the feds take you to court. You battle back. Then something happens you totally didn't foresee. The plagiarism charges. For the sake of discussion, we'll assume the Lex family sent the book to the feds. They wanted to get you off their back—what better way to do that than to ruin your reputation? So what did you do? How did you react to the charges of plagiarism?"

Stan kept quiet. Win said, "He disappeared."

"Correct answer," Myron said.

Win smiled and nodded a thank-you into the camera.

"You took off," Myron said to Stan. "Now the question again is why. Several things come to mind. It could have been because you were trying to protect your father. Or it might have been that you were afraid of the Lex family."

"Which would certainly fit Win's credo," Stan said. "Self-preservation."

"Right. You were afraid they'd harm you."

"Yes."

Myron treaded gently. "But don't you see, Stan? We have to think selfishly too. You're presented with this serious plagiarism charge. What choices did you have? Two really. You could either run off—or you could tell the truth."

Stan said, "I still don't see your point."

"Stay with me. If you told the truth, you would again look like a louse. Here you've been defending the First Amendment and your father and whoops, you get in trouble and you sell them out. No good. You'd still be ruined."

"Damned if you do," Win said. "Damned if you don't."

"Right," Myron said. "So the wise move—the selfish move—was to vanish for a while."

"But I lost everything by vanishing."

"No, Stan, you didn't."

"How can you say that?"

Myron lifted his palms to the skies and grinned. "Look around you."

For the first time, something dark flicked across Stan's face. Myron saw it. So did Win.

"Let's continue, shall we?"

Stan said nothing.

"You go into hiding and start counting your problems. One, your father is a murderer. You're selfish, Stan, but you're not inhumane.

You want him off the streets, yet you can't tell on him. Maybe because you love him. Or maybe there's Win's credo."

"Not this time," Stan said.

"Pardon?"

"Win's credo doesn't apply. I kept quiet because I loved my father and because I believe in protecting sources. And I can offer proof."

"I'm listening," Myron said.

"If I wanted to turn my father in—if that would have been in my best interest—I could have done it anonymously." Stan leaned back and folded his arms.

"That's your proof?"

"Sure. I didn't do the selfish thing."

Myron shook his head. "You got to go deeper."

"Deeper how?"

"Turning your father in anonymously wouldn't help you, Stan. Not really. Yes, you needed to put your father behind bars. But more than that, you needed to be redeemed."

Silence.

"So what would answer both those needs? What would put your father away and put you back on top—maybe even more on top than before? First, you had to be patient. That meant staying hidden. Second, you couldn't be the one who turned him in. You had to set him up."

"Set up my father?"

"Yes. You had to leave a trail for the feds to follow. Something subtle, something that would lead to your father, and something you could manipulate at any time. So you took a fake ID, Stan—the same way your father had. You even took a job where people would spot the disguise your father used and hey, maybe you could also tie in your dad's old nemesis the Lex family in the process."

"What the hell are you talking about?"

"You know what bugged me? Your father had been so careful in the past. Now all of a sudden he's leaving incriminating evidence in a locker. He rents the kidnap van on a credit card and leaves a red sneaker in it. It didn't make any sense. Unless someone was setting him up."

Stan's look of disbelief was almost genuine. "You think I killed these people?"

"No," Myron said. "Your father did."

"Then what—?"

"You're Dennis Lex."

Stan tried to look stunned, but it wasn't happening.

"You kidnapped Jeremy Downing. And you called me and pretended to be the Sow the Seeds killer."

"And why did I do that?"

"To have this heroic ending. To have your father arrested. To have yourself redeemed."

"How the hell does calling you—"

"To get me interested. You probably learned about my background. You knew I'd investigate. You needed a dupe and a witness. Someone outside the police. I was that dupe."

"The dupe du jour," Win added.

Myron shot him a look. Win shrugged.

"That's ridiculous."

"No, Stan, it adds up. It answers all my earlier questions. How did the kidnapper happen to choose Jeremy? Because you followed me after I left your condo. You saw the feds pick me up. That's how you knew I'd spoken to them. You followed me to Emily's house. From there, any old newsman worth a damn could have figured out her son was the sick kid I told you about. His illness wasn't a secret. So Jeremy's being taken is no longer a coincidence, see?"

Stan folded his arms across his chest. "I see nothing."

"Other questions get answered too now. Like why did the kidnapper wear a disguise and make Jeremy wear a blindfold? Because you couldn't let Jeremy identify you. Why didn't the kidnapper kill Jeremy right away, like he had the others? Same reason you wore the disguise. You had no intention of killing him. Jeremy had to survive the ordeal unharmed. Otherwise you're no hero. Why didn't the kidnapper make his usual demand not to contact the authorities? Because you wanted the feds in. You needed them to witness your heroics. It wouldn't work without their involvement. I wondered how the media was always in the right spot—in Bernardsville, at the cabin. But you set that part up too. Anonymous leaks probably. So the cameras could witness and replay your heroics—your tackling your father, the dramatic rescue of Jeremy Downing. Good television. You knew the power of capturing those moments for all the world to see."

Stan waited. "You finished?"

"Not yet. You see, I think you went too far in spots. Leaving that sneaker in the van, for example. That was overkill. Too obvious. It made me wonder how neatly it all came together in the end. And then I start realizing that I was your main sucker, Stan. You played me like a Stradivarius. But even if I hadn't shown up, you just would have kidnapped someone else. Your main dupes were the feds. For crying out loud, that photograph of your father by the statue was the only picture in the whole condo. It even faced the window. You knew the feds were spying on you. You threw the truth about Dennis Lex right in their faces. Surely they'd go to the sanitarium and put it together. And if not, you could somehow get it out in the end, when they had you in custody. You were all set to cave in and tell on your father when I came through in the clutch. Me, the dupe du jour, saw the truth up at the sanitarium. You must have been so pleased."

"This is crazy."

"It answers all the questions."

"That doesn't mean it's the truth."

"The Davis Taylor address you used at work. It was the same address as your father's in Waterbury. So we would trace it back to him, to Nathan Mostoni. Who else would have done that?"

"My father!"

"Why? Why would your father change identities at all? And if your father needed a new identity, wouldn't he shed the old one? Or hell, at least change addresses? Only you could have pulled it off, Stan. You could have hooked up the extra phone line with no problem. Your father was pretty far gone. He was demented, at the very least. You kidnapped Jeremy. Then you probably told your father to meet you at the house in Bernardsville. He did what you said—for love or because of dementia, I don't know which. Did you know he'd arm himself like that? I doubt it. If Greg had died, you'd probably look worse. But I don't know for sure. Maybe the fact that he fired shots just made you look more heroic in the end. Think selfishly, Stan. That's the key."

Stan shook his head.

" 'Say one last good-bye to the boy,' " Myron said.

"What?"

"That's what the Sow the Seeds killer said to me on the phone. The boy. I made a mistake when he called me. I told him a boy needed help. After that, I only used the word 'child.' When I spoke to Susan Lex. When I spoke to you. I said a thirteen-year-old child needs a transplant."

"So?"

"So when we talked in the car that night, you asked what I was really after, what my real interest in all this was. Remember?"

"Yes."

"And I said I already told you."

"Right."

"And you said, 'That boy who needs a bone marrow transplant?' You said, 'That boy.' How did you know he was a boy, Stan?"

Win turned toward Stan. Stan looked at Win's face.

"Is that your proof?" Stan countered. "I mean, is this supposed to be a Perry Mason moment or something? Maybe you slipped up, Myron. Or maybe I just assumed it was a boy. Or I heard wrong. That's not evidence."

"You're right. It's not. It just got me thinking, that's all."

"Thoughts aren't proof."

"Wow," Win said. "Thoughts aren't proof. I'll have to remember that one."

"But there is proof," Myron said. "Definitive proof."

"Impossible," Stan said, but his voice warbled now. "What?"

"I'll get to that in a moment. First let me back off on my indignation a little."

"I don't understand."

"At the end of the day, what you did was scummy, no question about it. But in its own way, it was almost ethical. Win and I often discuss the ends justifying the means. You could claim that's what happened here. You tried to turn your father in before he struck again. You did all you could to make sure nobody else was harmed. Jeremy was never in any real danger. You couldn't know that Greg would be shot. So in the end, you scared a boy, but so what? Next to the murder and destruction your father would have continued to wreak, it was nothing. So you did some good. The ends perhaps justified the means. Except for one thing."

Stan didn't bite.

"Jeremy's bone marrow transplant. He needs that to live, Stan. You know that. You also know that you're the match, not your father. That was why you slipped him that cyanide pill. Because once we dragged your father to the hospital and realized that he wasn't a match, well, we would have investigated. We would have realized that Edwin Gibbs was not Davis Taylor né Dennis Lex. So you had to have him kill himself and then you pushed for a quick cremation. I don't mean to make it sound as harsh or cold as all that. You didn't murder your father. He took the pill all on his own. He was a sick man. He wanted to die. It's yet another case of the ends justifying the means."

Myron took a moment and just looked into Stan's eyes. Stan did not look away. In a sense, this was more agenting work. Myron was negotiating here—the most important negotiation of his life. He had put his opponent in a corner. Now he needed to reach out. Not help him yet. He had to keep him in the corner. But he had to start reaching out. Just a little.

"You're not a monster," Myron said. "You just didn't count on the complication of being a bone marrow match. You want to do right by Jeremy. It's why you've gone so nuts trying to help the bone marrow drive. If they find another donor, it takes you off the hook. Because you're in this lie too deep now. You couldn't admit the truth—that you are the match. It would ruin you. I understand that."

Stan's eyes were wide and wet, but he was listening.

"Before I told you that I had proof," Myron said. "We checked the bone marrow registry. Know what we found, Stan?"

Stan didn't reply.

"You're not registered," Myron said. "Here you are telling everybody to sign up and you yourself aren't in their computer. The three of us know why. It's because you'd be a match. And if you matched, there would be those questions again."

Stan gave defiance one last shot. "That's not proof."

"Then how will you explain not registering?"

"I don't have to explain anything."

"A blood test will prove it conclusively. The registry still has the blood that Davis Taylor gave during the marrow drive. We can do a DNA test with yours, see if it matches up."

"And if I don't agree to a test?"

Win took that one. "Oh, you'll give blood," he said with just the slightest smile. "One way or another."

Something on Stan's face broke then. He lowered his head. The defiance was over. He was trapped in the corner now. No way to escape. He'd start looking for an ally. It always happened in negotiations. When you're lost, you look for an out. Myron had reached out before. It was time to do it again.

"You don't understand," Stan said.

"Strangely enough, I do." Myron moved a little closer to Stan. He made his voice soft yet unyielding. Total command mode. "Here's what we're going to do, Stan. You and I are going to make a deal."

Stan looked up, confused but also hopeful. "What?"

"You are going to agree to donate bone marrow to save Jeremy's life. You'll do it anonymously. Win and I can set that up. No one will ever know who the donor was. You do that, you save Jeremy, I forget the rest."

"How can I believe you?"

"Two reasons," Myron said. "One, I'm interested in saving Jeremy's life, not ruining yours. Two"—he tilted both palms toward the ceiling—"I'm no better. I bent rules here too. I let the ends justify the means. I assaulted a man. I kidnapped a woman."

Win shook his head. "There's a difference. His reasons were selfish. You, on the other hand, were trying to save a boy's life."

Myron turned to his friend. "Weren't you the one who said that motives are irrelevant? That the act is the act?"

"Sure," Win said. "But I meant that to apply to him, not you."

Myron smiled and faced Stan again. "I'm not your moral superior. We both did wrong. Maybe we can both live with what we've done. But if you let a boy die, Stan, you cross the line. You can't go home again."

Stan closed his eyes. "I would have found a way," he said. "I would have gotten another fake ID, given blood under a pseudonym. I was just hoping—"

"I know," Myron said. "I know all about it."

Myron called Dr. Karen Singh. "I found a matching donor."

"What?"

"I can't explain. But he has to stay anonymous."

"I explained to you that all the bone marrow donors remain anonymous."

"No. The bone marrow registry can't know about this either. We have to find a place that can harvest the marrow without knowing the patient's identity."

"Can't be done."

"Yeah, it can."

"No doctor will agree—"

"We can't play these games, Karen. I have a donor. No one can know who he is. Make it work."

He could hear her breathing.

"He'll have to be retested," she said.

"No problem."

"And pass a physical."

"Done."

"Then okay. Let's get this started."

When Emily heard about the donor, she gave Myron a curious look and waited. He didn't explain. She never asked.

Myron visited the hospital the day before the marrow transplant was to begin. He peeked his head around the doorjamb and saw the boy sleeping. Jeremy was bald from the chemo. His skin had a ghostly glow, like something withering from a lack of sunshine. Myron watched his son sleeping. Then he turned and went home. He didn't come back.

He returned to work at MB SportsReps and lived his life. He visited his father and mother. He hung out with Win and Esperanza. He landed a few new clients and started rebuilding his business. Big Cyndi handed in her wrestling resignation and took over the front desk. His world was wobbly but back on the axis.

Eighty-four days later—Myron kept count—he got a call from Karen Singh. She asked him to visit her office. When he arrived, she wasted no time.

"It worked," she said. "Jeremy went home today."

Myron started to cry. Karen Singh moved around her desk. She sat on the arm of his chair and rubbed his back.

• • •

Myron knocked on the half-open door.

"Enter," Greg said.

Myron did so. Greg Downing was sitting up in a chair. He'd grown a beard during his long hospital stretch.

He smiled at Myron. "Nice to see you."

"Same here. I like the beard."

"Gives me that Paul Bunyan touch, don't you think?"

"I was thinking more along the lines of Sebastian Cabot as Mr. French," Myron said.

Greg laughed. "Going home on Friday."

"Great."

Silence.

"You haven't visited much," Greg said.

"Wanted to give you time to heal. And grow that beard in fully."

Greg tried another laugh, but he sort of choked on it. "My basketball career is over, you know."

"You'll get over it."

"That easy?"

Myron smiled. "Who said anything about easy?"

"Yeah."

"But there are more important things in life than basketball," Myron said. "Though sometimes I forget that."

Greg nodded again. Then he looked down and said, "I heard about you finding the donor. I don't know how you did it—"

"It's not important."

He looked up. "Thank you."

Myron was not sure what to say to that. So he kept quiet. And that was when Greg shocked him.

"You know, don't you?"

Myron's heart stopped.

"That was why you helped," Greg said. His voice was pure flatline. "Emily told you the truth."

The muscles around Myron's throat tightened. There was a whooshing sound in his head.

"Did you take a blood test?" Greg asked.

Myron managed a nod this time. Greg closed his eyes. Myron swallowed and said, "How long . . . ?"

"I'm not sure anymore," Greg said. "I guess right away."

He knows. The words fell on Myron, smacking down like raindrops, beading and rolling off, impenetrable. *He's always known. . . .*

"For a while I fooled myself into believing it wasn't so," Greg said. "It's amazing what the mind can do sometimes. But when Jeremy was six, he had his appendix out. I saw his blood type on a chart. It pretty much confirmed what I'd known all along."

Myron didn't know what to say. The realization pushed down on him, swept away the months of blocking like so many children's toys. The mind can indeed do amazing things. He looked at Greg and it was like seeing something in the proper light for the first time and it changed everything. He thought about fathers again. He thought about real sacrifice. He thought about heroes.

"Jeremy's a good boy," Greg said.

"I know," Myron said.

"You remember my father? Screaming on the sidelines like a lunatic?"

"Yes."

"I ended up looking just like him. Spitting image of my old man. He was my blood. And he was the cruelest son of a bitch I ever knew," Greg said. Then he added, "Blood never meant much to me."

A strange echo filled the room. The background noises faded away and there was just the two of them, staring at one another from across the most bizarre chasm.

Greg moved back to the bed. "I'm tired, Myron."

"Don't you think we should talk about this?"

"Yeah," Greg said. He laid back and shut his eyes a little too tightly. "Maybe later. But right now I'm really tired."

At the end of the day, Esperanza stepped into Myron's office, sat down, and said, "I don't know much about family values or what makes a happy family. I don't know the best way to raise a kid or what you have to do to make him happy and well adjusted, whatever the hell 'well adjusted' means. I don't know if it's best to be an only child or have lots of siblings or be raised by two parents or a single parent or a gay couple or a lesbian couple or an overweight albino. But I know one thing."

Myron looked up at her and waited.

"No child could ever be harmed by having you in his life."

Esperanza stood and went home.

Stan Gibbs was playing in the yard with his boys when Myron and Win pulled into the driveway. His wife—at least, Myron guessed it was his wife—sat in a lawn chair and watched. A little boy rode Stan like a horsey. The other boy lay on the ground giggling.

Win frowned. "How very Norman Rockwell."

Myron and Win stepped out of the car. Stan the horsey looked up. The smile stayed on when he saw them, but you could see it starting to lose its grip at the edges. Stan hoisted his son off his back and said something to him Myron couldn't hear. The boy gave an "Aaaw, Dad." Stan jumped to his feet and ruffled the boy's hair. Win frowned again. As Stan jogged toward them, his smile faded away like the end of a song.

"What are you doing here?"

Win said, "Back together with the wife, are we?"

"We're giving it a go."

"Touching," Win said.

Stan turned toward Myron. "What's going on here?"

"Tell the kids to go inside, Stan."

"What?"

Another car pulled in the driveway. Rick Peck was driving. Kimberly Green was in the passenger seat. Stan's face lost color. He snapped a look at Myron.

"We had a deal," he said.

"Remember how I told you that you had two choices when the novel was discovered?"

"I'm not in the mood—"

"I said you could run or you could tell the truth. Remember?"

Stan's façade tottered, and for the first time, Myron saw the rage.

"I left out a third choice. A choice you yourself pointed out to me the first time we met. You could have said that the Sow the Seeds kidnapper was a copycat. That he had read the book. It might have helped you out. Taken some of the heat off."

"I couldn't do that."

"Because it would have led to your father?"

"Yes."

"But you didn't know your father had written the book. Isn't that right, Stan? You said you never knew about the book. I remember that from the first time we talked. I've been watching you say the same thing on TV. You claim you didn't even know your father wrote it."

"All true," Stan said, and the façade slipped back into place. "But—I don't know—maybe subconsciously I suspected something somehow. I can't explain it."

"Good," Myron said.

"Damn good," Win added.

"The problem was," Myron said, "you had to say you hadn't read it. Because if you had, well, Stan, you'd be a plagiarizer. All this work, all your big plans to regain your reputation—it would be for nothing. You'd be ruined."

"We discussed this already."

"No, Stan, we didn't. At least not this part of it." Myron held up the evidence bag with the sheet of paper inside.

Stan set his jaw.

"Know what this is, Stan?"

He said nothing.

"I found it in Melina Garston's apartment. It says 'With love, Dad.' "

Stan swallowed. "So?"

"Something about it bothered me from the beginning. First off, the word 'Dad.' "

"I don't understand—"

"Sure you do, Stan. Melina's sister-in-law called George Garston 'Papa.' When I spoke to him, he referred to himself as 'Papa.' So why would he sign a note like this 'Dad'?"

"That doesn't mean anything."

"Maybe, maybe not. The second thing that bothered me: Who writes a note like this—on the top inside of a folded card? People use the bottom half, right? But see, Stan, this wasn't a card. It was a sheet of a paper folded in half. That's the key. Then there are those tears along the left edge. See them, Stan? Like someone had ripped it out of something."

Win handed Myron the novel that had been sent to Kimberly Green. Myron opened it and laid the piece of paper inside it.

"Something like a book."

It was a perfect match.

"Your father wrote this inscription," Myron said. "To you. Years ago. You'd known about the book all along."

"You can't prove that."

"Come on, Stan. A handwriting analyst will have no trouble with this. The Lexes weren't the ones who found the book. Melina Garston did. You asked her to lie for you in court. She did. But then she started growing suspicious. So she dug around your house and found this book. She's the one who mailed it to Kimberly Green."

"You have no proof—"

"She sent it in anonymously because she still cared about you. She even tore out the inscription so no one, most especially you, would ever know where the book had come from. You had plenty of enemies. Like Susan Lex. And the feds. She probably hoped you'd think they did it. At least for a little while. But you knew right away it was Melina. She didn't count on that. Or your reaction."

Stan's hands tightened into fists. They started shaking.

"The victims' families wouldn't speak to you, Stan. And you needed that for your article. You ended up following the book more than reality. The feds thought it was to fool them. But that wasn't it. Maybe your father told you he was the killer, but nothing else. Maybe the real story wasn't as interesting, so you needed to embellish. Maybe you weren't that good of a writer and you really felt you needed those family quotes. I don't know. But you plagiarized. And the only one who could tie you to that book was Melina Garston. So you killed her."

"You'll never prove it," Stan said.

"The feds will dig hard now. The Lexes will help. Win and I will help. We'll find enough. If nothing else, the jury—and the world—will hear all you did in this. They'll hate you enough to convict."

"You son of a bitch." Stan cocked his fist and aimed it at Myron. With an almost casual movement, Win swept his leg. Stan fell down in a heap. Win pointed and laughed. Stan's sons watched it all.

Kimberly Green and Rick Peck got out of the car. Myron signaled them to wait, but Kimberly Green shook her head. They cuffed Stan hard and dragged him away. His sons still watched. Myron thought about Melina Garston and his silent vow. Then he and Win headed back to the car.

"You always intended to turn him in," Win said.

"Yes. But first I had to make sure he went along with donating the bone marrow."

"And once you knew Jeremy was okay—"

"Then I told Green, yes."

Win started the car. "The evidence is still marginal. A good attorney will be able to poke holes."

"Not my problem," Myron said.

"You'd be willing to let him walk?"

"Yes," Myron said. "But Melina's father has juice. And he won't."

"I thought you advised him against taking the law into his own hands."

Myron shrugged. "No one ever listens to me."

"That's true," Win said.

Win drove.

"I just wonder," Myron said.

"What?"

"Who was the serial killer here? Did his father really do it? Or was it all Stan?"

"Doubt we'll ever know," Win said.

"Probably not."

"It shan't matter," Win said. "They'll get him for Melina Garston."

"I guess," Myron said. Then he frowned and repeated, " 'Shan't'?"

Win shrugged. "So is it finally over, my friend?"

Myron's leg did that nervous jig again. He stopped it and said, "Jeremy."

"Ah," Win said. "Are you going to tell him?"

Myron looked out the window and saw nothing. "Win's credo about selfishness would say yes."

"And Myron's credo?"

"I don't know that it's much different," Myron said.

· · ·

Jeremy was playing basketball at the Y. Myron stepped into the bleachers, the rickety kind that shake with each step, and sat. Jeremy was still pale. He was thinner than the last time Myron had seen him, but there'd been a growth spurt over the last few months. Myron realized how fast changes take place for the young and felt a deep, hard thud in his chest.

For a while, he just watched the flow of the scrimmage and tried to judge his son's play objectively. Jeremy had the tools, Myron could see that right away, but there was plenty of rust on them. That wouldn't be a problem though. Again with the young. Rust doesn't stay long on the young.

As Myron watched the practice, his eyes widened. He felt his insides shrivel. He thought again about what he was about to do, and a swelling tide rose inside of him, overwhelming him, pulling him under.

Jeremy smiled when he spotted Myron. The smiled cleaved Myron's heart in two even pieces. He felt lost, adrift. He thought about what Win had said, about what a real father was, and he thought about what Esperanza had said. He thought about Greg and Emily. He wondered if he should have spoken to his own father about this, if he should have told him that this wasn't a hypothetical, that the bomb had indeed landed, that he needed his help.

Jeremy continued to play, but Myron could see that the boy was distracted by his presence. Jeremy kept sneaking quick glances toward the stands. He played a little harder, picked up the pace a bit. Myron had been there, done that. The desire to impress. It had driven Myron, maybe as much as wanting to win. Shallow, but there you have it.

The coach had his players run a few more drills and then he lined them up on the baseline. They finished up with the aptly named "suicides," which was basically a series of gut-heaving sprints broken up by bending and touching different lines on the floor. Myron might be nostalgic for many things connected to basketball. Suicides were not one of them.

Ten minutes later, with most of the kids still trying to catch their breath, the coach gathered his troops, gave out schedules for the rest of the week, and dispersed the boys with a big handclap. Most of them headed toward the exit, slinging backpacks over their shoulders. Some went into the locker room. Jeremy walked over to Myron slowly.

"Hi," Jeremy said.

"Hi."

Sweat dripped off Jeremy's hair, his face coated and flushed from exertion. "I'm going to shower," he said. "You want to wait?"

"Sure," Myron said.

"Cool, I'll be right back."

The gymnasium emptied out. Myron stood and picked up an errant basketball. His fingers found the grooves right away. He took a few shots, watching the bottom of the net dance as the ball swished through. He smiled and sat back down, still holding the ball. A janitor came in and swept the floor Zamboni-style. His keys jangled. Someone flipped off the overhead lights. Jeremy came back not long after that. His hair was still wet. He, too, had a backpack over his shoulder.

As Win would say, "Showtime."

Myron gripped the ball a little tighter. "Sit down, Jeremy. We need to talk."

The boy's face was serene and almost too beautiful. He slid the backpack off his shoulder and sat down. Myron had rehearsed this part. He had looked at it from all sides, all the pluses and minuses. He had made up his mind and changed it and made it up again. He had, as Win put it, properly tortured himself.

But in the end, he knew there was one universal truth: Lies fester. You try to put them away. You jam them in a box and bury them in the ground. But eventually they eat their way out of coffins. They dig their way out of graves. They may sleep for years. But they always wake up. When they do, they're rested, stronger, more insidious.

Lies kill.

"This is going to be hard to understand—" He stopped. Suddenly his rehearsed speech sounded so damn canned, filled with "It's nobody's fault" and "Adults make mistakes too" and "It doesn't mean your parents love you any less." It was patronizing and stupid and—

"Mr. Bolitar?"

Myron looked up at the boy.

"My mom and dad told me," Jeremy said. "Two days ago."

His chest shuddered. "What?"

"I know you're my biological father."

Myron was surprised and yet he wasn't. Some might say that Emily and Greg had made a preemptive strike, almost like a lawyer who reveals something bad about his own client because he knows the opposition will do it. Lessen the blow. But maybe Emily and Greg had learned the same lesson he had about lies and how they fester. And maybe, once again, they were trying to do what was best for their boy.

"How do you feel about it?" Myron asked.

"Weird, I guess," Jeremy said. "I mean, Mom and Dad keep expecting me to fall apart or something. But I don't see why it has to be such a big deal."

"You don't?"

"Sure, okay, I see it, but"—he stopped, shrugged—"it's not like the whole world's turned inside out or anything. You know what I mean?"

Myron nodded. "Maybe it's because you've already had your world turned inside out."

"You mean being sick and all?"

"Yes."

"Yeah, maybe," he said, thinking about it. "Must be weird for you too."

"Yeah," Myron said.

"I've been thinking about it," Jeremy said. "You want to hear what I've come up with?"

Myron swallowed. He looked into the boy's eyes—serenity, yes, but not through innocence. "Very much," he said.

"You're not my dad," he said simply. "I mean, you might be my father. But you're not my dad. You know what I mean?"

Myron managed a nod

"But"—Jeremy stopped, looked up, shrugged the shrug of a thirteen-year-old—"but maybe you can still be around."

"Around?" Myron repeated.

"Yeah," Jeremy said. He smiled again and *pow*, Myron's chest took another blow. "Around. You know."

"Yeah," Myron said, "I know."

"I think I'd like that."

"Me too," Myron said.

Jeremy nodded. "Cool."

"Yeah."

The gym clock grunted and pushed forward. Jeremy looked at it. "Mom's probably outside waiting for me. We usually stop at the super-market on the way home. Want to come?"

Myron shook his head. "Not today, thanks."

"Cool." Jeremy stood, watching Myron's face. "You okay?"

"Yeah."

Jeremy smiled. "Don't worry. It's going to work out."

Myron tried to smile back. "How did you get to be so smart?"

"Good parenting," he said. "Combined with good genes."

Myron laughed. "You might want to consider a future in politics."

"Yeah," Jeremy said. "Take it easy, Myron."

"You too, Jeremy."

He watched the boy walk out the door, again with the familiar gait. Jeremy didn't look back. There was the sound of the door closing, the echoes, and then Myron was alone. He turned toward the basket and stared at the hoop until it blurred. He saw the boy's first step, heard his first word, smelled the sweet clean of a young child's pajamas. He felt the smack of a ball against a glove, bent over to help with his homework, stayed up all night when he had a virus, all of it, like his own father had, a whirl of taunting, aching images, as irre-trievable as the past. He saw himself hovering in the boy's darkened doorway, the silent sentinel to his adolescence, and he felt what re-mained of his heart burst into flames.

The images scattered when he blinked. His heart started beating again. He stared again at the basket and waited. This time nothing blurred. Nothing happened.

ACKNOWLEDGMENTS

The author wishes to thank Sujit Sheth, M.D., Department of Pediatrics, Babies and Children's Hospital in New York, Anne Armstrong-Coben, M.D., Department of Pediatrics, Babies and Children's Hospital (and my love monkey), and Joachim Schulz, Executive Director, Fanconi Anemia Research Fund, all of whom offered up wonderful medical insights and then watched me take liberties with them; two fellow scribes, friends, and experts in their fields, Linda Fairstein and Laura Lippman; Larry Gerson, the inspiration; Nils Lofgren, for rocking me over the last hurdle; early reader and long-time bud Maggie Griffin; Lisa Erbach Vance and Aaron Priest for another job well done; Jeffrey Bedford, FBI Special Agent (and not a bad freshman dorm counselor); as always, Dave Bolt; and mostly, Jacob Hoye, my editor for all the Myron Bolitar books—and now a father. That dedication is for you, too, Jake. Thanks, dude.

For those interested in becoming a bone marrow donor and perhaps saving a life, I urge you to contact the National Marrow Donor Program at www.marrow.org or 1-800-MARROW2. For more information on Fanconi anemia, check out www.fanconi.org.

This book is a work of fiction. That means I make stuff up.

ABOUT THE AUTHOR

Harlan Coben is the author of six previous Myron Bolitar novels: *The Final Detail*, *One False Move*, *Back Spin*, the Edgar Award– and Shamus Award–winning *Fade Away*, *Drop Shot*, and *Deal Breaker*, which won an Anthony Award and received an Edgar Award nomination. He lives in New Jersey with his wife, daughter, and two sons. His e-mail address is bolitar@aol.com.